ONE WORLD OR NONE

A History of the World Nuclear
Disarmament Movement
Through 1953

VOLUME ONE

THE STRUGGLE AGAINST THE BOMB

ONE WORLD OR NONE

A History of the World Nuclear

Disarmament Movement

Through 1953

LAWRENCE S. WITTNER

Stanford University Press, Stanford, California, 1993

Stanford University Press, Stanford, California
© 1993 by the Board of Trustees of the Leland Stanford Junior University
Printed in the United States of America
CIP data appear at the end of the book

To the *hibakusha* of Hiroshima and Nagasaki

The Stanford
Nuclear Age Series

Conceived by scientists, delivered by the military, and adopted by policy-makers, nuclear weapons emerged from the ashes of Hiroshima and Nagasaki to dominate our time. The politics, diplomacy, economy, and culture of the Cold War nurtured the nuclear arms race and, in turn, have been altered by it. "We have had the bomb on our minds since 1945," E. L. Doctorow observes. "It was first our weaponry and then our diplomacy, and now it's our economy. How can we suppose that something so monstrously powerful would not, after forty years, compose our identity? The great golem we have made against our enemies is our culture, our bomb culture—its logic, its faith, its vision."

The pervasive, transformative potential of nuclear weapons was foreseen by their creators. When Secretary of War Henry L. Stimson assembled a committee in May 1945 to discuss postwar atomic energy planning, he spoke of the atomic bomb as a "revolutionary change in the relations of man to the universe." Believing that it could mean "the doom of civilization," he warned President Truman that this weapon "has placed a certain moral responsibility upon us which we cannot shirk without very serious responsibility for any disaster to civilization."

In the decades since World War II that responsibility has weighed heavily upon American civilization. Whether or not we have met it is a matter of heated debate. But that we must not fail and, moreover, that we are also responsible for preparing the next generation of leaders to succeed, can hardly be questioned.

Today, nearly half a century into the nuclear age, the pervasive impact of the nuclear arms race has stimulated a fundamental reevaluation of the role of nuclear armaments and strategic policies. But mainstream scholarly work in strategic studies has tended to focus on questions related to the development, the deployment, and the diplomacy of nuclear arsenals. Such an exclusively managerial focus cannot probe the universal revolutionary changes about which Stimson spoke, and the need to address these changes is urgent. If the academic community is to contribute imaginatively and helpfully to the increasingly complex problems of the nuclear age, then the base of scholarship and pedagogy in the national security-arms control field must be broadened. It is this goal that the Stanford Nuclear Age Series is intended to support, with paperback reissues of important out-of-print works and original publication of new scholarship in the humanities and social sciences.

Martin J. Sherwin
General Editor

Preface

> We have all been conditioned to go on living with the
> threatened dangers to . . . our civilization as we live with
> the inevitable personal catastrophe of our own death. . . .
> The difference is that while individuals can do little to alter
> their ultimate fate, a collective nuclear suicide can be
> prevented.
>
> Alva Myrdal, 1976

This may seem like an odd time to examine the struggle against the Bomb. Popular fears of a nuclear holocaust, so widespread only a decade ago that they sent millions of people into the streets in angry protest, have ebbed dramatically since that time. Moreover, the decline of public concern about the Bomb has some justification. Important arms control and disarmament treaties and the end of the Cold War do mean that, at present, the major powers are less likely to embark upon nuclear war among themselves than in the past. Furthermore, the United States and the Soviet Union (including its successor) have taken meaningful steps to dismantle substantial numbers of their nuclear weapons and to curtail production of new ones. Against this backdrop, the editors of the *Bulletin of the Atomic Scientists* recently reset the hands of their journal's "doomsday clock" at seventeen minutes to midnight—the most optimistic setting in its history.

Even so, the record of antinuclear attitudes and activities should receive our close scrutiny. One reason is that this reduction of the nuclear danger—like earlier ones—may have resulted, at least in part, from the struggle against the Bomb. Certainly the conventional explanation—that the Bomb itself has deterred nuclear war—is not entirely convincing. If nuclear deterrence alone has checked the drift to Armageddon, why has a weapon, unleashed so casually upon Japan, not been employed since that time against non-nuclear powers? For example, why did the United States not wage nuclear war against the Soviet Union, China, and other Communist states in the years when it had a nuclear monopoly and, later, a nuclear advantage? And why have nuclear-armed nations, possessing the weapons capable of deterring their foes, bothered with arms control and disarmament treaties? Furthermore, if the threat of nuclear war has led to some measure of nuclear caution, that merely underscores the importance of negative attitudes toward the use of nuclear weapons. Consequently, the deterrence theory provides an insufficient explanation for key developments in the nuclear age. An alternative—or perhaps supplementary—explanation for nuclear restraint, advanced in this book, is that opponents of the Bomb, by subjecting it to an onslaught of criticism, helped turn public sentiment against the weapon and thereby made it politically less acceptable as an instrument of war and diplomacy.

Another reason for taking the struggle against the Bomb seriously is that—despite new international treaties and the recent mood of harmony among the great powers—there is no sign that nations have abandoned nuclear weapons. Nearly half a century after the obliteration of Hiroshima, these weapons are exceptionally numerous, as well as more powerful, accurate, and widely dispersed than ever before. No nation that has developed the Bomb has renounced it, and other nations are constantly striving to develop it. This tendency toward nuclear proliferation may heighten in the aftermath of the Cold War, with the resurgence of nationalism and the possible employment of Soviet scientists in other lands. Thus, although the nuclear menace has been contained in important ways, it remains alive and well. We live in a world armed with nuclear weapons that, like poison gas, can—and perhaps will—be employed in future international crises. Annihilation continues to beckon.

My own life began to intertwine with these issues decades ago. Like millions of other schoolchildren mobilized by civil defense authorities, I periodically took cover under desks and in hallways to avoid incineration in a nuclear war; for a time, I wore a metal dog tag to identify my charred remains after the event. The contradiction did not entirely escape me. Accordingly, in the fall of 1961, I joined my first picket line, circling about a few trees in front of the White House. I was there along with about 80 other college students to urge President John F. Kennedy to resist the temptation to resume the U.S. government's testing of nuclear weapons. In previous months, the Soviet Union had broken the voluntary Bomb-testing moratorium it had initiated, and the nation was astir with talk about America's reentry into the race to have the world's biggest and best nuclear arsenal. I recall carrying a poster at the demonstration that declared: "Don't Mimic the Russians!" It was an appropriate (and clever) statement, I remember thinking. Moreover, I believed, as many others did, that preparations for nuclear war were irrational. A nuclear war, after all, would bring catastrophe upon the world. But the president soon ignored my advice and, over the passing decades, I grew accustomed to this phenomenon.

Nevertheless, something very curious happened. The nuclear disarmament movement grew into a seemingly irresistible force. By January 1962, thousands of American students, disturbed by nuclear testing and the prospect of nuclear war, were becoming acquainted with my White House trees. Meanwhile, in Great Britain, India, France, Japan, Scandinavia, Ghana, Australia, and elsewhere around the world, the pressure was mounting to stop the nuclear arms race. The atmospheric test ban treaty of 1963 seemed a logical consequence of this mass mobilization against the Bomb, which I expected would continue, as would further progress toward bringing the arms race under control. But instead, the movement faded rapidly, and the nuclear arms race continued. Only when the great powers began a new round of nuclear escalation in the late 1970s and early 1980s, accompanied by rhetoric about fighting and winning nuclear wars, did the movement revive and once again become a significant force. Indeed, with millions of people in motion in Stockholm and Sydney, London and Tokyo, Bonn and New York, Amsterdam and Rome—even in East Berlin, Budapest, Moscow, and Prague, where they defied Communist authorities—the nuclear disarmament campaign became the largest, most powerful reform movement of modern times. The only thing it could not do, it seemed, was to end the nuclear menace. Despite agreement on arms control treaties, nations clung to their nuclear tests, their nuclear weapons, and their options for nuclear war.

Why? On the one hand, there has emerged a very significant mass movement whose fundamental precept—nuclear disarmament—has inspired widespread public sympathy and support. Indeed, even the political leaders of nuclear-armed nations have proclaimed their desire to rid the world of nuclear weapons. Undergirding both phenomena is the genuine peril these weapons pose to human survival. On the other hand, the nuclear arms race has continued, and the world seems no closer to eliminating nuclear weapons than in 1945. To help myself and other people understand this paradox, I decided to embark upon a study of the subject. My goal was to provide the first history of the world nuclear disarmament movement and to grapple with the question of why, despite the clear necessity of freeing humanity from the threat of nuclear destruction, that movement has not been more effective.

It turned out to be a very ambitious project! Important books have been published on specific facets such as the struggle over the use of the Bomb during World War II and the activities of peace and disarmament movements in some individual countries. Naturally, I have drawn upon these studies whenever possible. But most of the story is located in a vast, uncharted wilderness. This is particularly true of the immediate postwar era, a time whose nuclear fears are now largely forgotten but which, in fact, produced the first worldwide wave of protest against nuclear weapons. Indeed, the full story of resistance to nuclear weapons encompasses millions of people, in dozens of countries, speaking many different languages, over more than half a century. To do the issue justice, one should have a large, multilingual research team, with ample resources, including substantial travel funds. But, alas, I am only one person, with limited language skills and little funding. Furthermore, few governments provide access to their records of recent decades. As a result, this study cannot be definitive. Rather, it is meant to serve as a trail-blazing work, beginning the process of uncovering the history of the worldwide struggle against the Bomb and of its effects on public policy.

Scholars usually treat national policymakers and peace movements separately. Diplomatic historians frequently depict policymakers as engaged in an intramural discussion whereas specialists on peace movements usually are content with providing organizational histories. But some interaction often occurs, both directly (in the form of confrontations between dissenters and power wielders) and indirectly (through such intermediate channels as the communications media and public opinion). Leaders of nation-states, of course, rarely admit that they are responding to public pressure, for to do so would subject them to the charge that they accommodate themselves to an "ill-informed," "emotional" populace—that they are "weak" rather than wise, unwavering guardians of the national security. To confess that the government is susceptible to popular pressure would also tend to encourage further citizen activism and, perhaps, embolden "the enemy." Accordingly, policymakers often cover their tracks, and the evidence for the impact of a disarmament movement on government policy tends to be minimal. In this context, it is all the more remarkable that, as this book demonstrates, there is considerable reason to believe that government officials have been painfully conscious of—and occasionally responsive to—public criticism of nuclear weapons.

One World or None is the first of three volumes, collectively entitled *The Struggle Against the Bomb*, devoted to the history of the world nuclear disarmament movement. Although it is tempting to cram everything into one book, the story is so vast, important, and little-known that I believe it deserves the more careful treatment that a multivolume work affords. In Volume 1, which examines the history of resistance to nuclear weapons through 1953, I have underscored the movement's ubiquity by looking at its progress and problems in numerous nations. Although many readers are unaccustomed to works with so broad a focus, I think they will recognize the necessity for examining events throughout the world if they are to see the global picture. Volume 2 will carry the history of the nuclear disarmament movement to 1970, and Volume 3 will bring the story up to the present. Because the volumes are divided chronologically, they may be read independently. Some of the characters and organizations, of course, run through the entire study.

The considerable research, translation, and writing necessary for this venture have been facilitated by financial support from a variety of sources. I would like to thank the American Council of Learned Societies for an ACLS/Ford fellowship and the National Endowment for the Humanities, the State University of New York at Albany, and the New York State/United University Professions Joint Labor/Management Committee for small grants-in-aid. In addition, the Nuclear Age History and Humanities Center of Tufts University and the History Department of the State University of New York at Albany have assisted me in numerous ways.

Many people have given generously of their help and time. Numerous archivists—too many, unfortunately, to list here—guided me to key records and documents. My daughter Julia Wittner served for two summers as my research assistant, and she was a joy to work with. Supplementing my limited language skills, Elisabeth Egetemeyr, Hans Fenstermacher, Mark Manassee, Anne Marfey, Adonios Mikrakis, Andrea Sherwin, Michael Weinberg, Julia Wittner, John Wolcott, and Joseph Zimmerman translated important materials for this volume. My colleagues Robert Frost and Gerald Zahavi overcame my Luddite resistance and helped me use a computer. Joseph Baratta, Graham Barker-Benfield, George Berger, Paul Boyer, Charles Chatfield, Garry Clifford, Blanche Wiesen Cook, Sandi Cooper, Richard Drake, Philip Everts, David Holloway, William Hoover, Michael Lutzker, Thomas Paterson, David Patterson, Michael Peristerakis, Kim Salomon, Melvin Small, Thomas Socknat, Todd Swanstrom, Peter van den Dungen, and Nigel Young assisted me with useful ideas, suggestions, or materials. Joseph Baratta provided me with the photos drawn from the World Federalist Association archives. Numerous persons read portions of the manuscript and recommended useful changes, including Graham Barker-Benfield, Donald Birn, Charles Chatfield, Carol Gruber, Norman Ingram, Ralph Summy, and Allan Winkler. My former student Donald Drewecki prepared the index. At Stanford University Press, Muriel Bell had the imagination and daring necessary to back a lengthy, unorthodox project, while Ellen Smith did much to transform my manuscript into its first volume. In addition, Martin Sherwin, the editor of Stanford's Nuclear Age series, has been connected with this work from its inception, and his broad knowledge, creative suggestions, and warm enthusiasm have done much to enrich it.

Finally, I have benefited enormously from the advice and encouragement of my partner, Dorothy Tristman, who, as a peace activist, intellectual, and friend, never doubted the importance of this endeavor.

L.S.W.

Contents

Sixteen pages of photos follow page 168.

A new type of thinking is essential
if mankind is to survive.

Albert Einstein, 1946

The Secret Struggle

Critics and the
International Crisis, 1913-43

> Certainly it seems now that nothing could have been more
> obvious to the people of the earlier twentieth century than
> the rapidity with which war was becoming impossible. And
> as certainly they did not see it. They did not see it until the
> atomic bombs burst in their fumbling hands.
>
> H. G. Wells, 1913

The Bomb had its critics long before it became a reality. Few in number but uncannily prescient, they foresaw the weapon's terrible consequences years before it was actually employed for the purpose of mass destruction. Yet they were unsure how to meet the challenge it posed to human survival. Deliverance from the threat of nuclear annihilation, it seemed, could be accomplished only by forgoing use of the weapon, a prospect that suggested the abolition of war or, at the least, a high level of military restraint. But how was this to occur in a world that, for thousands of years, had resorted to military force to resolve its most intractable conflicts? In the context of feuding nations, the Bomb—like previous scientific breakthroughs—would be developed and pressed into service by national leaders as a weapon of war. Indeed, in the late 1930s, as international conflict grew ever fiercer, even some of the Bomb's critics could not resist the temptation to build the weapon as a deterrent to its use by others. Caught up in the treacherous currents of a world at war, they became participants, albeit reluctant ones, in creating the very weapon they most feared.

Early Musings

If art occasionally prefigures life, that is because an artist may be unusually sensitive to contemporary developments. Certainly this was the case with H. G. Wells, one of the most popular and influential novelists of the early twentieth century. Obsessed with the rapid advance of science and technology, Wells was struck by the need for human institutions to change fast enough to cope with them. National sovereignty, particularly, seemed increasingly anachronistic—

an irrational carryover from the past that placed the future in jeopardy. In his novel *The World Set Free*, written in 1913 and published the following year, Wells portrayed a war fought with "atomic bombs." So devastating was this conflict that its survivors formed a world government that brought an end to war and, through the peaceful uses of science, ushered in an era of unprecedented social and economic progress. Throughout his long life, Wells argued that the nation was "incurably a war-making state" and that an "open conspiracy" of farsighted, rational people should move beyond it to build a genuine world community. "The directive idea of my life," he recalled, "was the creative World State." [1]

In his early warnings about atomic bombs, Wells was less original than has sometimes been imagined. Frederick Soddy, a British chemist to whom *The World Set Free* was dedicated, had declared in 1903 that the energy emitted by radioactivity made the world "a storehouse stuffed with explosives, inconceivably more powerful than any we know of." In 1905, the French physicist Pierre Curie, while lauding the benefits of radium, warned that it "could become very dangerous in criminal hands." Although British physicist Ernest Rutherford stated in 1915 that the production of atomic bombs, as envisioned by Wells, "does not seem at all promising," he conceded the following year that there was scientific interest in liberating atomic energy and that he hoped success would not be attained until humanity had learned to live peacefully. In 1920, the British astrophysicist Arthur S. Eddington wondered whether the use of atomic energy would be "for the well-being of the human race" or "for its suicide." Much of this theorizing was speculative, of course, and there is no sign that scientists deliberately avoided work related to atomic energy. But some, at least, had begun to raise the issue of social responsibility. The Russian mineralogist Vladimir Vernadsky wrote in 1922: "The time is not far away when man will take atomic energy into his hands. . . . Does man know how to use this power, to direct it to good and not to self-destruction? . . . Scientists must not close their eyes to the possible consequences of their work. . . . They must consider themselves responsible for the consequences of their discoveries." [2]

Wells's notion of a society of the righteous, committed to saving the world from its own folly, had even deeper roots in world history. It can be traced back at least to the fourth century, to the Babylonian Talmudic teacher Abbayah. According to this Jewish savant, in each generation there existed at least thirty-six righteous people (*lamed-vav tzaddikim*, in Hebrew) upon whom the future existence of the world depended. Jewish fiction and folklore took up the idea of these hidden saints, called in Yiddish *lamedvovniks*, and they played a prominent role in kabbalistic folk legend of the sixteenth and seventeenth centuries and in Hasidic lore after the late eighteenth century. Selfless love, righteous deeds, anonymity, and modesty characterized these *lamedvovniks*—true bene-factors of hapless humanity.[3]

Enter Leo Szilard

With the outstanding exception of modesty, Leo Szilard possessed all the traits of a genuine *lamedvovnik*. Born in 1898 into a Hungarian Jewish family of comfortable circumstances, Szilard was a sensitive, creative, and precocious child. From his father, he recalled, he received an early introduction to science and from his mother a sense of truth and moral purpose. After World War I, in which he served briefly as a draftee, Szilard studied in Berlin, where he took his Ph.D. in physics with Albert Einstein and Max von Laue. Writing to an associate, Einstein described Szilard as "a fine and intelligent man," who "may be inclined to exaggerate the significance of reason in human affairs." And, indeed, as the Weimar Republic disintegrated around him, Szilard hatched an abortive plan to create a small group of wise, unselfish men and women, which he called the *Bund*, to preserve civilization from the disaster that loomed. Szilard attributed what he termed his "predilection for 'Saving the World' " to the stories told to him by his mother. But the idea may also have been derived, or at least reinforced, by Szilard's reading of *The Open Conspiracy* by H. G. Wells, whom Szilard greatly admired. Curiously, Szilard did not read Wells's atomic war epic, *The World Set Free*, until 1932. But thereafter, he noted, "I found it difficult to forget." [4]

Szilard had good reason to remember the book. In late 1933, having fled from Nazi Germany, he was living in London, working to help other refugees and experimenting in nuclear physics. On September 12, he was pondering Rutherford's latest dismissal of the prospects for releasing atomic energy—heralded that day in the London *Times*—while stopped for a red light along Southampton Row. He recalled that, as the light changed to green and he crossed the street, he suddenly conceived the process that "could sustain a nuclear chain reaction, liberate energy on an industrial scale, and construct atomic bombs." Although Szilard remained uncertain of the necessary chemical element, the following month he applied for a patent "which described the laws governing such a chain reaction." Recognizing what this would mean—"and I knew it because I had read H. G. Wells"—he sought to keep the matter secret. As he explained to the British physicist F. A. Lindemann, he was "deeply concerned about what will happen if certain features of the matter become universally known. . . . An attempt . . . ought to be made to control this development as long as possible," either by "secrecy . . . among all those concerned" or by taking out patents. Perhaps at Lindemann's suggestion, Szilard sought to assign his patent to the British admiralty to preserve its secrecy. As he explained in his letter to the admiralty, information in his patent application "could be used in the construction of explosive bodies." These "would be very many thousand times more powerful than ordinary bombs, and in view of the disasters which could be caused by their use on the part of certain Powers which might attack this country, it appears very undesirable that such information should be published." At Lindemann's urging, the admiralty agreed to Szilard's unorthodox suggestion.[5]

Meanwhile, Szilard sought—without success—to draw some of the world's most important scientists into an arrangement to deal responsibly with nuclear fission. In June 1936, he told a correspondent that, given "the disaster to which this development can lead . . . an attempt will have to be made . . . to bring about something like a conspiracy of those scientists who work in this field." He wrote British physicist J. D. Cockcroft that he never considered "these patents as my property and the question now arises what to do with them." It was up to the leading physicists—Cockcroft, Rutherford, J. D. Chadwick, Frédéric Joliot-Curie, and Enrico Fermi—to decide "whether the patents should be withdrawn or maintained and in what form and by whom they should be administered." If a nuclear chain reaction proved feasible, the patents "might be used by scientists in a disinterested attempt to exercise some measure of influence over a socially dangerous development." Although Szilard corresponded with a number of top physicists on this issue, nothing came of it. He was, after all, a relatively unknown junior scientist. Furthermore, publication of research findings, not secrecy, was the norm in his profession. Symptomatically, in late December 1938, two German chemists, Otto Hahn and Fritz Strassmann, published the results of their successful experiment with nuclear fission. Asked many years later if he ever considered keeping the results secret, Hahn replied: "No. Never. . . . I was glad we were able to publish our paper so quickly." At the time, "all we knew was that we had done some good scientific work."[6]

Although Hahn claimed that "we didn't foresee the full consequences of what we had done," other scientists quickly understood the implications. Szilard, who had announced that he would leave England one year before the outbreak of World War II—and had somehow done just that—was now living in the United States; there he learned of the breakthrough from another Hungarian physicist, Eugene Wigner, in early January 1939. "All the things which H. G. Wells predicted appeared suddenly real to me," he later recalled. Writing to the financier Lewis Strauss on January 25, Szilard reported that the "very sensational new development" leads "perhaps to atomic bombs" and "revives all the hopes and fears in this respect which I had in 1934 and 1935." Szilard and Wigner agreed that it was "urgent" to confirm whether neutrons were emitted in the uranium fission process, for, if they were, a chain reaction seemed feasible. Working with an associate at Columbia University, Szilard performed the crucial experiment on March 3, 1939. When flashes of light appeared on their television tube screen, signaling the release of neutrons, it was clear to Szilard, as he recalled, that "the large-scale liberation of atomic energy was just around the corner. . . . That night there was very little doubt in my mind that the world was headed for grief." [7]

Once again, Szilard sought to generate a conspiracy of silence. During his discussion with Wigner, he had concluded that if neutrons were emitted by uranium fission, "this fact should be kept from the Germans." But how? Enrico Fermi, the great Italian physicist, had recently arrived at Columbia and was already conducting related experiments with results similar to Szilard's. Although Fermi wanted to publish his research paper, in part because he thought a chain reaction unlikely, Szilard and yet another Hungarian refugee physicist whom Szilard had mobilized, Edward Teller, finally prevailed upon the Italian to delay publication indefinitely. Meanwhile, in the spring of 1939, Szilard, Wigner, and émigré Austrian physicist Victor Weisskopf cabled to some of the most prominent British, French, and American physicists, urging that papers on nuclear fission be circulated only in private. Szilard and his associates also approached Niels Bohr, the distinguished Danish physicist, who was visiting the United States at the time. "We knew this was a hopeless thing, but . . . we had to try," Weisskopf recalled; "we were very much afraid of the Nazis." [8]

Szilard and his associates nearly succeeded. From Great Britain, the physicist P. M. S. Blackett reported that agreement had been reached to withhold publication. Physicists at the most prominent research centers in New York City and Washington also pledged to maintain secrecy. Although Bohr doubted the feasibility of using nuclear fission for explosives and thought the issue already too public to ensure secrecy, he made the initial effort to bring his Danish institute into line. But the French research team—headed by Joliot-Curie and including Lew Kowarski and Hans Halban—now balked. They had viewed Szilard's first telegram as a joke, but had taken later messages more seriously, especially after the German invasion of Czechoslovakia. Even so, like Fermi and Bohr, they considered it unlikely that an atomic bomb would be built for many years, if ever. Furthermore, they detested secrecy in science, felt that it would be impossible to maintain if papers were circulated privately, and worried that their own work would be overshadowed by the work of others that appeared in print. When a news release indicated, inaccurately, that scientists in Washington had published information on neutron emission, Joliot-Curie cabled that the French had decided to publish their research findings.[9]

The Atomic Arms Race Begins

Szilard's plan and its collapse had important consequences. The French team's publication of its report on neutron emission in *Nature* in late April 1939 precipitated the official atomic bomb programs in Germany, Great Britain, and, perhaps, the Soviet Union. Even so, the efforts of Szilard and his associates were not entirely in vain. Although the outbreak of war in September 1939 caused a blanket of secrecy to descend upon fission research in the belligerent countries, publication continued in the United States. Determined as ever to prevent the misuse of atomic energy, Szilard withheld publication of some of his own work and convinced other physicists—including Fermi, Herbert Anderson, and Louis Turner—to do the same. As it turned out, had their findings been published, German scientists would have acquired information crucial to the success of their atomic bomb project. Moreover, the American physicist Gregory Breit, awakened to the importance of secrecy through long conversations with Szilard and Wigner, used his position on the National Research Council of the Academy of Sciences to secure a total blackout on nuclear fission research in the United States.[10]

Ironically, fear of a German atomic bomb also led Szilard and his associates to initiate America's atomic bomb project. After the collapse of their secrecy plan in the spring of 1939, Wigner, particularly, argued that the U.S. government should be apprised of the ominous developments overseas. With the assistance of Wigner and Teller, mostly as chauffeurs, Szilard drove out to Long Island in July 1939 to discuss the issue with Einstein, who was vacationing there. One of the world's most eminent physicists, Einstein had also been a leading pacifist since the onset of World War I. Like Szilard, he had been horrified by the rise of fascism and the development of the Nazi war machine and, accordingly, had left Germany and become a proponent of collective security. Although Einstein did not work in the field of nuclear fission, he quickly grasped the situation outlined by Szilard. Therefore, on August 2, he signed a letter, drafted by Szilard, to President Franklin Roosevelt, warning that "extremely powerful bombs" might now be constructed by triggering a chain reaction in uranium. Einstein's letter, delivered to the president that fall by the financier Alexander Sachs, prompted Roosevelt to appoint a scientific advisory committee to investigate the matter. On October 21, Szilard, Teller, and Wigner appeared before the committee and, despite resistance from the U.S. Army representative, who thought the idea of an atomic bomb ridiculous, secured a small grant to enable Szilard to study the development of a chain reaction.[11] From this modest beginning, the vast Manhattan project developed. "I . . . chose the lesser of two evils," Szilard remarked years later. "I thought we must build the bomb, because if we don't, the Germans will have it first . . . and force us to surrender." [12]

The need to head off a Nazi military victory obsessed Szilard and others in the first years of the war. Although Einstein did no work on the Manhattan project, in 1940 he sent a second message to the president in an attempt to produce a stronger government commitment to the venture. Teller, who had serious qualms about engaging in weapons research, overcame his reluctance in the spring of 1940, when he heard a call to action from the president. He was soon employed by the Manhattan project and, within two years, was directing its component that dealt with the feasibility of a hydrogen bomb.[13] Working first at Columbia University and then at the Chicago Metallurgical Laboratory—or Met Lab, as it was called—Szilard played an important role in the development of the atomic bomb while, at the same time, demanding greater vigor from those persons he considered lackadaisical or incompetent government officials. In a letter of May 26, 1942, to Vannevar Bush, the Manhattan project's top scientific administrator, Szilard complained of "the slowness of the work" and concluded: "In 1939 the Government of the United States was given a unique opportunity by Providence; this opportunity was lost. Nobody can tell now whether we shall be ready before German bombs wipe out American cities." Among the many refugee scientists in America, as well as their native-born counterparts, there existed a fierce determination to win this first atomic arms race.[14]

But even in these first years of World War II, a strain of anxiety persisted in the United States about what the atomic bomb represented and portended. A few scientists, viewing it as a weapon of offense and mass destruction, refused to work on it at all.[15] I. I. Rabi, a Columbia physicist who had been an associate of Szilard's during the 1939 secrecy campaign, rejected a full-time post at Los Alamos because of his dismay that an atomic bomb would serve as the "culmination of three centuries of physics." [16] Some of those who did work on the Bomb project had ambivalent feelings. For a time, a few took comfort in the hope that further research would show that building atomic weapons was impossible. Fermi, who supervised the world's first nuclear chain reaction at the University of Chicago in December 1942, may have been among them. "Somewhere deep in his heart" Fermi believed that the war "did not really matter," Szilard recalled. "Even by the middle of 1942 Fermi thought that our work had no bearing on the war. . . . Whether he did not wish that there should be a 'bomb' or whether he did not make sufficient allowances for possibilities . . . I do not know." Robert Oppenheimer later observed that, after Fermi had attended one of his first conferences at Los Alamos, the Italian physicist turned to him in surprise and said, "I believe your people actually *want* to make a bomb." [17] Leo Szilard was surely one of the most ambivalent participants in the Manhattan project. After the successful chain reaction, he remained behind with Fermi, shook his hand, and said that he "thought this day would go down as a black day in the history of mankind." [18]

Despite the central role that Szilard and his émigré associates played in the development of the Manhattan project, U.S. government officials remained suspicious of them. In March 1939, when Fermi, a celebrated Nobel Prize winner, made a preliminary attempt to communicate their concerns to U.S. military authorities, they treated him in a patronizing fashion and casually dismissed him as "a wop." About a year later, Lyman Briggs, the chair of the president's Uranium Committee, decided that Szilard and Fermi should not attend one of its forthcoming meetings because "these matters are secret." The following month, Briggs disbanded a scientific advisory committee that Columbia chemist Harold Urey had convinced him to appoint; if a substantial research effort were launched without success, he explained, it would be embarrassing to have citizens of recent vintage—notably Szilard, Fermi, and Wigner—serving on it. Although Einstein was probably the world's most renowned scientist, his pacifist and other allegedly radical activities had led the Federal Bureau of Investigation (FBI) to gather information on him since 1932 and had given him a reputation as dangerously peace-minded. Consequently, despite Einstein's offer to do research on the atomic bomb, Bush ordered him excluded from the Manhattan project. "I am not at all sure that if I place Einstein in entire contact with his subject he would not discuss it in a way it should not be discussed," Bush informed the Institute for Advanced Study, Einstein's employer at Princeton. The project's scientific chief added that it was "utterly impossible" to "place the whole thing before" Einstein "in view of the attitude of people here in Washington who have studied . . . his whole history." [19]

Szilard experienced particularly chilly relations with U.S. officials. As early as 1940, U.S. Naval Intelligence reported, ludicrously, that he was "very pro-German" and a security risk; therefore, "it would be unwise to employ Mr. Szillard [sic] on secret work." Although the Bomb project's administrators ignored this recommendation, they disliked him intensely. James Conant, Bush's wartime assistant, contended that Szilard was "interested primarily in building a record on the basis of which to make a 'stink' after the war." [20] Finding Szilard's complaints about the project unbearable, Arthur Compton, the director of the Chicago Met Lab, sought to force his resignation in October 1942. Compton secretly suggested that the army "follow his motions" but take "no drastic action now." Eventually, however, fearful that the campaign against Szilard would stimulate "undesirable illwill" among Wigner and other important scientists, Compton backed away from this position. [21]

Szilard faced even greater difficulties with Major General Leslie R. Groves, the hard-driving director of the Manhattan project. An anti-Semite who considered Szilard a particularly obnoxious Jew,[22] Groves sought to have the physicist "apprehended" and "interned for the duration of the war" as an "enemy alien." Groves drafted an order to this effect, but the secretary of war refused to sign it, declaring—as Groves recalled—"that it was utterly impossible and he was sure that both of us knew it. . . . Neither a court nor public opinion would ever support us in such an action." The general did, however, manage to have Szilard, then at loggerheads with the government over one of his patents, removed from the Met Lab's payroll for all of 1943. Groves also continued to seek evidence that Szilard was a German agent through mail openings, wiretaps, and personal surveillance. "The investigation of Szilard should be continued despite the barre[n]ness of the results," the general ordered. "Until we know for certain that he is 100% reliable we cannot entirely disregard this person."[23]

Even had prejudices and personality conflicts been fewer, it seems unlikely that Szilard and his circle would have had much influence with U.S. policymakers, whose concerns differed from those of the émigré scientists in several important areas. Under the criterion of "wartime use"—the allocation of U.S. resources to activities that had a fairly rapid military payoff—government officials initially gave the Bomb project very limited support. When scientific developments in Great Britain finally convinced Roosevelt's top advisers that an atomic bomb was feasible in wartime, they persuaded him in the fall of 1941 to commit the vast resources necessary for the project. But behind the new U.S. commitment lay not merely the desire to deter Germany but the assumption that the U.S. government should use the Bomb in the war. Indeed, having earmarked more than $2 billion and some 120,000 people, including much of the nation's top scientific and engineering talent, for the Manhattan project in a situation of wartime scarcity, Roosevelt, Secretary of War Henry Stimson, and numerous other U.S. officials never doubted that they should employ the Bomb in wartime. Furthermore, after 1943, the Roosevelt administration began to conceive of the Bomb as an instrument to secure postwar diplomatic goals—an idea it bequeathed to its successor. As Stimson noted, the atomic bomb was the "master card" in America's diplomatic hand.[24] Consequently, at crucial points, Szilard and his associates were out of step with the official guardians of U.S. national security.

The British Role

In Great Britain, the atomic bomb project was initiated by scientists who, like their counterparts in the United States, had very uneasy feelings about nuclear weapons and, indeed, about warfare itself. Two refugee physicists, Otto Frisch and Rudolf Peierls, had done some calculations in the spring of 1940 on the production of uranium-235, which convinced them of the feasibility of an atomic bomb. They talked over their concerns with Marc Oliphant, an Australian physicist serving on the Maud Committee, a group of British scientists appointed to evaluate the feasibility of nuclear weapons. At Oliphant's suggestion, they drew up a report that proved decisive in the committee's recommendation, made in the summer of 1941, that an atomic bomb of great destructive power was "practicable" and that, given the likelihood of a Bomb project in Nazi Germany, "every effort should be made to produce bombs of this kind." Ironically, Frisch and Peierls were extraordinarily shy, gentle people, and Oliphant was a strict vegetarian to whom the slaughter of animals for food was repugnant. Like their counterparts in the United States, they viewed the atomic bomb—which Oliphant originally hoped the laws of physics would prove impossible—as "a deterrent" to a German atomic attack.[25]

Naturally, the spectrum of opinion among British scientists with knowledge of the Bomb was considerably greater. Some—like Max Born, a refugee from Germany, who had written a classic study of the nature of the atom—simply refused to work on the Bomb project. Although "I wished the downfall of Hitler with all my heart," Born recalled, "war work of this character seemed to me horrible." Joseph Rotblat, an émigré physicist from Poland, recollected that initially he sought to put the whole thing out of his mind, for "using my knowledge to produce an awesome weapon of destruction was abhorrent to me." But he "gradually worked out a rationale for doing research on the feasibility of the bomb"; like Szilard and others, he concluded that Allied possession of the weapon would deter its use by the Germans.[26] Other scientists—like Chadwick and Cockcroft, two members of the Maud Committee—hoped, as Cockcroft later remarked, "that the constants of nature might turn out so that the bomb was impossible." Once it became clear that a bomb was feasible, these people stayed with the project, although sometimes with uneasiness. "I had many sleepless nights," Chadwick commented twenty-eight years later. "I had then to start taking sleeping pills. It was the only remedy. I've never stopped."[27] Most Britons knowledgeable about the project, however, appear to have had few if any qualms about the production of the Bomb. Committed to the defeat of Nazi Germany, they viewed its development as essential. Sometimes, indeed, their fears carried over into plans for the postwar era. The Maud Committee, for example, argued that, even after the war, no nation "would care to risk being caught without a weapon of such decisive possibilities."[28]

As in the United States, those at the highest level of power in Great Britain placed the atomic bomb within a framework of traditional thinking about international conflict. Initially, Prime Minister Winston Churchill downplayed the importance of nuclear fission, contending in August 1939 that "the fear that this new discovery has provided the Nazis with some sinister, new secret explosive with which to destroy their enemies is clearly without foundation." Nevertheless, after the Maud Committee report emphasized the feasibility of producing the Bomb within a few years, Szilard's erstwhile confidant, F. A. Lindemann, now Lord Cherwell and the prime minister's top science adviser, told Churchill in 1941 that Britain "must go forward." Churchill quickly sent Cherwell's memorandum to the Chiefs of Staff, adding drily: "Although personally I am quite content with the existing explosives, I feel we must not stand in the way of improvement." Thereafter, Churchill never wavered from his belief that, if the Bomb were ready in wartime, it should be used. Moreover, like Roosevelt, he was committed to employing the Bomb as an instrument of postwar diplomacy. Indeed, meeting at Hyde Park in September 1944, the two world leaders signed a secret agreement for a postwar Anglo-American atomic monopoly.[29]

The German Bomb Project

Ironically, the German Bomb project, which did so much to engender the Anglo-American nuclear effort, began more auspiciously than it ended. In late April 1939, within a few days of the publication of Joliot-Curie's findings, two German physicists, George Joos and Paul Harteck, independently alerted government authorities to the military potentialities of nuclear fission. In his letter to the Wehrmacht, Harteck contended that the "country which first makes use of" nuclear explosives "has an unsurpassable advantage over the others." By that fall, the German army had taken command of a growing program of nuclear fission research, appropriating the Kaiser Wilhelm Institute for Physics and other scattered university institutes for the work. Werner Heisenberg (Germany's most prominent theoretical physicist after the purge of Jews from the sciences) and Otto Hahn oversaw Germany's research into the industrial and military applications of nuclear fission. Although German scientists made some progress toward the development of an atomic bomb, they never achieved a chain reaction. In part, their failure reflected a serious scientific error and, in part, the destructive effects of Allied sabotage and bombing during the last years of the war. But most significant, it was based on the relative lack of resources devoted to the Bomb project by the German government: approximately $10 million. Convinced that atomic weapons could not be built in time for use in the world war, the army gave the project a low priority after early 1942. Even Adolf Hitler, despite his apparent willingness to employ atomic bombs, believed that there was little immediate benefit to the Bomb project.

This opinion was reinforced by the führer's conviction that nuclear physics was "Jewish physics" and therefore of little value.[30]

The extent of resistance among German scientists to the building of the Bomb has long been in dispute,[31] at least in part because of the extraordinarily brutal, totalitarian nature of the Nazi regime. Who, in retrospect, wanted to admit that he or she had worked loyally, even zealously, to provide such a regime with nuclear weapons? In subsequent years, Hahn claimed that he had never done any work on atomic bombs; indeed, he would have "refused to work on an atomic bomb at any price." Heisenberg's team, he explained, "was making experiments with a view to utilizing nuclear energy, but not in order to make bombs."[32] Writing in a similar vein, Heisenberg contended only two years after the war that "Germany made no attempt to produce atomic bombs"; because the government had decided against a crash program in 1942, scientists "were spared the decision" as to whether to work on a Bomb project. Heisenberg and his wife maintained that, during a visit to Niels Bohr in Copenhagen in October 1941, he had sought to convey to the Danish physicist that Germany neither would nor could build atomic bombs and, consequently, the U.S. Bomb program should be abandoned. Unfortunately, they explained, it was impossible to speak directly about these things in wartime; therefore, even Bohr totally misunderstood his point and viewed him as a stooge of the Nazi regime.[33]

These protests smack of a postwar apologia. Admittedly, German scientists did not generally welcome the advent of war in 1939, in part because they feared being dispatched to the front. Furthermore, some disliked the Nazis, and others may have had secret qualms about military research. Nevertheless, almost all quickly rallied to the colors, supported the Nazi blueprint for a Greater Germany, and recognized the ramifications of their research for atomic weapons. Both Hahn and Heisenberg made important contributions to the military aspects of the nuclear fission project—a point they emphasized in their wartime reports to government officials. In 1942, the leading nuclear project scientists gave lectures and pep talks to representatives of the Nazi party, the German government, and German industry in which they stressed the utility of their research for war.[34] That year and thereafter, Heisenberg engaged in lecture tours in German-occupied Europe, lauding the German war effort. Because his visit to Copenhagen was part of a German cultural propaganda tour, there was little reason for Bohr to trust him, even if Heisenberg had said what he later claimed to want, which he did not. Indeed, it would be difficult, then or now, to put much faith in the dissident qualities of German Bomb project scientists and administrators; 56 percent of them were Nazi party members and 80 percent were members of either the party or its ancillary organizations.[35]

At best, it can be argued that the German scientists who engaged in nuclear research during World War II were less Nazi zealots than personal opportunists. Asked decades later about his initiation of the project, Harteck responded: "In those days in Germany we got no support for pure science. We were very, very poor. So we had to go to an agency where money was to be obtained. I was always realistic about such things." At this time, "the War Office had the money and so we went to them. If we had gone somewhere else, we would have got nothing." Echoing this interpretation, Heisenberg recalled that "for the first time we could get money from our government to do something interesting and we intended to use this situation." Scientists would "make use of warfare for physics." Heisenberg, of course, argued that in their reports to their superiors, project scientists emphasized the lengthy time period for the Bomb's development because "we definitely did not want to get into this bomb business." But he saw no reason "to idealize this." Talk of delays was "also for our personal safety. We thought that the probability that this [project] would lead to atomic bombs during the War was nearly zero." Thus, "if we had done otherwise, and if many thousand people had been put to work on it and then nothing had been developed, this could have had extremely disagreeable consequences for us." Moreover, "to be safe," they had to say that the Bomb could be made, for what would the regime think if, somehow, the Americans did develop the weapon? For such men, as for most German physicists, who during the Hitler era remained neither pro-Nazi nor anti-Nazi but merely eager to further their own careers, personal expediency apparently remained a driving principle.[36]

Those German scientists who did resist the Nazi juggernaut were generally far from the German Bomb project. For example, many scientists had fled from the Nazi regime and sounded the alarm about its nuclear research. There was also Paul Rosbaud, the editor of *Naturwissenschaften*, who stayed behind in Germany and provided British intelligence with valuable reports on his colleagues in the German Bomb program. There was also Wolfgang Gentner, a German scientist who risked his life by conspiring with Joliot-Curie in occupied France, thereby stopping the transfer of the French cyclotron to Germany for nuclear research and blocking German nuclear research in Paris.[37] Their daring resistance highlights the extent to which Bomb project scientists collaborated with the Nazi regime.

The Japanese and French Bomb Projects

The Japanese Bomb project was even smaller and less effective than the German. In April 1940, Lieutenant General Takeo Yasuda, a rising young army officer, ordered an investigation of the feasibility of producing an atomic bomb. That December, convinced that a bomb could be built, scientists in Tokyo began working on the project under the direction of Yoshio Nishina, a physicist of international stature. Responding to the intense interest of military and political leaders in the Bomb, Japan's top scientists met in a "Physics Colloquium" from December 1942 to March 1943 and concluded that, given the immense scientific and resource problems involved, it would be impossible for Japan—or the United States—to build a Bomb in time for use in the current war. The navy ceased support for the project, although army support continued, on a very modest scale, for nuclear research in Tokyo and Kyoto. With only a handful of researchers working on the project thereafter, it made little progress. Nishina was pessimistic about the war and prospects for the Bomb but remained committed to building the weapon. Similarly, some scientists worked desperately on the project in its final years, convinced that only nuclear weapons could save Japan from destruction. But other scientific participants were reportedly unenthusiastic. Their attitude may have reflected not merely a sense of futility but an uneasiness about the war and Japanese imperialism. Political dissidents among Japanese intellectuals, unlike their German counterparts, almost invariably remained in their homeland and contributed to a growing disdain for the war effort.[38]

If the French Bomb project never progressed very far, it was not for lack of scientific support. Shortly after the outbreak of war in 1939, Joliot-Curie, on his own initiative, visited Raoul Dautry, the French minister of armament, and explained that his uranium research could lead to a powerful new weapon, as well as to energy that could be used to propel submarines and fuel industry. Thus encouraged, the French government put money and resources behind Joliot-Curie's scientific team at the Collège de France, arranged for a daring theft of heavy water from Norway (where it was being manufactured for the Germans), and even marked out a plot of land in the Sahara Desert for experiments with an atomic bomb. After the collapse of the French war effort in 1940, Kowarski and Halban fled abroad, where they worked on the Anglo-American Bomb project, but Joliot-Curie stayed in Paris. Although forced by circumstances to cease his atomic bomb research, he remained an intense patriot. He not only helped sabotage German efforts to use his laboratory for uranium research but secretly became president of the National Front, the Communist-organized resistance movement, and a member of the Communist party. At his university, he supervised the making of Molotov cocktails and other explosives that were used in the popular uprising that hastened the German retreat from Paris. After the members of Joliot-Curie's team began returning to liberated France in 1944, he and Dautry revived the idea of a French atomic energy program and sold it to France's new political leader, Charles de Gaulle.[39]

The Soviet Union and the Bomb

Like most of its counterparts in other lands, the Soviet Bomb project received its initial impetus from nuclear scientists. When Hahn and Strassmann published the results of their nuclear fission experiments, great excitement arose among Soviet physicists, especially the younger ones, who conducted pathbreaking experiments of their own. Impressed by the potential but disappointed by the small scale of official support, two young physicists, Igor Kurchatov and Yuri Khariton, drew up a report to the presidium of the Soviet Academy of Sciences that called attention to the military and economic importance of atomic energy and appealed for additional funding. Senior scientists, however, convinced that an atomic bomb could not be produced in time to meet the immediate defense needs of the Soviet Union, rejected their proposal. Nevertheless, acting on behalf of his restless junior colleagues, Nikolai Semenov, the director of the Institute of Physical Chemistry, later wrote to the government about the possibility of creating a bomb with unprecedented destructive power. Before a reply could be received, the German invasion of June 1941 brought nuclear research to a standstill. Laboratories were evacuated and scientists assigned to the Red Army or to assorted types of war research.[40]

Eventually, however, the nuclear proponents had their way. Georgi Flerov, a 28-year-old physicist, pressed government agencies, Kurchatov, and other scientists to resume uranium research. Finally, in May 1942, he wrote directly to Soviet premier Joseph Stalin. Pointing to the suspicious absence of publication on nuclear research in America, he called for the immediate establishment of a nuclear laboratory in the Soviet Union. "It is essential," he wrote, "not to lose any time in building the uranium bomb." Shortly thereafter, Stalin conferred on the issue with top scientists and made the decision to push forward with a Soviet Bomb project. Although Stalin worried about the immense cost of the program and, warned by the scientists, had no expectation that the Bomb would be ready in wartime, reports on Bomb projects in Germany, Great Britain, and the United States convinced him that the Soviet state must possess nuclear weapons as soon as possible. Consequently, in February 1943 the Soviet Bomb project was formally launched under Kurchatov's direction.[41] By the end of 1944, Kurchatov had approximately a hundred researchers working on it in his Moscow laboratory. This was a very small-scale program by Manhattan project standards but was somewhat larger than Germany's.[42]

The opposition that emerged in the Soviet Union to the building of the Bomb does not appear to have been based on moral or political grounds.[43] Rather, it seems that some senior scientists, at least initially, may have resented the Bomb project as a diversion of resources from immediate military needs and, perhaps, from their own research.[44] One top Soviet scientist who is sometimes mentioned as an opponent of the Bomb is Peter Kapitza, then a very prominent physicist. After having lived, studied, and worked at Cambridge University since 1921, Kapitza visited his Soviet homeland in 1934 and was prevented by Stalin from leaving it. Making the best of the situation, Kapitza accepted a position in Moscow as the first director of the prestigious Institute of Physical Problems. Although he did not work directly on the atomic bomb,[45] this was not a matter of conscience. During the war, he served on official committees that advised the Soviet government on the Bomb project, tried to attract Niels Bohr to the Soviet Union, and promoted the idea of atomic weapons. "The recent past has provided new possibilities of using intra-atomic energy," he told an antifascist meeting of scientists in Moscow on October 12, 1941. "This matter is still very doubtful, but . . . there are great possibilities here" for "using atomic bombs which possess huge destructive force." Kapitza's nonparticipation in the actual project, like the absence of other senior scientists, may merely have reflected the low priority of the venture or, perhaps, a preference by Kurchatov for his own generation of young enthusiasts.[46] In early 1945, they were joined by a number of high-level scientists from the German Bomb project. Although some of the German recruits were probably not sanguine about their new employer, most freely offered their services to the Soviet government. Another German who volunteered his services to the Russians was Klaus Fuchs, an émigré to Britain, who, while working in Los Alamos, passed along important atomic information to Soviet agents.[47] His espionage provides but one additional indication of the willingness of most scientists, in wartime, to support their nation of choice.

Scientists and the Bomb

Despite the qualms felt by many scientists about the atomic bomb, they played a key role in spurring its development. This was not because they were more militaristic than other people. Rather, thanks to the advanced nature of their research in nuclear physics, they simply recognized earlier than did others that it might be possible to build an atomic bomb. And if it could be built, the Bomb would be developed for national arsenals. Consequently, with the drift toward world war, most atomic scientists considered an atomic bomb project necessary to defend their homelands from utter destruction. In this respect, they shared with their fellow citizens and with national leaders the view that, in the midst of violent world conflict, the preservation of national security made imperative the possession of the most destructive weaponry available. Confronted, then, with a situation of international anarchy, most scientists—including many with strong pacifist inclinations—opted for the development of the atomic bomb.

Many scientists, however, particularly those who feared a Nazi nuclear attack, supported the development of the Bomb as a deterrent. They did not necessarily favor its use as a weapon of war or as an instrument of postwar diplomacy. For this reason, they were at odds with the official guardians of national security, who—in line with the traditional relationship of force to statecraft—took the new weapon very seriously in these respects. Not surprisingly, then, in the final years of World War II, when it became clear that Nazi Germany did not have the Bomb after all, a rift would emerge between scientists and policymakers as to the new weapon's future.

Growing Resistance, 1943-45

The development of nuclear power . . . creates grave
political and economic problems for the future.

James Franck et al., 1945

Despite the key role that atomic scientists played in sparking the development of the Bomb, they were also the leading figures who called attention to the dangers it posed. Given their early ambivalence, this was hardly surprising, particularly after it became clear that they had nothing to fear from a German Bomb or from the tottering Japanese war effort. The absence of a clear necessity for the Bomb's use also colored the opinions of numerous U.S. military leaders, who proved remarkably skittish on the subject of an atomic attack. Nevertheless, leading figures in the Manhattan project and in the highest circles of the Allied governments remained determined to use the Bomb as a weapon of war and of postwar diplomacy. The result was a growing confrontation between critics and supporters of nuclear weapons.

Scientists Take the Lead

As early as September 1942, Szilard drafted a memo that outlined the Bomb's ominous portents. "What the existence of these bombs will mean we all know," he stated. "We cannot have peace in a world in which various sovereign nations have atomic bombs in the possession of their armies and any of these armies could win a war within twenty-four hours after it starts one." American policymakers must "take determined action near the end of the war in order to safeguard us from such a 'peace.' " Only two days later, in a memo to the Chicago Met Lab, Szilard revived his earlier call for a society of the righteous, a "group of intelligent men . . . who can, by repeated discussions, make clear . . . what the existence of atomic bombs will mean from the point of view of the post-war period." So worried was Szilard becoming about the fate of the postwar world that, momentarily, he slipped into advocacy of the Bomb's wartime use. On January 14, 1944, he argued in a letter to Bush that "it will hardly be possible" to secure "a peace that is based on reality" unless "high efficiency atomic bombs have actually been used in this war and the fact of their destructive power has deeply penetrated the mind of the public." Although this letter represented Szilard's only lapse from opposing use of atomic bombs, it underscored his continued fear that, with the development of atomic weapons, the world was careening toward disaster.[1]

These fears were shared by Niels Bohr, the Danish nuclear physicist whose eminence in science matched that of Einstein. Alerted by the Swedish am-bassador that the Germans were about to arrest him, Bohr escaped to Sweden in late September 1943. The following month, in response to entreaties from British atomic scientists, he flew to Great Britain, where he was briefed on the Anglo-American Bomb project. By December, Bohr was in the United States as part of the British scientific delegation. Although Bohr did some work in Los Alamos on the Bomb, his main reason for coming to the United States was to sound the alarm about the unprecedented dangers of a postwar nuclear arms race. It could be avoided, he believed, only if Churchill, Roosevelt, and Stalin agreed in wartime on international control of atomic energy. In Britain, Bohr had received a sympathetic hearing from Sir John Anderson, the cabinet mem-ber responsible for scientific research, and in the United States he greatly impressed Lord Halifax (the British ambassador) and Supreme Court Justice Felix Frankfurter. In early 1944, Frankfurter brought the matter to President Roosevelt's attention. According to Frankfurter, Roosevelt agreed with Bohr on the need for international control and promised to explore with Churchill the proper safeguards. Anderson followed up in England with a long memo to Churchill in which he posed the alternatives as a vicious arms race in which the United States and Great Britain would enjoy a temporary advantage or, as he recommended, "effective international control."[2]

Bohr's remarkable progress, however, proved illusory. Totally unsympa-thetic to the idea of international control, Churchill scrawled disparaging com-ments all over Anderson's memo, concluding: "I do not agree." The prime minister also rebuffed the advances of Cherwell, who wrote to him that he thought "plans and preparations for the postwar world or even the peace con-ference are utterly illusory so long as this crucial factor is left out of account." Although Bohr returned to London in April 1944 to talk with Churchill, the prime minister ignored him until entreaties from his advisers and from Sir Henry Dale, president of the Royal Society, finally broke his resistance. Pre-dictably, the meeting, which occurred on May 16, was a disaster. Churchill spent most of the thirty minutes in a harangue on an irrelevant matter and remained totally unmoved by Bohr's concerns. "I cannot see what you are worrying about," he told the Danish scientist. "After all, this new bomb is just going to be bigger than our present bombs. It involves no difference in the principles of war; and as far as any postwar problems, there are none that cannot be amicably settled between me and my friend President Roosevelt." Bohr remarked sadly, "We did not even speak the same language." [3]

Determined to pursue the issue, however, Bohr returned to the United States. On August 26, 1944, he had a lengthy meeting with Roosevelt in which he reiterated his point that, at this juncture in history, there was a superb opportunity to set an amicable course for future world relations by opening discussions with the Russians on international control of atomic energy. To move forward with development of secret weapons, he warned, would undermine international confidence and eventually plunge the world into a perilous nuclear arms race. The president was his usual affable self, agreeing that an approach to the Soviet Union should be tried and leaving Bohr with the impression that he might serve as Roosevelt's emissary to Russia. This, too, soon proved a fantasy. Meeting in Hyde Park on September 18, 1944, Roosevelt and Churchill explicitly dismissed Bohr's proposals and agreed that the Bomb "might perhaps . . . be used against the Japanese." They also resolved that "enquiries should be made regarding the activities of Professor Bohr and steps taken to ensure that he is responsible for no leakage of information." Irate at the activities of the Danish physicist, Churchill wrote Cherwell: "The President and I are much worried about Professor Bohr. How did he come into this business? . . . What is all this about? It seems to me Bohr ought to be confined or at any rate made to see that he is very near the edge of mortal crimes." Although Bohr continued to work within channels to secure international control of atomic energy, this idea continued to hold little appeal for the top political leaders of the United States and Great Britain.[4]

Bohr's mission, however, had some effect. If national leaders clung to traditional assumptions about weapons and world power, some figures at the lower levels of authority were beginning to ponder the alternatives. On September 30, 1944, apparently after consultation with Bohr and with some knowledge of the Roosevelt-Churchill plan for an Anglo-American atomic monopoly, Bush and Conant sent a memo to Secretary of War Stimson. Calling attention to the prospective dangers of the Bomb in a world of competing nations, they recommended that atomic energy be delegated to an international agency after the war. "There will be great resistance to this measure," they predicted, "but . . . the hazards to the future of the world are sufficiently great to warrant this attempt." Although Stimson remained noncommittal, he recognized the gravity of the problem posed by atomic weapons and sought to bring the State Department into the planning process. Bohr also had some impact on the thinking of Robert Oppenheimer, the project director at Los Alamos, with whom he spent considerable time discussing the idea of international control.[5]

At the same time, the unwarranted sense of progress that Bohr drew from his conversations served to demobilize others, most notably Einstein. Although Einstein did not work on the Bomb, he knew a good deal about it, in part because of his wartime conversations with Otto Stern, a former colleague who served as an adviser to the Manhattan project. After a discussion of theirs on December 11, 1944, Einstein became seriously alarmed at the prospects for a postwar nuclear arms race. Accordingly, he dispatched an impassioned letter to Bohr, arguing that, although politicians clearly did not understand the threat to humanity posed by the atomic bomb, influential scientists like Bohr, himself, and others in the United States, Great Britain, and the Soviet Union had the ear of political leaders. Could they not, together, press these leaders to place military power beyond the nation-state, in the hands of a supranational government? Hastening to Einstein's home in Princeton, Bohr spoke with him at length, assuring him that the implications of the Bomb had been called to the attention of "responsible statesmen in America and England" and that silence on the matter was essential. Einstein agreed, as Bohr recalled, to "impress on the friends with whom he had talked about the matter, the undesirability of all discussions which might complicate the delicate task of the statesmen."[6]

Ferment at the Met Lab

At the Chicago Met Lab, however, scientists were growing more outspoken. In the fall of 1944, a committee headed by Zay Jeffries[7] solicited views on the future of atomic energy among scientists working there. On November 18, the Jeffries committee produced a report, "Prospectus on Nucleonics," which it submitted to the lab director, Arthur Compton, and which he, in turn, passed along to higher authorities. Although much of the report was prepared by the committee secretary, Robert Mulliken, key sections on the social and political implications of atomic energy were written by Eugene Rabinowitch, a biophysicist. After leaving Russia as a schoolboy following the Bolshevik revolution, Rabinowitch had worked in Germany, Britain, and the United States. Humane, cosmopolitan, and a master of literary style, he provided some of the most prescient ideas in the report. "No lasting security against a national and international catastrophe can be achieved" through attempts to maintain U.S. atomic supremacy, he warned. "Peace based on uncontrolled . . . development" of atomic weapons "will only be an armistice" that will lead, eventually, to disaster. The conclusion was clear: the development of the atomic bomb "by some if not all, nations shows compellingly, because of its potential military consequences the necessity" for the immediate establishment of "an international administration with police powers which can effectively control at least the means of nucleonic warfare." [8]

By early 1945, the Met Lab was in ferment, not only over the question of a postwar nuclear arms race but over the prospective use of the atomic bomb. As the German war effort tottered toward collapse, it became clear that the Bomb, far from providing a deterrent to a Nazi atomic assault, might well become an offensive weapon against Japan. Szilard recalled that by the spring of 1945 he began to ask himself, "What is the purpose of continuing the development of the bomb, and how would the bomb be used if the war with Japan has not ended by the time we have the first bombs?" With the war nearly won, "it was not clear what we were working for." That spring, several "seminars" on the social and political implications of atomic energy were held among the restless younger scientists, who discussed international control, use of the Bomb against Japan, and the formation of a scientists' organization. A leading figure in these ventures was John A. Simpson, a 28-year-old physicist, although the somewhat older Szilard also emerged as a central intellectual force. In late April, James Franck, the distinguished refugee scientist who directed the chemistry section of the Met Lab, drew on Rabinowitch for a personal memorandum to higher authorities that stressed two of the themes now agitating the project scientists: the danger of a nuclear arms race and the necessity for international control of atomic energy. Although the memorandum apparently reached Bush and may even have influenced higher officials, Szilard had little patience with this procedure. "Men like Conant and Bush rendered the nation an immense service," he recalled, but "we were unable to accept them as our spokesmen." [9]

As he had in 1939, Szilard moved to alert the president of the United States to the impending danger. Once more, he turned to Einstein as an intermediary, although, he later claimed, "I was not free to tell him what the trouble was. All I could tell him was that . . . a serious mistake might be made unless the President intervenes." On March 25, 1945, Einstein gave Szilard an introductory letter to Roosevelt requesting that the president meet with the émigré physicist on a secret matter. Meanwhile, Szilard prepared his own memorandum, which warned that use of atomic bombs would "precipitate a race in the production of these devices between the United States and Russia," with the result that the United States would become increasingly vulnerable to attack and destruction. As alternatives, he recommended delaying use of the Bomb against Japan and working to establish nuclear arms controls. Roosevelt died before he could read the letter. But his successor, Harry Truman, suggested that Szilard meet with James F. Byrnes, an influential South Carolina politician and (unknown to Szilard) the new president's designee as secretary of state. Accompanied by Harold Urey (an important Bomb project scientist at Columbia) and Walter Bartky (the associate director of the Met Lab), Szilard talked with Byrnes on May 28 at his home in Spartanburg, South Carolina.[10]

Like the earlier encounter between Bohr and Churchill, this exchange between concerned scientist and power-wielding statesman merely highlighted their differences. When Szilard made his case against dropping the atomic bomb, Byrnes retorted that the use of the Bomb would help justify the enormous government expenditure on the Manhattan project and make the Russians "more manageable" in Eastern Europe. There would be no threat to an American nuclear monopoly for some time, Byrnes contended, for General Groves had assured him that the Soviet Union did not possess any uranium—a contention that Szilard contradicted but without much effect. Byrnes recalled that Szilard's "general demeanor and his desire to participate in policy making made an unfavorable impression on me." Indeed, he was glad that one of Groves's "intelligence agents had been following the three gentlemen." Szilard, in turn, later wrote that "I was rarely as depressed as when we left Byrnes' house. . . . I thought to myself how much better off the world might be had I been born in America and become influential in American politics, and had Byrnes been born in Hungary and studied physics. In all probability there would then have been no atomic bomb and no danger of an arms race between America and Russia." [11]

When Szilard returned to Chicago, the project was "in an uproar," as he recalled. Furious at the unauthorized approach to the White House and to Byrnes, General Groves grilled Bartky and denounced what he claimed was a breach of national security. To bring the issue back within official channels and, at the same time, fulfill a promise he had made earlier to James Franck, Compton appointed a Committee on Social and Political Implications of Atomic Energy, with Franck as chair.[12] Meeting in all-night sessions behind locked doors in early June 1945, the committee members—Franck, Szilard, Rabinowitch, Donald Hughes, James Nickson, Glenn Seaborg, and Joyce Stearns—felt their responsibility keenly. "By an accident of history," recalled Seaborg, "we were among a very few who were aware of a new, world-threatening peril, and we felt obligated to express our views." [13] On June 11, the Franck committee produced a report, largely written by Rabinowitch and influenced by Szilard,[14] that argued forcefully against combat use of the Bomb against Japan. "If the United States were to be the first to release this new weapon of indiscriminate destruction upon mankind," warned the committee, "she would sacrifice public support throughout the world, precipitate the race for armaments, and prejudice the possibility of reaching an international agreement on the future control of such weapons." As an alternative, the committee recommended revealing the Bomb to the world "by a demonstration in an appropriately selected uninhabited area." Rabinowitch later remarked that "we were all deeply moved by moral considerations" but "did not think that in the necessarily a-moral climate in which wartime decisions have to be made these would be effective." [15]

The fate of the Franck Report exemplifies the limited influence of the Bomb project dissidents upon U.S. government policy. Typically, Szilard wanted to send the report directly to the president. But Franck, committed to official channels, accompanied Compton to Washington with the intention of delivering it personally to Secretary Stimson. On June 12, Compton sought to arrange a meeting. Informed, untruthfully, by a Stimson aide that the secretary was out of the city, they settled for presenting the report to one of his assistants. Compton blunted its impact still further by attaching a cover letter criticizing the report for, among other things, not mentioning that the use of the Bomb would result in "the probable net saving of many lives." Meanwhile, recalled Rabinowitch, in Chicago "we waited for some reaction and we waited and waited and we had the feeling we could as well have dropped this report into Lake Michigan." [16] In retrospect, it seems unlikely that Stimson gave the report his careful attention, if he saw it at all, although his office did ask a Scientific Advisory Panel (composed of Compton, Ernest Lawrence, Oppenheimer, and Fermi) to evaluate the suggestion of a noncombat demonstration of the Bomb. On June 16, the panel responded that "no technical demonstration" was "likely to bring an end to the war." The panel's conclusion seems to have been the basis for Rabinowitch's later complaint that the Franck Report "was not supported by the leading scientists of the Manhattan project." [17] In any case, both the panel's assessment and the Franck Report seem to have been irrelevant to the policy adopted, for the U.S. government's decision to use atomic bombs on Japanese cities had been made more than two weeks before, on May 31.

The Government Decision

The decision to drop the Bomb on Japanese cities, without explicit warning, had been made, rather casually, by an innocuously named body, the Interim Committee. On April 25, 1945, Stimson had met with Truman and described to him what he called "the most terrible weapon ever known in human history." Impressed by the Bomb's devastating potential, Truman agreed to Stimson's proposal to appoint a special War Department committee to deal with the issue. This Interim Committee, which met several times that May, included Stimson, Bush, Conant, Byrnes, and U.S. Army Chief of Staff George Marshall.

Although Szilard later complained that many of the committee members "had a vested interest that the bomb be used," [18] this criticism, though valid, missed the larger issue that almost all these men believed employment of the Bomb in the war was, as Compton discovered at the crucial meeting, "a foregone conclusion." Stimson himself later wrote, "It was our common objective, throughout the war, to be the first to produce an atomic weapon and use it." Groves, too, later remarked, "There was never any question as to the use of the bomb . . . on the part of anyone who was in a top position on the project." Rather than focus on whether the Bomb *should* be used, the committee discussed *how* the Bomb would be used and how to deal with its ramifications in international affairs. At lunch one day, the issue of whether to use the Bomb finally came up, indirectly, when Compton asked if a nonmilitary demonstration of the Bomb could be arranged. No one thought it could be, and the committee soon turned to other matters. [19]

The ease with which the Interim Committee accepted combat use of the Bomb against Japan reflected the top priority that U.S. officials accorded military expediency in a world at war. Aerial bombardment of cities and the mass destruction of noncombatants, once considered hallmarks of fascist brutality, had become routine Allied practices by 1945. In this context, Stimson recalled, the atomic bomb seemed "as legitimate as any other of the deadly explosive weapons of modern war." [20] One leading scholar has written: "Nowhere in Stimson's meticulous diary . . . is there any suggestion of doubt or questioning of the assumption that the bomb should be used against Germany or Japan if the weapon was ready before the end of the war. . . . Bush and Conant never seriously questioned the assumption of the bomb's use either." These men were simply not concerned about "the moral implications of its military use." In later years, Stimson seemed surprised by the emergence of public controversy over the bombing of Hiroshima and Nagasaki. "The dominant objective was victory," he wrote. "If victory could be speeded by using the bomb, it should be used." Indeed, Stimson did report to Truman in wartime that employment of the Bomb probably would shorten the conflict, while Marshall championed its use to "shock" the Japanese into surrender. [21]

Furthermore, impressed by the new weapon at their disposal, top U.S. government officials were already dreaming of the power it would give them in postwar world affairs. Even Stimson, one of those most chastened by the dangers of a nuclear arms race, could not resist the allure of the Bomb as an instrument of postwar diplomacy. According to an entry in his diary, on May 14, 1945, he told Assistant Secretary of War John J. McCloy that "we have got to regain the lead" from the Soviet Union "and perhaps do it in a pretty rough and realistic way. . . . This was a place where we really held all the cards." Indeed, it was "a royal straight flush and we mustn't be a fool about the way we play it." The Soviet Union "can't get along without our help and industries and we have coming into action a weapon which will be unique." Byrnes, the incoming secretary of state, was equally enamored of the advantages the Bomb provided to the United States in the realm of international power politics. According to the president, Byrnes argued that "the bomb might well put us in a position to dictate our own terms at the end of the war." [22] As Rabinowitch had feared, among U.S. government leaders, moral concerns did not stand up well against considerations of military victory and postwar power.

Ironically, however, the military value of using the Bomb had dwindled considerably by mid-1945 and, for this reason, a small number of middle-echelon U.S. government officials did question U.S. policy. Arguing in late June that immediate use of the Bomb was unnecessary, McCloy suggested to Stimson and Truman that the Japanese should be explicitly warned that it would be used and, at the same time, offered retention of the emperor on a constitutional basis. But, according to McCloy, Byrnes opposed this idea "and wouldn't let it go." A similar position was taken by Under Secretary of the Navy Ralph Bard, a member of the Interim Committee, who initially favored the committee's decision but later changed his mind. On June 27, he sent a memo to Stimson, arguing that "Japan should have some preliminary warning," thus enabling her to surrender before the Bomb was employed. The following month, Bard remonstrated about the matter in an interview with Truman. Although the navy official cited his belief in the United States as "a great humanitarian nation," he was also strongly influenced by his knowledge that the war with Japan was virtually won.[23]

A group of U.S. military leaders also expressed doubts about the need to use the Bomb. Convinced that Japan would soon be defeated without a U.S. invasion of its home islands, top U.S. Navy officers—including Fleet Admiral Ernest King, Admiral William Leahy, and Admiral Chester Nimitz—were unenthusiastic about an atomic attack. Some top army officers also criticized U.S. bombing plans. General Dwight Eisenhower recalled that he told Stimson in July that he had "grave misgivings, first on the basis of my belief that Japan was already defeated and that dropping the bomb was completely unnecessary, and secondly because I thought that our country should avoid shocking world opinion." [24] Although some military officers may have resented the prospect of the Bomb eclipsing their role in securing Japan's defeat—just as, conversely, Groves had a vested interest in seeing the credit for that defeat given to the Manhattan project—the dubious necessity for its use provided a powerful argument against U.S. policy. Years later, Szilard contended that the Franck committee should have placed less emphasis on a nonmilitary demonstration of the Bomb and more on the lack of necessity for its use in combat.[25]

British and American Scientists

The most serious resistance to the use of the Bomb developed among scientists. In the spring of 1944, when Sir Henry Dale had approached Churchill on behalf of Bohr, he had been hoping for voluntary abstention from use of the Bomb in the interest of international control. After the collapse of the German war effort, doubts grew among British scientists about employing the Bomb in combat. Peierls recalled that he "felt very strongly that such a weapon should not be used lightly" and, therefore, favored "giving a demonstration, showing its power." At the same time, he recalled, "we felt the leaders were reasonable and intelligent people, and would make responsible decisions"—a belief he later conceded was "too optimistic." Having overheard Groves expatiating on the use of the Bomb to subdue the Russians and having conversed with Bohr on the dangers of the nuclear arms race, Joseph Rotblat felt a growing concern about his work at Los Alamos. In late 1944, when he learned that the German Bomb project had been a failure, he promptly resigned his position and returned to London to engage in nonmilitary work. Nevertheless, as foreigners, British scientists working in the United States felt inhibited from expressing dissenting opinions, a feeling reinforced by the British government's warning to stay clear of political issues in their host country. Indeed, after telling his supervisor of his plan to leave Los Alamos, Rotblat suddenly found himself accused by U.S. intelligence of being a Soviet spy. Other British scientists, like Oliphant, who denounced the atomic attack after it occurred, had no advance knowledge of U.S. bombing plans.[26]

American scientists and technicians, with greater knowledge and fewer inhibitions, became more active critics. At Los Alamos, the physicist Volney Wilson began to buttonhole project officials, asking if a noncombat demonstration of the Bomb could be arranged. Another project scientist, George Kistiakowsky, remembered that in the spring of 1945 the Los Alamos staff "began to discuss at great length . . . the issue of whether the bomb should be used militarily. . . . A great many people argued that Germany was near collapse, the Japanese were not able to wage the war . . . much longer and that therefore we should merely scare them by dropping the bomb in an uninhabited area." Other accounts, though, maintain that most scientists at Los Alamos were either too isolated or too busy to give much thought to the consequences of the Bomb,[27] although the testing of the weapon at Alamogordo in July 1945 produced a vague sense of dread.[28] Meanwhile, in New York City, Oswald Brewster, an engineer working on aspects of the project with the Kellex Corporation, dispatched a letter to the president warning of an atomic arms race and the potential for world destruction. In the letter, which was read by Stimson and, perhaps, by Truman, Brewster called upon U.S. leaders to stage a demonstration of the weapon and propose a plan for its international control.[29] As in the past, though, the Met Lab—whose work was largely completed and whose younger scientists were influenced by Szilard and Franck—remained the major locus of discontent. "In the summer of 1945," Rabinowitch recalled, "some of us walked the streets of Chicago vividly imagining the sky suddenly lit up by a giant fireball, the steel skeletons of skyscrapers bending into grotesque shapes." [30]

In early July 1945, Szilard launched a petition drive, directed to the president of the United States, against the atomic bombing of Japan. Surmising that the Bomb was about to be tested and convinced that "the cards in the Interim Committee were stacked" against restraint, he "thought that the time had come for the scientists to go on record against the use of the bomb . . . on moral grounds." When a strongly worded draft of the petition, dated July 4, garnered only a small number of signatures at the Met Lab, Szilard produced a more moderate draft on July 17. Using the Bomb "could not be justified," it argued, "unless the terms which will be imposed upon Japan have been made public in detail and Japan, knowing these terms, has refused to surrender." The petition also warned that "a nation which sets the precedent" of using atomic bombs "may have to bear the responsibility of opening the door to an era of devastation on an unimaginable scale." The petition was signed by 68 scientists at the Met Lab, mostly physicists and biologists.[31] Similarly, at the Oak Ridge Lab in Tennessee, Szilard's original draft made little headway, but a milder version was signed by 67 scientists, mostly physicists and chemists. The Oak Ridge petition urged that before the weapon was "used without restriction in the present conflict, its powers should be adequately described and demonstrated, and the Japanese nation should be given the opportunity to consider the consequences of further refusal to surrender." [32]

Angered by the petition drive, Manhattan project officials did their best to suppress it. The army was "violently opposed" to this effort, Szilard recalled, and "accused me of having violated secrecy by disclosing in the petition that such a thing as a bomb existed." In Chicago, Szilard and his associates, insisting on their constitutional right to petition, stood firm. At Oak Ridge, however, army pressure halted the petitioning process, despite the willingness of many additional scientists to sign. The petitioning never even began at Los Alamos, for Oppenheimer banned it from the outset. Furthermore, he sent Groves a copy of Szilard's explanatory letter and warned the general about "a further incident in a development which I know you have watched with interest." In this difficult situation, Szilard made a serious tactical error when, in deference to Franck, he agreed to send the Chicago and Oak Ridge petitions—addressed to the president—through official channels: from Compton, to Groves, to the president (then at Potsdam). Although Groves received the petitions on July 25, he kept them in his possession until August 1 and then passed them along to Stimson's office. There they remained until after the Bomb was dropped. One army officer, secretary to the Interim Committee, later explained that because the Bomb's use "had already been fully considered and settled by the proper authorities," it was decided that "no useful purpose would be served by transmitting . . . the petition" to the president. Although, in retrospect, it seems very unlikely that the scientists' protest would have altered the decision to drop the Bomb, it is significant that Manhattan project officials arranged matters so that President Truman remained unaware of it.[33]

Indeed, the Manhattan project director, General Groves, was implacably hostile to these critics of the Bomb. According to the minutes of the Interim Committee meeting of May 31, 1945, Groves complained "that the program has been plagued since its inception by the presence of certain scientists of doubtful discretion and uncertain loyalty," likely a reference to Szilard and his associates. In early July 1945, still seeking damaging information on Szilard, Groves wrote to Cherwell for details, noting that the dissident physicist "has not, in our opinion, evidenced wholehearted cooperation in the maintenance of security." To what must have been the general's chagrin, Cherwell replied that, though Szilard seemed concerned about "what sort of arrangements could be made to prevent an arms race," his "security" consciousness "was good to the point of brusqueness." Years later, Groves recalled telling Compton that he should "control his people a little bit more, particularly Szilard, who was continually a disruptive force." It was not so much what Szilard said, the general contended, "but his influence on others that made this difficult." Filled with self-pity, Groves considered himself besieged, surrounded by scientists who failed to appreciate him. "One of the big complaints made about me after the war was that scientists didn't like me," he told an interviewer decades later. "Who cares whether they liked you or not?" He added bitterly: "Nobody knew anything; remember that. Nobody knew anything at that time." Asked if he and the scientists had "started with the same base," Groves retorted contemptuously: "No, they had a little advantage. They could scatter some words around but they really didn't have any answers."[34]

The extent to which the dissenters' views represented those of most Bomb project scientists remains impossible to determine. With the exception of the

Chicago Met Lab, where Szilard's influence was substantial, there was little discussion at Manhattan project sites about the social and political implications of the Bomb. U.S. Army control of the project, the focus on narrow technical questions, and the determination of scientists themselves to maintain secrecy in wartime all served to inhibit debate on broader issues. Victor Weisskopf later contended that, had he known of the Franck Report at the time, he "certainly" would have supported it.[35] Furthermore, as circumstances and perceptions shifted, scientists occasionally altered their opinions. Teller, who refused to circulate Szilard's petition at Los Alamos, later regretted it.[36] Kistiakowsky, too, went from opponent, to supporter, to opponent of the Bomb's use, largely because of his changing view of Japan's readiness to surrender. Moreover, although Szilard mobilized only a minority of the scientists behind his petition, it is also true that he did so in the face of substantial interference from project officials and that organized opposition to the Szilard petition was virtually nonexistent among scientists. The only "counterpetition" mentioned by Compton as evidence for his later contention that most atomic scientists supported U.S. policy contained only two signatures.[37]

"In case somebody got to the White House with a claim that all scientists were against using the bomb," Groves recalled, he ordered Compton to take a poll of scientists at the Met Lab. According to Compton, the results of the July 12 poll were very reassuring, for the 150 respondents expressed "the same points of view" as the Interim Committee. But, in fact, the poll left much to be desired, both as an accurate barometer of scientific opinion and as a ringing endorsement of U.S. policy. Scientists later complained that the few minutes given them to respond were inadequate for them to think through an issue of such gravity and that the choices were unclear. The five options and the responses to them were as follows: (1) "most effective" military use (15 percent); (2) "a military demonstration in Japan to be followed by renewed opportunity for surrender before full use" (46 percent); (3) an "experimental demonstration" in the United States before Japanese representatives followed by an "opportunity for surrender before full use" (26 percent); (4) "an experimental demonstration" without "military use" (11 percent); and (5) "refrain from using them in this war" (2 percent). The choice of a plurality was "a military demonstration," but if this did not mean "full use" or the "most effective" military use, what did it mean? Some scientists, at least, assumed that it meant a less bellicose policy. Furthermore, even if all scientists who chose this option favored U.S. policy (i.e., atomic bombing of Japan's cities without warning), it is also clear that a substantial group (39 percent) did not.[38]

Of course, beyond a relatively small group of government leaders, military officers, and Bomb project scientists, the vast majority of people—including almost all persons employed by the Manhattan project—knew nothing of the atomic bomb during the war. Daring as some scientists were in challenging the direction of U.S. atomic policy, they did not choose to violate wartime secrecy and bring the issue to the public. But the idea crossed some minds. Years later, Rabinowitch wrote to a friend that, in 1945, he considered "revealing the coming of the atom bomb" to a prominent journalist such as Dorothy Thompson "so that, if a crime like the bombing of Hiroshima and Nagasaki were to be carried out in the name of the American people, these people would have at least known and not disapproved of it." His experience in the postwar era convinced him that "the vast majority of the American people would have enthusiastically favored the use of the bomb in Japan." Even so, he concluded, "they should have been given the opportunity to accept the responsibility for mass murder on an unprecedented scale—of which they now stand guilty before history without having known anything about it beforehand." [39]

"The Delicate Task of the Statesmen"

By late July 1945, control over the atomic bomb lay, in differing degrees, in the hands of the three Allied leaders meeting at Potsdam—Truman, Churchill, and Stalin—and none showed the least hesitation in using it against Japan. After a full description of the successful bomb test reached Truman and Churchill on July 18, they met to discuss the future. "Fair and bright indeed it seemed," Churchill recalled, with "the end of the whole war in one or two violent shocks." The prime minister observed: "There was never a moment's discussion as to whether the atomic bomb should be used or not." In fact, "the decision whether or not to use the atomic bomb to compel the surrender of Japan was never even an issue." [40] Although Truman appears to have been surprisingly ignorant about how the Bomb would be used,[41] his statements on numerous occasions confirm Churchill's account of an unwavering readiness to use it. "I regarded the bomb as a military weapon and never had any doubt that it should be used," he wrote in his memoirs. In a television interview taped in 1957, he declared: "I had no qualms about using it because a weapon of war is a destructive weapon. . . . When you have the weapon that will win the war, you'd be foolish if you didn't use it." [42] Stalin received a brief opportunity to discuss the Bomb with his professed allies on July 24, when, according to the president's account, he "casually mentioned to Stalin that we had a new weapon of unusual destructive force." Truman recalled that "the Russian Premier showed no special interest. All he said was that he was glad to hear it and hoped we would make 'good use of it against the Japanese.' " [43]

This ready acceptance of the Bomb's use in wartime was accompanied by exhilarating visions of postwar national power. Churchill was "completely carried away" by news of the successful U.S. bomb test, recalled Lord Alanbrooke, chief of the Imperial General Staff. "He . . . painted a wonderful picture of himself as the sole possessor of these bombs and capable of dumping them where he wished, thus all-powerful and capable of dictating to Stalin." Churchill's own published acount of the event, though more subdued, nonetheless attests to his newfound sense of national strength. With this "miracle of deliverance," he wrote, "we should not need the Russians. . . . We had no need to ask favours of them. . . . We seemed suddenly to have become possessed of . . . a far happier prospect in Europe." [44] Truman, too, was dazzled by the vistas opened up by the Bomb. "We were now in possession of a weapon that would not only revolutionize war," he wrote, "but could alter the course of history and civilization." Stimson observed that the president, after learning of the successful bomb test, "was tremendously pepped up by it and spoke to me of it again and again." Churchill noted that when Truman arrived at the Allied leaders' meeting, "after having read this report, he was a changed man. He told the Russians just where they got on and off and generally bossed the whole meeting." On July 25, Truman confided to his Potsdam diary: "It is certainly a good thing for the world that Hitler's crowd or Stalin's did not discover this atomic bomb. It seems to be the most terrible thing ever discovered, but it can be made the most useful." [45]

If Stalin was less exhilarated than frightened by the success of the Anglo-American Bomb project, he had a similar remedy at hand for Russia's international problems. When Truman informed him obliquely of the Alamogordo test, "I was sure that he had no idea of the significance of what he was being told," Churchill later remarked; "if he had had the slightest idea of the revolution in world affairs which was in progress his reactions would have been obvious." The British leader, however, totally misconstrued the meaning of the interchange, for Stalin understood only too well what was transpiring. Thanks to Soviet espionage, the Russian leader had known of the Manhattan project since 1942 and may have learned of the successful Bomb test before Truman raised the subject with him on July 24. In any case, Truman's remarks convinced Stalin to accelerate the pace of the Soviet Bomb project. "They simply want to raise the price," he complained to Marshal Georgi Zhukov and Foreign Minister V. M. Molotov. "We've got to work on Kurchatov and hurry things up." [46]

As the leaders of the Big Three laid plans for the future, the atomic bombing of Japan went forward on schedule. On the morning of August 6, a single American plane, flying unopposed over Hiroshima, loosed its atomic bomb over the city's crowded streets. In the ensuing blast and firestorm, perhaps

140,000 people were killed, 95 percent of them civilians. Although most were Japanese, some were Korean conscript laborers and a few were American prisoners of war. Among those who survived, countless people received hideous burns or fatal radiation poisoning. Three days later, at 1:00 A.M., Soviet armies entered what was left of the war in the Far East, shattering the Japanese government's hope for Soviet aid in securing a peace settlement with the United States and Great Britain and rendering the Japanese military position even more untenable. Later that same day, the U.S. government loosed its second atomic bomb over Nagasaki, killing an additional 70,000 people and wounding many others.[47] On August 10, the Japanese government, which had desperately sought a peace settlement since the spring of 1945 but had balked at the Allied demand for unconditional surrender, offered to surrender if the emperor and throne were spared. When the U.S. government implicitly accepted this offer, the war came to an end.[48]

Traditional Thinking and New Approaches

In the final years of World War II, a significant difference of opinion developed between a growing number of atomic scientists and most government officials. Viewing the Bomb as no more than a wartime deterrent, a substantial group of scientists opposed its unrestricted military use against Japan. Furthermore, given the Bomb's development, many of the scientists considered it futile to try to preserve national security on a long-range basis through weapons of war. Indeed, like Bohr and Szilard, they contended that in the context of competing nations, the Bomb would eventually undermine national security and bring the world to ruin. Convinced that traditional ways of thinking about international affairs would lead ultimately to a global holocaust, they argued forcefully for an agreement among the great powers to head off a postwar nuclear arms race. By contrast, national leaders—and particularly those at the apex of power— placed the atomic bomb within a framework of more traditional thinking about international relations. In their eyes, the Bomb was a legitimate weapon of war and a valuable instrument of postwar diplomacy. Although well aware of its unprecedented destructive power, they viewed its awesome might as beneficial, provided that the weapon remained in their hands rather than in those of their foes. In this fashion, they believed, the Bomb could be used to make other nations less threatening and to secure their own goals in world affairs.

From the moment of its birth, then, the atomic bomb—like earlier technological innovations in weaponry—pushed people in two different directions. To the official guardians of national security and to others who thought in traditional terms, it offered a splendid opportunity to bolster national military strength and to humble competing nations. To a growing number of others, and particularly to those farther from the levers of power, the Bomb represented a perilous lurch toward annihilation. Undergirding both perspectives lay the dangers inherent in violent conflicts among nations. Although national leaders were too structurally locked into those conflicts to resist the pull toward enhancing national military strength, others were beginning to wonder if, in an age of atomic weapons, the obsession with national military strength was not the siren song of global destruction.

The Nonaligned Movement, 1945-51

From the Ashes

World Peace Activism and the Movement in Japan

> We, the survivors, have come together . . . to
> contribute . . . to the peace of the world.
>
> Shinzo Hamai, 1948

Following the atomic bombing of Hiroshima and Nagasaki, a movement against the Bomb rapidly took shape in dozens of countries throughout the world. Alerted to the existence of the Bomb and to its catastrophic effects, thousands of people rallied behind a loose, popular crusade to save humanity from nuclear destruction. At its center stood those pacifist groups and constituencies that had survived World War II, as well as newer, rapidly growing organizations among atomic scientists and world government proponents. This movement argued that nations should end the traditional practice of securing their interests by marshaling superior military might—a practice that, with the advent of the Bomb, seemed fraught with new and terrible dangers. At other times, the campaign focused more narrowly on the need to eliminate or control nuclear weapons. In either case, this grass-roots struggle against the Bomb championed an alternative that, for a time, had considerable popular appeal: One World.

The emergence of a citizens' movement against the Bomb was particularly evident in postwar Japan. Horrified by the world war and by the atomic holocaust that had concluded it, the Japanese brought a new and powerful perspective to the nuclear disarmament issue. Millions of Japanese citizens became staunch critics of military force and, particularly, of nuclear weapons. Nevertheless, Japanese resistance to the Bomb remained somewhat muted during these years, for the American occupation of Japan placed severe limits on the development of an effective nationwide and international campaign. For some time, Japanese activists could bring the nuclear issue to world attention only with the assistance of another casualty of World War II: the world peace movement.

The World Peace Movement in 1945

World War II not only reshaped the landscape of international politics but seriously affected the world peace movement. Since the early nineteenth century, citizens' movements for peace, largely located in Europe and the United States, had agitated for alternatives to the policies of national aggrandizement and military buildup that had so often led to international conflict and war. In the twentieth century, particularly, these peace movements had started to develop a mass base, a trend that accelerated after the carnage of World War I produced a new wave of popular disillusionment with militarism.[1] World War II, however, revived the faith of many persons in armed force as the only effective guarantor of national security. Thus, although the war catapulted some peace organizations into new positions of influence, it had a devastating effect on most of them. Pacifist groups—those that refused to sanction any military activity— were especially hard hit by the conflict and underwent significant declines in membership and credibility.

The Pacifists

Of the three international pacifist organizations functioning at the end of World War II, the largest was probably the War Resisters' International (WRI). Founded in 1921 as Paco (Esperanto for "peace"), the WRI acquired its more enduring name two years later. In an effort to forestall another world conflagration, it sought to organize war resisters in all nations who would subscribe to the statement "War is a crime against humanity. We therefore are determined not to support any kind of war and to strive for the removal of all causes of war." Several hundred thousand persons—most of them socialists, anarchists, or other secular objectors to war—joined the organization, and at the outset of World War II, the WRI claimed 54 affiliated sections in 24 countries. The beginning of the war, however, led to dramatic losses and an almost complete disruption of contacts. In Allied nations, many WRI members—almost invariably staunch antifascists—became reluctant converts to the war effort. When resolute in their pacifist convictions, they were imprisoned by the thousands as conscientious objectors or increasingly isolated among their fellow citizens. In German-occupied Europe, the Nazis sent large numbers of WRI leaders and activists to prisons, to concentration camps, or to the scaffold.[2]

Although the WRI emerged from the war in an enfeebled condition, it managed to persevere and to revive. In 1946, at its first international conference since 1938, the WRI reaffirmed its credo, elected new leaders, laid plans for the protection of conscientious objectors, sent greetings to Mahatma Gandhi in India, and encouraged relief work in Europe. At the request of the American affiliate, the WRI conference also took up the issue of the international control of atomic energy.[3]

The religious counterpart to the War Resisters' International was the pacifist International Fellowship of Reconciliation (International FOR). It traced its roots to a dramatic farewell, on the eve of World War I, between two Christian pacifists, the English Quaker Henry Hodgkin and the German chaplain Friedrich Siegmund-Schültze. During the war, small FOR groups emerged in England, the United States, Holland, and Sweden, and, in the war's aftermath, the International FOR was launched at an October 1919 international conference in Holland. By rejecting violence and taking the way of Jesus, noted a conference report, "we too will be reconcilers and revolutionaries." Drawn for the most part from the Protestant clergy and laity, the FOR grew thereafter primarily in Europe, North America, and Japan.[4] Like the WRI, the FOR was devastated by World War II. It lost followers and credibility in Allied nations and its members suffered concentration camps, gas chambers, or imprisonment in those controlled by the fascist powers. Amid the ashes, however, it survived.[5]

The end of the war brought possibilities of renewal for the FOR. As might be expected, when, in March 1946, the International FOR Council met for the first time since the 1930s, the gathering was subdued. Siegmund-Schültze— arrested 27 times during World War I and in exile from his homeland during World War II—reported on the terrible things done in Germany and the general demoralization of European civilization. In the course of the proceedings, "the challenge to Christian pacifism" in a world "threatened by the atom bomb" provided one of the three major issues addressed. Although the International FOR—which claimed 30,000 members in fifteen countries—focused much of its energy at this time upon alleviating hunger and suffering in a devastated world, it continued its religious critique of warfare and, increasingly, championed nuclear disarmament.[6]

The third pacifist international, the Women's International League for Peace and Freedom (WILPF), grew out of an International Congress of Women in 1915 at the Hague. Presided over by Jane Addams of the United States and drawing together a thousand participants from twelve countries concerned about the carnage of World War I, the congress called for continuous mediation of the conflict by neutral nations and dispatched delegations to meet with government leaders. In May 1919, a second international congress, at Zurich, attracted women from sixteen nations who organized the WILPF, with headquarters at Geneva. Largely (but not formally) pacifist, the WILPF was active in a broad array of peace and social reform ventures in the interwar years and, at its height, could claim some 50,000 members in 40 countries. World War II, though, came as a heavy blow. Some WILPF members grew demoralized; others became active—albeit usually nonviolent—members of antifascist resistance movements. Meanwhile, WILPF leaders perished in fascist prisons, in extermination camps, or in exile, and WILPF sections in some European nations virtually disappeared.[7]

Despite its seriously weakened condition, however, the WILPF also survived the war and, in ensuing years, raised the demand for nuclear disarmament. In August 1946, when the WILPF held its first international conference since 1939, only thirteen sections sent delegates. Moreover, considerable division existed on national lines, particularly over the treatment of fascist nations, on economic and ideological issues, and on the appropriate attitude toward the Soviet Union. In these difficult circumstances, one representative, from the Netherlands, proposed that the organization be dissolved. Nevertheless, the gathering resolved to continue the WILPF, called upon world leaders to move toward world peace through cooperative action in a variety of areas (including atomic energy), and elected a new president—Emily Greene Balch, an American who received the Nobel Peace Prize later that year.[8]

In addition to the three pacifist internationals—indeed, to some extent overlapping with them—there existed, at the end of World War II, small pacifist groupings within the world's major religions. Preeminent among them were the Historic Peace Churches that had developed out of the Protestant Reformation: the Society of Friends (better known as Quakers), the Society of the Brethren, and the Mennonites. Although time and assimilation had undermined their corporate peace testimony and had left many of their followers uninvolved with peace activism, some members maintained the traditional pacifist "witness" of these denominations.[9] Most other Protestant denominations, as well as Jewish ones, had been strongly influenced by antiwar thinking after World War I. And although they were gradually drawn into support of their contending nations with the approach of World War II, they continued to harbor tiny pacifist minorities.[10] The Catholic church had officially renounced pacifism many centuries before, replacing it with a more accommodating "just war" doctrine. Even so, pacifism secured a small foothold in Catholic church circles through the activities of groups like America's Catholic Worker movement.[11] Furthermore, within Buddhism, Hinduism, and, to a lesser extent, Islam, the early pacifist concerns of these faiths continued to influence some believers.[12]

The situation was much the same in Labor, Social Democratic, and Socialist parties. Until the mid-1930s, pacifism had made considerable headway among democratic socialists. But the determination of these parties to resist fascism—by force, if necessary—had generally turned them into strong proponents of collective security and, eventually, war. Consequently, by 1945, as in the major religions, pacifism within democratic socialist ranks had been reduced to the faith of a tiny minority.[13]

In some ways, of course, World War II strengthened antiwar tendencies by illustrating the terrible consequences of military approaches to world problems. Trapped by shifting battle fronts, bombarded mercilessly from the skies, and brutally herded into concentration camps, some 60 million people, mostly civilians, were killed and countless others were crippled or otherwise injured. At the end of the war, numerous nations, victors and vanquished, lay in smoldering ruins, their economies shattered, their citizens reduced to beggary and starvation. Never before had the horrors of war been displayed so graphically and on such a worldwide scale.[14] Furthermore, the disastrous consequences of fascist misrule left many citizens of the former Axis nations disillusioned with flag-waving and militarism. At the beginning of 1946, one of the WILPF's international co-chairs called attention to "a really strong demand for our work in the anti-fascist circles in Germany."[15]

Overall, however, World War II weakened organized pacifism as a political alternative to war. Not only had the war badly mauled pacifist groups, but the movement's inability to stop fascist aggression or to halt the war itself had shattered its confidence and left it, in many instances, discredited and isolated from broader public currents. According to the same WILPF leader, its national sections in the former antifascist nations were experiencing "tiredness, disillusionment, discouragement," and "a sense of futility." On September 29, 1945, when representatives of the WRI, the International FOR, the Friends Peace Committee, and other pacifist groups met in England to consider the future, they readily acknowledged that the pacifist movement was in disarray in many nations. Furthermore, serious differences over strategy emerged at the meeting. According to *Peace News*, the major British pacifist journal, some participants "stressed the fact that the time is short: some form of 'pacifist sabotage' and speedy political awakening is necessary if further destruction is to be avoided." By contrast, others argued "that pacifists should not be concerned about the time factor, even in the face of the atomic bomb." Instead, "they should continue to work for a better relationship between nations and an awakening of the human spirit." There was no resolution of the issue or any sign that most Britons cared or even noticed.[16]

The Scientists

If World War II served to weaken organized pacifism, it had quite a different effect on the political influence of scientists. The scientific community had always been international in character but had usually been apolitical in nature.

During the 1930s, this apolitical norm began to change as left-wing currents propelled some scientists toward broader social concerns. The development of the British Social Relations in Science movement and the American Association of Scientific Workers exemplified this shift. World War II accelerated the politicization of the scientific community, for it not only demonstrated the interlocking nature of science and politics but pulled large numbers of scientists into nuclear fission research and thus into the struggle over the Bomb. Indeed, the networks formed among scientists during their wartime research and protest activities served as the basis for the postwar atomic scientists' movement.[17] Furthermore, unlike organized pacifism, which suffered in many Allied nations from the stigma of having opposed a war that most citizens supported, the scientists benefited from the popular impression that they had made an invaluable contribution to winning it. At the least, they possessed a special expertise in the area of atomic weaponry that other citizens—including most political leaders—lacked.[18]

The World Government Movement

The approach of World War II also substantially strengthened the movement for world government. Dating back at least to the Middle Ages, the idea of transferring sovereignty from warring nation-states to a global organization had inspired numerous thinkers, writers, and activists. In the aftermath of the unprecedented destruction wrought by the world wars, even many national policymakers proved willing to promote the development of the League of Nations and, later, the United Nations. But the popular demand to move beyond such loose associations of sovereign states to the creation of a genuine world authority grew in the 1930s. In 1933, H. G. Wells published one of the pioneering works of the world government movement, *The Shape of Things to Come*, and it inspired the formation of small "Wellsian societies" in various parts of the world. Although these world government groupings remained largely inactive and short-lived, in 1937 Rosika Schwimmer (a Hungarian pacifist, feminist, and journalist) and Lola Maverick Lloyd (the activist wife of a wealthy American publisher) founded a more durable movement in the United States: the Campaign for World Government. The following year, responding to the Munich crisis, a group of Britons organized Federal Union. Although favoring a "federation of free peoples," Federal Union viewed this as "the first step toward ultimate world government." [19] A similar idea animated *Union Now*, a federalist tract published by *New York Times* correspondent Clarence Streit in 1939 that sold more than 300,000 copies in the next decade.[20]

When the chaos and destruction of World War II brought the international system to the point of collapse, the idea of world government acquired considerable momentum. An avalanche of books and pamphlets addressed the subject, among them *One World* (1943), a best-seller by Wendell Willkie, the former Republican candidate for president of the United States. Serialized or printed in an abbreviated version in more than 100 newspapers in the United States and Canada, *One World* also sold two million copies in book form within two years of its publication. Rejecting "narrow nationalism" and "international imperialism," *One World* contended that "there can be no peace for any part of the world unless the foundations of peace are made secure throughout all parts of the world." Even more explicit about the necessity for world government was *The Anatomy of Peace*, a mordant account of the pathology of nations written by Emery Reves, a Hungarian journalist who had taken refuge from fascism in the United States. Published in June 1945 and on America's best-seller lists for the next six months, *The Anatomy of Peace* became the bible of the world government movement. By 1950, it had appeared in 20 languages and in 24 countries.[21]

At the same time, the world government movement began to burgeon dramatically. Meeting in mid-1944 in occupied Europe, representatives from resistance movements in France, Italy, the Netherlands, Denmark, Norway, Yugoslavia, Czechoslovakia, Poland, and Germany resolved that nations should "give up the absolute sovereignty of the State and unite in a single federal organization." Through a public petition, nearly a thousand prominent citizens of Brazil, Canada, Chile, China, Colombia, England, Mexico, Peru, and the United States also spoke out for world government. New organizations—including Streit's own Federal Union, Inc.—sprang up to preach the message of world peace through world federation. Their size and influence grew rapidly, particularly after the public learned that the final act of the war was also the most ominous: the unleashing of the atomic bomb.[22]

The Japanese People and Nuclear Weapons

Despite Japan's shocking introduction to the atomic era, the Japanese people generally expressed less criticism of the Bomb than of warfare during the late 1940s. This stance resulted, in part, from a widespread sense that they had been deceived by Japan's militarist leaders, whom they now blamed for Japan's terrible wartime suffering and destruction. Mothers of soldiers asked angrily, "For what purpose did I . . . let my son die?" Others were horrified by the devastating aerial bombardment of Japan's cities in the months before the atomic bombings or felt a sense of guilt for having succumbed to the Japanese government's war propaganda. Consequently, when an early poll asked about the atomic bombings, only 19 percent of Japanese respondents blamed the Americans for the act; 35 percent said the bombings were Japan's own fault, while another 29 percent replied that neither side was responsible, for they were the inevitable consequence of war.[23] Although American occupation officials appear to have been responsible for writing Article 9 of Japan's postwar constitution, which banned war and the maintenance of armed forces,[24] the provision was very popular with the Japanese people, most of whom turned resoundingly against militarism and embraced the cause of peace. As Robert Lifton has noted, in Japan, "peace came to symbolize . . . a new way for the future. It became a symbol for life." [25]

The relative absence of public discussion of nuclear weapons in Japan also reflected the censorship policy of U.S. occupation authorities, who governed Japan until 1952. Shortly after the beginning of the occupation, American officials adopted a press code that banned newspapers, magazines, or other print media from publishing anything that "might invite mistrust or resentment" of the occupation forces. This policy entailed the censorship of most Japanese material dealing with the Bomb, for U.S. officials feared that the publication of such material might tarnish the reputation of the United States both in Japan and in other nations. Furthermore, occupation authorities ordered the 8,734 staff members of their Civil Censorship Department to ban any mention of the censorship policy itself. Although inconsistent and waning during the final years of the occupation, U.S. censorship nevertheless had a significant impact on Japanese perceptions of nuclear weapons.[26]

Until August 29, 1949, when the Soviet Union exploded its first atomic bomb, this U.S. censorship policy resulted in a near blackout of unfavorable Japanese newspaper coverage of nuclear weapons. In September 1945, occupation authorities briefly suspended the operations of both Domei (the Japanese press agency) and the *Asahi Shimbun* (one of the nation's largest, most prestigious newspapers) for stories criticizing nuclear weapons, and thereafter, the Japanese press tamely submitted to the occupation's program of prepublication censorship. Stories on the Bomb or the Japanese peace movement were a favorite target of the censors, and only those news articles that portrayed the weapon as shortening the war or leading to peace were printed. Insisting on favorable coverage of U.S. nuclear weapons, American occupation authorities saw to it that Japanese newspaper readers received an upbeat appraisal of the Bomb and its effects. Thus, when a story reported that the U.S. Atomic Bomb Casualty Commission had concluded that sterility and altered genetic patterns might result from the bombing of Hiroshima, the censors suppressed it. By contrast, the censors routinely passed articles claiming (falsely) that the survivors of the Hiroshima and Nagasaki bombings enjoyed good health and had had their scars successfully removed through surgery.[27]

The occupation authorities also censored literature and the arts. After spending three nights in Hiroshima surrounded by disfigured bodies and moaning survivors of the atomic bombing, the writer Yoko Ota fled to the countryside, where she drafted her powerful novel *City of Corpses*. Although completed in November 1945, it could not be published until three years later, and then only in expurgated form. Another work on the atomic bomb, Tamiki Hara's *Summer Flower*, was also cut substantially before it was published in June 1947. Dr. Takashi Nagai, a physician from Nagasaki, completed his *Bells of Nagasaki* in 1946 but was barred from publishing it until he included material compiled by the U.S. intelligence division on Japanese atrocities in Manila. The book appeared in this Americanized form in 1949, two years before Nagai's death by radiation poisoning. Another censorship incident involved two artists, Iri Maruki and Toshiko Takamatsu, who had entered Hiroshima three days after the bombing and had begun drawings of the disastrous scene. In August 1950, a peace group published the first edition of their drawings, *Atomic Explosion*. But the book was seized subsequently by U.S. occupation officials, who suppressed further editions.[28]

Some writers on the Bomb proved more successful at outwitting the U.S. authorities. Determined to defy the censors, Shoda Shinoe, a survivor of the Hiroshima bombing, managed the feat with the assistance of a clerk at the Hiroshima prison. She brought him her volume of poems, entitled *Sange*, and he produced 150 copies of the work on his mimeograph machine. Thereafter, she secretly distributed them to survivors of the bombing. John Hersey's powerful novel, *Hiroshima*, also faced difficulties. When the *Nippon Times* requested permission to publish it in 1946, the censorship division objected that the book might create the impression that American use of the atomic bomb had been "unduly cruel." Only in 1949, after a public protest by the Authors' League of America, did the U.S. authorities relent and permit the publication of *Hiroshima* in Japan. Replying to a letter from the league's president, occupation commander Douglas MacArthur commented testily that those who claimed that censorship existed in Japan were engaged in "a maliciously false propaganda campaign."[29]

U.S. censorship of Bomb-related material operated in other areas of Japanese life as well. School textbooks, authorized by government authorities, rarely discussed the atomic bombings, and the occupation authorities placed sharp restrictions on medical and scientific research or publication dealing with bombing casualties. Indeed, only after the end of the occupation could Japanese scientific societies freely and independently conduct investigations of Bomb-related injuries. The extent to which U.S. occupation authorities went to control the flow of information on nuclear weapons is illustrated by their treatment of a lengthy documentary film, *The Effects of the Atomic Bombs on Hiroshima and Nagasaki*. Begun in the immediate aftermath of the bombing by the Japan Film Corporation under scientific direction, the film was quickly halted by American officials. Although U.S. authorities later reversed themselves and ordered its completion for the U.S. Strategic Bombing Survey, the film, when finished, was promptly impounded by the U.S. Army and shipped to the United States. There it remained (with the exception of ten reels hidden by determined Japanese cameramen) until 1967, when pressure from the Japanese public finally secured the release of what had by then become known as the "phantom film." Naturally, such policies limited the extent to which the Japanese people could reflect upon the meaning of nuclear weapons in the early postwar era. Even in Hiroshima, there was so little public discussion of the Bomb that, for the first ten years after it was dropped, the major newspaper did not possess movable type for the words "atomic bomb" or "radioactivity." [30]

The Role of the *Hibakusha*

Nevertheless, although limited by U.S. occupation policy, criticism of the Bomb did emerge in Japan during these years, particularly among the *hibakusha* (atomic bomb–affected persons) of Hiroshima and Nagasaki. [31] Immersed in death and suffering, they worked slowly and painfully to give meaning to their terrible experience. In Hiroshima, intellectuals gathered for poetry readings in memory of the dead and, in March 1946, launched *Chugoku Culture*, a magazine whose first issue was devoted to the effects of the atomic bombing. [32] On August 6, 1946, the Hiroshima branch of the Japanese Association of Religious Organizations sponsored a Memorial Day in Hiroshima, with ceremonies presided over by Shinto, Buddhist, and Christian clergy. This event added impetus to the establishment of the Hiroshima Peace Association, which brought together some 350 religious and civic groups that sponsored a citywide Peace Festival in 1947. At the ceremonies, which drew 10,000 people to Hiroshima's public park, a message was read from General MacArthur, who stressed that the development of the atomic bomb had completely changed war and, indeed, threatened the destruction of the human race. Sensitive to the reaction of occupation authorities, Hiroshima's new mayor, Shinzo Hamai, did not criticize the atomic bombing of Japan during the ceremonies. Instead, he organized prayers against the future employment of nuclear weapons and issued a Peace Declaration, appealing to the world to rid itself of war. By 1948, peace demonstrations memorializing the atomic bombings had become regular events in Hiroshima and in Nagasaki, where a movement against the Bomb was also developing. [33]

Indeed, the two ruined cities, as the first victims of nuclear war, became powerful symbols of world peace. In early 1948, the Reverend Kiyoshi Tanimoto, a Methodist minister portrayed in Hersey's *Hiroshima*, began a campaign to have nations around the world set aside August 6 as World Peace Day. Twenty nations responded to the call, holding prayer meetings and other public gatherings on August 6. Encouraged by the international ground swell of support, Mayor Hamai delivered a moving address on August 6, 1948, to 15,000 people at the new Hiroshima Memorial Tower of Peace and dispatched it to 160 cities in 68 nations. "A war of any kind is, at its best, inhuman and destructive by nature, only disgracing humanity," he declared. "Anything worthy of the peace of the world will come only out of" an "awakening against retaliation principles" and a "movement of laying down arms at any cost." Pointing to Japan's "peace constitution," he declared that if the same effort that went into creating atomic bombs "were applied to the promotion and preservation of peace, the realization of the dream of worldwide peace would not be impossible at all." And if peace were attained, "these lives which were sacrificed on August 6, 1945," would "not have been in vain." [34]

The idea that Hiroshima's terrible suffering could be redeemed through an end to war served as a powerful motivation for the survivors of the atomic bombing. Like Tanimoto, Hamai had been caught in the atomic attack but had miraculously survived. Throughout that day and those that followed, as he worked desperately to distribute food to other survivors, he had been surrounded by scenes of horror: burned and dying infants; corpses with their heads immersed in water they had tried to drink; parents digging frantically through ruins for the bodies of their children. As the first publicly elected mayor of Hiroshima, Hamai proved an unwavering opponent of nuclear weapons and war. Another Hiroshima resident who emerged unscathed from the atomic attack recalled: "I asked myself the question: 'Why was I saved?'" Although living, "I did not know why. . . . I thought there must be some mission for which I had survived." He, too, went on to become a leading peace activist in the city. Responding to the rising pacifist sentiment, the Japanese Diet voted in May 1949 to make Hiroshima a Peace Memorial City, a proposition approved in a referendum that July by 91 percent of Hiroshima's voters. The law was formally promulgated on August 6, when 30,000 people in Hiroshima and many others around the world gathered for what was now the annual observance of World Peace Day. [35]

As Hiroshima assumed a symbolic peace role, its peace leaders forged close ties with their American sympathizers. Sponsored by the Board of Missions of the Methodist church, Tanimoto toured the United States during a substantial part of 1948 and 1949, garnering support from religious and pacifist gatherings for a Hiroshima peace center. Thanks to the efforts of Norman Cousins (editor of the *Saturday Review of Literature*), Pearl Buck (novelist), John Hersey, and others, the center was established in New York City in March 1949; the following year, it opened in Hiroshima, where it arranged for the "moral adoption" of atomic bomb orphans by Americans and undertook welfare services for other victims of the atomic attack. Cousins himself visited Japan in 1949 for the August 6 memorial ceremony and returned with a Hiroshima Peace Petition, signed by 110,000 residents of the city. Although President Truman refused to accept the petition, Tanimoto eventually presented it to U.N. General Assembly president Carlos Romulo. Cousins also brought a message from Mayor Hamai to the people of the United States, thanking "those Americans who have helped us to bring a dead city back to life." Conceding that he did not consider it proper "to tell Americans what ought to be done," Hamai contended that it was appropriate "to tell them about what will happen to the world's cities if something is not done to stop war." Indeed, "the people of Hiroshima ask nothing of the world except that we be allowed to offer ourselves as an exhibit for peace. We ask only that enough peoples know what happened here . . . and that they work hard to see that it never happens anywhere again." [36]

Other Advocates of Peace and Nuclear Disarmament

Japan's traditional pacifist organizations underwent a revival in the postwar era and helped move the base for disarmament activism beyond the *hibakusha*. Composed largely of Christians and socialists, Japan's small pacifist movement had come under increasing attack from the government in the 1930s. During the war, it was formally suppressed.[37] But in the heady days of the war's aftermath and the adoption of the peace constitution, pacifism experienced a renaissance. In 1948, efforts began to revive the Japanese FOR, and the following year, with the assistance of American pacifists, it was reestablished, as was a section of the WRI. Both became champions of peace and disarmament in Japanese life.[38] Reorganized in 1946, the Japanese WILPF group grew rapidly and, in the spring of 1951, held a large public meeting featuring Hiroshima novelist Yoko Ota. The WILPF's president, Professor Tano Jodai, moved by books she had read on the atomic bombing, declared that "we Japanese women should unite ourselves more firmly and fight against the policy of rearmament." That same year, the Japanese WILPF group appealed to U.S. ambassador John Foster Dulles, then in Japan, to oppose Japan's loan of air and naval bases to the United States and to halt plans for the rearmament of Japan.[39]

Japan's world government movement also underwent substantial growth in the postwar era. Organized by Morikatsu Inagaki, a longtime proponent of the League of Nations, the Institute for Permanent Peace held fifteen meetings in Japanese cities during the month of January 1948 alone and arranged for the publication of fourteen newspaper articles and the broadcast of six radio programs on the idea of world federation. The institute also worked at producing a world constitution and published a monthly journal, *One World*. Later that year, Inagaki launched the Union for World Federal Government, which, by 1950, had some 4,000 members, organized in 50 chapters, and a monthly publication, *The World State*. Meanwhile, numerous peace and religious groups, including one led by the revered pacifist Toyohiko Kagawa, announced their support for world government. Moreover, a Parliamentary Committee for World Federation, founded in December 1949, soon claimed more than 180 members of the Japanese Diet, including Prime Minister Shigeru Yoshida. In November 1950, when the Union for World Federal Government held a public meeting in Tokyo of 5,000 people, mostly students, police had to turn away the overflow crowds.[40]

The rise of world federalism in Japan represented, at least in part, a response to the menace of the Bomb. Inagaki capped several years of speechmaking and writing by deliberately holding the founding meeting of the Union for World Federal Government on the third anniversary of the Hiroshima bombing. Two years later, on August 6, 1950, when a group of young people from Yokohama and Hiroshima began a fast in front of Hiroshima station, they adopted as their slogan "The way to realize 'No More Hiroshimas' is to build a world federation."[41] Attempting to draw a similar connection, the Union for World Federal Government proposed in 1950 that the city of Hiroshima serve as the site for the fifth assembly of the World Movement for World Federal Government. And, indeed, Hiroshima did host the international world federalist gathering in 1952. Albert Einstein's melding of the two causes appeared both in his "Message to the People of Japan," published in major Japanese newspapers in 1947, and in his telegram of support read at the union's 1950 meeting in Tokyo. "Only through world government," he declared on that occasion, "can our civilization be saved."[42]

Japan's scientists were somewhat less outspoken. Some, of course, were shocked by the destruction of Hiroshima, particularly those dispatched to the scene of the bombing to determine whether an atomic device had been used. Occasionally, they publicly questioned whether atomic power would bring peace or misery to the world. And at least one prominent atomic physicist, Satoshi Watanabe, became a leading proponent of world government.[43] Nevertheless, U.S. occupation restrictions on publishing scientific information dealing with the atomic bombing—accompanied by a U.S. ban on research in nuclear physics and by the U.S. Army's destruction of Japanese cyclotrons—appear to have had a chilling effect on the expression of dissenting opinions in Japan's scientific community. It is all the more remarkable, then, that in April 1950, a group of 120 top-ranking Japanese scientists and scholars issued a statement declaring that employment of atomic research for war was an "insult" to science, which should be devoted to peace.[44]

Although these organizations remained rather small, other forces—and particularly the powerful Japanese Socialist party, with strong support from the nation's labor movement—helped provide the peace and disarmament movement with a mass base. In November 1945, at its first postwar congress, the Socialist party declared that, as one of its three guiding principles, it opposed "all militaristic thought and action" and aimed "at the realization of perpetual peace through the co-operation of the peoples of the world." During parliamentary debates on the new constitution, party chair Tetsu Katayama strongly endorsed Article 9 and suggested that it be strengthened by a declaration of Japan's devotion to world peace. In 1949, the party officially proclaimed its support for a policy of permanent neutrality for Japan, based on its desire to avoid Japanese involvement in new wars. Despite American pressures for the rearmament of Japan, the party stuck to these principles in the ensuing years. In 1951, for example, the Socialist party came out strongly against rearmament and objected to an American-crafted peace treaty as inviting war with Communist nations.[45]

Working in alliance, these and other groups gave the peace and disarmament movement an increasingly important presence in Japanese public life. Returning from a speaking tour of Japan in early 1950, an American pacifist leader estimated that he had addressed approximately 9,500 persons in public meetings. He also reported on another rally, in Tokyo, of 10,000 persons, gathered to denounce rearmament and war. In July of the following year, a Religionists' Peace Movement organized the Japan National Congress for the Promotion of Peace, led by zealous Christian, Buddhist, and Shinto pacifists. Appealing to cultural groups, labor unions, and women's societies, the new movement claimed 3.5 million supporters. Although the Japan National Congress organized on a nationwide basis, in Tokyo alone it held numerous open-air meetings in parks and on temple grounds. On September 1, 1951, it organized a peace rally in Tokyo of 20,000 people, drawing heavily upon Socialist-led unions, the FOR, a new Buddhist group, and other antimilitary organizations. "Japan, as an absolutely dis-armed nation, has [a] special mission to fulfill," one veteran pacifist (and member of Japan's parliament) wrote proudly.[46]

The Japanese Public Confronts the Arms Race

During these years, the Japanese public, too, began to show signs of a strong aversion to the atomic bomb and a willingness to limit national sovereignty in the interest of preventing a nuclear war. The Soviet Union's testing of its first Bomb, in conjunction with speculation that the United States would move forward in the "atomic race," produced major headlines and editorial comments in all the important Japanese newspapers. As a *New York Times* correspondent reported from Tokyo, it was clear that "the situation is highly frightening to the Japanese." Some months later, news of President Truman's decision to manufacture the H-Bomb "commanded the closest attention of the Japanese press," the U.S. embassy reported anxiously from Tokyo. Combined with other Cold War developments, this added up "in the Japanese view to the frightening prospect of a super atomic war," with their home islands as "a battlefield." Symptomatically, suggestions from U.S. senators, the Federation of American Scientists, "and others advocating a peace offensive, disarmament, an end to the cold war, and even aid to the USSR have . . . been played up by the press." On February 2, 1950, the *Mainichi Shimbun* declared: "We only wish and pray that atomic power will never be used as a weapon of war in any way." Endorsing this idea, the *Asahi Shimbun* added: "Now is the time for all mankind to reconsider."[47]

Opinion surveys reinforce the impression of overwhelming hostility on the part of the Japanese public to the maintenance of armed forces and, particularly, to any use of nuclear weapons. In late 1951, a poll of 8,932 students enrolled in nineteen colleges throughout Tokyo reported that 81 percent opposed the rearmament of Japan. Only 12.2 percent of the students favored Japanese rearmament. The following year, an *Asahi Shimbun* survey concluded that only 38 percent of the general population supported the National Police Reserve, the predecessor of Japan's Self-Defense Forces. In January 1953, an opinion poll found that 73 percent of Japanese respondents opposed the suggestion that the United States use the atomic bomb to win the Korean War, while only 6 percent supported the idea.[48]

Development of a Movement

In the aftermath of the atomic bombing of Japan, key constituencies took the lead in campaigning for nuclear disarmament. Badly damaged by World War II, pacifist groups experienced severe losses in membership, morale, and credibility; nevertheless, with the coming of peace, they provided the disarmament cause with a committed, articulate following in many lands. Atomic scientists and world government proponents, whose influence expanded dramatically in wartime, also emerged as trenchant critics of nuclear weapons in the post-war era. Finally, the Japanese survivors of the atomic bombing—determined to alert humanity to the terrible dangers of modern war—threw themselves into the struggle against the Bomb. Working together in postwar Japan, these constituencies succeeded in overcoming the obstacles raised by the American occupation forces to fashion a growing movement for peace and disarmament. In Hiroshima, in Nagasaki, and, eventually, throughout the nation, the Japanese people were finding their voice as the world's most dedicated critics of the Bomb.

America's Nuclear Nightmare

The greatest obsolescence of all in the atomic age is
national sovereignty.

Norman Cousins, 1945

In the United States, the Bomb created a sensation that was unsurpassed throughout the world.[1] This reaction reflected the unique responsibility of Americans for the new weapon, which they alone had employed in war and, for a time, retained a monopoly on in peace. In addition, Americans recognized that the advent of the Bomb challenged the relative safety they had enjoyed in past conflicts. Although the continental United States had not been touched by a conventional war for more than a century, nuclear war had the potential for utterly annihilating America's cities. Emphasizing these new circumstances, movements of atomic scientists, world government advocates, and pacifists led a sustained and effective campaign to educate the public to the dangers confronting them. Addressing a CBS radio audience in early 1946, Robert Hutchins, chancellor of the University of Chicago, stated their message bluntly and concisely: "Those who now indulge in loose talk about settling international differences by force must realize that force means war. War means atomic bombs. And atomic bombs mean suicide."[2] As in Japan—and, indeed, around the world—these groups championed an alternative that resonated in the broader society: One World.

The Reaction to the Atomic Bombing

An overwhelming majority of Americans approved of the dropping of the atomic bomb on Hiroshima and Nagasaki. In a Gallup poll taken on August 8, 1945, 85 percent of American respondents expressed their support for "using the new atomic bomb on Japanese cities," as compared to 10 percent who stated their opposition.[3] The following month, another poll found somewhat less approval of the act among Americans; 4 percent would have refused to use nuclear weapons, 27 percent would have used them only after a demonstration on an unpopulated area, 43 percent would have used them on one city at a time, and 24 percent would have tried to wipe out as many cities as possible. But by December, approval of the bombing had increased somewhat, for a *Fortune* poll found that, although 4.5 percent would not have used nuclear weapons and 13.8 percent would have used them first on an unpopulated area, 76.2 percent would have used them one at a time or more quickly. In subsequent years, this pattern of overwhelming support persisted.[4]

Behind this support lay several key factors. The atomic bombing had been carried out by the American government in wartime and therefore appealed to patriotic sentiments. Explaining their position, supporters of the bombing invariably rallied behind the U.S. government's contention that it had saved lives. Furthermore, the war against Japan had great popularity among Americans, and vigorous support for the war often translated into approval of the atomic bombing. In addition, the mass media did little that might challenge the legitimacy of the atomic attacks. Covering events in Japan, the communications media generally told the story in a way that failed to contest the necessity or desirability of the bombing. They rarely, if ever, discussed the Bomb's victims or showed pictures of them; instead, they carried upbeat accounts of postwar reconstruction in the two Japanese cities.[5]

Conversely, critics of the war invariably condemned the atomic bombing. Writing to all members of the U.S. Fellowship of Reconciliation, A. J. Muste and John Nevin Sayre, the co-secretaries of the group, urged them to contact the president and members of Congress "to express moral revulsion against the resort to atomic bombing" and to call upon these officials to pledge never to use the weapon again. Dorothy Day, founder of the Catholic Worker movement, publicly rebuked the government with Christ's statement: "What you do unto the least of these my brethren, you do unto me!"[6] The atomic bombing shocked Emily Balch and the WILPF leadership. National secretary Dorothy Detzer remarked that they were "filled with shame" over it. That fall, the WILPF's national board declared that the atomic bombings had "shattered" the "moral authority of the United States."[7] The *Call*, newspaper of the tiny Socialist party, though long ambivalent about the war, assailed the use of the atomic bomb, as did the party's best-known spokesperson, Norman Thomas. "Our obliteration bombing and our use of two atomic bombs to destroy crowded cities," he wrote, "were atrocities of the first magnitude."[8]

Some prominent supporters of the war, including a substantial number of atomic scientists, also felt revulsion at the atomic bombing. Rabinowitch recalled: "The news of the Hiroshima strike was a terrible blow to many who had contributed most toward making the atomic bomb possible; the news of the bombing of Nagasaki was received by an even larger group with dismay and gloom." Viewing the atomic attacks as a catastrophe, Einstein later remarked that sending his letter to President Roosevelt was the "one great mistake" in his life.[9] The atomic bombing "is one of the greatest blunders of history," Szilard wrote on August 6. After the second bomb was dropped, he suggested to the chaplain at the University of Chicago that "a special prayer . . . be said for the dead of Hiroshima and Nagasaki" and that a collection be taken to aid the survivors. He also drew up another petition, declaring that "further bombings of the civilian population of Japan would be a flagrant violation of our own moral standards." [10]

Nor was the dismay among atomic scientists limited to the comparatively small group that had struggled actively to prevent atomic war. Otto Frisch, who worked at Los Alamos, recalled his "nausea" at the celebration of the Hiroshima bombing and commented that "few of us could see any moral reason for dropping a second bomb." On September 1, Samuel Allison, associate director of the Los Alamos lab, denounced the Nagasaki bombing at a meeting with the press. Alice Smith, the foremost chronicler of the atomic scientists, concluded that "most scientists who worked on the bomb reluctantly approved of the first bomb because it promised an early end to the war. But many who accepted Hiroshima were deeply shocked by the second bomb dropped on Nagasaki." [11] A sociological survey of Manhattan project scientists in September 1945 found that, although a slight majority approved the government's use of the Bomb, 42.5 percent said they would have demonstrated it first on an unpopulated area or not used it at all.[12]

Another sign that the atomic bombing repulsed some supporters of the war was the criticism it generated among religious leaders. Taking their cue from the pope's apparent condemnation of the Bomb, as well as from traditional conceptions of the "just war," leading Catholic theologians and publications deplored the atomic attack upon Japan. Writing in the *Catholic World*, one Catholic author declared that "the use of the atomic bomb, in the circumstances, was atrocious and abominable, and . . . civilized people should reprobate and anathematize the horrible deed." [13] Leaders of liberal Protestant denominations also reacted sharply to the bombing. In a joint statement issued on August 9, Bishop G. Bromley Oxnam, president of the Federal Council of Churches, and John Foster Dulles, chair of the council's Commission on a Just and Durable Peace, criticized the bombing and called for "a temporary suspension . . . of our program of air attack on the Japanese homeland." In a public message on August 20, 34 church leaders declared that the Bomb's "reckless and irresponsible employment against an already virtually beaten foe will have to receive judgment before God and the conscience of humankind. It has our unmitigated condemnation." The following year, *Atomic Warfare and the Christian Faith*—the official statement on the matter by the Federal Council of Churches—declared that "the surprise bombings of Hiroshima and Nagasaki are morally indefensible. . . . We have sinned grievously against the laws of God and against the people of Japan." [14]

None of the criticisms of the bombing had as much impact on the broader society as did John Hersey's article "Hiroshima." Published in the *New Yorker* on August 31, 1946, this 30,000-word account examined the effect of the atomic bombing on the lives of six people. Although written in a detached, restrained style, the story had great appeal in the United States. It was read over a major radio network, reprinted in its entirety by newspapers, featured in news articles and editorials, and republished as a best-selling book. Before beginning his research for the article, Hersey had approved of the atomic bombing. But his interviews in Japan produced in him "a kind of horror," he recalled. By recreating the event from the standpoint of the victims, Hersey transmitted his impressions to millions of Americans. A woman wrote to the *New Yorker*: "As I read I had to constantly remind myself that we perpetrated this monstrous tragedy. We Americans." Lamenting his earlier satisfaction at the bombing's success, one atomic scientist remarked: "I wept as I read John Hersey's *New Yorker* account. . . . We didn't realize." Nevertheless, although "Hiroshima" broke through the artificial silence surrounding the human effects of nuclear war, it did not change the minds of most Americans about the bombing. Instead, it reinforced the predominant emotions about nuclear weapons that had already become widespread among Americans: awe and, especially, fear. [15]

"Seldom, if ever," stated CBS radio commentator Edward R. Murrow on August 12, 1945, "has a war ended leaving the victors with such a sense of uncertainty and fear, with such a realization that the future is obscure and that survival is not assured." The mass media of all persuasions trumpeted the theme that, with the advent of nuclear weapons, the destruction of civilization lay at hand. From the conservative *Chicago Tribune* came the warning that atomic war would leave the world "a barren waste, in which the survivors of the race will hide in caves or live among the ruins." The liberal *New Republic* predicted that a nuclear war would "obliterate all the great cities of the belligerents, bring industry and technology to a grinding halt," and leave only "scattered remnants of humanity living on the periphery of civilization." In his Labor Day address, the president of the American Federation of Labor, William Green, declared that the atomic bombs had "struck terror into the hearts of human beings." That November, a prominent anthropologist remarked that America was gripped by a "fear psychosis"; atomic war, he said, had become "a nightmare in the minds of men." [16]

The nightmare of nuclear destruction, however, seemed to point in a pacific direction. As news commentator Raymond Gram Swing explained: "The weapons of war have now reached a power which can destroy us, so that if we wish not to be destroyed we must end the use of the weapons. And since the weapons cannot be effectively banned if war is to continue, there is no choice but to end war." Much the same case was made in November 1945 by the Synagogue Council of America, which argued that, with the advent of nuclear weapons, "our era of mutual suspicion and competition in international affairs must give way to an epoch of mutual trust and co-operation." In a radio broadcast of August 12, 1945, Robert Hutchins observed that the French philosopher Leon Bloy had referred to "the good news of damnation" on the theory that only the fear of perpetual hellfire would motivate moral behavior. "It may be," Hutchins noted, "that the atomic bomb is the good news of damnation, that it may frighten us into that Christian character and those righteous actions and those positive political steps necessary to the creation of a world society." [17]

The early critics of the Bomb were struck by the opportunities inherent in the situation. Amid the gloom surrounding the atomic bombings, Rabinowitch recalled, "a glimmer of hope appeared. . . . Was there not a chance—an off-side chance, but still a chance—that the fate of Hiroshima and Nagasaki would cause Man to turn a new leaf? Could we not spur this decision by buttonholing all who would listen and preaching to them our message of doom and our precept for survival: live in peace or perish?" The subsequent atomic scientists' movement, he noted, "was part of the conspiracy to preserve our civilization by scaring men into rationality." [18]

The Atomic Scientists' Movement

That conspiracy was soon in high gear. On July 12, 1945, Rabinowitch had suggested that once the Bomb became public knowledge, scientists should begin organized efforts "to create lasting security" against the "threatening devastation" of all nations by nuclear weapons. And, indeed, the campaign did commence in the aftermath of the attack on Japan, when atomic scientists' associations sprang up at numerous Manhattan project sites. At the Met Lab, the Committee on Social and Political Implications of Atomic Energy took the lead in forming the Atomic Scientists of Chicago, which Chancellor Hutchins assisted with a $10,000 grant and an impressive conference that fall on the nuclear dilemma. [19] On November 1, the groups from Chicago, Oak Ridge, Los Alamos, and New York joined together to launch the Federation of Atomic

Scientists, which, the following month, reorganized itself as the Federation of American Scientists (FAS). By early 1946, the FAS claimed seventeen local groups with nearly 3,000 members, including 90 percent of the scientists who had worked on the atomic bomb. Although some middle-aged scientists such as Harold Urey and Leo Szilard played important roles in FAS affairs, the vast majority of the FAS activists and leaders were remarkably young, including its first chair, William Higinbotham.[20] To the distress of some senior figures in the field, who argued that scientists should remain clear of politics,[21] the FAS committed itself from the start to freeing humanity from the threat of nuclear war.[22]

To secure this goal, the new movement developed several very effective means of outreach. In November 1945, the Federation of Atomic Scientists organized the National Committee on Atomic Information (NCAI), which drew together more than 60 leading civic, labor, religious, professional, and educational organizations in the United States. Working through these sympathetic groups, the NCAI distributed copies of materials on atomic energy, drawn up by the atomic scientists, to their millions of members.[23] Meanwhile, Rabinowitch—together, for a time, with his colleague Hyman Goldsmith—began editing the *Bulletin of the Atomic Scientists of Chicago* in December 1945. Although technically independent of the FAS, the new publication, renamed the *Bulletin of the Atomic Scientists*, provided what people regarded as the authoritative voice of the movement. Bearing its distinctive "doomsday clock," designed by Edward Teller and set at seven minutes to midnight, the *Bulletin*, by mid-1947, had a circulation of nearly 20,000, including scientists in seventeen countries.[24] In an effort to reach additional overseas scientists, the Cambridge association organized a Committee for Foreign Correspondence. Formally adopted by the FAS in 1946, the committee sent atomic information packets to 3,000 scientists, 275 libraries and scientific organizations, and 150 newspapers in 65 foreign lands. These packets included copies of FAS publications, the *Bulletin of the Atomic Scientists*, a widely discussed article by Urey ("I'm a Frightened Man"), and Hersey's *Hiroshima*.[25]

To secure the financial resources necessary to sustain these and other activities, Szilard conceived the idea of developing a separate organization to act as a fund-raiser for the movement: the Emergency Committee of Atomic Scientists (ECAS). Launched in May 1946 with Einstein as chair, ECAS drew upon a small group of prominent scientists, most notably Szilard, Urey, Victor Weisskopf, Hans Bethe, and Linus Pauling. Szilard, however, continued to dominate the new organization.[26] In the first ECAS press release, Einstein appealed for contributions to a $200,000 fund to support the "life and death struggle" to avert "humanity's destruction." Scientists, he said, "must let the people know that a new type of thinking is essential if mankind is to survive." These fund-raising ventures proved fairly successful for, by the fall of 1947, some $320,000 had been secured toward the new ECAS goal of $1 million.[27] Even more important, ECAS succeeded in putting the immense popular prestige of scientists such as Einstein squarely behind the struggle against the Bomb.

Why did the atomic scientists embrace the antinuclear crusade with such fervor? Some undoubtedly sought to atone for their wartime role. Oppenheimer suggested publicly that "the physicists have known sin; and this is a knowledge which they cannot lose." Einstein took a similar tack, arguing that, like Alfred Nobel, "the physicists who participated in producing the most formidable weapon of all time are harassed by a . . . feeling of responsibility, not to say guilt." In a variant of this theme, the FAS maintained: "Our country, the United States, has a peculiar responsibility. We first used the bomb. . . . *The bombs are marked 'Made in the U.S.A.'* "[28] Szilard, however, claimed that he "never felt any guilt" at his work on the Bomb project because developing the weapon seemed necessary at the time. But he did "feel a special responsibility" for coping with the ensuing arms race.[29] Certainly, guilt played a role for some—and perhaps even for Szilard[30]—but more widespread was a sense of social responsibility. As Weisskopf later observed, "maybe" a "feeling of guilt for having participated in devising this new weapon . . . drove us on," but "the most important reason was our nightmarish vision of an actual nuclear conflict, based on our particular understanding of the power of the weapon we had made." Or, as Rabinowitch contended, the scientists' participation in the Bomb project "convinced them that, with this discovery, a radical change had come in the role of science in public affairs," leaving humanity faced "with unprecedented dangers of destruction."[31]

But how was humanity to be saved from such a fate? From the outset, a substantial number of the atomic scientists thought the answer lay in world government. As Rabinowitch recalled, during one of their wartime discussions of the "implications of atomic bombs," a three-point program had been jotted down on the blackboard: "World government; if no world government, international control of atomic energy; if no international control of atomic energy, dispersal of cities."[32] Many scientists carried over these priorities to the postwar era. "The release of atomic energy has not created a new problem," Einstein told readers of the *Atlantic Monthly* in November 1945. "It has merely made more urgent the necessity of solving an existing one. . . . As long as there are sovereign nations possessing great power, war is inevitable." Consequently, both publicly and privately, Einstein argued that "world government" was "not just desirable" but "necessary for survival."[33] Addressing a gathering that November in Hollywood, Pauling claimed that, in the context of the atomic bomb, "the only hope for the world is to prevent war, and that war can be prevented only by a sovereign world government." Other leaders of the atomic scientists' movement—including Szilard, Urey, Rabinowitch, and Harrison Brown—made much the same case in the months after World War II.[34] Similar feelings infused the rank and file. A poll of the Association of Oak Ridge Engineers and Scientists, one of the most active FAS affiliates, found that 90 percent of the members favored the establishment of a world government.[35]

Nevertheless, given the need for rapid, effective action, the atomic scientists rallied around a stopgap measure. An organizing statement of the Atomic Scientists of Chicago, prepared by Rabinowitch in September 1945, contended: "Since world government is unlikely to be achieved within the short time available before the atomic armament race will lead to an acute danger of armed conflict, the establishment of international controls must be considered as a problem of immediate urgency." Addressing the Atomic Energy Control Conference at the University of Chicago later that month, Szilard argued that "if we could insure a period of peace for twenty to thirty years, this might give us enough time . . . to approach step by step . . . the ultimate goal of a world government." Einstein took up the same theme in 1946. "The only way out" of the atomic crisis lay in creating a "supranational organization," he maintained; but in the meantime, "mutual inspection" of military installations, combined with an interchange of technical data, would create a "breathing spell." [36] Furthermore, as Robert Oppenheimer and other supporters of international control of atomic energy often argued, the relinquishment of national sovereignty in this area would be an attainable first step toward world government. Responding to a leading world federalist, FAS president William Higinbotham made both points. "Atomic energy will not wait," he insisted. In addition, "the achievement of world control of atomic energy would open the door widely for further progress" toward "world government." [37] For the time being, then, the scientists' movement united around the idea of international control of atomic energy.

En route to this goal, the movement initiated some important ventures in public education and public policy. Outraged by the efforts of General Groves and the scientist-administrators of the Manhattan project to keep atomic energy in military hands, the FAS played a crucial role in the successful struggle for federal legislation ensuring civilian control of atomic energy.[38] The movement proved less effective in promoting another scheme—a conference of American and Soviet scientists that would discuss the prerequisites for safeguarding the world against the Bomb. The idea was pressed by Szilard or his surrogates in numerous meetings with U.S. government officials, including the secretary of state and the president, but proved fruitless because of the objections of U.S.

policymakers and, later, their Soviet counterparts.[39] Meanwhile, in early 1946 the FAS produced a hard-hitting book, *One World or None*, that sold more than 100,000 copies. Written by the movement's luminaries—including Einstein, Bohr, Urey, Bethe, Oppenheimer, and Szilard—the work clearly expressed their sense of urgency. "It all adds up to the most dangerous situation that humanity has ever faced," declared Harold Urey. "Time is short," concluded the FAS, "and survival is at stake." [40]

Those involved in the scientists' movement rejoiced at the appearance of the U.S. government's Acheson-Lilienthal Plan, which provided for the international control of atomic energy. In a statement issued on April 11, 1946, the FAS declared that "American scientists are overwhelmingly in favor" of its principles. An editorial in the *Bulletin of the Atomic Scientists* declared that the plan's publication "must be hailed by scientists, and by all who see in the international control of atomic energy the only hope for prevention of an atomic war." Writing that May to Bernard Baruch, the president's choice to present the plan to the United Nations, Higinbotham and other leaders of the FAS argued that the Acheson-Lilienthal proposal "furnishes the most constructive analysis we have seen of the technical questions of international control." Because of its potential for preventing an atomic arms race and the surprise use of the Bomb, "we believe it should be made the basis of your ultimate program in the United Nations Atomic Energy Commission." [41]

The scientists felt far greater ambivalence about the ensuing Baruch Plan. Dismayed by the appointment of Baruch and by his choice of advisers, leaders of the movement had "a great fear," as Higinbotham privately confessed, that Baruch would not recognize the virtues of the Acheson-Lilienthal report. "I am very worried," he told a correspondent.[42] This uneasiness only partially dissipated after Baruch announced his own proposals, which did, indeed, depart substantially from those of his predecessors. To be sure, the FAS overtly supported the Baruch Plan. Conversely, its leaders viewed Soviet counterproposals as valueless. Nevertheless, behind the scenes, numerous scientists questioned Baruch's insistence on scrapping the veto for enforcement procedures, his indifference to confidence-building measures, and, particularly, his rigidity. John Simpson, president of the Atomic Scientists of Chicago, found Baruch's U.N. performance "disheartening." Writing directly to Baruch, Urey claimed that "many" of his colleagues believed that the "one fault" of his U.N. statement was "that it leaves no leeway for bargaining." As the prospects dimmed for an American-Soviet agreement on atomic energy, an increasing number of scientists felt that Baruch bore some of the blame.[43]

The failure of the Baruch Plan destroyed the strategic unity that the atomic scientists' movement had forged around the concept of the international control of atomic energy. To be sure, the FAS pressed the U.S. government to continue atomic energy negotiations at the United Nations and, indeed, to undertake "detailed exploration of alternative plans."[44] Writing in the *Bulletin*, Rabino-witch argued that the "only . . . realistic blueprint for security" lay in "the sub-ordination of *all* nations to international law and order." Meanwhile, Einstein and the FAS, in a joint statement, maintained that "it is necessary to pursue every avenue toward one world." Nevertheless, the way forward had become unclear. A nasty controversy even erupted between the FAS and ECAS over the wording of a statement expressing the views of the scientists' movement.[45] On one extreme, Hans Bethe argued that the movement should cease to press for international control of atomic energy and, indeed, issue no public statements until it could develop another approach that it wholeheartedly supported. In the meantime, he thought, scientists should withdraw to their laboratories.[46] On the other, Einstein—convinced of "the craziness of the people who deter-mine the fate of homo sapiens"—grew impatient with delay and compromise. "If one realizes the implications of war preparations," he told Rabinowitch in August 1949, "one is virtually forced to become a rebel."[47]

For some scientists, this feeling of rebellion went as far as refusing to work on the Bomb. When FOR leader A. J. Muste queried prominent figures in the scientists' movement about the possibility of sparking conscientious objection to military employment, all of them rejected the notion. Such a walkout "would scarcely affect the situation" in the United States, Higinbotham argued, nor would it "stop the scientists in other countries who are developing new weapons of war."[48] Nevertheless, the *Bulletin* gave some attention to the idea, reprinting a 1946 letter by MIT mathematician Norbert Wiener in which he announced that he would no longer publish work that "may do damage in the hands of irresponsible militarists." Some two years later, the *Bulletin* printed another statement by Wiener urging scientists to assume "moral responsibility" for their work, as well as two lengthy articles by atomic scientists Cuthbert Daniel and Arthur Squires, who made the case for refusing to accept military employ-ment.[49] In November 1949, the *Bulletin* announced the formation of the Society for Social Responsibility in Science, designed "to foster throughout the world a tradition of personal moral responsibility for the consequences . . . of pro-fessional activity, with emphasis on constructive alternatives to militarism." Einstein joined the new group and, although most prominent activists in the scientists' movement did not follow his example,[50] by the late 1940s none of the leading figures in the FAS or ECAS was still working on atomic bombs.[51]

The waning prospects for international control of atomic energy also re-vived demands by scientists to focus on the goal of world government. Arguing in the spring of 1947 that the Bomb was not "an isolated issue," Szilard claimed that "what we need in this country now is a crusade—a crusade for an organized world community." [52] Support for this idea was tested in a conference at Lake Geneva, Wisconsin, of leaders of ECAS, FAS, and some FAS regional groups. Meeting from June 18 to 22, the conferees agreed on a compromise statement, endorsed by ECAS and FAS. It declared that the movement should "continue to urge the establishment of an effective international agency for the control of atomic energy" while, at the same time, recognizing "that our purpose— which is the elimination of war—requires the establishment of a government of the world with powers adequate to maintain . . . peace." This position soon unraveled, however, for ECAS issued a statement on June 30 criticizing U.N. atomic energy negotiations and calling forthrightly for "the creation of a supra-national government." [53] One more attempt to smooth over differences occurred in late November 1947, at another scientists' conference, in Princeton. Here, again, strong support emerged for continuing U.N. negotiations on international control while simultaneously working for world government; even so, most conferees felt that the FAS should avoid active agitation for a world state.[54] Frustrated by the situation, ECAS, in 1948, issued new calls for world government, funded a speaking tour in the United States by a leading British world federalist (Henry Usborne), and toyed with plans to establish a major foundation to bankroll the world government movement.[55] Although these measures led to the resignations of Bethe and Weisskopf,[56] their replacements (e.g., Hermann Muller, the geneticist) and the remaining ECAS members continued to emphasize world government as the solution to the nuclear arms race.[57]

Even so, much of the movement again closed ranks in February 1950, when President Truman announced his decision to develop a hydrogen bomb. Viewing the president's decision as a fait accompli, the FAS Council did not attack it frontally but issued a statement on February 5 that put it in a very dubious light. "If we make hydrogen bombs, the Russians will build them, too," the FAS declared; "we must have no illusions of security based on monopoly of a super weapon." Because "the kind of security we want can be had only by building a stable peace," there must be "a fresh start" toward "effective atomic control." [58] Shortly thereafter, Bethe—"terribly shocked" by the H-Bomb decision—pulled together twelve physicists at the convention of the American Physical Society for a press conference. In it, they declared that "no nation has the right to use such a bomb, no matter how righteous its cause. This bomb is no longer a weapon of war, but a means of extermination of whole populations. Its use would be a betrayal of all the standards of morality." [59] Szilard, Pauling, Brown, Weisskopf, and other prominent leaders of the movement also issued statements or otherwise warned about the terrible dangers inherent in the new weapon.[60] Speaking on the opening broadcast of Eleanor Roosevelt's television program on February 12, Einstein once again called for the creation of a "supra-national" government as the only "way out of the impasse." Until then, he declared ominously, "general annihilation beckons." [61]

The Growth of the World Government Movement

The emergence of the Bomb also spurred the development of a vigorous movement for world federation. "On August 6, 1945," Robert Hutchins recalled, "we all picked up our telephones to tell each other that there must never be another war" and that "we had to have world government." Although hyperbolic, Hutchins's statement contains elements of truth, for influential figures did begin to speak out on the subject in an unprecedented fashion. In early October 1945, twenty prominent Americans—including Supreme Court Justice Owen Roberts, U.S. Senators J. W. Fulbright and Claude Pepper, novelist Thomas Mann, Amvets leader Charles Bolté, and Einstein—joined to urge a "Federal Constitution of the World." Given "the new reality of atomic warfare," they declared, world government is an "immediate, urgent necessity, unless civilization is determined on suicide." [62] Later that month, a larger and more influential group, mobilized by Wall Street lawyer Grenville Clark for a meeting in Dublin, New Hampshire, swept aside a proposal by Clarence Streit for a union of democracies and called for the establishment of a world federal government. The alternative, they warned, was an atomic war, "which would destroy civilization and possibly mankind itself." [63] Riding the tide of nuclear concern, the world government movement soon attracted powerful supporters: businessmen such as W. T. Holliday, Robert Lund, and Owen D. Young; labor leaders Philip Murray, Walter Reuther, David Dubinsky, and A. Philip Randolph;[64] writers and intellectuals Stringfellow Barr, Carl Van Doren, E. B. White, and Lewis Mumford;[65] and news commentators such as Raymond Gram Swing.[66]

Perhaps the most effective of the new advocates of world government was Norman Cousins, the young, liberal editor of the *Saturday Review of Literature*. "When the news broke about the bombing of Hiroshima," he recalled, "it seemed to me that man overnight had come face to face with the problems of human destiny." Stunned by the event, he sat down that evening and penned a lengthy editorial, "Modern Man Is Obsolete." The dropping of the Bomb "marked the violent death of one stage in man's history and the beginning of another," he wrote. In the "new age" of the atomic bomb, "the first order of business is the question of continued existence." The "need for world government was clear long before August 6, 1945," he observed, but the atomic bombing "raised that need to such dimensions that it can no longer be ignored." [67] Certainly, Cousins did not ignore it for, in short order, he publicly challenged scholars to confront the issues raised by the Bomb, mobilized funding and support for the world government movement, criticized the use of the Bomb and supported nuclear arms control in the *Bulletin of the Atomic Scientists*, delivered speeches with such titles as "One World or None," and used the *Saturday Review* to develop a "moral adoption" program for 263 children orphaned by the Hiroshima bombing.[68] Meanwhile, he turned "Modern Man Is Obsolete" into a book that went through fourteen editions, appeared in seven languages, and had an estimated circulation in the United States of seven million.[69]

Robert Hutchins, the innovative chancellor of the University of Chicago, emerged as another outstanding proponent of world federalism. Young, handsome, and one of America's most influential educators, Hutchins was particularly useful to the cause. Within days of the atomic bombing, which he criticized privately and publicly, Hutchins told a radio audience of his hope that the Bomb might "frighten the peoples of the earth" into creating "a world society." [70] On repeated occasions, he made the same point. Later that year, for example, he argued that "the survival of mankind demands a world community, a world government, and a world state." [71] Alone among university administrators of his era, Hutchins provided the resources for intellectual efforts to cope with the dangers of the Bomb. Just as he encouraged the Chicago Met Lab scientists and subsidized the *Bulletin of the Atomic Scientists*, so he approved a request by two faculty members, G. A. Borgese and Richard McKeon, that the University of Chicago develop a committee to draft a world constitution. In this way, they argued, "the atomic discovery, Janus-faced, having shown its countenance of Death, might begin to lift the veil from its other visage, that is Life." [72] In March 1948, after lengthy discussions, the committee issued the Preliminary Draft of a World Constitution. Originally published in the committee's journal, *Common Cause*, it was reprinted several times in book and magazine form and translated into numerous languages. By late the following year, it had a worldwide circulation of 200,000 copies.[73]

As the idea of world government acquired momentum in the United States, new organizations sought to make it a reality. Although Streit's Federal Union disintegrated in late 1945, when most of its members concluded that his vision of a federation of democracies was too limited,[74] other organizations such as Americans United for World Government, World Federalists, USA, and Student Federalists—emphasizing the nuclear menace—enrolled thousands of new members. In February 1947, delegates from these and other world government groups met in Asheville, North Carolina, where six of the largest merged to form United World Federalists (UWF).[75] Committed to "work primarily to strengthen the United Nations into a world government," UWF claimed some 17,000 dues-paying members in more than 200 chapters. It also had an impressive galaxy of leaders, including Cousins, Clark, Holliday, Swing, and Van Doren, who served as vice-presidents, and a young marine combat veteran, Cord Meyer, Jr., who became the organization's first president. Appalled by the weakness of the United Nations, Meyer believed that the "vivid threat" of the atomic bomb might yet "overcome the ideological differences and narrow nationalism" that had previously blocked efforts toward world federation. Perhaps, he wrote in his new book, *Peace or Anarchy*, "fear would be able to accomplish what neither experience, reason nor religion had been able to do." [76]

Although UWF constituted by far the largest and most effective world government organization in the United States, some other federalist groups remained independent. World Republic, a student organization with about 2,000 members, kept aloof because it believed that a "people's convention," rather than established governments, should be the agency for initiating a world federation. This "people's convention" approach, developed by Georgia Lloyd, Edith Wynner, and Harris Wofford,[77] also had some appeal to the Chicago Committee to Frame a World Constitution. In addition, the "maximalist" Chicago committee disliked the "minimalist" approach of UWF, which favored only those curbs on national sovereignty necessary to prevent war.[78] Another holdout from UWF was the Citizens Committee for United Nations Reform, launched by the celebrated bridge expert Ely Culbertson. A revolutionary in his youth, Culbertson never lost his taste for social engineering and through his "quota force" proposal sought to reshape the international order. Although Culbertson's plan never had mass backing, it did draw considerable attention and influential support, ranging from American Civil Liberties Union director Roger Baldwin to the American Legion.[79]

Given the overshadowing importance of the nuclear menace to world federalists, it was hardly surprising that they developed an alliance with the atomic scientists' movement. Writing to Harold Urey in November 1945, the Executive Council of World Federalists, USA, expressed its "great satisfaction" at the formation of the Federation of Atomic Scientists. "This is the kind of development for which our group has worked and prayed . . . and we hasten to offer you our fullest support," they stated; indeed, they even suggested naming an FAS member to their governing body. In the ensuing months, Raymond Swing became one of the most vocal supporters of the scientists' movement and Norman Cousins ran fund-raising dinners for the atomic scientists in New York City. Meeting with the Atomic Scientists of Chicago in early 1946, Emery Reves discussed with them his ideas on world government.[80] The following year, UWF and FAS co-sponsored a luncheon forum in Washington, D.C., at which Cord

Meyer, Jr., spoke on the search for security. On another occasion, in Princeton, Meyer met with the leaders of ECAS, including Einstein, Szilard, and other prominent physicists. "The logic of their impassioned argument I found irrefutable," he recalled years later, "and their desperate sense of urgency reinforced my own conviction that we had little time left." Einstein, in turn, wrote an enthusiastic endorsement of *Peace or Anarchy*, which was placed on the book jacket. Soon thereafter, at the suggestion of a radio network, Einstein joined Meyer on a nationwide broadcast, moderated by Swing.[81]

The question of international control of atomic energy, however, proved trickier for world federalists than for atomic scientists, for many viewed it as an illusory solution to the problem of the Bomb. In September 1945, Reves warned Einstein that there was "only one way to prevent an atomic war and that is to prevent war"; but with the United Nations structured as "a league of sovereign nation-states," this was unlikely. To be sure, Americans United for World Government lauded the Acheson-Lilienthal report as an "advanced and constructive" proposal—"a first step" in the direction of "world law"[82]— and Norman Cousins and another prominent federalist, Thomas Finletter, publicly praised it as "a refreshing display of sanity." Nevertheless, Cousins and Finletter criticized the failure of the proposal to balance the surrender of sovereignty by other nations with the renunciation of the U.S. atomic stockpile. Meyer adopted an even tougher stance. "Before nations can be expected to give up weapons as decisive as atomic bombs," he wrote, "they must have a more reliable guarantee of their security than is provided in an international control of atomic energy which must degenerate into war at the first attempted evasion and which leaves uncontrolled the continuing competition for other types of weapons." He added: "Nations will never cease to compete for every weapon of war until they have a reasonable assurance that war is not possible and until they are given another method of resolving their inevitable differences."[83]

World government leaders expressed much the same qualms about the Baruch Plan. Although Grenville Clark supported it, arguing that it represented "a considerable beginning in federal world government,"[84] others were much less enthusiastic. Hutchins cited author Carl Dreher's comment that the Baruch Plan "seeks to prevent an atomic armament race by tying every other competitor to the starting post, while we forge still farther ahead by continuing to manufacture the bombs." The Baruch Plan did not go "far enough," observed UWF, for it failed to provide for "enforcement action" or to "include weapons other than the atomic bomb—weapons capable of destroying mankind as readily as the bomb." In an apparent concession, however, UWF added that "almost any world control of atomic energy is better than none. An international control plan would at least provide a period of truce." Privately, Meyer told William

Higinbotham of the FAS in early 1947 that "there is no hope in attempting to gain security by the one weapon at a time approach." Indeed, "the atomic control problem is not separable from the security problem as a whole." Therefore, "what is most to be desired is a working agreement between the United World Federalists, the atomic scientists, and as many other influential groups as possible on a minimum program" for world security.[85]

Not surprisingly, leading world federalists were deeply disturbed by the president's decision to build an H-Bomb. UWF used the occasion to argue that the only way to avoid war with the new weapons was "to eliminate war itself" by giving "the United Nations the power to prevent war." Other appraisals were far bleaker. Addressing a conference at New York University, Cousins warned that "life expectancy is about three years" if present trends continued.[86] In a letter to Hans Bethe, Erich Kahler, a member of the Chicago committee, declared that "we must not cease to speak up and to drive home to the people the picture of the impending moral and material catastrophe." Writing in *Common Cause*, Hutchins and Borgese argued that the Russians and the Americans were developing "a double suicide pact." Of course, there was "still liberty enough in this country for Cassandras to speak" and to warn "of doom." But, throughout history, they were rarely heeded.[87]

Despite the gloom, however, the world government movement made remarkable progress in the United States. By mid-1949, its largest organization, United World Federalists, had 46,775 members and 720 chapters throughout the nation.[88] The idea of transforming the United Nations into a world federation was endorsed by 45 important national organizations, including Americans for Democratic Action, the American Veterans Committee, the General Federation of Women's Clubs, the National Grange, the Farmers' Union, the United Auto Workers, the Junior Chamber of Commerce, the Young Democrats, the Young Republicans, and numerous Protestant, Catholic, and Jewish religious bodies. In early 1949, World Government Week was officially proclaimed by the governors of nine states and by the mayors of approximately 50 cities and towns (including Chicago, Minneapolis, and Miami).[89] Furthermore, thanks to a campaign led by North Carolina attorney Robert Lee Humber, by mid-1949 twenty state legislatures had passed resolutions endorsing world government.[90] That June, 91 members of the U.S. House of Representatives (64 Democrats and 27 Republicans) introduced a resolution putting their body of Congress on record as supporting world federation as the "fundamental objective" of U.S. foreign policy. The United Nations, declared the resolution—drafted by UWF—should be developed "into a world federation open to all nations with defined and limited powers adequate to preserve peace and prevent aggression." Within a short time, the resolution had 111 co-sponsors in the House and 21 in the Senate.[91]

This unprecedented challenge to nationalism actually lagged somewhat behind the surge of popularity world federalism experienced during these years. Although a UNESCO-sponsored poll of the late 1940s found that 42 percent of Americans favored world government, as against 46 percent who opposed it, other polls indicated a more positive response. A Roper poll in August 1946 found that 63 percent of Americans approved (and 20 percent opposed) the establishment of a world legislature with binding power over all countries. That same month, a Gallup poll reported that 54 percent of respondents were in favor of transforming the United Nations into a world government; only 24 percent opposed the idea. In August 1947, another Gallup survey placed support at 56 percent and opposition at 30 percent.[92] In two states where world government referenda appeared on the ballot, voters approved them by overwhelming margins—nine to one in Massachusetts and eleven to one in Connecticut. Some of this globalist outpouring undoubtedly sprang from the belief of Americans that their own experience with building a federal government pointed the way for the world—a belief skillfully played upon by world government proponents. But it also represented a response to the argument, as stated by Meyer, that "federation is the alternative to atomic war."[93]

American Pacifists and the Bomb

Pacifists, though also sharp critics of the Bomb, had considerably less appeal among Americans. Widespread popular commitment to World War II deprived pacifist groups of most of their influence in the broader society, particularly in wartime. Indeed, swept up by the draft law, some 6,000 American pacifists went to prison and another 12,000 performed unpaid labor in Civilian Public Service camps. Ironically, pacifist organizational membership actually grew somewhat during the war—in the FOR to an all-time high of 15,000 and in the War Resisters League (the WRI section) to nearly 2,500. These gains, however, appear to have reflected the need of pacifists to escape their overall isolation in American life. By contrast, the WILPF section, which had never been explicitly pacifist, lost nearly all of its nonpacifists, dropping from 15,000 to about 4,000 members, and the Catholic Worker organization also declined. Although the Friends, Mennonites, and Brethren still had several hundred thousand American members, they were not immune to the dominant trends; as a result, only dwindling minorities involved themselves in peace activities or refused military service.[94] In the immediate postwar years, membership in pacifist groups stagnated or declined somewhat, while pacifist influence in key constituencies, such as the churches, failed to return to prewar levels.[95]

Nor were all pacifists convinced that the advent of the Bomb was as revolutionary a development as some nonpacifists maintained. As long-term critics of war, they placed it within that general framework. Commenting on the new weapon in late August 1945, one member of the War Resisters League executive committee declared: "Our business is to destroy the institution of war itself. Let us not get lost in discussions of the particular frightfulness of this weapon or that." Another executive committee member thought the Bomb was not significant enough to warrant "any special letter or statement—it will not change our having more wars, only make them more horrible." A few months later, another pacifist observed that he did not think Cousins's book *Modern Man Is Obsolete* "has thrown any new or valuable light on the problem, which is, after all, the age old problem of war." Participating in a forum organized by *Fellowship* called "The Role of the Pacifist in the Atomic Age," a leading conscientious objector observed tartly that "pacifists are motivated by love, not fear, and the pacifist function in the atomic age remains the same as in the stone age." Even A. J. Muste, the FOR's co-secretary, remained uncertain as to how high a priority to accord the struggle against the Bomb. Only two weeks after the Hiroshima bombing, he reported himself "not entirely clear in my own mind whether our main emphasis ought to be on the atomic bomb or on stopping conscription." [96]

Most pacifists, however, recognized the altered circumstances of the post-Hiroshima world. Could the Bomb "ever be used 'in a good cause'?" asked Dwight Macdonald, a recent convert to pacifism, later that month; "the futility of modern warfare should now be clear." Writing to Muste only a day after the Hiroshima bombing, FOR staff member John Swomley claimed that the time had come to point out that, with human survival threatened by the new weapon, "disarmament is essential." On the West Coast, the pacifist journal *Pacifica Views* argued that "pacifist analysis . . . is forced into a new dimension. The elimination of war comes closer to the point where it is a practical necessity if the human race is to survive." [97] At the same time, pacifists recognized that individual war resistance—which many had championed in the past—now had less relevance. As one member of the War Resisters League executive committee remarked, because of the development of the Bomb, the conscientious objector does not "hold as strategic a position for the blocking of war regimes as he did when warfare wasn't as mechanized and atomic bombs hadn't been developed." Indeed, as a War Resisters League delegate told a WRI conference, "the atom bomb seemed to overshadow everything." Consequently, pacifist pronouncements began to sound remarkably like those of the atomic scientists' and world government movements. In 1945, the WILPF declared that the underlying message of the atomic bomb was simply "Make Peace or Perish." [98]

Not surprisingly, then, pacifist organizations came out strongly against nuclear weapons. In November 1945, the executive committee of the War Resisters League resolved that, "in view of the emergency created by the atomic bomb," it join with other groups in "an emergency pacifist campaign." Early the following year, it proposed an international agreement renouncing the manufacture or employment of nuclear weapons and providing for international inspection. When the U.S. government announced plans for nuclear weapons testing at Bikini, both the WILPF and the War Resisters League assailed the idea. "What should be vaporized is not an obsolete battleship," the WILPF declared, "but the whole process of the manufacture of the atomic bomb." [99] The FOR urged the U.S. government to work not only to reduce armaments but toward "total disarmament on a world scale." Arguing for unilateral nuclear disarmament, Muste claimed that "by holding on to the atomic bomb for our-selves . . . we force other nations into an atomic armament race." It was "psychologically sound," he contended, "to propose that the United States, which created the atmosphere of fear and suspicion by resorting to the use of the bomb, should take the initiative of creating the atmosphere of confidence by, in effect, confessing its sin and renouncing it." [100]

Pacifist efforts against nuclear weapons continued in subsequent years. In mid-1949, the American Friends Service Committee urged that the U.S. government employ a variety of measures to ease tensions with the Soviet Union, including placing the U.S. atomic bomb stockpile under United Nations seal. The following year, during August, pacifists gathered for a ten-day Hiroshima Fast in Washington. When, at the end of November 1950, President Truman discussed the use of the atomic bomb in Korea, pacifists in Chicago responded by organizing a Prayer Vigil for Peace that drew more than a thousand local participants. [101]

In the course of their campaign against the Bomb, pacifists sometimes had ambivalent feelings about their new allies in the atomic scientists' movement. Referring to a statement by the Federation of Atomic Scientists, Muste asked Einstein: "How can scientists who are building a stock-pile of atomic bombs 'teach men that they must abandon atomic weapons to preserve civilization?' " If the leaders of the scientists' movement were to refuse publicly to make nuclear weapons, he argued, the American people "would be shaken out of moral lethargy and despair and would become capable of inspired action to abolish war." Although Muste and some other pacifists continued to needle the scientists' movement along these lines, [102] relationships remained cordial. This situation reflected not only the fact that leaders of the atomic scientists' movement did not engage in military work but the recognition by pacifist leaders that these scientists remained consistent critics of the Bomb. Muste wrote to the FOR staff in early 1946, urging them to contact the atomic scientists, for "many of their utterances border closely on the pacifist position." At the end of that year, he noted his friendly relations with the Northern California Association of Scientists, including its dispatch of a scientist to address an FOR meeting. This scientist seemed "pretty close to our position," Muste remarked, and convinced him of the need to continue the dialogue between the two groups.[103]

Pacifists also felt some uneasiness about the new movement for world government. To be sure, the FOR, the WILPF, the War Resisters League, and the Society of Friends all formally endorsed the idea of world government, and a number of leading pacifists—including Tracy Mygatt, Vernon Nash, and Donald Harrington—devoted their efforts to the world government campaign.[104] The Bomb "has . . . laid on us a new obligation," John Nevin Sayre told readers of *Fellowship*: "prompt and extensive cooperation with non-pacifists in waging an educational campaign for national adoption of the idea of world law and government." [105] Nevertheless, disturbed by the prospect of a world government employing armed forces, pacifists often remained cautious about realization of the idea and about its supporters, most of whom, they noted apprehensively, had backed World War II.[106] "I am definitely in favor of federal world government," Muste contended, but "it could be that peace is the horse and world government the cart." As he told the journalist Dorothy Thompson, he did not "believe the world will get war out of its system save by a great moral decision and action—by renunciation of war. . . . World organization will come out of that moral act, not vice versa." This difference of approach was played out within the Society of Friends through a conflict between Federalists (who favored world political cooperation, including an international police force) and Functionalists (who championed other forms of world cooperation, such as the U.N. Relief and Rehabilitation Administration).[107]

And yet, for the most part, pacifists finessed the issue. "We do spiritually aim at 'one world,' a common humanity," wrote Muste. Sayre called for a world government "strictly limiting the use of force to restraint of *individuals* (not nations) by *police* (not armies, navies or bombs) operating under *law* and judicial process." As a result, pacifist groups maintained friendly relations with the world government movement.[108]

Even as they worked alongside new allies in the struggle against the Bomb, pacifists retained their own distinctive agenda. Appalled at the starvation in postwar Europe and Asia, the FOR urged a U.S. government food aid program, voluntary rationing, and a policy of personal restraint, including fasting. During the Chinese civil war, the American Friends Service Committee maintained a Friends Service Unit behind both Communist and Nationalist lines. It also engaged in postwar relief work in Japan and India.[109] Much pacifist energy went into demonstrating for the release of World War II draft resisters and against a new draft law.[110] Of course, in these and other ventures, pacifists did not abandon their critique of the Bomb. Conscription, they charged, was "preparation for atomic and bacterial war." In May 1946, as the U.S. government prepared for nuclear weapons testing in the Pacific, the *Catholic Worker* ran a full-page headline declaring:

PROTEST BOMB TESTS, FEED EUROPE AND ASIA
THERE CAN BE NO PEACE WHILE THE WORLD STARVES[111]

Muste, the most prominent pacifist of the era, provided a trenchant analysis of the Bomb issue that exemplified the general pacifist approach. Writing to Henry Wallace in September 1946, the FOR leader declared that sharing the secret of the Bomb with Russia alone "is inadequate and in some respects very dangerous." If the Bomb became "a weapon of the Big Three," it would only "enhance the arbitrary power they hold over others." Furthermore, there was no guarantee that "they may not some time fall out with each other and resort to atomic warfare." He also considered both the Baruch Plan and the rival Gromyko Plan seriously flawed.[112] The major problem with the Baruch approach "is that it attempts to deal with the problem of atomic weapons in isolation from the problem of war itself," Muste wrote in 1947. He added, cuttingly:

We cannot believe that any political or military leaders of whatever nation really think that if war occurs, nations will not resort to any weapons, atomic or other, which they deem necessary in order to ward off defeat and national extinction. Experience has amply demonstrated that the "outlawing" of a particular type of weapon . . . does not materially ameliorate the basic difficulty: the insecurity of all men in a world of armed, sovereign states.

As he told readers of *Peace News*: "The discussion of atomic control and of disarmament is not taking place in a vacuum" but "in the context of a terrific power-struggle between Russia and the United States." Therefore, the solution to the problem of the Bomb lay in a program of general disarmament and peace, enforced by the United Nations.[113]

As might be expected, pacifists deplored President Truman's decision to build the H-Bomb. On behalf of the FOR, Muste sent a letter to ministers urging them to protest to the president and congressional representatives, "preach about the hydrogen bomb issue and its implications," and "point out to the most earnest people, especially youth, that the evil logic of war . . . now becomes crystal clear." Calling for public protest, the War Resisters League recognized that it "may not halt the development of the bomb, but it may stimulate such thinking on the part of the government that the bomb may never be used even as a threat." The WILPF noted that even those who approved the decision to build the H-Bomb admitted that "this monstrous weapon provides no security" and argued, accordingly, that "America has an unparalleled opportunity now to lead the world not toward another stage of a stepped-up armaments race but in a determined effort to find constructive ways of resolving present problems." Although pacifists lacked the following to stage mass demonstrations, the War Resisters League, the FOR, and Peacemakers did sponsor a protest meeting attended by some 400 persons on February 24, 1950, at New York's Community Church. Condemning the decision to produce the H-Bomb as "morally hideous," the church's minister, Donald Harrington, declared: "Scientists should not make it. The people should not pay for or sanction the making of it. Legislators should not appropriate money for it." [114]

Thereafter, pacifists continued to assail the new weapon. "From flame-thrower to blockbuster to atomic bomb to Hell-Bomb—the nations, including the United States, march straight on," read a pacifist pronouncement. "No one draws a line and says: '. . . We are pulling out of this march of death.' " To dramatize their dismay, some 50 pacifists—including Dorothy Day of the *Catholic Worker*, Muste of the FOR, and a Hopi chief—descended on Washington, D.C. in April 1950 for a week-long Fast for Peace. During the event, they issued antinuclear appeals to both the White House and the Soviet embassy. That same year, Muste produced a pamphlet for the FOR, *Gandhi and the H-Bomb*, that made the case for the relevance of the Indian leader's program to the international crisis. "If the United States were to decide to try the way of nonviolence toward Russia, how would it go about it?" he asked. "Quite simply," he responded, "it would get out of the armaments race, whether Russia was prepared to come along at once or not, and devote its vast resources and skills and imagination in a great effort to bring about a world-wide improvement in the standard of living . . . and a brotherly, democratic world." If aggression occurred, "the Gandhian answer . . . would be nonviolent resistance. . . . The American people would be organized to refuse absolutely to transport Russian troops or munitions, to produce weapons for them, to work in mines or industries where foreign managers were put in charge, to publish papers for the invaders, to take police or other government jobs under them. They would carry on ceaseless propaganda," while showing "good will to all individual invaders." He concluded: "If the A-bomb and the H-bomb do not move us to achievements in the social and political realm as revolutionary as those that have taken place in the material, there is no hope left for civilization." [115]

American Society and the Bomb

Criticism of the Bomb also cropped up within the broader society. Just after the war, some of the sharpest came from disgruntled New Dealers, many of whom rallied around Henry Wallace, whom Truman dismissed as his secretary of commerce in 1946. Long a favorite among liberals, Wallace now sought to mobilize them for his third-party presidential campaign, which stressed resistance to the nuclear arms race and the Cold War. Despite an auspicious beginning, however, Wallace's Progressive party faded rapidly, and by the time of the 1948 election, he was left with a narrow base of Communists and a dwindling group of non-Communists still willing to work with them.[116] Socialist leader Norman Thomas, long a peace movement stalwart, did not support Wallace and, unlike the liberal leader, favored the Baruch Plan. Nevertheless, he, too, leveled sharp attacks upon nuclear weapons, which he—like the pacifists—felt could not be separated from the overarching context of international conflict and the arms race. Noting that "the nations drift dizzily toward a new world war," Thomas contended that "all our hope must lie in a successful appeal to the nations to accept universal disarmament under international supervision and international arrangements for security," including, eventually, a world federation. More mainstream figures also spoke up, on occasion, for nuclear disarmament, among them Maryland's Democratic senator, Millard Tydings. The powerful chair of the Senate Armed Services Committee, Tydings became alarmed after Truman, in early 1950, announced his decision to develop the H-Bomb and to abandon any further disarmament efforts. In speeches to the Senate, Tydings appealed to the president to call a world disarmament conference rather than leave Americans to "sweat out" a gathering crisis that might end in "total, incinerating war." [117]

The pronouncements of America's religious organizations also reflected persistent concern about the menace of the Bomb. Perhaps the strongest was the Federal Council of Churches' 1946 report, *Atomic Warfare and the Christian Faith*. Condemning methods of atomic warfare "that are intolerable to Christian conscience," the Protestant church body called upon the United States to cease "all manufacture of atomic bombs . . . pending the development of effective international controls" and to declare publicly that it would never be the first to use atomic weapons. But this report and more qualified statements in subsequent years did not rule out the use of nuclear weapons under all circumstances, a position also taken by the Catholic church, which adhered to its "just war" tradition.[118] Furthermore, major religious organizations did not challenge Truman's decision to develop an H-Bomb, and a statement by 30 theologians, ministers, and religious educators that did call it into question was signed almost exclusively by pacifists. Nevertheless, Protestant, Catholic, and Jewish bodies also championed disarmament efforts. Meeting in May 1950, the General Assembly of the Presbyterian church called for "immediate cessation" of the manufacture of H-Bombs by international agreement. The Synagogue

Council of America insisted that "our political leaders should face up to every possible rebuff" in a sincere effort to secure nuclear disarmament.[119]

Soundings of American public opinion also indicated significant misgivings about the Bomb. In late August 1945, in the first flush of American enthusiasm for the new weapon, a Gallup poll found that 69 percent of U.S. respondents regarded the development of the atomic bomb as a "good thing," while only 17 percent regarded it as bad. But by the fall of 1947, attitudes had changed substantially, for 38 percent now called the Bomb's development a bad thing, as compared to 55 percent who regarded it favorably. Indeed, in early 1947, another poll found that although 38 percent thought people "worse off" because of the discovery of nuclear fission, only 37 percent thought them "better off." [120] This growth in negative attitudes toward nuclear weapons apparently reflected a rising sense of their dangers for Americans. In May 1946, 75 percent of U.S. respondents told pollsters of their belief that, if the United States fought another war within the next 25 years, atomic bombs would be used against American cities. Early the next year, 53 percent said that, in the event of such a war, there was a "very real" danger that an atomic bomb would be dropped where they lived.[121] With the heightening of the Cold War, support for the Bomb revived somewhat, with the "good thing"–"bad thing" split growing to 59 to 29 percent by February 1949. But the explosion of the first Soviet atomic bomb that August apparently generated new apprehension about the weapon. In September 1945, a mere 12 percent of American respondents had told pollsters that the atomic bomb made another world war more likely and, as late as March 1949, only 25 percent made that claim; in the aftermath of the Soviet bomb explosion, however, the number increased to 45 percent. In August 1950, when Americans who believed the Soviet Union possessed the Bomb were asked if they thought that nation would use the weapon on American cities, 91 percent said "yes." [122]

For the most part, Americans did not favor unilateral action to deal with the menace of the Bomb. The closest they came to supporting such a course occurred in March 1946, when 37 percent of respondents reportedly favored (and 43 percent opposed) halting plans for U.S. nuclear tests on Bikini Island.[123] By contrast, asked in April 1946 if they favored continued American manufacture of the atomic bomb, 61 percent responded affirmatively and 30 percent negatively. In November 1946, when pollsters asked Americans if the United States should stop making atomic bombs and destroy its nuclear stockpile, 72 percent of respondents said no and 21 percent yes. The following October, when opinion surveys reverted to a question on continued American manufacture of the Bomb, 70 percent favored it, while 26 percent reported themselves opposed.[124]

Nevertheless, strong support existed for nuclear disarmament enforced by a world authority. In May 1946, a poll of Americans by the National Opinion Research Center found that 72 percent of respondents favored having the United Nations "pass a law and be given the power to enforce it so that no country in the world can make atomic bombs." Told that, under this provision, the United States would also have to stop making the Bomb and destroy its atomic stockpile, 56 percent still favored such a law. That September, asked if they preferred that the United States try to "keep ahead of other countries by making more and better atomic bombs" or work to strengthen the United Nations "to prevent all countries, including the United States, from making atomic bombs," 67 percent of respondents chose the latter.[125] Large majorities continued to support this position in 1947, with 79 percent that October telling surveyors that, in this context, they favored U.N. inspection of U.S. facilities. Indeed, 54 percent of American respondents to a Gallup poll in August 1946 supported (and 24 percent opposed) turning the United Nations into "a world government with power to control the armed forces of all nations, including the United States." Another poll that year found that 52 percent of Americans favored U.S. participation in a plan for liquidation of all national military establishments in favor of an international police force.[126]

Even after hopes for international control of atomic energy had faded and the president had announced the government's H-Bomb program, nuclear disarmament remained popular in the United States. "Public debate on the hydrogen bomb has resulted in a wave of pleas for 'fresh starts' and 'new approaches,'" reported a secret State Department study. "There is widespread concern that we are engaged in a dangerous race in weapons of mass destruction." On February 8, about a week after the official H-Bomb announcement, 48 percent of respondents in a Gallup poll favored (and 45 percent opposed) trying "to work out an agreement with Russia on control of the bomb before we try to make a hydrogen bomb." Queried about the same issue that March, Americans supported new efforts toward a control agreement by 68 to 23 percent.[127]

Ironically, despite the U.S. lead in the nuclear arms race, nuclear disarmament had substantial appeal among Americans.

A New Sense of Fear:

Great Britain, Canada, Australia, and New Zealand

> The only remaining alternatives are the end of humanity or the end of war.
>
> Vera Brittain, 1945

Great Britain and, to a lesser extent, the British Commonwealth nations of Canada, Australia, and New Zealand also experienced a postwar surge of uneasiness about nuclear weapons. As junior partners in the Manhattan project, the British and Canadians felt directly involved with the issue. Of course, because of their vested interest in the project, many citizens of these two countries took pride in its success. Furthermore, their firm commitment to the Allied war effort led large numbers of people in all these countries to support the Bomb's use against Japan. But these nations also had deeply rooted pacifist traditions, as well as new organizations among atomic scientists and advocates of world government, which provided an institutional basis for resistance to the Bomb. Furthermore, many Britons were aware that their country—a small island nation that continued to play the role of a great power—was particularly vulnerable to nuclear annihilation. For these reasons, criticism of nuclear weapons became a prominent feature of postwar British life and, to a lesser degree, also emerged in Canadian, Australian, and New Zealand affairs.

Britons and the Atomic Bombing of Japan

The bombing of Hiroshima caused an immediate furor in Great Britain, with the sharpest public criticism coming from pacifists and members of the clergy. Assailing the action, the British FOR journal declared that "war is now seen stripped of the last remnants of its tawdry glory and exposed in its naked and barbarous shame." The Bombing Restriction Committee, a British pacifist venture that had questioned the mass bombing of cities during World War II, immediately sent telegrams to Truman and Prime Minister Clement Attlee "emphatically" condemning the use of atomic bombs for "indiscriminate massacre of civilians."[1] In a front-page editorial, the *Catholic Herald* declared that use of the bomb was "not only utterly and absolutely indefensible in itself but . . . lights up for us all the immorality along the path we have all been treading." The archbishop of Canterbury, Geoffrey Fisher, called it "a terrible and shocking reminder that war is an unclean business," and the dean of St. Alban's described it as "a pitiless act of destruction." During the first days after the bombing of Hiroshima, the morning newspapers were filled with letters of disapproval. Protesting the bombing, several prelates refused to hold thanksgiving services in their churches on V-J Day. Indeed, the president of the Methodist Conference claimed that "the sense of horror at the devastating effect of the atomic bomb is almost universal."[2]

Actually, however, approval of the atomic bombing of Japan was quite widespread in Great Britain. A poll taken shortly after the action found that although 21 percent of British respondents opposed the bombing—more than twice the level in the United States—72 percent supported it. Crediting the Bomb with the defeat of Japan, British newspapers lavished praise upon the weapon. The *Daily Telegraph* asked heatedly: "Who can doubt that its use, which saved the lives of countless fighting men and put a sudden term to the suffering . . . was fully justified?" The Rev. C. L. Fogg praised God "for the work of the scientists" who had "shortened the war and saved thousands of lives," and the Very Rev. Lionel Blackburne, dean of Ely, expressed his indignation at those members of the clergy who had condemned the atomic bombing. "It is difficult to speak temperately," he explained, "of those who appear to value the lives of a cruel and barbarous people above the lives of those noblemen of our forces and our allies." In 1946, the British Council of Churches weighed in with an official study, *The Era of Atomic Power*, that—in contrast to the report of the Federal Council of Churches in the United States—contained no condemnation of the bombing.[3]

Like many Americans, however, Britons worried about what the Bomb portended. As Leonard Woolf, a leading intellectual and Labour party elder statesman, explained: "If you destroy the maximum number of people in the shortest possible time in the most painful way, you may induce the survivors to think about the possibility of preventing the same fate overtaking themselves." In a sardonic letter published in the London *Times*, George Bernard Shaw commented that it was "worth mentioning" that the explosion of atoms opened the prospect for the explosion of the world.[4] Speaking before an audience in Manchester, the Royal Air Force's official observer at the Nagasaki bombing was no less apocalyptic: "Britain is faced either with the end of this country or no more war . . . the choice between survival and extinction." H. G. Wells, whose nightmarish fantasy had become reality, sank into gloom. "There is no way out or round or through the impasse," he wrote. "It is the end." [5]

A new sense of fear even gripped the British establishment. On the day after the bombing of Hiroshima, the London *Times* editorialized that "the atomic bomb . . . carries the warning that another war will mean the destruction of all organized life." On August 8, contending that the Bomb "can speedily make an end of civilized life on earth," the *Times* maintained that there was "no alternative" to "the control of war itself." The following week, the *Times* returned to the theme, arguing that, with the development of the Bomb, "this defeat of Germany and Japan is in a most grim sense the last victory. . . . The outbreak of another war will be in itself the final defeat of civilized man. Ravage and ruin beyond imagination must be the fate of all who engage in it. . . . It must be made impossible for war to begin, or else mankind perishes." In the speech from the throne at the opening of Parliament on August 15, 1945, King George VI declared: "The devastating new weapon which science has . . . placed in the hands of humanity should bring home to all the lesson that the nations of the world must abolish recourse to war or perish by mutual destruction." [6]

Both major parties initially adopted the same somber tone. Churchill, now out of power but still the acknowledged Tory leader, declared with a lack of his characteristic ebullience that the Hiroshima bombing "should arouse the most solemn reflections in the mind and conscience of every human being." Attlee, the Labour party leader and the new prime minister, told the House of Commons on August 22: "I am certain that all of us in this House realize that we are now faced with the naked choice between world cooperation and world destruction." Incredulous at the sudden turn of the tide, Vera Brittain, a prominent novelist and leading pacifist, privately remarked: "Everyone, being now alarmed into realization, is saying exactly what pacifists said all through the war." [7]

Within a short time, these ideas pervaded British public opinion. Admittedly, in the immediate aftermath of the atomic bombing of Japan, most Britons took a rosy view of the new weapon, with 52 percent of respondents telling pollsters that it decreased the chances of war and a mere 12 percent saying that it increased them. But this mood soon shifted. In May 1946, a poll found that only 28 percent of British respondents thought that, in the long run, the release of atomic energy would do more good than harm, while 46 percent thought it would do more harm than good. [8] In the next few years, even heightened anti-Soviet feeling and talk of the alleged benefits of the "peaceful atom" did little to alter this negative assessment, which was bolstered by the radio broadcast of Hersey's *Hiroshima*. Asked the same question in October 1948, 41 percent of British respondents asserted that, ultimately, atomic energy would lead to more harm than good. Only 33 percent maintained the contrary.[9]

For most Britons, the solution to the problem posed by the Bomb lay in strengthening global institutions. In an editorial on August 8, 1945, the *Manchester Guardian* contended that, since the bombing of Hiroshima, those who still believed in unlimited national sovereignty "must wish the destruction of mankind. We are now drawn inexorably toward some form of world authority which all nations would accept for the control of a weapon which we dare not leave in national hands." Much the same assessment came from the more leftish *New Statesman*. "Public opinion in this country . . . is almost unanimous in demanding that the control of atomic armaments should be vested in a World Security Organisation and that national armaments should be outlawed," the magazine contended in mid-August. "Ten days ago such a proposal would . . . have been dismissed as utopian. Today . . . it is matter-of-fact statesmanship."[10] Asked in a January 1946 poll about their opinion of "the proposal to put the control of atomic energy under the United Nations Security Council," 74 percent of British respondents approved, while only 9 percent disapproved. Indeed, in the new circumstances, most Britons seemed ready to go much further toward limiting the traditional prerogatives of national sovereignty. In September 1945, 51 percent of respondents to a Gallup poll supported the statement that, "now that the atomic bomb has been invented . . . each country should abolish its armed forces, having them replaced by an international force under a world government."[11]

Despite the immediate furor over the danger posed by the Bomb, however, many Britons gradually distanced themselves from the issue. Perhaps because the United States had taken the lead with the wartime Bomb project and had employed only about 200 British scientists along the way, Britons did not feel the same sense of direct responsibility for the results. One observer reported that "piles of unsold copies" of Hersey's *Hiroshima* were languishing in British bookstores. Furthermore, many socialists and other reformers, traditionally the mainstays of British agitation for disarmament and world peace, were preoccupied with the transformation of Britain's domestic policy and its economy undertaken by the new Labour government, elected in July 1945. They had little time for, interest in, or influence on national security matters, which remained the bailiwick of more conservative forces.[12]

Finally, the British government kept its own postwar Bomb project shrouded in secrecy, giving very little information about it to Parliament or the press. During the entire tenure of the Labour government (1945–51), there was only one debate on atomic energy in the House of Lords and none in the House of Commons. Questions about the government's policy in this regard received an icy response. Emrys Hughes, a pacifist Labour member of Parliament, complained: "When an Hon. Member asks the Prime Minister about the atomic bomb he looks at him as if he had asked about something indecent." Through an arrangement between the leaders of Britain's two major parties, parliamentary questions about raw materials for atomic energy were usually avoided. Although the British press initially printed some serious background pieces about atomic weapons, it quickly lapsed into silence or pleasant fantasies about prosperity through atomic power. The result was an absence of sustained public debate about the Bomb.[13]

British Pacifists and Nuclear Weapons

Where criticism of the Bomb persisted, it often came from the depleted ranks of British pacifists. Before the war, Great Britain housed the world's largest, most influential pacifist movement. Gaining impetus from the popular revulsion against the carnage of World War I, the movement achieved its most dramatic expression in the formation of the Peace Pledge Union (PPU), which became a section of the WRI. Founded by the charismatic Anglican minister Dick Sheppard in 1936, the PPU enrolled people who formally renounced war and promised never to sanction another. By 1939, the PPU had 150,000 members, 1,000 local groups, and 30 full-time staff members. But the outbreak of World War II, which solidified support among conscientious objectors and other resolute pacifists, seriously undermined the PPU's morale and its prestige in the broader society. Indeed, many Britons, including some prominent in the interwar peace movement, became convinced that pacifism had invited aggression by the fascist powers. By the end of the conflict, the PPU's active membership had plummeted to no more than 20,000, and it continued to dwindle.[14] Although the British FOR stood at an all-time high point, with some 13,000 supporters, and the Society of Friends had about 20,000 members, much of this membership overlapped with that of the PPU. A pacifist visitor from overseas reported in 1947 that "the movement seemed to be in the doldrums." The circulation of *Peace News* (the PPU journal) was declining by 200 per week, pacifist literature centers were closing, there was "an almost total lack of young people" in the movement, and members themselves evinced "a sense of despondency."[15]

Nevertheless, if considerably less vibrant than in the heady days of the 1930s, British pacifism did serve as an important source of critical thinking about the atomic bomb. From the outset, it was recognized that the advent of nuclear weapons represented a dramatic turning point in human existence. "The production of the atom bomb is going to have unpredictable and revolutionary consequences," *Peace News* declared in its first comment on the obliteration of Hiroshima. Could the human mind "take control of this new form of energy and turn it to the service of life? Unless it can, human life at a civilised level lies under the dark shadow of . . . self-destruction." Pacifists also recognized the curious ramifications of the Bomb for their movement. As *Peace News* noted the following week, in light of the Bomb, "pacifism, conceived as mere war-resistance, may become obsolete." Pacifists were "faced with the duty of rethinking the whole of their position and separating what is eternal in it from what is ephemeral." Vera Brittain, elected chair of the PPU in 1948, recalled that "nuclear weapons immediately vitiated the campaigning methods of the secular pacifist societies, since the individual renunciation of war, while retaining its moral authority, had lost its political validity." Wars would no longer "cease if the common man refused to fight," for governing elites would henceforth rely less on soldiers than on nuclear weapons.[16]

Nevertheless, pacifists recognized that if nuclear weapons undermined notions of individual war resistance, they also provided a powerful argument for ending war. "Mass society reacts to the compulsion of circumstance," *Peace News* observed. "The atom bomb, which has certainly not convinced its millions of individual members of the necessity of pacifism, may quite well convince it of the necessity of peace." Commenting on the significance of the new weapon, the FOR's journal, the *Christian Pacifist*, stated that "the only safeguard is to abolish war utterly and finally." Around the world there was "a solemn realisation of the fact that now humanity must renounce war or perish." In an editorial on August 31, *Peace News* argued that "the bomb that closed World War II was the warning that it is no use preparing for World War III." With the coming of nuclear weapons, "the whole world has passed into a new dimension of experience," one that required "a total change of the human mentality." The "explosion of the atomic bomb was tremendous; but not so tremendous as will be the explosion in the human consciousness of the fact that there is no way out in war." [17]

Convinced, then, that the development of the Bomb bolstered the case for disarmament and peace, Britain's pacifist groups appealed to the British government for a dramatically new kind of leadership. On August 20, 1945, the British WILPF section told the prime minister that "the invention of the atomic bomb has rendered obsolete the weapons, conscript armies and strategic bases to which men cling." Would not the British government "make a dramatic appeal to the leaders of every country to turn wholly from the preparation . . . for catastrophic destruction and to seek security in worldwide cooperation for the satisfaction of human need?" Another appeal for new directions came in November 1945 from the National Peace Council (NPC), a coalition of Britain's peace groups, most of them pacifist. It formally called on the British government "to declare Britain's readiness in face of the challenge of the atom bomb, to join in a solemn renunciation of all war and in the progressive but rapid development of a system of world government." In addition, it asked that scientific advances be made available to all nations through the Economic and Social Council of the United Nations and that governments accept responsibility for relieving human distress in Europe.[18]

Pacifist groups also embarked upon a range of educational and agitational ventures. On August 31, 1945, the National Peace Council held an emergency meeting of 2,000 people in Central Hall, Westminster, around the theme "World unity or world destruction?" Sir John Boyd Orr (NPC president) warned the gathering that politics and economics had failed to keep up with scientific breakthroughs, while Dame Sybil Thorndike (actress) implored: "Before we have time to get used to the bomb, let us do something about it." [19] In the ensuing months and years, the Friends Peace Committee, the PPU, the FOR, and the National Peace Council worked singly and together to sponsor numerous meetings and other gatherings on the dangers of nuclear weapons, including a poster parade to Hyde Park in April 1948. At the latter event, which drew about 1,000 people, the Rev. A. D. Belden called for "a vast human revolt against this atrocity," adding: "Let every man and woman say 'No' to atomic war!" Speakers at these and other anti-Bomb gatherings included Alex Wood and Vera Brittain (both chairs of the PPU), Kathleen Lonsdale (a leading atomic scientist and pacifist), and Ritchie Calder (a prominent journalist).[20] In January 1949, the PPU held the largest pacifist demonstration since the war, drawing nearly 3,000 people to London's Central Hall for speeches by Laurence Housman (WRI chair), Alex Comfort (biologist and anarchist), a number of Labour M.P.'s, Michael Tippett (composer), Brittain, Thorndike, and others. That June, when the British government held a mock air battle, the PPU displayed a thousand posters in London declaring: "Cities Cannot Be Defended by Atom Bombs." In August, pacifists drew 3,000 people to a Hiroshima Day demonstration in Trafalgar Square.[21]

Pacifists also produced a good deal of literature criticizing nuclear weapons. In 1948, the Friends Peace Committee distributed a pamphlet, *The Challenge of the Atomic Bomb*, written by one of its leaders, Marion Parmoor. Challenging government plans for civil defense, the PPU in 1950 distributed more than 100,000 copies of a leaflet written by Comfort. Ridiculing official policy, he argued that, "if war comes, there will be no winner, no loser, and nothing to defend." There remained, he said, "only one course open—to see that war does not break out." Another PPU leaflet, *You and the Atomic Bomb*, produced in 1951, also lampooned precautions against atomic war, among them hiding under desks and crouching behind trees. One cartoon in the leaflet showed a mother diving under her baby carriage blanket as the infant looked on in astonishment. Civil defense, *Peace News* contended, "is . . . nothing but an elaborate preparation for national suicide." [22]

As an alternative, British pacifists consistently promoted disarmament. Under the editorship of John Middleton Murry, *Peace News* championed major disarmament initiatives with headlines like "The Only Defence Against the Bomb—Baruch Plan or Nothing." The FOR was also enthusiastic about the Baruch Plan, arguing that its "evident generosity" would "make for an all-round improvement" in East-West relations. At the same time, unlike Murry, it found merit in the Russian proposal to destroy all atomic stockpiles. In early 1947, Murry—growing ever more anti-Soviet—wrote bitterly that he regarded Russian rejection of the Baruch Plan "as a colossal crime against humanity." [23] Subsequently, when Murry left *Peace News* and the PPU as well, official pacifist reaction became more measured. In late 1948, *Peace News* depicted U.N. insistence on the American plan, in the face of stubborn Soviet resistance, as "futile and frivolous." Almost a year later, Kathleen Lonsdale praised the Baruch Plan as "a step forward in diplomatic relations" but suggested that "it failed because it tried to eliminate suspicion without substituting anything positive in its place." [24]

Naturally, British pacifists were also disheartened by the North Atlantic Treaty Organization (NATO) pact and by the Soviet development of the atomic bomb, which occasioned a new round of antinuclear activism on their part. In a letter to Britain's press, pacifist leaders reacted to the Soviet breakthrough by calling for the outlawing of war and war preparations. Vera Brittain argued that "this is the moment when the leaders of Britain and the United States of America should at least declare that they will destroy their stocks of atomic bombs and the formulas that produced them within a given period if the USSR will do the same, and submit to inspection by a neutral commission," which "will guarantee that this has been done. Not an armaments race in lethal weapons, but a supreme example of spiritual courage can now alone save humanity." [25] When the U.S. government instead announced plans to develop a hydrogen bomb, the PPU condemned Truman's decision as "a denial of fundamental moral principles and values and . . . an outrage against the conscience of mankind." The PPU was "convinced that this decision must lead to an intensification of the race in atomic weapons, the end of which is not peace but atomic war." The only way to secure peace and national security was by "the renunciation of the method of war, and abolition of conscription and of all armaments." [26]

Nevertheless, dwindling in numbers and influence, British pacifists provided the cause of nuclear disarmament with only limited assistance. The PPU's December 1, 1947, meeting—"No Atomic War!"—"had grand speeches," noted *Peace News*, "but only 50 people were there to hear them." In Glasgow the previous year, PPU staff member (and later chair) Sybil Morrison addressed "13 people at what was supposed to be a public meeting." In April 1947, at the PPU's annual general meeting, "the attendance was noticeably small compared with previous years, and many well-known faces were conspicuous by their absence," *Peace News* reported. "It was all too clear that English pacifism was going through a critical phase." Indeed, the circulation of *Peace News* was declining, and the PPU's annual budget stood at a mere 5,000 pounds. In April 1949, Morrison wrote that *Peace News* had "only 10,000 readers against the millions of the national press." Although the membership of the FOR rose slightly to 14,000, the once powerful PPU could claim no more than that number in a population of 40 million.[27]

Nor, despite their revulsion at the atomic bomb, did British pacifists make it the focal point of their activities. Although impressed by the significance of the new weaponry, pacifist leaders were often absorbed with other issues in these years. In September 1945, for example, in the immediate aftermath of the atomic bombing of Japan, the PPU executive committee resolved that Save Europe Now, a relief campaign for the war-torn continent, "was the most important form of activity during the next few weeks."[28] Indeed, throughout the postwar years, the PPU showed no more interest in the atomic bomb than in a broad range of issues, including conscription, relations among the Big Three, feeding Europe, decolonization, programs of the British Labour party, and the repatriation of prisoners of war. The FOR, too, preoccupied with starvation in Europe and peacetime conscription, gave the Bomb only intermittent attention.[29] Pacifists, after all, were not primarily critical of particular weapons or even of weapons per se but of the institution of war. Thus they took a more holistic, radical position than did many opponents of nuclear weapons. "The control or abolition of certain weapons, however desirable, is not all that is to be desired," the FOR maintained. Or, as Morrison insisted in a discussion of banning the atomic bomb and other current issues, "protest should be against the cause, not the symptoms of the disease." As a result, British pacifists did not place the problem of nuclear weapons at the top of their agenda.[30]

The Atomic Scientists

Britain's atomic scientists, if more restrained in style than the pacifists, focused more exclusively on the Bomb. Like their colleagues in the United States, British scientists who had worked on the Manhattan project were often deeply disturbed by the ominous implications of the atomic bomb, and these concerns came to the surface in the postwar era. In September 1945, a group of British scientists associated with the Bomb's development advised the British government that "the advent of this new weapon of destruction ought to be the signal for renewed efforts to achieve lasting world peace." They emphasized that "the remaining secrets of the uranium fission process are mainly of a technological and not fundamental character, and any advantages they give us in conducting negotiations are not likely to be long lived." Therefore, they urged "speed in endeavoring to secure some form of international control by the United Nations of the use of atomic energy." [31] Speaking before the PPU's "No Atomic War!" meeting, Kathleen Lonsdale argued that, "in atomic war, there can be no victors, only vanquished." Although Lonsdale, as a wartime pacifist, was not typical of British scientists, even former members of the Maud Committee, like Oliphant and Blackett, now emerged as vigorous opponents of the Bomb. Indeed, many of Britain's top atomic scientists felt a close affinity with groups like the Federation of American Scientists and the Emergency Committee of Atomic Scientists.[32] Consequently, they moved to form a British counterpart.

Joseph Rotblat played a key role in organizing the group. Upon his return to Great Britain in early 1945, Rotblat had deliberately chosen work on an aspect of nuclear physics—medicine—with no military applications. But he remained deeply concerned about the prospect of a nuclear holocaust, particularly because, at Los Alamos, he had worked next door to Edward Teller, then doing research on the feasibility of a hydrogen bomb. After the atomic bombing of Hiroshima seemed to set the process in motion, Rotblat began sounding out British scientists about the possibility of a moratorium on nuclear weapons research. To his regret, he encountered substantial opposition to this idea, especially from left-wing scientists, who argued that a research moratorium would leave the United States with a nuclear monopoly. Committed to "arousing the scientific community to the danger" of nuclear weapons "and to educating the public on these issues," however, Rotblat pressed forward with an alternative plan: the development of an arms control and disarmament organization among Britain's atomic scientists.[33]

Under the auspices of the British Association of Scientific Workers (AScW), an organization of 15,000 members with Blackett as president, an Atomic Scientists' Committee had been meeting to assess the significance of atomic energy. On February 23, 1946, the committee talked with John Simpson of the Federation of American Scientists, discussed the need for an international movement of scientists, and decided greatly to increase the scale of its work. At the following meeting, on March 8, the committee voted to form an association of atomic scientists that would "express opinions on policy regarding atomic energy development." Although the AScW suggested that the organization be continued under its auspices, most of the scientists involved, including Rotblat, rejected this idea. The AScW was a trade union and, furthermore, had a decidedly left-wing image. Consequently, in the spring of 1946, an independent Atomic Scientists' Association (ASA) was launched, with Nevill Mott as its first president. The ASA offered full membership to persons who had worked on the British, Canadian, or American Bomb projects and, by 1950, had about 140 full members and 500 associate members.[34] Although the AScW resented the ASA as a rival group, it also recognized its importance; consequently, a number of left-wing scientists joined the ASA's ranks. Indeed, drawing upon most of Great Britain's prominent atomic scientists, the ASA soon reflected a wide range of views. Both the pacifist Lonsdale and the hawkish Cherwell served as vice-presidents.[35]

Nevertheless, despite the diversity of opinion within the ASA, it emerged as a rough counterpart to the Federation of American Scientists, providing much of the information Britons received on the dangers of nuclear weapons. Through its small journal, the *Atomic Scientists' News*, the ASA reached scientific and other elite constituencies on issues of atomic energy control. Meanwhile, in the winter and spring of 1947–48, the ASA sponsored its major attempt at popular education, an Atomic Train exhibition. Organized by Rotblat and with ASA members serving as guides, the exhibition toured the entire country and was seen by an estimated 146,000 people. Thereafter, the ASA donated the Atomic Train to UNESCO, which deployed it in the Middle East and in Scandinavia. The published guide to the exhibit, prepared by the ASA, sold 53,000 copies, thus becoming the most widely distributed textbook in Great Britain on the subject of atomic energy and also subsidizing the ASA for years to come. Reflecting the thinking popular among most scientists at the time, the exhibit contrasted the dangers of nuclear weapons with the purported benefits of peaceful nuclear power.[36]

Britain's atomic scientists also devoted much attention to finding an appropriate policy for nuclear disarmament. Delighted by the Acheson-Lilienthal report, the Atomic Scientists' Committee gave it strong support, noting that it "contains all the proposals for the control of atomic energy that our committee considered essential." Oliphant told Oppenheimer that the report represented "a platform on which every scientist in our countries can fight, and I certainly will push it for all I am worth."[37] This enthusiasm dissipated somewhat with the announcement of the Baruch proposals, which provoked the opposition of Blackett and the AScW, although they probably satisfied most British atomic scientists.[38] When stalemate developed in the United Nations over the Baruch Plan, both the ASA and the AScW emphasized the need for compromise. The

AScW professed to find value in the Gromyko proposals, while the ASA acknowledged that "an effective system of control acceptable to all concerned is a very doubtful proposition in the present state of distrust between nations, since it must contain, at least in embryonic form, a measure of world government." [39] Throughout the balance of 1947 and the first half of 1948, the ASA sought what Oliphant called "compromise forms or alternative plans which might well be better than no agreed plan at all." In July 1948, however, the council of the ASA issued a pessimistic evaluation of the impasse. Noting "its continuing belief in some form of international control of atomic energy as the most desirable ultimate solution of the problem of atomic weapons," the council did not "consider that any good purpose will be served by pressing for it now. A substantial change in international relations is necessary before such plans . . . can be revived with any hope of success." A year later, Rudolf Peierls, the new ASA president, caustically reported to the organization that the recent debate in the United Nations over atomic energy controls "was conducted on all sides more with a view to its propaganda value than in any hope of agreement." [40]

Even as hopes for international control of the Bomb grew and then faded among British scientists, some were hard at work on Britain's own atomic weapons program. The secrecy of the British government's plans in this regard meant that there was no public debate on the issue, and officials gave the impression to many persons employed at the atomic research facility at Harwell that they were working on the peaceful uses of atomic energy. Nevertheless, a good number of scientists realized the significance of the project and either left it or, more usually, signed on willingly. [41] In the high-level committees of scientists that the government employed to consider the atomic program, Blackett's was the only voice of dissent. Replying to a scientist who upbraided him for working to develop atomic weapons, Cockcroft declared that the overwhelming danger of the time came not from the weapons but from the Soviet Union, "which has taken over the practices of the Nazi regime." He also believed that Great Britain, as the leader of Western Europe and the Commonwealth, should not be dependent upon the United States but should possess its own nuclear weapons. The ASA was bitterly divided over the British weapons program. [42]

Nevertheless, despite the ease with which the British government staffed its Bomb project, the atomic scientists' movement provided one of the most important voices in postwar Britain that spoke out for peace and nuclear disarmament. The ASA's executive vice-president, H. S. W. Massey, publicly argued that "the greatest social problem of the day is that of war"; therefore, scientists should "consider thoroughly their professional attitude to the whole question so that they may satisfy themselves that the work which they may be called upon to carry out is in the best interests of mankind." ASA president

Nevill Mott not only denounced nuclear weapons but assailed even the threat of strategic bombing. In a message to the ASA, he declared bluntly: "Let us at the outset be clear that the aim of our policy is to prevent war." Both ASA leaders were deeply troubled by the problem of the Bomb and opposed to Britain's entry into the nuclear arms race.[43] Furthermore, despite the traditional distaste for politics among British scientists and the attempts by its more "respectable" members to block ASA statements on public policy questions, the ASA cooperated closely with the National Peace Council and, in 1950, formally affiliated with it. These activities provided the backdrop to the petition, signed in April 1950 by 100 scientists at Cambridge University, calling upon the British government to "make a statement condemning production of the H-Bomb." In the ensuing months, individual scientists announced their refusal to work on the new weapon. "If I am personally asked to help in developing super-bombs," declared G. O. Jones of Oxford University, "I shall say, 'No, I am sorry, it is too disgusting.' "[44]

The World Government Movement

The menace of the Bomb also spurred the development of Britain's world government movement. Federal Union had managed to pull together a few thousand supporters during wartime, but the overall movement grew rapidly only after the bombing of Hiroshima. Newly organized federalist groups recruited prominent sponsors, published newsletters, and staged mass meetings focused on the nuclear danger. "We stand at the most perilous point in the whole history of humanity," a world government speaker told a large student federalist gathering in 1947. "War must be stopped now or it will destroy us all." In November 1948, a meeting on world government drew more than 2,000 people to Central Hall in London, where they heard Sir John Boyd Orr, the director of the U.N. Food and Agriculture Organization, declare that there would be neither victor nor vanquished in a new war; indeed, he argued, "any person advocating war as a solution to our difficulties is a homicidal maniac."[45] Naturally, longtime peace advocates welcomed such thinking. The National Peace Council changed the title of its journal from *Peace Aims* to *One World*; the new "Atomic World" section began with the observation of an American physicist that "the sooner we recognize the need for world government . . . the longer we will last." But world federalist sentiment moved considerably beyond the limits of the traditional peace constituency. In October 1949, for example, Boyd Orr addressed two "United World" gatherings in Scotland that drew some 13,000 people.[46]

Bertrand Russell provided Britain's burgeoning world government movement with one of its most influential—and controversial—figures. An eminent philosopher, mathematician, and peace proponent, Russell declared in the aftermath of the atomic bombing of Japan that "all the old disputes . . . have been rendered futile by the threat of the atomic bomb," which menaced humanity with "extermination." In a much publicized speech in the House of Lords in November 1945, he warned that society would "inevitably bring itself to destruction" unless the world agreed "to find a way of abolishing war." [47] The following year, Russell contended that there was "only one way in which great wars can be permanently prevented," and that was through "the establishment of an international government, with a monopoly of serious armed force." Nevertheless, unlike other advocates of world government, Russell was prepared to push the issue to a rapid showdown before other nations had the Bomb. The United States, he maintained, should join with other countries to form a world authority and should encourage the Soviet Union, through every reasonable concession, to join, too. Then, "if Russia acquiesced willingly, all would be well. If not, it would be necessary to bring pressure to bear, even to the extent of risking war." Although Russell professed "little doubt" that, under these conditions, the Soviet Union would join a world federation and thus avert a nuclear arms race,[48] pacifists—among others—were aghast at Russell's suggestion, which caused him some embarrassing moments in later years.[49] Meanwhile, he championed the Baruch Plan as "an immense advance toward sanity" and continued to promote the idea that, in an age of nuclear weapons, humanity's survival depended upon progress toward world government.[50]

By far the most effective leader of the British movement for world government was Henry Usborne, a handsome, dynamic young engineer who had established his own business on cooperative principles. Elected to Parliament in the Labour sweep of 1945, Usborne became interested in world federation after the atomic bombing of Hiroshima. In January 1946, he organized a small group of backbenchers into the Parliamentary Group for World Government, and in early 1947 they introduced a motion, drafted by Usborne and signed by 73 members of Parliament, affirming Britain's readiness to federate with other nations. Although the resolution failed to become official policy, it secured nearly 100 backers by the end of the year. Meanwhile, Usborne used his parliamentary base to launch the Crusade for World Government, which organized "World Government Week" in assorted cities, held mass meetings, secured favorable coverage in the press, and published a newsletter and other literature. Support for the crusade, which adopted the people's world convention approach, came not only from Russell and Boyd Orr but from top cabinet ministers, including Stafford Cripps and Ernest Bevin.[51] Immensely energetic and resourceful, Usborne himself barnstormed across the country and traveled also to Scandinavia, India and, in the fall of 1947, to the United States. Here, funded by the Emergency Committee of Atomic Scientists, Usborne met with Einstein, Cousins, Streit, Hutchins, Meyer, and other luminaries in the world government movement, conferred with top labor leaders and atomic scientists' groups, addressed 28 large meetings, gave 15 press conferences, and made 12 radio broadcasts.[52]

The key to Usborne's approach was his emphasis on the terrible destruction that loomed before humanity. "I think that the chances are 10 to 1 against my dying naturally, and then I am optimistic," he told the press in 1947. Only world government, he explained in a speech to Parliament reminiscent of H. G. Wells, could answer the question, "How can the scientific knowledge of our age be used for constructive purposes and prevented from destroying the world?" This was certainly the message of the Crusade for World Government when, in March 1950, its national council responded to the American decision to build an H-Bomb. Pointing to Einstein's statement that "the use of the H-Bomb might result in the extermination of all life on this earth," the national council reaffirmed "its belief in world federal government as the essential means whereby impending mass destruction may be averted." As Usborne put it in 1948, in a statement he drafted for overseas supporters: "The choice is indeed between one world or none."[53]

The extent to which Usborne's views outdistanced those of average Britons was tested by his campaign for reelection in early 1950. At the outset, it was clear that he would face an uphill battle to retain the seat that he had won by some 4,000 votes in the nationwide Labour landslide of 1945. In a reapportionment, Usborne had lost half of his former Birmingham district and acquired a heavily middle-class area that seemed unpromising territory for the Labour party. Furthermore, Usborne faced a young, attractive Conservative candidate, as well as Liberal and Communist opponents who seemed likely to siphon off some of the vote he might otherwise secure. Finally, Usborne's determination to make world government the centerpiece of his campaign opened the way for the Tories to garner votes through nationalist appeals. Not surprisingly, Labour viewed the seat as marginal, and the Conservatives expected to win. Sticking to his principles, Usborne ran a remarkably candid, unorthodox campaign, beginning with a letter to all voters declaring that world government was "the supreme task of our generation, which must take priority over everything." World federalist leaders from France and the United States came to his district and campaigned on his behalf, and public meetings were regaled with messages from prominent world government advocates from around the world. On election day, although the Labour party suffered defeats throughout the country, Usborne achieved an impressive triumph, winning reelection by the same margin as in 1945. As Harris Wofford, one of his American campaigners, wrote, Usborne's victory produced "for a moment an island of international comradeship, as if the ocean of nationalism had rolled back briefly."[54]

Although a surprising number of Britons seemed ready for world government, pacifists sometimes felt uneasy about it. A *Peace News* editorial in January 1948 stated that "we deplore the fact that so many sincere peace-workers are being drawn into" the Crusade for World Government. "An international police force is either a mechanism for waging war on dissident communities . . . or else it serves no purpose not adequately fulfilled by the police forces of sovereign states." A symbolic confrontation developed at the annual meeting of the Peace Pledge Union later that year, when Wing Commander Ernest Millington, chair of Usborne's parliamentary group, spoke of how world events had driven him from the military camp to the peace camp and of the progress of the Crusade for World Government. According to the record of the meeting, "there was general agreement with the view of the world which he outlined" but continued adherence to a resolution passed at the 1947 annual meeting "that the support or sanction of the use of armed force, whether controlled by an international or national authority . . . is not consistent with pacifism." The FOR, too, expressed its "conviction that only in some measure of world government can progress be made out of the present international anarchy" but remained cautious about any arrangement that might call for armed force. Although occasionally criticized from within pacifist ranks for its hostility to world government, *Peace News* stuck to this position, pointing, in further justification, to Russell's willingness to sanction military coercion to secure world federation.[55]

Despite the qualms of pacifists, however, in the five years after the Hiroshima bombing, world federalism made remarkable progress in Britain. By 1950, the Crusade for World Government had some 15,000 registered supporters, while other groups (among which Federal Union was by far the largest) claimed some 3,000. The National Peace Council, which represented 40 British organizations concerned with peace and international order, issued a statement declaring that, though its constituent groups had "differing judgements" on world government strategies, it was united "in its conviction that world unity and some form of world government are indispensable conditions of an ordered and settled peace." Boyd Orr, president of the National Peace Council, became the first president of the World Movement for World Federal Government. Opinion surveys also attest to the popularity of the idea. According to a UNESCO-sponsored poll in the late 1940s, 44 percent of Britons favored world government, as compared to 40 percent who opposed it.[56]

By the late 1940s, then, British pacifists, atomic scientists, and world government advocates were allied in the struggle against the Bomb. With the co-operation of the atomic scientists, pacifist groups used the occasion of visits by the Atomic Train to organize public meetings on the menace of nuclear weapons. At the August 1949 No More Hiroshimas Day rally in Hyde Park, a large crowd heard speeches by Daniel Posin (an American atomic scientist, who warned that there was no defense against the Bomb), Stuart Morris (PPU secretary, who talked of the global struggle to stop a future atomic war), and Frank Beswick (a Labour M.P., who spoke of world government as the alternative to atomic destruction). The following year, some 3,000 people turned out in Trafalgar Square for the August 6 World Peace Day rally, organized by the PPU and supported by the National Peace Council, the WILPF, the Friends Peace Committee, the Crusade for World Government, and other groups. Speakers included Vera Brittain, E. H. S. Burhop (of the ASA), Dora Russell (educator), and the Rev. Donald Soper (a prominent pacifist minister). Their joint position was voiced in the fall of 1949, after the first Soviet Bomb explosion, when a letter to world leaders and the press was issued by prominent pacifists (e.g., Vera Brittain and Stuart Morris), atomic scientists (e.g., Kathleen Lonsdale), and world government advocates (e.g., Henry Usborne) warning that "to put our faith in a race in atomic armaments . . . is to court disaster." They urged the British government "to give a new lead by deciding neither to make nor to borrow atom bombs, and to request the American government to withdraw its atom bombers from bases in this country." Contending that "agreement about atomic energy alone is not enough," they maintained that war itself "should be completely and effectively outlawed."[57]

Other Critics of the Bomb

Although these views were not adopted by Britain's mainstream institutions, they did secure a foothold within some of them. A small Labour Pacifist Fellowship, which included members of Parliament, championed nuclear disarmament and world government. The Labour party's left wing was particularly restive about British foreign and defense policy. Initially content with the Baruch Plan, it adopted a more dissident stance in the following years. In the summer of 1948, 34 Labour backbenchers from the party's pacifist and left-wing ranks issued a "Peace Letter" to Foreign Secretary Bevin that called for Britain's repudiation of atomic weapons, broad disarmament measures, a world food plan, and a policy of reconciliation between East and West.[58]

Sentiment for nuclear disarmament also made some inroads within the British churches, where pacifism remained an important ideological current, albeit a minority one. In the aftermath of World War II, both the British Council of Churches and its largest constituent body, the Church of England, issued reports on the atomic bomb that reflected a sharp division between those who favored banning it and those who supported retaining it as a deterrent. The report of the British Council of Churches, *The Era of Atomic Power* (1946), confessed that "we do not believe that the Church is able with its present insight to pronounce between the two alternatives." Two years later, the Anglican report, *The Church and the Atom*, declared that the use of nuclear weapons was immoral but that a majority of reporters favored their retention by the West. By contrast, the Methodists, whose ranks included some of the leading nuclear critics (e.g., the Rev. Donald Soper), took a more forthright stand in favor of the destruction of all atomic arsenals. Given these divisions, the British churches provided a voice of concern, albeit one without much substance, about the widening dangers of the nuclear arms race. In April 1950, for example, the British Council of Churches issued a statement calling on the government to take the initiative in promoting new international efforts to deal with the "appalling prospect" raised by atomic and hydrogen bombs.[59]

In the broader society, too, there was a growing concern about the dangers of nuclear weapons. Asked in October 1949 about Soviet development of the Bomb, a plurality of British respondents (35 percent) said that it made war more likely. Commenting on the same event, the *Times* recalled Dr. Samuel Johnson's observation that a man's knowing he was about to be hanged concentrated his mind wonderfully. The following February, observing that "the race to make these super bombs" had begun, the archbishop of York asserted that "it will only end either by their use in war or by international agreement to prohibit or control their manufacture. This is the only alternative—destruction or agreement."[60] In the summer of 1950, a Gallup poll found that 54 percent of British respondents believed that nuclear weapons would be used on civilian populations in a new world war and that only 21 percent thought there was any real protection against them. This rising uneasiness may explain why by 1950 British opinion on the U.S. atomic bombing of Japan had reversed itself. That summer, a poll found that only 41 percent of Britons still considered the atomic bombing justified, while 45 percent did not.[61]

Indeed, by 1950, British attitudes toward the use of nuclear weapons were becoming very negative. Although, beyond pacifist circles, there was a general sense of resignation at the American decision to build the H-Bomb, the prospect of employing such weapons aroused fierce opposition. At least some of it was provoked by President Truman's statement in late November 1950 about use of the atomic bomb in Korea. "Before the first reports of Mr. Truman's remarks . . . were toned down," reported a *New York Times* correspondent, "they caused something like consternation in the House of Commons" and "demands from the members that Britain should withdraw her forces from Korea." So great was what the newspaper called the "manifest horror at the thought of employing the atomic bomb" that Prime Minister Attlee announced his plan to fly immediately to Washington to meet with the president, prompting "cheers from both sides of the House." From London, the U.S. embassy reported that British public opinion was "deeply troubled" not only over the Far Eastern situation but over the "possibility that [the] atomic bomb might be used in Korea, thus setting off [a] general atomic war." This anxiety had been only "partly relieved" by Attlee's decision to go to Washington and by soothing statements from the White House.[62] Even before this, however, British attitudes toward the use of the atomic bomb by their NATO ally were rather cool. A public opinion poll in the summer of 1950 found that 47 percent of those British respondents who thought the United States might use the Bomb in a new war would oppose such action. In early 1951, a U.S. intelligence report concluded glumly that in Great Britain there existed "widespread popular alarm concerning the possible use of the A-bomb." [63]

Canada

Opposition to the Bomb was less prevalent in Canada, a nation that had been gravitating for years toward closer social, economic, and national security relations with the United States. Indeed, the initial Canadian reaction to the Bomb was very positive. Asked by pollsters in October 1945 about the atomic bombing of Japan by "the Allies," 77 percent of Canadians expressed their approval, 12 percent their disapproval, and 11 percent said they were undecided. In June 1946, 38 percent of Canadian respondents told the Canadian Institute of Public Opinion that they thought the discovery of atomic energy would do more good than harm, while only 26 percent thought the reverse. With the exception of the United States, this was the most favorable assessment of the prospects for atomic energy in any country surveyed.[64]

As might be expected, Canadian pacifists had a very different view of the situation. The Canadian FOR condemned the atomic bombing of Japan as an "atrocity" whose perpetrators "stand condemned before the bar of justice and mercy." Reflecting on the event some months later, *Reconciliation*, the FOR journal, argued that over all world problems "hangs the menace . . . of atomic power. Today we are all . . . living on the slope of a volcano which may erupt at any moment." It was necessary "to develop our social and political thinking to the point where it can safely cope with our scientific advance." Although some FOR members argued for patient opposition to all wars, Carlyle King, the group's first chair, told a meeting of the FOR national council that "the time at our disposal to avert an atomic war is very short." Consequently, there should be "a practical program of action to postpone, if not prevent, another war and work to remove the root causes of war." Pacifists should act as "a leaven" in other bodies: churches, U.N. organizations, and political groups.[65] But he argued some months later that "the difficulty is to get people to believe that the end is in sight. Life goes on as usual," even though the choices before humanity are "international control of atomic energy or extinction." The FOR vice-chair, the Rev. J. Lavell Smith, lamented to a church audience that humanity's procedures to set the world right "are patterned after those of all the generations of deluded men who have gone on believing, in spite of all the evidence, that the way . . . to eliminate violence is by a still greater show of violence. So we play the old game . . . with our terrifying stockpile of atom bombs."[66]

As the arms race accelerated, Canadian pacifists repeatedly assailed nuclear weapons. Convinced that "the single most important step towards preventing another war is disarmament," the Canadian FOR promoted literature stressing the dangers of the Bomb, including *One World or None*, and appealed to the Canadian government to "renounce war for all time," ban the atom bomb, work to halt global production of nuclear weapons, and place an embargo on Canada's export of uranium to the United States.[67] In March 1950, the FOR national council voted to issue a protest against the U.S. plan to move ahead with the production of the hydrogen bomb. "The time is ripe for fresh discussions" of nuclear disarmament, claimed the Canadian Friends Service Committee, "with the intention of proceeding as far and as rapidly as agreements can be achieved." When a proposal surfaced to use the Bomb in the Korean War, the FOR vigorously denounced the idea. "The proposal . . . to drop atom bombs on Chinese troops or elsewhere is a council of utter despair, ruthless, hopeless, uncivilized," it declared. The use of atom bombs "would mean the abandonment of all decency and the deliberate choice of death or ruination for millions." Commending British prime minister Attlee and Canadian minister of external affairs Lester Pearson for opposing the Bomb's use, the FOR called for "the complete outlawry of atomic and other weapons of violence."[68]

In fact, however, pacifists had minimal effect on Canadian public life. Here, as elsewhere, the abolition of nuclear weapons constituted only one item on their agenda. An FOR leaflet of 1946 talked of the organization's program as encompassing work "to feed the starving children of Europe and Asia," to transform the United Nations "into a genuine international government," to secure "universal disarmament," and to establish "an international commission to control the use of atomic energy so as to ensure that it will never again be used as an instrument of war."[69] Furthermore, implementing this agenda lay far beyond pacifist capabilities. In Canada, even more than in Britain, pacifists had been reduced to a marginal force in national life. Paid-up FOR membership stood at only about 300 in 1947, when its journal ceased publication for financial reasons. The Canadian WILPF group, which had endorsed World War II, dwindled in the postwar years and apparently had only one surviving chapter by the early 1950s. Not only was the strategy of individual war resistance substantially discredited by the war, but it appeared futile in an age of nuclear weapons. "Hiroshima changed everything," the director of the Canadian Association of Physicists told the readers of *Reconciliation*, and the pacifist "must now rethink all his most cherished concepts." Certainly, the movement seemed too weak to have much impact on events.[70]

Public concern about the Bomb was also limited by the Canadian government's early announcement that it would not develop nuclear weapons. Responding to a parliamentary inquiry in December 1945, Minister of Reconstruction Clarence Howe declared that "we have no intention of manufacturing atomic bombs." The reasons for this renunciation of nuclear weapons, reaffirmed thereafter, remain obscure but appear to have included the belief among policymakers that Canada faced no immediate threat, that the United States would protect Canada if such a threat materialized, that the cost was prohibitive, and that Canada was an unlikely candidate for great power status. Although this voluntary renunciation of nuclear weapons fed into later popular assumptions about the need to preserve a nuclear-free Canada, at the time it probably defused public anxiety that Canada might be drawn into the nuclear arms race.[71]

Even so, new forces were making themselves heard on the issue of the Bomb. Canadian radio broadcasts carried Hersey's *Hiroshima*, and ferment grew among atomic scientists. In November 1945, 122 members of the Canadian and British scientific staff engaged in atomic research at the laboratories of Canada's National Research Council sent a message to the political leaders of Canada and Great Britain expressing their "essential agreement with our American colleagues." The atomic bomb, they warned, was "the most destructive force known to mankind, against which there is no military defense and in the production of which no single nation can have an enduring monopoly." Indeed, "any effort to formulate foreign policies on the basis of a temporary superiority in atomic weapons will force all nations into an atomic armaments race" and create a situation in which "both great and small nations will face sudden destruction." Meanwhile, the Canadian Association of Scientific Workers (CAScW), which upon the bombing of Hiroshima had called for control of nuclear weapons by the United Nations, organized large public meetings on the subject in Montreal and Ottawa. The CAScW also showed film strips on atomic energy produced by the Federation of American Scientists and drew upon U.S. scientists as speakers for its meetings.[72]

For many Canadians, limiting national sovereignty seemed an appropriate way to deal with the nuclear menace. Advocates of the United Nations and of world government appealed to Canadians on these lines, often with some success. One small group, with offices in Toronto, circulated *One World or None* and placed the same slogan on the cover of its organizational brochure. Although organized world federalism in Canada remained a very small-scale phenomenon, world government organizations were formed in Winnipeg, Saskatoon, Toronto, Ottawa, and Montreal. In 1951, they merged to form the World Federalists of Canada.[73] Pacifists also championed the idea of world government while, at the same time, opposing any plan to provide it with armed forces.[74] Considerably more remarkable was the purported willingness of most Canadians to relinquish traditional aspects of national sovereignty for the purpose of securing conventional and nuclear disarmament. According to the Canadian Institute of Public Opinion, in July 1946, 59 percent of Canadian respondents approved having Canada "turn over control of all her armed forces and munitions, including atomic bomb materials, to a world parliament, providing other nations did the same." Leaders of Canada's political parties also endorsed the idea of world government.[75]

Australia

Thousands of miles away, in Australia, peace and disarmament groups also took some time to regain their footing after the setbacks of World War II. During that conflict, the vast majority of Australians were firmly committed to Allied military victory, particularly as Japanese forces advanced menacingly across the Pacific. Recognizing the futility of direct resistance to the war, Australian pacifists held small meetings, worked to ameliorate the war's consequences, and discussed plans for a peaceful future. These concerns were reflected in the *Peacemaker*, a pacifist newspaper established in 1939 by the Rev. Frank Coaldrake, an Anglican minister. In 1942, to coordinate their activities, pacifist groups formed the Federal Pacifist Council, which later became the Australian branch of the WRI and publisher of the *Peacemaker*.[76] Their influence upon the broader society, however, remained minimal. When atomic bombs exploded over Japanese cities, most Australians reacted with relief and thanksgiving. To be sure, in a letter published in the Sydney press, three Methodist clergymen condemned the bombing and concluded: "The atomic bomb is the logical outcome of a period of material development in which moral and spiritual values have been outpaced." Yet these sentiments were hardly typical. As one historian has noted, in Australia, "little sympathy existed for the first victims of nuclear warfare." [77]

For Australian pacifists, of course, the atomic bombing was not only an abomination but a confirmation of their stand against war. In the first issue of the *Peacemaker* to appear after the event, the Federal Pacifist Council reported optimistically: "Overnight, people have awakened to the truth of what pacifists have been crying in the wilderness for decades. . . . MANKIND CANNOT AFFORD ANOTHER WAR." In subsequent issues, the *Peacemaker* continued to hammer away at this theme. Writing in January 1946, a columnist pointed to the "ever-growing danger of a collision in the mists of nationalism which will loose the blinding light of the atomic bomb." The following month, the journal printed a cartoon on its front page showing Death standing with the Bomb suspended over the world, with a caption that read "The Last Warning." [78] For pacifists in Australia, as elsewhere, the problem was systemic. When news arrived that the Russians had the Bomb, a *Peacemaker* columnist returned to this point: "There is only one way of abolishing mass destruction . . . and that is by doing away with war." Some months later, in a discussion of the H-Bomb, he wrote: "If we are to have war, this, and worse, is the sort of thing we'll get. . . . The real problem . . . is to get rid of war." [79]

Given this holistic view, members of the Federal Pacifist Council—who numbered about 1,300 in 1947—continued their peace efforts along diverse lines. Some, especially the Quakers, worked on relief and reconstruction projects. The Federal Pacifist Council focused on peace education, opposition to conscription and military spending, and abolition of the White Australia policy, among other concerns. [80] World government provided a particularly lively issue at national conferences in 1947, 1948, and 1949, with Eleanor Moore, a leader of the tiny WILPF group and an ardent world federalist, heading up the discussion. "There is only one method that can create security against destruction by the atomic bomb," she noted; "it is the security given by a common sovereign order of law." Although Moore found, to her regret, that "governments, as such, are in disrepute in the minds of peace-loving people," the delegates at the 1948 conference did resolve to have the Federal Pacifist Council ask its constituent groups "to give serious study and constructive assistance to the programmes being pursued by movements for world government toward the achievement of the greater union of mankind and the removal of the causes of war." [81]

Like the pacifist movement, other peace-related movements in postwar Australia were weak. Supported by liberal internationalists and socially minded clergy, a new United Nations Association (which succeeded the League of

Nations Union) held regular informational and cultural meetings. But world federalism proved anemic, despite a UNESCO poll showing 35 percent of the Australian population favoring it (as against 58 percent who opposed it). By the summer of 1950, the Australian section of the World Movement for World Federal Government had only 700 members. Although members of the clergy were often prominent in peace groups, overall, as Eleanor Moore wrote in 1948, "there is a notable absence of anti-war efforts emanating from churches or carried on within their communities." [82]

As elsewhere, scientists worked to heighten concern about the Bomb. In 1946, for example, the Victorian Council of Scientific Societies convened a conference on atomic energy at which one of the three sessions focused on social implications. To add credibility to the venture, they arranged for messages of greeting from the atomic scientists' movements in the United States and Great Britain. The appeals of Einstein, Urey, Bohr, and Oppenheimer for control of the Bomb were also extensively quoted in late 1947 at the annual meeting of the Australian Association of Scientific Workers, in a speech by that organization's outgoing chair, T. Y. Harris. "We, as scientists, are facing the gravest responsibility we have ever known," she declared. "It is no exaggeration to say that our knowledge has reached such a stage that the misuse of science could now destroy . . . all forms of life upon the earth." [83]

Australia's best-known atomic scientist, Marc Oliphant, was also the most outspoken one on nuclear issues. Shocked and horrified by the atomic bombings, he became a fervent critic of nuclear weapons. His remarks were featured in the mass media of Great Britain (where he continued to work until 1950) and his native Australia (where he returned thereafter, as the first director of the Research School of Physical Sciences at the Australian National University). Despite his gadfly role, so great was Oliphant's prestige that Australian prime minister Ben Chifley appointed him as the technical adviser for Australia's U.N. delegation. Oliphant championed the Acheson-Lilienthal Plan and, later, the Baruch Plan, but he was determined that no opportunity be lost for international control of nuclear weapons. For this reason, once the Russians had rejected the U.S. proposal, he urged his country's delegation, unsuccessfully, to consider whether the Soviet plan was not better than none at all. Increasingly, he considered the issues of the Bomb and war inseparable. "Atomic weapons are now the supreme preoccupation of all countries and . . . render wars of the future suicidal and utterly indefensible," he declared. "It is essential that this problem be faced, not in isolation, but as part of the problem of the elimination of war." In 1948, he told readers of the *Bulletin of the Atomic Scientists*: "Control of atomic energy can be achieved only by so great a degree of political unification of the world that control is virtually a domestic problem. We must work for this unity—not for nice clean wars without weapons of mass destruction, but for elimination of war itself." Meanwhile, he vowed never again to work on scientific projects with military significance and, in 1950, told the press that any use of the atomic bomb would be a moral crime.[84]

Despite the weakness of the Australian peace movement, it maintained a continuous public critique of nuclear weapons. In August 1946, a group of Australian women, led by the editorial board of the *Women's Digest*, staged a protest meeting in Assembly Hall, Melbourne, against the further manufacture or use of atomic bombs. After listening to addresses by pacifist, scientific, and religious leaders, the gathering condemned the use of atomic energy for destructive purposes, called for the outlawry of all weapons of mass destruction, and demanded that scientific research be free from military and political control. Responding to Truman's November 1950 comments about using the atomic bomb in Korea, the WILPF issued a statement of protest to the secretary general of the United Nations. In a brochure entitled *Civil Defence*, the Federal Pacifist Council declared that "you already know, from the scientists themselves, that THERE IS NO DEFENCE AGAINST ATOM BOMBS EXCEPT PEACE." Australians also participated in World Peace Day events. Publicizing a meeting it was sponsoring in Melbourne on August 6, 1951, the WILPF called attention to the "6th anniversary of the first atomic bombing at Hiroshima" and asked, "Must it happen again?" In March 1952, the WILPF organized a protest meeting against the British government's plan to test an atomic bomb in Australia.[85]

The largest and most dramatic of the protests involved opposition to a government plan for the building of a rocket-testing range in central Australia. Begun in 1947 by church groups in an effort to protect the aborigines, the campaign soon condemned the military purposes of the rocket range as well. A widely distributed pamphlet, *Destroy the Rocket Project Now or It Will Destroy You*, argued that "guided missiles" were "for one purpose, and one purpose only—indiscriminate wholesale killing." Scientists had shown that "the rocket bomb and the release of atomic energy for human destruction" were "only the forerunners of frightful agencies" of death. "It is now, truly, One World Or None!" Addressed by church leaders, pacifists, and the president of the Australian Aborigines' League, a protest meeting of 1,300 people took place in Melbourne Town Hall on March 31. Here again speakers charged that the missile to be perfected would be "a robot carrier of atomic bombs." This demonstration, backed by similar activities in other parts of Australia, angered elements of the press, as well as the government, which passed legislation providing penalties for criticism of the Defense Department. Nevertheless, civil libertarians joined pacifists in condemning the new law. In addition, despite the official ban, activists continued their critique of the rocket range proposal, organizing a radio debate on the subject.[86]

Although it is impossible to trace the impact of these events and others—for example, the broadcast of Hersey's *Hiroshima* over Australian radio—public opinion in Australia does seem to have soured somewhat on the Bomb in the early postwar years. In August 1946, 31 percent of Australian respondents to an opinion poll declared that the Bomb had decreased the possibilities of another world war, as compared to 30 percent who thought the Bomb had increased such possibilities. Much the same balance was shown in July 1947, when 38 percent of Australian poll respondents reported that they viewed atomic energy as a benefit and 38 percent viewed it as a curse. But a November 1948 poll in Australia found that, while 36 percent of respondents thought atomic energy would do more good than harm, 46 percent thought the opposite.[87] The same growth in opposition to the Bomb can be seen in attitudes toward its control. According to a Gallup poll in October 1945, 60 percent of Australian respondents favored (and 40 percent opposed) retention of the Bomb's secret by the United States and Great Britain. Nevertheless, in January 1946, 44 percent of Australian respondents favored (and 41 percent opposed) giving the secret of the Bomb to a world government, and in December 1947, 48 percent of Australian respondents supported (and 27 percent opposed) giving control of all armed forces to a world government. By February–March 1949, the earlier attitudes were nearly reversed: 55 percent of Australian respondents favored (and only 28 percent opposed) giving control of all national armed forces to a world government. Furthermore, considerable resistance arose among Australians to future use of the Bomb. Polled in September 1950 about American employment of the atomic bomb in the Korean War, 18 percent of Australian respondents favored it, while 73 percent opposed it.[88]

New Zealand

In New Zealand, the peace movement was badly damaged by World War II. The governing Labour party, which had once worked vigorously against war and conscription, turned now—like its overseas counterparts—to staunch support of the Allied war effort, as did the churches. Consequently, the small Christian Pacifist Society paid a heavy price for its sharp public criticism of the war. By 1943, more than 70 members of the group were in prison for writings or speeches on peace. The founder of the society, the Rev. Ormond Burton, was not only imprisoned five times (for a total of two years and eight months) for pacifist speaking and journalism but dismissed from the Methodist ministry and reduced to scrubbing floors for a living.[89] In addition, some 800 conscientious objectors spent four to five years in prison or behind the barbed wire of detention camps. As a result, at the end of the war, pacifist groups in New Zealand were small, isolated, and exhausted. The Christian Pacifist Society claimed only 550 members, while the Peace Union and the No More War Movement (both WRI affiliates) were smaller and the WILPF near extinction.[90]

Naturally, pacifists in New Zealand were horrified by the atomic bomb. In an editorial on the issue in November 1945, the *New Zealand Christian Pacifist* cited approvingly an Auckland physicist who had written that "human affairs are rapidly moving to a crisis unparalleled in history. . . . This is a most fateful hour for the human race." Responding to the idea of outlawing the Bomb, the journal declared: "There is only one way to outlaw the use of the bomb, that is to outlaw war." A "new International of the Common People must arise," composed of men and women "who have renounced war and nationalism." Adopting a similar approach, the No More War Movement distributed literature of the Federation of American Scientists, claiming that such material is "a great help in our campaign against further war." Beginning in 1947, the Peace Union took the lead in organizing Hiroshima Day marches in Christchurch, while the Christian Pacifist Society handled these events in other urban centers.[91]

As elsewhere, however, pacifists in New Zealand were caught up with other peace issues as well. The Christian Pacifist Society focused on reviving pacifism within the churches, while the Peace Union worked to eliminate past disabilities imposed on conscientious objectors, to send relief parcels to Europe, and to block the imposition of compulsory military training. World government— a cause that had limited attraction in New Zealand—received some attention from pacifists. "The 20th century problem of peace," noted a writer in the *New Zealand Christian Pacifist*, "is a problem for which only a world solution will suffice." "The development of scientific warfare," left no alternative to "world citizenship."[92] By far the most salient issue for New Zealand pacifists, however, was conscription, which ignited a bitter public struggle in 1949. The major parties, press, and radio championed an enabling referendum, leaving the small pacifist groups and, among the churches, the Society of Friends, in lonely and beleaguered opposition. Speaking out that year against conscription in the otherwise sedate city of Nelson, a small band of pacifists was physically assaulted by a large crowd and pelted with eggs. Subsequently, the referendum carried, 78 to 22 percent.[93] In these difficult circumstances, New Zealand's pacifists could do—and did—little about the Bomb.

Even so, signs of apprehension about nuclear weapons and support for alternative security systems were emerging within the general population. Although many New Zealanders applauded the Bomb for ending the war, others looked askance at its destructive power. "I have felt disturbed about the consequences of this bomb and its effects in the future if war breaks out again," one legislator stated; "the atomic bomb is a frightful instrument against humanity." The two New Zealand scientists working on the Manhattan project at Berkeley both signed the petition to British prime minister Attlee calling for international control of atomic energy. On August 9, 1945, the *Evening Post* warned that "only temporarily can collective suicide weapons be retained" as "proprietary medicines belonging to one or two governments." Even while pronouncing itself hopeful about the future, the *Listener* made it clear that this was "partly because there is now . . . a chance that war has become too destructive to continue."[94] By 1950, two small branches of the World Movement for World Federal Government had emerged in New Zealand. That same year, a sample poll in the town of New Lynn found that 67 percent of its voters favored world government.[95] Thus, although few people publicly protested against nuclear weapons in postwar New Zealand, a current of concern was developing that would widen in the future.

New Thinking and Acting

Anti-Bomb sentiment made a significant debut in the postwar public life of Great Britain and played a lesser, but noticeable, role in the affairs of Canada, Australia, and New Zealand. As in Japan and the United States, critics of nuclear weapons called for limitations on the traditional prerogatives of national sovereignty as the most efficacious way to stave off what they feared was an impending nuclear holocaust. Here, too, the menace of the Bomb was stimulating new thinking and acting on war and international relations.

The Beginning or the End?

France, Germany, and Italy

> For pacifists and nonpacifists, Hiroshima can be the signal
> for the beginning or the end.
>
> *Volk und Friede*, 1948

Farther afield from nations directly associated with the atomic bombing of Japan, the Bomb stirred less of an immediate furor. For a time, many people in France, Germany, and Italy remained preoccupied with more immediate problems of postwar reconstruction. In addition, having undergone some of the worst horrors of World War II—including concentration camps, massive slaughter of civilians, and military occupation—they were not as shocked, at least initially, by the destructiveness of the atomic bomb as were the relatively unscathed Americans, British, Canadians, Australians, and New Zealanders. Furthermore, although the crushing defeat of fascist aggression and the public recognition of fascist misrule, including wholesale atrocities, discredited militarism in Germany and Italy, they tended to undermine pacifism and other nonmilitary approaches to international conflict in France. Consequently, although pacifist groups, atomic scientists, and world government advocates in these countries led the way in calling attention to the dangers of nuclear weapons, their statements sometimes lacked a popular resonance in the immediate postwar years.

Nevertheless, by the end of the decade, the Bomb was emerging as a source of substantial concern. Postwar relief and reconstruction projects alleviated hunger and homelessness while, at the same time, the growing Soviet-American confrontation raised the specter of a new, more devastating war. In this context, the failure to secure international control of atomic energy, combined with the Soviet Union's development of an atomic bomb and the American decision to build a hydrogen bomb, seemed particularly ominous.

Popular fears grew with the onset of the Korean War and the loose American talk of using the atomic bomb in that conflict. The result was a substantial rise in opposition to the Bomb, combined with the development of widespread support for the radical alternative of One World.

France

Support for nuclear weapons was widespread in France in the immediate aftermath of the Hiroshima and Nagasaki bombings. Indeed, a poll in October 1945 found that 85 percent of French respondents approved America's atomic bombing of Japanese cities, while only 10 percent opposed it—exactly the same percentages as in the United States. At the end of the year, another national survey reported that 56 percent of those polled thought that France should develop its own atomic bomb; 32 percent reacted negatively to this idea.[1] This relatively favorable attitude toward nuclear weapons reflected, in part, the militarization of public attitudes by World War II and the long, cruel Nazi occupation. At the least, it indicated the widespread assumption that there could hardly be a worse situation than the populace had already suffered.[2] In addition, the French thought that their scientists had contributed substantially to the development of the Bomb. Although resentment at the Anglo-American monopoly of the weapon surfaced quickly in France, this feeling also bolstered the idea that France, as a great power and a pioneer in nuclear research, should have its own.[3] Finally, both the French Right and the French Left took pride in their respective military traditions, leaving issues of disarmament to a small and not particularly reputable pacifist movement. Not surprisingly, in the fall of 1945 a "chanson" ridiculing America's atomic fears became a hit in Paris.[4]

Nevertheless, the vast destructiveness of the Bomb did have some chastening effect. Writing in *Combat*, the resistance leader Albert Camus condemned the Hiroshima bombing as "organized murder." Modern civilization had "reached the last degree of savagery," he declared, and henceforth it would be necessary to choose "between collective suicide or the intelligent utilization of scientific conquests." With nuclear weapons loose in the world, *Le Monde* editorialized on August 15, 1945, peace was not merely desirable but "absolutely necessary." Meeting at its first postwar national gathering, in mid-August, the French Socialist party unanimously adopted an appeal to the country which argued that the development of the Bomb left the world's nations with one choice: "Perish or unite." Survival demanded "a world organization for collective security based on justice and the cooperation of all free nations." Meanwhile, *L'Aube*, the official newspaper of the centrist Popular Republican

Movement, warned of "a sad destiny" if there were not, "among all the people of the earth, a mobilization of conscience in order to impose discipline in the usage of the great inventions." [5]

With the emergence of the Cold War and the nuclear arms race, French opinion grew more critical of the Bomb. The Communist party, initially enthusiastic about nuclear weapons, began to condemn them and U.S. nuclear testing when it became clear that the Bomb might be employed by the United States against the Soviet Union. The Socialist party, although much more sympathetic to the United States, nonetheless assailed U.S. nuclear tests. It also criticized both great powers for their failure to make peace, called for arms reductions, and again demanded strengthened international authority.[6] In early 1947, French peasants on the Saclay plateau, uneasy about a government plan for a local nuclear research center, circulated petitions against it and blocked the project for months. That November, a poll found that 83 percent of French respondents thought that the atomic bomb should be banned by the United Nations. Asked in December 1948 about the long-run impact of "atomic energy," only 34 percent of French respondents thought it would prove beneficial; 42 percent said it would be harmful.[7]

French pacifists initially played a marginal role in these developments. Pacifism had substantial appeal in prewar France but was weakened significantly by the advent of World War II and the vicious occupation regime. During the war, some pacifists tarnished their cause still further through defeatism or mild forms of collaborationism[8] although, ironically, others were imprisoned or executed by the Nazi and Vichy authorities for their resistance activities. Arrested in wartime, Jacques Martin, the postwar secretary of the French FOR, recalled that "we were in the very center of the clandestine resistance, and have endured what came in giving aid to Jews and others persecuted by the French police and the Gestapo."[9] Even in the aftermath of the war, lingering bitterness, desire for vengeance, and fierce patriotism made France particularly inhospitable to pacifism. Although the French section of the WRI was revived, it lacked members, financial support, and a permanent premises. The government played some role in this, for it banned the selling or advertising of its tiny newspaper, *Les Cahiers du Pacifisme*, to the general public, and meted out severe jail sentences to conscientious objectors.[10]

Nevertheless, French pacifism made a modest recovery in the late 1940s and early 1950s. Official restrictions eased somewhat in 1947 and by early 1948, thirteen small pacifist groups had drawn together into a Peace Federation (Cartel de la Paix). Working to foster reconciliation between East and West, the Peace Federation had about 20 constituent groups by the summer of 1951. In general, French pacifists championed unilateral disarmament, conscientious objection, Cold War neutrality, and world government. Andrée Jouve, co-chair of the small WILPF section, urged France to adopt "an independent position between the East and the West, without any military alliance." Writing in the April 1951 issue of *La Voie de la paix*, the pacifist Emile Bauchet contended that "we want the union of all the peoples, disarmed and in a world confederation," as well as "a code of real justice which will resolve pacifically conflicts between states, if need be with the help of an international police force recognized by all."[11]

Although the Catholic church was generally inhospitable to pacifism, French Protestantism provided a far more sympathetic constituency, including some of France's foremost pacifist leaders.[12] Perhaps the most prominent of these was André Trocmé, a Protestant minister, who during the war had mobilized his village of Le Chambon to assist thousands of Jews and other refugees fleeing the Nazi terror. Incarcerated for a time in a concentration camp and later threatened with death by the Gestapo, he had gone into hiding until the end of the war, when, together with his wife, Magda, he emerged as a leader of the small FOR group.[13] Like other French pacifists in these years, the Trocmés took on a variety of issues, including securing legal recognition of conscientious objection, publicizing the moral critique of war, and promoting the idea of world government.[14]

If French pacifists faced severe difficulties, French atomic scientists, by contrast, could criticize nuclear weapons from a position of unusual power and influence. Appointed high commissioner of the new French Atomic Energy Commission in 1946, Frédéric Joliot-Curie became the effective director of France's nuclear research program. In June of that year, the French delegate to the U.N. Atomic Energy Commission proclaimed that France had no intention of making atomic weapons, a position Joliot-Curie and his scientific cohorts repeatedly cited in justification of their work. "We assigned ourselves the task of developing only the peaceful applications of atomic energy," he explained in 1947 to readers of the *Bulletin of the Atomic Scientists*.[15]

This implicit rejection of the Bomb received powerful support from the French Association of Scientific Workers (Association Française des Travailleurs Scientifiques, FASW). Although the FASW had a decidedly left-wing orientation, this reflected, to a large degree, the left-wing sentiments of leading French scientists, including Joliot-Curie, who was an outspoken Communist. About 70 percent of French scientists became FASW members and, for a time, the organization's stance toward nuclear weapons seemed very much in line with that of the nonideological scientists' movement in the United States.[16] In November 1945, at a meeting called to discuss the problem of atomic energy, the FASW endorsed the call by American scientists for control of the atomic bomb by the United Nations. The following June, the secretary of the FASW wrote the Federation of American Scientists that it was "the primary duty of scientific workers the world over to support the campaign you have undertaken. . . . We are in complete agreement with you on the entirety of your activity." [17] In early July 1946, the FASW asked for authorization to translate and distribute numerous materials produced by the Federation of American Scientists, including its atomic energy study kit, articles from the *Bulletin of the Atomic Scientists*, assorted pamphlets, and *One World or None*. Other French scientists, inspired by the activities in the United States of the Emergency Committee of Atomic Scientists, promised to set up a counterpart in France. [18]

Only when the Baruch Plan failed to win Soviet support did the French and American scientists' movements begin to diverge substantially. At a Federation of American Scientists meeting in September 1946, Lew Kowarski of France said that he thought Henry Wallace's criticism of the Baruch Plan was justified, although he remained uncertain that a more conciliatory U.S. position would secure Soviet approval. At the same gathering, Joliot-Curie suggested that, if the United States stopped assembling bombs, that would ease world tensions considerably and strengthen America's moral position. On July 17, 1948, the FASW unanimously adopted a statement calling upon nations to cease manufacturing weapons of mass destruction, destroy existing weapons stockpiles, pledge not to resort to first use of such weapons against civilians, and resume international negotiations; scientists were urged collectively to refuse to build these weapons. In a letter sent to the *Bulletin of the Atomic Scientists* and printed shortly thereafter with careful disclaimers by the editors, four French scientists condemned the nuclear arms control proposal of the U.S. government, arguing that its conditions could be accepted "only by those who rely completely on the generosity of the U.S.A." The possessor of the Bomb, they charged, was "drunk with success." [19]

Despite his prominent position within the French nuclear "establishment," Joliot-Curie became one of the sharpest critics of U.S. policy toward the Bomb. In early 1946, at a meeting of scientists, he termed the American decision to maintain atomic secrecy "very dangerous" because it "appears as a means of pressure." He was more outspoken later that year, when he publicly attacked U.S. nuclear testing in the Pacific as "a miserable idea" and called upon the United States to stop making atomic bombs and join the rest of the world in applying atomic energy to peaceful pursuits. Joliot-Curie professed (and may have felt) great anguish at what he considered the perversion of science for means of mass destruction. [20] As his critics noted, however, his emphasis on the peaceful uses of atomic energy meshed well with the attempt by French Communists to undermine the American atomic monopoly and thereby head off a U.S. atomic attack on the Soviet Union. [21]

Even so, from 1945 to early 1949, Joliot-Curie walked a tightrope between his official, nonpartisan role and his commitments as a loyal Communist. His public statements, though critical of the United States, did not possess the full party-line flavor. In July 1947, a secret U.S. State Department analysis of an article he wrote reported that it was "not as much oriented toward the communist position as might have been expected from Joliot-Curie"; indeed, he "very neatly manages to dodge committing himself to either the Soviet position" or that of the French government.[22] As late as January 5, 1949, Joliot-Curie replied to those who raised doubts about his patriotism by publicly declaring that no honest French citizen, Communist or not, would deliver French atomic secrets to a foreign power. This statement reportedly led to sharp condemnation of Joliot-Curie within the French Communist party. In any case, a few weeks later, the party's secretary, Jacques Duclos, proclaimed a different version of national loyalty: "Every progressive man has two fatherlands, his own and the Soviet Union."[23]

National loyalty was viewed with considerably more suspicion by France's burgeoning movement for world government. Following the end of the war, French world federalist tracts had begun to appear in abundance, including some with such titles as *Destruction atomique ou gouvernement mondial* (Atomic destruction or world government).[24] World government groups sprang up quickly. Led by a former *maquis* commander, Colonel Robert Sarrazac, the Human Front of World Citizens (Front Humain des Citoyens du Monde), which for a time claimed 18,000 members, helped popularize Henry Usborne's plan for a people's world convention. A variety of other groups, vigorous but fragmented, took on additional roles, including the introduction of a world federalist bill into the French parliament. By mid-1950, the seven French branches of the World Movement for World Federal Government claimed over 38,000 members.[25] Nor was this the extent of globalist sentiment. According to a UNESCO-sponsored poll in the late 1940s, 45 percent of French respondents favored world government, while only 36 percent opposed it. In mid-1949, the federalist group in the French National Assembly numbered close to 200 members. In an interview published in *Combat*, the philosopher Jacques Maritain called upon France "boldly to assume leadership of a crusade for the establishment of a supranational organization of the world."[26]

Curiously, the activities of a young American war veteran, Garry Davis, provided the most important catalyst for France's postwar rejection of nationalism. The son of the popular bandleader Meyer Davis, Garry Davis had begun his career as an actor in Broadway comedies before becoming a U.S. bomber pilot during World War II. By the summer of 1944, he was growing disillusioned with his combat role. "How many bombs had I dropped?" he wondered. "How many men, women, and children had I murdered? Wasn't there another

way, I kept asking myself." After the war, Davis continued his career as a come-
dian but, as he noted, "offstage . . . I was a sober clown, indeed," watching
in horror "the march of nations toward World War Three." He recalled: "A
curious phrase beat faintly inside my mind, a phrase which seemed to echo
from nation to nation and . . . around the globe. 'One world or none,' wrote
Wendell Willkie; 'One world or none,' reaffirmed Bertrand Russell and Albert
Schweitzer; 'One world or none,' repeated Gandhi and Einstein." "Greatly excited" by Cord Meyer's *Peace or Anarchy*, Davis began working as a volunteer
for United World Federalists; nevertheless, he desired "a crusade, not a meeting," a chance to "practice 'one world.' " Accordingly, he decided that the time
had come to "secede from the old and declare the new." In September 1948,
he traveled to Paris, pitched his pup tent on a small strip of United Nations territory, renounced his American citizenship, and proclaimed himself a citizen
of the world.[27]

Davis created an enormous sensation. He was mobbed by journalists and
photographers, as well as by sympathizers, and mail poured in by the sackful
from all over Europe. On November 19, 1948, he began an unauthorized speech
from the balcony at the U.N. General Assembly session, only to be seized by
security guards. "Pass the word to the people," he called out as the guards bore
him away: "One government for one world!" In the ensuing confusion, his
message was continued by dozens of Davis partisans on the scene, including
Colonel Sarrazac, who declaimed to the assemblage: "Our common need for a
world order can no longer be ignored. We, the people, long for the peace that
only a world order can give. The sovereign states which you represent here are
dividing us and bringing us to the abyss of war." [28]

With this gesture, the "Little Man," as Davis was now called, became the
toast of Paris. Writing in *Franc-Tireur*, Georges Altman declared that "what
might be called the crazy act of a young American is the symbol of what all
peoples are thinking." Endorsements of Davis and of the idea of world citizenship flowed in from Albert Camus, André Gide, Jean-Paul Sartre, André
Breton, and numerous other French intellectuals, many of whom appeared
with him at press conferences or other public gatherings. A meeting featuring
Davis at the Salle Pleyel—with a seat on the platform left for Albert Einstein,
who telegraphed his endorsement of Davis and presided "symbolically" at the
event—filled the concert hall with 2,500 people, while thousands of others
stood outside in the rain. A week later, after Davis's young supporters had distributed a million leaflets in Paris, 15,000 enthusiasts packed a Davis meeting
at the Vélodrome d'Hiver. Wearing his old air corps flight jacket, Davis talked
of the need to abolish the "narrow nationalism which has always resulted in
war and death." [29]

Although pacifist and world government leaders had mixed reactions to Davis,[30] it was hard to deny, as Elisabeth Mann Borgese noted, that he had reached "for the first time in the history of the [world government] movement the imagination of the masses." In January 1950, the World Citizen registry, established by Davis, had neared the half-million mark, with signers from all over the globe.[31] Asked shortly thereafter what they thought of their towns becoming world territory, in accordance with the ideas of Garry Davis, French respondents gave their support to the proposal by 36 to 35 percent, with 29 percent expressing no opinion. By mid-1951, some 400 French communities had declared themselves "mundialized," or world territory. They included the hometown of President Vincent Auriol, who was told he had thereby become a world citizen—news that he took rather gracefully, in the circumstances.[32]

In war-weary France, threatened by a new conflict between the great powers, Davis had tapped a deep public concern. Claude Bourdet, a former resistance fighter and prisoner at Buchenwald who was now the editor of *Combat*, turned over a column in the newspaper to Davis's World Citizens movement and, soon, another one to French pacifists. Speaking in 1949 at a peace conference in London, Bourdet argued that the central appeal of world government— the unity of humanity—would provide an answer to the claims of both America and Russia and had the potential for mobilizing millions of people. In June 1950, celebrations were held in Cahors in honor of the 230 communes of the department of the Lot that had proclaimed themselves world territory. A gathering of 7,000 turned out for the dedication of the first milestone of the "World Road Without Frontiers" and, as a caravan moved along the highway between the mundialized villages, excited crowds gathered to light bonfires and greet the "world citizens." The following day, Lord Boyd Orr hoisted the "rainbow flag" of humanity and addressed another large crowd, including twenty local mayors and representatives of "mondialiste" or other world government groups from France, Germany, Great Britain, Italy, Austria, and the United States.[33]

In the context of the growing Cold War confrontation, Bourdet and some other French intellectuals were striving to carve out a nonaligned position. Focusing on survival, Bourdet used *Combat* and, later, *L'Observateur*, founded in mid-1950, to champion neutrality and France's role as a mediating force in Europe. French neutrality was also championed for a time by the Marxist-existentialists of *Les Temps Modernes*, who played the key role in the founding of the Revolutionary Democratic Rally (Rassemblement Démocratique Révolutionnaire, RDR), in the spring of 1948. Established by Sartre, Camus, Gerard Rosenthal, and David Rousset, the RDR disdained both the Soviet Union and the United States and worked for a European federation on democratic socialist principles. Efforts to foster nonalignment were also undertaken by Hubert

Beuve-Méry, the moderate Catholic and anti-Communist editor of the evening newspaper, *Le Monde*. The latter paper printed an influential article by Szilard, originally published in the *Bulletin of the Atomic Scientists* in October 1949, advocating a neutral Europe. Joining them in advocacy of nonalignment was the Catholic left-wing magazine *L'Esprit*, one of the organizational participants in the Peace Federation. Bourdet recalled that "pro-Americans treated us as disguised agents of international communism," while "the Communists violently accused us of failing to recognize the differences between 'the camp of peace' and 'the camp of war.' " Nevertheless, these "neutralists," as they were dubbed by their critics, advocated a genuinely independent position, a "Third Force" beyond the Cold War blocs.[34]

Such views flourished, of course, amid a growing French fear of nuclear destruction. Although the U.S. ambassador reported to Washington that the explosion of the first Soviet atomic bomb had little effect on French public opinion, a *New York Times* correspondent portrayed the response quite differently. "Everyone is asking," he wrote, "where is the exit?"[35] The U.S. decision to build a hydrogen bomb drew sharp criticism in France, not only from the Communist *L'Humanité* but also from the Socialist *Le Populaire* and the more conservative *Le Monde*. Speaking at a forum in New York City, Bourdet championed an international agreement to outlaw the use of nuclear weapons. The French ambassador to the United Nations reportedly told U.S. officials that, although "French public opinion had not formerly been much disturbed by the atom bomb question," the U.S. hydrogen bomb announcement and a recent warning by Einstein about radioactive poisoning of the environment "had created great nervousness in France."[36]

Numerous signs appeared of a profound dismay over nuclear weapons. French support for the U.S. atomic bombing of Japan fell to a new low in mid-1950, when a poll found that only 25 percent of respondents thought it justified, as against 48 percent who considered it unjustified. Noting that "two out of every three Frenchmen having opinions on the subject felt that the United States had been wrong in using the bomb against Japan," a U.S. intelligence report also observed that President Truman's November 1950 comment about possible employment of the bomb in Korea "created great concern throughout France." *Combat* talked of the moral issues posed by the Bomb, and *Le Monde* emphasized the pope's reference to the "feelings of horror aroused in all honest men by the new engines of destruction."[37] Only three hours after Truman's comment, the French government issued a statement opposing use of the Bomb in Korea. Recalling the flap among people in Paris and London over his remarks, Truman complained in his memoirs that "the slightest mention of atomic bombs was enough to make them jittery." With some justification, then, the U.S. intelligence analysis concluded that, in France, there existed "a general public repugnance to the use of this weapon under any but the most dire circumstances." [38]

Germany

In Germany, dominated from 1933 to 1945 by an extraordinarily militaristic, brutal, totalitarian regime, the organized peace movement suffered perhaps its greatest defeat. On taking power, the Nazi government immediately outlawed pacifist groups and arrested their leaders, many of whom died in concentration camps or were executed. Turning to the German Peace Society (Deutsche Friedensgesellschaft), founded in 1892 by Bertha von Suttner and claiming 30,000 members by 1933, the regime closed its offices, seized its records, banned its newspaper (*Das Andere Deutschland*), and arrested its leaders. Although initially spared, Catholic peace societies were later outlawed and their leaders arrested. Some peace activists escaped into exile, from which many never returned; others survived until they were executed for refusing military service or for urging resistance to the war effort. During its years in power, the Nazi regime largely succeeded in expunging the peace movement from German popular consciousness. This terrible devastation left the postwar movement, when it emerged after 1945, largely rootless and adrift.[39]

The postwar German peace movement faced other problems as well. As the scattered pacifist survivors regrouped, they found it difficult to obtain official authorization to function in occupied Germany. Despite their professed goal of eliminating German militarism, Allied authorities seemed remarkably indifferent or hostile to the antimilitarist activities of German pacifists. One German pacifist remarked: "We have a proverb . . . that everyone should sweep before his own door. . . . The Allies should let us have the broom to do it." Official obstacles were compounded by severe shortages of paper, pacifist literature, and financial resources.[40] Finally, pacifists encountered a widespread popular apathy toward " 'political' problems," which they attributed in part to the desperate scramble for economic survival in postwar Germany. They also considered it a reflection of political exhaustion in the grim aftermath of war and fascism.[41]

In these circumstances, German pacifist groups made a small-scale and muted revival in the postwar era. Reestablished under the chairmanship of Fritz Küster at a national conference in March 1946, the German Peace Society claimed 12,000 members in the three Western zones by 1950. Nevertheless, most were elderly, only about 3,000 paid their dues, and *Das Andere Deutschland*—revived amid postwar enthusiasm—temporarily collapsed because of its limited financial resources.[42] The program of the German Peace Society included the destruction of Prussian militarism, the education of youth for reconciliation between nations, and the creation of a ministry of peace. After 1948, it also focused on nuclear weapons. Its small monthly publications reported on the dire warnings of nuclear physicists in other lands, with Einstein prominently featured. "Every bullet does not strike," declared one of its leaflets, "but every atom bomb does."[43] Other German pacifist organizations also regrouped in these years, including the sections of the three pacifist internationals, but their membership remained small and their outreach limited. Like the German Peace Society, they took on a variety of issues, including nuclear weapons.[44]

Ferment among German scientists also remained relatively limited. Otto Hahn recalled that when he first learned of the Hiroshima bombing, "I was shocked and depressed beyond measure. The thought of the unspeakable misery of countless innocent women and children was something I could scarcely bear." Not surprisingly, Hahn continued to deny that there had ever been a German Bomb project, as did his wartime associates. Certainly in the years immediately after World War II, there seemed little prospect that Germany would further develop this research, which may have contributed to scientific complaisance. Max von Laue, the co-director of the Kaiser Wilhelm Institute for Physics in the postwar era, argued in an article in the *Bulletin of the Atomic Scientists* that to deal with the threat posed by nuclear weapons, a broad "spiritual change" was needed in the world. He thought there was no "universally valid" answer to the question as to whether scientists should continue to work on nuclear weapons.[45] Although a group of scientists in Germany did offer to undertake a program of education on the control of atomic energy if supplied with materials by their American counterparts, little seems to have come of the idea. As Joseph Rotblat observed, "In the post-war Federal Republic of Germany there was initially very little activity among scientists on matters relating to the nuclear arms race."[46]

The world government movement fared considerably better. Not only was world government supported by German peace groups,[47] but world federalist groups organized independently with some success in the postwar years. By mid-1950, the two German branches of the World Movement for World Federal Government—the League for World Government (Liga für Weltregierung) and the World State League (Weltstaat Liga)—claimed a total of 5,250 members.[48] Such numbers were dwarfed by registrants with the World Citizens movement of Garry Davis, which enrolled 125,000 Germans by late 1949. Indeed, a UNESCO poll in the late 1940s reported that Germans favored world government by 46 to 33 percent. In a sample ballot, conducted in the town of

Bad Kissingen in June 1949, 92 percent of voters expressed their support for a world parliament and a world government. A poll in West Germany in 1949 found that war refugees were particularly receptive to the idea.[49]

As indicated by the widespread appeal of world government, the limited organizational membership and activity of peace groups in postwar Germany provides an inadequate standard by which to measure the widespread popular revulsion to nationalism and war. According to opinion surveys conducted by the U.S. military government in the American zone of Germany in April 1946, December 1946, and August 1947, very large majorities rejected military values. Some 94 percent approved the statement "war does not pay," while 90 percent agreed that "a civilian is not less worthy than a soldier." Polled immediately after the popular Konrad Adenauer announced his support for a West German army in December 1949, only 26 percent of respondents in the U.S. zone favored the proposal, while 62 percent opposed it.[50] In early 1950, the Frankfurt *Allgemeine Zeitung* stated in a front-page editorial: "The simple truth is, all talk of a possible re-militarisation of Germany arouses deep anxiety in the hearts of millions of German mothers and a passionate repugnance in millions of German young men." The Frankfurt *Rundschau* reported a poll showing that 60.2 percent of Germans opposed military service under any conditions. Although young people were largely uninvolved in peace activism, they also struck observers as repulsed by the prospect of military service, a sentiment symbolized by the widely used youth slogan, "Without Us" (Ohne Uns).[51]

These attitudes acquired a more concrete form in the political struggle against German rearmament, led by the Social Democratic party (SPD). Under party chair Kurt Schumacher, the SPD adopted a policy of vigorous opposition. In 1946, Carlo Schmid, a rising star in the SPD, told a party rally that, though other countries "may continue to rearm, never again do we want to send our sons into the barracks. If the madness of war should break out again . . . then we should rather perish, knowing that it was not we who committed the crime." In 1947, at its national conference, the SPD passed a strong antiwar resolution. One delegate explained that the time had come to banish war and win German youth for the "heroism of peace." That fall, the SPD organized a "No More War" demonstration in Berlin. Although the rally, like other facets of German public life, proved rather small (with about 3,000 people) and dispirited, it nevertheless indicated the staunch opposition of the SPD to German rearmament.[52]

For a time, other important groups in German life seemed to share this perspective. In 1950, the Evangelical church, the largest Protestant denomination in West Germany, expressed its opposition to rearmament. The shocking experience of Nazi rule and, perhaps, a feeling of uneasiness at its general silence during the 1930s and 1940s, led the church temporarily to abandon its "just war" theology. One of its best-known leaders, Pastor Martin Niemöller, who had been imprisoned in concentration camps from 1937 to 1945 for his opposition to the Nazi regime, played a particularly prominent role in opposing remilitarization.[53] Although the Catholic church officially supported rearmament, a substantial Catholic minority remained antiwar and opposed the Adenauer program.[54] Furthermore, although a much smaller phenomenon, the Nauheim Circle, organized by Professor Ulbrech Noack, brought together a group of prominent Germans who raised questions about Germany's role in the growing East-West conflict.[55]

By 1950, then, pacifist groups, the Social Democrats, portions of the religious community, and other organizations had drawn the line against German rearmament. A declaration drafted by members of the German Peace Society, the world government movement, and the German branches of the WRI and the FOR contended that "the economic resources of Germany should not be diverted for the purpose of rearmament" but "should be used for the improvement of living standards." It opposed the reestablishment of a German army and called for a plebiscite to decide on rearmament. Together with religious, women's, and disabled soldiers' groups, they launched a petition drive for the plebiscite. In November 1950, a meeting of the coordinating council of German peace societies took a similar stand, arguing: "The German people would seal their doom by taking part in an armed conflict between East and West."[56]

Although the issue of nuclear weapons took a back seat to the more immediate concern of German rearmament in these years, Germany's peace groups did work to keep it alive. On August 6, 1948, now World Peace Day, peace groups in Hamburg (including the German Peace Society and the League for World Government), the SPD youth group, and cultural organizations sponsored a meeting at the university under the call "Never Again Hiroshima." That same day in Stuttgart, the German Peace Society, finding that Stuttgart Radio would not cover World Peace Day if it were associated with the Hiroshima bombing, distributed copies of the banned broadcast throughout the city. Early the following year, the German branch of the WILPF organized a women's meeting around the theme "We want peace, not atomic war."[57] In August 1949, World Peace Day was again celebrated in numerous localities. In Berlin, where eleven peace groups sponsored a large demonstration in the French sector, an "eternal fire" was lit in a large bronze lamp bearing the inscription, "Above all nations—humanity." Meanwhile, on August 5, the eve of the anniversary of the Hiroshima bombing, some 800 persons filled the University of Hamburg auditorium for a memorial meeting sponsored by the WRI branch and supported by 31 local groups, including the German Peace Society, the WILPF, the World Citizens, and the Crusade for World Government. "The impression produced by the meeting was tremendous," reported one pacifist leader; "the speakers were applauded over and over again." Reports of the meeting were carried on the radio and in the press.[58]

In 1950, German peace groups again made the link between the Hiroshima bombing and world peace. In Stuttgart, on the day of the bombing, some 600 people gathered for a Christian-Jewish remembrance service sponsored by the local sections of the WRI, the FOR, and other peace organizations. The situation proved stormy in Berlin, where an enlarged sponsoring committee for World Peace Day was denied permission to hold the event by the U.S. military government. Despite this rebuff, the sponsors sent a message to the citizens of Hiroshima and Nagasaki as "co-inhabitants of the earth, as survivors to survivors." They spoke now "because bloody experience has taught us that war does not solve but increases the problems of mankind." There was an "immediate danger to world peace" in "1) the preservation of national sovereignty; 2) the absence of organization to preserve international law; 3) the manufacture of armaments; 4) the use of economic resources and half of the world's revenue for the armaments race; 5) the fact that governments have not departed from the old ways which lead inevitably to war."[59]

These efforts by peace groups contributed to the development of very hostile public attitudes toward the Hiroshima bombing, in particular, and toward nuclear weapons, in general. A poll in June 1950 found that only 18 percent of West German respondents considered the American atomic bombing of Japan justified, 44 percent thought it unjustified, and 38 percent had no opinion. The major reasons given for rejecting the bombing were that it was inhuman and unnecessary. That same month, a poll reported that 53 percent of respondents in the Federal Republic disapproved use of the atomic bomb in any future war. Assessing the situation, a U.S. intelligence report in early 1951 concluded that, though American possession of the Bomb "is considered a safety factor," the people of West Germany "so far have evidenced little faith in the wisdom American statesmanship is likely to demonstrate in a decision on 'when' and 'where' to use the bomb." They have "frequently warned against an over-hasty decision to drop the bomb, particularly at the time of President Truman's much disputed A-bomb statement."[60]

Italy

The Italian peace movement, like its German counterpart, recovered slowly after the many years of fascist repression. In line with the glorification of war by Benito Mussolini's fascist regime, the government had banned all criticism of militarism and had suppressed Italian peace societies, some of long duration. With the collapse of fascist rule, Professor Giovanni Pioli and a tiny group of pacifists, some of whom had previously been imprisoned or otherwise persecuted, organized a section of the WRI in Milan. From there they reached out to other tiny pacifist groupings and stimulated a vigorous, if small-scale, campaign for the rights of Italian conscientious objectors. Pacifism and conscientious objection received a warmer welcome in the small Protestant denominations than in the dominant Catholic church, which viewed them as playing into Soviet hands. For very different reasons, the powerful Italian Communist party also took a jaundiced view of pacifism. In October 1947, when six small pacifist groups held their first joint postwar meeting, in Florence, the gathering was small and unimpressive. One participant wrote that, although some progress had been made toward united action, "the Italian pacifist movement is still quite 'up in the clouds,' "; its "main task is that of feeding itself with its own words." [61]

The Florence gathering was organized by the Movement of Religion (Movimento di Religione), established earlier that year by Professor Aldo Capitini of the University of Perugia and his friend Ferdinando Tartaglia, a Catholic priest. Dismissed in 1933 from his teaching post as one of thirteen Italian professors who refused to sign the fascist oath, Capitini subsequently worked at setting up antifascist groups of young people and workers before being imprisoned by Mussolini's regime. With the collapse of the fascist government in 1944, Capitini organized discussion groups in Italian cities on political, social, and educational questions. Together with his teaching in Perugia, this action scandalized the Catholic church, which was alarmed by his avant-garde ideas. Tartaglia also ran afoul of the Vatican, which excommunicated him from the priesthood for promoting internal reforms. Through the new Movement of Religion, which sponsored conferences in Italy's major cities, Capitini and Tartaglia attempted to draw together religious, moral, and social thought around a program of service to humanity. Often they focused on the problems of violence and war, as at the Florence conference of pacifist groups in 1947, when Capitini became head of the new Italian Association for Resistance to War. A prolific author and pacifist dedicated to Gandhian nonviolence, Capitini gradually emerged as the acknowledged leader of postwar Italian pacifism. [62]

Sentiment favoring world government grew more rapidly than pacifism in postwar Italy. According to a UNESCO-sponsored poll, in the late 1940s Italians approved of world government by a two-to-one margin. The largest of the Italian globalist organizations, the Italian Movement for European Federation and World Federation (Movimento Italiano per la Federazione Europea e Mondiale), claimed some 137,000 members in June 1949—a figure that seems too large to be accurate, but one considerably smaller than the estimate of more than a million in previous years.[63] Garry Davis's World Citizens movement reported receiving thousands of applications for World Citizens identity cards. Because many Italian political leaders were interested in world federation, a parliamentary committee to promote world government also emerged. Moreover, when Italy's new constitution was adopted, a provision was inserted that authorized limitations on Italian sovereignty necessary for an international organization to ensure peace and justice.[64]

The respectability of the federalist approach to peace in postwar Italy was underscored in the fall of 1947, when a federalist meeting convened in one of Rome's largest theaters. Organized by the Italian section of the Union of European Federalists, the gathering was chaired by Professor Ferruccio Parri, the former leader of the Italian underground and a recent prime minister, and was attended by members of the government and by foreign diplomats. Speakers included socialist leader and writer Ignazio Silone, Professor Gaetano Salvemini, and Italian finance minister Luigi Einaudi. They stressed repeatedly that Europe must renounce war and refuse to serve as a battlefield for rival power blocs.[65]

Italians proved particularly hostile to America's atomic bombing of Japan. *Osservatore Romano*, the Vatican newspaper, took a grim view of the Bomb, commenting that "this destructive weapon remains as a temptation for posterity." Reporting on the apparent papal condemnation, which was later officially denied, the Italian press also cited the remarks of liberal philosopher Benedetto Croce, who commented that, without humanity's moral and intellectual progress, the development of the Bomb would prove a catastrophe.[66] Enrico Fermi's sister Maria wrote to him from Italy: "Everyone is talking about the atomic bomb. . . . All are perplexed and appalled by its dreadful effects, and with time the bewilderment increases rather than diminishes." She recommended him "to God, Who alone can judge you morally." When, between July and October 1950, a poll surveyed Italian public opinion on the atomic bombing, only 14 percent of respondents considered it justified, as against 54 percent who thought it unjustified. This constituted the lowest level of approval in the five West European countries surveyed. According to a U.S. intelligence report, "to a large extent this attitude reflects the influence of such factors as the Italian experience with aerial bombardment in World War II, a revulsion against violence in general, the moral opposition of the Vatican to weapons of mass destruction, and, particularly among the poorer classes, Communist-Left-Wing Socialist peace propaganda." Also, of course, as American "enemies" during World War II, Italians had less reason than did U.S. allies to identify with American military conduct in that conflict.[67]

Many Italians also felt uneasy about the postwar nuclear arms race. In September 1949, shortly after the U.S. announcement that the Soviet Union had tested an atomic bomb, Italians—convinced that the pope would be an early target—began trying to sell buildings and apartments near the Vatican. The U.S. government's decision to build the hydrogen bomb, as a U.S. intelligence report noted, "brought forth the cry that this development was a 'last tragic warning to humanity' to find a path to peace or face complete destruction." In May 1950, Vittorio Orlando, a former Italian premier, led a group of top Italian political leaders in an appeal to the two nuclear powers to destroy their atomic bombs. Later that year, when Truman referred to the atomic bomb at his press conference, the conservative *Messaggero* expressed its hope, based on "elementary reasons of humanity," that the Bomb would not be used in the Far East. Indeed, according to the *New York Times*, Truman's remark, combined with an earlier statement by Dean Acheson on the gravity of the world situation, produced an "acute war scare in Italy." It noted that Communists and non-Communists alike "dread the possibility that Italy may become the target for atom bombs if war spreads to Europe." A public opinion survey in Italy from July to October 1950 found that, of those respondents who thought that the United States might use the Bomb in a new war, six out of ten opposed such action.[68] As in France and Germany, much of the populace had learned to regard nuclear weapons with fear and suspicion.

Confronting
"A Still Greater Catastrophe"

Elsewhere in Western Europe

> Hiroshima and Nagasaki were the manifestation of the most
> hellish kind of warfare. . . . If humanity does not find a way
> to use atomic power only for peaceful purposes, a still
> greater catastrophe lies . . . ahead.
>
> Johannes Hugenholtz, 1946

Elsewhere in Western Europe, antinuclear attitudes were also growing in the postwar era. As in France, war and fascist occupation had a brutalizing effect on much of the population, inflaming militarist and nationalist sentiments.[1] In many cases, they also resulted in the destruction or disruption of pacifist movements. Even in neutral nations like Sweden and Switzerland, antimilitarism emerged from the war in a weakened condition, thanks to the widespread assumption that only their strong military posture had saved them from foreign invasion. Furthermore, amid the rubble of bombed-out Europe, relief and reconstruction often assumed, at least initially, a higher priority than did defense against the nuclear menace. Nevertheless, in the aftermath of the Hiroshima bombing—and particularly as the arms race grew in intensity—the dangers of nuclear weapons were evident, especially to pacifists, atomic scientists, and world government advocates. Working together, they helped to mobilize the general public against the unprecedented threat of global annihilation.

Scandinavia

The Scandinavian countries experienced a rising tide of resistance to war and nuclear weapons in the postwar years. Before World War II, pacifist groups had fared relatively well among these nations' generally peace-loving populations. But as one postwar observer wrote: "During and after the war, pacifism has been under a cloud, and membership of the various pacifist societies has declined." The same was generally the case with broader peace organizations, which either lost support or grew more sedentary. Even so, opposition to the Bomb did develop and found expression through pacifist protests, statements by atomic scientists, and the dramatic burgeoning of the world government movement. In early 1951, a secret U.S. government intelligence report contended that in Scandinavia, although the Bomb was not "regarded as too horrible to be used under any circumstances," most people would justify its employment only if "civilization itself were at stake." [2]

Denmark

Denmark possessed perhaps the strongest peace movement in postwar Scandinavia. Unlike their counterparts in many other lands, Danish peace groups had not been suppressed during the Nazi occupation. That they were spared was particularly remarkable, for they assisted Jews in their escape from Denmark and published materials assailing Nazi interference with the churches, anti-Semitism, and educational practices. Indeed, members of pacifist groups like No More War (Aldrig mere Krig)—the WRI affiliate, founded in 1926—even engaged in underground resistance activities, including sabotage, although most could not stomach the violence this entailed. [3] In the postwar era, No More War, with some 3,000 members, participated in Quaker relief work, supported conscientious objectors, proposed mediation during the Korean War, and called for disarmament. [4] The FOR affiliate, the Christian Peace Society (Kristeligt Fredsforbund), founded in 1913, languished in these years but also engaged in relief activities. [5] Meanwhile, the large WILPF affiliate, with 22,000 members, aided relief efforts and worked to support UNESCO, revise textbooks, and secure ratification of the U.N. genocide convention, among other goals. [6]

As part of their antiwar program, these pacifist groups took up the issue of nuclear weapons. Preparing for the WILPF's international conference in 1946, the Danish section proposed early that year that the parent organization press for the "international control of atomic energy." It argued: "The invention of the atomic bomb has struck the world with stupefaction and terror." Indeed, "the end of civilization will be the result if atomic energy is not subjected to international control which will prevent its application for the purposes of war." Naturally, these groups had an agenda broader than nuclear weapons. Consequently, the top item on the Danish WILPF's "work program" for 1949–51 was "to fight the political, social and psychological causes of war." But further down the list came the goal "To work for the international control of atomic energy, as well as of all manufacture and trade in armaments." [7]

World government activism provided another important element in postwar Denmark's peace and disarmament movement. Founded in November 1946 by a young student, Thomas Hatt Olsen, One World (Een Verden) soon developed into a major crusade. In the winter of 1948–49, it conducted 200 public meetings throughout Denmark and established nineteen local chapters. By the summer of 1950, One World had some 13,000 supporters, including many members of the Danish parliament.[8] Henry Usborne reported that when he and Wing Commander Millington toured Denmark in 1948, at the invitation of One World, they attended a reception with Danish members of parliament, were received by the prime minister and members of the cabinet, addressed two "packed" public meetings in Copenhagen, and made a "highly success-ful" radio broadcast. The following summer, a vote on world government in the Danish town of Silkeborg produced a favorable response of 92 percent. In another sample ballot, conducted in October 1950, 77 percent of the voters in the town of Brande indicated their approval of world government.[9]

The menace of nuclear destruction clearly played an important role in stimu-lating this globalist thinking. In a 1949 newspaper feature on One World, one of its leaders, Professor Stephen Hurwitz, explained: "After the atom bomb, One World is the only defense." Kate Fleron, the editor of *Free Denmark*, defined the alternatives in the modern era as "One World or atom bombs and biological warfare. . . . By helping One World, we are doing something to save the future for the children." [10] That same year, One World sponsored "The Atomic Age," an exhibit presented throughout Scandinavia that was designed "to show the devastating powers of the atomic bomb." Its organizers ordered 3,000 copies of pamphlets from America's Emergency Committee of Atomic Scientists, in-cluding *Atomic War or Peace* and *Don't Resign from the Human Race*, and secured permission to translate them into Danish, Swedish, and Norwegian.[11]

The atomic scientists' movement had considerable prestige in postwar Denmark. *Politiken*, the nation's largest Liberal newspaper, published Harold Urey's anti-Bomb classic "I'm a Frightened Man," and Niels Bohr emerged as the nation's most influential critic of the nuclear arms race. To safeguard his credibility, Bohr remained independent of all peace and disarmament organi-zations. Nevertheless, he privately deplored the wartime use of the Bomb and publicly addressed the problem it posed. In an article he wrote that appeared in the London *Times* of August 11, 1945, Bohr warned: "Against the new destruc-tive power no defense may be possible, and the issue centers on world-wide cooperation to prevent any use of the new source of energy which does not serve mankind as a whole." Furthermore, no international control of the Bomb "can be effective without free access to full scientific information and the granting of the opportunity of international supervision of all [dangerous] undertakings." The "whole scientific community," he predicted, "will surely join in a vigorous effort to induce . . . an adequate appreciation of what is at stake and to appeal to humanity at large to heed the warning which has been sounded." [12]

Bohr himself worked persistently along these lines. As he explained to

Oppenheimer, he "felt it urgent to express views which might . . . invite confidence in scientific circles outside England and America." He published additional warnings—including one in *Science* and another (a reprint of his London *Times* piece) in the American best-seller, *One World or None*[13]—and privately lobbied the American government. After a discussion with Bohr at the U.S. embassy in Copenhagen, a U.S. official reported that the Danish physicist praised the Acheson-Lilienthal report as "a great advance . . . toward effective control of the use of the atomic energy" and urged its speedy implementation. When this proved a forlorn hope, he sent a lengthy letter in early June 1946 to Bernard Baruch, calling for "a genuine common effort aimed directly at averting a deadly menace to civilization." The existing situation called "for the removal of many barriers which present obstacles for mutual confidence." [14] That fall, he met with Baruch and Acheson to press his case for an open world, although without much effect. "The situation in the world is most deeply on my mind," he told Oppenheimer in the fall of 1947, and "I have thought very much of what steps might . . . pave the way for real progress." In 1948, Bohr again traveled to the United States and conferred on this matter with State Department officials, including Secretary of State George Marshall. According to a State Department record of one conversation, Bohr was "alarmed at the impasse in international control of atomic energy and claimed to understand and sympathize" with America's disarmament proposals. Nonetheless, he believed that Soviet fear of U.S. military superiority "would certainly prevent Russia's accepting them." Consequently, "some bold initiative" by the United States was "urgently needed." He suggested that President Truman propose "a mutual 'opening up' " of Russia and the United States, with "freedom of access and movement" and "a survey of atomic facilities." In a memo to Marshall, Bohr concluded: "The only way out of the crisis is to make a stand for free access, on a mutual and worldwide basis, to all information essential for an international relationship." [15]

Sweden

Concern about nuclear weapons also grew rapidly in Sweden. Shortly after the Hiroshima bombing, the newspaper *Dagens Nyheter*, while professing its relief that the bomb would shorten the war, declared: "Not even this gratifying result can hide the fact . . . that the old methods of destruction are suddenly being succeeded by a still more frightful one." Indeed, the world learned of the development of atomic weapons "with apprehension and even foreboding." Asked in a November 1948 public opinion poll about the long-run effects of atomic energy, 48 percent of Swedish respondents thought it would do more harm than good, while only 26 percent believed the reverse. Nor was there very much support for the U.S. bombing of Hiroshima. A poll taken in mid-1950 found that 61 percent of Swedish respondents considered the U.S. atomic bombing of Japan unjustified, as compared to only 34 percent who supported the action.[16] A U.S. government intelligence report in early 1951, observing "the rash of uniformly hostile editorial comment on the possible [American] use of the bomb in Korea," claimed that this criticism arose "primarily out of fear that this would bring about a world war" but "also implied moral condemnation of employment of the weapon in this area." Indeed, the U.S. embassy reported that Truman's statement about possible use of the atomic bomb in Korea produced a "sensational effect amounting to shock." Another opinion poll in Sweden, conducted in mid-1950, found that six out of ten of those Swedish respondents who thought the United States might use the atomic bomb in a new war opposed the idea.[17]

Swedish distaste for nuclear weapons probably owed at least something to the nation's neutral status during and after World War II, which limited Swedish identification with U.S. foreign policy.[18] It may also be true that, as Vera Brittain argued, Sweden preserved "certain moral values which belligerent nations inevitably lost." Even so, Sweden was certainly not a pacifist nation. Although the Swedish Peace and Arbitration Society (Svenska Fred- och Skiljedomsföreningen), founded in 1883, had once exercised considerable influence in Swedish life, it declined—as did other Swedish peace groups—in the late 1930s as fear of Nazi Germany grew. The labor movement and its political arm, the Swedish Social Democratic party, stopped criticizing military preparedness and instead began to champion the democratization of the armed forces. With the inception of the Soviet-Finnish War, the peace movement grew even more isolated. Consequently, Sweden moved toward a combination of strict neutrality and strong national defense—a policy that may have helped keep Sweden out of war but did not provide for the disarmament desired by peace groups.[19]

In this context, the traditional pacifist groups played a small, respectable, but fairly marginal role in postwar Swedish life. As one Swedish pacifist told an International FOR gathering in 1946, pacifism was "not taken very seriously in the country generally." The Swedish branch of the WRI, with about 2,000 members in 1947, engaged in relief work, support for conscientious objectors, and promotion of international cooperation and disarmament, as did the FOR branch (Förbundet för Kristet Sambällsliv), with its 900 members, many of them teachers and ministers.[20] The largest of the pacifist groups, the WILPF section (Internationella Kvinnoförbundent för Fred och Frihet), had more than 5,000 members and received a small annual subsidy from the government; it was particularly active in promoting the United Nations. Most of Sweden's pacifist groups worked closely together in a coalition, the National Peace Bureau, which published the journal *Freden*. Although these groups grew slightly just after the war, they were languishing by the end of the decade.[21]

The menace of nuclear war provided one of their major concerns. Writing in *Freden* shortly after the atomic bombing of Japan, the pacifist G. E. Dahlberg contended that the weapons' vast destructiveness showed conclusively that the only safety for people lay in the abolition of war. In a private letter at about the same time, one Swedish WILPF leader wrote: "What are we to say about the atom bomb? I think we have to warn and speak of it as we did of poison gas."[22] Not surprisingly, at an early date the WILPF assailed "the misuse of atomic energy for mass destruction." Some years later, in 1948, it sponsored an anti-Bomb talk by a leader of the WILPF's English section, the atomic scientist Kathleen Lonsdale, who spoke on the subject of nuclear ethics. Continuing as a sharp critic of the Bomb, Dahlberg cited the warnings of scientists that atomic bombs could be produced cheaply and in large numbers and that no defense against them was possible.[23] Nevertheless, because of the weakness of these groups, their message had a limited impact.

Here, as elsewhere, the world government movement exhibited greater dynamism and effectiveness than did pacifism. The idea of world federation had been discussed for decades within the Swedish peace movement,[24] but only in 1946 were steps taken to set up an organization. Visits by Henry Usborne, Bertrand Russell, Edith Wynner, and other dignitaries followed, resulting in large public meetings and membership campaigns. In the winter of 1948–49, for example, more than 500 people attended a meeting sponsored by the Swedish Group for World Federation (Svenska Arbetsgruppen av Världsfederation); the gathering was addressed by prominent educators and scientists, as well as by a Swedish member of parliament.[25] By mid-1950, the Swedish world government movement could point to several thousand members, an active parliamentary group, and the introduction into parliament of a bill designed to provide for Sweden's participation in a world government. The following year, activists scattered leaflets from helicopters over Sweden's major cities calling for the creation of "a popular movement for world law, world government, and world peace" and concluding, "One World or none."[26]

Other ventures in postwar Sweden also touched upon these themes. In December 1947, U.S. atomic scientist Harold Urey, interviewed on a Swedish National Radio broadcast entitled "One World—or None," warned that no military defense against nuclear weapons existed or could be imagined. Furthermore, he argued, "an adequate organization for the control of atomic energy or other means of making war . . . must be a world government." Reported in detail by the Swedish press, the program created a substantial stir and was twice rebroadcast. The Swedish Peace and Arbitration Society, eager to spread the message, published and distributed 50,000 copies of Urey's comments.[27]

Meanwhile, beginning in 1947, Vera Robert-Akesson, chair of a local WILPF group and with the backing of the Swedish branch, for several years produced concentrated, simultaneous radio, film, and press activities around the theme of world peace.[28] By 1948, her Swedish Peace Campaign Committee claimed the participation of 30 Swedish organizations and churches, representing more than three million people. In addition, she noted, the campaign had spread to Norway, Denmark, and Finland and had "gained followers in many other countries both in Europe and on other continents." The second "Proclamation" of the campaign, issued in 1948, began by pointing to "this time of greatest danger for a new global war, the combined atomic-, gas-, and bacteriological war," and went on to demand the development of the United Nations "towards a Federal World Government." Prudently, however, it added: "In the meantime, until this has been accomplished," there should be "immediate measures banning total war, atomic-, gas-, and bacteriological war." In 1949, the Swedish committee—now retitled the International Peace Propaganda Campaign—added to its pleas a call to supporters to participate in "World Peace Day, the Hiroshima Day, on August 6th." On that day, it issued a manifesto calling for an end to the arms race, the development of federal world government, respect for the new declaration of human rights, and international disarmament.[29]

Norway

World War II had more damaging effects on peace activism in Norway. The German invasion and occupation weakened the traditional opposition to armaments and military force among the general population.[30] At the same time, the Nazi conquerors and their collaborators badly mauled pacifist groups. They imprisoned or killed many Norwegian pacifists, including the chair of the WRI section, who died in a German concentration camp, and the chair of the WILPF section, who survived her concentration camp ordeal. The Quisling regime also seized the records, confiscated the funds, and banned the meetings of pacifist organizations. Nevertheless, here, as elsewhere, pacifists defied the authorities by meeting secretly, circulating illegal literature, and carrying on resistance activities. One activist recalled that Norwegian pacifists avoided violent ventures but engaged in "the form of sabotage in factories or the administration which hinders, stops, or makes impossible the Germans' war effort." Consequently, pacifism became a hazardous profession in Nazi-occupied Norway.[31]

In the aftermath of the war, Norway's pacifist groups underwent a muted revival. A reorganized WRI section, with fewer than 300 members, focused on relief work and opposition to compulsory military service, although its much smaller FOR counterpart was largely inactive. The strongest of the pacifist groups, the Norwegian WILPF section, with some 2,000 members, stressed support for the United Nations and the demilitarization of education.[32] In an effort to pool their limited strength, delegates from seven Norwegian peace groups met in October 1945 at Nobel House in Oslo and organized a liaison committee, the Norwegian Peace Council. By 1951, its twelve member organizations included the WRI, FOR, and WILPF sections, as well as the Friends, U.N. Youth Association, Norwegian Parsons Peace Committee, Norwegian Teachers Peace Committee, and Norwegian Peace Society. "Universal disarmament," argued the Norwegian Peace Council, "must be the aim of all peaceful foreign policy."[33]

The limited impact of these groups upon a nation traumatized by war and occupation was exemplified by the campaign opposing Norway's membership in NATO. Attempting to maintain Norway's traditional policy of neutrality, the WILPF took the lead in this campaign, which was also joined by the WRI section, the Norwegian Peace Council, the Communists, and some prominent members of the Labor and Liberal parties. Eventually, however, proponents of the treaty won an easy victory. Opposition proved unpopular in the general society and even within the ranks of the WILPF, which, as a consequence, dwindled substantially thereafter. In mid-1950, an English Quaker living in Oslo reported glumly: "The general support for defense measures and of the [NATO] Pact policy make propaganda for peace based on understanding, confidence, and a reduction of defense very unpopular and difficult." Privately, she conceded: "The peace movement has its back to the wall here."[34]

Newer peace currents were stirring, however. Spurred on by the arms race, sentiment for a world government gathered momentum in Norway during these years. The Norwegian world federalist movement began taking root in 1946, and in 1948, when Usborne and Millington barnstormed through Bergen and Oslo, they addressed crowded meetings and organized a parliamentary study group. By 1950, Norway's world government movement could claim nearly 2,000 members, mostly organized in One World (En Verden). According to a UNESCO-sponsored opinion survey of the late 1940s, 48 percent of Norwegian respondents favored world government, compared to 35 percent who opposed it.[35] Recognizing the importance of the issue, both the FOR and the WILPF organized study groups on Emery Reves's book *The Anatomy of Peace*.[36]

Pacifists also worked closely with atomic scientists and others to promote awareness of the dangers of nuclear weapons. In 1947, the Norwegian WILPF branch printed and distributed a translation of Urey's anti-Bomb article "I'm a Frightened Man," prepared by young atomic scientists at the University of

Oslo. That same year, the WILPF initiated a very large public meeting on nuclear weapons in Oslo, addressed by an atomic scientist and a military chief. The pacifist group also distributed an article by Robert Hutchins, "The Secret of the Atomic Bomb Does Not Exist," and a pamphlet entitled *The Biological Effects of the Atomic Bomb*, prepared by Dr. Leiv Kreyberg, a Norwegian physician. Meanwhile, local WILPF groups sponsored lectures with such titles as "Science and Peace" (with Marc Oliphant) and "The Atomic Bomb and World Peace." Responding to pressure from pacifists, the Norwegian state radio station aired a broadcast, on August 6, 1949, that centered on the Hiroshima Peace Festival. It included a talk by a physicist at Trondheim Technical College who spoke of the underdevelopment of moral values in the atomic age and warned of the horrors of nuclear war.[37]

The situation in Norway, then, eventually began to resemble that of its neighbors. In early 1950, the U.S. embassy in Oslo reported that Norwegian scientists were uneasy about the dangers of the "unrestricted development" of nuclear weapons and that the foreign minister "feels there is [a] definite undercurrent of defeatism and sense of futility in Norway as [a] result of [the] news of [the] H-bomb." In early 1951, a U.S. intelligence survey contended that, although "Norwegian opinion has been less articulate than that in the other Scandinavian countries on the immoral aspect of the use of the atomic bomb," the Norwegian position on this issue was not "fundamentally different." There had been "definite opposition among both military circles and civilians at the end of November 1950 to the possible use of the atom bomb in Manchuria," and the population had been "reported as 'uneasy' when these rumors were current."[38]

The Netherlands

Like its counterparts in other nations occupied by the Nazis, the once hardy Dutch peace movement suffered terribly during World War II. Even before the war, the movement had been declining, but with the inception of the German occupation, the conquerors proscribed peace groups and seized their resources. Because of their strong aversion to the Nazi New Order, pacifists threw themselves into clandestine activities, with all the resultant dangers. They met secretly in private homes and worked at a variety of resistance ventures, including the production of illegal newspapers and the hiding of Jews from their Nazi persecutors. In 1941, the Rev. Johannes Hugenholtz, the secretary of Church and Peace (Kerk en Vrede)—a religious pacifist organization of 5,600 members before it was banned—was sent to a concentration camp for assisting the Jews. Although Hugenholtz survived, the Nazis executed the secretary of the

WRI section. Other prominent pacifists spent lengthy periods in prisons, in concentration camps, or in hiding.[39]

Following the war, pacifist groups made a slow recovery, hindered, as in France, by the deep bitterness, poverty, and demoralization the population carried over from its wartime ordeal.[40] Always very small, the WILPF group remained so, in part because of a widespread belief that separate organizations for women were out-of-date.[41] By contrast, in June 1946, Church and Peace was reorganized as an FOR section, and by 1949 it claimed nearly 2,000 members. Meanwhile, the pacifist Hein van Wijk organized General Dutch Peace Action (Algemene Nederlands Vredes Actie, ANVA), which became a section of the WRI. Maintaining his leadership role in Church and Peace, Hugenholtz also served as the chair of ANVA and the editor of its journal.[42] At the initiative of the Red Cross, pacifist groups joined in 1948 with educational, labor, women's, and cultural organizations to establish a loosely structured peace federation, the Dutch Movement to Promote International Peace and Security.[43]

As elsewhere, pacifists in the Netherlands assailed the unprecedented dangers of nuclear weapons. Opposing the militarization of the two Cold War camps, Church and Peace claimed that, in a new war, "Europe will be completely lost. Preparation for this war means deliberate suicide for Europe." Hugenholtz told an American correspondent that Dutch pacifists hoped that "the atomic bomb danger" would lead people "to abolish armaments," although he feared that control of atomic weapons was "if not impossible, in any case very difficult." On a personal level, he felt most at ease in these circumstances with "non-violence defense"; and, for society in general, he favored "the reform of the UN" into a "federal world government." In a letter to Einstein in late 1945, Hugenholtz thanked the American physicist for championing world government, an international police force, and the international control of atomic energy. Warning, however, that little time remained before the Soviet Union developed the Bomb and "a super-war" erupted, Hugenholtz recommended organizing "all over the world a big total disarmament action."[44]

Dutch pacifists, however, faced a more immediate crisis in the form of their government's attempt to crush the newly independent Republic of Indonesia through force of arms. Church and Peace condemned Dutch military intervention as totally unjustifiable. Responding to the government's claim that the whole nation with the exception of the Communists approved its actions, Hugenholtz issued an opposition statement on behalf of ANVA that also cited criticisms by the Dutch Reformed church and by elements of the governing Labor party. A broadly based Committee for Peace in Indonesia was established at a large public meeting in Amsterdam that brought together pacifists and many other groups and individuals opposed to colonialism. Encouraged by the climate of resistance, about 2,000 young men refused to serve in the Dutch armed forces, and another 5,000 deserted rather than go to Indonesia. It was an effective display of renascent antiwar sentiment, although one that absorbed energies that might otherwise have been directed against the Bomb.[45]

For the most part, Dutch scientists played a more active role in promoting nuclear disarmament. Inspired by the efforts of their U.S. counterparts, 30 Dutch scientists formed a team to lecture on atomic energy control to civic leaders and public gatherings. Others published *Atoom*, a monthly magazine dealing with the question. The position taken by the U.S. government was replicated, to a great extent, in a resolution of the Christian Society of Scientists and Physicians in the Netherlands, which, in late 1947, adopted a resolution calling "international control and inspection of the atomic weapon . . . imperative." It rejected "prohibition of the atomic weapon without international control." By contrast, Professor M. Minnaert, president of the left-wing Dutch Association of Scientific Workers, argued for a compromise between the official U.S. and Soviet positions. "We can understand fairly well the motives which are at the bottom of the two rival proposals," he stated; "we think that they have sufficient in common to make an agreement possible." Many shared the impatience of one distinguished Dutch scientist who declared himself "thoroughly upset" by the continued U.S. production of atomic bombs. "It should have been the duty of the American people, or at least of its leaders, to say: we will not let ourselves be overpowered with fear; we value a righteous attitude and respect for civilization above all, and we will not increase our stock of atomic weapons. This might have meant a certain danger for the U.S., but it would have meant a relief to the world." [46]

The movement for world government also gathered momentum in the postwar Netherlands. To champion the cause, world federalist tracts appeared,[47] public meetings on the subject were convened (addressed by Henry Usborne and Bertrand Russell, among others), a parliamentary federalist group emerged, and a new political party (the Progressive Party for World Government) was formed. According to a UNESCO-sponsored poll of the late 1940s, 46 percent of Dutch respondents favored world government, as compared to 32 percent who opposed it.[48] By the summer of 1950, nearly 29,000 people had joined the six Dutch branches of the World Movement for World Federal Government. Several thousand citizens of the Netherlands also enrolled as World Citizens.[49]

As in France, the independent Left also turned to peace and disarmament activism. Uncomfortable with the demands of both the American and Soviet Cold War camps, radical newspapers like *De Vlam*, *De Groene Amsterdammer*, and *De Nieuwe Stem* championed a democratic socialist United States of Europe and, after the eruption of war in Korea, became convinced that the problem of war represented a major concern for builders of a new society. In January 1951, organized discussion of these themes commenced among Krijn Strijd of Church and Peace, Dirk Schilp of the *De Vlam*, and Johan Riemens of the now defunct movement against the Indonesian war. A conference followed that April—attended by representatives from Church and Peace, ANVA, *De Vlam*, and *De Nieuwe Stem*—which resolved to establish a more broadly based peace movement, one that would reject the military programs of the Eastern and Western blocs. This new movement, the Third Way (De Derde Weg), soon claimed the support of active groups in thirteen cities. One of its leaders, Jef Suys, a political scientist, proposed a manifesto for the Third Way contending that the two Cold War camps were leading the world to war not only because of their rigidly ideological approach to international issues but because of the nuclear arms race, which terrified both sides and made preventive war seem attractive.[50]

Alongside these indications of ferment among pacifists, scientists, world federalists, and independent leftists appeared additional signs of Dutch dismay over nuclear weapons. To be sure, U.S. intelligence tended to discount them. It reported that "there has been little public comment on the atom bomb as an immoral weapon. While recognizing it as an instrument with great destructive power, the Dutch have regarded it as another weapon," with expressions of revulsion over the use of the Bomb "limited mainly to Communist and pro-Communist groups."[51] This contention, however, is belied by a Gallup poll of November 1948, which asked the Dutch whether they thought that, "in the long run, atomic energy will do more good than harm?" In response, 52 percent of those polled indicated that they thought it would do more harm, while only 25 percent thought it would do more good. These proved to be the most negative views on atomic energy among the five countries surveyed. (In the United States, the response was, more good, 42 percent; more harm, 23 percent.) Even conservative Catholic newspapers expressed their anxiety at the U.S. plan to develop the hydrogen bomb.[52]

Belgium

Resistance to nuclear weapons was less common in postwar Belgium. Pacifism had never flourished in that country, and World War II, with its harsh German occupation, weakened it still further. In the war's aftermath, the WILPF retained little more than some individual members. Sections of the WRI and the FOR were revived in 1949, but they remained tiny and had little impact on political developments. Together with the Stop War Movement of

Baron Antoine Allard, a prominent pacifist, the war resisters group—led by the pacifist-anarchist Hem Day—focused on the rights of conscientious objectors. By mid-1949, twenty small peace groups united in a new movement called PAX.[53]

World federalism made somewhat greater headway in postwar Belgium. Enthusiasts published world government writings,[54] established a world federalist student camp, and organized a parliamentary federalist group.[55] Two world federalist groups—Federal Union (Union Fédérale) and World Coforces (Coforces Mondiales)—also provided the organizational base for the Stop War Movement. Although the Belgian branches of the World Movement for World Federal Government could point to a total of only 2,400 members by mid-1950, this did not reflect the extent of globalist sentiment. Maurice Cosyn, head of Federal Union, told Garry Davis in late 1948 that some 12,000 people in Brussels had joined the Friends of Garry Davis. In the summer of 1949, a test ballot on world government in the town of Nivelles found that 90 percent of the voters supported the concept.[56]

As part of their efforts for world peace, these groups took up the question of the Bomb. In a leaflet it distributed in 1948, World Coforces proposed working "against the atomic danger and the advent of a third war" by "taking atomic energy away from the politicians and giving it back to the scientists," creating "world federal forces," and using the U.N. Food and Agriculture Organization to feed the world. That same year, Federal Union sponsored a "Stop War" retreat at Heist, Belgium, for "all federalists" and "all individuals who are doing their very best to prevent a new war." Among the issues discussed were "atomic control and the organization of scientific research on a world basis" and "the production and use of atomic bombs." The latter included the "role of scientists," the "role of workers and unions," and "moral and practical aspects."[57]

For the most part, however, opposition to nuclear weapons in postwar Belgium remained below the surface of public discussion. According to a U.S. intelligence report, "only with reference to the manufacture of the hydrogen bomb has Belgian press comment touched on moral issues." The liberal *Le Matin* headlined a story "Manufacture of Superbomb Gravest Problem Posed to Human Conscience." But the conservative *La Libre Belgique* claimed that the weapon was immoral only if used for aggression. The independent *La Lanterne* remarked that moral issues were not a concern of the Soviet Union when choosing weapons, while the conservative *Het Nieuwsblad* did not see why the hydrogen bomb raised any moral issues when there had been no scruples over the production of the atomic bomb. Only in "Communist circles" did U.S. intelligence find any consistent opposition to the Bomb on moral grounds. A

New York Times correspondent reported that when news of the Soviet atomic bomb reached the people of Belgium and her small neighbors, they "seemed to feel that matters were completely out of their hands, so the less thinking the better." [58]

Switzerland

Peace activism fared somewhat better in postwar Switzerland. During World War II, Swiss pacifists had been relatively subdued, concentrating their efforts on assistance to refugee children. With the lifting of the war clouds, the Society of Friends sparked the formation of an umbrella organization, the Swiss Peace Council (Conseil Suisse des Associations pour la Paix). Organized in December 1945, it brought together 22 groups, including the Friends, the United Nations Society, and the FOR section, with more than 10,000 members. The Swiss Peace Council used this new strength and visibility to campaign for alternative service for conscientious objectors, prohibition of arms exports, and an end to the use of young people's sports organizations for paramilitary training. In addition, responding to pressures from British and American Quakers, it worked, unsuccessfully, to form a world organization of peace movements. Although peace groups favored the tradition of Swiss neutrality, they were dismayed by their country's high level of military preparations and by its complacent isolation from world affairs, including its refusal to join the United Nations.[59]

As part of their agenda, Swiss peace groups advocated nuclear disarmament. In September 1950, for example, six nonaligned peace groups, calling themselves the Committee of Determined Peace Organizations, proclaimed that they were "working for the prohibition of atomic weapons, for the destruction of the stocks of atomic bombs, and for a rigorous and effective international control of the products of atomic energy and atomic research." They recognized, they said, that "the prohibition of atomic weapons is . . . only one aspect of the general problem of world disarmament"; nevertheless, it was imperative. In line with contemporary thinking, they contended that "effective international control is only possible by limiting national sovereignty in favor of an international institution." Late the following year, the Swiss Peace Council sent an appeal to the Swiss government, urging it to call a world disarmament conference headquartered in Switzerland.[60]

As elsewhere, the world government movement became intertwined with these concerns. Like the United States, Switzerland was a nation in which federation had proved remarkably successful; consequently, the Swiss liked to point to their country as a model for the world. Not surprisingly, then, world government tracts appeared and world government groups became active in the postwar years.[61] By the end of 1950, Switzerland had some 2,000 registered World Citizens, although, as one activist admitted that year, participation in world federalist organizations remained low. In the meantime, prominent figures made the case that the Bomb had left humanity no choice but world government. "It is obvious that if we continue to think as we do today, it all will end in total explosion," wrote Denis de Rougement, a leading Swiss federalist. "And it is obvious that the great majority of men refuse to admit these evident truths. They harp the livelong day that people 'aren't ready for world government.' " He thought it time someone asked them "if they are ready for death." [62]

Austria

In the small neighboring nation of Austria, the situation differed in several respects. At the end of the war, the Allied powers viewed Austria as an Axis nation. Therefore, like Germany, Austria underwent four-power occupation, including demilitarization. To some degree, then, military force was discredited by the war and by the postwar occupation experience. Yet large numbers of Austrians viewed themselves as the victims of German aggression in 1938. Consequently, like many people in nations conquered by the Nazis, they tended to look upon military strength with a newfound respect. Moreover, little remained of the Austrian peace movement, which had been badly mauled by the fascist regime.[63]

The reestablishment of the Austrian peace movement was begun in 1945 by Professor Hans Thirring, a distinguished physicist, who had been dismissed from the University of Vienna in 1938 for his pacifist views. Returning to this post, Thirring organized the Austrian Peace Society, which recruited substantial numbers of intellectuals, as well as three cabinet ministers and the mayor of Vienna. In May 1947, it published a declaration against Austrian rearmament, contending that "a return to the old military tradition is apt to disturb peaceful relations with our neighbours and may . . . raise the suspicions of the occupying powers." Austria's integrity, it contended, could be defended by a small U.N. contingent.[64] Small WRI, FOR, and WILPF groups also resumed their activities.[65] In April 1949, on the initiative of the Austrian Peace Society and of the Society of Friends, thirteen Austrian peace groups met and reestablished the Austrian Peace Council, an umbrella group whose office had been raided and plundered by the Gestapo in 1938. Although the major political parties supported the introduction of conscription, the Austrian Peace Council reaffirmed the declaration of 1947. Following the lead of another prominent pacifist, Johannes Ude, the Peace Council demanded a plebiscite on conscription.[66]

Meanwhile, with Thirring's assistance, a world government movement also commenced activities in Austria. Although its major group, the World Citizens (Die Weltbürger), remained small, with a membership of 2,165, a Garry Davis World Citizenship Group claimed an additional 2,000. World citizenship, declared the tiny Austrian WILPF section, "seems to us capable of bringing us nearer to salvation" and "therefore we welcome it enthusiastically." [67]

Inevitably, the activities of these individuals and groups spilled over into the area of protest against nuclear weapons. Johannes Ude was an eminent Christian theologian and prominent prewar pacifist; indeed, only the end of World War II prevented his execution by the Nazis for military sedition. After 1945, he became a leading critic of conventional and nuclear war and repeatedly called for an end to the arms race. In 1948, he was a sponsor of the Hiroshima-based World Peace Day.[68] The Austrian Peace Council also took on the issue of the Bomb. In 1950, it demanded a ban on atomic weapons and condemned the H-Bomb as a purely offensive weapon.[69]

Thirring, who became the leading figure in the Austrian peace movement, was a theoretical physicist and a Socialist politician who wrote widely on issues of disarmament and peace for Austrian and foreign publications. In 1946, he published a book, *The History of the Atom Bomb*, that warned of nuclear holocaust. Praised by Victor Weisskopf in the *Bulletin of the Atomic Scientists* for its scientific and historical accuracy, the book also strongly supported all decisions taken by the U.S. government with respect to atomic weapons. These included not only what Thirring believed were Washington's attempts to secure international control of atomic energy but—curiously—the atomic bombing of Japan. Nevertheless, by the latter part of the decade, Thirring had grown more critical of U.S. policy, arguing that it was imperative for East and West to negotiate solutions to their conflicts. In the new world of nuclear weapons, he maintained, a third world war had to be avoided if humanity was to survive.[70]

On this point, at least, Austrian opinion seemed roughly to parallel that of the country's best-known peace leader. A 1949 report by an Austrian observer claimed that, though pacifist groups remained small and ineffective, within the general population there existed "a great and sincere desire for peace." Although many Austrians viewed U.S. possession of the Bomb as a deterrent to its use, a U.S. intelligence report commented in early 1951 that the weapon inspired "a general horror." The U.S. atomic bombing of Japan "has been condemned and there has been universal opposition against even the contemplation of its use against Chinese forces, either in Korea or Manchuria." Defensive employment of the weapon for such purposes as "retaliatory action for Soviet bombing of U.S. cities" would meet with Austrian approval, it concluded, but "generally, Austrian opinion would condemn the offensive use of the bomb." [71]

Ireland

Antinuclear sentiment also grew in postwar Ireland. Operating in a democratic nation that remained neutral in both World War II and the ensuing Cold War, Irish peace groups, like their Swedish counterparts, enjoyed a measure of respect and goodwill in the general society. To some degree, however, this was tempered by the generally unsympathetic attitude toward pacifism taken by the powerful Catholic church and by the popularity of the United States, a land to which many Irish citizens were tied by family connections. By the late 1940s, Ireland's three peace groups—the Irish Anti-War Crusade (the WRI section), the FOR, and the Church of Ireland Peace Fellowship—cooperated very closely with one another. In February 1950, at the monthly meeting of the Irish Anti-War Crusade, the members unanimously passed a resolution "to place on record their heartfelt dismay and horror at the recent decision of the American government to manufacture their latest lethal discovery—the hydrogen bomb." According to *Pax*, the journal of the group, the full resolution "subsequently appeared in all the leading Irish newspapers, provoking considerable correspondence." [72]

Indeed, public attitudes in Ireland remained consistently critical of nuclear weapons. In late 1946, the conservative *Irish Times*, a leading Dublin newspaper, carried the complete text of John Hersey's *Hiroshima* and added in an editorial: "All the crimes of the Goerings and the Himmlers, the horrors of the concentration camps . . . seem to be peccadillos in comparison with the supreme crime of the atomic bomb." A worried U.S. embassy reported that "the silence of the other Dublin papers indicates to us their assent to the views published by the *Times*." When the United States made its H-Bomb announcement, the embassy reported, it "created alarm, at least among leading groups." Even when newspapers accepted the necessity of the American decision, they argued that "the United States has been partly or mainly responsible for allowing this situation to develop." The *Irish Times* contended that the United States suffered from "a power complex springing from its unprecedented material superiority" and concluded that "the appalling armaments competition between the United States and Russia can only result in another world war." The time had arrived, the newspaper implied, "to bring the Americans and the Russians together in order to call a halt to this insane race for armed supremacy." [73]

Spain and Portugal

In Spain and Portugal, the situation differed substantially, for their right-wing dictatorships made peace activities impossible and, at least in the mass media, encouraged a climate of sympathetic regard for U.S. nuclear weapons. A commentator on Radio Madrid, while acknowledging the moral issue raised by the weapons, claimed that the Soviet Union would not hesitate to use them, unlike "civilized countries." Reacting to Truman's statement about the possible use of atomic weapons in Korea, the Nationalist *La Vanguardia* expressed its "sense of relief." When the U.S. government announced its plan to develop a hydrogen bomb, the Spanish press and government voiced their support for the decision. Meanwhile, in Portugal, noted a U.S. intelligence report, the people "tend to adopt a fatalistic attitude" toward nuclear weapons. They regarded them "as immoral" but considered it "essential for the United States to retain its supremacy in this field." [74] If nothing else, such attitudes underscored the invigorating effect that public advocacy of nuclear disarmament had had on popular consciousness elsewhere in Western Europe.

Muted Opposition

The Soviet Union, Eastern Europe, and the Third World

> Unless . . . the world adopts non-violence, it will spell
> certain suicide for mankind.
>
> Mohandas Gandhi, 1945

Opposition to nuclear weapons was considerably more limited elsewhere in the world. Dictatorship severely circumscribed the possibilities for peace and disarmament activism in the Soviet Union and much of Eastern Europe. In addition, the immense suffering that Nazi Germany and its allies inflicted on this region bolstered popular support for postwar military measures and undermined criticism of nuclear weapons. The Third World was affected by these factors as well, for portions of it were ruled by military dictatorships—externally imposed or home-grown—and some areas had been devastated by World War II. Furthermore, the Third World lacked the large educated middle class that provided the base for the peace and disarmament movements in many industrially developed nations. Finally, although most people in the Third World did not identify with the interests of the Cold War adversaries, their geographical distance from the nuclear confrontation and their overriding concern about national independence and economic development left them relatively uninterested in the question of the Bomb. The result was that, although a revulsion against nuclear weapons did develop among the people of these regions, the menace of the Bomb rarely became a significant issue in popular thought or public debate.

The Soviet Union

Dictatorship and war clearly dampened resistance to nuclear weapons in the Soviet Union. Initially, the Bolshevik regime had provided generous provisions for conscientious objection and had allowed pacifist groups to operate freely.

Subsequently, though, it began placing severe restrictions upon pacifist and antimilitarist propaganda. Finally, in 1929, the Soviet government closed down the last of the pacifist organizations—a Tolstoyan group, which contained subgroups affiliated with the WRI and the International FOR. Thereafter, faced with the certainty of brutal repression by Stalin's dictatorship, organized pacifist activities ground to a halt. Nor did they revive in the aftermath of World War II. Some individual pacifists maintained contact with the International FOR, but communication proved very difficult.[1]

The political climate proved just as forbidding for advocates of world government. Perhaps because America's atomic scientists provided important leadership for the world federalist movement, Soviet scientists were earmarked for the role of attacking it. Writing in Moscow's *New Times* in November 1947, the president of the Soviet Academy of Sciences and three other top Soviet scientists assailed Einstein and other "representatives of the intelligentsia of capitalist countries who are carried away by the seeming simplicity of the idea." In actuality, they argued, world government concealed "world domination of capitalist monopolies" and promised "new war orders and new profits." Proposals to establish it were "ridiculous" and "absurd." The "imperialist forces which aspire to world domination appear under a guise of allegedly progressive ideas which attract . . . scientists, writers and others." That was how Einstein had been led "to support plans and aspirations of the worst enemies of peace and international collaboration."[2] Given the dangers of public disagreement with this stand, which paralleled official Soviet policy, it was hardly surprising that no voices were raised in the defense of Einstein or world government.[3]

Unlike many scientists in the West, Soviet scientists—facing the prospect of severe reprisals—did not openly resist nuclear weapons or join the campaign for arms control and disarmament. Replying in June 1947 to the Committee for Foreign Correspondence of the Federation of American Scientists, the rector of Lvov State University contended coolly that "scientific workers" at his institution were "in complete agreement with Comrade A. A. Gromyko's viewpoint as expressed in his speeches at . . . the [U.N.] Security Council." I. V. Kurchatov, who directed the Soviet Bomb project, later claimed that Soviet scientists regarded such weapons work "as their sacred duty to ensure the safety of their country." Even less enthusiastic accounts, though stressing baser motives, do not suggest much scientific resistance. Yuri Orlov, who became a leading Soviet dissident, recalled that the physics department where he studied just after the war "was really a pact between scientists and the devil." It "prepared specialists mainly for fundamental nuclear and rocket research. Scientists badly wanted that for the sake of advancing science itself, and Stalin for the sake of producing bombs and rockets." Students, he noted, "were party to the pact, too. Most were untroubled by the idea of doing military work someday; others, like myself, believed we could manage to avoid paying that price for our education." [4]

Moreover, support for building nuclear weapons went beyond mere opportunism. Admittedly, many Soviet scientists were pressed into the Bomb program, and large numbers of other participants were slave laborers or prisoners.[5] Nevertheless, in the aftermath of a bloody fascist onslaught and in the emerging context of the Cold War, many Soviet citizens sincerely believed in the necessity for a Soviet Bomb. Even Andrei Sakharov, in later years perhaps the sharpest critic of his country's nuclear weapons policy, was enthusiastic about his early work on the Soviet H-Bomb, which began in mid-1948. "I had no doubts as to the vital importance of creating a Soviet superweapon for our country and for the balance of power throughout the world," he recalled. "Carried away by the immensity of the task, I worked very strenuously." In his memoirs, he wrote: "We began our labors convinced that our enterprise was absolutely vital for our national security and the preservation of peace." [6]

Of course, there probably were Soviet scientists who secretly disliked the atomic bomb project or who preferred nuclear arms controls to a nuclear arms race. The distinguished physicist Mikhail Leontovich, who had worked on military projects during World War II, did his best thereafter to avoid military work. The FAS Committee for Foreign Correspondence learned from a U.S. scientist returning from the Soviet Union that its material did reach Soviet scientists. According to the committee, this scientist found "that their response to it was favorable" and "that at least one Russian scientist had forwarded the committee's letter to the President of the Soviet Academy of Sciences." [7] In later years, Sakharov reflected on the curious behavior of Igor Tamm and Lev Landau, two of his associates on the Soviet Bomb project. Strolling privately about the garden of the Institute of Physical Problems with Landau in the mid-1950s, Sakharov recalled that the latter told him, "I don't like any of this." Sakharov took this reference to mean "nuclear weapons in general, and his involvement with them in particular." When Sakharov asked him why, Landau replied, "Too much noise." Sakharov wondered if this was a joke but noticed that Landau seemed "grave and melancholy." Yakov Zeldovich, another physicist working on the Soviet Bomb project in the 1940s, later told Sakharov that when he saw the finished plutonium, he thought not only of "the prisoners who worked in the uranium mines and at the nuclear installations, but also the potential victims of atomic war." [8]

Other incidents suggest that there may have been some direct resistance. According to *New York Times* reporter Harrison Salisbury, who interviewed U.S. scientists returning from a 1956 visit to Moscow, "several . . . physicists" employed on the Bomb project ran afoul of Stalin's regime. And Colonel G. A. Tokaev, a Soviet military expert who later defected to the West, also reported that "a number of specialists who had been working on atomic projects were arrested in 1947 for negligence and lack of results."[9] But did their difficulties reflect principled objections to the Bomb?

The limits of dissent seem well illustrated by the case of Peter Kapitza. When, in the aftermath of the Hiroshima bombing, Stalin instituted a crash program to produce nuclear weapons, he appointed Kapitza—director of the Institute of Physical Problems and perhaps the Soviet Union's best-known scientist—to the high-level committee chosen to oversee the Bomb project. Genuinely fearing United States aggression, Kapitza had no objection to accepting this position. The committee, however, was directed by Lavrenti Beria, the head of the secret police, and Kapitza soon found him impossible to work with. In a letter to Stalin of October 3, 1945, Kapitza asked to be relieved of his work on the atomic project, explaining that Beria lacked "respect for scientists." When Stalin ignored this appeal, Kapitza complained about Beria again in another letter to the Soviet dictator. Beria, in turn, pressed Stalin for permission to arrest the physicist, an act that probably would have resulted in his liquidation. Eventually, Stalin arranged for a milder form of punishment. Kapitza was denounced on trumped-up charges related to his other work and, in August 1946, dismissed from his post at the institute. Although Kapitza continued his research work at his country house just outside Moscow, he was for the next eight years under virtual house arrest and, according to his son Sergei, "in great despair and close to a nervous breakdown."[10]

Following Stalin's death, the Soviet government reinstated Kapitza as institute director. In this capacity, he wrote to Nikita Khrushchev, outlining his relation to the Bomb project and addressing the rumor, spread by Beria, that he had been unpatriotic. "The sole reason I was forced to refuse this work was the insufferable relationship of Beria to science and scientists," he explained. "So there is no basis for the accusations against me that I, as they said, was a pacifist and therefore refused to work on the atomic bomb." That Kapitza was not making this disclaimer to curry favor with the new Soviet ruler is evident from his next words, which would hardly endear him to the government of any great power: "I personally do not see why it follows that a person is assumed to be guilty if he, true to his own convictions, refuses to make weapons of destruction and murder." Having thus rebuffed Stalin, Beria, and Khrushchev, Kapitza maintained to the end of his life that he supported the building of the Soviet atomic bomb. In later years, Sakharov concluded that Kapitza's "soft-pedaling" of the "moral issues" was "not simply a ruse." His son also thought that in the 1940s Kapitza did not oppose the Bomb.[11]

Like the scientists, most Soviet citizens expressed few, if any, qualms about nuclear weapons during these years. The explosion of the American atomic bombs over Japan received low-key coverage in the nation's mass media and subsequent government propaganda efforts were directed to avoiding popular panic. Stalin himself reassured the population that it had nothing to fear from America's nuclear arsenal; not only was the Bomb of little military significance, he argued, but—ostensibly as part of the Communist effort to harness atomic energy for peaceful purposes—the Soviet Union would soon possess it as well. Consequently, "the coming of the atomic age" affected the average Soviet citizen "only slightly," a *New York Times* correspondent reported from Moscow in June 1946. "He knows that there is such a thing as the atomic bomb, but in the newspapers and in lectures he has been told that the bomb is . . . not as effective as the bombs used by most of the powers in World War II." When the Soviet explosion of an atomic bomb was announced in September 1949, crowds in Moscow gathered around loudspeakers "with obvious elation," the *New York Times* reported. Russians interviewed professed no surprise that the Soviet Union possessed an atomic weapon. "Of course we have," said a housewife; "I have never doubted it." A female university student, commenting on the official announcement, said that she was "sure it will be welcomed by all people here and many abroad." [12]

The same picture of calm, popular support for the Soviet nuclear weapons program was drawn by the U.S. embassy in Moscow. Samples gathered by U.S. reporters "correspond to our guess about [the] general attitude of Soviet citizens" to the Soviet nuclear breakthrough, the embassy reported. There was "little excitement, some pride in Soviet achievement, [and] perhaps [a] slightly greater sense [of] security due [to the] diminution [of the] American atomic 'threat.'" Because most Russians accepted Molotov's 1947 assurance that the Soviet Union possessed the atomic secret, the recent announcement was "not [a] major surprise." Moreover, the embassy added, with a trace of envy, the "Soviet press has never whipped up apocalyptic hysteria about [the] importance of [the] bomb as has [the] US press since 1945." Soviet citizens were "constantly assured" by their leaders that U.S. "warmongers will not succeed [in] launch[ing] war" and are "very much absorbed in problems [of] daily life." [13]

Eastern Europe

Before the solidification of Communist governments in Eastern Europe, peace and antimilitary groups in that region seemed to be making some headway. Admittedly, World War II devastated Eastern Europe, including its small pacifist groups, and stimulated a climate of fear and hatred that augured poorly for their revival. From Poland, the sole survivor of the WRI section reported in 1947 that "pacifism is not popular here, chiefly because [the] systematic murder and cruelty" of the Nazis had awakened "self-preserving instincts" rather than "more peaceful feelings." She did claim, however, that people were beginning "to realize that it is necessary to unite the world if we want to avoid other wars." Indeed, in mid-1947, the secretary of the WRI noted that, although its Bulgarian section could not organize openly, contact had been made with 160 individual pacifists in Bulgaria. WRI or International FOR contacts were also resumed with Romanian, Czech, Yugoslav, Polish, and East German pacifists, although local groups could not operate openly in most of these countries. In Czechoslovakia, the relative political freedom before the Communist takeover enabled the WILPF and the FOR to reestablish a small-scale presence in the postwar years. By the beginning of 1948, the Czech WILPF group was holding regular meetings, assisting hungry children, and attempting to serve as a bridge between women in East and West.[14]

This focus on non-nuclear issues typified pacifist activity in this war-devastated region. In Czechoslovakia, for example, the postwar government gave Premysl Pitter, a pacifist leader and social worker, the use of four country mansions for the rehabilitation of children released from the concentration camps. Pitter not only nursed hundreds of Czech-Jewish children back to health but soon did the same for hundreds of German children residing in Czech internment camps. The need for this rehabilitation work was obvious, and Pitter managed to continue these operations even under the Communist regime, at least for a time.[15]

Despite the political and social constraints, however, the nuclear weapons issue did surface on occasion in Eastern Europe. In Bulgaria and Czechoslovakia, scientists held meetings to discuss the literature on international control of atomic energy sent to them by their U.S. counterparts, although without any significant results. Speaking at an international scientific gathering in late 1947, a prominent Czech biologist and member of parliament declared that "the fright of the new war, which we already call atomic war . . . weighs on us, on all our activities, our work and all our life." He added, presciently, "There cannot be any real freedom in a small country which feels that its future lies in the hands of the quarrelling Great Powers." [16] This same bitterness was reflected in the attitude of a Hungarian transport worker, who, asked about the Bomb, replied: "We are immune to fear. . . . We've been run over by our enemies and friends." At the same time, small groups of Hungarians, Poles, Yugoslavs, Czechs, and East Germans showed interest in the world government movement. In Czechoslovakia, *The Anatomy of Peace* had a wide circulation, and reviews appeared in almost all Prague newspapers during 1947. Later that year, Czech students organized a world federalist group. Adding engineers, lawyers, and business-men to its ranks, the group drew federalist speakers from the United States to address its meetings and also invited Henry Usborne to appear in Prague under its sponsorship. The federalist group applied to the Office of the President for legalization and endorsement of its activities in early 1948, just before the Communist coup put it out of operation.[17]

Although peace groups in Eastern Europe were crushed by the advent of Communist totalitarianism,[18] antimilitary attitudes persisted. In 1949, for example, a young man in Czechoslovakia assembled a group of 42 young people who desired to spread pacifism throughout their country and those surrounding it. Although harassed by the police, they continued their activities. Conscientious objection to military service also continued in Communist-ruled Czechoslovakia. In August 1951, a survey of East German young people attending a Communist youth festival in East Berlin found them startlingly hostile to East bloc military measures. Although 70 percent were members of the Free German Youth (the Communist party youth group), most made negative comments about the East German People's Police, largely on the basis that it was a camouflaged army. The following year, the Free German Youth succeeded in recruiting only a third of their expected quota of "volunteers" for East Germany's paramilitary forces, leading to an official purge of the organization.[19]

The Third World

In the years after World War II, relatively little antinuclear activism emerged in the nations of the Third World. In part, this reflected geographical distance, for nuclear weapons were not developed or deployed in these countries and, therefore, it seemed unlikely that they would become nuclear battlefields. In addition, however, Third World peoples often had more immediate concerns—most notably, national independence (particularly in colonized lands) and economic development. Furthermore, Third World nations often had authoritarian governments (either home-grown or colonial) that limited the opportunities for social criticism and protest movements. Finally, Third World societies did not possess the large, educated middle class that served as the primary constituency for movements of pacifists, world government advocates, and atomic scientists in the industrialized nations.

In those small footholds in Third World nations secured by organized pacifism, criticism of nuclear weapons was often mingled with other, more immediate concerns. By the late 1940s, tiny pacifist groups had emerged in some Latin American nations, including Argentina, Mexico, and Uruguay, but they worked primarily on issues of conscientious objection and military expenditures. In Mexico, the small FOR group, with 285 members, published a pacifist periodical (*Fraternidad*) and antimilitary pamphlets, among them a translation of Harold Urey's anti-Bomb article, "I'm a Frightened Man." It also sponsored lectures on a variety of subjects, including atomic energy and the future of civilization.[20] In Argentina, where pacifists also worked against assorted forms of militarism, the FOR journal featured a story by Einstein entitled "World Government or War of Extermination?" Elsewhere, pacifist efforts were also scattered, emphasizing reconciliation among religions (as in Israel) and among races (as in South Africa).[21] Even in India, where pacifists addressed the nuclear menace more directly, they frequently subordinated it to other concerns. Although World Peace Day, the anniversary of the Hiroshima bombing, was observed in pacifist ceremonies at New Delhi in 1949, speakers discussed India's conflict with Pakistan and Mohandas Gandhi's call to cleanse oneself of hatred.[22]

Ironically, despite his immense importance to the world peace movement, Gandhi did little to build a peace movement in India. Although his method of *satyagraha*, or nonviolent resistance, provided an inspiration to pacifists in India and around the world, it was not in practice directed toward achieving peace but toward securing independence and justice, two primary concerns of Third World nations. At the same time, the existence of Gandhi's dynamic movement and the strong support for it by Western pacifists preempted the development of a movement focused on peace. Consequently, at the time of Gandhi's assassination in 1948, no viable pacifist organization existed in India—a source of some concern to Western peace activists.[23] Only in November 1950 did an FOR section, organized by Gandhians at the urging of English and American pacifists, emerge in India. Led by C. S. Paul and K. K. Chandy, the Indian FOR remained small and without much influence. Nor did it concentrate its efforts on nuclear weapons.[24]

Nevertheless, though Gandhi did not organize a powerful Indian peace and disarmament movement, he did help foster a critical attitude toward the Bomb. In 1946, he declared: "I regard the employment of the atom bomb for the wholesale destruction of men, women, and children as the most diabolical use of science." Combining one of his own themes with another prevalent one, he added that, when he first heard of the Hiroshima bombing, he said to himself: "Unless now the world adopts non-violence, it will spell certain suicide for mankind." The following year, Gandhi remarked that "he who invented the atom bomb has committed the gravest sin in the world of science," concluding once again: "The only weapon that can save the world is non-violence." As for the Bomb, that "will not be destroyed by counter-bombs," he wrote. "Hatred can be overcome only by love."[25]

If pacifist and antinuclear ideas were starting to take root during these years in the Third World, so were plans for world government. Although nationalist, anti-imperialist sentiments among Third World peoples limited their participation in world government organizations,[26] demands for One World were occasionally voiced. In Latin America, advocates of world government produced hortatory literature[27] and established active world federalist groups in Argentina and Brazil. The Argentina Pacifist Association (Asociacion Pacifista Argentina), which became an affiliate of the World Movement for World Federal Government in 1947, publicized world federalism in its journal, *Pacifismo*, sponsored lectures in Argentina's major cities, and displayed photos of the Atomic Train exhibition in Great Britain. Calling upon Argentine legislators to form a federalist parliamentary group, the organization began by stressing "the menace of atomic destruction which hangs over all humanity." Although hindered by what one of its leaders called a "rather totalitarian regime," the Argentina Pacifist Association had 1,100 members by 1950.[28]

Elsewhere in the Third World, the world government movement could also point to some small-scale progress. In Mexico, a poll in the late 1940s found that 19 percent of respondents favored the creation of a world government (as against 72 percent who opposed it). Although most residents of the Middle East showed few signs of supporting world government, small branches of the World Movement for World Federal Government developed in both Turkey and Pakistan.[29] Meanwhile, from Africa, a leader of the Nigerian independence struggle reported that he had interested "multitudes of people in Nigeria" in the world government cause; indeed, they elected him as the Nigerian delegate to an international world government convention in 1950.[30] In India, the idea of world government had the backing of leaders of the ruling Congress party, as well as of the Socialist party, its major competitor. After the Indian Association for World Government was formed with the support of the Indian government, it grew quickly into an organization of over a thousand members, headed by the deputy speaker of the Indian parliament.[31] In 1949, the world government movement also established itself in the Philippines, where it was led by the former president of the University of Chicago chapter of United World Federalists. Plagued by all the problems of an impoverished Third World society (including Communist revolution), the Filipino movement nevertheless made progress through talks in crowded meeting halls, town plazas, and remote villages. By the summer of 1950, the Philippine World Federalists claimed 550 members, largely educators and students, and looked forward to what its president called the creation of "One World."[32]

Although scientists—and particularly atomic scientists—were less numerous in the Third World than in industrialized nations, their voices were also raised during these years in efforts to control the Bomb. Having published articles on the "problem of the atomic bomb" in "almost all the great newspapers of our country," reported a prominent Argentine physicist, he had read *One World or None* "with great emotion." Writing to his American counterparts, he proposed an international organization of physicists to help avert a future war and offered to help spread the message of nuclear disarmament in Latin America.[33] In December 1945, the Science Society of China issued a public statement declaring that, "as the secrets of atomic energy cannot be kept for long, and so monopoly at present by any single nation or a limited number of nations will only arouse international distrust," all information about atomic energy "should be placed under the control of the United Nations Security Council." The following month, a message issued by the Natural Science Society of China and the Chinese Association of Scientific Workers, warning that "an atomic armament race would lead to the total extermination of the human race," called for an international scientific conference under the jurisdiction of UNESCO or the U.N. Security Council to deal with the Bomb. Similar statements followed from the Council of the Chinese Physical Society and the joint annual conference of seven Chinese scientific societies. Writing to the Federation of American Scientists in the fall of 1947, leaders of the Chinese Association for the Advancement of Science reported not only that "a number of our members have been very concerned about the use of atomic energy" but that some of the literature of the U.S. movement had been published in their monthly journal, *Science*.[34]

In the Third World, as elsewhere, the atomic bombing of Japan created a tremendous sensation. Press comments in India were harsh, with the *Statesman* writing that "the atom bomb raids have shocked all but the unthinking or the heartless. . . . Is the new discovery to revolutionize the world peacefully or to tear civilization to tatters, annihilate the people?" The *Hindustan Times*, a leading Congress party newspaper, maintained that the Bomb could not be justified on any basis but reprisal. The Argentine public was "profoundly impressed by the news of the atomic bomb," the U.S. embassy reported, adding, "The tremendous shock to public opinion occasioned by the use of the bomb and its fateful future potentialities has been mitigated only by thankfulness that it is . . . a secret shared solely by the United States and Great Britain." In Peru, "the imagination of the entire populace has been captured," the U.S. embassy declared. Although no comments critical of the United States had been voiced, "there has been below the surface some feeling that the bomb should not have been used because of its catastrophic consequences."[35] From Brazil, U.S. officials reported that the Bomb had made "a profound impression" upon the populace; although editorial opinion "unanimously upheld the use" of the Bomb, it also warned "against the future dangers to humanity which it presents." [36]

Indeed, however opinions might vary within the Third World as to the wisdom of the Bomb's use against Japan, there was a general dread of its portents. As the U.S. embassy reported from Venezuela, "the most widespread comment is some variant of the idea, 'Well, the world *must* keep the peace this time; we must get along together; otherwise we shall all be consumed in the holocaust.' " For this reason, public sentiments in the Third World paralleled those in the industrialized nations on how to deal with the Bomb. Asked in August 1947 if they thought that manufacture of atomic bombs should be continued or prohibited by international agreement, 66 percent of Mexican respondents favored prohibition, while only 26 percent supported continued production. [37]

Nevertheless, public opinion in the Third World—unlike opinion elsewhere—apparently grew more indifferent to nuclear weapons in subsequent years as other issues took precedence. The news of the Soviet atomic bomb "aroused no deep or widespread reaction," the U.S. embassy reported from Burma. From Iran came news from U.S. officials that because that country was "not in [the] atomic bomb league, public opinion is entirely disposed to permit other countries to worry about this gigantic question." A few weeks later, the U.S. embassy commented that "Iranians [are] entirely apathetic." From Mexico, U.S. officials contended that the public showed "limited interest" in an "event which apparently seems far removed [from] their immediate field of concern." In Hong Kong, the U.S. embassy claimed that "all reports indicate [that] few people here [are] thinking about [the] atomic bomb. They are much more concerned with [their] own affairs." [38] In the Philippines, Ethiopia, Lebanon, Saudi Arabia, Nicaragua, India, and Syria, the reaction to the Soviet nuclear breakthrough was substantially the same. [39]

Most of the Third World also proved relatively indifferent to the U.S. government's announcement of plans to develop an H-Bomb. In antinuclear India, to be sure, the volume of press comment was "heavy and sustained," worried U.S. officials reported, with a primary reaction of "horror and shock" coupled with the general view that the decision "is one more step in [the] US-USSR struggle for world power." But apathy reigned in most other areas of the Third World. In Argentina, according to U.S. officials on the scene, the average citizen, "while much mentioning [the] bomb, feels [that] he [is] far away and neither he nor [the] country will be affected directly." From Taiwan, the U.S. embassy reported that "people here are almost entirely wrapped up in [their] own problems and feel [the] H-bomb has no meaning for them personally." According to a report from the U.S. embassy in Honduras, the average citizen of that country believes that the H-Bomb "has little relation to his daily life." [40]

Such comments suggest that the salience of Third World concern about the Bomb declined somewhat in the years after 1945, although there is no evidence of a shift in opinion.

A Limited Critique

In the Soviet Union, Eastern Europe, and the Third World, concern about nuclear weapons did develop in the postwar era but was more limited than elsewhere. As in other countries, this concern usually manifested itself through the activities of pacifists, scientists, and world government advocates. Nevertheless, a variety of factors offset the impact of these constituencies upon their broader societies. In the Soviet Union and Eastern Europe, the combination of wartime suffering, totalitarianism, and commitment to the Cold War drastically circumscribed the possibilities for antinuclear activism. Furthermore, the impoverished, nationally dependent condition of the Third World was such that, although criticism of the Bomb was fairly acceptable, other issues often appeared to have greater immediate relevance. The result was that the movement against the Bomb, though emerging for the first time in these regions, was at least temporarily relatively weak.

The International Dimension

Man's rebellion against his Creator has reached such a point
that, unless stayed, it will bring self-destruction upon him.

World Council of Churches, 1950

The worldwide upsurge of protest against the Bomb prompted several international organizations to make the issue a key item on their agenda. Prominent among them were the three pacifist internationals, which, in the shadow of nuclear war, acquired a new strength and reason to persist. Other internationals made up of scientists and world government activists developed in the aftermath of the Hiroshima bombing, largely as a response to it. In addition, worldwide religious bodies—most notably the World Council of Churches and the Roman Catholic church—were drawn into the nuclear debate and occasionally served as important sources of criticism of the nuclear arms race. Together, these organizations provided the basis for an independent, nonaligned, worldwide citizens' movement for nuclear disarmament. Assailing the nuclear buildup in both Cold War camps, this movement promoted the new thinking about international conflict as the key to human survival.

The Pacifists

By the late 1940s, the three leading pacifist organizations—the War Resisters' International, the International Fellowship of Reconciliation, and the Women's International League for Peace and Freedom—had made substantial progress toward reviving their international networks and developing international programs. New WILPF groups arose in Iceland, India, Italy, Japan, and Palestine, and the WILPF's international journal, *Pax International*, which had last appeared in 1940, reemerged in 1949. That year, thirteen countries sent delegations to WILPF's international congress in Copenhagen, including eight delegates from Germany, now restored to membership in the world body after an absence of seventeen years. The WILPF's international co-chairs reported a much better atmosphere in 1949 than at the divisive international conference of 1946. Another impressive revival was made by the WRI, whose 1948 international conference drew delegates from 20 nations, and claimed 56 sections in 30 countries. Together with the International FOR, these resurrected pacifist internationals took on a broad range of peace campaigns, from supporting the rights of conscientious objectors to strengthening the United Nations.[1]

These peace campaigns included persistent attempts to rouse the people of the world to halt the nuclear arms race. In 1948, for example, the War Resisters' International circulated the Declaration of Peace that had been read at the foot of the Memorial Tower of Peace in Hiroshima by the mayor of the city. The International FOR organized its 1950 world conference around the theme "Reconciliation in an 'Atomic World'—The Task of the Christian Pacifist." That year and the following one, the WILPF championed the idea of an armaments "truce," in which nations would pledge to cease the production and use of all weapons. As part of this plan, a world disarmament conference would be convened to consider, as an initial measure, the replacement of national armed forces by an international police force under U.N. direction. In May 1951, Emily Balch wrote to the WILPF International Executive Committee that she assumed that "all of us would agree that there must be no recourse now, or ever, under any circumstances, to atom bombs and similar hellish devices."[2]

In December 1949, pacifist leaders from these organizations and others attended an important international gathering—the World Pacifist Meeting, in Santiniketan and Sevagram, India—to discuss matters of mutual concern. Gandhi's rising international stature in the postwar years had inspired British pacifists to promote the idea of holding a conference on world peace under his auspices. But Gandhi decided to delay the conference until after India's independence, and soon afterward he was assassinated. Nevertheless, Gandhi's disciples in India and pacifists elsewhere were determined to persist with plans for the project. Consequently, the conference finally convened in December 1949 with approximately 100 top pacifist leaders from 34 countries in attendance. Although largely ignored in most nations, it drew a great deal of attention from the Indian mass media and was addressed by India's prime minister, Jawaharlal Nehru, who pledged to work for the removal of the causes of war.[3]

Like many pacifist conclaves during these years, the World Pacifist Meeting addressed a variety of peace and disarmament issues, among them the menace of nuclear weapons. One evening, after a discussion of the relationship between science and peace, Tomiko Kora—a professor of psychology and a member of the upper house of the Japanese Diet—movingly described the destruction of Hiroshima, her conversations with Mayor Shinzo Hamai, and her hope that nuclear war would never recur. A Chinese delegate, chairing the meeting, called for a moment of silence as an expression of contrition for the sufferings of the Japanese people. Throughout the proceedings, the conference ranged over numerous matters, including the heightening Soviet-American confrontation. Although the conference resolution on disarmament did not specifically mention the atomic bomb, it did state that "work against armaments gives concrete opportunity to the people to express their desire to build their security on truth and non-violence." Contending that "unilateral disarmament is possible," the resolution urged pacifists, "as a major project, to develop the moral power which would take away the occasion for armaments and to cooperate with all genuine attempts to bring about disarmament, general or unilateral."[4]

Because of the influence of Gandhi and his disciples on the World Pacifist Meeting, much of the conference discussion focused on nonviolent resistance in India and other lands. Most of the delegates were greatly impressed by the potential of employing nonviolent resistance as an alternative to war, and some organized themselves into an International Liaison Committee for Satyagraha Units. This committee—which included A. J. Muste and Richard Gregg of the United States, Michael Scott of Great Britain, Henri Roser of France, Heinz Kraschutzki of Germany, Riri Nakayama of Japan, and Diderich Lund of Norway—circulated a memo, "Satyagraha Units or The Peace Army," that portrayed nonviolent resistance as particularly appropriate in the nuclear era. "The Atomic Age is proving the futility of military protection," the memo declared. "It is, therefore, necessary to organize defence based on Soul-force or non-violence." Suggesting the establishment of nonviolent resistance units in different countries, the committee also observed that "the need of effective and total resistance to war and conscription in the Atomic Age is so great and urgent that civil disobedience to these evils is . . . imperative."[5] Unlike many a committee memo, this one—and some of its sponsors—would set the agenda for subsequent events.

The Atomic Scientists

The atomic scientists proved somewhat less successful than the pacifists at organizing their constituency on the international level. In late July 1946, at the suggestion of the British Atomic Scientists' Association, an international conference of atomic scientists met at Oxford, where it agreed that the creation of a loosely knit organization for the exchange of information would be beneficial. Accordingly, the conferees decided to establish an international information bureau in New York City, under the auspices of the Federation of

American Scientists, and designated representatives from the United States, France, Norway, India, Holland, Sweden, Switzerland, and Great Britain to develop further plans. But, although the FAS Council voted in September to launch the information bureau, the project came to nought.[6]

Two factors, at least, undermined efforts to establish an international organization of atomic scientists. The existence of the World Federation of Scientific Workers (WFSW), founded in late 1946, preempted the possibilities for establishing yet another organization. But the WFSW had little appeal for most nonaligned scientists, particularly those from Great Britain and the United States. Some considered it under Communist control.[7] Others, like Rabinowitch, had argued from the start that "the kind of organization we want is one . . . which would concentrate all efforts on the atomic bomb problem"—a condition the WFSW did not meet.[8] An additional difficulty lay in the barriers erected by the Soviet and American governments to meetings or other contacts between scientists from their respective nations. These barriers repeatedly frustrated Szilard and other advocates of an international scientists' movement against the Bomb.[9]

Nevertheless, with considerable effort, an informal network of concerned scientists and groups eventually transcended national frontiers. Determined to "promote an interchange of information and ideas" leading to "international atomic energy control" and "to counteract the present trend toward an armament race," the Committee for Foreign Correspondence of the FAS mailed over 10,000 pamphlets on the nuclear issue to scientists in more than 60 nations. Among these publications were the Acheson-Lilienthal proposal, the Baruch proposal, the Gromyko proposal, the U.N. Atomic Energy Commission report, and *One World or None*. The FAS committee also solicited the scientists' views on atomic energy control and asked for suggestions on "cooperative efforts" among scientists of different nations.[10] The two most powerful of the nonaligned scientists' groups, the American FAS and the British ASA, remained particularly close, printing each other's statements in their publications and holding occasional joint meetings.

The state of their accord and their mutual concerns were evident in a conference they held at Oxford, England, in mid-September 1950. Rudolf Peierls, the ASA president, had proposed the idea to the FAS in March, remarking that "the rapid development of the atomic arms race" had put British scientists "in a state of bewilderment and frustration." In response, FAS president William Higinbotham told Peierls that the FAS would send a delegation to a meeting in Britain and that the ASA should also try to attract some scientists from continental Europe, including Niels Bohr. The latter, indeed, had already told Oppenheimer that there must be more "scientific collaboration . . . aimed at breaking down the idiotic barriers" and that "the main theme will have as always to be peace and with it freedom." Although Bohr did not attend the gathering, it did draw Kowarski from France, as well as respectable delegations from the ASA and the FAS. According to Higinbotham's account, those attending the meeting agreed that "political considerations" stood in the way of great power accord on control of atomic energy and that "it was not worth while discussing the technical aspects of the problem or trying to stimulate further discussions" in the U.N. Atomic Energy Commission. If the "Iron Curtain" could be breached, they thought, "then perhaps it would be possible to build an area of understanding among the peoples themselves." But they were gloomy about this possibility, as well as about the new restrictions placed on travel to the United States. What the world needed, they agreed, was "greater openness," and the meeting ended "with plans for closer cooperation in the future." [11]

The discussion of openness by atomic scientists reflected, in part, the continuing efforts of Niels Bohr. After 1948, Bohr had grown increasingly disillusioned with the responses of governments to atomic weapons and to his own proposals for dealing with them. Consequently, he decided to put forth his views to the general public through an "Open Letter to the United Nations." Delivered to the U.N. Secretariat on June 12, 1950, and announced simultaneously at a press conference in Carlsberg, Denmark, Bohr's Open Letter adumbrated the themes he had stressed so persistently in the past. Indeed, for the first time, he published sections of his wartime and postwar memos to the government officials of the United States and Great Britain. Bohr concluded that, in light of the development of nuclear weapons, "a radical adjustment of international relationships is . . . indispensable if civilization shall survive." Not only was "proper appreciation of the duties and responsibilities implied in world citizenship . . . more necessary than ever before," but "full mutual openness, only, can effectively promote confidence and guarantee common security." He predicted that "the efforts of all supporters of international cooperation, individuals as well as nations, will be needed to create in all countries . . . the demand for an open world." [12]

Because of the deteriorating international situation, Bohr's Open Letter had only a modest impact on the public, but it did underscore the existence of an international scientists' movement. In Denmark, as might be expected, the Open Letter drew banner headlines. The youth organizations of six Danish political parties endorsed Bohr's stand, and it also had some appeal elsewhere in Scandinavia. Nevertheless, although Bohr's plea received some coverage in the rest of Western Europe, it was largely ignored elsewhere [13]—except among the scientists. Both the ASA and the FAS distributed the Open Letter to their members, and Peierls took the lead in defending it against press criticism in Great Britain. Privately, Higinbotham complained, at least initially, that the Open Letter seemed unclear and impractical, but it was a major topic of discussion at the international meeting in September 1950. Here the conferees "all concurred in the philosophy expressed in the letter and thought that it should receive continued study by our members." Although they agreed that "a policy of 'openness,' if adopted by the West solely for propaganda purposes, would do more harm than good," they also thought that, "if adopted as a goal toward which this policy is continually directed, this concept holds great promise." One FAS activist reported that it was "wonderfully encouraging . . . to hear this calm and challenging statement from a man of Professor Bohr's stature" and that the Danish physicist stood "at the vanguard of scientists today." [14]

Proponents of World Government

Of all the nonaligned groups concerned with nuclear weapons, the most effective in developing a significant international organization during these years were the world federalists. In September 1946, at the instigation of the British group, Federal Union, an international meeting of federalists convened in Luxembourg. The delegates, representing 37 organizations from fourteen countries, voted to establish the World Movement for World Federal Government (WMWFG) and unanimously resolved: "Conscious of the increasing perils which threaten mankind and of the functional incompetence of the Sovereign State to solve these difficulties, we appeal to men and women everywhere to join with us in this great campaign for the creation of a world federal government, embracing all the peoples of the globe." When, in August 1947, the WMWFG was officially launched at another international conference in Montreux, Switzerland, it was an organization of substance. Some 300 delegates and observers from 24 countries participated, including members of the British, French, and Italian parliaments, a representative of the Turkish government, and many university students. In addition, messages of support arrived from Einstein, British foreign secretary Bevin, and Italian foreign minister Carlo Sforza. In ensuing years, the world government movement continued its remarkable progress, holding larger and more impressive international conferences in Luxembourg (1948) and Stockholm (1949).[15] Meanwhile, the World Citizens movement of Garry Davis and an influential movement for European federation also gained momentum.[16] By the summer of 1950, the WMWFG claimed 52 member groups in 22 countries, another 21 affiliated groups in 9 countries, and a distinguished leadership, including its president, Lord John Boyd Orr (the first director-general of the U.N. Food and Agriculture Organization and Nobel Prize winner in 1949); chair of the Executive Committee, Elisabeth Mann Borgese (editor of the Chicago committee's journal, *Common Cause*); and chair of the Standing Committee, Abbé Grouès-Pierre (member of the French Chamber of Deputies).[17]

Although the Bomb was not the only issue discussed by the WMWFG, it was certainly viewed as among the most important. To be sure, like the pacifists, world federalists had a systemic view of international conflict and, as they resolved at Stockholm, rejected the notion "that control of atomic energy can be usefully discussed as an isolated problem." Indeed, they argued that the failure of U.N. negotiations "was due primarily to the basic difficulty of treating disarmament as a subject separate from the establishment of world law." Nevertheless, the rhetoric and genuine concerns of world federalists were clearly linked to the nuclear menace. "The tremendous powers which science has placed in the hands of governments can . . . destroy human society as we know it," Boyd Orr declared at Montreux, adding, "The best scientific brains are being drawn in to devise improved atomic bombs." At Stockholm, as well, he warned of "a third world war with atomic bombs and bacteriological weapons of death, which will put an end to our civilization." Addressing the same gathering, the Abbé Pierre argued that world government was "a matter of the survival of humanity, or its self-destruction." Professor Brandt Rehberg of Denmark (a member of the WMWFG Executive Committee) contended: "Science cannot be arrested." It had "reduced the world to one indivisible unit, and . . . more than ever before we are linked to the other by a common destiny." Appropriately, at the closing session of the Stockholm conference, delegates stood while Morikatsu Inagaki, chair of the Japanese Union for World Federal Government, read a message of encouragement from the mayor of Hiroshima.[18]

Typical of contemporary world government thinking was an advertisement signed by Einstein, Boyd Orr, Camus, Thirring, Hutchins, Kagawa, Lord Beveridge (British economist), Yehudi Menuhin (Israeli violinist), Hu Shih (Chinese philosopher), John Steinbeck (American novelist), Jacques Maritain (French philosopher), Roberto Rossellini (Italian filmmaker), Leopold Senghor (Senegalese politician), Thomas Mann (German novelist), and other world federalist celebrities. "Confronted by the means of destruction that are now in the hands of men," they stated, "all differences of politics, race and creed are beside the point. These things will virtually cease to exist along with the human race unless mankind agrees to the establishment by peaceful means of a world government." It was "only in this way" that "war can be averted and the peace and plenty for humanity which we all desire, be made possible." They concluded with rhetoric typical of the time: "The choice is indeed between one world or none."[19]

Despite the impressive strength and élan of world federalism on an international level, it suffered from some serious difficulties. For one thing, the movement was divided, to some extent, between "minimalists" and "maximalists." The former, often from the United States, sought a world government with powers limited to preventing war, while the latter, often from Europe and the Third World, favored granting it greater powers. Although the question was hardly settled by 1950, the minimalists were making headway. Another division among federalists had to do with the area to be federated: some favored the establishment of regional bodies, and particularly a united Europe, while others supported nothing less than the federation of the world. Although there were attempts to finesse the issue by pressing for regional federations as "a first step," at a fairly early stage the most zealous advocates of a united Europe formed their own organizations and thereafter had relatively little to do with the WMWFG and its affiliates. A variant of this conflict focused on the issue of including the Soviet Union in the world federation, a tricky issue because the Kremlin seemed so adamantly opposed to participation in any world government. On this point, the "universalists" triumphed once again. Finally, federalists were divided over the appropriate route to world government. Some (most notably, America's United World Federalists) favored pressing national governments to strengthen the United Nations. Others (particularly Usborne's Crusade for World Government), skeptical that national governments would voluntarily relinquish sovereignty, championed the direct popular election of delegates to a "people's world convention." [20]

Ironically, for a movement emphasizing unity, world federalism was actually rather divided. Although most of the controversies remained, for the time being, within the organizational framework of the WMWFG, Garry Davis, the titular head of the World Citizens, insisted on keeping his group totally independent. Calling world citizenship "a new type of faith," Davis contended that it must "remain completely free of all existing organization." Great difficulty existed in getting "the many international organizations working for world unity to work together on a common front," Boyd Orr privately complained in 1950. "Every attempt I have made to get them together ends in an argument—each body thinking that its own method is the only method and any other movement is subversive." He was "not yet clear how we can get over this, and whether indeed it is possible to get over it." [21]

Nor were these the only problems facing the world federalist movement. The WMWFG was "unmistakably green," G. A. Borgese noted, and lacked seasoned leadership. His wife, Elisabeth Mann Borgese, privately conceded in late 1948 that the WMWFG still contained "numerous crack-pots," although she thought the situation was improving. Even more disturbing, the world federalist movement was, in G. A. Borgese's words, an "Amer-European enterprise, strikingly occidental and white." Of the 22 countries with member groups in the WMWFG in 1950, only 5 were nonwhite (Argentina, India, Japan, Pakistan, and the Philippines) and only 2 others lay outside of Europe and North America: Australia and New Zealand. Moreover, neither the World Citizens nor the WMWFG had made any headway within Communist nations.[22]

Despite these weaknesses, however, the world government movement could point to some impressive gains. Between 1946, when it was founded, and 1950, the WMWFG grew into a global organization of 56 member groups with some 156,000 members. Millions of other people, although not members, had been converted to the idea of world government, including an estimated one million from 78 countries who had registered as World Citizens. UNESCO opinion polls in 9 nations during 1948 and 1949 found that world government was favored by a majority or plurality of respondents in 6 of them (France, Great Britain, Italy, Netherlands, Norway, and West Germany) and rejected in only 3 (Australia, Mexico, and the United States).[23] World Protestant bodies called for strengthening the United Nations, and the pope delivered a very positive assessment of world government (and of the WMWFG) at the WMWFG conference in early 1951.[24] This tide of support contributed to the development in 11 countries of parliamentary world federalist groups, some of them quite large. In Sweden, the parliamentary group had some 100 members; in Japan, 110; in France, over 200; in Italy, nearly 300. In addition, by 1950 approximately 400 communities in France, Belgium, Denmark, West Germany, and India had adopted the Charter of Mundialization, and the constitutions of France, Italy, the Netherlands, and West Germany were amended to permit limitations on national sovereignty for the purpose of joining a regional or world federation.[25]

Religious Organizations

The traditional role of religious bodies in addressing moral questions, combined with growing public concern about nuclear weapons, led the new World Council of Churches, representing most of the world's Protestant denominations, to grapple with the issues posed by the Bomb. It found itself seriously divided, however, for there was no greater consensus among church leaders than among most people of the world on how to respond to the atomic crisis. In 1948, at the first meeting of the World Council of Churches, in Amsterdam, pacifists were seriously outnumbered and, therefore, unable to rally much support for a resolution unconditionally condemning "modern warfare, with its mass destruction." Nevertheless, significant debate ensued as to whether modern war, with its obliteration bombing and nuclear weapons, could any longer fulfill the criteria of the "just war." In addition, although the Amsterdam meeting did not endorse the concept of unilateral disarmament, it did call upon Protestant churches to promote reduction of armaments on a multilateral basis.[26]

With the development of the hydrogen bomb, the sense of urgency within the Protestant churches quickened. Meeting in Geneva from February 21 to 23, 1950, the executive committee of the World Council of Churches declared that the hydrogen bomb represented "the latest and most terrible step in the crescendo of warfare" that had transformed it from a limited conflict into "mass murder. . . . Man's rebellion against his Creator has reached such a point that, unless stayed, it will bring self-destruction upon him." Claiming that "all this is a perversion," the statement added that "it is against the moral order by which man is bound; it is a sin against God." The world church body appealed to governments to "avert the danger of world suicide" through "a gigantic new effort for peace." Although the World Council of Churches left the contents of that effort vague, its Central Committee followed up in July with a call for international discussions to bring an end to nuclear and bacteriological weapons, which caused "destruction of life on so terrible a scale as to imperil the very basis on which law and civilization can exist."[27]

Like the world Protestant body, the Catholic church, if inconsistent in its views, was groping toward a general condemnation of nuclear weapons. In official and semiofficial statements, the Vatican criticized the atomic bombing of Japan, while, at the same time, denying their significance or privately assuring American officials that it understood the necessity for a U.S. atomic monopoly.[28] Nevertheless, traditional Catholic notions of national self-defense and the just war were being undermined by a growing belief among church leaders that nuclear war was futile and immoral. Speaking to the Pontifical Academy of Sciences on February 8, 1948, Pope Pius XII called for outlawing the atomic bomb, that "most terrible weapon." And shortly after the Soviet Union tested its first atomic device, *Osservatore Romano*, the semiofficial Vatican newspaper, warned of World War III unless the Bomb, a "terrible and inhuman" weapon, was outlawed. Both the United States and the Soviet Union should renounce use of the Bomb, the journal said, for it placed humanity on the brink of suicide. Similarly, papal encyclicals of July 26 and December 6, 1950, which called on Catholics to pray for peace, referred to the development of "murderous and inhuman weapons" that raised "horror in the souls of all honest persons."[29]

Although the fierce anti-Communism of the Vatican and assorted Catholic church officials sometimes diluted the impact of such statements, Catholic peace sentiment was beginning to acquire an institutional form through the emergence of a new organization, Pax Christi. Founded in the aftermath of World War II, Pax Christi developed out of attempts by the archbishop of

Lourdes, Pierre-Marie Théas, to foster Franco-German reconciliation. For a time, Pax Christi, endorsed by the pope in 1948, remained closely tied to the official Catholic hierarchy and, therefore, reflected the cautious, ambiguous stance of the church on issues of war and peace. Nevertheless, Théas and other activists in the organization were deeply concerned about the atomic bomb. Thus, in later years, as Pax Christi spread across Europe and Asia, it became an important force within the Catholic church for discussions of nuclear disarmament.[30]

During these years, efforts were also made among Buddhist leaders to establish an international peace organization. Attempting to combine the strength of Buddhism in India, China, and Japan into a "peace front," prominent Buddhist educators, officials, and abbots of various temples met in 1951 in Japan and formed the Buddhists' Association for a Round Table Conference on Peace. In a resolution adopted by the gathering, the delegates agreed that "it is high time that we Buddhists firmly observed the creed of ahimsa, the basic principle of life, and condemned warlike violence as an unpardonable crime." On this basis, they launched an "appeal to our fellow believers and the peoples of the world." The Rev. Riri Nakayama, a Buddhist monk who attended the 1950 World Pacifist Meeting in India, reported that Buddhists were readying themselves for nonviolent resistance against Japanese rearmament.[31]

Problems and Opportunities

Despite its impressive growth in the postwar years, the international movement for nuclear disarmament faced some serious problems. Most obvious among them was that, even in its strongholds of the United States, Western Europe, Japan, and Australasia, it attracted fairly small numbers of adherents. Consequently, it was unable as yet to spark mass mobilization, much less majority movements that could transform national and international policy. Furthermore, the movement was divided not only organizationally but strategically. Pacifists, for example, remained suspicious of atomic scientists who continued to do weapons work and of a proposed world government that would employ military power. Atomic scientists sometimes saw little need to go beyond plans for nuclear arms controls and therefore often thought far less systemically than did pacifists and world government advocates. For these same reasons, world government proponents sometimes considered pacifists hopelessly naive and atomic scientists foolishly narrow. In turn, religious groups remained uncertain of how far to carry their critique of the Bomb and sometimes hesitated at forming alliances with more uncompromising opponents of nuclear weapons.[32]

Even so, the dangers of the Bomb proved a strong stimulus to mutual appreciation and cooperative action. Because of the common commitment to stopping the nuclear arms race, organizational membership was often overlapping, and the names of leaders such as Einstein, Boyd Orr, Russell, Bourdet, Hugenholtz, Trocmé, Brittain, Capitini, Lonsdale, Thirring, Kagawa, Cousins, and numerous others often adorned the letterheads of numerous organizations. Relations among peace groups were friendly, and greetings often were sent from the international convention of one group to the world gathering of another.[33] After Bohr issued his Open Letter, the international office of the WILPF dispatched it to all the WILPF's national sections.[34] Atomic scientists enlivened pacifist and world government meetings, while the WMWFG and the World Citizens worked side by side with pacifist organizations. Einstein, the very symbol of the concerned scientist and world federalist, remarked that, "if civilization survives, Gandhi will go down as the greatest man of our time." And in a "Dedication to Gandhi," *Monde Fédéré*, the journal of the WMWFG, printed a story by the Chicago Committee which argued that the Indian pacifist leader had "died as the presumptive first president of One World." [35]

To give some formal structure to the natural alliance of peace and disarmament groups in the postwar era, the pacifist internationals joined with church, women's, and world federalist groups to establish the International Liaison Committee of Organizations for Peace (ILCOP) in 1949. By the early 1950s, its constituent organizations included nine national peace councils (one with 40 member groups) and two other national organizations, as well as nine international organizations: Friends Peace Committee, International FOR, Pax Romana, International Movement of Roman Catholic Intellectuals, Service Civil International, WRI, World Citizenship Movement, World Movement for World Federal Government, and the World Youth Friendship League. It also maintained contact with some 30 other organizations.[36]

Although ILCOP remained a rather loosely structured, poorly funded body, it did hold annual international conferences that addressed issues of importance to peace organizations, including the Bomb. In September 1949, the ILCOP conference at the small village of St. Cergue, in Switzerland, brought together delegates from fourteen countries to grapple with the perils of modern warfare, the problem of world famine, and the effective mobilization of moral and spiritual forces for world peace. After presentations by Brock Chisholm (the director general of the World Health Organization) and Lew Kowarski (of the French atomic energy authority) on the menace of atomic war, the gathering, led by Ritchie Calder, agreed to a short-term program. It would work for a "truce" among the great powers in extending their spheres of influence; "functional cooperation" of East and West through the agencies of the United Nations; and reopening the question of international control of atomic energy, including a period of phased disarmament. The meeting sent an appeal along these lines to the United Nations, but at the same time maintained that "mankind is confronted with a crisis of the spirit," in which "a revolutionary change is required not only in the mind, but also in the heart." [37]

The growing alliance of diverse groups around the nuclear issue was evident in the development of August 6, the anniversary of the Hiroshima bombing, as World Peace Day. Pacifist organizations, world government groups, churches, and atomic scientists all cooperated in organizing commemoration ceremonies, which were held on a global basis. In 1949, the largest event occurred in Hiroshima, where 30,000 people attended a ceremony led by Mayor Hamai. But there were also meetings in Berlin and Hamburg, a peace manifesto in Sweden and a demonstration in Great Britain, church sermons and services in the United States, gatherings in Budapest and New Delhi, and additional events in the Philippines, Nigeria, Australia, New Zealand, the Gold Coast, and nineteen other countries. With some justification, activists took pride in having developed a worldwide movement against the Bomb. [38]

The movement's international progress could also be measured by the widespread public acceptance of its contention that the emergence of the Bomb necessitated extraordinary changes in the way nations dealt with one another. Specifically, it secured broad popular support for an attack on one of the most jealously guarded prerogatives of the nation-state: the right to wage war. By emphasizing the prospect of nuclear holocaust, peace and disarmament groups helped generate a shift in popular thinking toward the approval of limits on national sovereignty, ranging from the international control of atomic energy to outright world government. Admittedly, pacifists, atomic scientists, and world government advocates, sometimes joined by religious leaders, played the leading role in voicing such ideas, but poll after poll showed that such concepts were taking root in the broader society. Confronted by the unprecedented danger of nuclear war, people showed a remarkable willingness to accept an idea with radical implications: One World.

Some Observations and Some Doubts

But would they hold to it? Observing this phenomenon, the British writer Aldous Huxley—a sharp critic of war since the 1930s—privately told an American pacifist leader that "the best large-scale peace policy to support at present is a reasonable system of atomic control, which, if put into force, may become the opening wedge for wider international collaboration and waivers of sovereignty in particular fields." The creation of world government at one stroke was "chimerical," he thought, but people "do want immediate protection from the bomb—and if they want it more than they want flags, brass bands, and the sentiments of exclusive nationalism, there is a chance that the first renunciations of sovereignty may be made in that one limited field." Despite his hopes, however, Huxley retained some doubts. After all, he had lived through the widespread renunciation of war after World War I, only to see nations once again plunge into mass slaughter. "Do people want protection from the atom more than indulgence in nationalistic idolatry?" he asked. "Their words say, yes; but their behavior, too often, says, no." [39]

Albert Einstein and Leo Szilard reenact the drafting of their letter of August 2, 1939, warning President Franklin Roosevelt that Germany might be developing the atomic bomb. Photo courtesy Archive Photos and Council for a Livable World.

The key U.S. official responsible for the atomic bomb in wartime: Secretary of War Henry L. Stimson. Photo courtesy U.S. National Archives.

Below: U.S. President Franklin Roosevelt and British Prime Minister Winston Churchill meet in Quebec, September 12, 1944. Six days later they rejected Niels Bohr's plea for nuclear arms controls. Photo by U.S. Army Signal Corps, courtesy Franklin D. Roosevelt Library.

General Leslie Groves and physicist Robert Oppenheimer reenact their preparations for the first test of the Bomb, conducted at Alamogordo, New Mexico, July 16, 1945. Photo courtesy Harry S. Truman Library.

Soviet and American government leaders at the Potsdam conference, where U.S. President Harry Truman and Soviet Premier Joseph Stalin exchanged cryptic comments on the atomic bomb, July 1945. Left to right (foreground): Stalin, Truman, Soviet Ambassador Andrei Gromyko, U.S. Secretary of State James Byrnes, and Soviet Foreign Minister V. M. Molotov. Photo by U.S. Army, courtesy Harry S. Truman Library.

Above: Emily Greene Balch, international president of the Women's International League for Peace and Freedom. Photo courtesy Swarthmore College Peace Collection.

At right: Shinzo Hamai, mayor of Hiroshima, reads the Declaration of Peace at the August 6, 1948, ceremonies commemorating the atomic bombing of the city and calling for an end to nuclear war. Photo copyright *Chugoku Shimbun*.

Some 15,000 people attend the August 6, 1948, ceremonies in Hiroshima. The "Atomic Bomb Dome," which survived the attack to become its symbol, looms in the background. Photo copyright *Chugoku Shimbun*.

The Rev. Kiyoshi Tanimoto, a *hibakusha* and prominent peace activist from Hiroshima. Photo courtesy Fellowship of Reconciliation.

Morikatsu Inagaki, leader of Japan's world government movement, before the Atomic Bomb Dome, January 1952. Photo courtesy World Federalist Association.

The Emergency Committee of Atomic Scientists, November 17, 1946. Seated, left to right: Harold Urey, Albert Einstein, and Selig Hecht. Standing, left to right: Victor Weisskopf, Leo Szilard, Hans Bethe, Thorfin Hogness, and Philip Morse. Photo courtesy World Federalist Association.

Eugene Rabinowitch, founder and editor of the *Bulletin of the Atomic Scientists*. Photo courtesy University of Chicago Archives.

Above left: Robert Hutchins, chancellor of the University of Chicago, who took up the intellectual challenge posed by the Bomb. Photo courtesy University of Chicago Archives. *Above right:* Norman Cousins, editor of the *Saturday Review of Literature*. Photo courtesy Swarthmore College Peace Collection.

World federalist rally, White Plains, New York, December 1948. Photo by James Nevins, courtesy World Federalist Association.

A student orator advocates world federation as the alternative to world destruction, Bronx, New York, circa 1948. Photo by John Grifalconi, courtesy World Federalist Association.

A. J. Muste, co-secretary of the U.S. branch of the Fellowship of Reconciliation. Photo courtesy War Resisters League and A. J. Muste Memorial Institute.

UWF president Alan Cranston testifies before the Foreign Affairs Committee, U.S. House of Representatives, October 12, 1949. Photo courtesy World Federalist Association.

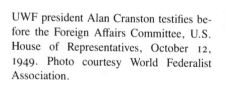

American pacifists gather after picketing the Soviet embassy during their week-long "Fast for Peace," Washington, D.C., April 6, 1950. Photo by U.S. Information Agency, courtesy U.S. National Archives.

Norman Thomas, peace activist and standard-bearer of the Socialist Party of America. Photo courtesy World Federalist Association.

Above left: Vera Brittain, British writer and leader of the Peace Pledge Union, February 1940. Photo by Margery Goodkind, courtesy Vera Brittain Archives, William Ready Division of Archives and Research Collections, McMaster University Library. *Above right:* Nevill Mott, first president of the British Atomic Scientists' Association, circa 1945. Photo by Lisa Meitner-Graf, courtesy Sir Nevill Mott and Niels Bohr Library, American Institute of Physics.

Kathleen Lonsdale, a vice president of the Atomic Scientists' Association and a prominent pacifist, conducts a scientific demonstration, circa 1947. Photo courtesy Fankuchen Collection, Niels Bohr Library, American Institute of Physics.

French pacifist leader André Trocmé. Photo courtesy Swarthmore College Peace Collection.

Henry Usborne, British world federalist leader and Labour M.P., arrives in the United States for a speaking tour, 1947. Photo courtesy World Federalist Association.

P. M. S. Blackett, president of the British Association of Scientific Workers, 1948. Photo by Lotte Meitner-Graf, courtesy Niels Bohr Library, American Institute of Physics.

French pacifist leader Magda Trocmé. Photo courtesy Swarthmore College Peace Collection.

Garry Davis is ousted from the U.N. General Assembly in Paris after beginning his unauthorized speech demanding "one government for one world," November 19, 1948. Photo by Robert Cohen, courtesy World Federalist Association.

At right: Czech pacifist refugee Premysl Pitter. Photo courtesy Fellowship of Reconciliation.

Below left: Niels Bohr in Denmark, during the 1950s. Photo courtesy Niels Bohr Institute and Niels Bohr Library, American Institute of Physics.

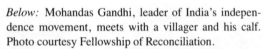

Below: Mohandas Gandhi, leader of India's independence movement, meets with a villager and his calf. Photo courtesy Fellowship of Reconciliation.

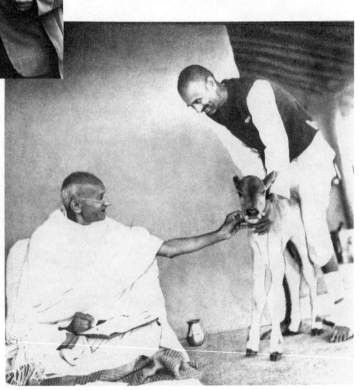

John Boyd Orr, president of the World Movement for World Federal Government, addresses world federalist youth, 1949. Photo courtesy World Federalist Association.

Organizing the Communist-led peace movement: Frédéric Joliot-Curie (at the podium), Pietro Nenni, and Pablo Picasso at the World Peace Congress, Paris, April 1949. Photo courtesy *The Guardian*.

W. E. B. Du Bois, distinguished American scholar and champion of racial equality, at the Buffalo Stadium rally that concluded the World Peace Congress, Paris, April 1949. Photo courtesy *The Guardian*.

Below: The Rev. Hewlett Johnson, the "Red Dean" of Canterbury, England, during a visit to Australia to address the Australian Peace Congress, April 1950. Photo courtesy Ralph Summy.

Below: The opening rally of the Australian Peace Congress, held in Melbourne's Exhibition Hall, April 16, 1950. Photo courtesy Ralph Summy.

Above: President Harry Truman, U.S. Secretary of State Dean Acheson, and U.S. Secretary of Defense George Marshall reassure British Prime Minister Clement Attlee (seated, right) that they had not been planning to use the Bomb in the Korean War, December 4, 1950. Photo by National Park Services–Abbie Rowe, courtesy Harry S. Truman Library.

At right: Jawaharlal Nehru, India's Prime Minister, and Carlos Romulo, U.N. delegate from the Philippines and U.N. General Assembly president, during a visit to the United States, October 11, 1949. They are flanked by Indira Gandhi (Nehru's daughter) and Lakshmi Pandit (Nehru's sister and India's ambassador to the United States). Photo by U.S. Department of State, courtesy Harry S. Truman Library.

Students at St. Joan of Arc Parochial School, Queens, New York, practice taking cover from the Bomb while nuns pray, November 28, 1951. Photo by Bill Stahl, courtesy Fellowship of Reconciliation.

The U.S. government keeps its lead in the nuclear arms race by exploding "Mike," the world's first thermonuclear device, at Eniwetok, November 1, 1952. Photo by U.S. Air Force, courtesy Fellowship of Reconciliation.

The Communist-Led Movement, 1945-51

"Against the Warmongers"

The Development of the Communist-Led Peace Movement

> Our desire for peace will not be expressed by a passive pacifism.
>
> Frédéric Joliot-Curie, 1949

During these years, there also developed another kind of nuclear disarmament movement—one aligned with Soviet foreign policy. As the Cold War heightened to the point of military confrontation, Communist leaders in the Soviet Union and elsewhere organized a mass movement to condemn Western foreign and military policy. A key component of this campaign was an effort to stigmatize nuclear weapons and thereby undermine the military advantage of the United States in this area. Furthermore, by directing their own peace movement, Communist leaders hoped to project the image of the Soviet Union as a peace-loving nation, attract new recruits to their party, and overshadow nonaligned nuclear disarmament campaigns, which raised embarrassing questions about the Soviet Union's role in the Cold War and the arms race. These efforts to develop a pro-Soviet peace movement achieved some success, for millions of people, Communist and non-Communist, within Communist nations and without, genuinely believed that the Soviet Union was a peace-loving nation and feared that a belligerent United States was about to attack it with nuclear weapons. But the one-sidedness of this Communist-directed peace campaign limited its appeal outside the circle of Soviet sympathizers. Indeed, the campaign was soon at odds not only with Western military and defense policy but with the nonaligned nuclear disarmament movement as well.

Communist Parties and the Atomic Bombing of Japan

Initially, world Communist leaders fully supported the dropping of the Bomb. Told at Potsdam about a new weapon that he realized was an atomic bomb,

Stalin expressed his hope that the United States would make "good use of it" against the Japanese. Even after the Bomb was revealed to the world on August 6, 1945, Communist leaders showed no qualms about the atomic bombing of Hiroshima. According to a London *Daily Worker* correspondent, Marshal Josip Broz Tito of Yugoslavia told him that "the atomic bomb is a splendid weapon when used against aggressors." [1] Indeed, the day after the obliteration of Hiroshima, the British Communist newspaper editorialized: "The employment of the new weapon on a substantial scale should expedite the surrender of Japan" and save "valuable lives in the Allied nations." In subsequent days, it displayed no sympathy for the victims of the atomic bombing. On August 9, amid further hosannas to the Bomb, the *Daily Worker* headlined a news story: "'LET'S HAVE A RECONCILIATION,' JAPS SQUEAL." When the second bomb was dropped on Nagasaki, the Communist newspaper again applauded the action: "The use of the atomic bomb has mercifully shortened the war, with a consequent saving of human life." Subsequently, the London *Daily Worker* called for an end to Allied "delay" in employing additional atomic bombs against the Japanese. [2]

The Communist press in other nations voiced similar opinions. When the Vatican indicated dismay at the atomic bombing of Hiroshima, *L'Humanité*, the French Communist newspaper, expressed its "astonishment" at this churlish attitude. It added that "the work of Professor Joliot-Curie was of enormous assistance in the realization of this wonderful conquest of science." In Rome, the Communist *L'Unita* argued in an editorial, "On the Service of Civilization," that condemnation of the atomic bomb represented "a curious psychological perversion and a doctrinaire obedience to a form of abstract humanitarianism" that "we do not share." [3] Canada's Communist newspaper, the *Canadian Tribune*, greeted the atomic bombings—as well as Soviet participation in the Far East war—with enthusiasm, running the headline "U.S.S.R., ATOM BOMB K.O. JAPAN WARLORDS." The "universal rejoicing in Canada," it noted, was clouded only by the "mass lay-offs" caused by "cut backs in war production." In the United States, the New York *Daily Worker*, in its first editorial comment on nuclear weapons, praised "these latest scientific miracles" and declared that "the United States is justly proud of its own work in developing the fissure of the uranium atom." Writing in the same issue, a columnist concluded: "Let us greet our atomic device not with a shudder, but with the elation and admiration which the genius of man deserves." [4]

Some of the world's leading Communist intellectuals shared this enthusiasm for nuclear weapons. Commenting publicly on the use of the Bomb against Japan, J. B. S. Haldane, a distinguished scientist and a member of the British Communist party's executive committee, concluded: "I welcome the atomic bomb." In an article on the weapon published within days of its dramatic debut, J. D. Bernal—one of Great Britain's most eminent scientists and Communists—expressed not a word of criticism regarding its use but instead proclaimed his satisfaction that "the democratic countries have finished their first task of liberating all countries from domination by reactionary forces." Pointing to the vast energy sources provided by nuclear fission, he painted a bright picture of the future. "With unlimited possibilities for expansion and open frontiers," he contended, "mutual suspicion . . . will give way in a new universal constructive effort full of excitement, uncertainty, hope and promise."[5]

Even so, as Communist fears grew of what a U.S. atomic monopoly might augur for the Soviet Union, Communist pronouncements became more cautious. On August 13, the London *Daily Worker* reported caustically that the disclosure of the Bomb has "caused something like an explosion in the heads of irresponsible politicians and commentators, who are now joyously announcing that the balance of power . . . has shifted in favor of Britain and the United States at the expense of the Soviet Union." That same day, U.S. Communist party chair William Z. Foster warned that "the control of such a terrific power cannot be left in the hands of reactionaries, who would surely do the peoples of the world immeasurable harm with it. . . . The masses must see to it without fail that the governments holding such an incredibly powerful instrument . . . are safely controlled by democratic forces who will not abuse its use."[6]

As the Cold War heightened, Communist rhetoric underwent a total reversal on the issue of nuclear weapons and portrayed the atomic bombing of Japan as symptomatic of America's ostensibly fascist leadership. In his New York *Daily Worker* column of November 21, 1946, Mike Gold reported that "the Hiroshima bombing was a sample of what the American Nazi imperialist is ready to do." He added: "Both the atom bomb and the Hitler program can be proven to be part of the same world forces." The London *Daily Worker*, which had previously praised use of the Bomb for its merciful "saving of human life," experienced a dramatic conversion (or perhaps historical amnesia) on this point. On the seventh anniversary of the Hiroshima bombing, the newspaper insisted that "the excuse that, in the long run this bestial action saved lives, is worthless." This "rotten excuse," stated the *Daily Worker*, "was always a favorite with Hitler and the Nazi sadists."[7]

The World Federation of Scientific Workers

The Communist mobilization against the Bomb gathered momentum in part because of the pivotal role Communists had acquired in the scientific community, particularly in Great Britain and France. Near the end of World War I, the National Union of Scientific Workers had been launched in Great Britain as a trade union. In 1927, it was partially reorganized and renamed the Association of Scientific Workers (AScW). Floundering in the early 1930s, the AScW was revived by Bernal and other left-wing scientists at Cambridge, who transformed it into a force championing applied science and Popular Front politics. Bernal became friendly with Joliot-Curie in the mid-1930s and during World War II both men plunged enthusiastically into their countries' military efforts. During the German occupation of France, Joliot-Curie joined the Communist party and became a leader of the resistance. Bernal, in turn, worked at the highest levels of the British war effort and was possibly its most important scientific participant. As a result, both men emerged from the war not only as staunch Communists but as exceptionally influential scientists.[8]

Combined with the rising importance of science in wartime, these circumstances led directly to the formation of the World Federation of Scientific Workers. In June 1945, Joliot-Curie and Bernal met again, this time in Moscow, during an anniversary celebration of the Russian Academy of Sciences. Impressed by the emergence of scientists' associations in numerous nations, they discussed with Soviet scientists the idea of forming an international scientists' organization. Further discussions of this idea took place during February 1946 at an international conference, "Science and the Welfare of Mankind," organized by the AScW in London. When Joliot-Curie received a favorable reaction to the idea from scientists of nine countries, the AScW agreed to draft a constitution for the new body and to sponsor an inaugural conference. In July 1946, the conference convened in London with delegates or observers from fourteen countries. According to one observer, Bernal was "the outstanding personality throughout the proceedings." A few days after the delegates voted formally to launch the WFSW, the new executive council selected Joliot-Curie as president and Soviet scientist N. N. Semenov and Bernal as vice-presidents of the new organization.[9]

Although Communist-led, the WFSW initially avoided taking doctrinaire positions. This probably reflected, at least in part, the leadership's recognition of the need for caution when dealing with a predominantly non-Communist membership. In Great Britain, the country that in the early years possessed two-thirds of the members of the world body, the AScW claimed some 16,000, a figure far larger than the number of Communist scientists and technicians in that nation. Another moderating influence was the desire of WFSW leaders to secure the affiliation of influential nonaligned scientists' groups such as the American FAS, which sent observers to the founding meeting. Indeed, one observer reported that "everything consistent with a middle of the road policy" was being "done to make federation attractive to the FAS." Another American scientist at the founding conference noted the "deference" paid to the American group; when discussion began on the trade union connection, which the Americans did not want, "it was immediately dropped."[10] Nevertheless, despite these blandishments, the FAS—like the British ASA—remained stubbornly independent of the WFSW. As one FAS leader wrote, "Anything that could be interpreted in this country as a tie-up with a pro-Soviet outfit would be ruinous."[11]

Despite its early moderation, the WFSW eventually became an auxiliary, albeit a cautious one, of the Communist-led campaign against the Bomb. At the WFSW's founding conference in July 1946, Bernal, who wrote its charter, established the atomic energy issue as the organization's top priority. This would have caused little difficulty had the organization not adopted Soviet positions on Cold War issues and insisted upon what the Dutch, New Zealand, and South African branches criticized as "political affiliations." The WFSW sought out alliances with the Communist-dominated World Federation of Trade Unions and gave its enthusiastic support to the conferences that launched the Communist-led peace movement. At the same time, its most prominent leaders—first Joliot-Curie and, later, Bernal—assumed the top posts in two decades of Communist-led agitation against the Bomb. These activities seriously embarrassed many non-Communist scientists, who, within a few years, were deserting the WFSW by the thousands. Eventually, their places were filled by the scientists' associations of Communist nations, an influx that funded the organization and kept it alive but gave it an ever more pro-Soviet coloration.[12]

The Wroclaw Congress (1948)

The mobilization of scientists and other intellectuals behind the Communist-directed peace campaign took a leap forward in August 1948, with the opening, in Wroclaw, Poland, of the World Congress of Intellectuals for Peace. Hopeful that the conference might bridge Cold War divisions and provide for a serious discussion of intellectual and cultural issues, a number of prominent non-Communists attended, including Julian Huxley, the director general of UNESCO, who chaired the meeting. But, as Huxley later wrote, "there was no discussion in the ordinary sense of the word." After a warm welcoming speech by the Polish foreign minister, the Soviet novelist Alexander Fadeyev launched into a vitriolic attack on the United States that, in the words of Kingsley Martin, editor of the *New Statesman* and a delegate at the gathering, "sounded like a declaration of war." Assailing the works of Eugene O'Neill, André Malraux, Jean-Paul Sartre, and other Western writers, Fadeyev declaimed that "if hyenas could type and jackals could write, they would write such things." "All the evils of the world were put down to American imperialism and the British were not much better," Martin recalled. "The world was divided into the heroes of the Soviet Union (with only their less heroic followers) and the small group of reptilian Fascists who were plotting war." This was the theme of nearly all speakers thereafter, who delivered lengthy, insulting denunciations of all things Western and hymns of praise to the Soviet Union, usually to wild applause.[13] In its final resolution, softened to conciliate disconcerted Western delegates, the congress proclaimed that war was being prepared by "a new fascism," a "small group of people in America and in Europe prompted by the desire for profits and guided by the idea of race superiority and negation of progress inherited from Nazism."[14]

Although many of the delegates from non-Communist countries were either Communists or otherwise sympathetic to the Soviet Union and, therefore, not averse to this line of thought, some delegates from Western countries found the one-sided, vituperative nature of the proceedings unbearable. Huxley warned the gathering that "a good deal of what has here been said has been destructive. In place of attempts at mutual comprehension, there have often been attacks on all other systems than one's own." Such behavior "cannot lead to peace, and may help to promote war." Angered by the tone and content of the gathering, Professor A. J. P. Taylor of Great Britain responded with his own address, which protested the flood of propaganda and concluded that proponents of "culture" should criticize all the great powers, especially the governments of their own countries. Taylor's speech "met with a very strong reaction," a Polish delegate recalled, and was followed by icy silence. Indeed, it probably reached the conference floor only because Taylor, when asked to submit it for approval beforehand, said that he would speak extemporaneously. Behind the scenes, French philosopher Julien Benda asked one of the Soviet delegates if it was fair to refer to Sartre and O'Neill as jackals. "And why do we have to clap every time Stalin's name is mentioned?" he asked. "I'm all in favor of co-operation, but what I'm being asked to do is swear allegiance."[15]

The organizers of the Wroclaw conference had a particularly ugly confrontation with Albert Einstein. Invited to address the gathering, Einstein sent a friend, Otto Nathan, with his prepared message. At the meeting, the organizers pressed Nathan to change or omit parts of Einstein's speech, particularly those calling for the establishment of a world government. When Nathan refused to make the suggested changes, the conference officials read an earlier Einstein letter as the American physicist's purported "Message to the Congress." Not surprisingly, both Nathan and Einstein felt badly used. Remarking tartly that "such practices cannot contribute to the creation of an atmosphere of mutual trust," Einstein released the text of his actual speech to the *New York Times*.[16]

Despite these rebuffs, world Communist leaders were pleased with the

Wroclaw Congress, for it had inaugurated their own peace campaign. The September 15, 1948 issue of *For a Lasting Peace, for a People's Democracy*, the elegantly named Cominform journal, declared that the decisions at Wroclaw "confront the Communist parties and especially the Communist intellectuals with the important and honorable task of being in the forefront—in bringing together the intellectuals of their countries for the defense of peace and culture." In fact, the Wroclaw conference had provided for the creation of the International Liaison Committee of Intellectuals for Peace, with headquarters in Paris and embryonic national committees in each of the 46 countries represented at the meeting. To be sure, some persons at Wroclaw had refused to sign the final declaration, but these, claimed Soviet delegate Ilya Ehrenburg, were "idiots and imbeciles." In a letter that September to the *New Statesman*, Bernal extolled the gathering and its conclusions, maintaining that the United States was being readied for "a war for complete world domination," in which "nothing of the old panoply of Fascism is lacking." Communist commitment to the development of an appropriately aligned peace movement was reinforced on October 29, when *Pravda* published an interview with Stalin. On this occasion, the oracle of the world Communist movement denounced the leaders of the United States and Great Britain for their "policy of unleashing a new war" and called upon the "forces in favor of peace" to unseat them. In a speech delivered a week later, Soviet foreign minister V. M. Molotov reiterated this theme.[17]

April in Paris: The World Peace Congress (1949)

Plans now moved forward to establish a massive, worldwide, Communist-led peace movement. Meeting in Budapest in December 1948, the Bureau of the Women's International Democratic Federation (WIDF)—a Communist-controlled body—expressed its support for the convocation of a large peace conference that would launch an international organization. Joliot-Curie accepted an invitation to head up the gathering. Although the French physicist had been unable to attend the Wroclaw Congress, his wife had attended in his place. Moreover, he remained gravely concerned about what he feared would be the onset of a war against the Soviet Union. By February 1949, the International Liaison Committee of Intellectuals, formed at the Wroclaw Congress, had joined the WIDF in issuing a formal call for a World Peace Congress that April in Paris. Not only did Joliot-Curie, Bernal, and French Communist officials work zealously to organize it, but much of the powerful world Communist apparatus was called into play to ensure its success. Writing of the forthcoming event, the Cominform bulletin confidently predicted that "the Peace Congress will become an historic landmark."[18]

It was certainly a memorable event. Although the French government refused visas to 384 delegates, on April 20, 1949, nearly 2,000 people crowded into the Salle Pleyel in Paris, festively adorned with Picasso doves, while their excluded counterparts gathered for a simultaneous meeting in the friendly environs of Prague. The two gatherings, Joliot-Curie claimed, represented 600 million people in 72 countries—a figure apparently derived by counting the entire population of Communist nations and adding on the memberships of Communist parties and Communist-controlled groups elsewhere. Welcoming the unprecedented gathering—now called the World Congress of the Partisans of Peace—Joliot-Curie spoke of the need to launch a great "peace offensive" against the forces of war. "We are not here to ask for peace," he said, "but to impose it. This congress is the reply of the peoples to the signers of the Atlantic pact. To the new war they are preparing, we will reply with a revolt of the peoples." Although nuclear weapons did not receive much attention in Joliot-Curie's welcoming message, he did declare that "one of the most spectacular misappropriations of science is the atomic bomb, produced . . . as a weapon of mass destruction." [19]

Other addresses that day were even more strident. In a wildly applauded speech, Paul Robeson, a member of the U.S. delegation, denounced "the policy of the United States government, which is similar to that of Hitler and Goebbels." Black people, he said, would never fight a war against the Soviet Union. Instead, the world's peoples would continue their battle for "peace and liberty . . . along with the Soviet Union, the democracies of Eastern Europe," and China. Much the same message came from Prague, where Jan Drda, the president of the Czech Writers Union and the chair of the meeting, contended that "while atomic pirates of Wall Street, their auxiliaries, and lackeys in other countries secretly agree upon new plans for aggression . . . and new massacres, the peoples of the whole world now clearly and resolutely raise their voice." [20]

In the five days that followed, the peace congress continued along similar lines. Fadeyev charged that the "drunkenness and corruption" among American youth showed that the United States was "preparing for a future war a framework of criminals" and "petty crime fuehrers." Partway through the proceedings, the announcement of the Chinese Communist capture of Nanking sent the delegates into five minutes of delirium. "The forces of the camp of peace and democracy are growing in numbers and strength," proclaimed Professor Kuo Mo-jo, head of the Chinese Communist delegation. "The war for national liberation is springing up vigorously in one place after another in the East. . . . Led by the Soviet Union, the camp of peace and democracy . . . is capable of sending the warmongers to the grave." [21] On the final day of the Paris conference, its organizers drew a crowd they estimated at 500,000—but which, more likely, numbered under 50,000—for a rally at the Buffalo Stadium. Addressing the assemblage, W. E. B. Du Bois, a distinguished American scholar and head of the U.S. delegation, charged that the United States was "leading the world to hell . . . with the same old human slavery . . . and to a Third World War." Meanwhile, in Prague, the delegates finished up with what a *New York Times* dispatch called "an hour's hearty cheering, including 'Long live Stalin, Mao Tse-tung, people's democracies, progressive Germany, and progressive America.' " [22]

Observing the Paris gathering with some awe, French writer Jean Genêt considered it "the most concentrated inflammatory anti-American propaganda effort in this part of Europe since the beginning of the cold war." [23]

Ebullient and determined, the participants in the Paris Peace Congress did not take kindly to deviant views. When a British speaker, Harvey Moore, suggested that, as supporters of peace, the delegates call for a halt to the war in China, he received a chilly reception. A Polish delegate recalled that "the silence of the listeners was a proof that they rejected pacifism as an anachronistic idea, out of keeping with the requirements of the times." [24] When O. John Rogge of the United States, in an otherwise acceptable speech, said that the Soviet Union shared responsibility with the United States for the development of world tensions, he drew boos and hisses from the crowd. Garry Davis, at the time the toast of Paris for his World Citizens efforts, asked the conference organizers for fifteen minutes to address the six-day assemblage but was refused admission. The conference was not "a marketplace where anyone could offer his wares," explained Abbé Jean Boulier, one of its organizers. Davis did "not make any distinction between the two blocs into which the world is divided, whereas the Congress sees the world as a non-aggressive Soviet group and a war-minded imperialistic group, headed by the United States government." [25]

Naturally, the Paris conference did not create much enthusiasm among those not already favorably inclined to the Soviet Union. Although Du Bois lauded it as "the greatest meeting of human beings united in a great cause which I have ever seen," a former leader of the Spanish Communist party recalled acidly that the new movement did not go "beyond the normal political and social sphere influenced by the Communists." The new "Peace Committees" spawned by the Paris conference "were made up—with a few exceptions—of Communists and their sympathizers." [26]

Despite the limitations of the first World Congress of the Partisans of Peace, Communist leaders professed enormous satisfaction at the outcome. *Izvestia* crowed that this "demonstration of solidarity with the bulwark of international peace, the Soviet Union, is evidence that the attempts of the organizers of military-political alliances to set the peoples of America and Western Europe against the Soviet Union are failing utterly." Writing in *Pravda*, Ehrenburg—

a leading Soviet author and journalist—claimed that the Paris conference had provided a "turning point," for the imperialist "howling" about the atomic bomb had at last "been drowned by human voices." In later years, Joliot-Curie also lauded the Paris conference, claiming that its call for the "banning of atomic weapons" was "probably the first great public expression of the will to put an end to the atomic danger." Meanwhile, in May 1949, the Soviet *New Times* reported happily on "the rise of an unprecedented movement of the peoples," in which "hundreds of millions in all parts of the world have united their efforts to foil the plans of the warmongers." [27] Although such contentions were substantial exaggerations, Communist leaders had launched the world's largest "peace" organization, the World Committee of the Partisans of Peace, and had placed it securely under their control.

Strengthening the Movement

In the aftermath of the Paris meeting, a Permanent Committee of the Partisans of Peace met to coordinate the activities of national groups and to hammer out a program. Among its first orders of business was the expulsion of the Yugoslav section, which, it charged, was "wholly subordinate" to the Yugoslav government, a regime that "has openly embarked on more and more open and hostile action against the U.S.S.R. and the people's democracies." Fadeyev, head of the Soviet delegation, explained: "Tito and all his clique are hirelings in the hands of the warmongers." In addition, the Peace Partisans called for outlawing the atomic bomb and staged another anti-American congress, at Rome. At this new gathering, in October 1949, Ehrenburg again charged Americans (those "Chicago pork dealers") with fomenting war against the Soviet Union, Fadeyev accused the United States of "invading Italy with rivers of Coca Cola," and the Rev. Hewlett Johnson, the pro-Communist dean of Canterbury, assured listeners that religious persecution did not exist in the Soviet Union. [28] That month, commenting on the Peace Partisans' campaign, *Pravda* reported happily that "this movement for peace has nothing in common with bourgeois pacifism." Meeting in Budapest in late November, the Cominform was equally enthusiastic. It adopted a resolution presented by Mikhail Suslov, the Soviet official responsible for international Communist affairs, that lavished praise on this "mighty movement of the partisans of peace." [29]

Indeed, the Suslov resolution directed Communist parties and other Communist-controlled groups to make Communist-led peace campaigns their top priority. "The struggle . . . for the organization and consolidation of the forces of peace against the forces of war should now become the pivot of the entire activity of the Communist parties and democratic organizations," the Cominform declared. Specifically, Communist parties should "work even more persistently to consolidate organizationally and extend the movements of the partisans of peace" and devote "particular attention . . . to drawing into this movement trade unions, women's, youth, co-operative, sports, cultural, educational, religious and other organizations, and also scientists, writers, journalists, cultural workers," and political leaders "who act in defense of peace." In fact, "the paramount task of the Communist and Workers' Parties is to draw the broadest sections of the working class into the ranks of the fighters for peace." [30]

How does one account for the decision of world Communist leaders—and certainly those in Moscow—to place the development of the Communist-led peace movement at the top of their agenda? Although little is known definitively about Communist motives, it seems clear that, by the late 1940s, Communist leaders feared war with the United States, and not without some justification. The brutal extension of Communist control in Eastern Europe had been followed, in 1948–49, by a hardening of U.S. military policy toward the Soviet Union, as exemplified by the military confrontation over Berlin, the signing of the NATO pact, and plans for an arms buildup in Western Europe. Furthermore, although the Soviet Union exploded its first atomic device in August 1949, the United States enjoyed substantial advantages in numbers of nuclear weapons and delivery systems and might, Communist leaders feared, launch a preemptive strike. "The North Atlantic bloc envisages outright aggression against . . . Eastern Europe and . . . the Soviet Union," Suslov warned the Cominform. The United States and Great Britain were "carrying on their preparations for war at top speed." Early the following year, French Communist leader Maurice Thorez told a congress of the French Communist party that "peace hangs by a thread." [31]

In this increasingly dangerous context, Communist leaders believed, a peace campaign under their direction could play a very useful role. By encouraging popular resistance to Western military programs, the Soviet Union and its Communist supporters might reduce the risks of war by the United States ("the warmongers") and, especially, undermine the ability of the U.S. government to employ its deadliest weapon, the atomic bomb. In addition, a Communist-led peace campaign would have a strong appeal to the war-weary and antinuclear masses of the world. Within Communist nations, therefore, it would bolster the popularity of Communist governments ("the camp of peace") and provide such governments with the necessary justifications for military programs ("the defense of peace against the warmongers"). Elsewhere, a Communist-led peace campaign would provide a useful mechanism for recruitment or, at the least, the encouragement of pro-Soviet opinion. [32]

Finally, a Communist-led peace campaign would seize the initiative from the nonaligned peace and nuclear disarmament movement ("bourgeois pacifism"), thus weakening its ability to challenge Soviet military policy, including Soviet development of nuclear weapons. Certainly, Communist leaders did not look kindly upon existing peace organizations. In 1947, a resolution of the Women's International Democratic Federation condemned the WILPF for alleged fascist propaganda. The following year, Bernal charged that "a peace movement that is not an exposure and a fight against the heirs of fascism and their ideas is an illusion; worse, it is a diversion of effort that helps the war makers." Communist disdain for nonaligned elements was also evident in an article ("The Great Battle of the Peoples for Peace") that Pierre Cot, a French politician prominent in the Communist-led movement, wrote in 1951 for *Pravda*. "In certain circles" in Western countries, "resistance to war preparations takes a mainly passive form—neutralism, the 'without us' movement in Germany, and religious pacifism," he noted derisively. "The same can be said of India and the Arab countries. Such partial forms of resistance to war are too weak-kneed to merit recommendation. . . . If they become widespread, they could atrophy the entire peace struggle." The bottom line, of course, was that, unlike his own movement, such movements remained fiercely independent and nonaligned. Cot charged, with rhetoric typical of Soviet (and Western) military proponents: "No one has the right to neutrality between peace and war, between enslavement and liberty." [33]

The Stockholm Peace Appeal (1950)

The most ambitious venture in the Communist-led peace campaign was undoubtedly the Stockholm Peace Appeal. On March 15, 1950, the Permanent Committee of the Partisans of Peace convened in Stockholm under the leadership of Joliot-Curie. Beginning his welcoming address on an upbeat note, the French scientist declared that the development of the Soviet atomic bomb, "the victory of People's China," and the creation of East Germany had "considerably strengthened the Peace Front." Even so, in the aftermath of President Truman's announced decision to develop an H-Bomb, Communist leaders were apparently ready to focus on the nuclear issue. In his report, Joliot-Curie delivered what he called "a grave warning" that "the human race" faced "destruction by the hydrogen bomb" and called for the abolition of all nuclear weapons. After numerous anti-American speeches, the meeting adopted an ingenious resolution, written by Ilya Ehrenburg. Subsequently known as the Stockholm Peace Appeal, it demanded "the unconditional prohibition of the atomic weapon," "strict international control" to enforce this measure, the branding of the government that first used the weapon as "a war criminal," and signatures on this appeal by "all people of good-will." [34] Using the Stockholm Peace Appeal as a petition, the Partisans of Peace subsequently embarked upon a vast, well-publicized, international effort to gather signatures.

The Stockholm peace petition campaign was in many ways well suited to Communist goals. Its moderate tone reflected not only the mandate of the Suslov resolution to carry the efforts of the Peace Partisans beyond the friendly circles of Communists and their sympathizers but the cautious, defensive nature of Soviet "peace" policy. As Stalin commented, approvingly, "the current peace movement has the aim of drawing the popular masses into the struggle to preserve peace and avert a new world war. It does not, therefore, seek to overthrow capitalism and establish socialism." At the same time, as political scientist Marshall Shulman has noted, "by attaching a moral stigma exclusively to the atomic weapon . . . the appeal would neutralize the very form of military power in which the West still had an advantage." The Stockholm Peace Appeal also neatly sidestepped the complexities of how to ban the Bomb. Although it talked of "strict international control," the Soviet Union also paid rhetorical obeisance to this idea—without, however, ever getting around to supporting a plan that implemented it. *Pravda* claimed that the Stockholm meeting had "charted a program of further action . . . against the imperialist warmongers." [35]

The Stockholm peace petition drive reflected both the strengths and weaknesses of the Communist-led peace movement. Drawing upon the substantial efforts of the Peace Partisans—and behind them the staunch support of governments within Communist nations and of Communist parties in other nations—the Stockholm petition campaign claimed 500 million signatures from 79 countries by the end of 1950. Although this was a remarkable record, it was not as impressive as these figures imply. More than 400 million of the alleged signers, for example, came from Communist nations, including what were purportedly the entire adult populations of the Soviet Union and the "People's Democracies." Indeed, at one point the announced number of signers from Bulgaria exceeded that country's population, and in other countries, such as Hungary, children under five years of age would have had to be included to justify the figures. To be sure, there were millions of signers in Western nations, including an estimated 14 million from France and nearly 17 million from Italy. But these were nations with very large, popular Communist parties, and in countries with smaller ones the figures fell off very sharply. Furthermore, of course, the petition was a mildly worded one, which many people motivated by "goodwill" could—and did—sign. Only when the nature of the Stockholm petition campaign became apparent did the rate of signing in Western nations decline. Indeed, at that time, many early signers began to request the withdrawal of their names from the petition.[36]

The World Peace Council

Plans by the Peace Partisans for another world conference were under way when, in late June 1950, the Korean War added a new dimension to the situation. The Secretariat of the Permanent Committee quickly expressed its "ardent sympathy and solidarity with the Korean people, which is winning its national unification in a struggle against foreign intervention," and it demanded the withdrawal of U.S. troops. Although it claimed that the Stockholm appeal remained "the surest way to ease international tensions and to establish peace," the Korean crisis was rapidly moving to the fore of Communist concerns. Calling for a "new phase" in the peace campaign, the Cominform journal proclaimed that the time was ripe for an "extension of the program of the movement."[37]

Having encountered governmental obstacles in organizing a meeting in Italy and, later, Great Britain, the Peace Partisans finally convened what they called the Second World Peace Congress in November 1950 in Warsaw. In this immensely supportive environment, the 2,000 delegates were greeted by cheering crowds (who threw flowers and money at them) and by the president of Poland (who told them of his "profound joy" at "this most illustrious assembly in the history of man"). Renaming their movement the World Peace Council (WPC), the delegates elected Joliot-Curie its first president by acclamation. The new organization claimed that it comprised more than 75 national peace committees and 150,000 local groups.[38]

Although outlawing the Bomb remained a priority of the delegates at Warsaw, new issues of more immediate concern to Communist nations now superseded it in importance. In a blistering speech that drew loud and prolonged applause, Fadeyev charged that the United States was transforming Korea "into a desert of ruins and ashes, flooding the country with the blood of children, and performing all sorts of fascist bestialities, similar to those that led to the Nuremberg Trial." Declaring that U.S. warplanes had repeatedly crossed the Manchurian border and indiscriminately bombed Chinese mothers and children, Kuo Mo-jo of China condemned General Douglas MacArthur for attempting to launch a third world war. Eventually, the resolution adopted by the Warsaw delegates, who termed themselves "the genuine voice of peace-loving mankind," charged that "the United Nations does not justify the main hope placed in it" and called, instead, for the convening of a five-power conference as the route to peace. The first item in a ten-point program adopted at Warsaw demanded "termination" of the Korean War and "the withdrawal of foreign armies from Korea" and the sixth called for the convening of an international commission to "investigate the crimes perpetrated in Korea, and specifically the question of General MacArthur's responsibility." Only in point seven did the Warsaw resolution address the issue of nuclear weapons, and then as part of a package: "the unconditional banning of all means of atomic, bacteriological and chemical weapons, poisonous gases, radio-active and all other means of mass extermination."[39]

In subsequent months, nuclear weapons continued to be displaced by other items on the World Peace Council's agenda. Launching another petition drive, this time behind the "Warsaw Appeal," the WPC eventually claimed signatures from 562 million people, more than 90 percent of them from Communist countries. Another WPC petition drive, in 1951, netted a purported 600 million signatures endorsing a five-power peace pact. When the WPC met in Vienna in November 1951, its resolutions included one calling for "the absolute prohibition" of nuclear weapons. But it was buried in a list that dealt with a five-power pact, the Korean War, the German question, a Japanese peace treaty, the Near and Middle East, Southeast Asia and Vietnam, and cultural exchanges.[40]

WPC attacks on U.S. policy in Korea, however, maintained the emphasis on scientific horror that had characterized its earlier denunciation of the Bomb. In February 1952, after both the Chinese and Soviet governments alleged that the United States was practicing germ warfare in Korea, Kuo Mo-jo—a vice-president of the WPC and president of the Chinese Committee for the Defense of Peace—took up the cry. In a message to Joliot-Curie, he claimed that "the U.S. armies of aggression, in a treacherous effort to wipe out the civilian population of Korea, as well as the armed forces of the Korean and Chinese people, have spread . . . large quantities of insects carrying the germs of plague, cholera, typhus, and other contagious diseases." The governments of China and North Korea would not allow the International Red Cross or the World Health Organization to conduct an inquiry, he stated, for these organizations were not impartial. But he hoped that the WPC would take up the issue. Without conducting an inquiry of its own, the WPC promptly trumpeted Chinese allegations. In a widely distributed letter of March 8, Joliot-Curie claimed that these germ warfare charges were valid and demanded that "public opinion . . . denounce this crime."[41]

Indeed, the World Peace Council made the germ warfare issue the center of a new campaign. On April 3, 1952, arguing that Joliot-Curie was "prostituting science," the U.S. ambassador to the United Nations, Warren Austin, had sharply rebutted the contention that his country practiced germ warfare.

Nevertheless, the WPC pressed forward with the attack. On May 3, in an open letter to Austin, the WPC president reiterated charges of American "use of the bacteriological weapon in Korea and China," contending that Kuo Mo-jo and others producing such reports "are scientists . . . whose professional capacity and moral integrity cannot be doubted." Moreover, he claimed that such action represented only "a first step" toward America's employment of weapons "capable of obliterating all life on our planet." In September 1952, the WPC issued the 330,000-word report of its commission of inquiry, which claimed to have investigated 13 Korean and 27 Chinese incidents involving allegations of germ warfare. To no one's surprise, the commission validated all of the Chinese and North Korean charges. Meanwhile, captured U.S. pilots "confessed" to the crimes. "The utilization of biological weapons by the armed forces of the United States," proclaimed Joliot-Curie, constitutes "one of the most sinister chapters in the history of humanity."[42]

The Response of the Nonaligned Movement

The world pacifist leadership, while maintaining its commitment to interpersonal reconciliation, took a firm stand against organizational collaboration with the Communist-led movement. The December 1949 World Pacifist Meeting resolved that "towards individual Communists or Communist sympathizers, pacifists will cultivate the same attitude of goodwill and love as toward all other human beings." In this light, "serious discussion between Communists and pacifists, in which each tries to understand the other more deeply . . . is to be encouraged." Furthermore, pacifists should "oppose all attempts to arouse anti-Communist hysteria" and seek "to rule out any policy of preparation for war with Russia." Nevertheless, "it is our judgment that at the present time it is unwise for pacifists and pacifist organizations to collaborate organizationally . . . for limited objectives with the Communist Party or with organizations in which its members have a substantial influence." Given Communist support for wars of their own choosing, "groups collaborating with Communists in an anti-war campaign one day may find the next day that the Communists have withdrawn and wrecked the organization. Not only is precious effort thus wasted, but the pacifist witness is confused and weakened."[43]

Although individual pacifists sometimes participated in Communist-led peace ventures—for example, by signing the relatively innocuous Stockholm Peace Appeal—the pacifist internationals adopted a critical stance. As two WILPF members recalled, "it was difficult, and sometimes painful, to cast doubts on expressions of solidarity in the cause of peace, freedom and democracy that claimed a mass following" through the WPC and its affiliates, "but impossible not to do so when these movements were so at variance with the real conditions of life behind the Iron Curtain and so lacking in criticism of provocative actions by Communist governments." After considerable discussion of the problem, the WILPF left its local groups free to decide whether or to what degree cooperation was possible, but its international organization followed a policy of noncooperation with Communist-led peace campaigns.[44]

Much the same attitude prevailed in the WRI and the International FOR. In a "personal" statement to the WRI—but one that expressed the consensus of WRI affiliates—the chair and secretary of the WRI declared in February 1951 that they refused to associate with the WPC "because we know that those who control this organisation . . . do not believe in peace fundamentally, and advocate it only when it suits their political ends." Furthermore, "we know that they are prepared to advocate and support war and violent revolution in certain circumstances and that at any moment, at the bidding of Moscow, they may reverse their present policy. They do not deny that their . . . primary concern is to support the U.S.S.R. in its world power conflict with the U.S.A." Finally, "we feel that it is impossible for us to ally ourselves with, or have confidence in, those who frankly and systematically use lies for political ends and are prepared at a moment's notice to turn on those whose support they now seek. Such an alliance would, we are certain, in no way further the cause of peace."[45] Similar views animated the leadership of the International FOR, which, like the other pacifist internationals, refused to send delegates or otherwise to support the world conferences organized by the Communist-led movement.[46]

Reports from pacifist observers at these events did little to alter pacifist wariness about the World Peace Council and its motives. Attending the Berlin WPC meeting in early 1951, a British FOR observer claimed that the delegates were "desperately anxious to avoid war" but did not seem to have a "full appreciation of what peacemaking involved." She concluded that "little positive peacemaking was to be found." Later that year, another British FOR member observed the WPC's Vienna conference. Although he thought the gathering important and expressive of a genuine desire for peace, he noted that "many speeches were violently critical of the 'West' and not least of the U.S.A.; none were critical of the 'East.' " In these circumstances, the world pacifist bodies continued to avoid sending delegates to WPC gatherings.[47]

Like the pacifists, the nonaligned movement of atomic scientists kept its distance from the Communist-led peace campaign. "Peace will only come as the result of reconciliation and not as a by-product of condemnation," wrote Kathleen Lonsdale of the British ASA. She was "therefore convinced that campaigns, such as that accusing the USA of experiments in germ warfare, are harmful to peace." Asked to send a message to the 1949 World Peace Congress in Paris, Einstein replied that, in view of his "experience with the first congress of this kind at Wroclaw" and a similar venture in New York, he had "the strong impression that this kind of procedure does not really serve the cause of international understanding. The reason is that it is more or less a Soviet enterprise and everything is managed accordingly." In itself, this would "not be so bad" if Soviet and other East bloc delegates "were really free to express their personal opinions rather than having to express what is currently the official Russian point of view." But they were not. Thus he refused to associate himself with such ventures.[48]

The leaders of the atomic scientists' movement took a particular interest in—but had little respect for—the Stockholm Peace Appeal. Responding to a request from a Danish Communist newspaper that he sign the Stockholm petition, Bohr issued a public statement that he could not "join any appeal . . . which does not include the clearly expressed demand of access to information about conditions in all countries and of fully free exchange of ideas within every country and across the boundaries."[49] In an issue of the *Bulletin of the Atomic Scientists*, Rabinowitch did print an appeal by Joliot-Curie for support of the Stockholm petition, but he accompanied it with his own editorial criticizing the scheme. "When Professor Joliot-Curie addresses sympathetic writers, actors, and movie stars in 'peace congresses,'" Rabinowitch remarked, "he may assume that they do not know where the matter of atomic energy control stands, and are ready to believe that the principal obstacle on the way to its establishment is the refusal of the American government to renounce atomic weapons; but he cannot presume such lack of information when he speaks to American scientists." Similarly, according to a report on the September 1950 meeting of delegates from the American FAS and the British ASA, the Stockholm Peace Appeal was "judged a very effective piece of propaganda," which provided "no help" on the crucial issue of how to control nuclear weapons.[50]

The Communist-led peace campaign also generated virtually no sympathy or support among world government leaders. They were, of course, vitally concerned with securing Soviet participation in any future world government. For this reason, the ever-energetic Henry Usborne talked vaguely in 1947 of "plans for getting a deputation to fly to Moscow to explain both world government in general and our plans in particular to Stalin and such of [the] Polit-Bureau as we can get to." But this venture apparently never materialized, and the subsequent wave of Communist-led peace congresses left world federalist groups cold. Their alienation may have resulted, in part, from the bitter attacks on the idea of world government by the Soviet Union and Communist parties. So sharp was the confrontation that *Common Cause* entitled one article on the subject "World Federalism vs. Communism." In addition, however, federalists shared the views of other groups that the Communist-led peace movement was a bogus venture, which, for principled and tactical reasons, they wanted to avoid. When, in early 1951, the WPC seemed on the verge of sending several observers to the forthcoming WMWFG conference in Rome, both the executive council and the delegates voted to bar their admission.[51]

Nor did the Communist-led peace movement make much headway among church bodies. In July 1950, the Commission on International Affairs of the World Council of Churches sent a letter to religious leaders in 70 countries criticizing the Stockholm Peace Appeal and declaring that it was being used by Communist groups to further their own ends. Early the following year, in an exchange of letters with Joliot-Curie, the executive secretary of the commission, Richard Fagley, rebuffed the WPC leader's proposals for arms reductions. The Catholic church, too, adopted a hard line toward Communist-led peace ventures. Denouncing the 1949 Paris conference as a Moscow-inspired maneuver, *Osservatore Romano* contended that it was designed to undermine the solidarity of Western nations and lay the groundwork for Soviet domination of Europe. A few years later, in an obvious reference to the Communist-led movement, Pope Pius XII warned that "pacifist efforts or propaganda originating from those who deny all belief in God" were "always very dubious." [52]

Sharp criticism of the Communist-led peace campaign also came from the non-Communist Left. In June 1950, a conference of Europe's Socialist parties denounced the Stockholm petition and dismissed the pro-Soviet peace movement as camouflage for a totalitarian policy of militarism and domination. Three months later, in an acknowledged effort to counter the Stockholm Peace Appeal and "Communism's phony peace talk," a European Socialist assembly at Strasbourg drafted its own plan for "peace without appeasement." In early 1951, the labor parties and labor federations of Norway, Sweden, Denmark, and Iceland put forward a ten-point peace program designed in part to offset the Stockholm appeal. "Any act of aggression, no matter what kind of weapon is used . . . is a crime against the peace and security of the entire world," declared its first point. Furthermore, the United Nations must "decide all international disputes threatening the peace," and "all governments must respect resolutions adopted by the U.N." This social democratic manifesto insisted that "fear of the atom bomb can be removed only if all major powers manifest a sincere will to solve the problems of international control." [53]

Recognizing the political isolation of the Communist-led peace campaign, its organizers occasionally reached out to nonaligned peace groups. In an address to the Warsaw conference of November 1950, Joliot-Curie declared that "we ought to consider helping other international organizations when they take just and effective initiatives in favor of peace." He mentioned the Society of

Friends, the Red Cross, and the world government movement. These groups, he suggested, "would be able to find points of agreement with our Movement." Bernal, too, used the occasion of the Warsaw conference to call for "the closest cooperation" with other groups supporting peace.[54]

When such cooperation failed to materialize, activists in the Communist-led campaign reverted to bitter recriminations. Ivor Montagu, who chaired the WPC's British affiliate, claimed that "so-called peace-supporters who think they are for negotiation between Communist and non-Communist countries, and their peaceful coexistence, but refuse to work with Communists to get it, or even discuss with them how to get it, are deceiving themselves." Montagu maintained that "to pretend to want peace, or a peace movement, without Communists is not a contribution towards peace at all, but a declaration of war on half the world." One of the Communist-led movement's luminaries, the Rev. Hewlett Johnson, recalled his "deep sorrow" that "the Christian Church in the West did not welcome the Peace Campaign and even, in its political blindness, opposed it. To that extent the spirit of Christianity departed from this institution and took concrete form elsewhere." Where this "spirit" reemerged he did not specify, but his overall orientation—like that of the Communist-led peace campaign—suggested Moscow as the appropriate locale.[55]

The New Movement: Success and Failure

By the early 1950s, the world Communist movement had organized a large, highly visible peace and disarmament organization—the World Peace Council—under its control. In light of the initial Communist enthusiasm for the atomic bombing of Japan, the WPC's later condemnation of nuclear weapons, including their employment at Hiroshima and Nagasaki, was surely hypocritical. Nevertheless, the Communist-led peace movement did have a genuine fear of the Bomb, for—as Soviet-American relations deteriorated—it viewed the weapon as a likely instrument of U.S. attack on the Soviet Union and other Communist states. Assailing nuclear weapons and nuclear war, the new movement hoped to hobble U.S. military policy by unleashing a tidal wave of popular protest against the Bomb. But the WPC met with no more than modest success, for its strident Cold War partisanship severely undercut its appeal. As a result, the new movement remained confined primarily to Soviet sympathizers—a substantial group in the aftermath of World War II but one with waning influence in most non-Communist nations.

"Comrades, Turn East"

The Communist-Led Campaign in France, Great Britain, and the United States

> Comrades, turn East—not West.
>
> A delegate at the founding conference
> of the British Peace Committee, 1949

France

Of all non-Communist nations, France provided the best terrain for the Communist-led peace campaign. In the wake of the Molotov-Ribbentrop Pact, the French Communist party (PCF)—like others around the world—had scuttled its support for collective security and had sharply condemned national defense measures, even after the Nazi invasion and conquest of France. But the German attack on the Soviet Union in June 1941 caused another turnabout in PCF policy, with Communists now taking the lead in the French resistance and emerging as some of its most heroic, respected figures. In the postwar era, trading heavily upon these patriotic, antifascist credentials, French Communists reaped substantial benefits. Large numbers of enthusiastic recruits flocked to the PCF, while millions of others, viewing it as a "progressive" force, turned it into France's strongest political party, supported by one out of every four voters. The French also felt a large measure of sympathy for the Soviet Union, which they viewed as the principal liberator of Europe from Nazi slavery. PCF and Soviet ventures generated particular respect among French intellectuals, who, in addition to their loathing for fascism, rarely felt much enthusiasm for the United States.[1]

A Communist-led peace movement soon took root. In February and March 1948, Yves Farge, a former leader of the resistance and a figure close to the PCF, had organized Fighters for Liberty (Combattants de la Liberté) as an extension of the wartime movement. Impressed by the potentialities of the group to link antifascism with opposition to Western defense measures, the Cominform encouraged PCF participation. Two PCF leaders, Laurent Casanova and Charles Tillon, helped transform the group, which was recast as Fighters for Liberty and Peace (Combattants de la Liberté et de la Paix). In November 1948, after a massive congress held by the new organization, the editor of the PCF newspaper, L'Humanité, declared enthusiastically that the gathering "confirms the basic idea of Comrade Stalin, the greatest strategist of the struggle for peace, that the peoples will compel the instigators of a new war to retreat." With some fanfare and compromises engineered by the PCF, the Fighters for Liberty and Peace reemerged in 1949 as the Movement for Peace (Mouvement de la Paix, MDP), the French affiliate of the Partisans of Peace and, later, of the World Peace Council.[2]

Enhanced by the MDP's non-Communist antecedents, as well as the leadership of Tillon—a very creative and independent Communist who had gained fame in the wartime resistance—the organization embarked on a number of nondoctrinaire ventures, acceptable to large sectors of public opinion. In the fall of 1949, it promoted a "peace ballot," which opposed German rearmament, nuclear weapons, the Vietnam War, and a large military budget. In the spring of 1950, the MDP threw itself into the Stockholm peace petition campaign and generated an enormous response. Jean Genêt reported from Paris that June that the Stockholm Peace Appeal "has already been signed by a hardly credible galaxy of prominent anti-Communist Frenchmen." These included prominent politicians, members of the French Academy, and "a mass of university professors, popular writers, star actors, and famous artists." Fifty percent of the population of Calais had already signed, and some towns "signed en bloc." He concluded that "Communist propaganda" was "enjoying the most extraordinary success, especially among non-Communists, that it has ever had in France." Eventually, some fourteen million people in France signed the petition.[3]

From its inception, however, the Communist peace campaign had alienated a substantial number of nonaligned groups and individuals. Responding to the early activities of Garry Davis, L'Humanité had sneered at his "revolution in a handkerchief" and criticized him for placing the United States and the Soviet Union on the same level. When, shortly before the opening of the April 1949 conference of the Partisans of Peace in Paris, it became evident to organizers that the meeting needed a broader political base, they invited the participation of antiwar figures from the groups around the Catholic Esprit, the non-Communist Left Franc-Tireur, Davis, and Claude Bourdet. By this time, however, feelings were already too strained for them to accept; indeed, a rival peace congress, organized by the non-Communist Left, was already

scheduled for April 30.[4] Sponsored by the Revolutionary Democratic Rally
(Rassemblement Démocratique Révolutionnaire), led by writers David Rousset and Jean-Paul Sartre, this International Day of Resistance to Dictatorship
and War had the support of the pacifist Peace Federation, the Socialist party,
the non-Communist trade unions, and many liberal groups. The Day of Resistance—dismissed as the work of "Trotskyist agents" by *L'Humanité*—drew
some 6,000 Parisians to the Vélodrome d'Hiver, where they heard a broad
range of speakers. Some, like Sartre, U.S. novelist Richard Wright, and French
journalist Maurice Merleau-Ponty, assailed as warlike both "the more or less
disguised annexation of Central Europe by the Soviet Union on the one hand
and the North Atlantic pact on the other." When U.S. atomic scientist Karl
Compton praised U.S. atomic weapons as a force for peace, the audience responded with boos, catcalls, whistles, and hisses. Partway through the event,
groups of anarchists and other *enragés* in the crowd sought, through disruption,
to break up the gathering. But Davis leaped on a table, pacified the tumult, and
brought the evening to a reasonably successful conclusion.[5]

The following year, as the Stockholm petition drive surged forward, tensions persisted between aligned and nonaligned critics of nuclear weapons.
Although FOR leader André Trocmé remained willing to talk with MDP
leaders on a personal basis, he refused organizational cooperation. Henri Roser,
another FOR leader, agreed to participate in a Communist-led peace conference
only if he could raise questions about Soviet deportations and concentration
camps; when an MDP leader responded that this could not be arranged, Roser
declined to attend. In late May 1950, French Socialist leaders criticized the
Stockholm Peace Appeal and pointed out that their party was supporting legislation in the National Assembly that would not only condemn atomic bombs
but commit the government to arms control and disarmament under an international body. Counterattacking, the PCF declared that the Socialists supported
"Marshallization and war."[6]

Although the Catholic church, for the most part, dodged the issue of the
Bomb, occasionally it was drawn into the controversy provoked by the Stockholm petition. On June 19 a group of French cardinals and archbishops made
public a letter noting that, "in this atmosphere of confusion," the petition had
"deceived many good people." But they added that "whoever has a 'true sense
of humanity' . . . can only condemn the use of all modern weapons which
strike without distinction both combatants and civil populations"; indeed, "we
condemn them with all our strength." This distaste for the petitioners, as well
as for the Bomb, was evident in the complaint by an editor of *Témoignage Chré-
tien*, who regretted that the petition proponents, "not content with demanding
the outlawing of the atom bomb, did not demand also some other little items

which might have been painful for the USSR and the Communists." These items included "acceptance of a plan for the control of atomic energy such as the United States has proposed; acceptance of a commission of inquiry on Soviet concentration camps; acceptance of a plan of progressive and universal disarmament and the establishment of a true system of collective security, or the evacuation of the countries of Eastern Europe."[7]

The fervently pro-Soviet orientation of the PCF, however, made a nonaligned position out of the question. When President Truman announced that the Soviet Union had exploded its first atomic bomb, *L'Humanité* criticized not the development of the Bomb but the announcement. "It is part of an ingeniously organized campaign to develop a war psychosis," the French Communist journal explained. "The United States government needs to justify the creation of a whole series of pacts against the Soviet Union and the people's democracies in order to hold in check the peace movement, which is sweeping the world." *L'Humanité* applauded Soviet development of the Bomb because, it claimed, the Soviet Union was interested solely in peace.[8] Indeed, party secretary Maurice Thorez declared that, if war erupted, the French people would welcome the arrival of Soviet troops. Nor did the PCF show much respect for the neutralist and nonaligned movement in France. "Every class has the literature it deserves," wrote the PCF's Roger Garaudy, denouncing "the intellectual fornications" of Jean-Paul Sartre. PCF leader Waldecq Rochet claimed that "all those who are not communists . . . but who nevertheless do not want war, can . . . fight for the defense of peace at the side of the Soviet Union and the communists." But "those who really want to prevent war cannot hold an equal balance between the Soviet peace policy and the war policy of the American imperialists and their valets."[9]

Such Cold War partisanship also doomed any independent tendencies within the MDP, which was soon reduced to serving as a mouthpiece of Soviet policy. Under PCF pressure, the MDP joined in the Cominform campaign against Tito, branding him a fascist. When one non-Communist MDP leader showed too much independence on this issue, he was expelled. The PCF also closed down the MDP's journal for its resistance to the Soviet endorsement of German rearmament. Indeed, the MDP had been engaged in a major campaign against German rearmament until the World Peace Council, in line with Soviet policy, insisted upon changing the movement's emphasis to securing a five-power peace pact. Aghast at this shift, Tillon—who vigorously opposed German rearmament—took this occasion to argue for transforming the MDP into a movement independent of Moscow. From the standpoint of the PCF, such treasonous behavior could not be tolerated. In September 1951, Tillon was removed as general secretary of the MDP and, after a "trial" by his fellow Communists in France, expelled from the PCF as well.[10]

To remain at the forefront of the Communist-organized peace campaign, leaders had to hew considerably closer to the party line. Ever since January 1949, when he had publicly declared that "a French Communist, like any other French citizen in a government position," was loyal to his nation, Joliot-Curie had been under a cloud within the PCF. To be sure, he had convened the April 1949 meeting of the Partisans of Peace in Paris and had taken on the presidency of the resulting world organization. But Joliot-Curie remained the top official in France's nuclear program at a time when the Bomb was becoming the centerpiece of the shrill, Communist-led peace campaign. For this reason alone, anything he said on the subject was fraught with great significance to the PCF and to the French government.[11] In his speech of April 5, 1950, before the PCF national congress, at Gennevilliers, he clearly passed the test, at least the one administered by the PCF.

On this occasion, punctuated by repeated warnings of imperialist war and enlivened by a huge red banner proclaiming that the French people "never shall make war against the Soviet Union," Joliot-Curie provided the PCF with what it wanted. "How happy are the scientists who do research in the Soviet Union," he declared, for in that country "exploitation of man by man no longer exists. They have a tranquil conscience as they work in their laboratories, for they know that the results they obtain will serve for the betterment of human conditions and in the defense of acquired liberties." Furthermore, "they know their government . . . has solemnly and many times proposed to the governments of other nations the banning of the atomic weapon" and that if "the war criminals decide to throw atomic bombs at their country . . . their science and technology are sufficiently developed to deliver blows which would be decisive." In France, though, scientists played a different role. Here, in the midst of Western plans for "a war of aggression," the "progressive scientists, Communist scientists, will never give a scrap of their science to make war against the Soviet Union. And we shall stand firm, upheld by our conviction that in acting in this way we are serving France and the whole of mankind."[12]

Secretly, Joliot-Curie and his wife moved even further toward Cold War partisanship. In 1949, when the Chinese Communist government dispatched a top physicist abroad to purchase China's first nuclear instruments, the Joliot-Curies helped arrange the transaction in France and England. Their ambitions for China's nuclear program apparently ran considerably beyond the exclusively peaceful uses they recommended for the West. Conversing with the Chinese radiochemist Yang Chengzong in Paris during October 1951, Frédéric

Joliot-Curie urged him to "tell Chairman Mao" that China "should own the atomic bomb"—advice the Chinese government took very seriously when, a few years later, it made the decision to build the weapon. As a follow-up to this admonition, Irène Joliot-Curie gave Yang ten grams of radium salt, standardized for radioactive emissions, "to support the Chinese people in their nuclear research." [13]

Even without full knowledge of the activities of the PCF and of Joliot-Curie, most of the French public remained unmoved by the Communist-led peace campaign. To be sure, the Stockholm peace petition and the opposition to German rearmament had substantial resonance in French public life. Nevertheless, the MDP remained too closely tied to Soviet foreign policy to enable it to break out of the same political cul de sac that increasingly isolated the PCF from French public opinion as the Cold War advanced. For its part, the nonaligned peace movement showed no signs of warming toward the Communist-led peace campaign. In June 1951, the pacifist *La Voie de la paix* claimed that Communist peace activism "is merely circumstantial and occasional; it is neither honest nor sincere. . . . For us, pacifism is internationalist and could never be a means of manipulating public opinion to the advantage of a state." [14] Thus, despite its ability to attract unprecedented numbers of people to peace petition drives and rallies, the Communist-led peace campaign in France proved incapable of inspiring a majority movement. Instead, after an extravagant debut, it found itself largely confined to the ranks—large but dwindling—of France's Soviet sympathizers.

Great Britain

In Great Britain, where the Communist party was far weaker, its approach was much the same. It mobilized its membership for peace rallies—including one in November 1948 at Trafalgar Square that drew 10,000 of the faithful—and could count on occasional peace and anti-Bomb speeches by prominent Soviet sympathizers, most notably British M.P. Konni Zilliacus and the "Red Dean" of Canterbury, the Rev. Hewlett Johnson. [15] A Congress of Peace it held in June 1949 resolved that the Soviet Union "is a progressive people's state of a kind for which the British people can and must entertain feelings only of friendship." As elsewhere, the Communist party's view of nuclear weapons was thoroughly in line with Soviet foreign policy. Charging that the Atlantic Pact would catapult Great Britain into atomic war, the party warned the British government in March 1949 that "British working people will never allow themselves to be used as tools of Wall Street and the key for war against Socialist Russia." That September, party secretary Harry Pollitt declared that the first explosion of an atomic bomb by the Soviet Union represented a "tremendous gain for the peace-loving forces of the world." [16]

This same partisanship and much the same constituency characterized the British Peace Committee, formally launched in late October 1949 at a conference in London by persons who had attended the World Congress of the Partisans of Peace that spring in Paris. According to a pamphlet published by the new group, one delegate, after denouncing the "imperialist warmongers," could barely be heard "above a storm of applause" as he concluded: "Comrades, turn East—not West." Zilliacus, on hand for the occasion, pointed to the "basic difference" between the treaties signed by the Soviet Union ("consistent with the [U.N.] charter") and those concluded by the Western powers ("inconsistent with the [U.N.] charter"). Another ubiquitous figure, J. D. Bernal, told the gathering that "the future of British culture is tied up with the struggle for peace." He also brought the good news that the Peace Partisans had suspended the Yugoslav Peace Committee from their ranks, a decision supported by the British Peace Committee. According to the official account, "the delegates stood and cheered" when a fraternal delegate from the Soviet Peace Committee rose to speak. "In our country there are no exploiting classes," he stated. "History is on our side. . . . What possible motive can we have for aggressive war?" The only speaker to receive a mixed reception was Sybil Morrison of the PPU, who presented the pacifist approach to world affairs. A pacifist observer reported that "there was a roar of applause when she said that . . . the idea of Communism would not be destroyed by killing Communists; when the ovation died away, she remarked that, by the same token, neither would the idea of capitalism be destroyed by killing the wicked capitalists." This comment "was received in cold and deathly silence!" [17]

As the local affiliate of the Peace Partisans [18] and, later, of the WPC, the British Peace Committee became a leading proponent of outlawing nuclear weapons. At the October 1949 conference, a resolution had called for "the banning of the Atom Bomb," and the following February Bernal was praising scientists in America who took a stand "against the criminal lunacy of the hydrogen bomb." [19] Finally, in the spring of 1950, the British Peace Committee joined its overseas counterparts in launching the Stockholm peace petition campaign. "Tens of thousands of people throughout Great Britain . . . are convinced that a concerted national struggle is absolutely essential," the committee explained in a press release. Focusing on the need to "Ban the Bomb" and "Declare the First User a Criminal," the committee instructed its followers not to spend time on questions concerning the sponsors of the campaign, but to say, "Sign the petition and join the British Peace Movement." [20]

Although the Stockholm Peace Appeal was rather bland and the official pronouncements of the British Peace Committee vague, the Communist cat kept peeping out of the new movement's bag. On May 7, 1950, thousands of Communist-organized peace demonstrators surged through London, clashing with police and bearing signs that ranged from the inoffensive "Peace" to the more strident "Halt the American Warmongers." That July, after the inception of the Korean War, the British Peace Committee did manage to stage a large and efficient peace conference, with some attempts at balanced political presentations. But it featured speeches by the usual galaxy of Soviet supporters—Ilya Ehrenburg, the Abbé Boulier, and the dean of Canterbury—and one delegate commented frankly: "Some of us think that the struggle in Malaya, Indo-China, Indonesia and Korea is a struggle for peace." A pacifist observer noted with surprise that "the BPC appears to be undaunted by the seeming inconsistency of their peace professions with the launching of aggressive war by their friends in North Korea." [21]

In fact, the consistency of the British Peace Committee lay not in its pacifist proclivities but in its leaders' pro-Soviet approach to world affairs. Shortly after the German invasion of the Soviet Union, the Rev. Hewlett Johnson had issued a "Message to British Workers," declaring: "Russia stands for all that is progressive: for justice and equality between classes and races; for the ending of exploitation between man and man; for a juster and nobler economic and social order. That is why she has been so hated. That is why Hitler now attacks her." Disdaining pacifism, Johnson declared in a wartime broadcast that "war . . . is the supreme test of men and things. War demonstrates, as nothing else can demonstrate, the strength and weakness of men and nations." In 1943, the *Daily Worker* gave him an honorary place on its editorial board, and thereafter he became a regular contributor to the Communist newspaper. As the Cold War grew, Johnson, who continued his lavish praise of the Soviet Union, served as a luminary of Britain's Communist-led peace movement and one of its best-known speakers. In May 1949, he publicly assailed America's atomic bombing of Japan, arguing that the action had been directed against the Soviet Union. He charged that the United States, unlike the Soviet Union, had either to face mass unemployment or to consume its wealth through war. Thereafter, Johnson led the British campaign against alleged American germ warfare in Korea and China, publicizing Communist charges on this score in the press and in a pamphlet he produced on the subject, entitled *I Appeal*.[22]

The chair of the British Peace Committee, Ivor Montagu, exhibited the same Cold War partisanship. Americans were "Hitler's heirs," he charged in a vitriolic pamphlet, *Plot Against Peace*. "America today is an instrument for aggression and world-conquest more powerful and perfectly adapted than Hitler's Germany." Its "economy, state structure and intellectual life" are "controlled and integrated for war; the opposition to war crushed and denied elementary rights; the ideas and habits of the citizenry intensively molded to justify world conquest" and "to become habituated to cruelty." Indeed, "the mantle of Goebbels has descended upon the warmongers." When American leaders plan war "to halt the progress of the U.S.S.R. and China and the People's Democracies, it is because they fear the competition of truth. . . . They know well enough the growing life, the joy, the serenity, the moral stature of the millions on the other side of the iron curtain they strive desperately to keep closed." Communists were "not afraid of the future. They, and they alone, are certain of it. Where else in the world can the people foresee such a future as that framed before the Soviet people in the Fifth Five-Year Plan?" That was why U.S. leaders "threaten war on the world. They dare not wait." [23]

Despite the one-sided nature and strident tone of the Communist-led peace campaign, its organizers made occasional efforts to broaden its appeal. In November 1950, at the Warsaw conference, Bernal called upon "pacifists, world government supporters, men of goodwill with Liberal or Socialist views, and genuine patriots, however conservative their views," to join the new movement. The *Daily Worker*, too, advocated building "an even bigger peace front," and the British Peace Committee regularly invited pacifist groups to attend its conferences and those sponsored by the World Peace Council. Furthermore, by circulating the relatively innocuous Stockholm appeal, the British Peace Committee reached a substantial number of well-meaning and non-Communist Britons. Eventually, the committee claimed that it had garnered more than a million signatures. [24]

Nevertheless, Britain's Communist-led peace campaign generally remained isolated, even in circles where it hoped to secure some support. In early 1949, the British Trades Union Congress labeled the forthcoming World Peace Congress in Paris "part of a Communist campaign" and sent warnings about it to affiliated bodies. Later that year, Bernal was dropped from the Council of the British Association for the Advancement of Science for a particularly insulting speech he delivered before the Soviet Partisans of Peace. [25] In June 1950, the Labour party threatened to expel those of its members who joined affiliates of the Partisans of Peace, and the Cooperative Women's Guild shunned the Stockholm peace petition as a Communist device. That same month, at the annual conference of the United Nations Association of Great Britain, a motion calling for banning the H-Bomb was defeated; expressing his doubts about "prohibiting particular weapons," Professor Gilbert Murray argued that "the thing is to prevent war, because a country in despair will use any weapon it can find." Viewing the British Peace Committee as little more than a Soviet device, many Britons shunned it. [26]

Although the Wroclaw and Paris conferences had sought to mobilize intellectuals, the new peace movement attracted few British intellectuals outside the Communist orbit. Typical of the recalcitrant Britons was J. B. Priestley, a writer shocked by the Hiroshima bombing into a determined quest for international understanding and peace. Responding in the *New Statesman* to Ilya Ehrenburg's "Open Letter to Writers of the West," Priestley suggested that "if you mean what you say" and "are not writing propaganda bosh," then "organize a congress, or edit a book, in which Russian writers will be as frankly critical of their government as some of us western writers will be frankly critical of ours. Let me read or hear you and your colleagues openly denouncing the size and power of the Red Army, the creation of a huge submarine fleet, the work on the bombs and the rockets and the other horrors." Priestley expressed his agreement with Ehrenburg that "the Soviet Union does not want war," and he was certain that the Soviet "people—bless them—are horrified at the thought of it. But it is not obvious to me that your leaders genuinely desire . . . a real peace, a world community of people living their own life without constant interference from other peoples, all open and friendly, enjoying what they can contribute to a world civilization. Or, alternatively, they are not free from the hysterical fear that is now so common in America." Peace would be secured, he concluded, only "when men in power . . . regard this world as a home and not as a potential battlefield. I will do what I can in London if you will begin to attempt something in Moscow." [27]

The Communist-led peace campaign also made few inroads among pacifists. To be sure, during the dangerous early years of the Cold War, the Peace Pledge Union did adopt a policy that opened the door for limited forms of cooperation with nonpacifists, including Communists. At its meeting of September 26, 1948, the national council of the PPU resolved that "the PPU is ready to co-operate in the present urgent situation, where possible, with all who are endeavoring to avoid a third world war." In practice, this meant that a representative of the PPU would attend rallies and other gatherings sponsored by Communists (and other nonpacifists) and make pacifist speeches.[28] Responding to criticism of this practice by some PPU members, including Vera Brittain and Frank Lea (the editor of *Peace News*),[29] Morrison wrote that she did not think that PPU speakers would be "contaminated" by Communists; indeed, Communists might "be shown the real way to peace." Dismay with this practice grew, however, as the one-sided nature of the Communist-led peace campaign became more apparent. Raising the issue at the annual meeting of the PPU in April 1949, PPU leader Michael Tippett argued that he did not want his colleagues and friends in Soviet bloc nations to "think that I have stood with their torturers." Morrison, too, was approaching the limits of her tolerance.

In December 1949, she complained to readers of *Peace News* that "the chief concern of the British Peace Committee is to prove that the USSR, being perfect, cannot possibly be held responsible in any respect either for the present tension or for any future war." Its "unquestioning hero-worship" of Russians "belongs to the world of school-children and adolescents, not to adults in an adult world." As the Stockholm peace petition campaign heated up, pacifist organizations were ready for a total break.[30]

On June 21, 1950, the national council of the PPU issued the following statement:

Recognizing the danger to peace in any confusion between pacifism and Communism, and in attempts to avert a third world war being identified with pro-Russian sentiment, and in order to prevent misunderstanding and even misrepresentation, the National Council of the Peace Pledge Union desires to make clear its attitude to the Communist Party and the British Peace Committee. . . .

The National Council is convinced that fundamental differences of principle make it neither possible nor desirable for the PPU as a movement to have any connection with the Communist Party or the BPC, and render it necessary to discourage members of the PPU from signing the BPC petition (which originated at the Stockholm meeting . . .) which, in its judgment, obscures the real issue.

The National Council urges [PPU] groups to make certain of the actual origin and motive of local peace councils, and advises PPU members not to join such local peace councils when they are dominated by Communists. It urges groups instead to take the initiative in themselves forming local peace councils in co-operation with others with whom there is more fundamental agreement about constructive peacemaking as an end in itself, and not as a means to some other end.

The National Council also requested that PPU officers and staff not take part in gatherings arranged by the British Peace Committee.[31]

Thereafter, although debate raged within the pages of *Peace News* on the appropriate policy for pacifists when dealing with Communist peace advocates, the PPU stuck to this position,[32] which was also adopted by other nonaligned peace groups. Shortly thereafter, the British FOR branch announced that it was "unable to co-operate" with the British Peace Committee, which was "not, in fact, prepared to oppose all forms of intolerance, violence, tyranny, and materialism wherever they are found." The FOR concluded that "this is not peacemaking as we understand it."[33] Similarly, in November 1950, the National Peace Council rejected the British Peace Committee's invitation to send delegates to the proposed World Peace Congress at Sheffield, citing its own "critical attitude and reservations regarding the nature and origin" of that gathering. The National Peace Council, wrote one of its leaders, did not consider the British Peace Committee's gatherings "to be in fact 'peace' meetings."[34] Committed to civil liberties and freedom of travel, the PPU publicly protested the British

government's denials of visas to persons wishing to attend the Sheffield conference or one arranged the following year by the British Peace Committee. But it
refused to send delegates to either event.[35]

The United States

Nowhere, of course, did Communist leaders consider it more important to
build a properly oriented peace movement than in the United States. Not only
was the need to restrain the American "warmongers" a guiding principle of the
Communist-led movement, but the peace movement already in place seemed
politically unreliable. In 1948, American Communists had thrown themselves
into Henry Wallace's third-party campaign for the presidency, focused on
peace, but had little success at rallying support among Americans, in general,
or among leading peace activists, in particular. A. J. Muste, considered the
dean of American pacifists, had argued in the FOR journal that "a vote for
Wallace is a vote for the Communist party," an option he opposed. Another
peace movement leader, the Socialist Norman Thomas, had long been a sharp
critic of Stalinism and, accordingly, the Communist party despised him.[36]
American Communists were particularly hostile to the burgeoning world government movement. World federalism "weakens the struggle for progress and
strengthens the hand of reaction," the *New Masses* charged; "it is the ideology of imperialism." The *Daily Worker*—which attacked Norman Cousins's
Modern Man Is Obsolete for beautifying "the betrayal of peace"—claimed that
world government was "but a reflection . . . of the aspirations of American
foreign policy to dominate the world." [37]

From 1949 to 1951, as the Cominform's peace campaign grew more intense, the American Communist party moved from one party-sponsored peace
venture to another. "The Party's Peace Campaign is our major task," an official
policy statement declared in early June 1950. "It is primary and transcends all
other issues and struggles. . . . Every issue before us . . . must be thought
through and presented in terms of the overriding issue: PEACE." Meanwhile,
the Stockholm Peace Appeal "opens up new possibilities of bringing into our
ranks new thousands of the best fighters for peace and security and socialism."
This was not a self-interested matter, the Communist policy statement claimed,
for "without this growth of a strong, vanguard Party, no peace movement can
grow to its necessary breadth." [38]

As it turned out, neither American Communists nor the movement gained
very much from the Communist-led peace campaign. According to W. E. B.
Du Bois, the 60 Americans who attended the April 1949 peace congress in
Paris procrastinated for nearly a year thereafter "because in the state of hysteria

and war-mongering we found in the United States, it was not at all clear as to what could be done legally." Finally, in early April 1950, after the Stockholm conference, a gathering of figures within the party orbit organized the Peace Information Center, an organization chaired by Du Bois and headquartered in New York City. Focusing its efforts on circulating the Stockholm appeal, the Peace Information Center printed 750,000 pieces of literature, issued periodic *Peacegrams*, and assured its supporters that "THE CALL FOR PEACE AND AN END TO ATOMIC WEAPONS HAS SWELLED TO A MIGHTY CHORUS." The reality, however, was less encouraging. In October, facing what it claimed were "severe and pressing financial difficulties," as well as a Justice Department demand that the leaders of the center register as agents of a foreign principal, the center's executive board voted to dissolve the organization.[39] To fill the vacuum, in early 1951 the party helped launch a new group, the American Peace Crusade, headed by Willard Uphaus, active at the Wroclaw conference and other party-organized peace ventures, and Thomas Richardson, a black trade unionist. It called for an end to the fighting in Korea, peace with China, and efforts to "ban the atom bomb." Privately, however, the leaders of the American Peace Crusade conceded its weakness.[40]

Nor did the Stockholm Peace Appeal rally the support of most Americans. Leaders of the Protestant, Catholic, and Jewish faiths, in a joint statement, publicly denounced it, as did the executive council of the American Federation of Labor, which called it "spurious" and "a rank fraud."[41] Unconvinced by or unaware of these criticisms, a significant number of Americans did circulate the petition and sign it. Du Bois eventually claimed that his campaign had garnered 2.5 million signatures. Nevertheless, the Stockholm petition remained generally unpopular, and this number, if corrrect, fell substantially short of the party's goal of five million. Moreover, upon reflection, some signers (like Emily Greene Balch of the WILPF) withdrew their earlier endorsement.[42]

In addition to providing the only substantial force behind the Stockholm petition drive in the United States, the American Communist party also mobilized its supporters behind a number of world peace conferences. These included the Cultural and Scientific Conference for World Peace (March 1949) at New York City's Waldorf Astoria Hotel and the American Continental Congress for World Peace (September 1949) in Mexico City. As two important components in the worldwide Communist peace campaign, these gatherings were large and controversial, with an obvious pro-Soviet orientation. The party apparently played a lesser role in the Conference on Peaceful Alternatives to the North Atlantic Pact (May 1949) in Washington, D.C., and the Mid-Century Conference for Peace (May 1950) in Chicago—two ventures in which large numbers of non-Communists participated and which, therefore, had a rather innocuous tone. With the exception of the Mexico City meeting, at which anti-American invective was common, the conference resolutions were usually vague and inoffensive. At the Waldorf conference, the resolutions expressed support for strengthening the United Nations, cooperating with peace movements around the world, and rousing Americans to "protect the peace." Such moderation apparently represented an attempt by Communists to broaden their base of support in a very hostile environment.[43]

Despite the appealing vagueness of the Stockholm petition and the peace conference resolutions, the underlying partisanship of the campaign's leaders surfaced on occasion. Responding in September 1949 to the news of a Soviet atomic bomb, the *Daily Worker* chortled: "The 'cold war' madmen simply don't know which way to turn. They had everything all neatly planned. . . . From a safe distance, crazy generals would push buttons to wipe out hundreds of millions." But "this profit-drunken stupidity can't hold water any more." The Soviet Bomb, explained the *Daily Worker*'s foreign affairs editor, was "a contribution to peace." The weapon had "already eased the crisis by confounding the war-makers. And it can open up a whole new avenue for enforcing a settlement upon the imperialists." Irked by criticism of the Stockholm Peace Appeal from U.S. Secretary of State Dean Acheson, Du Bois retorted that "hundreds of millions of people may be pardoned for interpreting your statements as foreshadowing American use of the atom bomb in Korea." Indeed, Du Bois sometimes implied that the United States was unique in villainy. In a pamphlet entitled *I Take My Stand for Peace* issued in June 1951, he claimed that, "of all nations of earth today, the United States alone wants war, prepares for war, forces other nations to fight and asks you and me to impoverish ourselves, give up health and schools, sacrifice our sons and daughters to a Jim-Crow army, and commit suicide for a world war that nobody wants but the rich Americans who profit by it." The United States, he declared the following year, was becoming "the greatest warmonger of all history." [44]

Sometimes, even insiders found this one-sidedness hard to bear. A case in point was that of O. John Rogge, a former assistant attorney general of the United States, who was a prominent U.S. delegate at numerous Communist-organized international peace conferences. In September 1949, he caused some consternation at the Mexico City conference when, after sharply attacking U.S. foreign and domestic policy, he delivered some criticisms of Soviet policy as well. In March 1950, during an address before the Supreme Soviet on behalf of the Partisans of Peace, Rogge suggested that the two sides in the Cold War stop exploiting differences and start exploring areas of agreement. "The Americans must stop blaming the Communists, and the Russians must stop blaming the capitalist imperialists," he told what must have been an astonished audience.[45] Angered by the North Korean invasion of South Korea, he joined Henry Wallace in denouncing the attack and, at a meeting of the Peace Partisans' executive committee in August 1950, called for the adoption of resolutions that would criticize the invasion, amend the Stockholm appeal to condemn all aggressors, and readmit the Yugoslav delegation. None of these resolutions reached a committee or was even discussed. The finale came in November 1950, when Rogge spoke before thousands of delegates at the Warsaw Congress. Here he told them that Communist nations, and not the United States, had resorted to wars in Korea and Tibet "to give the revolution a violent shove." Condemning the Stockholm Peace Appeal and the expulsion of the Yugoslavs amid loud cries of derision from the audience, he concluded that progressives "will not accept the Cominform position that progress is to be identified with the policies of the Soviet Union—at least not for long." It was "the end of the road," he told a reporter. "The two things I found here were hate and violence." [46]

The rejection of the Communist-led peace campaign by American peace activists was equally decisive, as typified by their response to the Waldorf conference of March 1949. Organized by the National Council of the Arts, Sciences, and Professions, this Cultural and Scientific Conference for World Peace drew almost entirely upon Soviet sympathizers and the dwindling band of liberals still willing to work with them. In his opening address, Harlow Shapley, a Harvard astronomer, who chaired the conference, did seek to maintain some balance of blame for the Cold War. But his view was brushed aside by the ubiquitous Fadeyev, who argued that "while there are elements in the United States responsible for the menace to peace, there are no such elements in *our* country." Although the conference organizers refused to give Muste and other pacifist leaders places on the conference agenda, a small group of pacifist authors attended the session on writing and publishing and stirred the audience into a fury by directing embarrassing questions at the speakers. Dwight Macdonald inquired about missing Soviet writers: "Are they alive or dead? Are they in concentration camps or free?" After asserting that they were in good health and "not persecuted," Fadeyev added mockingly that "in Russia writers don't stop writing merely because they are criticized." Dimitri Shostakovich— pale, tense, and unsmiling—was asked by poet Robert Lowell about how criticism from the party's central committee had helped him compose better music and responded, "The criticism brings me much good." Lowell also inquired about Soviet provisions for conscientious objection, to which Soviet novelist P. A. Pavlenko, after a long pause, replied: "I don't know, because whenever my country has called, I have fought. . . . I hope to be still able to fight for my country when I am a hundred!" Muste did deliver a pacifist speech, but at a large counter-rally organized by a rival group, Americans for Intellectual Freedom.[47]

The best-known rebuff to the Waldorf conference came from Norman Cousins. Invited by Shapley to speak at the gathering, Cousins had initially declined, stating that he did not think the meeting would serve a useful purpose because of the auspices under which it was held. Later, however, Cousins changed his mind, apparently because he believed it worthwhile to deliver a more direct challenge to conference organizers and participants. Shapley, in turn, restored Cousins to the program and, although he did not like the speech when he read an advance copy, gave him a warm introduction. Speaking before 2,000 people on the opening night, Cousins claimed that Americans, by criticizing the conference, "are not speaking out against the idea of peace or the need of peace or the possibility of peace." Rather, "they are speaking out against a small political group in this country which has failed to live up to the rules of the game in a democracy." In the view of most Americans, this group "owes its primary allegiance and duty not to America but to an outside government" and, therefore, "is without standing and without honor in its own country." By contrast, most Americans were determined to "work for peace with justice in the world" and "believe this can best be done—indeed, that it can only be done—by a supreme effort behind the United Nations, giving it the form and substance of world law." Indeed, "the time has come for all peoples everywhere to produce a volcanic eruption of public opinion" behind this cause. "The time has come for all nations—and when I say all, I mean all—to recognize a higher law." It was not a talk that pleased most of the audience, which interrupted it a dozen times with hissing and booing, but it did indicate the attitude of most members of the nonaligned peace movement in the United States.[48]

Certainly there was little enthusiasm for the Communist-led peace campaign in the leadership of the established peace movement. John Haynes Holmes, a prominent pacifist minister, praised Cousins's speech as an effective rebuff to it, and Norman Thomas deplored "the so-called Stockholm peace petition," which he dismissed as "a communist document and . . . very unrealistic." According to the minutes of a War Resisters League administrative meeting in June 1950, "much concern" was expressed "over the current Communist peace drive and it was felt that an attempt should be made to interest the pacifist and non-Communist peace and liberal groups to combine in producing an alternative." Addressing the question of pacifist cooperation with Communist peace ventures, Muste argued that "in Russia and Communism we have very real evil" and "deceitfulness." Moreover, he did not see an inconsistency in calling for U.S.-Soviet negotiations and refusing to work with Communist peace groups because "the practice of love and fellowship toward human beings does not imply collaboration with them in wrong which they may be doing." Indeed, "these elements are not truly or objectively working for peace," and to "argue that human fellowship requires working with Communists in peace fronts without analyzing the objective political and social significance of this kind of collaboration" was foolish and counterproductive.[49]

Although some pacifists did not share these opinions, all U.S. pacifist groups adopted policies of nonparticipation in Communist-organized peace ventures. In October 1950, the WILPF national executive committee agreed to draw up a statement explaining why it could not take part in the Stockholm petition campaign, a venture it viewed as motivated by politics rather than a sincere concern for peace and freedom. Later that year, the War Resisters League declined an offer from Frédéric Joliot-Curie to participate in the Second World Congress of the Partisans of Peace. The appeal to the congress, it stated, "while expressing many noble sentiments, is in our opinion so inadequately worded and so partial to one side in the present big power struggle that little hope exists that genuine strides toward lasting peace can be made on that basis." There must be a way to break "through the impasse wherein the aggressiveness of one side only incites the other to intensified military preparations and actions." Peace "must be approached in a spirit of renunciation and humility and dedication to the task of building a world moral order based on the dignity of the individual, on respect for his economic, political, and civil rights, and on mutual action to promote the material security and cultural freedom of all."[50]

In 1951, an official FOR policy statement contended that "Communist-inspired 'peace' campaigns are not genuine" and only lead "to building up the Communist party rather than pacifism or peace." It believed that "the best way to test any 'peace' project or joint effort which is proposed is to discover whether its promoters will place a clear statement in its public program that it is opposed to militarism and war preparations *both* in Russia and in the United States, that it is critical of the foreign policy of both countries, and opposed to all forms of totalitarianism." It stated, however, that "while we must decline to be fooled . . . in connection with 'peace fronts,' we must do our utmost to avoid contributing to anti-Communist hysteria and must continue, even at cost to ourselves, to defend the civil rights of Communists and other elements." Only by supporting a non-Communist peace program, the FOR concluded, might people "not be confined . . . to a choice between this 'peace' propaganda and that, coming from behind an atomic stockpile here or in Russia, but might have a chance to reject all the varieties of propaganda and choose peace itself."[51]

World federalists were at least as hostile. Numerous activists lauded Cousins's speech at the Waldorf,[52] while others attacked the Communist-led peace drive more directly. In a sermon he delivered in May 1950 at the Community Church of New York, the Rev. Donald Harrington, a world federalist leader, excoriated the fact that, while "the international Communist movement is waging war, both hot and cold," American Communists "have launched an exceedingly widespread and well-financed campaign for 'peace.' " They were not "really interested in peace," he charged, "but in appeasement." Meanwhile, the president of United World Federalists, Alan Cranston, warned the executive council that, through Communist-sponsored peace campaigns, the Soviet government was seeking to use the peace issue for its own purposes. Condemning the Stockholm petition as a cynical maneuver designed to undermine American power, UWF sent a memo to its chapters urging members—and "all Americans"—to refuse to sign "the Communist-inspired" document.[53]

America's atomic scientists also kept their distance from the new movement. Writing to Shapley some two weeks before the Waldorf conference, Victor Weisskopf expressed his regret that the meeting no longer looked like an attempt "to rally the liberal intellectuals here and abroad, in order to further our common aim: peace and freedom." Instead, "in the selection of the participants . . . there was a heavy emphasis on those groups who constantly condoned the Russian attacks on freedom." Consequently, he did not plan to attend. In a message to Joliot-Curie in late 1950, Einstein rejected participation in the Communist-sponsored peace meeting planned for Sheffield, England. "I must confess frankly," he told the French physicist, "that I cannot believe that in the present situation manifestations of such kind will help to bring genuine peace nearer."[54]

The only prominent U.S. atomic scientist—and the only major U.S. peace movement leader—who played a significant role in the Communist-led campaign was Linus Pauling, a distinguished chemist. Although not himself a Communist, Pauling argued that people "must learn how to get along with Communists"; therefore, he belonged to what he called "a number of organizations that are described as Communist-Front organizations" and was willing to work with Communists on peace activities, including the Progressive party campaign of 1948. He became a vice-president of the WFSW and, along with Du Bois, a U.S. vice-president of the September 1949 Continental Congress for World Peace in Mexico City. At the same time, he remained a member of the Emergency Committee of Atomic Scientists and an outspoken proponent of world government.[55]

Pauling's positions overstepped the normal boundaries of both movements.

His unusual attempt to bridge the two was evident at the Mexico City conclave, where he delivered one of the few relatively balanced speeches. Although he charged that "the time seems to be approaching when a scientist must express hatred for Russia in order to be allowed to carry on government-sponsored research," he went on to say that "there is one significant basis for hope now in existence—the United Nations." He contended that "the principal reason for the failure of the move toward international control of atomic energy seems to be opposition by all nations to the abandonment of national sovereignty to any degree." But "the nations of the world need to transfer more of their sovereignty to the United Nations, and in the course of time convert it into an effective world government." For a meeting dominated by anti-American rhetoric, it was a very unorthodox address. Pauling also "jolted his listeners noticeably," the New York Times reported, "when he declared that science was 'not free in the United States or Russia.'" In addition, Pauling signed a letter of protest to Joliot-Curie when the WPC leader charged the United States with practicing germ warfare in Korea.[56]

By the early 1950s, then, it had become apparent that the Communist-led peace campaign in the United States had fallen far short of its goals. Assessing the situation in May 1951, Communist party secretary Eugene Dennis noted glumly that the party was "creating . . . united front peace organizations and campaigns in [its] own image." And though this new movement had adopted "an advanced program"—that is, "the immediate program of the party"—its organization and activity involved "at best only a narrow circle of workers and progressives already under the party's influence."[57]

Mass Movement and Mass Disdain

Overall, then, the Communist-led peace campaign produced limited results in the three major NATO powers. In France and, to a lesser extent, Great Britain, it generated a vigorous mass movement that criticized Western military measures and, especially, nuclear weapons. Even in the United States, where organized Communism was far weaker and more isolated, the campaign received substantial publicity and reached millions of people through the Stockholm petition. But despite the unpopularity of the Bomb and occasional efforts by Communist leaders to moderate their tone and tactics, the organized movement rarely spread very far beyond the orbit of the Communist party and other Soviet sympathizers. Powerful political parties, unions, and church groups condemned the Communist-led campaign. Furthermore, organizations of pacifists, scientists, and world government supporters—themselves critics of militarism and the Bomb—rejected it as well. At times, this stand resulted from their desire to avoid being stigmatized as Communists. But more fundamentally, it reflected their belief that the Communist-led campaign was hypocritical, one-sided, and, therefore, profoundly harmful to the cause it claimed to represent.

"We Are Not Pacifists"

The Communist-Led Campaign in Other Non-Communist Nations

> The Soviet Union does not and cannot want war. . . . The
> Anglo-American imperialist powers are the real instigators.
>
> V. Chakkarai Chettiar, 1949

Canada

During the late 1940s, a Communist-led peace movement also emerged in Canada. The 1946 arrest and conviction of top leaders of Canada's Communist party—the Labour Progressive party—on charges of espionage for the Soviet Union did enormous damage to Canadian Communism. Nevertheless, convinced that the United States would stop at nothing to destroy the Soviet Union and other Communist states, the party threw its diminished resources into the struggle for peace, which it accorded the highest priority.[1] This struggle began to take shape in October 1948, when Harry Ward, a professor emeritus at New York's Union Theological Seminary, who held a very sympathetic view of the Soviet Union, addressed a gathering of friends and former students in Toronto. Alarmed at the foreign policy of the United States, which he claimed was preparing to attack the Soviet Union with nuclear weapons, and inspired by what he had read of the Wroclaw conference, Ward urged the development of a powerful Canadian peace movement. Ward's exhortation appealed to both Communists and non-Communists present at the meeting, and a provisional committee was formed to organize the venture. To establish the movement on a national basis, the committee turned to the Rev. James Endicott, a former United church missionary, who, during his lengthy sojourn in China, had become a keen supporter of the Chinese Communist revolution and of Communism in general. In May 1949, after months of preparatory work by Endicott and others, 530 delegates met in Toronto and officially launched the Canadian Peace Congress (CPC), with Endicott as chair.[2]

Although the central role of Communists and other Soviet sympathizers in the developing movement was clear enough, it seemed for a time that the CPC might be able to attract a more substantial constituency. Organizers invited Canadian FOR leaders to address early gatherings and to appoint delegates to participate in the coordinating bodies of the new organization. Although Endicott, in his first speeches, attacked U.S. "war propaganda" and praised the "Chinese democratic revolutionary forces," he also proclaimed that the new movement "welcomes all points of view." Indeed, he assured Canadians that the CPC was not designed to defend Soviet foreign policy. An early statement of the organization declared that "differences between nations . . . can and must be resolved without recourse to war" and that "the cause of world peace is greater than party, greater than class, and greater than political expediency." The CPC's first resolutions were not inflammatory and included one calling for "the immediate prohibition of the atomic bomb as a weapon of warfare."[3]

Despite these early attempts to develop a broad base of support, the CPC never managed the feat, for it plunged enthusiastically into the worldwide Communist-led peace campaign and eventually became the Canadian branch of the World Peace Council. Representing the CPC at the Paris, Mexico City, and Stockholm gatherings of the Peace Partisans, Endicott served on the committee that drafted the Stockholm Peace Appeal. At Paris, he told the delegates that U.S. air bases on Canadian territory were being readied for an atomic attack on the Soviet Union. In Moscow, according to *Pravda*, he announced that "democratic liberties have been destroyed in America and . . . the warmongers hold sway there." Assisted by appearances of the Rev. Hewlett Johnson and by the work of local affiliates, Endicott and the CPC eventually obtained the signatures of some 300,000 Canadians on the Stockholm petition. Most of the petition effort, though, came from the Communist party. According to his son, Endicott developed a close "personal relationship with the leaders of the Canadian party," who secured "a working agreement" with him, which he understood "was communicated to local party committees." Meanwhile, in February 1950 the party's national committee ordered "the entire energy and activity of the party into the fight for peace." Endicott's son has maintained that, despite this close relationship and his Communist sympathies, the CPC leader never formally joined the party because he believed that he could "be most effective" in this way.[4]

The efficacy of Endicott and the CPC were sorely tested during the Korean War, when they took up the cry of germ warfare. In a broadcast from China via Radio Peking in April 1952, Endicott corroborated Chinese claims that the U.S. government had been deploying germ-laden insects; "in fact," he added, "I have caught some myself." He would not provide a "detailed and specific account," though, "because I do not wish to make available to the American germ war criminals any useful facts." Returning to Canada to deal with a storm of criticism, Endicott defended his charges in a fighting speech before CPC supporters in Toronto. Here he again charged that "lawless American militarists" in Korea were using germ warfare against the people of China but added that "the greatest, most universal, most effective movement of the people of the world" would defeat these "homicidal maniacs." In another speech to the CPC's Toronto affiliate, Endicott claimed that the U.S. government's "degenerate warmongering" included not only "the attempt to re-build a Nazi army in Europe" but "use of germ war" in China and Korea, which "has been proved to all who have ears to hear or eyes to see." In response, Lester Pearson, Canadian minister of external affairs, denounced the germ warfare charges as a "clumsy hoax." The Soviet government was apparently more impressed, for later that year it named Endicott as a recipient of the Stalin Peace Prize.[5]

Most Canadian pacifists kept their distance from these ventures, particularly as the Communist tone of the CPC became more intrusive. Anxious to offset the weakness of Canadian pacifism and acquainted with Endicott through their ministries in the United church, a few individual pacifists had helped recruit him to head the new movement.[6] But most pacifists and their organizations were soon repelled by his support for Communist revolutions and by the CPC's development as a champion of Soviet foreign policy. In response to an early invitation by the Toronto Peace Council, one of the CPC's early affiliates, to send delegates to its meetings, the national council of the Canadian FOR discussed the issue for months. Some FOR leaders argued that the political orientation of the Peace Council could be modified from within. But others contended that the group was already regarded as Communist by all shades of opinion and that the FOR had a fundamentally different approach to the question of peace. Eventually, the FOR national council passed along the invitation to its Toronto branch with a "strong recommendation" that no official representatives be appointed. Reflecting some years later on his relations with pacifist groups, Endicott remarked bitterly that he had been "extremely disappointed with the American FOR"—which, he charged, took "its direction from the American State Department"—and "somewhat disappointed with the Canadian FOR." He had concluded, he said, that "a large number of people in the FOR do not seek reconciliation with the Communists but secretly hate them."[7]

Certainly, most Canadians showed little love for the CPC and for the Stockholm Peace Appeal, which many repudiated once their Communist orientation and sponsorship became apparent. With the exception of the Communists, all of Canada's political parties denounced the CPC, even the most left-wing among them, the social democratic Cooperative Commonwealth Federation.

Although a few of its local activists supported the new peace movement, the leadership strongly opposed it. M. J. Coldwell, the national leader of the party, described the Stockholm appeal as a "cruel deception," an "instrument of Russian policy." The 1950 national convention of the Cooperative Commonwealth Federation unanimously condemned the Stockholm petition, and its national office urged members to have nothing to do with the Communist-led peace movement. Meanwhile, newspapers denounced the CPC as a "Communist front," and groups of Canadians—often composed of recent immigrants from Europe—harassed and disrupted CPC meetings. Thus, although the CPC developed a strong network, capable of handling petition drives and of organizing large meetings (including Endicott's Toronto rally of 1952, which drew 10,000 people), it ended up largely isolated beyond the ranks of Communists and their sympathizers.[8]

Australia

Initially, a different pattern emerged in Australia. In May 1948, at its first postwar congress, the Australian Communist party declared that "the Anglo-American imperialists" had "assumed the role of Hitler and the Japanese military fascists" in the world. Therefore, it was the "duty of communists to lead the resistance to the warmongers and to organize peacelovers around a broad program of peaceful cooperation among the nations," including "the outlawry of atomic weapons." Perhaps because party leaders doubted the imminence of war, however, for some years the party did fairly little along these lines. Instead, it concentrated on strengthening its position within the labor unions and exerting pressure on Australia's Labor government. Only the Communist party's intellectuals, disturbed by the sectarian attitudes of some of its leaders, worked to develop a peace campaign.[9]

Nevertheless, in the aftermath of the Paris conference of April 1949, the party mobilized its resources behind the formation of a new movement. Reporting to the Communist party's Central Committee Plenum that June, party leader L. L. Sharkey declared that "our party, and all friends of peace, have a tremendous responsibility to bring before the Australian masses the findings of the Peace Congress and to organize a corresponding peace movement and peace sentiment throughout Australia." That July, in Melbourne, a more diverse group laid plans for an Australian Peace Council (APC), and in September the APC was officially launched at a public rally in the Melbourne Town Hall, attended by some 3,000 people.[10] The APC grew rapidly and soon claimed 150 local peace committees affiliated with APC branches in all states except Tasmania. In late 1949, the APC organized a widespread "Peace Ballot" which, the following year, reemerged in the form of the Stockholm peace petition. According to the APC, it drew more than 200,000 signatures. Moreover, in the spring of 1950 the APC convened an Australian Peace Congress, attended by some 10,000 people, with delegates allegedly representing 549,000 Australians. The congress issued an "Australian Peace Manifesto," which called for banning the atomic bomb, promoting disarmament, renouncing conscription, opening diplomatic relations with Communist China, and preventing military intervention in Southeast Asia.[11] The driving force in these ventures was the Communist party and especially its intellectuals. Three of the ten members of the APC's executive committee were Communist party members, as were the first three national organizing secretaries of the APC.[12]

Despite the prominent role of Communists within the APC, it drew a substantial number of non-Communists as well. The best-known of them were the "three peace parsons": the Rev. Victor James, the APC's first secretary; the Rev. Alfred Dickie, its first chair; and the Rev. Frank Hartley, who soon joined James as co-secretary. Alarmed by the bellicose pronouncements and policies of the early Cold War years, they felt considerably greater sympathy for Communism and for the Soviet Union than did most Australians. So did another founder and leader of the APC, Jessie Street, who was a former president of the Australian Soviet Friendship Society and a warm supporter of the Soviet Union. The influential role that non-Communists played within the APC may also have reflected the need of the Australian Communist party, then in the process of disintegration, for allies. Indeed, the party was reeling from external attacks, including government arrest of its leaders, official outlawry (until the measure was overturned by Australia's high court), and a proposal to outlaw it by constitutional amendment. Moreover, the Communist party remained unconvinced that a peace campaign should be its top priority. Consequently, the party gave the APC only intermittent support and a rather loose rein.[13]

Nevertheless, in the first years of its existence, the APC adopted an unmistakeably pro-Soviet orientation to world affairs. It focused on the dangers of America's nuclear weapons, placed all blame for the Korean War on the United States and South Korea, and repeatedly tacked party slogans onto its resolutions. Protesting against the APC's one-sided interpretation of the Korean conflict, three of its more prominent members announced their resignations in June 1950. In September 1950, the APC's Victoria affiliate contrasted the "attempted terrorism" against the peace movement in the United States with government support for it in Communist nations.[14] The featured speaker at the APC's Peace Congress, the Rev. Hewlett Johnson, sharply assailed the "war" policies of the United States, from the Marshall Plan to nuclear deterrence, and called for "smashing the power of the warmongers." Nuclear war, he said, was desired only by "a few profiteers and magnates." As for the Russians, "they plan peace; they think peace; they speak peace." He had "seen the glorious things they are doing there," believed that Stalin was totally sincere, and was "convinced that the Soviet Union will never be the first to drop an atomic bomb." To no one's surprise, the APC joined the World Peace Council, which it called "the organized international peoples' movement for peace," and, at the WPC's founding meeting in Warsaw, one APC leader chaired a session and three were elected to its presidium. The APC also assailed the United States for practicing germ warfare in Korea.[15]

The APC's pro-Soviet stance soon generated widespread antipathy in Australia. The press bitterly denounced its activities, and many cities and municipalities refused to allow it to use public meeting halls. When the Rev. Johnson arrived to address the April 1950 Peace Congress, the *Church Standard*, official publication of his denomination in Melbourne, denounced the congress as "part of the world-wide attempt to identify the cause of Russian communism with the cause of international peace"—an identification that was "completely false and dangerously misleading." [16] The APC faced not only the bitter antagonism of the conservative parties but, in early 1950, proscription by the executive bodies of the New South Wales and Victoria Labor parties. In response, the leaders of the APC issued a statement (*You Can't Ban Peace*) declaring that "the Communist Party did not establish the Australian Peace Council, does not control its policy or activities, and cannot use it for ends other than advancing world peace." But a year later, the Labor party's triennial national conference officially banned the APC. Dominated by fervent anti-Communists, the conference resolved that no one could remain a Labor party member who associated with the APC, which it described as a "subsidiary organization of the Communist Party." [17]

Australian pacifists, though less virulent in their anti-Communism, generally stayed clear of the Communist-led peace campaign. As civil libertarians, pacifists spoke out against the arrest of Australian Communist leaders for allegedly subversive statements and against the government plan to dissolve the Communist party.[18] At the same time, recalling past Communist tactics and shifts of position, many pacifists doubted the APC's sincerity. In January 1950, the annual Pacifist Conference rejected pacifist organizational affiliation with the APC. In addition, although the conference asked the *Peacemaker*, the most prominent pacifist journal, not to attack the new organization, the conference requested that it not publish APC material. The editor thoroughly agreed with this stand, as did regular columnists. Sometimes pacifists evinced a more sympathetic attitude. In October 1950, one subscriber to the *Peacemaker*, complaining that "the peace journals are neck and neck with the Red baiters," argued that this would not save them from being discredited. But in the following issue, another reader replied: "It is of little account that pacifists are continually pronounced supporters of the enemy. Of paramount importance is that the charge should never be justified." [19]

Europe and Japan

In Italy, the Communist-led peace drive produced mixed results. With an unusually large and popular Communist party at its disposal, the peace campaign in Italy easily developed as a mass movement. Condemning the United States and other Western "imperialist" nations in late 1949, the Italian Partisans of Peace promised to organize peace demonstrations "in each family, in each district, in each village" throughout Italy. Some progress toward this goal was apparently made, for the Stockholm petition, largely circulated by the Communists, drew nearly seventeen million signatures. In his memoirs, the Rev. Johnson recalled speaking before an "immense audience" at a WPC-sponsored gathering in Rome. Furthermore, with such overwhelming Communist involvement, the movement invariably adopted the proper approach. A Communist-sponsored peace conference in Milan proclaimed proudly: "We are not pacifists. We will fight to maintain peace." Yet Communist-organized peace meetings were sometimes thinly attended, drawing far more heavily on middle-class intellectuals than on the party's working-class base. Similarly, party-led efforts to stage protest strikes against "American imperialist aggression" fizzled when workers gave them no more than lukewarm support.[20] If the Italian Communists were able to reach millions of people with their "peace" message, they had less success in mobilizing them to support it.

Communist parties also led vigorous peace campaigns in Scandinavia. In Sweden, the Communist party took the lead in forming the Swedish Peace Committee and set the tone of its subsequent activities, including circulation of the Stockholm petition, affiliation with the WPC, and accusations of U.S. germ warfare in Korea. Although one party leader claimed that "a united front in the struggle for peace" was forged "from below," this merely put the best face on the fact that the new movement had limited appeal to leading non-Communists. The non-Communist press and political parties, including the ruling Social Democrats, either deliberately ignored or roundly condemned the Stockholm peace conference and the ensuing peace petition.[21] In neighboring Denmark, the Communists took the lead in organizing the Partisans of Peace, which, under the direction of Professor Mogens Fog (a party member) and Elin Appel (a former Liberal member of parliament), circulated the Stockholm appeal. Fog and Appel were attractive figures and, initially, many non-Communist Danes signed the petition. Nevertheless, with growing recognition of the petition's sponsorship, the campaign lost momentum. Its decline was accelerated by the Communist party's clumsy handling of the popular Niels Bohr, whom, that spring, the party falsely accused of working on the U.S. hydrogen bomb and, therefore, being akin to Hitler. When, only a few weeks later, Bohr released his Open Letter, the party reversed itself and claimed Bohr as a supporter of the Stockholm Peace Appeal. Bohr, in turn, publicly repudiated the appeal. By July 1950, nearly 10,000 Danish signers of the Stockholm appeal—about 10 percent of the total—had formally requested that their names be removed from the petition.[22]

In the Netherlands, too, the Communist party organized a peace and disarmament campaign firmly under its control. Delegations of Communists and some non-Communists attended the Communist-led international peace conferences of 1948–49. Although the non-Communists were disturbed by what they saw at Wroclaw and Paris, the Communists evinced great enthusiasm. Pushing ahead, they organized the Dutch Peace Council, which affiliated with the WPC and—powered by the country's strong Communist party—soon had branches throughout the country. The activities of the Dutch Peace Council initially inspired a flurry of support, including a circulation of 20,000 for its newspaper and half a million signatures on the Stockholm peace petition. Nevertheless, the Communist character of the Dutch Peace Council scared away the vast bulk of the country's population. Although the Dutch party and the Soviet Union had won substantial popular sympathy thanks to their wartime antifascist role, this fund of goodwill ebbed in the postwar years, particularly after the Communist coup in Czechoslovakia. The population also looked askance at the Dutch Communist party's adulation of the Soviet Union, epitomized by party leader Paul de Groot's 1949 statement that Communists would greet with cheers the liberating Soviet army. As a result, support for the Dutch Peace Council remained largely confined to Holland's dwindling number of Soviet sympathizers.[23]

Elsewhere in non-Communist Europe, the pattern was much the same. In the aftermath of the Paris conference, members and sympathizers of the Swiss Labor party (Switzerland's Communist party) organized the Swiss Movement for Peace, which gathered 250,000 signatures on the Stockholm petition and affiliated with the WPC. Widely viewed as a Soviet mouthpiece, the Swiss group soon aroused considerable popular hostility,[24] as did its Belgian counterpart, the Belgian Union for the Defense of Peace, which was established under similar auspices.[25] During 1950, in the inhospitable circumstances of post–civil war Greece, young members of the outlawed Communist party founded the Democratic Front for Peace, which they transformed the following year into the United Democratic Youth of Greece.[26] Communists also organized the German Peace Partisans, which, in mid-July 1950, reportedly dispatched some 10,000 Germans from East and West Germany into West Berlin to circulate the Stockholm petition. Here, according to *Pravda*, "the savage fascist morals of the Anglo-American warmongers" became evident, for "the American gangsters" set "several thousand fascist thugs," including the police ("that band of neo-S.S. men") upon them; some were deported to the East, while others languished "in American dungeons." Pacifists in West Germany were not impressed, and one complained that some of the people preaching peace would have no qualms about establishing a German armament industry after the Red Army took over the country.[27]

In those few non-Communist countries where the Soviet Union had some leverage, the new movement fared somewhat better. Austria, still under four-power occupation, for a time provided the Communist-led peace campaign with a friendly environment and even the site for the WPC headquarters. In June 1950, a largely Communist gathering of some 2,000 people in Vienna launched an Austrian peace crusade. Addressing the assemblage, the chief speaker, Ernst Fischer, a Communist member of the Austrian parliament, warned that "powerful single groups of greedy millionaires, political adventurers, and hysterical agitators are preparing for war." Although the turnout at the conference's mass rally proved much smaller than predicted, in its subsequent campaign for the Stockholm appeal the new movement gathered half a million signatures among Austrians.[28] The picture was also somewhat brighter for the Communist-led peace campaign in Finland, which, after its defeat by the Soviet Union in World War II, sought to remain on good terms with its powerful neighbor. Viewing the struggle for peace as its primary task, the large Finnish Communist party established and sustained the Finnish Peace Committee, founded in 1949. Like its counterparts, the Finnish Peace Committee adopted a very favorable stance toward Communist-bloc nations while excoriating the United States and other NATO countries. Unlike most of its counterparts, the Finnish Peace Committee enjoyed some success in public life and, indeed, became the largest peace group in Finland.[29]

If Japan had not been under the U.S. occupation regime, the Communist-led peace campaign might have flourished there as well. Although occupation authorities prevented Japanese delegates from attending the April 1949 conference in Paris, members of the Japanese Communist party and other left-wing intellectuals later that year established the Society for the Defense of Peace. Thereafter, this group was renamed the Japan Peace Committee and became an affiliate of the WPC. Under its auspices, Communist party members and front groups threw themselves into the growing agitation against nuclear weapons, especially the Stockholm peace petition campaign. Alarmed by this turn of events, as well as by the onset of the Korean War, U.S. occupation authorities banned the 1950 peace ceremony in Hiroshima and stepped up their growing "Red Purge." The petitioning, however, continued. In late March 1951, a year after the campaign's inception, its organizers claimed that nearly 6.5 million Japanese had signed the Stockholm Peace Appeal.[30]

The Third World

Appealing to revolutionary nationalism and condemning Western colonialism, the Communist-led peace campaign also made significant strides in the Third World. Communists successfully organized groups under their control in the Middle East, Latin America, Africa, and large parts of Asia. In August 1950, *Izvestia* claimed that "the movement of partisans of peace" had been expanding rapidly in Iran, Turkey, Israel, Syria, Egypt, Lebanon, Iraq, Sudan, Algeria, Tunisia, and Morocco. In Israel alone, where the Permanent Committee in Defense of Peace had been formed, the Stockholm Peace Appeal allegedly had been signed by some 260,000 people, more than 35 percent of the adult population. According to Moscow radio broadcasts, Africans were being summoned from their jungle fastnesses by means of drums to win their support for banning the atomic bomb. "Since many people cannot write," one broadcast noted, "they sign the peace petition by impressing finger marks. Heads of families sign with their thumb print while the last-born of a family signs with his hand."[31] Although such accounts may have been fanciful, Communists did succeed in building WPC affiliates in many Third World nations that the established peace groups had never reached.

Even so, there were limits to the progress of the Communist-led peace campaign in the Third World, as illustrated by its experience in India. Deeply committed to the antibourgeois strategy and violent tactics of Indian Communist party leader B. T. Ranadive, Indian Communism had difficulty shifting gears and developing an all-class movement for international peace. Consequently, although the party did manage to organize the First All-India Peace Congress in Calcutta in November 1949, it drew together only those organizations under party control. The conference established an All-India Peace Committee (AIPC), with V. Chakkarai Chettiar as president. He confidently told the delegates that "the Soviet Union does not and cannot want war," of which "the Anglo-American imperialist powers are the real instigators." Catching the drift of proceedings, *Pravda* and *Izvestia* headlined stories on the conference "We Will Never Fight, Under Any Conditions, Against the U.S.S.R."[32] This pure party line, however, seems to have had relatively little popular appeal. Although the AIPC predicted that it would collect "millions" of signatures on the Stockholm peace petition, by September 1950 it had gathered only 300,000, a figure which the party conceded represented a dismal failure. Among those prominent advocates of peace who refused to sign the Stockholm appeal was Jayaprakash Narayan, a disciple of Gandhi who led the Indian Socialist party.[33]

Meanwhile, pressure mounted on the Indian Communist party to moderate its position toward peace. In January 1950, the Cominform told the Indian party that "the peace movement . . . must be developed throughout the country along the line laid down in *The Defence of Peace and the Struggle Against the Warmongers*." This meant that peace "must become the pivot of the entire activity of the party and the mass organizations. It is our duty to merge the struggle for national liberation with that for peace." Having inspected the Indian peace movement that April, J. D. Bernal also chided the AIPC for narrow-minded sectarianism. Indian peace workers, he wrote in *Crossroads*, the Communist weekly, "are all too few" and had "demanded of their followers perhaps too much understanding and too far-reaching political agreement." In this context, conflict between leftists and moderates dominated an October 1950 All-India Peace Convention, convened in Bombay, and later that year two leaders of the Indian party traveled to Europe to seek advice on the growing crisis. Interviewing British Communist leader R. Palme Dutt, they asked him whether the peace campaign should dominate party activities. Dutt replied that "the peace movement must become the main activity of the party" and that it should be based on "a broad front of all sections of the Indian people." Meanwhile, P. C. Joshi, a former general secretary of the party who had been expelled for reformism, began to seize upon the peace issue as a means of ousting the current leadership.[34]

In response to these pressures, the Indian Communist party and the peace movement were reorganized in 1951. At the end of March it was announced that *Crossroads* would drop its "narrow sectarian outlook" and would "be devoted above all to the cause of Peace." An All-India Peace Convention met in Bombay in May 1951 and established an All-India Peace Council, with Saifuddin Kitchlew, who had a long record of leadership in the Indian National Congress, as president. During the conference sessions, well-known Communists kept in the background and, in their place, put forward prominent figures from the Congress party, artists, and writers. As another means of broadening the movement's appeal, the convention voted "to make special approaches at all organizational levels to all sections of opinion which are still outside the movement, including the large body of pacifist opinion, led by the close Ashram disciples of Mahatma Gandhi, and to the various religious bodies which stand for peace." According to an AIPC publication, the May 1951 convention represented "a historic milestone in the history of the Indian peace movement. In some ways, one can call this convention the real starting point of a fully national movement." [35]

Nevertheless, the AIPC continued to be closely tied to Communist policy, for the new party leadership and strategy remained thoroughly aligned with the ambitions of Communist nations. The peace movement, the party leadership declared, "must explain to the people how the liberation of Tibet is not a threat to peace, but a decisive blow against the instigators of war, and uphold the heroic action of the Chinese volunteers who, by smashing the plans of the American warmongers to enslave the Korean and Chinese peoples, strengthened the cause of world peace." Echoing this interpretation, the new AIPC, in one of its first publications, said nothing of Gandhianism. Instead, citing "the million dead of Korea" and "the slaughter in Malaya and Vietnam," it proclaimed that "our hearts beat in warm solidarity with the victims of aggression." Avoiding the implication that Communist nations bore some responsibility for the wars then raging, the AIPC called for rescinding the U.N. resolution branding the People's Republic of China as an aggressor in Korea. The Bomb received a token nod as "the peril which hangs over humanity," but, in line with WPC priorities at this time, "the unconditional prohibition of all manner of atomic weapons" rated no more than ninth place on the AIPC agenda. Instead, as a loyal affiliate of the World Peace Council, the AIPC championed the WPC's petition for a five-power peace pact, which it predicted would draw the signatures of eleven million people in India. Given the AIPC's subservience to Cominform policy—and its consequent isolation—it is not surprising that, a year after the target date, the petition had been been signed by fewer than one-fourth this number.[36]

The Nonaligned and the Aligned

As in other parts of the non-Communist world, nonaligned peace groups in these nations almost invariably kept their distance from Communist-led peace ventures. Distributing a peace appeal in 1950 in the Netherlands, Church and Peace, while condemning preparations for "a new war" as "deliberate suicide for Europe," also criticized Communist-organized peace activity. "Communists say . . . 'Don't unload American weapons, dockers,' " it noted. "But would they say this of Soviet weapons? Do not support the Communist party, whose peace efforts are one-sided only." Neither Church and Peace nor ANVA proved willing to cooperate with the Dutch Peace Council. To counteract the supposition that it had anything to do with the Communist-led peace campaign, the Swiss Peace Council officially changed its name to the Union of Non-Communist Peace Groups in Switzerland.[37] In Denmark, the WILPF group agreed to do no more than send an observer to the WPC's Sheffield conference in November 1950. Early the following year, the WILPF held a joint meeting with other Danish peace groups to discuss their attitude to the Partisans of Peace. A WILPF leader reported that, although a majority favored "keeping our minds open and hearing what the partisans had to say," it also opposed "letting down the iron curtain (excuse me) in our own country." The Danish WILPF decided to remain open-minded but "not to take political action together." In 1952, it summarized its position toward Communist-led peace movements as "willingness to meet and discuss problems with them but no political cooperation."[38]

Serious tensions between nonaligned and Communist-led peace groups also developed in New Zealand. A pacifist minister wrote that he had signed the Stockholm petition "because I'm prepared to object to any weapon so horrible as to destroy the God-given gift of life"; but "active co-operation" with its Communist-organized sponsor, the New Zealand Peace Council, "is exceedingly difficult, if not altogether impossible." In February 1951, an editorial in the *New Zealand Christian Pacifist* reported that some of its readers "feel qualms . . . regarding active co-operation in the work and witness of the New Zealand Peace Council." These qualms, it added, arose "much less from fear of being smeared as associates of undesirables than from doubts as to whether we have to any real extent a common goal." Later that year, at the annual conference of the New Zealand Christian Pacifist Society, a discussion took place about the relationship of the organization with the Peace Council. Conference participants decided that, though the pacifist group might send "observers" to Peace Council meetings, it was "unable to affiliate," for it had a "special responsibility" to propagate its "own 'peculiar' point of view."[39]

A similar attitude prevailed among nonaligned peace groups in West Germany. According to *Peace News*, the German section of the WRI "had a lively discussion on their relationship with Communist inspired organizations" in late 1950. "It was agreed to avoid co-operation with such organizations, but to show the same goodwill, understanding, and friendship towards individual Communists and fellow travellers as would be extended to any other individual." About the same time, the group issued a statement condemning the government's decision to dismiss Communists and fellow travelers from government employment.[40] At its annual meeting in September 1950, the German Peace Society resolved to dissociate itself "from organizations that, under the name of peace, are following policies of force or are allowing themselves to be misled by such aims." It also declared that it regarded "the 'banning of the atomic bomb' as insufficient as long as the abolition of all other means of warfare is not demanded at the same time." This implicit critique of the Stockholm

Peace Appeal informed an August 1950 message from the sponsors of World Peace Day in Berlin, who wrote that they refused "to sign a call to outlaw the atomic bomb so long as it is not linked with the outlawing of civil war." [41]

Nonaligned peace groups in Sweden also took a firm stand against cooperation. Rejecting the Swedish Peace Committee and the Stockholm appeal, they issued their own calls for peace. In November 1950, for example, a "Swedish Peace Appeal" was issued by the Swedish Peace Council, the WILPF, the Swedish Peace and Arbitration Society, the World Peace Mission, the Teachers Peace Association, the Mothers' Peace League, the Youth Peace Society, the FOR, the Group for World Government, the Parliamentary Group for World Federal Government, the Workers' Central Organization, the Union of Cooperative Women's Guilds, and other non-Communist organizations. The signatories appealed for an end to the arms race; disarmament, safeguarded by international control; the creation of an international force to replace national military forces; an international court to settle conflicts between nations; and "the creation of a supra-national authority equipped with adequate powers, preferably by strengthening and expanding the United Nations to become a world government based upon international law." These were, they said, "the demands of the free democratic peace movement" and "must not be confused with the so-called Stockholm Appeal." They emphasized that "our peace work is independent of the interests of power politics and that the demands of this Appeal are directed to all people and all countries." The Swedish Peace Committee dismissed these groups as "the bourgeois peace movement," and they dismissed the Peace Committee as "the Communist peace movement." [42]

Only in exceptional cases and to a limited degree were these distinctions muddied. The most dramatic contrast to the pattern in other countries emerged in Finland, where one of the nonaligned movement's luminaries, Felix Iversen, as well as the group he led, the Finnish Peace Union, assisted in founding the Communist-dominated Finnish Peace Committee. Iverson also became an official of the WPC and a recipient of the Stalin Peace Prize. Furthermore, some Finnish WILPF members worked closely with the new Communist-led group. But these developments inspired substantial controversy within Finland's peace community. A sharp debate broke out inside the Peace Union which, as a result, lost about one-third of its members. Eventually, most pro-Soviet activists chose to mobilize through the Peace Committee and most nonaligned activists through the Peace Union, Finland's second largest peace organization. [43]

A more modest exception emerged in Austria. Although Professor Johannes Ude, a distinguished pacifist, publicly refused to sign the Stockholm Peace Appeal, a group of nonaligned peace organizations did agree to participate in the June 1950 Communist-led peace congress in Vienna. Their official statement of participation emphasized their belief that "the manufacture of atomic weapons is a crime against humanity"; however, it added that "the atom bomb is not the only means of mass destruction; and a war does not begin in the first place with the dropping of bombs; it has already begun when the spirit of hatred and mistrust is spread." Hans Thirring, who had attended the Paris congress of April 1949 and had been disappointed by its anti-Western tone, agreed to serve as a member of the presidium for this congress. Nevertheless, he stirred a furor shortly before it began when, in an open letter, he condemned the Communist-led peace campaign as hypocritical. Thereafter, addressing the gathering, he pointed out that millions of people in the West would not support a peace movement while Eastern countries "are known only for their iron military discipline, their determination to destroy capitalism, the uncompromising and irreconcilable speech of their statesmen and press, and their almost stereotyped voting in the United Nations." He told delegates from the East that "if you want to end the cold war and the war hysteria, see that the words and deeds of your statesmen confirm" the claims "that the Soviet Union does not need war, does not want war, and . . . is ready to cooperate . . . in the United Nations." [44] To activists in the Communist-led campaign, this must have served as yet another illustration of how unreliable the nonaligned peace movement remained.

A Movement Contained

Throughout the balance of the non-Communist world, the Communist-led peace campaign usually met with little success in moving beyond the party's regular constituency. As the beneficiary of widespread resentment at Western colonialism and racism in Third World nations, it did make some progress in this region. And it developed some influence in Finland and Austria, then under the shadow of Soviet power. But these were exceptions to the rule. For the most part, the World Peace Council could rely only on those forces already fond of the Soviet Union: Communist parties and their sympathizers. Committed to very different values and goals, nonaligned peace groups almost invariably kept their distance, while the general public often grew hostile. Here, as in the United States, Great Britain, and France, the Communist-led peace campaign was stigmatized and contained by its obvious Cold War partisanship.

"Stalin Is Our Peace"

The Communist-Led Campaign in Communist Nations

> By signing the Stockholm appeal, Soviet citizens will express . . . their unqualified devotion to the great standard-bearer of peace, the leader of all peoples, Comrade Stalin.
>
> Soviet Peace Committee, 1950

The Soviet Union

Naturally, the Communist-led peace campaign received an enormously favorable send-off in the Soviet Union. An all-star cast of Soviet delegates was dispatched to the many Communist-led peace conferences in other lands, leading Soviet writer Ilya Ehrenburg to remark, in retrospect, that he devoted more of his time "to congresses, conferences, and council meetings than to my professional work." To lay the groundwork for a Soviet peace movement, a meeting in early July 1949 initiated, on August 25, an All-Soviet Congress of Supporters of Peace in Moscow, addressed by pro-Soviet luminaries of East and West. Warning that "the imperialists intend to go on with unleashing an aggressive war," Soviet writer Nikolai Tikhonov contrasted this with the Soviet "struggle for peace." In its search for peace, he said, "the Soviet government two and one-half years ago proposed that the atomic weapon should be outlawed." But "in the name of war, the ruling circles of the U.S.A. and Britain are still thwarting the implementation of this proposal." On hand for the occasion, J. D. Bernal brought the greetings of foreign scientists to the Soviet people and to "the great protector of science, Stalin." He predicted that, "soon, in the United States, no one who has not been an inveterate enemy of the Soviet Union will be allowed to teach or engage in scientific research." According to *Izvestia*, another Soviet participant suggested that "our best answer to the instigators of war should be intensification of the struggle for communism, an upswing in labor productivity, and strengthening of the economic and military might of our country." [1]

Inspired by such messages, the All-Soviet Congress elected a Soviet Peace Committee, chaired by Tikhonov, and dispatched a message to Stalin. "The common people throughout the world have faith in the ultimate victory over imperialist barbarism," the gathering declared. "Our friends from abroad have assured us that the peoples of their countries are determined to struggle against warmongers and consolidate friendship with the peoples of the Soviet Union." Having established the Soviet Peace Committee, the congress "entrusted it with the task of strengthening friendship among peoples, unmasking warmongers, and fighting for peace." [2]

The Soviet Peace Committee's first major task was to launch a vast, nation-wide mobilization around the Stockholm Peace Appeal, which had been written by Ehrenburg.[3] After several months of preparatory work, Soviet Peace Committee leader V. V. Kuznetsov kicked off the campaign on June 19, 1950, in an address before the Supreme Soviet, nominally the ruling body of the Soviet Union. Lauding the Partisans of Peace, which he claimed "unites more than 800,000,000 people in 76 countries," Kuznetsov went on to draw a sharp contrast between Soviet virtue and Western villainy:

Comrade Deputies! The great Soviet people—the builder of a communist society—marches in the first rank of the fighters for enduring peace and friendship among the peoples. The Soviet people ardently approve the peace-loving foreign policy of our government. . . . Throughout its entire existence, the Soviet Union has undeviatingly followed the Leninist-Stalinist policy of peace and friendly relations with all states and peoples on the basis of mutual respect and complete equality of rights.

Our wise leader and teacher, the leader of the Soviet government, the great Stalin, has emphasized more than once that "the foundation of our relations with the capitalist countries lies in admitting the coexistence of the two opposite systems" and that the Soviet Union . . . really does pursue a policy of peace.

The Soviet "policy of strengthening an enduring peace," however, was "opposed by the policy of preparing a new world war followed by the imperialists." Calling upon the Supreme Soviet to resist Western warmongers by adopting the Stockholm Peace Appeal, Kuznetsov drew stormy applause. Even more prolonged applause followed when he concluded: "The peoples of all countries know that when it is a matter of defending peace they can confidently rely on the Soviet people led by the Communist Party and the great Stalin." To what was reported as "thunderous applause," the Supreme Soviet unanimously endorsed the Stockholm appeal.[4]

The Soviet peace campaign now surged forward. On June 24, *Pravda* reported that "millions of agitators" were explaining the Stockholm appeal "to the masses of workers." In this fashion, they would "aid Party organizations in the development of socialist competition to achieve fulfillment of plans ahead of schedule." Indeed, the press trumpeted stories of workers planning to fight for peace by overfulfilling their production quotas. According to *Pravda*, Stalin Prize winner N. V. Ugolkov told a meeting at the Red Proletarian Factory that "all Soviet people warmly approve the historic decision of the Supreme Soviet," but, for workers, "the strengthening of our motherland, bastion of world peace, is our contribution to the struggle for peace and against the warmongers." Therefore, he promised "to fulfill three years' quota by the anniversary of the great October revolution." Meanwhile, on June 29, Soviet Peace Committee chair Tikhonov pointed out that the Supreme Soviet expected the Stockholm petition to be signed by all Soviet citizens. On the following day, when it began the petition drive, the Soviet Peace Committee expressed its own "firm conviction that all Soviet citizens will respond to this call." Indeed, "by signing the Stockholm appeal, Soviet citizens will express their devotion to the cause of peace, their readiness to defend peace throughout the world, their monolithic solidarity around their own Bolshevist party and their unqualified devotion to the great standard-bearer of peace, the leader of all peoples, Comrade Stalin."[5]

Clearly, this was an offer that could not be refused. During the first week of July 1950, *Pravda* and *Izvestia* carried 173 appeals, declarations by prominent Soviet citizens, news items, editorials, and reports of meetings held throughout the Soviet Union related to the Stockholm petition. In one of them, a letter to "all working men and women," the Central Council of Trade Unions called upon all workers to sign the Stockholm peace petition, thus "averting the war being prepared by the imperialists." On July 1, the day after the drive began, *Pravda* reported: "Workers of Capital Unanimously Sign Stockholm Petition." A welder in the S. N. Kirov Dynamo plant allegedly explained: "Can we forget that the imperialists, the ferocious enemies of our motherland and of all progressive humanity, are openly carrying on preparation for a new war and have already gone over to direct acts of aggression in Korea?" From Stalingrad, on July 5, came the news, via *Pravda*, that "the working people of this heroic town are unanimously signing the Stockholm manifesto." In what *Pravda* described as "moving letters," two schoolteachers announced: "We joyfully place our signatures to the Stockholm manifesto. Stalin is our peace. Stalin is our happiness." People's Artist Cherkasov, a member of the Soviet Peace Committee, argued that "the signature of every Soviet citizen is a powerful rebuke to the base machinations of the Anglo-American imperialists." On July 10, ten days into the campaign, *Pravda* reported enthusiastically that 96,360,866 Soviet citizens had signed the Stockholm peace petition. At mass meetings and gatherings everywhere, the Soviet people "are condemning the activities of the American warmongers . . . and are demanding an end to the aggression against the freedom-loving Korean people." In "factories, collective farms, machine and tractor stations, and state farms the working people are keeping a Stakhanovite peace watch, overfulfilling production plans . . . and lowering costs." [6]

Indeed, prodding Soviet citizens to work harder provided a key aspect of the campaign. In its message to Soviet workers, the Council of Trade Unions expressed its "firm confidence that the working people of our country, in signing the appeal for banning atomic weapons, will develop wider socialist competition for pre-schedule fulfillment and overfulfillment of national economic plans and for further strengthening the might of our socialist motherland, vanguard of the worldwide front of peace, democracy, and socialism." To what extent this actually happened remains debatable, but success stories soon abounded in the nation's press. According to *Pravda*, "collective farmers, combine operators and tractor drivers" decided to "pledge excellent harvesting and more grain for the country and thus contribute to the cause of peace." Proclaiming that his signature represented "serious obligations," one worker purportedly swore "to devote every day, every hour to consolidating the might of the motherland." In Tbilisi, *Pravda* reported, "the workers of . . . the Stalin Railroad Repair Yard have resolved to strengthen their signatures of protest against war by new labor exploits. About 1000 workers in this enterprise are overfulfilling their quotas." [7]

Everywhere, it seemed, the people's message was the same. From Kuibyshev province came word of declarations in the local newspaper by people who, to further the peace petition drive, were embarking on new Stakhanovite tasks. "Knowing that the best answer to the warmongers' machinations is our concern for the strength of the Soviet state," declared a locomotive engineer, "I will work with still greater determination and effort and fulfill at least three quotas per shift." Another "Stakhanovite peace watch" occurred in Minsk, where lathe tender Maria Gur reportedly managed to "fulfill her norms 300% to 350% regularly." She allegedly told *Pravda*: "The better we employ the equipment we have on hand and the more we produce the more dependable and lasting will the peace be." According to an editorial in the Soviet newspaper, "the glorious daughters of the Soviet people are actively backing up their determination to defend peace by their inspired work for the good of the great socialist motherland. They know well that the stronger the Soviet Union . . . the more secure will be the cause of peace throughout the world. Millions of women patriots are working selflessly at enterprises and construction sites," while "women collective farmers stand in the front ranks of . . . the Stalinist plan for the transformation of nature." *Pravda* argued that "Soviet citizens well know that the stronger and more powerful their motherland, the more successful will be the struggle for peace and the stronger will be the camp of peace." [8]

Intellectual workers, of course, also did their part. In an anthology, *For Peace, for Democracy*, produced for the occasion by Soviet writers, Hero of

Socialist Labor Yelena Khobta cursed "the sub-men of America and Britain who again want a war." Speaking to newspaper correspondents at her collective farm, she asked them to "write about it in the newspapers so that he himself—what's his name? The American warmonger?" "Acheson?" a newsman suggested helpfully. "No, Truman himself. Write that we, the Soviet people, don't want to fight," but "let nobody touch us! . . . As Lenin pointed out, as Comrade Stalin says . . . it's toward communism we are going, and let no one stand in our way!" In "About the Atom Bomb," another story from the anthology that *Pravda* thought "deeply permeated by the people's wisdom," Ostap Vishny told a tale about Svirida, a grandfather on a collective farm. Asked what he thought of the atom bomb, the old man responded: "The thought and the will of the Bolshevist Party and of Comrade Stalin are also composed of atoms, and these atoms also possess atomic energy. And not just an ordinary energy, but Stalinist!" He continued: "If you were to multiply this Stalinist atomic energy by the people's love for Stalin and for the Bolshevist Party, what an atomic bomb would result! Ha! Don't you think so? That's why I fear nobody's atom bomb." "I shook grandfather Svirida's hand firmly," Vishny concluded.[9]

Scientists, too, were mobilized for the cause. In an article for *Pravda* entitled "It Is the Duty of Every Soviet Citizen to Sign the Stockholm Manifesto," geneticist Trofim Lysenko declared that Soviet scientists were joining the peace campaign "with complete unanimity." It was "impossible," he wrote, "to speak without anger of the Anglo-American warmongers," who "wish to destroy the greatest achievements of civilization." In the West, "the black forces of the warmongers have set up a venal science, the representatives of which are as much the enemies of mankind as their imperialist masters." Through their signatures on the Stockholm petition, however, Soviet scientists showed "their resolve to develop and enrich advanced Soviet science—science serving the cause of peace and progress." A similar distinction was drawn that July, when a group of Soviet scientists issued an open letter to American microbiologists. "On whose side are you?" they asked. "That of the band of imperialist conspirators, dreaming of the destruction of civilization . . . or that of those who are fighting for the entire world?" In the current situation, "it is impossible to be neutral. Planes of your country are destroying the peaceful cities of Korea and killing thousands of women, old people, and children. American pilots are dropping the Colorado beetle on democratic Germany, trying to pave the way for starvation in Europe." The letter concluded that "all honest scientists of America must arise under the banner of the fighters for peace!"[10]

Given the enormous Soviet mobilization around the Stockholm petition, it came as little surprise that, on November 6, 1950, Nikolai Bulganin, vice-chair of the Council of Ministers, officially proclaimed that the appeal had been signed by more than 115 million Soviet citizens, "the entire adult population of our country." Clearly, he said, "the Soviet people stand for peace" and would "resolutely uphold the cause of peace." According to the Soviet *New Times*, through their response to the Stockholm petition, "the Soviet people demonstrated their wholehearted and unanimous approval of the Soviet government's Stalin peace policy." It showed that "the peoples of the Soviet Union will, under the leadership of their government, continue to march in the front ranks of the fighters against war." [11]

Among the themes developed by the Soviet peace campaigners, the strongest was the contrast between the diabolical evil of the American government and the unsullied virtue of their own. Ehrenburg, deputy chair of the Soviet Peace Committee and perhaps its busiest traveler, writer, and speaker,[12] developed this into something of a new art form. When "the whole world" was "blessing the Soviet people" for defeating Nazi Germany, he wrote in early 1950, "who could think at the time that, before a year was out, fascist werewolves would crawl out into the light—new aspirants to world domination . . . the spiritual successors of the Führer?" "Blind in their selfishness and impotent in their rage," the Americans had "been brandishing the atomic bomb" without success, for the Soviet Union "stood vigilantly in defense of peace" and, thereby, "destroyed the plans of the frenzied Yankees." Commending the Soviet Union for saving "mankind from fascist slavery and annihilation," Tikhonov assailed "the newly manifest pretenders to world domination," who were "hastening to enact fascist laws under which any American who thinks like an honest and peaceful person can be thrown into a concentration camp." By contrast, the Soviet Union was "marching boldly along the path of peace because the immortal genius of the great fighter for peace and the happiness of peoples—the great Stalin—lights our way." [13]

Leaders of the Soviet peace movement frequently assailed U.S. nuclear weapons policy as a means of highlighting this Manichean picture. Denouncing the "atomic sharks" of America, Ehrenburg claimed that "their dreams, their calculations, their delirium is devoted to the mass extermination of humanity." Another Soviet peace movement leader, Academician Eugene Tarle, claimed that the American bombing of Hiroshima "was essentially baser than the loathsome Hitlerite misdeeds." [14] Returning to the attack in September 1950, Ehrenburg contended that the Partisans of Peace had been successful in stopping the "criminals" from dropping an atomic bomb on Korea, "but this does not mean that they will not drop it on Korea or on any other country if the people are not vigilant. . . . Criminals remain criminals; they have been restrained, but not halted." The Soviet Union, of course, had "stood for peace since the first days of our republic" and continued to "stand firmly for peace." Like Tikhonov,

Ehrenburg publicly attributed this situation to "the great and noble man who brought our ship through the storm, who stands at the helm, guiding us to the green shores of happiness—Stalin." [15]

As nonpacifists—indeed, as supporters of their country's military policies—Soviet Peace Committee leaders were not above issuing threats about what a nuclear war would do to the United States and its allies. Occasionally, therefore, they stopped describing how the Partisans of Peace would defeat the "warmongers" and grew more menacing in their pronouncements. "If the American beasts of prey . . . start a new war," Ehrenburg warned in October 1949, "it will not linger in the Old World—the war will reach America, too." Speaking at a Communist-organized conference in Vienna in November 1951, Alexander Korneichuk, a dramatist and a leader of the Soviet Peace Committee, admonished Americans not to "be deceived into new adventures which will involve you and other peoples of the world in untold suffering." At the same meeting, Ehrenburg warned that Soviet bombs would be "sufficient" to turn a British aggressor "into a new Hiroshima." "Atomic warfare," he added ominously, would "bring to densely populated countries . . . desolation and ruin." [16] Like Soviet and American policymakers, the leaders of the Soviet Peace Committee apparently believed that threats of nuclear holocaust had a salutary deterrent value, at least for their Cold War opponents.

Not surprisingly, they had little use for nonaligned peace activists. After Fyke Farmer, a leading world federalist, invited Ehrenburg to visit him in Tennessee during the Soviet writer's 1946 tour of the United States, Ehrenburg wrote scornfully in the Moscow press of such "provincial utopians," working for this "fantastic" project. "They talk a great deal about a 'world government,'" Ehrenburg wrote in 1950, but "so far they cannot come to terms with one another. . . . They live in brutal hostility toward people of different nationality. Some burn Negroes; others hound Jews. . . . We despise their hatred, their barriers, their haughtiness." [17] Another leader of the Soviet Peace Committee, Alexander Surkov, warned that "the warmongers carry on their black banner the perfidious slogan of cosmopolitanism. For the propagation of bourgeois cosmopolitanism they are mobilizing 'the creative legacy' of all the traitors and turncoats of the past." There was, for example, "that preacher of moral filth, treachery, and cynicism, Jean-Paul Sartre," not to mention other nonaligned intellectuals drawn from "the cesspools of the world." Fresh from his peace junket to the United States and Europe, Shostakovich reported that, while "the forces of fighters for peace are growing," writers like Sartre had joined "the camp of the warmongers" and, consequently, had "lost honor and conscience." [18]

Indeed, the leading proponents of the Soviet "peace struggle" adopted an unrelentingly hostile attitude toward those advocates of peace who distanced themselves from the Communist-led movement. The Metropolitan Nikolai, speaking on behalf of the Russian Orthodox church at the All-Union Peace Conference of 1949, no sooner pledged his church to "resist the temptation" of the "Washington Cain" than he denounced the pope as "an agent of American imperialism." Responding to John Rogge's contention that it was necessary to remove "the mountains of fear which divide the American and Soviet peoples," S. Gerasimov, another Peace Committee leader, declared that millions of Americans "distinguish the heinous aim of the warmongers behind all the provocative clamor." The "Soviet people have already proved repeatedly in deeds that fear is a feeling little known among them"; indeed, among citizens of the Soviet Union, "so-called 'mountains of fear' have never existed and never will arise." Ehrenburg professed to be "surprised and hurt" when J. B. Priestley, replying to his open letter, called for an effort to restrain military measures in their respective countries. Some of what Priestley said "sounds like a joke," Ehrenburg told his Soviet audience, which, of course, did not have the opportunity to read the amusing missive. The Soviet Peace Committee leader concluded: "It seems to me that Priestley's quarrel with me is only an echo of his quarrel with himself. Priestley is undoubtedly undergoing a drama of inner doubts." He was "like many decent intellectuals in Britain who hate war but do not know how to avert it and who, losing themselves on their own doorstep, await with fatalism the awful denouement." [19]

In retrospect, it seems clear that the leaders of the Soviet Peace Committee were not free agents. Fadeyev, to be sure, addressing the Western press en route to the Waldorf conference, claimed that "we have no instructions from our government." The Soviet delegates, he said, were "going to the conference to speak freely as free individuals. We are not restricted in any way." Others, however, were somewhat more candid about intellectual life in Stalin's Russia. "I was told that I must go to Paris for the World Peace Congress," Ehrenburg wrote years later in an otherwise upbeat account. "The defense of peace seemed to me a splendid thing," he added, softening the admission. But then he continued: "I was asked to write a speech and submit it for approval." Having secured this approval, Ehrenburg headed off for Paris on the first leg of his extensive travels to Communist-led peace gatherings. In the much freer atmosphere of 1989, an official of the Soviet Peace Committee conceded that, under Stalin, "a public organization was not an independent body; its role was secondary, to help and serve." Or, as the WPC journal put it that year, the Soviet Peace Committee "had two main tasks: to illustrate abroad that the Soviet people supported their government's foreign policy; and to ensure support of Soviet foreign policy from the public abroad." [20]

Nor was this loyal management of the "peace struggle" at the behest of the regime out of character for some of its leaders. Ehrenburg, for example, despite his occasional difficulties with the authorities, exemplified opportunism during the Stalin era, leading George Orwell to dismiss him as a literary prostitute. Remembering the Soviet Peace Committee leader years later, Nikita Khrushchev remarked that, although Ehrenburg was a major writer, "somehow he managed to reconcile himself to Stalinist methods." Khrushchev recalled that the author Galina Serebryakova, who had spent almost twenty years in a labor camp and had seen two of her husbands die in Stalin's purges, had given Ehrenburg "a tongue-lashing for having been a toady to Stalin. . . . She said that while Stalin was chopping off heads and carting writers off into exile, Ehrenburg had been going around giving speeches in support of Stalin's treatment of the intelligentsia." Even Ehrenburg conceded in later years that during Stalin's regime, he had lived "with clenched teeth" because he knew that so many of those arrested were innocent. Such discretion and service to the regime provided him with a very comfortable existence. Indeed, in his final years, Ehrenburg lived in relative luxury, surrounded by souvenirs of his foreign travels, including paintings worth millions of dollars.[21]

If Ehrenburg was compromised, Fadeyev, as Khrushchev recalled, served as "chief prosecutor against the creative intelligentsia." As general secretary of the Soviet Writers' Union from 1946 to 1953, Fadeyev authorized all arrests of Soviet writers in this period; indeed, according to Khrushchev, Fadeyev played a faithful role as "Stalin's agent, even to the point of giving false evidence against people accused of committing crimes." For his loyal service to the Soviet dictator, Fadeyev received great wealth, numerous honors, enormous bureaucratic power, and membership on the party's Central Committee. After Stalin's death, however, and the rehabilitation of virtually all the writers arrested on his personal authorization, Fadeyev "couldn't take it," Khrushchev recalled. He "couldn't get over the fact that he had so often . . . played the role of Stalin's henchman." Guilt-ridden and alcoholic, Fadeyev shot himself in 1956.[22]

Nevertheless, the Soviet "peace struggle" may have had deeper roots than opportunism and more lasting effects than disillusionment. Given the immense death and destruction World War II brought to the Soviet Union, it seems likely that millions of Soviet citizens—including many leaders—genuinely feared a new war and, particularly, a nuclear war. Therefore, the Stockholm petition and other aspects of the Soviet "peace struggle" may have enjoyed some genuine popularity and, indeed, provided a means acceptable to the regime through which Soviet citizens could voice their dismay at the prospect of new mass destruction. In addition, through its denunciation of the atomic bomb and nuclear war, the campaign behind the Stockholm Peace Appeal helped undermine the regime's earlier assurances that Soviet citizens had nothing to fear from U.S. nuclear weapons. After all, it was impossible to have it both ways: either the Bomb posed a threat to survival, or it did not. In this fashion, then, the "peace struggle" in the Soviet Union probably had the unintended consequence of spreading concern about the Bomb even within the land where fear, allegedly, did not exist.[23]

Hungary

The Communist-led peace campaign took a similar form in Communist-ruled Hungary. On June 17, 1949, a Hungarian Congress in Defense of Peace convened in the Conference Hall of the Hungarian parliament, with delegates present from numerous officially supported groups, including the Democratic People's Army. In a report to the gathering entitled "Hungary in the Struggle for Peace," Geza Losonczi, a member of the National Committee of the Hungarian Intelligentsia, outlined the tasks of the campaign: increasing Hungary's political, economic, and military strength; waging a merciless struggle against the agents of imperialism; inculcating in the population, including the armed forces, a healthy patriotism and vigilance; strengthening national unity; and standing firmly in the ranks of the peace front led by the Soviet Union.[24]

Naturally, mobilization behind the WPC's assorted peace appeals became a high priority. Plunging into the Stockholm peace petition drive, the official Hungarian We Will Defend Peace movement called upon the Hungarian people to establish peace committees "in every city, village, farmstead, factory, shop and office." By mid-1950, it claimed that some 7.5 million Hungarians had signed the Stockholm Peace Appeal—a remarkable feat because Hungary's total population (including infants and children) then stood at about 9.2 million. In 1951, the petitioning resumed as part of the WPC's campaign for a five-power pact, gathering 1.8 million signatures in the first six days. According to an official campaign statement, the petition drive would "help the entire Hungarian people to understand . . . who wants war and why" and "what is the purpose of the rearmament of Western Germany and of the war preparations of the Tito gang." The drive would also explain to Hungarians "the sense and aim of the peace policy of the Soviet Union" and deepen "their fraternal alliance with the People's Democracies and the Soviet Union."[25]

"This fight is not just weak pacifism, not a formal refusal of force, nor an unmanly retreat from war," explained *Szabad Nép*, a Hungarian Communist journal. Indeed, "the fight for peace is not directed theoretically and generally against war." According to the Soviet *New Times*, by late July 1950, as the invading North Korean armed forces poured into South Korea, about two million Hungarians, "in the name of peace and the triumph of Socialism," had made large financial contributions to equip them with field hospitals. Committed to the traditional formula of peace through military strength, the leaders of the Hungarian "peace struggle" considered a thoroughgoing rejection of war to be totally unacceptable. "Pacifism is the imperialist poison by which an attempt is made to weaken the people's resistance," Major-General Istvan Szabo told the Hungarian Peace Congress in November 1950. "Anyone who professes that Hungary should not prepare for the defense of peace is a traitor and an agent of the imperialists, an enemy of our people." [26]

Poland

The "peace struggle" in the Polish People's Democracy was equally responsive to the ruling Communist party's national priorities. In a publication titled *The Tasks of the Party in the Struggle for Peace*, issued in April 1949, Boleslaw Bierut, the chair of its Central Committee and president of Poland, outlined a campaign against the "warmongers" that excluded what he called "barren pacifism." What was needed, he stated, was "a national struggle, the struggle of patriots to preserve sovereignty." One participant recalled that, soon, "there was no sphere of life—political, economic, social, or ideological—which was not linked with slogans of the struggle for peace." Campaigns developed to "oppose cosmopolitan trends in art and ideology," to forge "closer ties with the Soviet Union and other socialist countries," and to introduce "voluntary overtime in an effort to exceed production norms." Indeed, "everything that could be a decisive factor in strengthening People's Poland was included within the framework of the struggle for peace." At the least, this seemed good for national morale. The peace movement "gave people a feeling of strength and hope," she recalled. It "helped to overcome fatalism and a feeling of helplessness in the face of what then seemed an imminent cataclysm." [27]

The "peace struggle" in Poland quickly mushroomed into a vast totalitarian effort. Founded on March 24, 1949, the Polish Committee of Defenders of Peace (PKOP), headed by Professor Jan Dembowski, took charge of the Stockholm petition campaign. According to an official history, the PKOP put 136,000 three-person canvassing teams into the field to visit every home, organized 88,000 local peace committees, and sponsored 80,000 rallies, meetings, and lectures. In addition to printing four million copies of the Stockholm Peace Appeal, the PKOP printed one million booklets entitled *Sign the Peace Appeal*, as well as numerous other inspirational ventures in publishing: *We Vote for*

Peace (500,000 copies), *Peasants in Defense of Peace* (500,000 copies), and *Struggle for Peace, We Shall Win the Struggle for Peace*, and *Before the Polish Peace Congress* (each printed in the tens of thousands). Meanwhile, the Polish post office instituted a special Stockholm appeal cancellation on all letters and telegrams.[28]

As elsewhere in the Soviet bloc, these efforts were accompanied by more innovative devices. Polish poets contributed their talents to the cause, including five volumes of peace poetry appearing during 1950 alone. Meanwhile, as one participant recalled, "countless production commitments were undertaken both in factories and on farms." According to the Soviet *New Times*, " 'Peace Watches,' that is, an extra production effort as a contribution to the struggle for peace, were organized extensively in factories and mills . . . and the workers taking part showed splendid results as regards both output and quality. Miners and steelworkers in Silesia, textile workers in Lodz, engineers and railwaymen, have pledged pre-schedule fulfillment of their annual production plans" in the cause of peace. This "good example," a participant recalled, "was followed by school children." A Pathfinders' resolution adopted in an elementary school declared that, "as a token of solidarity with the PKOP," the pupils would "work so hard that no one need ever repeat the same year," make "shoes and clothes last longer, collect scrap metal," and "put in 300 hours work on the construction site of a machine depot." [29]

On paper, at least, the Polish campaign behind the Stockholm Peace Appeal was an enormous success. In late June 1950, when the campaign officially closed, the PKOP reported that eighteen million Poles had signed the Stockholm petition. By contrast, only 190,000 had failed to do so. According to a Polish newspaper, these ne'er-do-wells consisted chiefly of "Kulaks, urban speculators, and the episcopate, heading the reactionary section of the clergy, and members of Jehovah's Witnesses." Some of the nonsigners tried to clear their names by pathetic letters published in the press or in *Peace Is Winning*, the PKOP journal. Here they described how, through sickness or isolation, they had missed contact with the signature collectors. "I have been ill since 1943 and have not been able to walk for three years now," wrote an invalid from Slezany. "Wishing to have a clear civic conscience, I ask the Polish Peace Committee to send a canvassing group to me so that I can add my modest signature, as a condemnation of the American warmongers." [30]

In later months, new ventures followed in the Polish peace campaign. The first Polish Peace Congress, held in late 1950, demanded "the cessation of American aggression in Korea," as well as "a ban on nuclear weapons." Addressing the gathering, Adam Rapacki, deputy chair of the PKOP and a high-level official in the Polish government, declared that "the defenders of peace all over the world have chosen the right weapon in their peace struggle." They were "working enthusiastically to accelerate the growth of . . . the defensive, political, and moral forces of the socialist world and the peace camp on the one hand, and to paralyze the aggressive preparations of the imperialists and unmask the despicable, deceptive imperialist campaign on the other." New peace petition drives followed, accompanied by the usual massive circulatory apparatus and stepped-up production schedules for hapless workers. Acknowledging the interaction of the peace campaign and government priorities, President Bierut entitled a February 1951 address, delivered to the sixth plenary session of the Communist party, "The Struggle of the Polish Nation for Peace and the Six-Year Plan." [31]

East Germany

In neighboring East Germany, the Communist-led peace movement also emerged with considerable fanfare. Launched in May 1949 by prominent intellectuals and rising political leaders (among them Erich Honecker), the German Committee of Fighters for Peace organized a panoply of publicity and events for October 2, 1949, designated by Communist nations as their first World Peace Day. At the Berlin opera house, Burgomeister Friedrich Ebert, mayor of the eastern sector, told an audience of 2,000 that this "democratic capital of Germany" anticipated "the formation of a German government which does not work for the aims of imperialist warmongers but for all of Germany and for the peace of the world." Although Soviet authorities relaxed border restrictions in anticipation of the arrival of a flood of West German participants in the Peace Day festivities, the tide moved the other way, for large numbers of East Germans crossed into the American and British zones for the purpose of shopping or just catching a glimpse of the comparatively luxurious West. [32]

Shrugging off such setbacks, the new East German government, organized in October 1949, proceeded with the peace campaign. To bolster the Stockholm petition drive, Walter Ulbrecht, the Communist party secretary, announced in April 1950 that it was "the future task of the party to organize Peace Committees at the state, district, town and factory level." By September 1950, an official report claimed the existence of 27,708 such committees. They collected signatures on the Stockholm Peace Appeal, provided the population with information on the allegedly peace-loving policies of the Soviet Union and East Germany, and warned of the "war-triggering policy" of the West. Meanwhile, apparently recognizing their mistake of the previous year, officials organized mass demonstrations of East German youth within the confines of East Berlin. Under the slogan "Peace, Freedom, and a United Germany," a purported 700,000 members of the Free German Youth paraded about wearing blue shirts and carrying vast banners. Reorganized in December 1950, the new German Peace Committee also agitated against a West German army, promoted its East German counterpart, and encouraged workers to labor harder in the interests of peace. Anna Seghers, a prominent East German writer and a leader of the German Peace Committee, told a group of steelworkers: "Each ton of steel is a blow in the face of the warmongers!"[33]

Other Communist Nations

Elsewhere in the Soviet bloc, the story was much the same. In Bulgaria, campaign leaders gathered astounding numbers of signatures on the Stockholm Peace Appeal and instituted special work days for the defense of peace in factories and at construction sites.[34] According to the Soviet *New Times*, "a conference in defense of peace" was held on March 24, 1949, in Pyongyang, North Korea, and was attended by 1,500 delegates representing organizations in North and South Korea. A post office employee in Shanghai, China reported that the Stockholm appeal had been circulated "all over this country, in every village, every town, every city and every province. . . . Women and girls are delivering imploring speeches asking all citizens to sign for peace." After the two Asian Communist nations plunged into the Korean War in 1950, the nature of their peace campaigns became particularly apparent. In the fall of 1951, Peking radio proudly reported that the Chinese Peace Committee had raised enough money to purchase 2,000 warplanes and 200 tanks.[35]

In Communist Yugoslavia, of course, the situation was somewhat different. Having been expelled from the Cominform and, accordingly, from the Communist-led world peace movement, the Yugoslavs had little patience with either of them. On October 2, 1949, taking advantage of the Soviet bloc's World Peace Day, the Yugoslav government organized mass peace meetings throughout the country. At these gatherings, speakers stressed Yugoslavia's desire for peace and the threat of war posed by the Kremlin's hostility to the government of Marshal Tito. This new Yugoslav peace movement—soon named the Yugoslav National Committee for the Defense of Peace—became increasingly important to the Yugoslav government as Tito sought to carve out an independent position in world affairs. Convening in the parliament building in Belgrade in November 1950, the Yugoslav National Committee launched a counteroffensive against the World Peace Council. Speaker after speaker argued that Soviet imperialism was the major threat to the peace of the world and that the WPC, on behalf of the Soviet government, was seeking to create a war psychosis.[36]

Nevertheless, just as Tito's government practiced a form of Stalinism without Stalin, so the Yugoslav movement bore some similarity to the affiliates of the WPC. Certainly, like other Communist-led peace movements, it lacked independence.

The Critics: Pacifists and Churches

The new, officially sponsored peace movements did not impress those small clusters of pacifists that survived in Communist nations. In China, to be sure, a few former members of the FOR supported the Communist-led peace campaign.[37] But they were an exception. Two Polish pacifists who managed to contact the WRI cast doubts on the value of the signatures gathered on the Communist-led campaign's peace petitions. They also professed their desire for a new social order with characteristics very different from those lauded by the official movement: "Civil liberties, control of government, a cooperative basis of economy, and decentralization." From East Berlin, one young WRI member wrote that "there is much talk about peace in this Eastern Republic," but pacifists "realize that an idea is a danger when there is too much loud talk about it." Indeed, "the idea is fed with the well-known stuff: People, fatherland, human rights, uniforms, badges, etc. No wonder that many fanatics are already willing to fight for such an idea. . . . Even the idea of peace serves as propaganda for war."[38]

Another negative assessment came from the pacifist Premysl Pitter, who fled from Czechoslovakia in 1951. "Pacifists living behind the 'iron curtain' can work only from man to man," he declared. "They avoid being drawn into [official] peace actions . . . because they do not believe in them—and do not want to help in creating a smokescreen for red militarism." Pitter argued that there was "no doubt that the common people sincerely want peace" but contended that "their peace-longing is misused for a policy of hatred against the Western powers that are stamped as the only war-mongers."[39]

A somewhat more charitable—albeit unflattering—interpretation was advanced by Heinz Kraschutzki, a distinguished pacifist, who, after East German authorities dismissed him from his position as a history lecturer, moved to West Berlin. "You cannot prepare the people for an aggressive war by preaching that war is hell and that peace is the highest of all ideals," he told the WRI. "I am sure they mean peace and so are friends of mine with a long pacifist record who are living in Eastern Germany." East German Communists "are firmly convinced that the West is preparing to attack the East and, in their opinion, the only possible means of defense is armaments." The tragedy, he thought, lay in the latter assumption, which, in East and West alike, narrowed the chances for peace.[40]

The official peace campaign in Communist nations drew some support from the area's churches. The Bulgarian Orthodox church lauded Stalin's "political acumen" for creating the Russian church, which had led its counterparts into "the active ranks of those who stand for peace and democracy." The Albanian Autocephalous Orthodox church also claimed that it had joined "the camp of peace," while, in Romania, the Patriarch Justinian called on all believers to "support the fight for peace, which is being menaced by the enemies of human life, the Anglo-American rich." In China, Christian church leaders signed formal statements, publicized in the West by the Rev. Hewlett Johnson, charging the U.S. government with practicing germ warfare.[41]

Elsewhere, some Protestant and Catholic churches also rallied behind the Communist-led campaign. Echoing the latter, the Czech Brethren, the largest Protestant church in Czechoslovakia, passed a resolution, framed in part by the anti-Western Joseph Hromadka, that promised "to recognize what forces are threatening the cause of peace." According to the official Czech news service, in July 1950, at a church conference in Moravia, clergymen of "all Christian churches and religious societies" denounced the West's "godless plans" for war and affirmed the Stockholm appeal. Shortly afterward, the same agency announced that 453 Roman Catholic priests had condemned "the imperialist policy of the warmongers." In Hungary, where the Protestant churches were "democratized" by the Communist regime, they sent their "sincere greetings and good wishes" to the 1949 Paris conference of the Partisans of Peace. The following year, after the World Council of Churches issued its warning against the Stockholm appeal, Hungary's Reformed Bishop Albert Bereczky responded with an open letter on the subject: "You repudiate the Stockholm Appeal, because you see it as a propaganda action. I sincerely support the Stockholm Appeal, and likewise the propaganda for it." [42]

Nevertheless, the churches also produced Eastern Europe's most effective opponents of the Communist-led peace campaign. Although invited to participate in official Peace Day rallies on September 1, 1949, East Germany's Protestant Evangelical church and its Roman Catholic church refused to do so. Both churches also spurned the Stockholm appeal, and the Evangelical church issued its own independent peace statement that May. On August 6, in the midst of the campaign to convince Germans that the Soviet Union was the "bulwark of peace," the Protestant bishop of Berlin told a congregation in East Berlin that "the church is the only power which really stands for peace." Meanwhile, in a statement read from all East German Catholic pulpits, that church announced that it could not "join committees and campaigns which use the name of peace, but serve political purposes." Such statements left Communist leaders fuming. "Certain church leaders," complained the Politburo, "have undertaken one reactionary attack after another against the movement of the fighters for peace."[43]

Church resistance also cropped up elsewhere but encountered a harsher reaction from the authorities. Refusing to sign the Stockholm appeal, Roman Catholic clergy in Romania had their ranks purged by the regime. In Hungary, too, Catholic clergy refused to sign the petition, prompting the leaders of the campaign to denounce them as "against peace." Indeed, when Bishop Josef Peteri refused to receive a petition delegation, the Hungarian National Peace Committee charged him with "unlawful and warmongering activities" and called for his trial on charges of violating the constitution. Angered by church resistance to the Communist-led peace campaign, the Hungarian government arrested almost a thousand priests, monks, and nuns in a single night and, the following year, reportedly arrested Archbishop Josef Groess, Bishop Endre Hamvas, and Bishop Peteri for refusing to sign the WPC's petition for a five-power peace pact.[44]

In Poland, too, the Stockholm petition drive provided the occasion for a bitter confrontation between church and state. By June 1950, newspapers throughout the country were featuring stories and editorials condemning the Catholic church hierarchy because not a single bishop had signed the appeal. "They have not joined the ranks of the whole Polish nation on the side of peace," charged one Polish official, who singled out seven bishops as "blind instruments carrying out the orders of the Anglo-American imperialists." The government used a church-state agreement in early 1950, in which the church had pledged its support for peace, to intimidate the clergy—telling priests, for example, that they could no longer teach if they did not sign the Stockholm petition. Eventually, to avoid further difficulties, the church hierarchy gave its oblique approval to the Stockholm appeal. Jehovah's Witnesses, who also refused to sign the petition but never made an accommodation with the government, met a crueler fate. Some 80 percent of them were arrested for participation in an alleged "spy ring"; their resistance to the Stockholm appeal was cited as one count in the indictment.[45]

A Movement as Mouthpiece

In Communist nations, where less need existed than in Western countries to court suspicious public opinion or governments, the Communist-led peace movement emerged in its starkest simplicity as a mouthpiece for Soviet foreign and military policy. The movement portrayed that policy in the most adulatory of terms, just as it depicted the policy of the West as unremittingly aggressive, warmongering, and fascist. Devoting enormous propaganda resources to the peace campaign—highlighted by a shrill attack on the Bomb—Communist governments had every reason to assume that it would have some effect. And it probably did. In the short run, the campaign seems likely to have enhanced the willingness of citizens of Communist nations to support Soviet bloc military measures. At the least, it spurred some to work harder and helped isolate others from pacifism and other nonaligned critiques of military power. But, by emphasizing military dangers, the Communist-led peace campaign probably made many people more jittery about war in general and about nuclear war in particular. To judge, however, from the fervent support Communist governments accorded their official peace campaigns, this last phenomenon received little attention at the time.

Consequences

The Uneasy Leader

The U.S. Government and the Bomb

> We had no alternative . . . but . . . to maintain, if we could,
> our initial superiority in the atomic field.
>
> Harry S. Truman, 1953

After the atomic bombing of Hiroshima, secrecy, compartmentalization, and other wartime security procedures no longer insulated American officials from the new thinking about war and national sovereignty. To the contrary, the enormous destructiveness of atomic weapons and the furor about them that emerged in the United States and overseas made a strong impression on key American policymakers. Some, at least, became acutely conscious that the development of the Bomb had created a new and dangerous situation that could not be handled satisfactorily by the traditional methods of war and diplomacy. At the same time, American policymakers were increasingly disturbed about the growing power of the Soviet Union. Other problems, of course, confronted them, but, as Dean Acheson recalled, "overshadowing all loomed two dangers . . .—the Soviet Union's new-found power and expansive imperialism and the development of nuclear weapons." [1] How would American officials balance these concerns, particularly if they seemed to pull in opposite directions?

New Thinking About War and Diplomacy

From the outset, U.S. government leaders were shaken by the enormous destructiveness of the Hiroshima bombing and by the sharp criticism that it generated. At President Truman's cabinet meeting of August 8, 1945, according to one record of that gathering, he "expressed concern" about apparent papal condemnation of the Bomb and "pointed out that the cooperation of the Vatican is needed in days to come, particularly in dealing with the Catholic countries of Europe." [2] To the president's dismay, on August 9 he received word from the general secretary of the Federal Council of Churches that it, too, was about to issue a public condemnation of the atomic bombing.[3] When top U.S. officials gathered in the White House the following morning, Secretary of War Stimson suggested that the bombing be halted. According to one of those present, "he cited the growing feeling of apprehension and misgiving as to the effect of the atomic bomb even in our own country." Truman, who before the atomic bombing may not have fully comprehended its dreadful ramifications for the civilian population, took Stimson's advice. Later that day, he told his cabinet meeting that he had ordered a halt to the use of atomic bombs in the war. According to Secretary of Commerce Henry Wallace, the president "said the thought of wiping out another 100,000 people was too horrible. He didn't like the idea of killing, as he said, 'all those kids.' "[4]

As debate grew over the wisdom and morality of the bombing, the Truman administration became increasingly embarrassed and defensive. When Leo Szilard sought to publish his antibombing petition of July 17, 1945, signed by 68 Manhattan project scientists, the U.S. Army threatened to have him fired from his job at the University of Chicago and prosecuted under the Espionage Act.[5] In November 1945, attempting to counter disturbing reports about deaths in Japan from radioactivity, General Groves, director of the Manhattan project, informed a congressional committee that doctors had assured him that radiation poisoning actually provided "a very pleasant way to die."[6] Shortly afterward, Robert Oppenheimer accompanied Acheson to the White House and remarked that some atomic scientists felt they had blood on their hands. Incensed by the incident, Truman told Acheson: "I don't want to see that son of a bitch in this office ever again." Oppenheimer, he claimed, had "turned into a crybaby. I don't want anything to do with people like that."[7]

At the same time, the widespread public uneasiness about nuclear weapons gave concerned American officials the opportunity to press for a new approach to international issues. Although the new secretary of state, James Byrnes, sought to use the U.S. atomic monopoly to pressure the Soviet Union into diplomatic concessions, others, such as Stimson, began to champion alternatives. On September 11, he appealed to Truman for direct discussions with the Soviet Union on the Bomb. "If we fail to approach them now," he wrote, "and merely continue to negotiate with them, having this weapon rather ostentatiously on our hip, their suspicions and their distrust of our purposes and motives will increase." He explained: "If the atomic bomb were merely another . . . weapon to be assimilated into our pattern of international relations, it would be one thing. We could then follow the old custom of secrecy and nationalistic military superiority." But "the bomb instead constitutes merely a first step in a new control by man over the forces of nature too revolutionary and dangerous to fit into the old concepts. . . . It . . . caps the climax of the race between man's growing technical power for destructiveness and . . . his moral power." [8]

Although Stimson did a poor job of making his case at a subsequent cabinet meeting, other officials took up the issue. On the night of the Hiroshima bombing, Under Secretary of State Dean Acheson had concluded that "if we can't work out some sort of organization of great powers, we shall be gone geese." Accordingly, he sought to reinforce Stimson's argument. The creation of the atomic bomb was "a discovery more revolutionary in human society than the invention of the wheel," he wrote in a September 25 memorandum to the president; "international controls . . . should be sought to prevent a race toward mutual destruction." That same day, Vannevar Bush sent the president a memorandum stressing the necessity for reaching an accommodation with the Soviet Union on the Bomb. "Down one path lies a secret arms race," he contended, "down the other international collaboration and possibly ultimate control." The United States, he said, could not evade the choice, for "we live in a new world." Although these officials remained vague on how to achieve international control of atomic energy—sometimes suggesting a direct approach to the Soviet Union and at others calling for U.N. action—they were united in their assumption that the U.S. government should take the lead in proposing a plan to spare the world a nuclear arms race and nuclear war. [9]

Despite his failure to move beyond traditional assumptions in wartime, Truman showed signs of adapting to the new climate of thinking. As late as his radio address of August 9, 1945, he continued to cling to the certitudes of the past. Proclaiming that "we must constitute ourselves trustees of this new force," he added, "We thank God that it has come to us, instead of our enemies." But by the time of his October 3 message to Congress, drafted by Acheson, Truman was moving in a different direction. "The release of atomic energy constitutes a new force too revolutionary to consider in the framework of old ideas," he said. "The hope of civilization lies in international arrangements looking, if possible, to the renunciation of the use and development of the atomic bomb." Conceding that "the difficulties in working out such arrangements are great," the president argued that "the alternative . . . may be a desperate armament race which might well end in disaster." Truman also raised the specter of annihilation four days later, in a speech at a county fair in Missouri: "We can't ever have another war, unless it is total war, and that means the end of our civilization as we know it. We are not going to do that." [10]

In November 1945, when the leaders of Great Britain, Canada, and the United States met to consider the question of the Bomb, they adopted a statement—the Truman-Attlee-King Declaration—that brought these new ideas into focus. "The application of recent scientific discoveries to the methods and practice of war has placed at the disposal of mankind means of destruction hitherto unknown, against which there can be no adequate military defense, and in the employment of which no single nation can in fact have a monopoly," it declared. Of course, "the only complete protection for the civilized world from the destructive use of scientific knowledge lies in the prevention of war." Nevertheless, to prevent the use of atomic energy for destructive purposes, the declaration called for the establishment of a U.N. commission to prepare recommendations "for the elimination from national armaments of atomic weapons and of all other major weapons adaptable to mass destruction." If the Truman-Attlee-King Declaration, like its signers, remained vague about how these goals were to be attained, it nevertheless provided a ringing statement of principles very much in line with those of the burgeoning movement against nuclear weapons.[11]

Truman also toyed in these months with the idea of world government. Meeting with Fyke Farmer for a discussion of the subject on October 11, 1945, he brushed aside Farmer's argument that world federation was essential to avert an atomic arms race and, eventually, nuclear war. World government was "nothing more than a theory at the present time," Farmer quoted him as saying. Nevertheless, Truman also talked at length that fall with world government proponent Ely Culbertson to discuss his memorandum "How to Control the Atomic Threat." Encouraged by the meeting, Culbertson and journalist Dorothy Thompson submitted a plan in December that proposed strengthening the U.N. charter to provide for "effective international controls of scientific weapons and of armed aggression." They suggested reorganization of the Security Council and World Court, limitation and inspection of all scientific weapons, and creation of a "world police force." Apparently intrigued by these ideas, Truman proposed "a special message" on the subject to his White House speechwriter.[12]

This unprecedented receptivity to new approaches to world order provided the backdrop for a very innovative policy proposal: the Acheson-Lilienthal Plan. Convinced of the urgency of the atomic bomb issue, which he termed "the most serious cloud hanging over the world," Acheson prevailed upon Byrnes and the president to appoint a committee to formulate the American position. That committee, headed by Acheson but with important input from TVA director David Lilienthal and particularly from Robert Oppenheimer, met during the early months of 1946 and crafted an ingenious formula for the international control of atomic energy. Announced in March 1946 and soon known as the Acheson-Lilienthal Plan, it provided for the creation of an international body, an Atomic Development Authority, that would maintain a monopoly of fissionable material and distribute it only in "denatured" form for peaceful purposes. Meanwhile, existing nuclear weapons would be destroyed and a system of international inspection would alert nations to any violations of the agreement. Although the Acheson-Lilienthal Plan could not prevent a nation from developing nuclear weapons if it were determined to do so, it would rid the world of those weapons then in existence, and its provisions for international ownership and inspection would make the building of new ones difficult and dangerous.[13]

As Victor Weisskopf noted at the time, the Acheson-Lilienthal Plan was a direct result of the new climate of thinking fostered by critics of the Bomb. Referring to the plan, Lilienthal observed that he had received his "initial acquaintance with . . . the atomic energy problem" from the conference organized by Szilard and the scientists' movement at the University of Chicago. Oppenheimer, particularly, had been deeply influenced by that movement and especially by Niels Bohr, whereas Acheson felt the public pressure for nuclear disarmament keenly. Drawing on the ideas of the Franck report, Bohr, and the postwar campaign against nuclear weapons, the Acheson-Lilienthal report emphasized not only the immense danger posed by the Bomb but the hopelessness of military defense against the new weapon and the futility of national attempts to maintain a nuclear monopoly. As Bush and Acheson stated in a radio broadcast announcing the plan, America's nuclear advantage "is only temporary. It will not last. We must use that advantage now to promote international security" through "international agreement."[14]

Even more striking, the plan provided for unprecedented limitations on the traditional prerogatives of the nation-state. Seeking "to make explicit some of the things left implicit" in the Acheson-Lilienthal Plan, Oppenheimer wrote privately shortly after its appearance that the report "proposes that in the field of atomic energy there be set up a world government, that in this field there be renunciation of national sovereignty." For this reason, he stated, the development of nuclear weapons not only "intensifies the urgency of our hopes" but "provides new and healthy avenues of approach" for "the problem of preventing war." Oppenheimer made the same points about nuclear weapons and the necessary approach to them in the fall of 1945 in a letter to Einstein.[15]

The Baruch Plan

The Acheson-Lilienthal Plan represented the zenith of the movement's impact on American public policy for, in March 1946, the U.S. government's position on the Bomb began to move toward a more traditional approach. In part, this shift resulted from Truman's appointment that month of Bernard Baruch, a crusty, 75-year-old South Carolina financier, to serve as the U.S. representative to the U.N. Atomic Energy Commission. Acheson, considering Baruch a shrewd stock market speculator whose reputed wisdom was "entirely self-propagated," immediately protested to Byrnes, but without effect. Lilienthal recalled that, when he heard the news, he felt "quite sick." The United States needed "a man who is young, vigorous, not vain, and whom the Russians would feel isn't out simply to put them in a hole, not really caring about international cooperation." Disgusted by the appointment and fearful that their plan would be subverted, the members of the Acheson-Lilienthal committee refused for a time to work with Baruch.[16] In turn, Baruch heaped scorn upon "the Acheson-Lilienthal crowd" and demanded that he be given a free hand in shaping the American proposal.[17] Wary of the repercussions in the Senate if Baruch were not pacified, Truman gave the financier what he wanted. Byrnes also proved very accommodating. At the end of May, when Baruch asked Byrnes what his atomic policies were, the secretary of state replied: "Oh hell, I have none. What are your views?"[18]

Nevertheless, Baruch, like Acheson, Lilienthal, and Oppenheimer, was affected by the new climate of opinion. Therefore, despite his mediocre qualifications for the task confronting him, he proved remarkably willing to consider innovative approaches to the problem of world security. In a draft of May 7 on the atomic energy question, Baruch affirmed "the broad outlines of the Acheson-Lilienthal proposal" but went further, proposing "the elimination of war." After all, he wrote, "if it is possible to eliminate the atomic bomb effectively, we can eliminate all the instrumentalities for war." There would have to be a "super agency" in command of force, while each nation would "be permitted a certain amount of arms to be used in its police force." "This may seem like an ambitious program," he noted, "but here is the opportunity to go towards the light at the end of the tunnel—peace." Somewhat later that month, in another memo, he noted that "eliminating the atomic bomb carries with it the thought that if it can be done, why not do the same with biological warfare and the rocket?" Indeed, "why not go a step further and outlaw war?" Once again, he proposed reducing national military strength and developing "an international police force." As late as May 26, he was still writing of his desire to "eliminate all instrumentalities of destruction" and concluding: "Why not try to do the thing which must be done rather than to do something piecemeal which would raise the hopes for peace, but never quiet the fears of war?"[19] Eventually, Truman and the State Department prevailed upon Baruch to narrow his focus to the abolition of nuclear weapons. Baruch, however, continued to chafe at this limitation.[20]

But though Baruch was strongly attracted by the idea of disarmament under world control, he was also deeply suspicious of the Soviet Union. In a letter to Byrnes of March 13, Baruch complained that a U.S. proposal to the United Nations would "have to be based upon a better observance of promises" than provided for in the Acheson-Lilienthal Plan. "In the present circumstances that would be worth very little, judging by your notes to Russia." If the United Nations were to control atomic energy, there would have to be "a better understanding . . . with other countries, particularly Russia," including some assurance that "all contracts and promises" were "lived up to." Frightened of Soviet power in the world and pressed to adopt a hard line by U.S. military officials, Baruch insisted upon what he called "automatic punishment" for violators of the treaty. "It seems to me that a certainty of punishment is essential," he told General Eisenhower in late May. He did not want the U.S. proposal to be left "as a pious declaration like the Kellogg-Briand pact," he recalled, but one that "provided a punitive, swift, sure and condign punishment." [21] The Acheson-Lilienthal Plan did not take this approach and thereby exacerbated Baruch's scorn for its proponents. Indeed, Baruch remained convinced that Acheson was pro-Soviet and "soft on communism." Nor did he have much confidence in the plan's antecedents. "I think that Messrs. Truman, Attlee and King got stampeded into making their original proposals," he wrote privately.[22]

Therefore, when Baruch appeared at the United Nations on June 14, 1946, to present his plan for the international control of atomic energy, it differed substantially from its predecessor. To be sure, Baruch's address contained the rhetoric made popular by critics of the Bomb, including a reference to the choice of "World Peace or World Destruction," and even touched upon his earlier theme of abolishing war. It also proposed to strengthen world authority through unprecedented limitations on national sovereignty. But the Baruch Plan departed from the Acheson-Lilienthal Plan by providing for the creation of a U.N. control body that, among other things, would make an initial survey of raw materials, punish offending nations (presumably through nuclear war), and—for enforcement actions—lack the Security Council veto. Because the United States then enjoyed a large, built-in majority in the United Nations and would also, as in the Acheson-Lilienthal Plan, retain its nuclear weapons until the final stage of international control, this plan was heavily weighted toward what Baruch considered the security needs of the United States.[23]

In the context of the growing Soviet-American fear and suspicion that characterized the Cold War, no agreement on these or other lines was reached. Rejecting the Baruch Plan, Soviet diplomatic officials proposed instead that the United States destroy its nuclear stockpile as the first step toward nuclear disarmament. In the view of U.S. officials, this proposal heavily favored Soviet interests and, consequently, they quickly dismissed it. Truman told Baruch that July: "We should not under any circumstances throw away our gun until we are sure the rest of the world can't arm against us." Instead, the U.S. government clung doggedly to the Baruch Plan, refusing to accept its modification. Earlier, Baruch had succeeded in scrapping the idea that the U.S. plan serve as a "basis" for negotiations. Consequently, he now insisted that the United States "stand firm on the position we have taken" and accept "no compromise." Conversing with Australian foreign minister Herbert Evatt, Baruch turned off his hearing aid when he decided he had heard enough. Then he lectured Evatt on why the American proposal could not be changed. On December 30, 1946, Baruch secured official U.N. endorsement of his plan, but this represented little more than a propaganda victory, for the Kremlin remained uninterested in it.[24]

Behind the rigidity of the U.S. stance lay not only growing fears of the Soviet Union but an unwarranted comfort some officials took in the U.S. nuclear monopoly. The scientists and the State Department had agreed that this monopoly was temporary and would last five years or less. But others were emboldened by a greater sense of security. "America can get what she wants if she insists on it," Baruch told David Lilienthal. "After all, we've got it and they haven't and won't have for a long time to come." His notes for a June meeting with Truman are consonant with this assumption. "Anyway," he wrote, "we've got the Bomb." Truman, too, was beginning to take heart at the notion that America's exclusive possession of the weapon guaranteed U.S. security, an idea he imbibed from General Groves, who predicted that the U.S. monopoly would last for up to twenty years. So convinced was the president of the Soviet Union's backwardness in this area that, in 1949, when it exploded its first atomic bomb, he refused, for a time, to accept the event as a reality.[25]

Returning to Business as Usual

If the Baruch Plan represented a clumsy and unproductive compromise between the new thinking and the old, subsequent U.S. policy signaled a substantial reversion to traditional norms of international behavior. An accelerated buildup of the U.S. nuclear arsenal provided one indication of the trend. In the first postwar months, the U.S. government had done little to develop a nuclear stockpile and, by November 1946, possessed only two atomic bombs. Baruch and his aides, however, argued that, until a treaty for international control was signed, the United States should continue to manufacture the Bomb. Truman, too, considered U.S. nuclear weaponry insufficient and gave orders to expand it. Consequently, by June 1947, the U.S. arsenal had grown to thirteen atomic bombs, with a production rate of two per month. The Czech coup and the Berlin crisis spurred a substantially greater buildup. The government added nuclear reactors at Hanford in 1948 and 1949 and, at Truman's orders, produced large numbers of nuclear weapons, bringing the U.S. nuclear stockpile to approximately 200 atomic bombs by late 1949. That July, Truman secretly told a group of diplomats from friendly countries that "we'll never obtain international control" and, therefore, "we must be strongest in atomic weapons."[26]

Although discussions of international control of atomic energy continued at the United Nations, they did so without much enthusiasm from American officials. Baruch's successor, Frederick Osborn, recalled that, in December 1946, shortly after he assumed his duties, Acheson called a committee meeting at which the "Army and others" opposed any further negotiations on the subject. Privately, Acheson told Osborn "that there was quite a question in the State Department whether the negotiations should continue because they had been turned down so definitely by Russia, and it might be foolish for us to be . . . suppliants." Nevertheless, Osborn spoke forcefully for continuing the U.N. process, pointing out that representatives of other countries (especially Great Britain, Canada, and France) thought that Baruch himself might have been an impediment to agreement. "For this reason," Osborn noted, the committee agreed to continue negotiations, although it did not think "there was likely to be any breakthrough." Acheson emphasized that the United States should not appear to have "refused to negotiate."[27]

Appearances were maintained, but the U.S. negotiating position grew increasingly inflexible. In July 1947, for example, the British delegate suggested privately to Osborn some minor modifications in the Western negotiating position. Osborn recalled that "I rather lost my temper and told him that the British government apparently did not know what they wanted, and that if they were trying to force us to accept a weak treaty they were trying something contrary to the interests of their own people." In late 1948, he stated, "almost every country" on the U.N. Atomic Energy Commission "urged us to compromise and the question was constantly debated within the United States delegation." But believing that "any compromise whatsoever would be dangerous to the security of the United States," Osborn insisted, successfully, upon an unyielding position. Sometimes this brought him into direct conflict with the U.S. delegate to the United Nations, Warren Austin. That same October, Osborn fumed that Austin had done "tremendous injury" to the U.S. position by his talk of compromise. Austin "has been entirely loyal to his instructions, but very deep in his heart he rebels against carrying them out and . . . gets things balled up." Angry at Austin's assistants, Osborn charged that one was "guilty of actual sabotage," while another showed a distressingly "compromising spirit," which "leads to his making a dangerous impression." Osborn became infuriated when, at a press conference, Austin stated that the atomic energy situation was "not hopeless" and that "a way will be found to reach agreement." After Austin left,

Osborn corrected these "extremely dangerous" remarks by adding that "the impasse was really hopeless until the Soviet [leaders] changed their entire attitude." The U.S. position "cannot be compromised," he wrote privately in early 1949, "for a too weak plan would be worse than none." [28]

By this point, of course, there were signs that, public declarations to the contrary, the U.S. government had little interest in nuclear disarmament under almost any circumstances. On February 9, 1949, noted Atomic Energy Commission (AEC) chair David Lilienthal, the president told him "that the atomic bomb was the mainstay and all he had; that the Russians would have probably taken over Europe a long time ago if it were not for that. Therefore, he had to guard it very carefully." That spring, Truman secretly decided to make the Bomb the centerpiece of future U.S. strategic planning. When the Soviet Union tested its first atomic bomb in the fall of 1949, the State Department's Policy Planning Staff reviewed the U.S. position on international control of atomic energy, but without much interest in developing a disarmament approach that would appeal to the Kremlin. Karl Compton, the director of the Research and Development Board of the Defense Department, told the group that "abolition of the atomic process . . . would menace our security, as the Russians have a great advantage over us in conventional weapons." Uncomfortable with U.S. hypocrisy in the area of nuclear weapons, Acheson—now secretary of state— told Lilienthal in late December that "if we keep saying we want the control policy when we don't, we are perhaps fooling others, but we shouldn't commit a fraud upon ourselves." In late 1952, McGeorge Bundy reported that the State Department's disarmament panel thought that "no real negotiation in this area would at present be fruitful or even desirable." [29]

American policymakers also adapted themselves to nuclear proliferation, at least when it bolstered their Cold War camp. The powerful impetus provided by the first Soviet nuclear weapons test, Acheson recalled, brought Anglo-American-Canadian negotiations about sharing the Bomb near fruition. Indeed, negotiators agreed that "fabrication of atomic weapons would be concentrated on this side of the Atlantic with arrangements for a certain number to be allotted to the United Kingdom." But in early 1950, the British arrest of Klaus Fuchs for espionage stirred up a hornet's nest in Congress, and the plan was scotched. The situation proved even trickier in France, where, in the spring of 1949, American officials considered the atomic energy field "rather badly tainted with Sovietism." Any information supplied to Joliot-Curie "would undoubtedly be passed on promptly to the Russians," they complained. Consequently, they looked for "means of putting leverage on the French to clean their atomic house." For the time being, the United States sought "to slow down the French program." By contrast, the Defense Department argued that, in Japan, then shaping up as a promising Cold War ally, "any attempted imposition of post-treaty atomic energy controls would be objectionable." After full restoration of Japanese sovereignty, "political negotiations might well be undertaken with the Japanese government . . . with the view of reaching a mutually acceptable agreement concerning Japan's interest and activity in the field of atomic energy, particularly in regard to the military applications." [30]

On to Armageddon

In this climate of Cold War thinking, the nuclear arms race rapidly accelerated. On October 5, 1949, shortly after the president announced the first successful test of a Soviet atomic bomb, AEC commissioner Lewis Strauss sent a memo to his fellow commissioners calling for "an intensive effort" to build a hydrogen bomb, a weapon with a thousand times the power of the bomb that had destroyed Hiroshima. "That is the way to stay ahead," he insisted. A self-made businessman who had publicly argued against the possibility of eliminating atomic bombs, Strauss believed that "the only thing that retires a weapon is a superior weapon." In his vigorous campaign for the H-Bomb, Strauss was joined by the Joint Chiefs of Staff, Senator Brien McMahon (chair of the Joint Committee on Atomic Energy), and scientists Edward Teller, Ernest Lawrence, Karl Compton, and Luis Alvarez. "I believe it unwise to renounce, unilaterally, any weapon which an enemy can reasonably be expected to possess," Strauss told the president. "My opinion . . . based upon discussions with military experts is . . . that the weapon may be critically useful against a large enemy force both as a weapon of offense and as a defensive measure." [31]

Unexpectedly, though, substantial resistance to producing an H-Bomb developed within the Atomic Energy Commission. The General Advisory Committee (GAC), chaired by Oppenheimer and composed of scientists, unanimously opposed such a policy. Six members declared their belief that "the extreme dangers to mankind inherent in the proposal wholly outweigh any military advantage that could come from this development." Given its unlimited destructive power, the H-Bomb could "become a weapon of genocide." If it refused to develop the weapon, the United States could provide "by example some limitations on the totality of war"; at the same time, it would remain protected by its large stock of atomic bombs. Two other GAC members, Enrico Fermi and Isidor Rabi, also warned of "genocide" and noted that the United States already possessed sufficient atomic bombs for its defense. Why not, they asked, use this opportunity to halt the arms race by securing a pledge from all nations to renounce production of the H-Bomb? [32] Responding to the GAC report, the AEC split three to two in its November 9 recommendation to the president. The minority, led by Strauss, championed a crash program to build the new weapon, but the majority, led by Lilienthal, opposed it. "To launch upon a program of Superbombs," Lilienthal declared, "would set us upon still another costly cycle of misconception and illusion about the value to us of weapons of mass destruction as the chief means of protecting ourselves and of furthering our national policy."[33]

Despite the stand of the AEC majority and of the General Advisory Committee, the outcome was heavily weighted toward proponents of the new weapon. Although Truman appointed a special committee of the National Security Council to consider the question of the H-Bomb, he was predisposed to build it. As he recalled in his memoirs, "I believed that anything that would assure us the lead in the field of atomic energy development for defense had to be tried out." The committee—composed of Acheson, Lilienthal, and Secretary of Defense Louis Johnson—did not see eye to eye; indeed, as Acheson recalled, Johnson and Lilienthal had "a head-on confrontation" over the issue, after which Acheson shuttled back and forth between them. In mid-January 1950, seeking to circumvent the machinery of the National Security Council committee, Johnson sent a memo from the Joint Chiefs of Staff directly to the president. Arguing that "military considerations outweigh" any possible "moral objections," the Joint Chiefs claimed that renunciation of the H-Bomb would be "foolhardy altruism." Truman informed his Central Intelligence Agency (CIA) director that this memo "made a lot of sense and that he was inclined to think that was what we should do." Meanwhile, within the committee, Acheson—by this point soured on plans for nuclear disarmament and reconciled to production of the H-Bomb—lined up with Johnson. On January 31, the three committee members met with the president and presented him with a report that favored development of the new weapon. Lilienthal tried once again to make the case for a new disarmament initiative, but the president interrupted him and, as the AEC chair recalled, said that "people are so excited he really hasn't any alternative but to go ahead and that was what he was going to do." Lilienthal felt that he had stood up to "a steamroller" and that the president was "clearly set on what he was going to do before we set foot inside the door." The entire meeting lasted seven minutes.[34]

Those few hopes that this lurch forward in the nuclear arms race might spur new disarmament initiatives were soon scotched by the administration. In the aftermath of Truman's H-Bomb decision, Acheson delivered a series of public and private addresses to rebuff talk by Senator McMahon of a "world-wide atomic peace," by Senator Tydings of a world disarmament committee, and by U.N. Secretary General Trygve Lie of a ten-point program of negotiations with the Soviet Union. "No approach from the free world . . . will help to resolve our mutual problems," Acheson declared. The U.N. leader, he complained privately, was "more eager than aware." Meanwhile, the administration secured the resignation of key opponents of the H-Bomb from the AEC's General Advisory Committee and developed immense nuclear construction projects on an unprecedented scale. Within a few years, this nuclear program absorbed approximately one-tenth the electricity produced in the United States. On November 1, 1952, the U.S. government set off its first thermonuclear device in the Pacific. A thousand times as powerful as the bomb that had devastated Hiroshima, the weapon obliterated an entire island, one mile in diameter, and left a vast crater on the ocean floor.[35]

Plans for using atomic and hydrogen bombs emerged somewhat more slowly, at least in part because key U.S. policymakers had developed some qualms about waging nuclear war. In June 1947, for example, Marshall told Osborn that he "would hesitate to use the bomb except as a final act of self-preservation." Despite the administration's much heralded dispatch of 60 "atomic capable" B-29 bombers to Great Britain in July 1948, during the Berlin blockade, the planes carried no nuclear weapons. On July 21, in a meeting with U.S. officials, Truman declared: "I don't think we ought to use this thing unless we absolutely have to. It is a terrible thing to order the use of something that"—and here he paused, looking reflectively at his desk—"that is so terribly destructive, destructive beyond anything we have ever had." Touching the same theme he had struck immediately after the Hiroshima and Nagasaki bombings, he added: "You have got to understand that this isn't a military weapon. . . . It is used to wipe out women and children and unarmed people. . . . So we have got to treat this differently from rifles and cannon and ordinary things like that."[36]

This uneasiness about nuclear war faded somewhat as the Soviet-American confrontation grew more intense. Responding in September 1948 to a question from Secretary of Defense Forrestal about whether he would use the Bomb, Truman said that "if it became necessary, no one need have a misgiving but that he would do so." That same month, the National Security Council agreed that, in the event of "hostilities," the U.S. military "must be ready to utilize promptly and effectively all appropriate means available, including atomic weapons." Truman, to be sure, retained sole authority to order use of the Bomb, and privately he continued to express his distaste for it. People who "think this is just another bomb . . . are making a very serious mistake," he told Lilienthal in February 1949. Launching into a discussion of the destructiveness of atomic war, he again concluded: "This isn't just another weapon." Significantly, though, when Lilienthal added his own comments along these lines, Truman shifted his stance somewhat: "Dave, we will never use it again if we can possibly help it. But I know the Russians would use it on us if they had it."[37]

Subsequently, the U.S. government evinced an increased willingness to employ nuclear weapons. In August 1949, at a meeting of top State Department officials, George Kennan expressed his "uneasy feeling" that the United States was "traveling down the atomic road rather too fast" and declared that it "might be best for this country if it were decided that atomic bombs would never be used." In response, the secretary of state maintained that "it would be difficult to justify any such approach, particularly if our failure to use atomic weapons meant a great loss of lives or a defeat in war." Later, Acheson also rejected Kennan's proposal for "no first use" of nuclear weapons. That December, to the alarm of the British government, the U.S. secretary of state secretly told the Atlantic Defence Committee "in very strong terms the intention of his government to use the atomic bomb" in a future war. By the end of the meeting, during which he raised strong objections to this position, the British secretary of defense was relieved to find that officials agreed "that nothing they did now could commit governments to the use of the atomic bomb." [38] Nevertheless, employment of the Bomb was clearly becoming more acceptable to American officials.

With the onset of the Korean War, this slide toward use of the Bomb accelerated. Admittedly, Truman's heavily publicized remarks at his November 1950 press conference about employing the atomic bomb in Korea raised a false alarm as to the imminence of nuclear war. British prime minister Attlee told his cabinet that, in their subsequent meeting, Truman "assured" him that he "had never had any intention of using the atom bomb in Korea." [39] But this reassurance was not entirely justified for, in fact, the Truman administration had been discussing the use of nuclear weapons in the war. As early as June 25, 1950, the first day of the conflict, the president had inquired if the United States could "knock out" Soviet air bases in the Far East. Told that it "could be done if we used A-Bombs," the president authorized the U.S. Air Force to draw up plans for such an attack. On December 1, after Chinese intervention in the war, there was further discussion—this time at a high-level meeting in the Pentagon—about the use of atomic weapons in Korea. Later that month, in the context of possible Soviet air action against U.S. forces in Korea, the administration again discussed employing nuclear weapons. [40]

One of the factors that militated against using the Bomb was strong opposition from foreign governments and peoples. In a "Top Secret" memo, the State Department's Far East specialist warned that a "unilateral decision by the United States to use the atomic bomb against China would in all likelihood destroy the unity preserved thus far in the combined UN action in Korea." Indeed, "it is probable that U.S. use of the A-bomb would be deplored and denounced by a considerable number of nations who had up to that time supported the action in Korea." Moreover, "should the Soviet Union be prepared to launch a third World War, atomic bombing of China would encourage Soviet participation in war under conditions by which the U.S. moral position would be irreparably damaged while the Soviets would suffer the minimum condemnation." Finally, use of the Bomb on an Asiatic population would cause a "revulsion of feeling" to "spread throughout Asia. . . . Our efforts to win the Asiatics to our side would be cancelled and our influence in non-Communist nations of Asia would deteriorate to an almost non-existent quantity." From Ceylon, a U.S. diplomat warned that use of the Bomb in non-Soviet Asia would "create such [a] wave [of] horror and antipathy toward [the] USA in Asia . . . that we thereby run serious risk of losing [the] support of most Asiatic peoples if war with [the] USSR results." In his memoirs, Truman recalled the great difficulty he had in quieting the foreign uproar over his November 30 pronouncement on nuclear weapons, as well as the opposition of all U.S. allies in Korea to General MacArthur's proposal to extend the war to the mainland of China.[41]

Nevertheless, the administration continued to give serious consideration to using the Bomb. In April 1951, the president called in the new AEC chair, Gordon Dean, and told him that a heavy concentration of Communist military forces in North Korea, China, and the Soviet Union might portend an attempt to push U.S. troops out of Korea and, perhaps, seize Japan. Although he had not yet decided to use nuclear weapons, he was dispatching them to the Pacific. The following month, Paul Nitze, director of the State Department's Policy Planning Staff, told the Canadian ambassador that "our preliminary thinking was that a massive Soviet entry into the Far Eastern situation would lead to the [American] use of atomic weapons."[42] This situation never materialized, and such action was not taken, but the atmosphere remained ominous. In a conversation with General Matthew Ridgway that June, Secretary of Defense Marshall stated that the situation in Korea had deteriorated to the point that he was going to recommend to the president that they warn Chinese leaders that, unless the fighting ended, "we are going to give them a taste of the atom." By 1952, Truman himself had apparently come around to this view, for he told aides that he would consider use of the Bomb if the North Koreans and Chinese did not agree to an armistice. "The proper approach now would be an ultimatum," he wrote, "threatening all out war."[43]

Ultimately, of course, cooler heads prevailed and the Korean conflict did not escalate into a nuclear catastrophe, but, in later years, Truman reflected on how very dangerous the situation had become. Recalling his resistance to the pressures of the generals to use nuclear weapons on Chinese cities and thus unleash a global holocaust, he wrote that "I could not bring myself to order the slaughter of 25,000,000 noncombatants. . . . I just could not make the order for a Third World War."[44] His recognition of the temptation to employ nuclear weapons in a time of military crisis may explain why, in a televised interview with Edward R. Murrow on February 2, 1958, Truman made one of the most somber forecasts of his career. Expressing his hope that the H-Bomb would never be used, he added a grim warning: "If the world gets into turmoil, it will be used. You can be sure of that."[45]

Handling Critics of the Bombing of Japan

Increasingly committed to maintaining U.S. military superiority, American officials reacted with growing hostility to public criticism of nuclear weapons. The continuing popular uneasiness about the atomic bombing of Japan was particularly irritating. Lamenting the appearance of Hersey's "Hiroshima" in the *New Yorker*, one of Baruch's aides suggested that the magazine print a piece about the sufferings of allied prisoners of war in Japan "to counter the feeling that the use of the bomb against Japan was a bad thing." In September 1946, when Admiral William F. Halsey was quoted in an Associated Press dispatch as criticizing use of the Bomb against Japan, Baruch complained bitterly to Forrestal that this gave "aid and comfort to the minority in this country who seek to weaken our national security by putting America in the wrong on moral grounds in the eyes of the world." Forrestal, no less irked, responded that Halsey was "wrapped up in the same package as Henry Wallace,"[46] then the navy secretary's arch demon. Convinced of the need for a counterattack, Truman asked Stimson "to assemble the facts" that would present the administration's case to the public.[47]

Stimson's brief for the administration, entitled "The Decision to Use the Atomic Bomb," was published in the February 1947 issue of *Harper's*, and excerpts were carried in newspapers, on radio networks, and in mass circulation magazines. Making the case for the atomic bombing, the former secretary of war argued that it had averted a bloody invasion of Japan at a cost of "over a million casualties" to American forces, "much larger" casualties to the "enemy," and "additional large losses" to U.S. allies.[48] In fact, this was a gross exaggeration and, during wartime, neither Stimson nor other top American officials ever predicted casualty levels of this magnitude.[49] Privately, Stimson attributed the article's appearance to the fact "that Jim Conant felt very much worried over the spreading accusation that it was entirely unnecessary to use the atomic bomb." In a letter to Truman, Stimson maintained that "the criticisms which it has been intended to answer were made mainly by Chicago scientists, some of whom had been connected with the development of the project. The article has also been intended to satisfy the doubts of that rather difficult class of the community which will have charge of the education of the next generation, namely educators and historians." [50] Naturally, administration officials—past and present—applauded the results. Secretary of State Marshall was enthusiastic about the article, reported Acheson, who added that it "was badly needed and . . . superbly done." Byrnes, the outgoing secretary of state, expressed his hope that it might "stop some of the idle talk." [51]

This effort to counter the critics of the Hiroshima bombing represented not merely a defense of past activities but an attempt to maintain America's nuclear options in the future. Conant—who had submitted eight pages of editorial changes for the article—told Stimson that "if the propaganda against the use of the atomic bomb had been allowed to grow unchecked, the strength of our military position by virtue of having the bomb would have been correspondingly weakened." The Russians had to be "convinced that we would have the bomb in quantity and would be prepared to use it without hesitation in another war." Writing in a similar vein, Bush informed Stimson that the article was necessary "not only for the purposes of history, but also in connection with the current thinking in this country." Stimson himself told Baruch of his hope that the article would be useful "in meeting the ill-informed and sentimental criticisms which might, if continued, produce a dangerous climate of opinion." [52]

As nuclear disarmament groups turned the bombings of Hiroshima and Nagasaki into symbols of the horrors of nuclear war, U.S. government officials grew ever more sensitive about the issue. Convinced that any discussion of the atomic attacks would redound to the disadvantage of the United States, American occupation authorities in Japan censored or blocked publication of relevant newspaper stories, as well as literary, artistic, and scientific works.[53] In 1950, U.S. officials also banned the annual atomic bomb commemorative ceremonies in Hiroshima. In occupied Germany, too, U.S. authorities acted to block public references to the atomic bombing of Japan and formally prohibited Hiroshima Day events. In 1948, U.S. authorities refused to allow radio mention of an August 6 pacifist demonstration in Stuttgart if it was associated with the atomic bombing of Hiroshima. In 1950, Berlin pacifists and world government advocates, who had held large peace celebrations in the French sector of that city on August 6, 1949, planned to hold a similar demonstration in the American sector. But although German authorities granted permission, U.S. officials refused to allow it to occur.[54]

The Problem of the Scientists' Movement

U.S. government officials formulating American policy toward nuclear weapons viewed the atomic scientists' movement as particularly dangerous. Baruch told Lilienthal: "The only thing the scientist does is to frighten the public about atomic energy, and [this] may force something foolish to be done." As he put it, "the scientists take an extreme view" of the Bomb. On another occasion, Baruch argued that "the scientists should keep to their field and not go into ethics or politics except to give such judgments and opinions as they are trained for to men who know how to make the practical and social applications of atomic energy." Not surprisingly, Baruch decided to "drop the scientists" from the planning process for international control of nuclear weapons "because," as he recalled impatiently, "I knew all I wanted to know." [55] Osborn, Baruch's successor as U.S. delegate to the U.N. Atomic Energy Commission, publicly attacked the atomic scientists in late 1947. "When the scientist . . . sets forth his views on the causes of war and the means of peace, he is traveling far from home and his morals are apt to suffer accordingly," Osborn argued before a university audience. If, as a result of "the wantonness with which he deals with the facts," the American people "do not think honestly and clearly, how can we expect to win in this great debate with Soviet Communism?" Osborn also made arrangements for press criticism of the Emergency Committee of Atomic Scientists. [56]

State Department officials shared this jaundiced view of the scientists' movement. In August 1946, reporting on a speaking tour he had recently undertaken for the State Department, George Kennan wrote that the atomic scientists he had met at Berkeley "seemed to combine a grudging approval of Mr. Baruch's proposals . . . with an unshakeable faith that if they could only get some Soviet scientists by the buttonhole and enlighten them about the nature of atomic weapons, all would be well." He added, sarcastically:

Politically, these people are as innocent as six-year-old maidens. In trying to explain things to them I felt like one who shatters the pure ideals of tender youth. But . . . they didn't believe much of what I said and left, I am sure, unshaken in the comfortable con-viction that such evil as exists in the world has its seat in the State Department, which doesn't want to understand, and not by any chance in the breasts of upstanding foreign statesmen who await only the generous hand of friendship from our side and a pledge of faith in the form of the secrets of the manufacture of atomic weapons. [57]

Although the atomic scientists did not favor giving atomic bomb secrets to the Russians, Szilard and other leaders of the movement did propose a meeting of American and Soviet scientists—an early version of the Pugwash confer-ences—that same year. But Secretary of State Byrnes blocked the meeting. [58]

The hostility to the atomic scientists was particularly ferocious within the U.S. Army. Despising the movement's leaders and particularly Szilard, Gen-eral Groves worked feverishly to destroy their influence. In September 1945, he sought to derail the conference on the atomic bomb that they had organized at the University of Chicago. In 1946, probably at the urging of Groves, the army secretly arranged to have Szilard's employment by the Manhattan project terminated. That same year, Groves vetoed the award of a proposed Certificate of Appreciation for Civilian War Service to the scientist. "It was quite evident" that Szilard "showed a lack of support, even approaching disloyalty, to his superiors," the general charged. Referring contemptuously to the activist scientists, Groves told an interviewer in 1967: "They started to find that they were looked upon as experts. So just like . . . college students today they started to say, 'We should be running this. We know everything.'. . . But they knew nothing about international affairs, nothing about management, nothing about anything else." Groves claimed: "I was very bitterly opposed by this group because I didn't want to give all of our information to the Russians. That was the key to the opposition"—that and "the fact that they were trying to get control." [59]

The scientists' movement enjoyed a less consistently hostile relationship with the Atomic Energy Commission, an agency that, through their postwar campaign for civilian control of atomic energy, they had helped to create. For a time, the movement had a powerful friend in Lilienthal, the AEC's first chair. Not only did he play a key role in pressing their views, from the time of the Acheson-Lilienthal Plan to his spirited fight against the H-Bomb, but he remained a direct supporter of the scientists' movement. But upon Lilienthal's departure from the post in early 1950, Truman chose an individual with quite different views as his successor: Gordon Dean, one of the two AEC commissioners who had supported the H-Bomb's development. Thereafter, the AEC's relationship with the scientists' movement rapidly deteriorated. Later that year, the AEC seized and burned 3,000 copies of the *Scientific American* for publishing an article on the H-Bomb by one of the weapon's leading scientific critics, Hans Bethe. Because the article contained no secrets, the publisher (Gerard Piel) concluded that the AEC was attempting to intimidate opponents of the Bomb. [60]

Perhaps as a result of the negative image of the scientists' movement within policymaking circles, Robert Oppenheimer, the government's top scientific adviser on atomic energy matters, never gave it his wholehearted support. To be sure, Oppenheimer served as a member of the Advisory Panel of the Federation of American Scientists and chair of the Board of Sponsors of the *Bulletin of the Atomic Scientists*. Even so, he kept his distance from the movement. In conversations with government officials, he criticized some of its leaders and its popular publication, *One World or None*. On repeated occasions, he declined invitations from the Emergency Committee of Atomic Scientists, citing doubts about its plans or disagreements with them. Writing to William Higinbotham, president of the Federation of American Scientists, in May 1947, he argued bluntly that the movement should abandon its political activities. "Our role can no longer be that of the prophets of doom," he contended, "but rather that of a group of specialized and, in their way, competent men . . . who are after all intellectuals and not politicians." [61]

The U.S. government took a particularly hard line toward politically active scientists in other nations. Based on a study he did for the Federation of American Scientists, Weisskopf estimated in April 1952 that "at least 50% of all the foreign scientists who want to enter the U.S. meet some difficulties." These difficulties included lengthy delays in obtaining visas or outright denials of them. Although the State Department usually failed to provide explanations, scientists in the field of nuclear physics or whose political activity was "suspected of being unorthodox by U.S. standards" were the most frequently rejected group. Some of these people were probably Communists, but they also included a large number of scientists whose only political indiscretion appears to have been their criticism of nuclear weapons. Among them were Lew Kowarski of France (whose statements on the dangers of the arms race had alienated U.S. officials and who was barred from entering the United States for scientific meetings from 1951 to 1957) and H. S. W. Massey of Great Britain (the executive vice-president of the British Atomic Scientists' Association). Rudolf Peierls, president of the Atomic Scientists' Association, who had no left-wing connections, encountered repeated difficulties acquiring a visa when he sought to visit the United States. [62]

Marc Oliphant, Australia's most distinguished physicist and a prominent opponent of the Bomb, was also barred from traveling to the United States for scientific meetings. According to Oliphant, the U.S. consul general "assured me that I was not accused of having any Communist affiliations or of subversive activity. But my public speeches . . . and my campaigning for peace 'were providing bullets for the Russians and other enemies to fire back at the U.S.' " [63]

America's own atomic scientists became the subjects of intense loyalty-security investigations and experienced repeated attacks upon their patriotism. In September 1946, as part of its plans for emergency detention of alleged subversives, the FBI told the Justice Department that "existing scientific groups have been infiltrated by Communists with the view in mind of propagandizing the relinquishment of the secret of the atomic bomb." Four years later, Senator Joseph McCarthy charged that the Federation of American Scientists was "heavily infiltrated with communist fellow-travellers." Harold Urey, one of many scientists unjustifiably denounced by McCarthy, responded: "Because we told disagreeable truths, we have been accused of wishing to give up our progress because we are impractical dreamers or plain traitors." As one historian has observed, although no American atomic scientist was ever shown to be guilty of treasonable activity, "No group was more closely inspected or forced so often to prove their loyalty. Because of this special attention, physicists and mathematicians made up more than half of the people who were identified as Communists in congressional hearings. Hundreds of scientists were mercilessly pursued, often losing their jobs, some of them ending in exile or suicide." In connection with AEC employment alone, the U.S. government investigated in detail some 150,000 people by the end of the 1950s.[64]

Although much of the loyalty-security program was purportedly an attempt to prevent espionage, in practice it led to attacks on critics of the Bomb, for government officials sometimes regarded their criticism of the weapon as evidence of subversive intent. When Leo Szilard published a "Letter to Stalin" in the December 1947 issue of the *Bulletin of the Atomic Scientists*, the Justice Department explored the possibilities of prosecuting him under the Logan Act.[65] Hans Bethe, a leader of the Emergency Committee of Atomic Scientists and a prominent foe of the H-Bomb, was placed under surveillance by the FBI. With the issuance of the report of the AEC General Advisory Committee opposing development of the H-Bomb, AEC commissioner Lewis Strauss immediately suspected committee chair Robert Oppenheimer of disloyalty to the United States.[66] According to Ralph Lapp, then a young physicist, his own writings criticizing AEC secrecy and nuclear weapons testing turned him into "public enemy number one." In the fall of 1952, the acting secretary of state told the president that he, the secretary of state, and the CIA director considered a forthcoming article in the *Saturday Evening Post* by Lapp and journalist Stewart Alsop "a most serious breach of national security and one of a series of such breaches." The article, "The Inside Story of Our First Hydrogen Bomb," was a most unlikely candidate for this designation. Although it called attention to the dangers of the nuclear arms race, it provided little more than a history of the decision to build the weapon. The article had also been cleared for publication by the AEC.[67]

Albert Einstein, chair of the Emergency Committee of Atomic Scientists, had long irritated U.S. government officials by his well-publicized statements calling for peace and disarmament. In late 1947, one of Baruch's aides told his boss that, after reading an article by Einstein on those subjects, he thought someone should propose that Einstein "stick to the field of mathematics." Although Einstein had never shown any signs of being a Soviet agent or a Communist, in 1950 the FBI launched an investigation of the famed scientist to explore both possibilities. In part, this action was a response to a request from the Immigration and Naturalization Service, which suggested the appealing prospect of canceling his citizenship. Eventually, J. Edgar Hoover's minions gathered some 1,500 pages of evidence on Einstein's allegedly subversive activities, including articles he had written for the *Bulletin of the Atomic Scientists* and other publications calling for nuclear arms controls and world government. Only after the scientist's death in 1955 did the FBI close the Einstein case.[68]

Another scientist critical of the Bomb, Niels Bohr, received gentler handling by U.S. officials, but they consistently spurned his proposals. Impressed by Bohr's eminence in nuclear physics and by his great prestige in his native Denmark, State Department representatives maintained an appearance of respect for his opinions by meeting with him on numerous occasions. Even so, they rejected his call for greater "openness" about nuclear weapons as a means of alleviating fear between the superpowers. "I could not agree that the mutual lack of confidence between the West and the Soviet Union rested on . . . mere fear," one State Department official reported in 1948. Later that year, Marshall endorsed a recommendation that "no 'offer' in the sense of the Bohr proposal should be made."[69] After Bohr, dismayed by the failure of the United States to advance new proposals for international control of nuclear weapons, issued his June 1950 Open Letter, the Danish government lobbied U.S. officials on behalf of his new proposal. Nevertheless, with Secretary Acheson firmly opposed to the Bohr plan, the State Department again rejected the advice of the Danish physicist. Years later, Groves claimed that Bohr "was at times a thorn in the sides of everyone dealing with him."[70]

Coping with Other Critics

Foreigners, of course, could be troublesome, for they often exhibited less enthusiasm for the U.S. role in the nuclear arms race than did Americans. India's prime minister, Jawaharlal Nehru, proved particularly irritating in this regard, for he consistently denounced nuclear weapons. Asked his opinion of the H-Bomb shortly after Truman announced plans to develop it, the Indian leader replied that, if one thought the world worthwhile, the H-Bomb had to be abandoned. Nehru did not have a "reasonable view" of the U.S. nuclear weapons program, reported the American embassy, which warned Washington that "similar remarks" by Nehru "may be made at any time and contribute to further distortion of [the] Indian perspective on this subject."[71] U.S. government officials also appear to have found British pacifism objectionable for, in the early 1950s, they seized Stuart Morris, chair of the Peace Pledge Union, when he entered the United States to begin a speaking tour arranged by American pacifists. Offered release on the condition that he abandon his tour, Morris refused to do so and, after being detained for two weeks on Ellis Island, the doughty pacifist was finally allowed to continue.[72]

U.S. government officials also reacted coolly to the burgeoning world government movement. In May 1946, Richard Tolman, Baruch's top scientific adviser, reported that he had told Harold Urey that, although "we appreciated and welcomed his support," the Baruch group "did not want him to tie us up with the job of working for 'world government.'" In November, Baruch complained to Acheson that abolition of the veto "has been enlarged by the 'One Worlders' to mean something different than the language" of the U.S. atomic energy proposal; indeed, "the 'One Worlders' have made more of this thing than we intend to." By May 1947, Baruch was still attacking promoters of world government, but this time for recognizing the limitations of his plan. "I am rather chagrined by your inability to grasp the problem that was presented to us," he wrote tartly in a draft letter to Cord Meyer, Jr., the UWF president. "I do not think you have clarified but have confused the issues and confused the people."[73] Upon assumption of his atomic energy post, Osborn publicly proclaimed that it was "a fallacy to believe that the effort to control atomic energy for peaceful purposes only requires some sort of world government, or is a step toward world government." In 1950, he complained to a correspondent that "world government under the present retarded conditions of many of the world's peoples would lead either to war or else to the loss of all those values towards which Western European civilization is striving."[74]

Indeed, as the movement for world federation gained momentum, the State Department firmly rejected it. In January 1946, veteran State Department official Sumner Welles publicly assailed Einstein's plea for world government, arguing that it was "wholly impracticable." As presently constituted, the United Nations could find "an effective solution" to the problem of the atomic bomb. Appearing before the House Committee on Foreign Affairs on May 5, 1948, Secretary of State Marshall testified against proposals to strengthen the U.N. charter, arguing that problems of peace were not "solvable merely by new forms of organization." Instead, "it is to changes of substance we must look for the improvement of the world situation."[75] Although Under Secretary of State Will Clayton accepted membership on the UWF Advisory Board in March 1948, policy differences with the organization led him to resign in January 1949, after which he threw his efforts behind the harder-line Atlantic Union Committee. Meeting with an impeccably respectable group of proponents of "limited world government" in April 1949, Secretary Acheson was cordial but unenthusiastic, pointing out "many of the practical difficulties in dealing with the Soviet Union and the numerous barriers to any further limitations on sovereignty in the present world situation."[76]

State Department thinking on how to cope with world federalist activities is captured in a memo of July 29, 1949, drawn up by its Bureau of International Organization Affairs. "There is a real danger that, unless positive action is taken . . . further concentration of public attention on world government movements in the United States will prevent public realization of the present value of the United Nations," it argued. Although the bureau recommended that the "statements of the Department with respect to world government movements should be positive and constructive," making it appear that their viewpoint "is being given intelligent and comprehensive consideration," they should be warned that "the world government movement could defeat its own purposes if its activities result in jeopardizing the United Nations." The State Department should "not discourage" these groups, but "rather guide and afford information" to them. "Responsible officers of the Department" should "maintain informal contact with the major organizations" to "keep the Department aware" of their activities and channel them in the proper direction.[77]

Nevertheless, relations remained tense. In the spring and summer of 1949, Warren Austin, the U.S. ambassador to the United Nations, publicly attacked world federalism. Prominent world federalists, in turn, criticized Austin's "campaign against the world government idea." In an apparent attempt to soothe ruffled feathers, Austin had what UWF described as a "friendly and cooperative meeting" with Cord Meyer, Jr., to whom he claimed that he had been misquoted in recent newspaper accounts.[78] But conflict came to the surface again in early 1950, when State Department officials spoke out strongly against UWF and other federalist proposals in House and Senate committee hearings. Deputy Under Secretary of State Dean Rusk testified in February that "it would be disastrous if, by turning in any irresponsible or whimsical fashion to new forms of organization or glittering formulae for perfection, we were to set ourselves back." In the face of sharply divided testimony, UWF resolutions became stalled in the Senate Foreign Relations Committee and the House Committee on Foreign Affairs. Meyer recalled that when he applied for a position with the State Department in the spring of 1951, "some friends" there "were not encouraging. They explained quite frankly that my prominent association with the world federalist movement had made me so controversial that the department could not risk the public criticism that my appointment might cause."[79]

Like the State Department, Truman now provided little encouragement to world government groups. As a good politician, of course, he occasionally received delegations of prominent federalist leaders.[80] But when Norman Cousins, who had led one of these delegations, proposed in late January 1948 that he establish a presidential committee to study the problem of strengthening the United Nations, Truman rejected the proposal out of hand. "In the light of existing political conditions, both domestic and foreign, there are limits beyond which the administration cannot usefully go at this time," the president explained; "the creation of a Presidential committee would, I feel, be definitely premature." In August, when Meyer asked Truman to send a message of interest and encouragement to the second convention of the World Movement for World Federal Government, the president—on the advice of the State Department—declined to do so.[81] On October 18, 1948, in a public address, Truman warned about the dangers of "atomic weapons and bacteriological warfare" but cautioned that it would "be a long while before the great powers constitute the friendly family of nations which is often described as 'One World.' " Years later, Meyer wrote of a meeting he and other UWF leaders had with the president in the late 1940s. Truman "listened attentively, with his head cocked to one side," Meyer recalled, "and then asked a few questions that showed considerable skepticism." [82] Thus, although the president remained on reasonably good terms with UWF and some of its leaders,[83] he never provided them with any support for their political goals.

Other elements of the federal government gave the world federalist movement a more difficult time, particularly as the heightening Cold War stirred up a new climate of strident nationalism and intolerance. Conducting an investigation of UWF in 1948, the House Committee on Un-American Activities charged that sixteen persons whose names appeared in its literature were affiliated with other groups cited as "Communist-front and/or subversive." When the Truman administration submitted the name of Thomas K. Finletter to Congress as the president's designee for secretary of the air force, legislators assailed his former role as a UWF vice-president. In 1952, a rider tacked onto federal legislation by Senator Pat McCarran of Nevada barred the distribution of funds to federal agencies that promoted, directly or indirectly, "one-world government or one-world citizenship." In accordance with its provisions, the federal government removed numerous books from its overseas information centers, including Clarence Streit's Union Now. Meanwhile, Senator McCarthy and his cohorts repeatedly attacked the "one-worlders." [84]

Defeating "the Trojan Dove"

As might be expected, the U.S. government adopted a very aggressive policy toward the Communist-led movement against the Bomb. In March 1949, when the Cultural and Scientific Conference for World Peace convened in New York City, the FBI spied on its leaders and the State Department denied visas to all foreign delegates from non-Communist countries whom it believed held Communist views.[85] What the U.S. ambassador to France called a "counter-offensive" picked up momentum the following month, when the State Department sought to discredit the first World Congress of the Partisans of Peace in Paris by disseminating hostile material in labor, intellectual, and religious circles and by encouraging the organization of the competing non-Communist rally, which included obtaining speakers for the event.[86] Thereafter, the State Department barred a Peace Partisans delegation from visiting the United States,[87] pressed friendly governments to block the holding of Communist-organized peace conferences in their countries,[88] and launched its own peace propaganda campaign.[89] Secretary Acheson denounced "the Trojan dove from the Communist movement" and charged that the Stockholm peace petition was no more than "a propaganda trick in the spurious 'peace offensive' of the Soviet Union."[90] Joining the attack, the House Committee on Un-American Activities blasted the petition as "Communist chicanery" that would "prepare the path for treason." Among other things, the petition would provide "a gigantic and invaluable Red mailing list for the Communist party" and would "serve as a means of blackmailing for years to come those who may have innocently lent their names" to it.[91]

During the ensuing furor and government investigations, participants in the Communist-led peace campaign might have wondered who was doing the blackmailing. In the summer of 1950, the State Department barred Paul Robeson, a prominent figure at Communist-led peace congresses, from overseas travel. Passport officials told Robeson and his attorneys that, unless he pledged not to make any speeches while abroad, his case would not be reconsidered. As a result, Robeson lost his right to cross international borders.[92] In February 1951, the U.S. government indicted five leaders of the Peace Information Center, the principal organizer of the Stockholm petition in the United States, for failing to register as agents of the Partisans of Peace and its successor, the World Peace Council. Among those indicted, fingerprinted, and handcuffed was its 83-year-old chair, W. E. B. Du Bois, who faced five years' imprisonment, a $10,000 fine, and loss of civil and political rights. Although a federal court dismissed the case against the Peace Information Center in late 1951, the following year the State Department denied an application by Du Bois and his wife to travel to a peace conference in Brazil. "Your proposed travel," it stated, "would be contrary to the best interests of the United States."[93]

Indeed, federal, state, and local authorities conducted a vendetta against participants in Communist-led peace efforts for years thereafter. Linus Pauling, for example, active in a number of Communist-led peace ventures,[94] signed several non-Communist affidavits, but the State Department produced a list of suspect meetings he had addressed, petitions he had signed, and conferences he had endorsed to argue that he had followed the "Communist Party line." [95] Consequently, on three occasions it denied him a passport to attend scholarly meetings abroad. Only in late 1954, when Pauling received the Nobel Prize for Chemistry, did the State Department relent and restore his right to travel.[96] In New York State, the state police worked secretly with local school board officials to arrange the firings of teachers in the public schools who, in the early 1950s, had been active in Communist-led peace ventures.[97]

Soothing Public Opinion

The U.S. government's sensitivity to criticism of nuclear weapons reflected, in part, its determination to control the terms of any public discussion of the Bomb. In the opinion of the Truman administration, a genuine debate on nuclear weapons would undermine their credibility as instruments of war and diplomacy. "Were the United States to . . . publicly debate the issue of the use of the bomb on moral grounds," observed the National Security Council in 1948, "this country might gain the praise of the world's radical fringe and would certainly receive the applause of the Soviet bloc, but the United States would be thoroughly condemned by every sound citizen in Western Europe, whose enfeebled security this country would obviously be threatening." Furthermore, by 1950, when it made its decision to develop the H-Bomb, the administration was growing skittish about public sentiment at home and abroad. "Ideally, it would be desirable in view of the upsurge of the Soviet peace propaganda campaign to say nothing whatever about the H-bomb program," one State Department official advised the secretary of state. Truman himself told Acheson in February 1950 that "the least said about the so-called hydrogen bomb by officials in the position that you and I are in, the better it will be for all concerned." [98]

Increasingly, the administration shaped those statements that it did make about nuclear weapons with the intention of soothing public opinion. " 'The soul searching' minority element of our population, who ultimately have so much influence on the public," noted one U.S. official, "must be addressed in terms of reassuring them that . . . we are still open to proposals whereby this devastating weapon could be controlled by international means." At a meeting of the U.S. delegation to the United Nations in September 1950, Ambassador Austin "asked whether there should not be some recognition of the suspicion which prevails in the Assembly among all nations that we have not been sincere in our [disarmament] offers." Senator Henry Cabot Lodge, Jr., fretted that the U.S. stand "was not clear at all in the mind of the average man, judging from the Stockholm Appeal," and the American position, he believed, "should be advertised to offset this effect." Only John Foster Dulles seemed contemptuous of shaping U.S. statements to meet popular fears about the Bomb. Noting the "principal reliance" of the American government on nuclear weapons, he dismissed any U.S. disarmament proposal as "simply a propaganda move." Although Dulles "favored such propaganda when it could be gotten away with, he did not believe this field should be selected" for the "main propaganda effort." [99]

The advocates of tailoring American pronouncements on nuclear weapons to the needs of Cold War propaganda apparently won the battle. Austin later informed America's U.N. delegation that Truman's October 24, 1950, speech to the United Nations had been "psychological warfare to meet the Stockholm Peace Petition." In 1952, the president approved the recommendation of the government's Psychological Strategy Board that "we must be extremely careful in our public statements about atomic weapons." Before issuing such statements, officials should ask themselves if this information would "strengthen the morale of the free world" or "create the fear that the U.S. may act recklessly in the use of these weapons." In the future, "as new developments in these weapons transpire, we must so present that information . . . as to buttress the confidence of the free world." [100]

A New Ambivalence

In the aftermath of the atomic bombing of Japan, American policy toward nuclear weapons at first paralleled and then began to diverge from the postwar climate of critical thinking about the Bomb. The Acheson-Lilienthal Plan and, to a lesser extent, the Baruch Plan, reflected the influence of grass-roots nuclear disarmament campaigns, particularly those conducted by atomic scientists and world government proponents. But as fear of the Soviet Union became the driving force in American foreign policy, this influence diminished accordingly. Within the American government, the balance shifted from the new thinking to the old, from the pursuit of One World to the pursuit of military superiority.

Nevertheless, despite their commitment to developing and stockpiling nuclear weapons, as well as their occasional consideration of using them, American officials remained uneasy. Their ambivalence was captured in the president's January 1953 State of the Union address. Nuclear war "would be one in which man could extinguish millions of lives at one blow, demolish the great cities of the world, wipe out the cultural achievements of the past—and destroy the very structure of a civilization that has been slowly and painfully built up through hundreds of generations," he warned. "Such a war is not a possible policy for rational men. We know this, but we dare not assume that others would not yield to the temptation science is now placing in their hands." [101]

By the end of the Truman administration, then, American policymakers, while deeply enmeshed in the nuclear arms race, had grown more thoughtful and somber than in the halcyon days of 1945, when the Bomb had seemed a "royal straight flush." Learning of the obliteration of Hiroshima, the president had rushed about the ship carrying him back from Potsdam, declaring proudly: "This is the greatest thing in history!" By the 1950s, the mood had changed substantially. Writing to Acheson in early 1954, Truman remarked grimly: "Our tribal instinct has not been eliminated by science and invention. We . . . haven't caught up physically or ethically with the atomic age. Will we?" [102]

In Hot Pursuit

British and Soviet Nuclear Policy

> We have got to have this thing over here whatever it
> costs. . . . We've got to have the bloody Union Jack flying
> on top of it.
>
> Ernest Bevin, 1946

> It is necessary to speak . . . about the atomic bomb. . . . We
> will catch up. . . . We will have atomic energy also.
>
> V. M. Molotov, 1945

In national and international affairs, appearances can be deceptive. On the surface, at least, it seemed more likely that a program to develop nuclear weapons
would be forestalled in Great Britain than in the Soviet Union. The postwar
diplomatic and military alliance between Great Britain and the United States
meant that the British government had little reason to fear the American nuclear
monopoly and reasonable grounds to assume that it would remain safe under the
American nuclear umbrella. Furthermore, Great Britain was a freely functioning democracy, with opportunities for critics of nuclear weapons to challenge
their country's entry into the nuclear arms race. By contrast, after 1945 the
Soviet Union was engaged in a bitter Cold War confrontation with the nuclear-
armed United States. Moreover, Stalin's ruthless dictatorship afforded limited
opportunities for dissent or resistance to any Soviet plan to develop the Bomb.
Nevertheless, the public policy trajectory of both countries proved fairly similar. In the aftermath of the war, Great Britain and the Soviet Union plunged
ahead with ambitious nuclear weapons programs, resulting in the explosion
of the Soviet Union's first atomic bomb in August 1949 and in a similar breakthrough by Great Britain some three years later. Both governments were well
aware of the public uproar about nuclear weapons, and both made some accommodations to it. Nevertheless, convinced that their acquisition of the Bomb
was of supreme importance to their role in the international arena, the leaders
of Great Britain and the Soviet Union subordinated other concerns to this overriding consideration.

Great Britain

Ironically, Great Britain's new Labour government began with an attitude toward nuclear weapons very similar to that of the Bomb's sharpest critics. Impressed by the gravity of the situation, Prime Minister Clement Attlee penned a startling note to himself on August 28, 1945. "A decision on major policy with regard to the atomic bomb is imperative," he wrote. "Any attempt to keep this as a secret in the hands of the U.S.A. and U.K. is useless. . . . The only course which seems to me to be feasible and to offer a reasonable hope of staving off disaster for the world is joint action by the U.S.A., U.K. and Russia based on stark reality." What action? He continued: "We should declare that this invention has made it essential to end wars. The new World Order must start now." Attempts to prevent the further development of the Bomb "will be futile unless the whole conception of war is banished from people's minds and from the calculations of governments." He concluded: "Only a bold course can save civilization." [1]

On September 25, after consulting with his cabinet colleagues (who agreed with him) and with Churchill, now the opposition leader (who did not), Attlee dispatched a lengthy letter to Truman that was nearly as apocalyptic. Ever since the explosion of the atomic bomb, "I have been increasingly aware of the fact that the world is now facing entirely new conditions," he wrote. "If mankind continues to make the atomic bomb without changing the political relationships of States sooner or later these bombs will be used for mutual annihilation." To rid itself of "this menace," humanity would have "to make very far-reaching changes in the relationship between States." Indeed, "in the light of this revolutionary development," there would have to be "a fresh review of world policy and a new valuation of what are called national interests." On this basis, Attlee asked for a meeting with Truman "so that we may agree what the next step should be." [2]

Under what the U.S. State Department called "heavy public pressure, manifested in the press and in Commons," for international control of atomic energy, numerous British political leaders championed the new thinking during the fall of 1945. Referring to the atomic bomb, Sir Stafford Cripps, a member of the cabinet, declared that "it is absolutely vital and essential that we should not allow this new form of destruction to be let loose on the world. . . . War has become certain national and international suicide—there can be no victory. . . . We must find the way by which we can settle world differences without war." On November 22, Anthony Eden, the Conservative foreign affairs spokesperson, told the House of Commons that "by the discovery of this atomic energy, science has placed us several laps ahead of the present phase of international political development, and unless we can catch up politically . . . we are all going to be blown to smithereens." There was no way, in the long term, to make the world safe from the atomic bomb "save that we abate our present ideas of sovereignty." Responding for the government the following day, British foreign secretary Ernest Bevin declared that, with "the coming of the atomic bomb," the world was "driven relentlessly along this road" to "a greater sovereignty." There would have to be "a world law with a world judiciary to interpret it, with a world police to enforce it," and with "a world assembly" to enact it. He was ready, he said, "to sit down with anybody, of any nation," to draw up the plans.[3]

By this time, however, American, British, and Canadian leaders had already held the meeting called for by Attlee, and its outcome presaged a different course of action. To be sure, the ensuing Truman-Attlee-King Declaration of November 1945 made some of the same points. "Faced with the terrible realities of the application of science to destruction," it declared, "every nation will realize more urgently than before the overwhelming need to maintain the rule of law among nations and to banish the scourge of war from the earth." It also called for "extending" the authority of the United Nations and, specifically, for the creation of a U.N. atomic energy commission. But no plans were laid out at the meeting either for effective international control of atomic energy or for strengthening the United Nations. Instead, much of the talk and actual agreement centered on sharing atomic information among the three nations. In the context of Truman's disinterest in Attlee's grander visions and of a spiraling Cold War, British leaders began to fall back upon more traditional ideas of national defense. Indeed, as indicated by the focus on sharing nuclear information, an alternate route to postwar British security was beginning to emerge: an independent nuclear deterrent.[4]

Throughout late 1945 and 1946, pressure mounted within the British government to develop Britain's own Bomb. Contending that the best defense against nuclear weapons was the threat of nuclear retaliation, the Chiefs of Staff argued in October 1945 that "to delay production pending the outcome of negotiations regarding international control might well prove fatal." This argument took on added force when it became clear that the U.S. government, despite earlier assurances, was cutting off the British from key nuclear information. Asked years later about the decision to have Britain build the Bomb, Attlee replied: "We couldn't get cooperation with the Americans. That stupid McMahon Act prevented our acting fully with them." In addition, although publicly supportive of the Baruch Plan, British officials privately felt skeptical about its desirability and practicality.[5]

Underlying these factors was a more fundamental belief of British policy-makers—redolent of Churchill's views during World War II—that a great power required the most advanced weapons available. Speaking at a meeting of the Defence Sub-committee of the British cabinet on October 26, 1946, Foreign Secretary Bevin sharply rebuffed those who said that Britain could not afford the Bomb and expostulated: "That won't do at all. . . . We have got to have this thing over here whatever it costs. . . . We've got to have the bloody Union Jack flying on top of it." In January 1947, at the meeting of the subcommittee that gave the go-ahead for the Bomb project, Bevin once again argued forcefully that Britain, as a great power, "could not afford to acquiesce in an American monopoly of this new development." Attlee himself later declared: "For a power of our size and with our responsibilities to turn its back on the Bomb did not make sense." [6]

Within official ranks, the only substantial dissent came from Professor P. M. S. Blackett, a member of the government's Advisory Committee on Atomic Energy. In a carefully argued ten-page memorandum of November 5, 1945, the physicist contended that an atomic weapons program would be both costly and of limited value to Great Britain's defense. Accordingly, he recommended that Britain proclaim that it would not manufacture them for a specified period of years, would not acquire them from the United States, welcomed inspection by the United Nations, and invited other countries to do the same. Returning from a disheartening visit to the United States in late 1946, Blackett met with Attlee on two occasions and submitted another cautionary memorandum. In it, he championed a neutralist foreign and defense policy for Great Britain, including its continued abstention from production of nuclear weapons.[7]

These arguments met with a brusque rejection by the British government. Dismissing Blackett as a "layman" on "political and military problems," the prime minister referred his November 1945 memorandum to the Chiefs of Staff, who expressed their "complete disagreement" with its assumptions and conclusions. Attlee concurred. Blackett's later proposals encountered even fiercer resistance. The Foreign Office called them "dangerous and misleading rubbish," and Bevin penciled in the observation that Blackett "ought to stick to science." Commenting on the same matter, the minister of state opined that the only issue requiring action was Blackett's continued presence on the government's advisory committee.[8]

A milder criticism of the British Bomb program—albeit one that political leaders also disregarded—was voiced in 1949 by Sir Henry Tizard, the government's chief adviser on defense research policy. In a memo to the defense minister, he confessed that he had "always had some doubt" about whether it was wise for Great Britain to plunge into the costly business of building its own atomic bombs, particularly if the weapons and the know-how could be obtained from the United States. On another occasion that year, he observed: "We persist in regarding ourselves as a Great Power, capable of everything and only temporarily handicapped by economic difficulties." But "we are not a Great Power and never will be again," and "if we continue to behave like a Great Power we shall soon cease to be a great nation." As might be expected, however, this view won few converts within policymaking circles, where Great Britain's role as a great power remained sacrosanct.[9]

Meanwhile, as the British Bomb program moved forward, government leaders encouraged the deployment of American nuclear weapons. In July 1948, during the Berlin crisis, the U.S. government dispatched 60 B-29 bombers capable of carrying nuclear weapons to East Anglia. Visiting Washington in late October 1948, Sir Stafford Cripps, then chancellor of the exchequer, told Defense Secretary Forrestal, as the latter recalled, that "Britain must be regarded as the main base for the deployment of American power and the chief offensive against Russia must be by air." When Forrestal visited Britain that November, he jotted in his diary, Attlee told him that "there is no division in the British public mind about the use of the atomic bomb—they were for its use." Clearly, Attlee was. So was the leadership of the Conservative opposition, which returned to power in the fall of 1951. In this respect, the explosion of Britain's first atomic bomb over Australia's Monte Bello Islands in October 1952, though satisfying to British officials, was anticlimactic.[10] Over the years, they had acclimated themselves to the presence of nuclear weapons and the prospect of nuclear war.

Containing the Critics

Perhaps because Britain's Labour government had played no role in the atomic bombing of Japan, it left the public defense of the action to the British political leader who had authorized it: Winston Churchill. Like his American counterparts, Churchill expressed no qualms about the nuclear destruction of Hiroshima and Nagasaki. Quite the contrary, during the remainder of his life, most of which he spent in Parliament as Tory leader, he did everything possible to justify it. In late August 1945, he publicly defended the atomic bombing, contending that it had saved the lives of a million American and 125,000 British troops. By 1953, when his *Triumph and Tragedy* appeared, he had raised the number of British lives saved by the action to half a million—an increase of 300 percent. The number of American lives saved remained the same.[11] Britons, of course, unlike Americans, vote in British elections—a thought that may have crossed Churchill's mind when his party contested elections in 1950 and 1951, following which he resumed office as Britain's prime minister.

For its part, the Labour government of 1945–51 apparently feared criticism of Britain's postwar Bomb program and, consequently, did its best to limit public knowledge of that program's existence. Indeed, until the explosion of Britain's first atomic bomb in 1952, the existence of the program was concealed not only from the public but from Parliament and most of the cabinet.[12] Symptomatic of the administration's distaste for public scrutiny was the prime minister's reply to a 1949 proposal from the minister of supply. The latter recommended that "non-secret material" be "made into a brief, non-technical film" showing the progress of Britain's atomic energy program, then allegedly civilian. Attlee retorted sharply: "I doubt whether there is any popular demand, and do not see what good you could hope to achieve by it."[13] Attlee's biographer has suggested that the government secrecy policy might have been designed to avoid criticism from the left wing of the Labour party or from Churchill. With the same issue in mind, Cherwell referred vaguely to "political opposition from pacifists or pseudo-Communists." Both explanations point, at least in part, to the attack Attlee might have faced from elements within his own Labour party had his decision to build a British Bomb become public. Indeed, Bevin frequently faced a revolt by these forces, including one in October 1950, when they tried, unsuccessfully, to get the annual Labour party conference to adopt a resolution calling on the government to encourage efforts to outlaw the atomic bomb.[14]

Not surprisingly, the Attlee government also looked askance at the nuclear disarmament activities of some of the leading British atomic scientists. Like Churchill, Bevin publicly berated those atomic scientists whom he claimed sought to supersede the state. This kind of criticism and others led Oliphant to conclude that "the task of enlightening public opinion has made some of us unpopular, and therefore somewhat unsuccessful in official circles."[15] His surmise was accurate enough. Within official channels, J. D. Cockcroft, the director of the Atomic Energy Research Establishment, warned that, unless more civil servants participated in the Atomic Scientists' Association, "the initiative" was "apt to pass into the hands of the very leftwing scientists." Commenting on his "regular and extensive contacts" with ASA leaders, one of Attlee's top aides warned: "It is a curious, but none-the-less important fact, that extreme brilliance in scientific research is very frequently coupled with immaturity of outlook. . . . Many of the young men engaged on atomic research, who are hand-picked for their brilliance, are adolescent in their approach to political and similar questions." As a result, "their fears about the government's attitude towards scientific research," while "often felt deeply and with something of the passionate fervour of youth," might be "unreasoning." [16]

This dismissal of ASA leaders as immature and irrational occurred in the context of an intragovernmental dispute over how to relate to the Atomic Train exhibition, the ASA's most important attempt at popular education on atomic energy. Informed in the fall of 1947 that the minister of supply planned to re-lease photos of atomic research facilities for the exhibition, Attlee responded tartly that "the train can go on but we should not supply photographs or take any responsibility." In response, the minister of supply remonstrated that the ASA "includes practically all the leading scientists in the country in this field," and the photos had "all been carefully examined to ensure that they revealed noth-ing which could not be made public." Apparently irate, Attlee refused to budge and added: "I do not understand why, when your Ministry was approached on this matter, I was not notified." [17]

Although the minister resigned his position, a counterattack quickly gath-ered momentum. The new minister of supply pointed out that "the press had already been told that the exhibition was being organised with full co-operation of the Ministry of Supply and that we had given a limited financial guarantee against loss." To back off from these commitments "would lay us open to a charge of breach of faith." It would also "alienate the nuclear physicists in this country on whom our technical progress in atomic energy depends and con-firm their fears about the government's real attitude towards the dissemination of information on this subject. This might lead to an open contest with the Atomic Scientists which could do much harm both in this country and over-seas." The prime minister's chief aide reinforced this case, arguing that "much harm might be done both in this country and overseas, if action were taken which resulted in an open breach between the Government and the Association which represents the Atomic Scientists." When the defense minister and the foreign secretary indicated their concurrence with this position, Attlee finally gave way and the Ministry of Supply, as well as the Treasury, did provide important cooperation. [18]

Nevertheless, government officials deliberately kept their cooperation to a minimum. As one Ministry of Supply official informed Cockcroft, thanks to the prime minister's instructions, he and his colleagues "did what we could to dissociate ourselves from the exhibition without involving ourselves in a charge of breach of commitments. The exhibition was not opened by a Minis-ter, and senior officials of the Department declined invitations to the opening." In March 1948, when Joseph Rotblat invited Attlee to visit the Atomic Train during its stay in London, both the defense minister and the foreign secretary advised him to reject the offer, which he did.[19] Only a bit later that spring, after the exhibit had received a very successful public reception, did the government relent somewhat. Contending that it was "very desirable" that the Ministry of Supply "should be on good terms with the A.S.A., who could otherwise be somewhat troublesome," one official urged the relevant minister to accept an invitation to visit the train and dispel a "feeling of discouragement" among the project's organizers about the government's attitude. In response, the minister of supply finally put in an appearance at the exhibit. Shown around by Rotblat, the minister wrote the atomic scientist, with a sincerity that in hindsight might well be questioned, of his hope that the train "will continue to have great success."[20]

As might be expected, the Attlee government adopted a considerably more hostile approach to the Communist-led peace movement. According to a U.S. embassy official in Paris, one of the few dissenting speeches at the April 1949 World Peace Congress, that of Harvey Moore, "was prepared by the British Foreign Office." The following year, the issue came closer to home. In September, Bevin complained to the cabinet that the forthcoming Sheffield conference, scheduled to draw a large number of Communist delegates from abroad, "would be widely misrepresented as showing weakness on the part of the government." The cabinet believed that it "would not be practicable to ban the conference," both because it had no formal power to do so and because the Soviet government "would exploit the situation to the full." Therefore, "it would be preferable to take all practicable steps to expose the hypocrisy of the Communists in posing as supporters of world peace."[21] The first step apparently came in October when, addressing the Labour party's annual conference, Bevin denounced the Communist-led peace campaign as "a fraud." The BBC, especially in its foreign broadcasts, also began a steady campaign against Communist-organized peace conferences.[22]

On November 1, 1950, Attlee followed up with a well-publicized speech to the Foreign Press Association, in which he condemned plans by "adherents of the Cominform" to hold "a bogus peace conference" in Sheffield. Through "the precious Stockholm Peace Appeal" and other measures, he charged, the Communist organizers of the gathering sought "to paralyze the efforts of the democracies to arm themselves." For the same reasons, "the armed robber baron of the end of the Middle Ages had the strongest objection to cannons and gunpowder in the hands of the government." In this speech, Attlee also revealed the government's decision to deny visas to at least some of the overseas delegates. The British government, he declared, would "refuse admittance to those whose intention one knows is to burn the house down."[23]

By denying admittance to approximately half the conference delegates, including its scheduled chair, Joliot-Curie, the Attlee government incurred some criticism in Parliament but also secured several of its goals. Confronted with this latest obstacle, the conference organizers gave up the struggle and moved the meeting to the far more inviting environs of Warsaw, where it opened later that month. This pleased the British government as well as the American, which had been pressing Bevin to "throttle the forthcoming congress." Indeed, pressure from the United States, combined with the rumblings of opposition Conservatives, may have been behind Bevin's earlier fear of exhibiting "weakness." In early 1950, Klaus Fuchs had confessed to atomic espionage, thereby exposing the British government to the charge, particularly from the United States, that it could not be trusted with atomic secrets. This may explain Attlee's warning, at the cabinet meeting of November 9, 1950, that the admission of peace conference delegates on a large scale would "be likely to provoke further attacks on the efficiency of the security services." [24] In this sense, disrupting the Sheffield conference seemed likely to help safeguard Great Britain's nuclear options in more ways than one.

If the British government refused to accommodate itself to pressures from the Communist-led peace movement, it was considerably more chary about public opinion. Although it managed to avoid agitating the public by keeping the existence of the British Bomb program a secret, other Bomb-related issues sometimes caused serious difficulties. The most significant of these erupted when, at President Truman's press conference of November 30, 1950, he implied that the U.S. government was considering the use of the Bomb in Korea. According to the record of a British cabinet meeting later that day, in the context of "great alarm in the House of Commons," Attlee proposed to announce his intention to go to Washington to consult with Truman. Although he remarked that "the responsibility for deciding on the use of the atom bomb would have to be defined," the prime minister seemed more concerned about how to deal with public opinion, for he "said that urgent action was necessary in order to allay popular anxiety." This point was later reiterated by Acheson, who recalled that the British ambassador told him that "the principal pressure was from the British domestic political situation and increasing public anxiety over present developments." Fortunately for both governments, these problems could be addressed fairly easily. Avoiding any promises to consult the British government about future American use of the Bomb, U.S. officials drew up a statement designed to soothe the British public. [25]

To their discomfort, British officials considered themselves trapped in the middle between unsatisfactory public attitudes toward nuclear weapons in both countries. In the United States, they maintained, the public viewed the atomic bomb as a Cold War panacea that posed little danger and, therefore, was inclined to be too anxious to use it. By contrast, the British public viewed the Bomb as an immoral weapon or, at the least, too dangerous for first use. The task of statesmanship, British officials believed, lay in convincing the public to accept a middle ground, in which the Bomb would be employed only for vital objectives. When the British ambassador suggested as much during Anglo-American talks in 1952, U.S. officials remarked that it might be a good idea to reeducate the British public. The Foreign Office retorted that it would be better to disabuse U.S. public opinion of its excessively lighthearted attitude toward nuclear warfare. And here the matter rested[26]—uncomfortably, secretly, and certainly far short of Attlee's erstwhile vision of a new World Order.

The Soviet Regime and the Bomb

Although the Soviet nuclear project was well under way by August 1945, the atomic attacks on Hiroshima and Nagasaki convinced the Soviet leadership to initiate a crash program to obtain the Bomb. In the middle of that month, shortly after Stalin's return from Potsdam, he called together the people's commissar of munitions, his deputies, and Kurchatov for a meeting at the Kremlin. "A single demand of you, comrades," the Soviet leader said. "Provide us with atomic weapons in the shortest possible time. You know that Hiroshima has shaken the whole world. The balance has been destroyed. Provide the bomb— it will remove a great danger from us." Long profoundly suspicious of the capitalist West, Stalin was concerned not only that the Bomb's vast power lay in hands other than his own but that the U.S. government seemed perfectly willing to use it as a weapon of war and diplomacy. These fears and suspicions were exacerbated by Anglo-American wartime secrecy. As Margaret Gowing, the official historian of the British Bomb project, has remarked, failure to consult Russia about the Bomb "guaranteed that the attempts made just after the war to establish international control . . . were doomed."[27] Soviet leaders trusted American leaders no more than the latter trusted them.

Indeed, in his memoirs, Khrushchev claimed that Stalin was not merely suspicious of Anglo-American leaders but "frightened to the point of cowardice." According to Khrushchev, Stalin knew "that we faced the possibility of still another war—one which would be fought with modern weapons, a war of intellects and of science. He knew that the outcome of the next war would depend on which side could manufacture the latest weaponry faster and better. And he also knew that in this sphere we lagged behind the West." Consequently, "Stalin trembled with fear," Khrushchev recalled; "how he quivered!" Terrified that "the capitalist countries would attack the Soviet Union," Stalin "ordered that the whole country be put on military alert. . . . Guns were set up around Moscow, loaded with shells, and manned around the clock by artillery crews ready to open fire at a moment's notice." Obsessed with Soviet vulnerability, Stalin "completely monopolized all decisions about our defenses, including—I'd even say *especially*—involving nuclear weapons and delivery systems." Khrushchev recalled that "we were sometimes present when such matters were discussed, but we weren't allowed to ask questions." If anyone showed an interest in the subject, "Stalin would say the reason for that person's interest was his desire to inform his 'real masters'—the catchphrase we used at that time for enemies." [28]

Spurred on by Stalin, the Soviet Union made great efforts to match America's nuclear achievements. Under the direction of Lavrenti Beria—the chief of the secret police to whom Stalin had entrusted the venture—the atomic bomb project recruited leading Soviet scientists, engineers, and industrial managers; large numbers of others came from the ranks of political prisoners, who performed approximately half of the nuclear research. Prison laborers carried out most of the widespread mining and construction work. Disturbed that the Bomb was not ready by 1947, Stalin initiated a purge of the nuclear scientists. Aimed especially at Jews, this scientific purge probably delayed progress on the project. Finally, on August 29, 1949, the Soviet Union tested its first atomic bomb, thereby performing the feat in only a little more time than the United States had taken. [29]

Although Soviet scientists (including Andrei Sakharov) began work on the theoretical possibilities of a hydrogen bomb in 1948, this project, like the race to develop an atomic bomb, was stimulated—at least in part—by American efforts. Klaus Fuchs had told his Soviet contact about studies of the H-Bomb at Los Alamos in wartime, and Truman had announced the American decision to build an H-Bomb in January 1950. Furthermore, the first American thermonuclear test, in 1952, apparently played a role in accelerating Soviet research and suggesting technical breakthroughs. Consequently, just as the production of the first Soviet atomic bomb encouraged the U.S. government to develop a hydrogen bomb, so U.S. hydrogen bomb efforts encouraged Soviet leaders to proceed with the development of their own. It was tested less than a year later, in 1953. [30]

Despite the anxious, even desperate, attitude of Soviet leaders toward nuclear weapons, they adopted a public stance toward them that varied from ridicule to sangfroid. Dining with Stanislaw Mikolajczyk of the Polish Provisional Government on the night after the Hiroshima bombing, Molotov told him that the event was "American propaganda. From a military point of view, it has no meaning whatsoever." That September, at the London conference of foreign ministers, Molotov joked with Byrnes about the Bomb, and in December, at their Moscow meeting, he belittled the issue by insisting that it be relegated to the bottom of their agenda. Asked about the Bomb by a London *Times* correspondent in September 1946, Stalin replied coolly that he did "not believe the atomic bomb to be as serious a force as certain politicians are inclined to regard it." He added: "Atomic bombs are intended for intimidating weak nerves, but they cannot decide the outcome of war." [31]

Soviet communications media reinforced this notion that nuclear weapons were of little significance. Indeed, after August 8, 1945, when *Pravda* carried Truman's announcement of the dropping of the Bomb, that newspaper and *Izvestia* entirely dropped the subject, including the bombing of Nagasaki, which went unreported in the Soviet Union. Not until September 6 did either newspaper again mention the Bomb; and even then, *Izvestia* merely stated that Byrnes had claimed that "the atom bomb was in the same class as any other weapon of war." This curious phenomenon continued, leading the American Russian Institute to conclude in mid-1946: "The Soviet press has not indulged in sensational speculations of the bomb's destructiveness; on the contrary, there has been a tendency to quote American sources to the effect that the bomb is not an 'absolute' weapon." The American embassy in Moscow reached similar conclusions. In January 1950, it reported: "The Soviet press continues . . . to play down the destructiveness of the atomic bomb." Although the Soviet government distributed civil defense manuals to the populace, they did not mention the existence of nuclear weapons. [32]

This refusal to admit publicly the dangers of nuclear weapons apparently met important political needs for Soviet leaders. First, by hiding their weakness in the context of the Bomb, they might discourage the attempts of their Cold War adversaries to conduct "atomic diplomacy." Certainly, it would have been much out of character for Stalin—or, indeed, for any world statesman— to confess fear in the face of his enemies. In addition, by conveying an attitude of calm self-assurance, they could help maintain the morale of the Soviet public and of Soviet allies in Eastern Europe. Indeed, the Kremlin's leaders faced the gloomy prospect that, if threatened with America's nuclear weapons, even the Soviet armed forces might prove unwilling to fight. Only by minimizing the extent of the nuclear danger could popular loyalty and military discipline be maintained. [33]

Given the Soviet regime's sharp fear of America's nuclear monopoly, commentators have remained uncertain why the Soviet Union did not react more favorably to the Baruch Plan. The uncertainty is exacerbated by the lack of any access to relevant Soviet records. Some observers have speculated that the Soviet government could not tolerate the abolition of the veto—and thus dominance of the control process by a Western majority—entailed in the American proposal. Others, such as Baruch, claimed that Soviet leaders' "real objection isn't the veto but rather the whole idea of permitting their country to be subjected to inspection from without."[34] Both objections seem implicit in the counterproposal made by the Soviet Union's U.N. ambassador, Andrei Gromyko, which provided for destroying U.S. atomic stockpiles without inspection or enforcement. Although subsequent Soviet proposals did accept the principle of control mechanisms, such proposals never moved, in these years, from general support of the idea to its practical implementation.[35]

The key to understanding Soviet policy may be that Soviet leaders, like their American and British counterparts, had decided to head off what they perceived as threats to their national security by the traditional method of amassing military strength. This approach certainly provided the basis for their crash program to build a Soviet atomic bomb, which, by the time of the debate over the veto and inspection, was well under way. Because they expected to possess nuclear weapons in the near future, the Baruch Plan, which would terminate their nuclear development program while leaving the United States in possession of its atomic bombs for an undetermined period, had relatively little appeal. Indeed, to overcome the U.S. nuclear monopoly, all they had to do at the U.N. atomic energy talks was to stall, making deferential gestures to international control of nuclear weapons, until the Soviet Bomb was ready. Then they could negotiate, if they desired to do so, on considerably more advantageous terms than provided by the Baruch Plan.[36]

In retrospect, a number of U.S. officials have conceded that the Soviet rejection of the Baruch Plan made sense in terms of traditional great power diplomacy. "The Baruch Plan may have asked too much of the Soviets," recalled Dean Rusk, then the director of the State Department's Office of Special Political Affairs. "We wanted them to agree to international controls after we had already demonstrated our ability to make atomic weapons, but before they had the ability." If the situations had been reversed, Rusk added, the United States would probably have done the same thing: "Had the Soviets been the first to develop and use a nuclear weapon and had they made exactly the same proposal, before we ourselves had cracked the secret of the Bomb, it is most unlikely that President Truman or Congress would have accepted it."[37]

The limited Soviet interest in bargaining over U.N. control of nuclear weapons was very apparent to American officials. "Gromyko has no independent discretion in negotiation but is just playing the record over and over again," Baruch privately complained. Baruch's successor, Frederick Osborn, also concluded that the Russians "had no intentions of negotiating." Osborn recalled one particularly striking encounter. Gromyko, he noted, was almost always accompanied by suspicious-looking assistants and "never let down on his official demeanor." In mid-1947, though, the Soviet ambassador seemed "very tired" and "approaching a nervous breakdown." Osborn collared him alone in the hall one day and, referring to "all these public debates which have been largely propaganda," asked him if they could sit down by themselves somewhere and talk about reaching an agreement to prevent the use of nuclear weapons. According to Osborn, "Gromyko leaned against the wall . . . and he was quiet for quite a long while and looked at me. Then he said, 'Mr. Osborn, you may be sincere, but governments are never sincere.' " Then the world-weary Soviet ambassador trudged off down the hall.[38]

In the aftermath of its first successful atomic test, the Soviet regime still apparently felt little incentive to eliminate the Bomb, at least on American terms. Although Soviet foreign minister Andrei Vishinsky championed a resolution at the United Nations for the immediate adoption "of practical measures for the unconditional prohibition of atomic weapons and the establishment of strict international controls," this apparently was put forward as a propaganda measure, designed to strengthen the one-sided appeals of the Partisans of Peace. Symptomatically, it included a gratuitously offensive reference to "the mighty popular movement in all countries for peace and against the warmongers." *Pravda*, of course, contended that "all supporters of peace welcome the Soviet Union's possession of atomic weapons as a victory for the cause of peace, because they firmly believe in the peaceful policy of the U.S.S.R." A similarly upbeat, if somewhat more threatening, position was advanced in a speech by Soviet deputy premier Georgi Malenkov on November 6, 1949. Noting that the Soviet Union "possesses the atomic weapon," he declared that "we do not want war and we shall do everything possible to avert it." But he added: "Let no one imagine that we are intimidated by the fact that the warmongers are rattling their weapons. It is now not we, but the imperialists and aggressors who should fear war." According to *Pravda*, "stormy, prolonged applause" followed.[39] In the ensuing years, the Soviet government—like the American—plunged forward with its atomic and hydrogen bomb programs while, at the same time, insisting that its weapons were purely defensive and, at the United Nations and elsewhere, publicly calling for the outlawry of nuclear arms.[40]

The Soviet government's adaptation of the nuclear issue for propaganda purposes was evident in its dealings with the Red Cross. In 1946, a preliminary conference of National Red Cross Societies adopted a resolution calling for the prohibition of the atomic bomb. Two years later, the International Committee of the Red Cross extended this resolution to cover all nondirected weapons and asked nations to "prohibit absolutely all recourse to such weapons and to the use of atomic energy or any similar force for purposes of warfare." By 1949, when the Communist-led campaign to ban nuclear weapons was moving into gear, the Soviet delegate submitted a resolution to an international Red Cross conference at Geneva to outlaw the atomic bomb, along with "other weapons intended for the mass extermination of peoples." Arguing that this resolution went beyond the conference mandate for care of war victims, Western nations derailed the proposal. But it was revived at the International Red Cross conference of 1950, which voted to propose the prohibition of atomic weapons to the 62 signatories of the Geneva conventions on rules of war. Sensing the potential for a propaganda breakthrough, the Soviet delegation led an all-out campaign at the October 1950 Red Cross Board of Governors conference for the adoption of constitutional changes that would have aligned the organization with the efforts of the Partisans of Peace. But the delegates, responding to what they called the "political abuse" of the Red Cross, defeated the move by a vote of 40 to 5. "All weapons are inhuman, and the Red Cross is opposed to killing human beings altogether," an angry Bolivian delegate commented. "The Russian proposal is a political matter which has no place in this conference." [41]

The most direct Soviet propaganda efforts, of course, went into furthering the activities of the Communist-led peace movement. Rallying behind the idea that, in the words of *Pravda*, "the people will be able to check the hand of the criminal warmongers," the Soviet press produced a flood of adoring stories about the Partisans of Peace and its successor, the World Peace Council. The Paris Peace Congress "has stirred the hearts of millions and millions," the Soviet *New Times* reported, and "the might of the Soviet Union infuses them with new strength for a successful struggle against the warmongers." Admittedly, there were some renegades. As *Pravda* noted, "by adopting an openly hostile attitude to the Partisans of Peace movement, the Yugoslav Titoite ruling clique has exposed itself to an even greater degree as a band of militant fascists on the payroll of the American warmongers." [42] Indeed, the official party journal declared that anyone in any country who refused to sign the Stockholm petition automatically proved himself "an accomplice and henchman of the warmongers." Fortunately, however, this phenomenon represented what *New Times* called a "vain effort to turn back the wheel of history." "The front of peace is invincible," it chortled; "the warmongers are suffering defeat after defeat in their struggle against the mighty movement of the partisans of peace." [43]

Soviet support for the worldwide Communist peace campaign went substantially beyond accolades in the mass media. Under intense pressure from the Soviet government, press, and official peace movement, "the entire adult population of the country" signed the Stockholm petition, or so officials announced. In addition, the campaign mobilized large numbers of Soviet agricultural and industrial workers to put in additional shifts or to overfulfill their production quotas. "Having signed the Stockholm appeal," reported a worker at the Yerevan tire factory, "I devote all my strength to increasing the might of our beloved motherland. Working a Stakhonovite peace watch in July, I fulfilled the monthly plan 150%; I will do even better in August." To encourage the population further, the Soviet government installed large, brightly painted "peace" signs along the highways outside Moscow. They bore such inspirational slogans as "U.S.S.R, pillar of peace" and "Under the banner of communism to peace." [44] The Soviet government also began awarding Stalin Peace Prizes worth about $25,000 each to people for "outstanding services in combatting the warmongers and promoting peace." The Soviet *New Times* thought this perfectly appropriate, for "the international peace front" drew its "inspiration" from "the genius of the great Stalin," the "man who heads the world front of struggle for peace." The first round of prizes went to the illuminati of the Communist-led peace campaign, including Frédéric Joliot-Curie, Kuo Mo-jo, and the Rev. Hewlett Johnson. In later years, the Soviet government also awarded them to James Endicott, Yves Farge, and Ilya Ehrenburg.[45]

Kremlin officials took a considerably less favorable view of pacifists. "Pacifist ideology," Malenkov declared contemptuously in late 1949, "usually combines a verbal condemnation of war with total inaction." He contrasted this with the Paris Peace Congress's "firm determination to struggle actively against warmongers and to block their insidious plans and schemes." In similar fashion, an article in *Pravda* the following year argued "that well meant pacifist wishes cannot curb the subversive policy against peace." [46] Apparently hostile to the WILPF, the Soviet Union worked to deny that international pacifist group status as a nongovernmental organization at the United Nations. Furthermore, like their American counterparts, Soviet officials were dismayed by the activities of pacifists within their own Cold War camp. When dozens of members of Jehovah's Witnesses, a pacifist religious sect, were arrested by the Polish government for their refusal to sign the Stockholm Peace Appeal, *Izvestia* headlined a story on the event "Warmongers' Accomplices Are Caught Red-Handed." The Soviet newspaper reported proudly that "this band of American spies and diversionists has been liquidated. . . . The Polish people are defending themselves and the well-being of their country and strengthening the cause of peace." [47] *Pravda* insisted: "With the fighters for peace or with the warmongers—there is no third way!" [48]

Atomic scientists also came in for sharp criticism. Writing in *New Times* in June 1946, Soviet military affairs specialist Modest Rubenstein produced a slashing attack on the FAS book *One World or None*. Out of well-intentioned zeal for international control of atomic energy, he charged, the scientists had exaggerated atomic destructiveness. Furthermore, their "florid talk about a 'world state' is actually a frank plea for American imperialism." In June 1947,

Andrei Zhdanov, a member of the Politburo and reputedly second in command to Stalin, publicly condemned "the Kantian vagaries of modern bourgeois atomic physicists," thereby launching a heated ideological campaign against Western and Soviet scholars.[49] Over the next few years, Soviet newspaper or magazine articles attacked Niels Bohr (a "western bourgeois idealist"), Albert Einstein (a proponent of "world domination"), Ralph Lapp (a " 'scientist'-cannibal"), and Linus Pauling (a "bourgeois scientist . . . hostile to the Marxist world view"). In his June 1947 speech, Zhdanov had denounced the "many followers of Einstein," and numerous articles now condemned "reactionary Einsteinism." [50]

Although some of these attacks on Western critics of the Bomb did not discuss their peace proposals, it seems likely that these and other strictures were designed to sever the connections of Soviet scientists with a Western scientific community that was promoting nuclear disarmament. During these years, the Kremlin launched repeated attacks on Soviet atomic scientists for "reactionary idealism" and other "Western" influences. In March 1949 the Soviet *Literary Gazette* charged that cosmopolitanism was being propagated in the Soviet Union by an "anti-patriotic group among us which attempted to undermine the foundations of socialist culture." In part, the journal claimed, this resulted from American scientists who met "last year [and] addressed a new sermon of cosmopolitan 'ideas' to scientists of the world. They declared that they were all 'citizens of the world' and that only a single world science existed for them." [51] Soviet films, too, warned against Soviet scientists becoming "homeless cosmopolitans" or "passportless wanderers in humanity." Most tellingly, in 1948, when the Emergency Committee of Atomic Scientists sought to arrange a conference of leading scientists from East and West to discuss the failure to secure nuclear arms controls, the Soviet government shut the door firmly on the proposal.[52]

At least some of this resistance by the Soviet regime to scientific "cosmopolitanism" was based on a growing fear of the idea of world government. Although *Pravda* criticized the notion of world government as early as December 2, 1945, when it contended that the international confidence necessary for a global authority did not exist, the Soviet position on the issue did not harden into bitter hostility until the summer of 1946. Thereafter, apparently connecting the world government idea with the more modest Baruch Plan, the Soviet government launched a shrill attack. Molotov warned that October of "world domination by way of . . . world government," and the following month the *Bolshevik* condemned the idea as "thoroughly reactionary." In September 1947, Zhdanov devoted considerable attention to the issue in an address to the founding meeting of the Cominform. The purpose of the campaign for world government "is to mask the unbridled expansion of American imperialism," he charged. "The idea of world government has been taken up by bourgeois intellectual cranks and pacifists, and is being exploited not only as a means of . . . ideologically disarming the nations that defend their independence against the encroachments of American imperialism, but also as a slogan especially directed against the Soviet Union."[53]

This became the official Soviet position. "In order to cover up their aggressive plans," claimed Radio Moscow, "the monopolists and ideologists of the bourgeoisie . . . propagate all sorts of theories of the world state." An editorial in *Voprosy Filosofii* made a similar point: " 'I am for the world nation,' says the fascist of the Anglo-Saxon doctrine, but 'precisely my nation is the world nation.' " The American "imperialists" who advocated world government, *Izvestia* contended, were "following the model of the Hitlerite racialists . . . exalting the Anglo-Saxons as a 'superior race.' "[54] *Pravda*, in turn, claimed that United World Federalists wanted "disarmed nations throughout the world under the surveillance of armed American police," a plan "copied from the filthy utopian sketch of Hitler's 'New Order.' " On September 13, 1948, Radio Moscow repeated a charge in the Soviet *Literary Gazette* that the program of the Chicago Committee to Frame a World Constitution "embodies the ambitions of the American war-mongers," those "promoters of the American age of world atomic empire." The Kremlin's attack on world government merged easily with its campaign against "cosmopolitanism." In an article published on April 7, 1949, entitled "Cosmopolitanism: Ideological Weapon of American Reaction," *Pravda* charged that "cosmopolitanism is the gospel of so-called 'world citizenship,' the abandonment of any allegiance to any nation whatsoever, the liquidation of the national traditions and culture of the peoples under the screen of creating a 'world' culture."[55]

Prominent world federalists came under sharp attack from officials and the press in the Soviet Union. Robert Hutchins was denounced as "one of the ring-leaders of the American cosmopolitans," whereas UWF leaders Cord Meyer, Jr., and Vernon Nash were labeled, respectively, a "cosmopolitan gangster" and a "cosmopolitan Judas." In October 1947, Soviet delegate Andrei Vishinsky departed from the text of his speech at the United Nations to assail Henry Usborne for "making a junket around the United States in connection with the campaign for the notorious idea of a world government." Two other prominent British Labour party proponents of world government, Kingsley Martin and Harold Laski, were denounced as advocating a "world union of imperialist monopolists." After Garry Davis turned up in Paris, *Pravda* portrayed him as a "debauched American maniac" who brought from America the idea of world government, "along with powdered eggs and gangster novels."

Izvestia dismissed another prominent proponent of world government, Bertrand Russell, as "the English fascist Malthusian philosopher." [56]

Soviet commentators attacked Russell with particular vehemence. Hitler had "found worthy successors in England," wrote one. "Bertrand Russell urges the atom-bombing of the Soviet Union. That is only natural, for he hates socialism; under socialism, life would lose all its attractions for him, for there would be no one to hate, no one to kill." Fortunately, though, humanity was not compelled to take "the path of degeneration along which fascist creatures like Bertrand Russell are leading it." Commenting on the forthcoming non-Communist peace demonstration in Paris, *New Times* predicted in April 1949 that "a number of reactionaries . . . will sing the praises of the new bidders for world supremacy and vilify the camp of democracy." Topping the list was "Bertrand Russell, the pro-fascist philosopher." These "bankrupt ideologists of the rotting capitalist world present a miserable spectacle," the Soviet journal noted. "The stage settings and falsifications of these myrmidons of the warmongers are . . . impotent." [57]

Other nuclear disarmament proponents at odds with the Communist-led peace movement also came under withering attack. After O. John Rogge's critical address at the November 1950 Warsaw Congress, Radio Moscow denounced him as a money seeker with a "divided soul." Norman Cousins, who had rebuffed the Communist-led peace campaign at the Waldorf conference of 1949, was condemned by *Pravda* for "a malicious speech against the organizers of the congress." In 1949, after Jean-Paul Sartre had headed up the nonaligned peace rally in Paris, the Soviet press attacked him as the creature of "imperialist masters," the "servile executor of a mission confided to him by Wall Street." [58] *Pravda* claimed that the Vatican, "unmasked" as a "warmonger" by its criticism of the Stockholm petition, had "showed itself once again in the imperialist camp," while "the leaders of the right-wing socialist parties have shown themselves as enemies of peace and aides to the warmongers." Indeed, the socialists were "warmongers and servants of American imperialism who screen their treachery with a pseudo-socialist label, with the teaching of cosmopolitanism." [59]

The Soviet government's scorn for nonaligned peace advocates was exemplified by the reaction of the official communications media to British writer J. B. Priestley. With his published rejoinder to Ilya Ehrenburg in the *New Statesman* ("A Letter to a Russian Colleague"), Priestley had "openly gone over to the warmongers' camp," charged the Soviet *Literary Gazette*. Ostensibly, this was of little consequence. The journal noted: "On the one hand there are hundreds of millions of people fighting for peace and on the other there is Mr. Priestley," this "little Philistine." It added contemptuously: "The thousandth slander, the thousandth slanderer—all of this is of too little interest to consider at length." But, significantly, it found the motivation to conclude: "A defender of peace and an enemy of peace are not colleagues. They are adversaries." [60]

Competition and Accommodation

Despite their recognition of the new thinking and new movements that had been inspired by the advent of nuclear weapons, both the British and Soviet governments moved rapidly to join the nuclear arms race. In the context of fierce international rivalries in which they played a major role, their leaders could not resist the temptation to acquire and stockpile nuclear arms. To be sure, they did not wage nuclear war, a risky policy in a world where others had the Bomb, as well as one that was also discouraged by the worldwide climate of fear that nuclear weapons and their critics had begun to generate. Although neither government showed much sympathy for opponents of the Bomb, both made some accommodations to them, ranging from peace propaganda, to disarmament proposals, to attempts to defuse situations in which nuclear war seemed likely. It was not much to become enthusiastic about, but perhaps all that nuclear disarmers could expect from governments that, overcome by traditional notions of national security, had embraced the Bomb.

Restive Onlookers

The Public Policy Response Elsewhere

The atomic bomb should be abandoned.

Jawaharlal Nehru, 1950

Although the United States, Great Britain, and the Soviet Union launched extensive programs to improve or develop their own nuclear weapons, other nations had more modest ambitions and, on occasion, promoted efforts to curb the growing nuclear arms race and its concomitant menace of nuclear destruction. The relative lack of enthusiasm among policymakers of the lesser powers for developing the Bomb did not always reflect the activities of nuclear disarmament movements. Often, it resulted from the inability of their nations, which had limited resources, to produce such weapons, as well as from their assumption that their countries remained reasonably safe under the protection of one or another of the nuclear powers. The most common criticism of the Bomb that they did initiate largely reflected their fear that the nuclear powers would use the weapons casually or aggressively. Not surprisingly, in the nations most firmly locked into the Cold War camps of the United States and the Soviet Union, policymakers often exhibited—and tolerated—little deviation from the official national defense programs. But at the edges of the Cold War alliances and beyond—and particularly in the new and uncharted political territory of the Third World—government leaders sharply criticized the nuclear arms race and, on occasion, maintained cordial relations with peace and nuclear disarmament groups.

Inside the American Cold War Camp

In the war's aftermath, some of America's Cold War allies adopted public positions that seemed to indicate substantial resistance to the Bomb. The Canadian government, for example, announced in December 1945 that, despite Canada's past role in the Manhattan project, "we have no intention of manufacturing atomic bombs." In 1948, the Canadian government reiterated its decision to explore only the peaceful uses of atomic energy. Furthermore, Canadian officials publicly championed international control of atomic energy through the United Nations.[1]

France, too, seemed to take a principled position of resistance to the development of the Bomb. Shortly after its employment at Hiroshima, French president Charles de Gaulle warned that, "if the atomic bomb is accepted internationally as a normal instrument of war and if no organization controls it, it will be a terrifying element in future wars, such as to change the material and moral aspects of mankind." Speaking at the first meeting of the U.N. Atomic Energy Commission in June 1946, Alexandre Parodi, head of France's delegation, proclaimed that France's nuclear research efforts were "purely peaceful" and "our wish is that the nations of the world take the same attitude as speedily as possible." Furthermore, France's new constitution, adopted in October 1946, provided that, "on condition of reciprocity, France consents to the limitation of sovereignty necessary to the organization and defense of peace."[2]

Behind the scenes, as well, the issue of nuclear weapons led to some early skirmishing between the United States and its Cold War partners, particularly with respect to the Baruch Plan. Baruch recalled that Russian and Polish attempts to delay adoption of his proposal by the U.N. Atomic Energy Commission "at times were aided and abetted by the English, Canadians and sometimes the French and the Dutch." Indeed, he noted that "at one time the British representative told me that his Majesty's government had told him that he could not support me."[3]

The reality, however, fell somewhat short of these antinuclear proclamations and of Baruch's sense of Western betrayal. Behind the Canadian government's decision not to initiate its own nuclear program lay not only the immense cost of such a program for a nation of Canada's size but its assumption that the U.S. government would defend it against whatever military threat might emerge. Consequently, although Canada never developed its own nuclear weapons program, it sold plutonium and uranium to the United States and British governments for the production of their nuclear weapons.[4] Furthermore, Canada's high-profile work on behalf of nuclear arms controls reflected, at least in part, its desire to soothe public opinion. Reporting to the State Department on his meeting in early 1950 with Canadian diplomatic officials, U.S. ambassador at large Philip Jessup declared that their wish "to resume more formal conversations with the Russians" resulted "largely from the point of view of public relations." In May, Acheson recalled that, at another diplomatic meeting, Lester Pearson, Canada's minister of external affairs, suggested U.N. talks on atomic energy "not with any idea that any substantive progress would be made, but because the so-called Vishinsky proposals of last fall were being used by Communist propaganda" to give the impression that the Soviet Union favored international control of nuclear weapons while the United States opposed it. That September, Canadian officials renewed this argument. According to Jessup, "Pearson thought that . . . we could really go ahead and discuss things like disarmament" if the Russians were sincere about "effective international control." But "he was under no illusions that such a change had really taken place and was stressing the debating value." [5]

The French government's opposition to nuclear weapons was also far less substantial than it appeared. In July 1944, three top French nuclear scientists working on the Manhattan project in Canada had met with de Gaulle and alerted him to the significance of the Bomb. One of them, Bertrand Goldschmidt, recalled: "We wanted him to be aware of the momentous advantage that possession of this weapon would represent for the USA, and therefore to be ready to recommence atomic research as soon as possible." This "contributed to the creation" of the French Atomic Energy Commission (CEA) in October 1945. Indeed, de Gaulle later stated that he established the CEA above all to enable France to produce her own nuclear weapons. At the time, of course, the government kept this intention secret, and the CEA director, Joliot-Curie, apparently believed that the CEA existed solely to develop a new source of industrial energy. This confusion about the purpose of the French nuclear program could persist not only because the government genuinely wanted to develop civilian nuclear power but because France, hampered by severe financial and resource constraints at the end of the war, could not afford a crash program to produce the Bomb. Rather, it gradually constructed its nuclear reactors and increased its stocks of plutonium so it would be able to build nuclear weapons at a later date. François Perrin, Joliot-Curie's successor, recalled that de Gaulle "did not insist that it be done at once" but believed that the Bomb would be produced "in a rather distant future." [6]

For the time being, then, the French government remained reasonably comfortable under the American nuclear umbrella, concerned primarily with fashioning for itself a useful public relations image. Jules Moch, a French cabinet minister in the late 1940s, later recalled that he had "absolutely" no fear of war at that time; the United States possessed an "atomic monopoly," and therefore he "thought it was impossible for the Soviets to attack, and also that they had no intention to attack." France eventually supported U.S. insistence upon the adoption of the Baruch Plan and, even after Soviet development of the Bomb, showed little sign of straying from the fold. Jean Chauvel, France's ambassador to the U.N. Atomic Energy Commission, remarked privately to American officials in March 1950 that the French, British, and Canadians had "followed the American lead" and "that this had been, and remained, necessary." Although the French public was developing a "great nervousness" about nuclear weapons, France "would, of course, continue to follow the lead" of the United States. That July, when the French ambassador, Henri Bonnet, met with State Department officials, he also combined a dismay at antinuclear attitudes with a determination to resist initiatives toward nuclear disarmament. "A common approach" to the disarmament issue was necessary, he remarked, "because Soviet 'peace' propaganda had made certain inroads in Europe and elsewhere." He added that "it was also necessary to consider methods of dealing with impracticable proposals for atomic energy control." Such proposals "might be made from the most generous motives" but could "be extremely dangerous." [7]

Nevertheless, leaders of America's NATO allies did grow jittery, on occasion, at the prospect that the U.S. government might prove too eager to use the Bomb and thus launch a nuclear holocaust. In late 1950, shortly after Truman's loose talk about employing the atomic bomb in the Korean War, the Canadian government publicly warned against escalation of that conflict. Reacting to the same incident, the French Foreign Office released a statement declaring bluntly that "the Korean objectives are not important enough to justify the use of the atomic bomb." A U.S. official at the United Nations secretly reported that "many European and Commonwealth delegations" had expressed "great apprehension with respect to the President's statement and the hope that it didn't mean what it seemed to mean." Although Truman's clarifying message eased the situation, it did not entirely remove the "great shock" that his original remarks had caused. Reviewing developments in Korea shortly thereafter, the Danish foreign minister declared that use of the atomic bomb could be justified only if "freedom itself" was at stake.[8]

America's Allies and the Nuclear Disarmament Movement

Attitudes toward nonaligned nuclear disarmament groups varied widely within the ranks of America's postwar allies. In Scandinavia, where peace groups had long been accorded some measure of respect, government policies were rather friendly to them. Although the postwar Norwegian government often disregarded pacifist advice—for example, by joining NATO—it appointed pacifists to important posts and assisted their work in small ways. Halvard Lange, Norway's foreign minister and a former assistant secretary of the International FOR, smoothed the path for Norwegian delegates to attend the 1946 International

FOR meeting. Among other political leaders, he also saw to it that the government's yearly grant to peace groups ($1,400) was continued.[9] In neighboring Denmark, Prime Minister Hans Hedtoft issued a public statement of support for Niels Bohr's Open Letter of June 1950. Privately, the Danish government informed the U.S. State Department that it attached "very great importance to the thoughts expressed in Professor Bohr's Open Letter and would deeply deplore it should Professor Bohr's initiative be looked upon by the public merely as an expression of the good intentions of a purely theoretical scientific mind." It contended that "an early clear American declaration to all countries in favor of an open world and a renewed American offer to place all military scientific inventions at the disposal of all countries under the safeguard of mutual appropriate international control would be of the greatest value in the effort to surmount the present international stalemate."[10]

Elsewhere—and particularly in countries with more militaristic traditions —U.S. allies reacted with more hostility to nonaligned peace and disarmament activism. In late 1950, police raided the offices of the Argentina Pacifist Association, confiscating its records and seizing the latest issue of its journal, *Pacifismo*. A report on Argentina at the 1951 WRI conference stated that "public work for peace is dangerous. . . . Any movement for peace is labelled Communistic. . . . Members are being watched." In Turkey, where a peace society composed primarily of intellectuals was formed in 1950, the government moved quickly to suppress it.[11] Suspicious of groups refusing military service, the right-wing Greek government arrested large numbers of Jehovah's Witnesses, sentencing some to long jail terms and executing others. Numerous other Western nations imprisoned conscientious objectors, and Spain provided death without trial for open rejection of military training. In France, according to Claude Bourdet, "neutralism" quickly stirred up a reaction among powerful forces. "A campaign was launched against *Le Monde* by the French right-wing press, the Quai d'Orsay and the U.S. Embassy and . . . nearly succeeded in ousting Hubert Beuve-Méry from the editorship." Bourdet claimed that because of his own "neutralism" and "anti-colonialist policy" at *Combat*, he was forced to resign his editorship of that journal in 1950.[12]

The situation also grew difficult for peace activists in West Germany, where the authorities had banned Hiroshima Day events in 1950. In the fall of 1951, two police officers visited FOR leader Friedrich Siegmund-Schültze one night to arrest him. Although the aging pacifist managed to have this order countermanded, he believed his arrest—and that of four other pacifists—represented part of a government campaign to intimidate peace activists. He pointed out that West German officials had also published lists of Communists and, he claimed, had added pacifists to these lists with the intention of stirring up threats and reprisals against them.[13]

The governments of U.S. allies reacted particularly sharply to the Communist-led peace campaign. In 1951, when the World Peace Council sought to establish its headquarters in Paris, the French government barred the organization from doing so. Enraged by the activities of the Australian Peace Council, the Australian government canceled the passports of all its citizens attending the Warsaw Peace Congress. In 1951, the Greek government arrested six members of the Democratic Front for Peace, formed by young members of the Communist party, and sentenced two to life imprisonment, executed another, and tortured another to death.[14] In the spring of 1950, after the Rev. James Endicott made a particularly inflammatory statement in the Soviet Union, Lester Pearson warned Canadians to "be on guard against . . . the individual who, wearing the mantle of the Peace Congress, has knowingly or unknowingly sold his soul to Moscow." Endicott, said Pearson, was "beneath contempt," and the Canadian Peace Congress was the "agent of a foreign aggressive imperialism." Meanwhile, Canadian police trailed Endicott, photographed people attending CPC meetings, and harassed circulators of the Stockholm petition. In Quebec, Communists going door-to-door with the petition adopted the practice of placing a lookout at the end of the street to sound the alarm when the police arrived.[15]

Probably the best-known confrontation between the Communist-led peace campaign and a Western government occurred in France. The situation there was particularly volatile because the French government's atomic energy program lay in the hands of Joliot-Curie—not only an outspoken Communist but the chair of the WFSW and of the World Peace Council. The United States and, increasingly, the French government feared that Joliot-Curie would deliver atomic secrets to the Soviet Union. They certainly viewed him as unreliable. The French Communist party, in turn, may have feared that Joliot-Curie would produce findings useful for the United States, desired to impose discipline upon its large crop of unruly intellectuals, or, at the least, considered the eminent physicist more useful as a martyr than as a government official.[16]

Consequently, the situation headed ineluctably toward a showdown. Pressed by Communist leaders to take a party-line stance, Joliot-Curie finally obliged by proclaiming at the April 1950 PCF convention that "progressive scientists" would "never . . . give a particle of their knowledge for a war against the Soviet Union." In response, Premier Georges Bidault dismissed Joliot-Curie from his CEA post. As his non-Communist colleague Lew Kowarski summarized the event: "When he became the leader of people who went about the country and Europe proclaiming, 'if the government orders us to make weapons, we will say no,' he obviously was no longer a suitable person to be in charge of an establishment which, among other things, had to make weapons." To say that Joliot-Curie's dismissal "was sudden" is, "shall we say, naive."

In parliament, all parties except the Communists supported the action. Subsequently, the government, which did not draw fine distinctions, moved to purge Kowarski and other CEA scientists whom it believed, in his case erroneously, were hindering the military potential of the French atomic energy program.[17]

Inside the Soviet Cold War Camp

The Soviet Union's Cold War allies adopted a position on nuclear weapons paralleling that of the "socialist motherland." During the period of America's nuclear monopoly, Communist nations—anxious to maintain morale at home and to avoid encouraging America's "atomic diplomacy"—joined the Soviet Union in publicly belittling the importance of the atomic bomb. On January 6, 1949, for example, the Romanian newspaper *Romania Libera* published an article purporting to show that atomic weapons had no strategic significance. When popular attention shifted to H-Bombs, Communist nations continued to put up a brave front. In February 1950, shortly after Truman's declaration that the United States would commence building a hydrogen bomb, the Warsaw press responded by casting scorn upon the power of U.S. nuclear weapons. One newspaper claimed that the "entire world press" considered the American president's announcement a "gigantic bluff." [18]

Naturally, the leaders of Communist nations were overjoyed by the Soviet Union's atomic breakthrough and consistently portrayed it as a force for peace. "In the past," noted the Chinese newspaper *Ta Kung Pao*, "the atomic bomb used to be the secret weapon of imperialism, monopolized by war-lovers to cow peoples of other nations in order to blackmail them." But "the Soviet Union is a veritable home of world peace, and . . . once a dangerous weapon is mastered by the Soviet Union, it is forthwith turned into an instrument of peace." Indeed, "as a result of the Soviet Union's righteous announcement, the world's forces of peace are assured of ultimate victory, and the schemes of the warmongers have become totally frustrated." By "winning the liberation war the Chinese people have defeated American imperialist intrigues in China," claimed *Jen Ming Jih Pao*; "we now believe that Soviet possession of the atomic bomb will smash the new war plans of American atomic militarists." [19]

Other Soviet bloc nations adopted the same position. One Hungarian newspaper noted that the Western masses, heretofore misled to believe that the atomic bomb would give an advantage to the imperialists, now would side with the "devoted safeguard of peace," the Soviet Union. In Bulgaria, *Otechestven Front*, the semiofficial government newspaper, took up the issue in an editorial entitled "New Contribution of USSR to the Consolidation of Peace." It contended that "in the hands of imperialists the atomic weapon is a threat to peace and serves in the preparation of a new war." Fortunately, though, "the Soviet Union, possessing atomic arms, defends peace and international collaboration." Another Bulgarian newspaper, *Zemedelsko Zname*, noted that the Soviet Union "shall never abuse this weapon"; rather, with the defeat of atomic diplomacy, "the world movement for peace will receive a new impulse." In East Germany, the press greeted the news of the Soviet nuclear breakthrough gleefully, and the Czech, Romanian, and Polish governments shared this enthusiasm. In fact, the Polish Foreign Affairs Ministry formally announced that Soviet possession of the Bomb would greatly facilitate finding a solution to the problem of international control of atomic energy.[20]

Those who challenged this benign vision of Communist military might incurred the intense hostility of Communist governments. "We are not, we cannot be pacifists," declared General George Palffy at the Hungarian Communist party conference of June 1948. With the horrors of World War II still fresh, people cherished the idea of peace and, therefore, argued Palffy and party leader Matyas Rakosi, the "danger of pacifism" was serious. In 1949, the Hungarian minister of defense complained that "a certain pacifism has appeared within the ranks of our party," with "slogans like 'We want no more wars!' . . . We have to overcome this feeling in order to suppress it in the masses."[21] Reporting to the WRI in the summer of 1950 on events in East Germany, Heinz Kraschutzki noted that "recently, pacifism and the idea of a neutralized Germany have been put on the list of those movements that are officially considered as dangerous." Communist authorities, he said, "firmly believe that the capitalist world has got to attack them before succumbing. And, using a very old argument . . . they say that everybody who is not willing to take arms is practically helping the 'enemy.' " The idea of world government also came under fire, with *Free Bulgaria* charging that its impetus came from "the most power-hungry imperialists."[22]

When they considered it necessary, Communist governments supplemented this propaganda barrage with direct repression. In Bulgaria, the government imprisoned one WRI leader and barred others from traveling to international meetings.[23] In Hungary and Czechoslovakia, WILPF groups were officially disbanded and outspoken Christian pacifists were forced to resign their ministries.[24] From China came word that the small FOR group had dissolved; after "our 'Liberation,' " noted one member, "it seemed rather fruitless and unwise to hold FOR meetings."[25] In East Germany, one pacifist reported, the authorities "seemed to grow more ruthless." They disbanded the German Peace Society and also prevented the FOR from operating; indeed, by 1951, the level of government intimidation in East Germany had become so severe that the remaining FOR members asked their parent group to cease sending them the

FOR newspaper. Throughout Eastern Europe, an observer remarked, world federalist organizing efforts were "prevented by government action." [26]

One of the best-known pacifists to come under government attack was Premysl Pitter, the Czech social worker who had been a member of the WRI Council from 1925 to 1939. For a few years after the inception of the Communist government in Czechoslovakia, Pitter was able to continue his work at Milicuv Dum, the social settlement for children he had established in the slums of Prague. Although he told the new school inspector that he did not agree with the "violent methods" employed by the party, that official responded that, although "your idealistic philosophy hinders you from being one of us," that "need not prevent you from working with us." Eventually, however, it did. In 1951, the local Communist party demanded his dismissal, claiming that he incited "against the order of the People's Democracy and only individuals who are absolutely reliable politically and ideologically are acceptable as educators." More denunciations followed, police searched his home and seized his records, and he was dismissed from Milicuv Dum. On the brink of arrest and forced labor, Pitter fled from Czechoslovakia in August 1951.[27]

Accepting exile in West Germany, where he worked at aiding refugees, Pitter continued his nonaligned pacifist commitments. The Communist regime had "brought positive achievements" to Czechoslovakia, he reported to Western pacifists. Nevertheless, people's "souls are starving." He told a pacifist gathering in London some months after his arrival in the West that religious believers "have proclaimed love and justice but not applied them. That is why others came, who . . . want to carry through by violence the justice that we should have realised with love. . . . At the same time, we must see clearly that the Communists with their methods cannot succeed in bringing more happiness. . . . They are building on sand." Thus pacifists needed "to prepare even now a new world." [28]

Nations on the Edges

Nations on the periphery of the Cold War camps and beyond it assumed a stance more critical of nuclear weapons. Although Yugoslavia began as a staunch supporter of Soviet policy, after the Tito-Stalin split of 1948 it shifted rapidly to a position of Cold War neutrality. In this new role, it organized peace conferences and promoted nuclear disarmament.[29] Another neutral, Sweden, initiated talks among the Scandinavian nations at the outset of the Cold War about a mutual defense pact. Because Sweden insisted on strict nonalignment while Norway favored some linkage to the other Western powers, these negotiations ended unsuccessfully in 1949. Norway and Denmark then joined NATO but showed little enthusiasm for nuclear weapons and nuclear war.[30] The Swedish government adopted a policy of armed neutrality and began an atomic energy program that, though civilian in orientation, did not exclude the possibility of later weapons production.[31] Even so, as a U.S. intelligence report complained, Sweden was "even more sensitive than the Danish government to the possible international repercussions arising out of the use of the atom bomb." Sweden's foreign minister, Osten Undén, called for the elimination of nuclear weapons and declared that, meanwhile, the Bomb should be employed only in a "cataclysmic case."[32]

Other nations, though under the shadow of one or another of the Cold War antagonists, kept themselves more or less free of Cold War military ventures. Defeated by the Soviet Union during World War II, Finland signed a Treaty of Friendship, Cooperation, and Mutual Assistance with the Soviet Union in 1948 and made good relations with that neighboring nation the cornerstone of its postwar foreign policy. Nevertheless, it managed to develop a free society at home and to avoid military entanglements abroad. Finland's government also became a sharp critic of nuclear weapons.[33] Like Finland, Japan also had its postwar role shaped, at least in part, by one of the great powers. Under the American occupation regime, Japan adopted a new constitution in 1947 that, in Article 9, renounced "war . . . and the threat or use of force as a means of settling international disputes." American authorities soon changed their minds about the desirability of this provision; but, together with the Japanese peace movement, Article 9 remained an important factor inhibiting government action to remilitarize Japan and to acquire nuclear weapons.[34]

Of these governments, only the Finnish showed any sympathy for the Communist-led peace movement. Pursuing its policy of good relations with the Soviet Union, Finland's Center government, led by Urho Kekkonen, gave its support to that movement, and almost all its leaders signed the Stockholm Peace Appeal against the atomic bomb.[35] By contrast, the Swedish government was deeply embarrassed by the Stockholm conference and appeal. Expressing his "considerable disgust" at the use of the name "Stockholm" on the document, Sweden's Social Democratic prime minister, Tage Erlander, publicly denounced it as "international Communist propaganda." Shortly thereafter, Swedish foreign minister Undén expressed his regret at the United Nations, leading *Pravda* to retort that Undén had become "the myrmidon of American atomic diplomacy."[36]

The reaction of these governments to the nonaligned peace movement varied considerably. Although the Swedish government maintained a substantial military force for national defense, it also remained on fairly good terms with peace groups. In fact, it granted small financial subsidies to some of them, including the Swedish section of the WILPF. In Japan, some local governments, such as the one in Hiroshima, promoted peace activities. On August 2, 1950, Japanese authorities—apparently at the behest of U.S. occupation officials— abruptly canceled the Hiroshima peace memorial ceremony and all other events linked to the atomic bombing, but they were resumed the following year.[37] In Yugoslavia, Tito's new government dissolved independent pacifist groups and, like Greece and Poland, initiated trials of Jehovah's Witnesses, in this case for their resistance to military service. Nevertheless, after its break with the Soviet Union, the Yugoslav government not only established its own nonaligned Yugoslav National Committee for the Defense of Peace but brought pacifists and other peace activists to Yugoslavia for conferences on peace and disarmament. The October 1951 Conference for Peace and International Cooperation, held at Zagreb, provided official positions for Kenneth Ingram of Great Britain, Johannes Hugenholtz of the Netherlands, Martin Niemöller of West Germany, Hans Thirring of Austria, and other prominent pacifists.[38]

Third World Governments and the Bomb

Some of the sharpest condemnations of nuclear weapons came from the leaders of Third World nations. Incapable of developing such weapons on their own, distrustful of Cold War alignments, beset by widespread domestic poverty, and sensitive to the fact that, thus far, nuclear war had been waged exclusively against people of color, they often looked askance at the nuclear arms race. In November 1949, Carlos Romulo of the Philippines, then U.N. General Assembly president and working zealously for a nuclear truce between the United States and the Soviet Union, called for the temporary suspension of atomic bomb production and for the prohibition of the use of existing bombs. Even though the great powers spurned his proposals, he insisted that "complete agreement" on nuclear disarmament could and should be reached through the United Nations.[39] Third World opposition to nuclear weapons heightened after Truman's remarks about using them in Korea. According to the record of a meeting between U.S. and Saudi Arabian U.N. delegates, the Saudi official "said that the delegations representing the Near East and Asia were profoundly distressed and disturbed over the President's announcement. . . . The people of the whole Asiatic continent would never understand why the American people had decided to use the atomic bomb against them" but "would regard it as an action of the white race against the colored races." Thus the Bomb's use "would have a disastrous effect upon the relations of the United States with the rest of the world for years to come" and "everything possible should be done to prevent such a disaster." Newspaper accounts at the time confirm the bitterly hostile nature of the Asian response to the suggestion of using the Bomb in Korea and the long-term demand for rechanneling the money from development of weapons to peaceful pursuits.[40]

Perhaps the most eloquent and persistent critic of nuclear weapons was India's first prime minister, Jawaharlal Nehru. As early as 1946, he expressed his hope that "India, in common with other countries," would "prevent the use of atomic bombs." Speaking before a dinner audience in New York City in 1949, he declared that India rejoiced at not having the Bomb. A fear complex governed the world, he complained; "when nations become afraid, others get afraid," and "a crescendo of fear rises," leading to "deplorable consequences." Replying to a parliamentary inquiry as to his views on the American decision to develop an H-Bomb, Nehru replied that, if one thought the world worthwhile, the H-Bomb should be abolished; a decent world and the H-Bomb, he said, could not coexist.[41] Later that year, shortly after Truman broached the subject of using nuclear weapons in Korea, Nehru publicly condemned the use "anywhere at any time" of the Bomb, which he characterized as the "symbol of incarnate evil." Speaking at a press conference in New Delhi on March 13, 1951, he asked: "Exactly what are we trying to do by atomic warfare? . . . I cannot for a moment think of any objective which would not be swept away by 1,000 million people being destroyed or disabled." Nuclear war would lead to the "physical collapse of the world, and what is no doubt worse," the "moral collapse of humanity."[42]

In addressing the issues of the nuclear arms race, some key Third World leaders clearly adopted the prescriptions and rhetoric of the nuclear disarmament movement. Starting in 1946, for example, Romulo—in his capacity as the U.N. delegate of the Philippines—delivered direct pleas for "world government" to the United Nations. His 1946 speech called for a U.N. General Assembly with powers "fully adequate to the great purpose, the prevention of war." Romulo also championed a favorite idea of the atomic scientists' movement: the convocation of a world conference of scientists to develop a new approach to the international control of atomic energy.[43] Nehru, too, became a champion of world federation. "The world, in spite of its rivalries and hatreds and inner conflicts, moves inevitably towards closer cooperation and the building up of a world commonwealth," he declared in 1946 in an important policy address. "It is for this One World that free India will work." Despite the disinterest of the great powers, he continued to articulate this position. "We talk of world government and One World and millions yearn for it," he told a radio audience in April 1948. "I have no doubt in my mind that world government must and will come, for there is no other remedy for the world's sickness."[44]

Although peace and disarmament groups remained weak in the Philippines and India, other factors magnified their influence. Both nations gained their independence in the aftermath of World War II and, consequently, their leaders sometimes viewed themselves as natural spokespersons of an emerging Third World, with all the attendant concerns and obligations. Furthermore, in India at least, the independence struggle, led by Gandhi, had employed a nonviolent, pacifist strategy which had a substantial impact on the politics of the postcolonial era. In addition, Western peace activists frequently championed decolonization and, thereby, sometimes established friendly relations with the leaders of newly emerging Third World nations.[45]

They certainly had close ties with both Romulo and Nehru. Romulo's 1946 speech, for example, was written by Alan Cranston and Grenville Clark, two leading world federalists from the United States. Norman Cousins also cultivated his contacts with Romulo—among other means, by publishing his poetry in the *Saturday Review of Literature*—and assured the Filipino leader of his "enthusiastic applause for your urgently needed and dramatically stated recommendations on atomic control." With an apparent eye to future action, Cousins assured Romulo that "there are perhaps only two men in the world today who speak from a platform which would assure them of a sympathetic hearing from the overwhelming preponderance of the world's peoples. One is Nehru. The other is yourself." Cousins also developed excellent relations with the Indian prime minister, whom he interviewed at length in 1951 for his book *Talks with Nehru*. Feeling a natural kinship with the Indian leader, numerous Western peace activists sought to mobilize him, sometimes successfully, on behalf of disarmament and peace. In 1948, for example, Einstein, Pearl Buck, and Clarence Pickett (of the American Friends Service Committee) cabled to Nehru proposing that he take some initiative to improve the world situation.[46] Often at odds with their own governments, Western advocates of nuclear disarmament could usually count upon a readier welcome among Third World leaders.

A Modicum of Influence

By 1951, then, in nations other than the three nuclear powers, nuclear disarmament activists had achieved a modest degree of influence in the realm of government policy. To be sure, the Communist-led peace movement—for all its size and fury—apparently had very little effect on nuclear weapons programs. In Communist nations, it mirrored rather than initiated government policy, and elsewhere it led to little more than arrests, government purges, and the upgrading of Cold War propaganda. Only in Finland could it be said to have the support of a non-Communist government and that was because the government sought good relations with the Soviet Union. The nonaligned nuclear disarmament movement made greater progress. Admittedly, the nations of the two Cold War camps generally remained content with the nuclear policies of their respective paladins. And particularly (but not exclusively) in Communist nations, officials moved to repress nonaligned disarmament organizations and activities. But the governments of NATO countries—and probably those of Soviet allies as well—did grow jittery over the prospect of nuclear war and, in a few nations (e.g., Denmark), nuclear disarmers spurred government officials to independent action. More significantly, in other countries on the periphery of the Cold War—such as Japan, Yugoslavia, and Sweden—the nonaligned movement achieved official recognition and bolstered tendencies to support disarmament. Furthermore, in some Third World nations, where its preachments were reinforced by factors endemic to these countries, the nonaligned nuclear disarmament movement could count on key policymakers to articulate its proposals. Although clearly unsuccessful with its full agenda, the movement did have some impact on the public policy of the non-nuclear powers.

Crisis and Decline of
the Movement, 1950-53

The movement is in crisis.

Elisabeth Mann Borgese, 1950

Despite the upsurge of opposition to nuclear weapons in the immediate after-math of the atomic bombing of Japan, criticism of the Bomb tapered off in the late 1940s and especially in the early 1950s. To be sure, most of the new organizations among scientists and world government advocates continued to function during these years, as did the older pacifist groups. And these groups continued to provide the focal point for evaluating and publicizing the dangers posed to human survival by nuclear weapons. But at the same time, severe problems buffeted the nuclear disarmament movement. Preeminent among them was the growing popular commitment to the Cold War, which left little room for ideas of disarmament and One World. Beyond this, moreover, loomed the popular suspicion of disarmament engendered by the Communist-led peace campaign and the difficulty in sustaining a movement based on the fear of destruction. In these circumstances, it was remarkable that the movement for nuclear disarmament survived as well as it did.

The Impact of the Cold War

The major factor behind the decline of the nuclear disarmament movement was the growing public commitment to employing nuclear weapons for national defense. As early as 1947, Norman Thomas had criticized the "peace through fear" approach, observing that if the Bomb really was an absolute weapon, then people would conclude that "our best defense is not disarmament, but scientific armament." Of course, this notion that the Bomb might deter aggression against one's own country or its allies soon provided the basis for the strategic policies of the great powers. Furthermore, as the Cold War grew more confrontational, nuclear deterrence and possible nuclear war began to form an article of faith for their publics as well. Returning from a trip across Canada in 1951, the Canadian FOR secretary reported that many people "cling to the old patterns of violence in their attempts to protect themselves from . . . whatever they think is evil." At the moment, "Russia seems to be the big bogey, and although people admit you can't destroy an ideology with bombs, they seem to feel they have no other recourse." Surveying the situation that year, Eugene Rabinowitch concluded gloomily that the scientists had helped influence not only "those who are horrified at the very idea of the use of atomic weapons" but "those who now clamor for the use of atomic weapons in Korea—in the mistaken belief that this weapon can win for its wielder any war, any time." Andrei Sakharov recalled that, working on the H-Bomb in early 1953, he felt "committed to the goal which I assumed was Stalin's as well: after a devastating war, to make the country strong enough to ensure peace." [1] Millions of people on both sides of the "Iron Curtain," perceiving themselves as besieged by dangerous enemies, reconciled themselves to the presence of the Bomb.

In Great Britain, the adjustment proved fairly easy. Churchill popularized the notion that, without the Bomb in American hands, "it is certain that Europe would have been communized . . . and London . . . under bombardment." Like Churchill, British newspapers championed not only the American Bomb but a British one as well. The *Daily Express* explained in July 1950 that "the only certain protection against the atom bomb" is for Britain to develop her own "so that any potential assailant will know that his cities would receive our bombs in return for his." [2] Over the protests of a pacifist minority, the British churches also rallied behind the Bomb. The Oldham report, a 1946 pronouncement on atomic weapons by the British Council of Churches, contended that the nation's responsibility to wage war could not be "diminished or altered by technical advances and the introduction of new weapons, even though the resulting problems may be far more acute." The Bomb should be employed as a deterrent and for "reprisals" against "a nation which attempted to use it for aggressive purposes." In 1948, a Church of England commission declared that "the possession of atomic weapons is generally necessary for national self-preservation, [and] a government . . . is entitled to manufacture them and hold them in readiness." Asked about the development of the British atomic bomb in early 1952, shortly after it was announced by the government, British respondents expressed approval of the action by 60 to 22 percent. A pacifist member of Parliament conceded that peace groups in Britain had stirred up "little popular response." [3]

In France, as well, the developing Cold War eroded opposition to nuclear weapons. Although the powerful Communist party continued to thunder at the Bomb—or at least the one possessed by the United States—the Socialists joined more conservative parties in supporting the maintenance of the American nuclear arsenal. Placing the onus of responsibility for the nuclear arms race upon the Soviet Union, the Socialist party argued that the American Bomb was a necessary evil that should be ready for defense against a Soviet attack. Whatever their qualms about nuclear weapons, much of the French public seemed to agree. In May 1952, a poll found that, of all France's political parties, only the Communist party had a majority that believed the American lead in nuclear weapons increased the possibility of war. Among the Socialists, a clear plurality (41 percent) thought the American lead decreased the possibility, and substantial majorities in the other parties agreed.[4]

In West Germany, too, support for the military and for nuclear weapons grew with the hardening of the Cold War. Although large majorities had opposed the development of a West German army, shortly after the outbreak of the war in Korea opposition dropped to 45 percent, and by 1952 rearmament had secured both Catholic and Protestant church backing. Curiously, the previous majority support for West German participation in NATO eroded somewhat during the first year of the Korean War, but it bounced back to majority status in July 1951.[5] Polls in June and December 1950 did find that majorities of West Germans opposed the use of nuclear weapons in the Korean War. But West Germans seemed less inclined to forgo use of the Bomb in a context of greater importance to them. According to a U.S. government poll in July 1951, 35 percent of West German respondents favored immediate use of the Bomb in the event of a Soviet invasion of Western Europe and another 36 percent sanctioned use of the weapon if it were employed first by the Soviet Union.[6] Concluding a lecture tour, one pacifist bemoaned the widespread acceptance of what most West Germans "consider as inevitable rearmament, with a final clash with Russia." After a sweeping election victory by his Christian Democratic party in 1953, Konrad Adenauer crowed: "The 'count me out' standpoint . . . has yielded to a realistic assessment of the German situation."[7]

The shift toward popular acceptance of nuclear weapons occurred most dramatically in the United States, one of the two leading Cold War antagonists. Polls found that by 1947, 66 percent of Americans viewed the Soviet Union as an "aggressive" nation and 77 percent expected a war within two decades. Fearful of Soviet power, Americans clung to their nuclear monopoly and, later, to their advantage in the nuclear arms race. In the summer of 1949, a Gallup poll found that 70 percent of respondents opposed any pledge of no first use of nuclear weapons in a future war. Shortly after the president's announcement that the United States would begin building an H-Bomb, an opinion survey reported that 69 percent of Americans favored the decision, 9 percent expressed "reluctant approval," and 14 percent disapproved. By July 1950, a poll revealed that 77 percent of respondents thought the United States should use the Bomb in any future world war.[8] People "really are very shortsighted," Einstein wrote his friend Max Born in September. Returning to the United States later that year, Supreme Court Justice William O. Douglas was aghast at the situation. "It was disquieting to find . . . the prevalence of the belief that full-scale world war is inevitable," he told a convention of United World Federalists. "Many men of good will have lost hope for any solution short of war."[9]

Certainly, hard-line views seemed on the ascendant. Senator Brien McMahon, chair of the Joint Committee on Atomic Energy and once a proponent of nuclear arms controls, pressed relentlessly for more and bigger nuclear weapons; the United States, he argued in July 1951, needed "thousands and thousands" of atomic bombs. Although the members of the AEC's General Advisory Committee had opposed an H-Bomb program in late 1949, all of them contributed at least marginally to it in subsequent years. In *The Christian Conscience and Weapons of Mass Destruction*, a 1950 report of the Federal Council of Churches, this Protestant federation declared: "For the United States to abandon its atomic weapons, or to give the impression that they would not be used, would be to leave the non-Communist world with totally inadequate defense." Furthermore, "if atomic weapons or other weapons of parallel destructiveness are used against us or our friends in Europe or Asia, we believe that it could be justifiable for our government to use them in retaliation." Popular opinion outran even these constraints. In November 1951, with the Korean War bogged down on the battlefield, 51 percent of Americans favored dropping the Bomb on "enemy military targets" in that conflict.[10] There had developed "a political and intellectual climate which has been learning to spurn or, even worse, to ignore" the idea "of one world," noted G. A. Borgese. "The chief fact of life, in the overwhelming opinion, is that the worlds are two" and "they cannot join in peace."[11]

Naturally, this situation undermined peace and disarmament organizations. In West Germany and France, pacifist leaders feared that their groups stood on the brink of government repression. In Great Britain, where pacifist-government relations were more relaxed, the Peace Pledge Union nonetheless encountered growing difficulties with private groups and with the mass media. After the PPU produced a leaflet criticizing civil defense measures, its printer refused to continue publishing its materials. Sybil Morrison complained that the PPU faced "not misrepresentation so much as a complete, and apparently deliberate, boycott of pacifist views and activities by the national newspapers."

She recalled one PPU meeting in London during 1949, addressed by some of Great Britain's cultural luminaries. Although "about 30 press representatives" attended, "no single word about the meeting . . . appeared in the London press." She speculated: "Perhaps it is considered bad for the British public to know that some of its most distinguished exponents of the arts and science are pacifists." [12]

The heightening Cold War atmosphere generated particularly serious problems for proponents of world government. At the winter 1950–51 meeting of the World Citizens International Secretariat, the Swiss delegate reported that the Swiss people resisted involvement in something they considered "indefinite or outside immediate Swiss actualities." Making much the same point, the German delegate reported that "the German people did not believe in something which had no apparently feasible basis." In the United States, where 22 states had passed resolutions supporting the establishment of a world government, by June 1951—under intense pressure from "patriotic" groups—all but 8 of these states had voted to rescind them. In early 1950, a bill supporting American membership in a world government had passed the California assembly unanimously and the state senate by nearly two to one. But a surge of nationalist hysteria led to the measure's repeal and to the introduction of a bill to investigate United World Federalists.[13] Journals of general interest "just do not discuss the issue" of world government, G. A. Borgese complained in April 1951, "because, with the Korean War . . . the goal seems remote indeed." UWF president Alan Cranston wrote that federalists were finding that, like the Red Queen in *Through the Looking Glass*, "it takes all the running you can do to keep in the same place." [14]

Recognizing that the nuclear disarmament movement's difficulties flowed in large part from the heightening Cold War, Leo Szilard suggested a dramatic reorientation in strategy. He explained this in the form of a story about a drunkard looking for his house key in Trafalgar Square. Asked by a policeman if he had lost it there, the drunkard responded that he had lost it in Soho. "If you lost it in Soho," the policeman remarked, "why, then, do you look for it here under this lamp?" The drunkard replied: "There is light here, and in Soho it is dark." Szilard maintained that the point of the story was "that the key to the control of atomic bombs does not lie in the narrow area of atomic energy on which the spotlights of public discussion are focused, but rather in the dark fields of our overall foreign policy." [15]

Adopting this new approach, Szilard began to discuss what he called "an overall East-West settlement" with other ECAS leaders. "In the absence of such an overall settlement," he wrote Einstein in early 1950, "international control of atomic bombs is not likely to be agreed upon, or if it is agreed upon, it is not likely to be maintained for very long." The Acheson-Lilienthal proposal had "dealt with atomic energy as an isolated issue," he noted, but "overall negotiations with Russia" might prove more fruitful. For this purpose, he proposed that ECAS sponsor the creation of a citizens' committee "for the study of the possibility of peace with Russia" and arrange for a meeting with Soviet scientists to consider the kind of settlement needed for international control of atomic energy. Although Pauling and other scientists were interested in the plan, this eventually proved another of Szilard's many ideas that went unrealized.[16]

Similar ideas bubbled to the surface elsewhere. At a two-day forum in April 1950 sponsored by the *Nation*, most of the assembled peace activists, scientists, and liberals reportedly agreed with the observation of Clark Eichelberger, a veteran internationalist, that "weapons of mass destruction cannot be dealt with apart from the entire armaments problem . . . and the armaments problem cannot be dealt with apart from the basic causes of the Cold War." Hans Thirring, too, argued for replacing "disarmament proposals" and "war-resister movements" with a settlement of international issues. Writing in March 1953 in the *Bulletin of the Atomic Scientists*, the Austrian peace movement leader maintained that this could be done by securing agreement on definitions of international aggression. Even if governments failed to reach such an agreement, "a movement from below . . . could improve the international situation." All peoples, he stated, should be invited to join "in a non-Communist—and even non-pacifist—peace movement with the one clear and unambiguous target of rejecting and resisting aggression."[17] Although nothing came of this proposal either, it provided an additional indication that some peace movement leaders, at least, recognized that the issue of nuclear disarmament had become trapped in the web of international power politics.

The Movement Confronts the Cold War

The Cold War undermined the idea of disarmament not only within the general populace but within the camp of the nuclear disarmers themselves. As the Soviet-American confrontation intensified, a substantial number of nonpacifists began to abandon the idea of disarmament and to champion some form of military defense. Within months of the Baruch Plan's unveiling at the United Nations, noted Harold Urey, the ECAS vice-president, he "concluded that the Soviet Union would agree to no effective control" of the Bomb. Accordingly, much to the distress of many activists in the atomic scientists' movement, in 1947 he began advocating a federation of those nations willing to resist Soviet might, and in 1950 he supported building the H-Bomb.[18] Meanwhile, turning its back on the idea of world government, a new Atlantic Union Committee (AUC) sought to transform the NATO alliance into a political union opposed to the Communist bloc. Founded by U.S. Supreme Court justice Owen Roberts, former secretary of war Robert Patterson, and former under secretary of state Will Clayton in 1949, the AUC absorbed Streit's Federal Union chapters in the United States and attracted significant elite support in Canada, Great Britain, and Western Europe. Although Atlantic Union never inspired the enthusiastic, mass following that rallied behind the idea of world government, it did provide a means for some people to retreat from the apparently unattainable ideal of One World.[19]

Growing support for military measures also played an important role in hobbling the British Atomic Scientists' Association. According to the minutes of its annual meeting of June 30, 1951, Lord Cherwell—a leading proponent of nuclear weapons—"urged very strongly that the Association should refrain altogether from expressing views on political matters." The ASA should give advice on "technical matters such as, for example, civil defense arrangements," he stated; but "expressing views on whether atomic bombs ought or ought not to be used in warfare was not our job, and could do harm." Outgoing ASA president Nevill Mott, voicing the position adopted by the ASA Council during the year, agreed with Cherwell that the ASA "ought not to make political pronouncements" but did think that scientists needed a "forum" to "discuss . . . the social and political implications of their work." Objecting more firmly to a retreat from politics, Joseph Rotblat rejoindered that "in its early days the Association was preoccupied with the question of international control—a problem which certainly embraced both science and politics." Although Mott and the editor of the ASA journal argued that it should provide for a discussion representing all viewpoints, Cherwell and other speakers objected vehemently, deprecating "the idea of conducting a sort of political forum in the *News*." Badgered by its "respectable" vice-presidents, the ASA lapsed into relative silence.[20]

For many disarmament activists, the Korean War proved a decisive turning point. Opposing any "surrender" to "Stalin's imperialist communism," Norman Thomas backed the war as a U.N. police action.[21] Indeed, within the United States, there was remarkably little opposition to the war, and even some top leaders of the Progressive party, including Henry Wallace, broke with their former associates and endorsed U.S. policy.[22] In August 1950, the National Executive Council of United World Federalists declared that "the total military effort of the UN must be sustained until the aggression is repulsed." In November, UWF proclaimed that "the United States must continue with all speed to muster its full strength in the cause of freedom until the defenses of the free world are so strong that they will deter aggression. . . . The immediate survival of freedom depends on this." [23] Nor were these sentiments limited to the United States. On July 28, 1950, Henry Usborne told the British House of Commons that world government supporters were "four square behind the United Nations" in the Korean War. Previously a bulwark against rearmament and Cold War alignment, the Japanese Socialist party split over these questions in late 1951, and two competing parties functioned thereafter until 1955. A U.S. intelligence study in early 1951 reported happily that the papacy and its support groups seemed to be reconciling themselves to nuclear weapons. [24]

This support for military measures, though, was often sharply qualified. Norman Thomas considered the Korean War badly mishandled by the U.S. government and strongly opposed its escalation. In its November 1950 pronouncement, UWF argued for "some purpose to this program of military power other than war or a continuing arms race" and stated that it "must be a United Nations vested with the power to enforce disarmament and with the sole right to use force among nations." [25] Even though he supported U.S. policy in Korea, Norman Cousins argued against expansion of the conflict, opposed the use of the atomic bomb, and continued to champion world government as the only long-term solution to international problems. [26] Moreover, UWF leaders strongly opposed plans for a federation excluding the Soviet Union, lobbying in Congress against proposals for Atlantic Union and defeating a proposal along these lines at its 1950 convention after a confrontation so bitter that it almost destroyed the organization. [27] When Great Britain entered the Korean War, the Crusade for World Government urged its members to emphasize the need to restructure the United Nations, support mediation by the Indian government, and "make it crystal clear . . . that we stand above the East-West struggle." Privately, Usborne wrote that "to save further massacre and misery we should aim for an armistice as quickly as possible." He did not "accept the view," he added grimly, "that the situation since Korea is fundamentally any different from what we faced in earlier times. It is only that more people have begun to understand that we are—and always have been—at war." Only a "world federal constitution," he argued, could bring peace. [28]

Nevertheless, in these conditions of international confrontation, a small group became clear partisans of one or the other Cold War camp. Breaking with his friends in America's atomic scientists' movement, Edward Teller became a staunch Cold Warrior and one of the key proponents of building a hydrogen bomb. [29] In 1949, Cord Meyer, Jr., the president of UWF, became increasingly disturbed by Soviet policy and disillusioned with world federalism as an alternative; "my repetitive warnings of approaching nuclear doom echoed hollowly in my head," he recalled. Later that year, he resigned his post and, by 1951, had commenced a lengthy career with the U.S. Central Intelligence Agency.[30] A few threw in their lot with the other side. Alienated by the Korean War, Europe's shift rightward, and McCarthyism, Jean-Paul Sartre began a close relationship with the French Communist party and with the Soviet Union that lasted from 1952 to 1956.[31]

By contrast, though, most of the disarmament movement—and especially its pacifist wing—did not take sides in the Cold War but, rather, strongly resisted its escalation. In both West Germany and Japan, peace groups threw themselves into struggles against the rearmament of their countries.[32] Szilard advocated the neutralization of "those nations which are at present caught between the strategic aspirations of America and Russia," and Einstein sought to dispel what he called "the widespread hysterical fear of Russian aggression."[33] With the inception of the Korean War, the international WILPF agitated for a cease-fire, the withdrawal of foreign troops, and a negotiated settlement of the conflict. In numerous nations, pacifist groups joined in assailing the bloodshed in Korea. Appealing for "the cessation of strife," the Canadian FOR urged an armistice and the continuation of "negotiations toward mediation on the lines suggested by Prime Minister Nehru."[34] As the war escalated, the Swiss peace movement, calling for "an immediate cease-fire," protested against rapidly rising Swiss weapons exports. New Zealand pacifists campaigned against their country's dispatch of troops to Korea.[35] In Great Britain, the National Peace Council organized an ad hoc body, the Peace with China Council, which held large peace meetings throughout the country. In the United States, pacifist organizations sharply criticized the conflict, which they feared was a preliminary to World War III. What the Korean War means, the FOR warned, "is that Russia and the United States are now engaged in an unlimited atomic and biological armaments race and are locked in a military power-struggle around the entire world."[36]

Yet their staunch opposition to Cold War policies also distracted these peace organizations from the issue of the Bomb. Caught up in the struggle against German rearmament, FOR leader Siegmund-Schültze reported in the fall of 1950 that "nearly all letters which I . . . write have to do with remilitarization." There was "hardly a day" when he did not "speak about this subject at a meeting or with visitors." In the United States, the *Bulletin of the Atomic Scientists* gradually broadened its concerns to other world issues.[37] After the inception of the Korean War, the PPU focused almost entirely on that conflict and largely dropped the nuclear weapons question. "PEACE WITH CHINA!" drew three-quarter-page headlines in *Peace News* and became the theme of mass meetings throughout Great Britain. These meetings attracted many nonpacifist peace activists as speakers, including Kingsley Martin and Victor Gollancz.[38] Recalling British peace activity in the 1950s, Sybil Morrison later wrote: "Korea, Suez, Cyprus, Malaya, Indonesia, Kenya, Quemoy, Berlin; there seemed no end to the conflicts, and in respect to each one there were letters and deputations, lobbyings, meetings, demonstrations and special leaflets."[39] In this context, there was little time or energy left to confront the menace of the Bomb.

Even in Japan, where the peace movement was fiercely antinuclear, new concerns linked to the heightening Cold War kept coming to the fore. To be sure, World Peace Day rallies resumed in Hiroshima on August 6, 1951, and they occurred annually thereafter. In 1952, a mass citizens meeting in Hiroshima sponsored by 42 organizations called for a ban on the production and use of nuclear weapons. Disarmament activism also grew during the early 1950s in Nagasaki, which held a widely attended exhibition of atomic bomb drawings and organized a Society to Protect A-Bomb Victims. Nevertheless, other issues sometimes crowded out the anti-Bomb message. In the early 1950s, the Japanese WILPF chapter gave top priority to defending Japan's "peace constitution." Preparing for World Peace Day on August 6, 1951, Japanese pacifists announced their platform: "(1) No rearmament of Japan; (2) No amendment or emasculation of the war-renouncing clause of Japan's constitution; (3) No treaty, until one can be obtained with all the powers that were at war with Japan; (4) An end to the occupation." Strikingly, their statement did not mention nuclear disarmament.[40] Whether or not disarmament groups compromised with the Cold War, it posed a major obstacle to the struggle against the Bomb.

The Communist Stigma

Proponents of disarmament in Western nations also labored under the heavy burden of being identified with Communism. Traditionally, fierce nationalists had accused advocates of peace of siding with the enemy; therefore, it was not surprising that in the Cold War context, rabid patriots accused them of Communist sympathies. But in addition, as Vera Brittain recalled, "international Communism chose that moment to wave a banner called 'Peace,' " thus making it a particularly "dirty word."[41] The results were devastating. "Communist propaganda for peace has discredited . . . preaching for peace and made suspect . . . pacifist action," noted an International FOR report from Argentina. In West Germany, pacifist leaders attributed their difficulties in organizing meetings and drawing members to the identification of peace workers with Communists.[42] On a nationwide speaking tour during 1951, the Canadian FOR secretary found that "great confusion" existed everywhere she went as to the relationship of the FOR with the Communist-led CPC and that "most church people" were "afraid of any possible connection." The administrative secretary of the American section of the WILPF reported that "the mass hysteria started by the government but now out of control . . . is making our work difficult and presenting us with new problems."[43] In France, Sweden, Austria, and Canada, nonaligned peace activities acquired a debilitating Communist stigma.[44]

Naturally, nonaligned peace groups did their best to challenge this image. "This leaflet is issued by the Peace Pledge Union, founded by Dick Sheppard (not by Joe Stalin)," stated a PPU handout on civil defense; "it has nothing to do with the Communist peace campaign."[45] Given "the activity of the peace movement that is conducted by the Eastern countries," reported the Swedish WILPF, the group emphasized "the word 'freedom' in our name and we have stressed the importance of human rights." But "people in general can often not differ[entiate] between our league and the Women's Democratic Federation." Charged by a major newspaper and by a prominent member of the nobility with Communist subversion, Britain's National Peace Council initiated legal action in both cases and secured published apologies. The National Peace Council, it turned out, had been confused with the British Peace Committee. Meanwhile, in the United States, activists in the atomic scientists' movement spent a great deal of time defending outspoken members of their profession from a McCarthyite onslaught. "Is PEACE a bad word?" asked an American FOR leaflet. "Because the Communists misuse the word, are Americans going to agree that they prefer war?"[46]

As one Australian peace activist noted, doing " 'peace' work" in these circumstances became "very difficult." In the United States, Monogram Pictures canceled plans for a film on the life of the Indian chief Hiawatha, fearing that the story of his peace efforts might be construed as Communist propaganda. On crowded streets in New York City, pacifists found people so afraid to accept their leaflets that sometimes twenty minutes would elapse before they could distribute one.[47] In Great Britain, the Truro City Council voted to ban the PPU newspaper, *Peace News*, from the city library. The Communist-led peace campaign "has further intensified the ignorant popular confusion of Communism with pacifism," a *Peace News* editorial complained. In New Zealand, "the word 'Peace' has become suspect—to use the word is to be branded a dupe of Moscow," stated a February 1951 editorial in the *New Zealand Christian Pacifist*. "No daily paper can refer to a meeting called for the purpose of discussing the prevention of war without putting the word 'peace' in inverted commas."[48]

Confused with their Communist rivals, WILPF sections took a battering in many nations. The Norwegian section reported that "it is not easy to work for peace in Norway today and difficult to get new members, even though lots of people actually are in accordance with our aims and work." Such people "are afraid of being suspected of communistic sympathies, as we have now and again . . . been accused of communism. . . . These accusations have done much harm to our work." In its yearly report for 1950, the Swedish WILPF bluntly declared: "The Peace Partisans have made it more difficult to work for peace. People think that everything with the word peace in it is communistic." From neighboring Denmark, the WILPF section reported simply: "The activity of the 'Partisans of Peace' . . . tends to make all peace work unpopular." Attacked as a Communist organization, the Vancouver, Canada, chapter even had its records destroyed by a would-be patriot. According to the official WILPF history, "the activities of the World Peace Council and its subsidiaries . . . often constituted as great a handicap to the established peace movement in the West as the Atlantic Pact."[49]

World government groups encountered a barrage of anti-Communist abuse, particularly in the United States. Beginning in 1949 and escalating thereafter, articles and editorials in right-wing and purportedly patriotic magazines and newspapers charged that world federalism was part of a Communist conspiracy. The world government movement, claimed the Daughters of the American Revolution, provided "the key to Russian domination of America." American Legion posts in Hagerstown, Maryland, sought to block the performance of a world government play by repeated charges that United World Federalists was engaged in subversive, pro-Communist activities. In Texas, UWF was banned from the campus of Texas Tech, and a public high school teacher was forced to sever his UWF affiliations to retain his job.[50] In Connecticut, the *Bridgeport Telegram* ran an editorial headed simply "World Government Means Communism." So vicious did attacks by the Veterans of Foreign Wars (VFW) become in Minnesota that UWF nearly initiated a libel suit against the state organization. Meanwhile, in Wisconsin, U.S. Representative Lawrence Smith told a VFW meeting that world government was "just as dangerous as the communism we are fighting."[51]

Leaders of world government groups received much the same treatment. Assailed by the Hearst press, the *Brooklyn Tablet*, and other publications as pro-Communist, news commentator and prominent world federalist Raymond Gram Swing found himself targeted for blacklisting by *Counterattack* and investigated for subversion by Senator McCarthy. In its depiction of Norman Cousins as a leader of un-American activities, the American Legion publicized the fact that he had addressed the Waldorf conference but omitted mentioning that he had attended to deliver an indictment of the Communist-led peace movement. The *Chicago Tribune* charged that the federalist cause, "ostensibly a movement for the establishment of a world government," was led by dangerous liberals and radicals, while "quietly in the background are veteran followers of the Communist party line." The objectives of Alan Cranston, UWF president, did not "differ materially" from those of Communist party leaders recently convicted under the Smith Act, the newspaper maintained.[52]

The association of peace activism with Communism also proved debilitating in Eastern Europe. Although initially the idea of a peace campaign had some genuine appeal to the war-weary people of the region, the one-sided, propagandistic nature of the enterprise that emerged within these Communist states chilled most of the popular enthusiasm for the project. Gradually, East Europeans became cynical and apathetic about the state-sponsored peace movement, just as they grew cynical and apathetic about what government officials billed as "socialism." Two Hungarians recalled that, as the official " 'peace struggle' . . . became a euphemism for armament, expansion and a policy of intimidation," suspicion grew among Hungarians "towards any version or goal of the peace movement." Here, too, then, the Communist-led peace campaign helped to undermine peace activism and leave it "fundamentally discredited."[53]

In addition to damaging peace and disarmament groups in their relations with the public, Communist-led peace activism also put severe strains on these groups internally. Although nonaligned groups almost always resisted organizational cooperation with the Communist-led peace campaign,[54] some members did not approve of this policy, while others felt it was not implemented strictly enough.[55] Numerous questions remained unanswered or, if answered, matters of dispute. Should "observers" from nonaligned groups attend Communist-led gatherings? Should members of nonaligned groups participate as individuals?[56] What was the proper attitude to take toward the participation of Communists or Communist sympathizers in nonaligned groups? The chair of the Danish WILPF section worried lest the typical WILPF chapter "dwindle into a small, mainly Communist, handful of women." In the United States, the WILPF section mailed out material to its branches on how to deal with both left-wing infiltration and right-wing attack, acknowledging that the job would be difficult. "In our effort to keep our organization free from subversion and to defend it from overt attacks, we must neither abandon our basic principles and program nor stoop to the totalitarian methods we abhor," it explained. Rather than establish a policy restricting membership, WILPF branches should "make as clear as possible to our fellow citizens that we act from our own consistent and long-established principles and not from consideration of political expedience dictated to us by any political group or faction."[57] But how, exactly, was this to be done?

Movements in other nations experienced similar problems. A British WILPF leader, noting the numerous disputes between and within national WILPF sections in 1951, contended that "at the root of all these conflicts . . .

is the personal attitude toward Communism." Within the British executive committee, she added, "we are certainly not all of one mind." According to the official WILPF history, attempts by the Communist-led Women's International Democratic Federation to use WILPF "for its own partisan aims, even though unsuccessful, were a considerable embarrassment to WILPF national sections." Indeed, "rifts caused by the Communist peace campaigns . . . halved the membership in Scandinavia and Switzerland." [58] Communist peace activism thus posed a problem for the nonaligned nuclear disarmament movement not only with respect to the Cold War but as a matter of its own internal dynamics.

Exhaustion and Escapism

Because most reform movements have a natural life cycle, it is hardly surprising that, after a period of intense activity, the movement against nuclear weapons would show signs of ebbing vitality. Most people have only so much time and energy to devote to public concerns before their private lives again demand precedence or, at least, some attention. This phenomenon became apparent in the atomic scientists' movement, where a growing impatience developed among activists to return to their laboratories and classrooms. "For many of us," wrote John A. Simpson in November 1946, the movement "has meant the postponement or complete loss . . . of valuable research time out of the productive part of our lives." Although "this has been justified," it "cannot be justified over longer periods of time." Commenting on "the retreat into private lives" that characterized the United States in 1949, an organizer for the War Resisters League worried that Americans were "waiting for the world to explode." But he conceded that part of the withdrawal from public concerns was "necessary and healthy, for we can't live all of the time with great, complex problems of mankind and the world." The following year, in Great Britain, a writer for *Peace News* pointed to the declining sales of that journal and asked: "What has gone wrong?" His answer was that "for pacifists, no less than other people, these last five years have been a time of re-habilitation," which included "catching up on disrupted careers, home building," and "coping with the urgent tasks of reconstruction in every sphere of life." [59]

Moreover, the movement's feeling of exhaustion was magnified by a sense of futility. After all the efforts to awaken national populations and their leaders to the dangers of nuclear weapons, what had been accomplished? As war and the arms race lurched forward, the morale of their sharpest opponents ebbed substantially. Attempting to explain the "very weak state" of the pacifist movement in New Zealand in 1951, one of its leaders pointed to "a feeling of helplessness in face of what appears to be . . . a hundred years war." In the

United States, a pacifist conclave that same year concluded that FOR members shared the "same sense of defeatism prevalent in the country with regard to war."[60] For a time, the scientists' movement maintained its hopes for international control of atomic energy, focusing on continuing efforts in the United Nations. But after late 1946, international control began to appear increasingly unlikely, and a mood of pessimism gradually engulfed the movement. Writing to Niels Bohr in late 1950, Leo Szilard commented with his usual gallows humor: "Theoretically I am supposed to divide my time between finding out what life is and trying to preserve it by saving the world." But "at present the world seems to be beyond saving, and that leaves more time free for biology."[61]

Another component of the movement's waning fortunes apparently lay in what psychiatrist Robert Lifton has called "psychic numbing": the deadening of feelings in the face of mass destruction.[62] Fear of a nuclear holocaust, of course, had played a key part in the struggle against the Bomb. This feeling was symbolized by the movement's most popular slogan, "One World or None," and by the clock on the front of the *Bulletin of the Atomic Scientists*, registering the number of minutes before the midnight of nuclear war. But could this intense fear be sustained? To judge from numerous barometers of public sentiment, it could not. In Great Britain, noted one PPU leader, "when the atom bombs fell the terrible news did momentarily create a great fear. Everywhere people were deeply shaken and moved." Yet "the mood passed. The human mind began to accommodate itself to this development. The terror subsided." A government-sponsored civil defense survey in 1951 found that, despite all the public furor about nuclear weapons, Britons displayed remarkably little knowledge of the Bomb or desire to face the issues it raised. A quarter of the women surveyed claimed that they did not know it had been used in Japan. According to a summary of the British survey, "the immediate reaction" of "a large part of the population to the very idea of a possible war" was "to wish not to hear about it."[63]

Other surveys also found substantial portions of the public apparently determined to avoid confronting the nuclear menace. Opinion pollsters reported that when asked questions about foreign affairs, people did not mention nuclear weapons. If the pollsters themselves raised the issue, respondents would declare that they were not worried, for God or the government would take care of them. But when the interviewers pressed beyond the nonchalant responses, terror would begin to creep out. In 1950, an American worker told an interviewer that the Russians could never bomb the United States. Then, after his confidence was gently questioned, he reversed himself. "Their planes could get through," he admitted; "I hate to think of what would happen." People elsewhere also seemed bent on evading the issue. When the Soviet Union exploded its first atomic bomb, it seemed very likely that there would be considerable consternation, at least among U.S. allies. But a secret U.S. government study reported that, around the world, "the popular reaction has been generally calm and in some areas apathetic."[64]

Surveys of American opinion during the late 1940s and early 1950s reinforce this picture. Although postwar polls found that virtually every American had heard of the atomic bomb, in 1946 half of the respondents declared that they were not worried about it and only one out of eight reported deep personal concern. In the face of the scientists' repeated contention that there was no defense against nuclear weapons, 54 percent of respondents to a June 1946 poll declared that the United States would be able to develop such a defense; by December 1949, 60 percent made this prediction. Indeed, over time, Americans seemed to grow more complacent about the nuclear menace. In September 1946, 53 percent of those polled stated that in the event of "another war" there was "a very real danger" that an atomic bomb would be dropped in a place where they lived. Polled in December 1950, only 25 percent said there was "a good chance" that "in case of another world war" their community would be attacked with atom bombs. In the fall of 1950, when Americans were asked if there were anything in the national or international realm that disturbed them, only 1 percent spontaneously raised the issue of the Bomb. Yet, remarkably, as one survey noted, "half the people who say they are not worried indicate a recognition that the bomb is a threat—often that it is a very grave threat." Impressed by this contradiction, scholars have written of the American public's "evasion," "escapism," and "fear suppression." They have also pointed to a widespread sense of powerlessness Americans felt with respect to the Bomb. This feeling, combined with fear, led to their "turning away from the entire topic."[65]

Massive public relations programs encouraged the popular retreat from reality. Publicizing the "peaceful uses" of atomic energy, governments and corporations generated books, films, radio programs, exhibits, comic books, and fairs with a cheery message of atomic-based prosperity for all. In the CBS program "The Sunny Side of the Atom," the narrator, in a trancelike reverie, declared: "I saw a great light, more luminous than the sun, flooding out over the darkness of the earth. Its rays were lighting up the innermost recesses of life, searching out secrets never revealed by the light of the sun." He "saw all men standing straight and tall and confident, facing without fear their future, urged forward by a new hope, by the infinite wonder and possibility of a new life." Amid the popular euphoria about "peaceful" nuclear power, government officials dismissed warnings of radiation hazards or environmental damage and did a generally effective job of soothing public fears through a combination of misinformation and unruffled optimism.[66]

Organizational Decline

Organizational decline was particularly evident within the once flourishing atomic scientists' movement. In the United States, where the movement had begun, the Committee for Foreign Correspondence voted to dissolve in early 1948, and the Emergency Committee of Atomic Scientists tottered toward collapse at the end of the year. In November, the discouraged leaders of ECAS, faced with internal disagreements and an empty treasury, met and agreed that there was little point in continuing on an active basis. Although ECAS maintained a twilight existence until 1951, it served as little more than a forum for the ideas of Leo Szilard.[67] The Federation of American Scientists, which had reached a peak of 3,000 members in 1946, also decayed, dropping to little more than 1,000 by mid-1949. Although FAS membership recovered somewhat in later years, after 1948 its core of activists numbered only about 100. Under the able editorial guidance of Eugene Rabinowitch, the *Bulletin of the Atomic Scientists* continued to provide a vital resource for the scientists' movement and for the public, but it faced serious difficulties securing adequate funding and constituency.[68]

In Great Britain, the atomic scientists' movement was grinding to a halt. In the fall of 1953, one of the ASA's leaders reported that, in recent years, the group had "largely concentrated its efforts in the production of the *Journal*," its revised publication, "and this is now almost its sole activity." Within the organization, he noted, there was a "general lack of enthusiasm," which was "reflected in the paucity of full members at the annual general meetings . . . and in the difficulty in finding successors to its retiring active officers." Few young people joined the organization. Furthermore, all branch activities had ceased. At the last general meeting, only fifteen full members attended, and some of them were retiring council members. Consequently, he suggested disbanding the ASA and turning its periodical into "a semi-popular technical journal giving some preference to articles on atomic energy." In fact, the ASA managed to limp along into the latter part of the decade but with little energy or activity.[69]

The world government movement was also in trouble. The most powerful of the new globalist organizations, the World Movement for World Federal Government, underwent a substantial decline. United World Federalists, the American branch and by far the largest, had peaked at nearly 50,000 members in 1949, but the number dropped to 38,000 in 1950 and to 22,000 by June 1951. Hemorrhaging members, abandoned by its student affiliate, and torn by internal dissension, UWF contributed far fewer financial and other resources than in the past to keeping the world movement afloat. Not surprisingly, these cutbacks and others sent the WMWFG reeling. So difficult did it become to support the WMWFG's activities that the small staff at its Paris headquarters sought private loans to purchase office supplies, and leaders of its student affiliate auctioned off their personal belongings. Remarking on the overall "crisis" in the movement, the chair of the WMWFG executive committee, Elisabeth Mann Borgese, told a friend that she was "terribly upset and would . . . like to quit." [70]

Although the WMWFG weathered the crisis and survived in weakened form, the same could not be said of other world government campaigns. From December 31, 1950, to January 5, 1951, the much discussed Peoples World Convention—to be chosen in unofficial elections by the people of the world for the purpose of establishing a world government—met in Geneva, chaired by Henry Usborne. It proved a fiasco. Although supporters of the idea had introduced bills for the election of delegates into numerous parliamentary bodies— including those of France, Italy, Belgium, Brazil, and Turkey—only the legislature of Tennessee had taken positive action. Consequently, when the Geneva meeting convened, there were 500 observers from 43 nations at its sessions but only 3 official delegates: 2 from the United States (elected by 290,000 voters in Tennessee) and 1 from Nigeria (supported by tribal chiefs). Even the election of the Tennesseeans was suspect, for the authorizing legislation had been repealed. The convention did choose a continuations committee to prepare for a genuinely representative Peoples World Convention in the future. But as the years passed with no progress toward this goal, the project seemed increasingly farfetched and lost whatever credibility it had once enjoyed. [71]

The World Citizens movement of Garry Davis became another casualty of the era. Exhausted and craving time for contemplation, Davis returned to the United States in the spring of 1950. There he married, studied Indian philosophy and religion, and in September 1950 applied for restoration of his American citizenship. A few years later, Davis traveled to India to study with a guru. In these travels, Davis used a self-created World Passport, a practice that provoked repeated conflicts with government officials, and he continued to preach the idea of world citizenship. But he abandoned all efforts to create an organized movement. Garry Davis "knows how to stir up opinion with symbolic, striking acts," noted a French pacifist leader. "But he seems unable to keep a track for more than a few months, continually unsatisfied by his own achievements and by others . . . and no force nor friendship can keep him, if his imagination is dreaming of something new and different." Meanwhile, the World Citizens movement crumbled. At a meeting of its international secretariat in the winter of 1950–51, Robert Sarrazac reported that the World Citizens registry was moribund and needed "further 'motor' action" to "give it a real vitality." [72] None, however, materialized.

Other antinuclear forces also lost momentum. The 1949 World Peace Day celebration in Hiroshima drew only "a few thousand," an observer reported, and the atmosphere was strangely lighthearted and diffuse, characterized by fireworks, confetti, and the appearance on stage of a "Miss Hiroshima." The following year, in response to orders from the authorities, the ceremony was canceled.[73] In the United States, the membership of pacifist organizations declined substantially in the early 1950s, leading to cutbacks in staff and office space. Membership in the Fellowship of Reconciliation, which had been generally stable since 1942, dropped by 21 percent between 1950 and 1953.[74] In the Netherlands, the Third Way deteriorated rapidly, exhausted by fruitless internal wrangling. When the independent Left *De Vlam* ceased publication in September 1952, the movement lost its principal forum outside of pacifist circles and faded thereafter into insignificance. By the mid-1950s, the Dutch peace movement had reached a nadir, with a small number of participants, often of advanced age.[75]

The story was much the same elsewhere. In Switzerland, the nonaligned Swiss Peace Council went through an internal crisis in the early 1950s that caused the departure of some constituent groups and left the remainder largely paralyzed. The Swiss WILPF group declined in size by some 50 percent. In Scandinavian nations, the WILPF also lost approximately half its membership, and the Swedish Peace and Arbitration Society found it impossible to mobilize support for its own nonaligned position. Noting that in France there existed only two organized FOR chapters, a 1951 report concluded that "the Christian pacifist in France is very lonely." [76]

Fading from Significance

By the early 1950s, the nonaligned movement against nuclear weapons had faded substantially—if not from sight, then from significance. Surveying the wreckage, Hans Thirring reported in early 1953 that, "on the other side of the ideological gulf," lay "the very large and efficient Communist-sponsored movement of the World Peace Council." It was "well organized" and "well equipped with periodicals and propaganda means," but hardly a genuine peace movement. And "on this side of the gap" lay "a multitude of well-meaning but uncoordinated, tiny peace societies which, being partly ridiculed, partly suspected as communists or fellow travellers . . . have absolutely no influence on the foreign policy of their respective countries." For quite different reasons, the Austrian peace movement leader was not greatly impressed by either.[77]

How, despite the movement's early promise, had this state of affairs come about? Certainly its decline did not result from any diminution of the nuclear menace. Indeed, by this time, both the United States and the Soviet Union had embarked upon crash programs to produce new weapons of unprecedented destructiveness: hydrogen bombs. Instead, the dwindling of the movement and of popular support for its core ideas largely reflected the difficulties in separating nuclear weapons from the harsh world of power politics and its contemporary manifestation, the Cold War. By the fall of 1949, Szilard had concluded that "we cannot have an agreement which will eliminate the atom bomb from the national armaments without a general reduction of armaments" and "we cannot have reduction of armaments without a settlement of the political issues." [78] The onset of the Korean War, which further damaged the movement both internally and externally, confirmed this dilemma, making it all too clear that no campaign for nuclear disarmament could progress very far in a world torn by fierce international conflict. In addition, the ferocious reaction against the Communist-led peace movement and the nonaligned movement's own gathering exhaustion weakened the struggle against the Bomb to the point of marginality.

One World might well provide the answer to the nuclear menace. But in the early 1950s, relatively few people seemed ready for it.

Conclusion and Epilogue

The New Thinking and the Old

> Though with the top of their mind people don't wish to be
> destroyed, on the deeper levels they seem determined not to
> give up the modes of thought and feeling that make war,
> which now means destruction, inevitable.
>
> Aldous Huxley, 1946

As this book has demonstrated, the Bomb inspired substantial opposition in the years through 1953. Even before the weapon's shocking debut, Wells, Szilard, and a growing number of scientists warned about its immense potential for destruction and sought to create alternatives that would guarantee humanity's survival. And following the atomic bombing of Japan, the secret struggle against the Bomb, waged largely by a small group of scientists, blossomed into a popular crusade on a global basis. Although pacifist organizations such as the War Resisters' International, the International Fellowship of Reconciliation, and the Women's International League for Peace and Freedom had been badly damaged by World War II, they retained a presence in many nations and served as a key component of this popular movement. Their efforts received powerful reinforcement not only from Japanese survivors of the atomic bombings but from new organizations among scientists and world government advocates that, responding to the advent of the Bomb, became influential forces in many societies. Although the priorities and favored instrumentalities of these groups differed somewhat, they had enough in common to enable them to work effectively together in the cause of nuclear disarmament. Nuclear weapons, they warned repeatedly, rendered obsolete the traditional policy of guaranteeing national security through overwhelming military strength. The real alternatives, they insisted, were One World or None.

Socially and politically, this struggle against the Bomb developed somewhat unevenly. Like most peace and disarmament movements of the preceding century, it drew disproportionately upon the educated middle class. Scientists, of course, played a very prominent role in agitation for nuclear disarmament. But other well-educated persons—economically secure but intellectually alarmed—were also disproportionately represented, including teachers, writers, and prominent cultural figures. Traditionally active in peace and disarmament campaigns, women's and religious groups also played an important part in this one, which touched upon their moral concerns.[1] Politically, the movement appears to have had relatively little appeal to conservatives or right-wing forces, perhaps because of its direct challenge to nationalism and because of its failure to satisfy their virulent anti-Communism. Instead, it tended to attract reformers of a more liberal persuasion. Even so, only the social democratic parties of the former Axis nations (where military priorities had been discredited by fascism) gave it their wholehearted support. For the most part, the movement could count on little more than small numbers of recruits from liberal and social democratic constituencies and occasional backing from some of their elected officials.

The nonaligned nuclear disarmament movement also proved geographically uneven. Although it experienced occasional stirrings in Eastern Europe, the Soviet Union, and (more often) the Third World, dictatorship and—in the latter case—a very different set of priorities muted its appeal in these regions. The real strongholds of the movement lay in Japan, North America, Western Europe, and Australasia. To some degree, this reflected the direct relationship that some of the nations in these areas (e.g., Japan, the United States, Great Britain, and Canada) had with the development and use of the atomic bomb in World War II. More significantly, though, it appears to have resulted from their relatively high level of political freedom and industrial development. Political freedom provided an environment in which reform movements could emerge and flourish, while industrial development generated not only weapons of mass destruction but an educated middle class[2]—two important factors behind the creation of the nuclear disarmament movement. Calling attention to this curious aspect of industrial modernization, H. G. Wells once remarked that human history was becoming a "race between education and catastrophe."[3]

Whatever its limitations, however, the nonaligned nuclear disarmament movement also showed clear signs of strength. Formed, for the most part, in the immediate aftermath of the atomic bombing of Japan, the new movement could soon draw upon several hundred thousand participants, in hundreds of groups, located in dozens of nations. They generated an enormous quantity of literature on the subject of the Bomb and distributed it widely. In addition, they held public meetings, participated in radio broadcasts, and sometimes took to the streets for demonstrations. The movement also attracted individuals of great eminence and international renown who spoke out publicly on behalf of its vision of a world without the Bomb. A few, like Nehru and Romulo, were influential statesmen. Although not a mass movement capable of mobilizing millions of people, it was a lively, visible, worldwide phenomenon.

Furthermore, through its activities, the nuclear disarmament movement helped to focus public attention on the menace of the Bomb and thereby contributed to the remarkable radicalization of popular thinking about international relations that characterized the immediate postwar era. Horrified by the prospect of a future nuclear holocaust, millions of people came to welcome the idea of nuclear disarmament. To attain this goal, many favored unprecedented limitations on national sovereignty, ranging from international control of atomic energy to world government. In either case, it added up to something approximating the movement's prescription of One World.

Of course, it can be argued that public opinion, even without the prodding of these groups, might have taken this direction. But this seems less likely than the conclusion that peace and disarmament groups, by sounding the alarm about nuclear weapons, helped generate an outpouring of popular concern and a demand for globalist solutions. Certainly, the public discussion that ensued—including the rhetoric, arguments, and proposed solutions—closely paralleled their pronouncements, particularly the well-publicized statements of the atomic scientists. Furthermore, if the nuclear disarmament movement had no impact on public opinion, it is hard to understand why the governments of so many nations took it as seriously as they did. Indeed, convinced that peace and disarmament groups constituted a force to be reckoned with, public officials in numerous countries made vigorous efforts to counter or silence their criticism of the Bomb. Sometimes they even sought to co-opt disarmament forces. Uneasy about the criticism its nuclear weapons program might provoke, the British government kept that program totally hidden from public scrutiny. For their part, Communist governments suppressed nonaligned activism wherever they could and devoted enormous resources to building an alternative movement.[4] Also, in places where nonaligned peace and disarmament organizations did not exist—as in the Communist dictatorships of the Soviet bloc, the right-wing dictatorships of the American bloc, and large portions of the Third World—public opinion remained considerably less agitated about the Bomb.

Somewhat belatedly, Communist leaders developed their own campaign against nuclear weapons. Drawing upon the substantial resources afforded them by Communist governments and mass-based political parties, they pulled together a very large, vigorous, and widespread movement—far larger than its nonaligned counterpart. Yet, despite the Communist-led campaign's clear superiority in resources and numbers, it also faced a very serious problem: most people in non-Communist nations (and many in Communist nations as well) intensely disliked Communism. At the least, they were repelled by the one-sided, pro-Soviet nature of the Communist-led campaign against the Bomb. As a result, the new World Peace Council and its affiliates never managed to move very far beyond the ranks of Soviet sympathizers.

J. D. Bernal, who succeeded Joliot-Curie as president of the World Peace Council, offered a very different interpretation of the organization's difficulties. In 1961, conceding that the WPC was not "adequately representative of peace sentiment in the West," Bernal maintained that this resulted from "the fact that our movement was born at the height of the cold war, and 'peace' immediately became a dirty word." Pinning the "communist label" on the World Peace Council "was the result of a deliberate policy of 'smear,' fostered by advocates of the cold war and only too easily accepted by some of its opponents. Liberal minded and peace loving people in Britain and the United States argued that it was dangerous for the success of movements in their own countries to be associated with any international organizations to which communists were admitted." In that way, they "helped to split the world peace movement into two." [5]

This interpretation, however, is belied by the facts. As this book demonstrates, the World Peace Council began as the direct result of efforts by Communist leaders and other Soviet sympathizers. Furthermore, it failed to expand beyond these confines largely because of its own internal limitations. Around the world (rather than only in Great Britain and the United States), nonaligned peace groups and their leaders objected not to the admission of Communists to peace organizations but to the control of the peace movement by partisans of one side in the Cold War. At times, to be sure, nonaligned groups were concerned with avoiding a Red taint. But their major reason for resisting the entreaties of the World Peace Council was their recognition that they had little in common with it. As Fernando Claudin, the former leader of the Spanish Communist party, recalled, persons other than Soviet sympathizers took "no real part in it for the simple reason that the [Communist-led] peace movement had to be strictly subservient to every twist of Soviet foreign policy." [6] Moreover, the stigmatizing process went the other way. Far from being the victim of Red-baiting by its non-Communist rivals, the World Peace Council, by making the struggle against the Bomb appear to be a "Communist issue," helped undermine the nonaligned movement.

Whatever their differences, however, the nonaligned and the aligned struggles against the Bomb had an important feature in common: the motive of fear. Although pacifists as well as some nonpacifists were also driven by a broad humanitarianism, the upsurge of nonaligned nuclear disarmament activism clearly reflected the Bomb's enormous destructiveness. This was not a new phenomenon, for the development of peace movements during the nineteenth and twentieth centuries had resulted, at least in part, from the ever-greater destructive capacity that science and technology had imparted to modern war.[7] Naturally, the advent of the Bomb reinforced the popular tendency to seek alternatives to war and, therefore, strengthened peace and disarmament movements. Communist leaders—as proponents of revolutionary violence, wars of "liberation," and Soviet military policy—did not share this revulsion toward modern war. But in the late 1940s and early 1950s, they were genuinely alarmed by the prospect of a U.S. nuclear attack upon the Soviet Union and its allies. Therefore, despite the one-sided nature of their campaign, it had a defensive character. They, too, felt threatened by the Bomb.

Even the leaders of the great powers shared these concerns, at least to some degree. To be sure, like the statesmen of the past, they were also motivated, on occasion, by a desire for national aggrandizement and by the hubris that so often afflicts the powerful. Yet from the beginning of the nuclear arms race to the development of the H-Bomb, national leaders had been disturbed by the prospect that their enemies would use nuclear weapons to intimidate or destroy their countries. When they contemplated the Bomb (or other powerful weapons) in the hands of their foes, policymakers—from the most humane and democratic to the cruelest and most authoritarian—invariably felt fear and suspicion. Nor was this feeling irrational. Thousands of years of war and global plunder had convinced the official guardians of national security that, in the anarchic world of international relations, they had good reason to fear other nations. Faced with this dangerous situation, they could respond in two quite different ways. The traditional way was to maintain or to attain the lead in the arms race, in this case the nuclear arms race. The alternative, considerably more daring, was to change the structure of international relations. In the aftermath of the terrible destruction of World War II and the shocking advent of the nuclear age, it seemed for a time that national leaders might actually choose the latter.

And yet the moment was lost. After a brief accommodation to the anti-nuclear tide, national leaders resumed their traditional orientation to weapons and national power. They geared up their armies, threw down the gauntlet to their adversaries, and spurred their nations forward in the nuclear arms race. Once strongly attracted by the idea of nuclear disarmament, the public gradually came to terms with these developments or deliberately ignored them. The Bomb, of course, was not used again in war. But national leaders threatened its use and laid plans for new atomic attacks. By the late 1940s, the Bomb had become an integral part of the world of international rivalry and great power conflict.

Looking back upon the struggle against the Bomb of the late 1940s and early 1950s, critics of the weapon differed on what had been accomplished. For the most part, leading nonaligned activists—pointing to the ongoing nuclear arms race—felt dispirited and defeated. Pacifists were "but 'voices crying in the wilderness,' " recalled the PPU's Sybil Morrison. "All their propaganda, leaflets, demonstrations, and deputations seemed to be ineffective." Surveying the years since 1945, Eugene Rabinowitch was equally morose. "Scientists— whose profession requires a recognition of facts, however unpleasant—cannot but admit the fact that their campaign has failed," he wrote in 1951.[8] By contrast, the choreographers of the Communist-led peace movement evinced fewer doubts about the efficacy of their efforts. A Polish activist maintained that the Communist-led movement, by overcoming "the pacifist ballast of the thirties" and "supporting the policy of the USSR and the socialist commonwealth," had "helped bring about a diminution of the cold war." Ivor Montagu took a similar view. "The world must thank the [Stockholm] appeal," he claimed, for the fact "that the bomb was not . . . used in Korea, that we are not already plunged in world war, and that at least the bomb is not yet the accepted normal weapon." Decades later, the newsletter of the World Peace Council maintained that the Stockholm appeal "helped to prevent imperialism's use of atomic weapons." [9]

Where does the reality lie?

The nonaligned nuclear disarmament movement can take credit for exerting some influence on the development of official disarmament proposals. During World War II, the top leaders of the American and British governments had shown no interest in ridding themselves of the Bomb; quite the contrary, they had laid plans for a postwar atomic monopoly. But in the aftermath of the war and in the midst of the furor about nuclear weapons, their position shifted considerably. The Truman-Attlee-King Declaration, the Acheson-Lilienthal Plan, and even the harder-line Baruch Plan showed clear indications of having been influenced by the nuclear disarmament movement. Even if these proposals represented a concession to public opinion rather than to the movement, that opinion had been shaped, in part, by the critics of the Bomb. Nor, despite the later belief of U.S. officials that disarmament proposals were futile and perhaps dangerous, did they break off all discussion of the subject—one more sign of an official policy adaptation to public pressure.

Elsewhere, too, the nonaligned movement helped frame the terms of discussion and debate. In some nations, and particularly within those least enthusiastic about the Cold War, the movement enjoyed a measure of influence. Sometimes, indeed, leaders of the nonaligned peace movement suggested or even drafted what became official policy proposals. Although it had less impact on Soviet policy, the movement did affect it in some ways. Soviet proposals for international control of atomic energy, as well as the development of the Communist-led peace movement, apparently reflected, at least in part, what

Western leaders also knew: that opposition to the Bomb represented a far from negligible phenomenon in world affairs and, therefore, had to be courted.

The movement—both nonaligned and aligned—also helped prevent further use of the Bomb. Discussing the Hiroshima and Nagasaki atomic attacks in wartime, top American, British, and Soviet leaders had shown no interest in avoiding them. Nevertheless, the public outcry over these actions apparently chilled any impulse by Truman to use the Bomb again in the war and, in subsequent years, continued to leave administration leaders on the defensive. Furthermore, in the aftermath of the war, world statesmen—including Truman, Churchill, and Stalin—never reverted to their easy wartime talk about employing nuclear weapons. To judge from his private remarks, Truman, at least, seems to have become remarkably sensitized to the issue. Moreover, at various junctures, foreign government leaders lectured American officials about why it was imperative to avoid using the Bomb. In part, their caution may have reflected their own independent qualms, but many cited public pressures to avoid a nuclear war.

In the absence of documentary evidence, it is impossible to say why the Soviet government did not employ the Bomb as a weapon of war. Perhaps, as some observers have argued, the American nuclear arsenal deterred leaders of the Kremlin from taking this dangerous step. But other factors also may have been at work. It does not appear unreasonable to assume that, given the worldwide uproar about the Bomb, including the Communist-led campaign against it, Soviet leaders—like their Western counterparts—had begun to believe that the use of the Bomb should be reserved for extreme circumstances. Conscious of the severe propaganda losses entailed in launching a nuclear war and, perhaps, newly sensitized to the dangers of waging it, Soviet officials may have scuttled more ambitious scenarios and settled for possessing the Bomb as a deterrent to foreign attack.

At most, however, the movement's influence in these years can be viewed as a braking action—albeit an important one—in the nuclear arms race. In the postwar era, after an initial period of hesitation, the U.S. government sought to improve upon its atomic monopoly by stockpiling large quantities of atomic bombs, while the governments of the Soviet Union and Great Britain scrambled to build their first atomic weapons and eventually succeeded. Within a short time, all three nations were competing to build, stockpile, and deploy hydrogen bombs—weapons with a thousand times the destructiveness of the bomb that had destroyed Hiroshima. Meanwhile, producing plutonium through "peaceful" uses of the atom, France and other nations laid the groundwork for their own nuclear weapons programs. In public pronouncements, national leaders warned of nuclear war while privately they made plans for it. Indeed, few people could have much confidence that the nuclear powers would forgo use of the Bomb if their leaders viewed its employment as absolutely vital to their national security. For a movement that sought to rid the world of the danger of nuclear war, the situation in 1953 did not look at all promising. That year, the editors of the *Bulletin of the Atomic Scientists* placed the hands of their famous "doomsday clock" at the most alarming setting in its history: two minutes to midnight.[10]

Why—despite the nonaligned movement's strength and the broad popular support for its position—did it have such a limited impact on events? A variety of factors surely played a role. Emerging with great fanfare in the late 1940s and early 1950s, the Communist-led movement discredited the struggle against the Bomb and produced severe stresses, external and internal, among non-aligned peace organizations. In addition, the catalytic agent—the widespread fear of total destruction—proved difficult to sustain over a lengthy period. Indeed, as the years passed, it proved hard enough to sustain such a movement among its exhausted core constituency. Finally, and most significant, it proved exceedingly difficult to separate the Bomb from the contemporary international context. Although the vast majority of people and policymakers looked upon a future nuclear war with dread, they were unwilling to forgo a weapon that might be useful to their countries in situations of international conflict. Frightened of nuclear war, they also feared national humiliation or defeat.

As H. G. Wells had argued in his fantasy about atomic war, *The World Set Free*, the Bomb confronted humanity with a radical alternative to the traditional way nations and their populations had related to one another. Much in line with this viewpoint, Einstein and other advocates of One World had called for new thinking and behavior to meet the unprecedented challenges raised by the destructiveness of modern technology. Nevertheless, although many persons recognized the logic of this position, they found such changes difficult to accept, personally and institutionally. They found it easier to fall back upon older, familiar—and more dangerous—patterns of behavior. Consequently, instead of restructuring international relations to cope with the unprecedented peril of the Bomb, they incorporated the Bomb into the traditional framework of international relations. Surveying the situation from the vantage point of the mid-1950s, Eugene Rabinowitch concluded: "Nations were not ready, at the end of World War II, to change radically their way of thinking, their political institutions, and their international relations to enter a new, permanently war-less era." The failure to control the Bomb "was not a failure of scientists," he maintained. "It was . . . a failure of conviction by both the leaders and the led."[11]

It might be argued, of course, that the fault lay with the nuclear disarmament movement itself. Was not the choice it posed much too stark? After all, the failure to create One World did not result in none; nor were nuclear weapons used again in war after the destruction of Hiroshima and Nagasaki. Furthermore, by insisting upon globalist solutions—from international control of atomic energy to world government—was the movement not setting before nations a Herculean task that was unlikely to be fulfilled? In addition, given the pacifist proclivities of at least part of the movement, was it not ignoring other, more practicable alternatives to participating in the nuclear arms race, such as a conventional military defense?

Though certainly debatable, these points are not convincing. Of course, nuclear weapons have not destroyed a divided world. But the continued progress of the nuclear arms race has made this prospect increasingly feasible. Moreover, it is hard to imagine that the problem of weapons of mass destruction, like many others plaguing the international community, will not require a solution that is global in scope. Indeed, the leaders of the great powers—hardly the paragons of fuzzy-minded, utopian thinking—have adopted this very orientation for their arms control and disarmament proposals. Finally, a conventional military defense has little advantage over a nuclear defense if both are geared to inflict maximum destruction upon an enemy country. And why would they not be geared toward this goal? Those who place their faith in military restraint by desperate nations may be at least as naive as pacifists are sometimes reputed to be.

Ultimately, as Szilard had realized, the problem faced by the nuclear disarmament movement was systemic. There was no magic formula that would secure nuclear disarmament as long as nations remained at one another's throats. In 1929, Salvador de Madariaga, the former head of the disarmament section of the League of Nations, drew much the same conclusion. "It is . . . hopeless to try to solve the problem of armaments in isolation from the remaining problems of the world," he wrote glumly. The arms race was "a world symptom," which "must be cured by curing the world disease, which is anarchy." Indeed, "no general disarmament is possible in the absence of a well organized World Community." [12] A quarter-century later, this same prognosis seemed all too appropriate.

The problem of nuclear weapons, then, had not been solved and would not go away. In the following decades, the Bomb—caught up in the fierce international conflict that characterized the Cold War—would become ever more menacing. Determined to perfect their nuclear arsenals, the great powers would conduct nuclear weapons tests that spewed radioactive fallout across broad portions of the globe. Determined to maximize their nuclear strength, they would stockpile vast numbers of H-Bombs for use in war. Determined to attain the capability to destroy enemy populations more effectively, they would perfect intercontinental ballistics missiles with unprecedented velocity and accuracy. Although the world would avoid nuclear war, it would teeter on the brink of catastrophe, for—in a showdown over nuclear missiles in Cuba—American and Soviet leaders, staring "eyeball-to-eyeball," would move dangerously close to triggering a war of annihilation.

And, in response, a new wave of struggle against the Bomb would emerge. Fiercely committed to the survival of humanity, it would grow into a far larger, more influential movement than in the past. This new movement of the 1950s and 1960s would mobilize mass marches in dozens of countries, launch startling campaigns of civil disobedience, galvanize a generation of youthful idealists, generate a surge of women's peace activism, spawn peace parties and candidates, rally the support of the world's leading intellectuals, and carry the struggle for nuclear disarmament into Third World and Communist nations. Riding a new tide of popular concern about nuclear weapons, the movement would have a significant impact upon the leaders of numerous nations. Indeed, hard-pressed by the rising demand for banning the Bomb, the leaders of the great powers would declare a moratorium on nuclear testing and, eventually, negotiate the world's first nuclear arms control agreements. Once again, the unprecedented peril of nuclear destruction would inspire an unprecedented popular response—one of great moral and political power.

Reference Matter

Notes

For complete authors' names, titles, and publication data on works cited in short form in these Notes, consult the Bibliography. The following abbreviations are used:

BAS	*Bulletin of the Atomic Scientists*
CC	*Common Cause*
CDSP	*Current Digest of the Soviet Press*
DOS	Department of State
ECAS	Emergency Committee of Atomic Scientists
FAS	Federation of American Scientists
FOR	Fellowship of Reconciliation
FRUS	*Foreign Relations of the United States*
NYT	*New York Times*
PN	*Peace News*
PPU	Peace Pledge Union
SASSAE	Special Assistant to the Secretary of State for Atomic Energy
SecState	Secretary of State
WILPF	Women's International League for Peace and Freedom
WMWFG	World Movement for World Federal Government
WPC	World Peace Council
WRI	War Resisters' International

Preface epigraph: Myrdal, *Game of Disarmament*, p. 319.

Book epigraph: Emergency Committee of Atomic Scientists press release of May 22, 1946, Box 57, Albert Einstein Papers.

Chapter 1

Epigraph: H. G. Wells, *The World Set Free*, p. 117.

1. Earle, "H. G. Wells"; Wagar, *H. G. Wells and the World State*, p. 274; Dickson, *H. G. Wells*, pp. 228–29; H. G. Wells, *The World Set Free*; H. G. Wells, *The Open Conspiracy*; G. P. Wells, ed., *H. G. Wells in Love*, p. 235.

2. Badash, Hodes, and Tiddens, "Nuclear Fission," pp. 196–201; Weart, *Nuclear Fear*, pp. 17–35. For literary fantasies of nuclear war that appeared before the writing of *The World Set Free*, see Franklin, *War Stars*, pp. 41–44, 50–51.

3. *Encyclopaedia Judaica* (New York: Macmillan, 1972), 10: 1368; Nathan Ausubel, *The Book of Jewish Knowledge* (New York: Crown Publishers, 1964), p. 256; Nathan Ausubel, ed., *A Treasury of Jewish Folklore* (New York: Crown Publishers, 1972), pp. 104, 204.

4. B. Bernstein, "Introduction," pp. xxiii–xxv; Weart and Szilard, eds., *Leo Szilard*, pp. 3–4, 16, 22–30; Shils, "Leo Szilard," p. 38; Einstein to H. Noel Brailsford, Apr. 24, 1930, in Nathan and Norden, eds., *Einstein on Peace*, pp. 103–4; Leo Szilard, "Memoirs (Dictated 1960)," pp. 1–4, Box 40, Szilard Papers.

5. Szilard, "Memoirs (Dictated 1960)," pp. 7–8, Box 40, and Szilard to Lindemann, June 3, 1935, Box 12, Szilard Papers; B. Bernstein, "Introduction," pp. xvii, xxvi; Rhodes, *Making of the Atomic Bomb*, pp. 13, 27–28, 224–25; Weart and Szilard, eds., *Leo Szilard*, pp. 17–18; Szilard to C. S. Wright, Feb. 26, 1936, in Feld and Szilard, eds., *Collected Works of Leo Szilard*, pp. 733–34.

6. Szilard to Singer, June 16, 1935, Box 18, Szilard to Cockcroft, May 21, 1936, Box 6, and Szilard to M. L. Oliphant, May 27, 1936, Box 14, Szilard Papers; Weart, *Scientists in Power*, p. 97; Hahn, *My Life*, p. 164.

7. Hahn, *My Life*, p. 164; B. Bernstein, "Introduction," p. xxvii; Weart and Szilard, eds., *Leo Szilard*, pp. 53–55, 62; Szilard to Strauss, Jan. 25, 1939, Box 18, Szilard Papers.

8. Weart and Szilard, eds., *Leo Szilard*, pp. 53–54, 56, 69–73; Weart, "Scientists with a Secret," pp. 24–28; Weart, *Scientists in Power*, pp. 78, 87–89; Teller, *Energy*, pp. 142–43; Szilard to Joliot-Curie, Feb. 2, 1939, Wigner to P. A. M. Dirac, Mar. 30, 1939, Weisskopf to Hans Halban, Mar. 31, 1939, Weisskopf to P. M. S. Blackett, Mar. 31, 1939, and Szilard to George Pegram, Mar. 27, 1939, Box 6, Szilard Papers.

9. Blackett to Weisskopf, Apr. 8, 1939, Joliot-Curie, Halban, and Kowarski to Weisskopf, Apr. 5, 1939, Joliot-Curie to Szilard, Apr. 6, 19, 1939, Box 6, and Szilard to Blackett, Apr. 14, 1939, Box 4, Szilard Papers; Weart and Szilard, eds., *Leo Szilard*, pp. 73–74, 77–79; Weart, "Scientists with a Secret," p. 28; Weart, *Scientists in Power*, pp. 88–91; Goldsmith, *Frédéric Joliot-Curie*, pp. 73–74.

10. Weart, "Scientists with a Secret," pp. 28–30; Breit to Szilard, June 5, July 16, 1940, Szilard to Breit, June 7, July 6, 1940, Box 5, Szilard Papers.

11. Weart and Szilard, eds., *Leo Szilard*, pp. 82–85, 87, 94–96; B. Bernstein, "Introduction," pp. xxix–xxx; Einstein to Roosevelt, Aug. 2, 1939, and Szilard to Einstein, Oct. 17, 1939, Box 55, Einstein Papers; Szilard to Sachs, Aug. 15, 1939, Box 2, and Sachs to Roosevelt, Oct. 11, 1939, and Roosevelt to Einstein, Oct. 19, 1939, Box 1, Atomic Bomb File; Teller, *Legacy of Hiroshima*, pp. 10–11; Rhodes, *Making of the Atomic Bomb*, pp. 303–8.

12. "Excerpt from a Television Interview with Mike Wallace (February 27, 1961)," in Hawkins, Greb, and Szilard, eds., *Toward a Livable World*, p. 337. For similar assessments of the motives of U.S. scientists, and particularly those fleeing Nazi conquest of their homelands, see Grodzins and Rabinowitch, eds., *Atomic Age*, p. 3.

13. Einstein to Alexander Sachs, Mar. 7, 1940, and Sachs to Roosevelt, Mar. 15, 1940, Box 55, Einstein Papers; Josephson, "Albert Einstein," p. 136; Teller, *Energy*, pp. 145–46; Teller, *Legacy of Hiroshima*, pp. 12–13; Hans A. Bethe oral history interview, Oct. 27, 28, 1966, p. 59.

14. Feld, "Leo Szilard," pp. 681–82; Szilard to Bush, May 26, 1942, Box 5, Szilard Papers; Weart, *Scientists in Power*, p. 185; Compton, *Atomic Quest*, p. 8. For Szilard's continued fear of German progress on the Bomb, see Szilard to Lord Cherwell, Aug. 18, 1944, Box 5, Szilard Papers.

15. Among them were Merle Tuve, Richard Fowler, Joseph Platt, Alexander Langsdorf, and Volney Wilson. After the Japanese attack at Pearl Harbor, Wilson changed his mind and worked on the Bomb project at Chicago and Los Alamos, although, as his supervisor recalled, "the conflict in his soul was still there." Badash, Hodes, and Tiddens, "Nuclear Fission," pp. 221–22; Compton, *Atomic Quest*, pp. 41–43.

16. Although Rabi eventually became a visiting consultant, in early 1945 he warned against working "merely to see that the next war is bigger and better." Oppenheimer to Rabi, Feb. 26, 1943, in A. Smith and C. Weiner, eds., *Robert Oppenheimer*, pp. 250–51; Kevles, *Physicists*, pp. 334–35; Rhodes, *Making of the Atomic Bomb*, pp. 452–53.

17. A. Smith, *A Peril and a Hope*, p. 4; Szilard, "Book: Apology (in lieu of a foreword)," pp. 4, 6, Box 40, Szilard Papers; N. Davis, *Lawrence and Oppenheimer*, p. 182.

18. Weart and Szilard, eds., *Leo Szilard*, p. 146.

19. Rhodes, *Making of the Atomic Bomb*, pp. 294–95, 635–36; Sherwin, *A World Destroyed*, pp. 29–30; Josephson, "Albert Einstein," pp. 133, 136–37; Schwartz, "The F.B.I. and Dr. Einstein," p. 168.

20. B. Bernstein, "Introduction," pp. xxxi, xxxiii. For additional material on Bush and Conant's objections to Szilard, including his "foreign origin," see Bush to Roosevelt, Mar. 7, 1944, Box 1, Atomic Bomb File; Leslie R. Groves interview, Nov. 7, 1967, in Ermenc, ed., *Atomic Bomb Scientists*, p. 246.

21. Compton to Leslie R. Groves, Oct. 26, 1942, and Nov. 10, 1943, "201 (Szilard, Leo)" folder, Manhattan Engineering District Records.

22. For indications of Groves's anti-Semitic, nativist views, see Rhodes, *Making of the Atomic Bomb*, pp. 502, 828; B. Bernstein, "Introduction," p. xxxii; Blum, ed., *Price of Vision*, p. 471.

23. Leslie R. Groves, Draft of Secretary of War to the Attorney General, Oct. 28, 1942, Groves to Compton, Nov. 25, 1943, and Groves to District Engineer, Manhattan District, June 12, 1943, "201 (Szilard, Leo)" folder, Manhattan Engineering District Records; Leslie R. Groves, "Re: Szilard" (Oct. 17, 1963), Box 9, Groves Papers; B. Bernstein, "Introduction," pp. xxxii–xxxiii; Rhodes, *Making of the Atomic Bomb*, pp. 503, 506–7.

24. Sherwin, *A World Destroyed*, pp. 5–6, 13, 27–29; Rhodes, *Making of the Atomic Bomb*, p. 405; Giovannitti and Freed, *Decision to Drop the Bomb*, p. 106; Stimson Diary, May 15, 1945. According to Stimson, "at no time, from 1941 to 1945, did I ever hear it suggested by the President, or by any other responsible member of the government, that atomic energy should not be used in the war." Stimson and Bundy, *On Active Service*, p. 613.

25. Frisch, *What Little I Remember*, pp. 126–27; Peierls, *Bird of Passage*, pp. 154–55; Weart, *Nuclear Fear*, p. 84; Cockburn and Ellyard, *Oliphant*, pp. 97–98, 140; Pierre, *Nuclear Politics*, pp. 16–17; Gowing, *Britain and Atomic Energy*, p. 43.

26. Badash, Hodes, and Tiddens, "Nuclear Fission," p. 222; *NYT*, Aug. 10, 1945; Clark, *Birth of the Bomb*, pp. 81–82; Joseph Rotblat, "Leaving the Bomb Project," *BAS* 41 (Aug. 1985): 16–17.

27. Cockcroft to Wigner, Apr. 15, 1940, Box 6, Szilard Papers; Clark, *Birth of the Bomb*, p. 62; James Chadwick oral history interview, Apr. 15–20, 1969, p. 105.

28. Clark, *Birth of the Bomb*, pp. 60–63, 83, 197–200; Gowing, *Britain and Atomic Energy*, pp. 78, 85–89.

29. Churchill, *Gathering Storm*, pp. 386–87; Gowing, *Britain and Atomic Energy*, pp. 37–39, 96, 106; Sherwin, *A World Destroyed*, pp. 110–11, 284; Aide Mémoire of Conversation between the President and the Prime Minister at Hyde Park, Sept. 18, 1944, Byrnes Papers.

30. Irving, *German Atomic Bomb*; M. Walker, "Uranium Machines," pp. 30–36, 78–

83, 272–73; Rhodes, *Making of the Atomic Bomb*, pp. 296, 311, 344–45, 404–5; Speer, *Inside the Third Reich*, pp. 225–28; Allen W. Dulles to Alvan L. Barach, Feb. 23, 1959, Box 80, Dulles Papers.

31. The idea of a conspiracy among German scientists to avoid producing atomic bombs was first broached by the participants themselves and later promoted in a best-seller by German journalist Robert Jungk. It has also been sharply repudiated by numerous scientists from other lands, including Samuel Goudsmit, the Dutch refugee physicist who conducted an extensive investigation of the German Bomb project for the U.S. government, and Eugene Rabinowitch, the founding editor of the *Bulletin of the Atomic Scientists*. S. A. Goudsmit, "Heisenberg on the German Uranium Project," *BAS* 3 (Nov. 1947): 343; Philip Morrison, "ALSOS: The Story of German Science," *BAS* 3 (Dec. 1947): 354, 365; Max von Laue, "The Wartime Activities of German Scientists," *BAS* 4 (Apr. 1948): 103–4; Jungk, *Brighter Than a Thousand Suns*, pp. 87–104; Rabinowitch to Kurt Rosenwald, Mar. 3, 1971, Box 2, and S. A. Goudsmit, review of *Brighter Than a Thousand Suns*, Box 3, Rabinowitch Papers, Albany.

32. Hahn, however, distanced himself from the Bomb project even farther than he distanced Heisenberg, claiming that he was the only one of the German nuclear scientists interned in England at the end of the war "as a result of a misunderstanding." O. Hahn, *My Life*, pp. 173, 185–86.

33. W. Heisenberg, "Research in Germany," p. 214; Werner Heisenberg, "The Third Reich and the Atomic Bomb," *BAS* 24 (June 1968): 34–35; E. Heisenberg, *Inner Exile*, pp. 75–81; Irving, *German Atomic Bomb*, pp. 102–3, 295–96.

34. M. Walker, "Uranium Machines," pp. 68, 72, 82–93, 387–88; Irving, *German Atomic Bomb*, pp. 50, 118–21, 296–97; Rhodes, *Making of the Atomic Bomb*, p. 404; Speer, *Inside the Third Reich*, pp. 225–26.

35. M. Walker, "Uranium Machines," pp. 162–83, 310–11, 375, 380–82; Rhodes, *Making of the Atomic Bomb*, pp. 383–85. For a more general discussion of the collaboration of German scientists with the Nazi regime, see Eugene Rabinowitch, "The Virus House: The German Atomic Bomb Project," *BAS* 24 (June 1968): 34.

36. Paul Harteck interview, July 6, 1967, in Ermenc, ed., *Atomic Bomb Scientists*, p. 97; Werner Heisenberg interview, Aug. 29, 1967, ibid., pp. 23–24, 27, 34; Beyerchen, *Scientists Under Hitler*, pp. 199, 206–10.

37. Irving, *German Atomic Bomb*, p. 182; Weart, *Scientists in Power*, p. 157; Goldsmith, *Frédéric Joliot-Curie*, pp. 98–100.

38. Dower, "Science, Society, and the Japanese Atomic Bomb Project"; Shapley, "Nuclear Weapons History"; Pacific War Research Society, *The Day Man Lost*, pp. 18–20, 23–44, 48–49, 93–94, 126–27, 183–84; Hideki Yukawa oral history interview, p. 4; Coox, "Evidences of Antimilitarism in Prewar and Wartime Japan," p. 513; Ienaga, *Pacific War*, pp. 203–28.

39. Weart, *Scientists in Power*, pp. 130–37, 157–59, 165–66, 204–6; Goldsmith, *Frédéric Joliot-Curie*, pp. 99–101, 106–9, 122–23; Scheinman, *Atomic Energy Policy in France*, pp. 3–7. As early as 1939, Kowarski recalled, "we did know that at some moment there would be explosives." Lew Kowarski oral history interview, p. 87. See also Lew Kowarski interview, Mar. 16, 1970, in Ermenc, ed., *Atomic Bomb Scientists*, pp. 177–78.

40. Holloway, "Entering the Nuclear Arms Race," pp. 160–72; Holloway, *Soviet Union and the Arms Race*, pp. 15–17; York, *Advisors*, pp. 29–30; Rhodes, *Making of the Atomic Bomb*, pp. 500–501.

41. Holloway, "Entering the Nuclear Arms Race," pp. 172–75, 187; Holloway, *Soviet Union and the Arms Race*, pp. 18–19; A. P. Alexandrov, "The Heroic Deed," *BAS* 23 (Dec.

1967): 11–12; Igor Golovin, "Father of the Soviet Atomic Bomb," *BAS* 23 (Dec. 1967): 15–16; Golovin, *I. V. Kurchatov*, pp. 39–40.

42. Holloway, "Entering the Nuclear Arms Race," p. 178. Smaller figures on the size of the Soviet project, albeit for January 1944, are given in York, *Advisors*, p. 31; Rhodes, *Making of the Atomic Bomb*, p. 502.

43. For an early argument—which has not been substantiated by later research—that the Soviet scientific community was divided over the moral-political issues, see Kramish, *Atomic Energy in the Soviet Union*, pp. 100–104. Although a lengthy study of the Soviet Bomb project by U.S. intelligence agencies remains classified, a respected U.S. journalist who had the opportunity to read it maintains: "There is nothing in that report to suggest, even remotely, any Soviet opposition to the building of the bomb." Tad Szulc to the author, May 23, 1988.

44. See, for example, Holloway, "Entering the Nuclear Arms Race," pp. 168–69, 187.

45. Parry, *Peter Kapitsa on Life and Science*, pp. 6–7, 13–16; Cockcroft, "Kapitza at the Cavendish," p. 740; McElheny, "Kapitsa to Visit England," p. 744; *NYT*, July 15, 1956.

46. York, *Advisors*, p. 38; Kapitza to Bohr, Oct. 28, 1943, Box 77, SASSAE, DOS Records; A. Bohr, "The War Years," p. 205; Holloway, "Entering the Nuclear Arms Race," p. 172; personal interview with Sergei Kapitza, June 28, 1990.

47. Irving, *German Atomic Bomb*, pp. 290–92; *Los Angeles Times*, Aug. 26, 1984; Williams, *Klaus Fuchs*.

Chapter 2

Epigraph: James Franck et al., "A Report to the Secretary of War," p. 26.

1. Weart and Szilard, eds., *Leo Szilard*, pp. 154, 161–63; Szilard to Metallurgical Lab, Sept. 23, 1942, Box 68, and Szilard to Bush, Jan. 14, 1944, Box 5, Szilard Papers; Shils, "Leo Szilard," p. 40. For Szilard's concern about the dangers of the Bomb in 1943, see Lord Cherwell to Leslie R. Groves, July 12, 1945, "201 (Szilard, Leo)" folder, Manhattan Engineering District Records.

2. J. R. Oppenheimer to Secretary Marshall, Mar. 20, 1948, Box 77, SASSAE, DOS Records; Gowing, "Niels Bohr and Nuclear Weapons," pp. 268–71; Rhodes, *Making of the Atomic Bomb*, pp. 54, 482–83, 526–28; Gowing, *Britain and Atomic Energy*, pp. 346–51.

3. Churchill later told Cherwell: "I did not like the man when you showed him to me, with his hair all over his head." Gowing, "Niels Bohr and Nuclear Weapons," p. 271; Gowing, *Britain and Atomic Energy*, pp. 352–55; Rhodes, *Making of the Atomic Bomb*, pp. 528–31; A. Bohr, "War Years," pp. 204–5; Jones, "Meetings in Wartime and After," pp. 284–85.

4. Gowing, "Niels Bohr and Nuclear Weapons," pp. 272–76; A. Bohr, "War Years," pp. 205–10; Niels Bohr, untitled memorandum (July 3, 1944) and "Addendum to Memorandum of July 3rd 1944" (Mar. 24, 1945), Box 21, Oppenheimer Papers; Rhodes, *Making of the Atomic Bomb*, pp. 531–38; Gowing, *Britain and Atomic Energy*, pp. 356–65; "Tube Alloys" (Sept. 18, 1944), PREM 8/116, Prime Minister's Records.

5. Hewlett and Anderson, *New World*, pp. 329–30; A. Smith, *A Peril and a Hope*, p. 13; Rhodes, *Making of the Atomic Bomb*, pp. 561–62, 832–33; Hans Bethe oral history interview, Oct. 27, 28, 1966, p. 62.

6. Clark, *Einstein*, pp. 314–16; Gowing, *Britain and Atomic Energy*, pp. 360–61; Nathan and Norden, eds., *Einstein on Peace*, pp. 303–4.

7. The other members of the Jeffries committee were Fermi, James Franck, Thorfin Hogness, Robert Stone, Charles Thomas, and Robert Mulliken.

8. "Prospectus on Nucleonics (the Jeffries Report)," in A. Smith, *A Peril and a Hope*, pp. 539–59; ibid., pp. 22–23; Hewlett and Anderson, *New World*, pp. 324–25. For what looks like a rough draft of the report by Rabinowitch, see Rabinowitch draft of Metallurgical Laboratory statement, Box 8, 1972 Addenda, Rabinowitch Papers, Chicago.

9. Weart and Szilard, eds., *Leo Szilard*, p. 181; A. Smith, *A Peril and a Hope*, pp. 24–27, 30–33; John A. Simpson, "Some Personal Notes," *BAS* 37 (Jan. 1981): 26–27; "The Story of a Petition," Box 73, Szilard Papers.

10. "Dr. Szilard (Record S-10), 5/22/56," Box 40, Szilard Papers; Einstein to Roosevelt, Mar. 25, 1945, President's Personal File 7177, Franklin D. Roosevelt Papers; Szilard, "Atomic Bombs and the Postwar Position of the United States in the World (Spring 1945)," Byrnes Papers; Weart and Szilard, eds., *Leo Szilard*, pp. 181–83, 205–8; Rhodes, *Making of the Atomic Bomb*, pp. 635–37; A. Smith, *A Peril and a Hope*, pp. 27–29.

11. Weart and Szilard, eds., *Leo Szilard*, pp. 183–85; B. Bernstein, "Introduction," p. xxxv; Szilard, "A Personal History of the Atomic Bomb," pp. 14–15; Byrnes, *All in One Lifetime*, pp. 284–85; Alice Kimball Smith, "Behind the Decision to Use the Atomic Bomb: Chicago, 1944–45," *BAS* 14 (Oct. 1958): 296. For another Szilard lobbying venture against use of the Bomb, see Szilard to J. Robert Oppenheimer, May 16, 1945, Box 14, Szilard Papers.

12. Weart and Szilard, eds., *Leo Szilard*, p. 186; A. Smith, *A Peril and a Hope*, pp. 41–42. Franck had been a dissenter in other contexts. For example, he had resigned his German university position rather than serve under Nazism—an act that led 33 of his faculty colleagues to denounce him publicly for sabotaging the new Germany. Eugene Rabinowitch, "James Franck, 1882–1964, Leo Szilard, 1898–1964," *BAS* 20 (Oct. 1964): 16–17.

13. Ralph Lapp, address to luncheon meeting of the Conference on Peace Research in History; Grodzins and Rabinowitch, eds., *Atomic Age*, p. 4; Seaborg, *Stemming the Tide*, p. 60.

14. Rabinowitch to Linus Pauling, May 18, 1957, Pauling Papers; Weart and Szilard, eds., *Leo Szilard*, p. 186.

15. James Franck et al., "A Report to the Secretary of War," pp. 19–27; A. Smith, *A Peril and a Hope*, p. 53.

16. B. Bernstein, "Introduction," p. xxxv; Sherwin, *A World Destroyed*, pp. 212–13; Compton, *Atomic Quest*, p. 236; Giovannitti and Freed, *Decision to Drop the Bomb*, pp. 116–19.

17. A. Smith, *A Peril and a Hope*, pp. 46, 48–51; Sherwin, *A World Destroyed*, pp. 213–14; Giovannitti and Freed, *Decision to Drop the Bomb*, 119–23, 142–43; Eugene Rabinowitch, "The Virus House: The German Atomic Bomb Project," *BAS* 24 (June 1968): 34; Rabinowitch to Michael Kasha, May 30, 1972, Box 1, Rabinowitch Papers, Albany.

18. Rhodes, *Making of the Atomic Bomb*, p. 624; A. Smith, *A Peril and a Hope*, pp. 34–40, 70–71; Weart and Szilard, eds., *Leo Szilard*, p. 185.

19. Compton, *Atomic Quest*, pp. 238–39; Compton to Hughston M. McBain, Feb. 14, 1947, Box 7, Hutchins Papers; Stimson, "Decision to Use the Atomic Bomb," p. 98; W. Laurence, "Would You Make the Bomb Again?" pp. 8–9.

20. B. Bernstein, "Roosevelt, Truman, and the Atomic Bomb," pp. 59–60; Schaffer, *Wings of Judgment*, pp. 3–189; Stimson, "Decision to Use the Atomic Bomb," p. 98.

21. Sherwin, *A World Destroyed*, pp. 194–95; Stimson and Bundy, *On Active Service*, p. 629; Pogue, *George C. Marshall*, pp. 19, 23.

22. Stimson Diary, May 14, 1945; Truman, *Year of Decisions*, p. 87. For another illustration of the power orientation of Byrnes and of the Interim Committee, see Byrnes, *All in One Lifetime*, pp. 283–84.

23. John J. McCloy interview, May 18, 1980, Box 121, Toland Papers; Ralph Bard, "Memorandum on the Use of S-1 Bomb" (June 27, 1945), in Strauss, *Men and Decisions*, p. 192; A. Smith, *A Peril and a Hope*, pp. 52–53; N. Davis, *Lawrence and Oppenheimer*, p. 247.

24. King and Whitehill, *Fleet Admiral King*, pp. 598, 605n, 621; Leahy, *I Was There*, p. 441; Eisenhower, *Mandate for Change*, pp. 312–13. See also Eisenhower, *Crusade in Europe*, p. 443; Stimson Diary, May 15, 1945.

25. Weart and Szilard, eds., *Leo Szilard*, p. 186.

26. Gowing, *Britain and Atomic Energy*, p. 371; Clark, *Birth of the Bomb*, p. 200; Giovannitti and Freed, *Decision to Drop the Bomb*, pp. 332–33; Peierls, *Bird of Passage*, p. 204; Frisch, *What Little I Remember*, pp. 175–76; Joseph Rotblat, "Leaving the Bomb Project," *BAS* 41 (Aug. 1985): 18–19; personal interview with Joseph Rotblat, July 12, 1990; *PN*, Sept. 28, 1945.

27. Compton, *Atomic Quest*, p. 233; A. Smith, *A Peril and a Hope*, p. 62; Giovannitti and Freed, *Decision to Drop the Bomb*, pp. 164–67; Fermi, *Atoms in the Family*, p. 242; Lamont, *Day of Trinity*, pp. 83–84. For additional material on anti-Bomb activism at Los Alamos, see Schaffer, *Wings of Judgment*, p. 161.

28. Oppenheimer recalled that the scene after the blast was "entirely solemn. We knew the world would not be the same. . . . I remembered the line from the Hindu scripture, the *Bhagavad-Gita* . . . 'Now I am become Death, the destroyer of worlds.' I suppose we all thought that, one way or another." Rhodes, *Making of the Atomic Bomb*, pp. 675–76; N. Davis, *Lawrence and Oppenheimer*, pp. 240–41; Lamont, *Day of Trinity*, p. 235.

29. Hewlett and Anderson, *New World*, p. 355; A. Smith, *A Peril and a Hope*, pp. 38–39; Knebel and Bailey, "Fight Over the A-Bomb," pp. 20–21.

30. John A. Simpson, "Some Personal Notes," *BAS* 37 (Jan. 1981): 30–31; N. Davis, *Lawrence and Oppenheimer*, p. 243; Eugene Rabinowitch, "Five Years After," *BAS* 7 (Jan. 1951): 3.

31. Weart and Szilard, eds., *Leo Szilard*, pp. 186–87, 211–12; "A Petition to the President of the United States" (July 17, 1945), enclosure in Matthew J. Connelly to James Byrnes, Sept. 6, 1945, Document No. 345, Miscellaneous Historical Documents; Szilard to Oppenheimer, July 23, 1945, Box 70, Oppenheimer Papers.

32. Smith claims that the Oak Ridge petition had 88 signatures; Knebel and Bailey give the total as 68. Charles D. Coryell et al. to the President of the United States, n.d., enclosure in Arthur H. Compton to K. D. Nichols, July 24, 1945, Box 6, Szilard Papers; A. Smith, *A Peril and a Hope*, p. 55; Knebel and Bailey, "Fight Over the A-Bomb," p. 22.

33. Weart and Szilard, eds., *Leo Szilard*, pp. 187–88, 213; A. Smith, *A Peril and a Hope*, pp. 55–56, 71; Oppenheimer to Groves, July 17, 1945, Box 36, Oppenheimer Papers; B. Bernstein, "Introduction," pp. xxxvi–xxxviii.

34. "Notes of the Interim Committee Meeting, May 31, 1945," in Sherwin, *A World Destroyed*, p. 302; Groves to Cherwell, July 4, 1945, and Cherwell to Groves, July 12, 1945, "201 (Szilard, Leo)" folder, Manhattan Engineering District Records; Leslie R. Groves interview, Nov. 7, 1967, in Ermenc, ed., *Atomic Bomb Scientists*, pp. 248, 250.

35. A. Smith, *A Peril and a Hope*, pp. 59–62; Weisskopf, *Privilege of Being a Physicist*, p. 207.

36. Teller to Szilard, July 2, 1945, Box 18, Szilard Papers; Teller, *Legacy of Hiroshima*, pp. 13–14, 20; Teller, *Energy*, pp. 149, 155.

37. Giovannitti and Freed, *Decision to Drop the Bomb*, pp. 170–71; A. Smith, *A Peril and a Hope*, p. 57; Compton, *Atomic Quest*, pp. 241–42; "A Petition to the Administration of Clinton Laboratories" (n.d.), Box 73, Szilard Papers.

38. Two investigative journalists, Fletcher Knebel and Charles Bailey, reported: "The phrase 'military demonstration in Japan' was promptly interpreted by pro-bomb officials as meaning an attack without warning, though many of the poll participants later contended they meant just the opposite, and that the phrase 'before full use of the weapon is employed' clearly implied that they first wanted an atomic demonstration that would not kill large masses of people." Compton, *Atomic Quest*, pp. 243–44; Farrington Daniels to Compton, July 13, 1945, Box 7, Szilard Papers; Arthur H. Compton and Farrington Daniels, "A Poll of Scientists at Chicago, July, 1945," *BAS* 4 (Feb. 1948): 44, 63; A. Smith, *A Peril and a Hope*, pp. 56–59; Knebel and Bailey, "Fight Over the A-Bomb," p. 23.

39. In July 1945, Rabinowitch briefly considered "a petition to tell the American people about the problem" but decided against it. One relative outsider who apparently knew of the Bomb and of the struggle to prevent its use was the chancellor of the University of Chicago, Robert Hutchins. In an apparent reference to Szilard's July 1945 petitioning efforts, he told the physicist: "The petition looks good to me. I hope it may be effective." Personal interview with Ralph Lapp, June 28, 1987; Rabinowitch to Ruth [Adams?], July 15, 1971, Box 1, Rabinowitch Papers, Albany; Rabinowitch, "Memo on 'The Impact of Nucleonics' " (July 12, 1945), in Sherwin, *A World Destroyed*, pp. 333–35; Hutchins to Szilard, July 26, 1945, Box 10, Szilard Papers.

40. Churchill, *Triumph and Tragedy*, pp. 638–39. See also Truman, *Year of Decisions*, p. 419.

41. During the Potsdam conference, Truman wrote in his diary: "I have told the Sec. of War, Mr. Stimson, to use it so that military objectives and soldiers and sailors are the target and not women and children. . . . He & I are in accord. The target will be a purely military one and we will issue a warning statement asking the Japs to surrender and save lives." This statement indicates that Truman did not realize that the target would be predominantly civilian and that it would be destroyed without specific warning. Truman Diary, July 25, 1945, in Ferrell, ed., *Off the Record*, pp. 55–56. See also Robert L. Messer, "New Evidence on Truman's Decision," *BAS* 41 (Aug. 1985): 51, 56.

42. Truman, *Year of Decisions*, p. 419; *NYT*, Feb. 3, 1958; B. Bernstein, "Roosevelt, Truman, and the Atomic Bomb," pp. 61–62. See also Schaffer, *Wings of Judgment*, pp. 171–73.

43. Memoirs may be inaccurate. But even at the time, Truman told Clement Attlee that, in Attlee's words, Stalin "had not cross-examined him on this matter." Moreover, one scholar has suggested that Truman, in his remarks to Stalin, actually may have been more specific about the Bomb than his ghostwritten memoirs imply. If so, there is even less reason to doubt the Soviet leader's support for the atomic bombing of Japan. Truman, *Year of Decisions*, p. 416; Churchill, *Triumph and Tragedy*, pp. 669–70; Attlee to Churchill, Aug. 1, 1945, PREM 8/109, Prime Minister's Records; Mark, " 'Today Has Been a Historical One,' " p. 319.

44. Bryant, *Triumph in the West*, pp. 363–64; Churchill, *Triumph and Tragedy*, p. 639.

45. Truman, *Year of Decisions*, p. 415; Sherwin, *A World Destroyed*, pp. 223–24; Truman Diary, July 25, 1945, in Ferrell, ed., *Off the Record*, p. 56.

46. Churchill, *Triumph and Tragedy*, p. 670; *Los Angeles Times*, Aug. 26, 1984; York, *Advisors*, p. 31; Zhukov, *Memoirs*, p. 675.

47. The number of deaths caused by the bombings remains a matter of conjecture. Robert J. Lifton has written of the death count at Hiroshima: "Variously estimated from 63,000 to 240,000 or more, the official figure is usually given as 78,000, but the city of Hiroshima estimates 200,000." The U.S. Strategic Bombing Survey claimed that the deaths

at Hiroshima ranged "between 70,000 and 80,000, with an equal number injured." Rhodes, *Making of the Atomic Bomb*, pp. 734, 740, 742; Dower, *War Without Mercy*, pp. 47, 298, 325; Lifton, *Death in Life*, p. 20; U.S. Strategic Bombing Survey, *Effects of Atomic Bombs*, p. 15.

48. Stimson and Bundy, *On Active Service*, pp. 626–27; Sherwin, *A World Destroyed*, pp. 234–37; U.S. Strategic Bombing Survey, *Japan's Struggle to End the War*.

Chapter 3

Epigraph: Shinzo Hamai, mayor of Hiroshima, delivered this message on the third anniversary of the atomic bombing of his city. Shinzo Hamai, "The Declaration of Peace" (Aug. 6, 1948), Hiroshima Peace Society Records.

1. Some of the most important studies of the development of peace movements in Europe and the United States are Beales, *History of Peace*; Curti, *Peace or War*; Brock, *Pacifism in the United States*; Brock, *Pacifism in Europe to 1914*; DeBenedetti, *Peace Reform in American History*; Cooper, *Patriotic Pacifism*.

2. Beaton, *Twenty Years' Work*, pp. 4, 8–17; Brock, *Twentieth Century Pacifism*, pp. 110–11; *PN*, Jan. 10, 1947.

3. Minutes of the meeting of the International Council, WRI, Dec. 28–31, 1946, Box 1, WRI Records.

4. Stevenson, *Towards a Christian International*, pp. 1–5; *Forty Years for Peace*, pp. 3–4, 11; Brock, *Twentieth Century Pacifism*, p. 110.

5. *News Letter*, no. 51 (June 1946), pp. 1–3; Brittain, *Rebel Passion*, p. 61.

6. Brittain, *Rebel Passion*, pp. 61–63; "Stockholm," *Christian Pacifist*, no. 53 (May 1946), pp. 842–43.

7. Frank J. Gordon, "A Brief History of the Women's International League for Peace and Freedom" (1981), pp. 2–4, WILPF International Office Records; Bussey and Tims, *Women's International League for Peace and Freedom*, pp. 17–22, 25–33, 180–88; Foster, *Women for All Seasons*, pp. 22–23, 25; "Data on the Women's International League for Peace and Freedom" (May 1, 1947), Reel 50, WILPF (International) Records.

8. Bussey and Tims, *Women's International League for Peace and Freedom*, pp. 179, 188–89; Brittain, *Testament of Experience*, p. 412; Randall, *Improper Bostonian*, pp. 404–5, 411.

9. The record of the Historic Peace Churches is recounted at length in Brock, *Pacifism in Europe to 1914*; Hirst, *Quakers in Peace and War*; Brinton, *Sources of the Quaker Peace Testimony*; Bowman, *The Church of the Brethren and War*; Hershberger, *War, Peace, and Nonresistance*.

10. For Protestant peace sentiment between the wars, see Van Kirk, *Religion Renounces War*; Bainton, *Christian Attitudes Toward War and Peace*, pp. 212–20; DeBenedetti, *Origins of the Modern American Peace Movement*, pp. 98–106. Church positions thereafter are discussed in Abrams, "The Churches and the Clergy in World War II," pp. 110–19.

11. For differing aspects of Catholic thought on peace, see Musto, *Catholic Peace Tradition*; Piehl, *Breaking Bread*.

12. Ferguson, *War and Peace in the World's Religions*, pp. 28–61, 124–37.

13. Pacifism's declining influence within the French and British parties is discussed in Gombin, *Les socialistes et la guerre*; Brock, *Twentieth Century Pacifism*, pp. 134–35; Gordon, *Conflict and Consensus in Labour's Foreign Policy*, pp. 47–101.

14. The number of World War II–related deaths cited by authorities varies from 40

million to 60 million. I have chosen the highest figure—given by Quincy Wright—which includes war-caused disease and starvation. Dyer, *War*, pp. 89–96; S. Brown, *Causes and Prevention of War*, p. 70; Wright, *A Study of War*, pp. 1541–43.

15. Gertrude Baer to J. Repelaer van Driel, Jan. 2, 1946, Reel 75, WILPF (International) Records. Further substantiation of this point is provided in those portions of Chapters 3 and 6 dealing with postwar Japan and Germany.

16. At a conference of pacifists and other sympathetic peace activists in late 1946, the secretary of the Swiss Peace Council lamented that "there is no effective international peace movement." Ibid.; *PN*, Oct. 5, 1945; Laszlo Hamori, "The International Peace Movement's Achievements in 1946 and Perspectives for 1947" (1946), Conseil Suisse des Associations pour la Paix Records.

17. Rotblat, "Movements of Scientists," pp. 124–25; Strickland, *Scientists in Politics*, pp. 12–14; Badash, Hodes, and Tiddens, "Nuclear Fission," pp. 223–24.

18. With his usual sardonic humor, Szilard wrote in 1947: "If it is remarkable that all these scientists should have found their voice, it is even more remarkable that they should be listened to. But mass murders have always commanded the attention of the public, and atomic scientists are no exception to this rule." Szilard, "Physicist Invades Politics," p. 7.

19. Kuehl, *Seeking World Order*, pp. 3–37; Wynner and Lloyd, *Searchlight on Peace Plans*, pp. 31–492, 544; Baratta, "Bygone 'One World,' " pp. 3–5, 9, 285–86; Schuman, *Commonwealth of Man*, pp. 432–34.

20. Streit, *Union Now*; Wooley, *Alternatives to Anarchy*, p. 91.

21. Baratta, "Bygone 'One World,' " pp. 79, 134; Willkie, *One World*, pp. 202–3; A. Lilienthal, *Which Way to World Government?*, p. 16; Reves, *Anatomy of Peace*.

22. Baratta, "Bygone 'One World,' " p. 372; *World Government Highlights*, p. 42; A. Lilienthal, *Which Way to World Government?*, p. 7; Baratta, "International History of the World Federalist Movement," pp. 374–75.

23. Bamba and Howes, eds., *Pacifism in Japan*, pp. 269–70; K. Tsurumi, *Social Change and the Individual*, pp. 258–59, 263–65, 271–73, 280–83; Lifton, *Death in Life*, pp. 99–100; Asada, "Japanese Perceptions of the A-Bomb Decision," pp. 202–3.

24. At the very least, General Douglas MacArthur and other U.S. occupation officials strongly supported the constitutional provision. McNelly, " 'Induced Revolution,' " pp. 79–80; Schonberger, *Aftermath of War*, pp. 57–59; Harries and Harries, *Sheathing the Sword*, pp. 213–19.

25. Lifton, *History and Human Survival*, p. 243.

26. Ibid., p. 140; Braw, *Atomic Bomb Suppressed*, pp. 14, 45–47, 69, 137; Nishi, *Unconditional Democracy*, pp. 87–90; Committee for the Compilation of Materials, *Hiroshima and Nagasaki*, p. 14.

27. Nishi, *Unconditional Democracy*, pp. 100–102; Braw, *Atomic Bomb Suppressed*, pp. 97–98, 104–7.

28. Rubin, "From Wholesomeness to Decadence," pp. 88–91; Koschmann, "Postwar Democracy," pp. 6–7; S. Tsurumi, *Intellectual History of Wartime Japan*, p. 103; Lifton, *Death in Life*, pp. 402–7; Kamata and Salaff, "Atomic Bomb and the Citizens of Nagasaki," p. 44; *Meaning of Survival*, p. 87.

29. *Meaning of Survival*, pp. 64–65, 68; Thurlow, "Atomic Bombing of Hiroshima and Nagasaki," p. 227; Braw, *Atomic Bomb Suppressed*, pp. 108–9; Kamata and Salaff, "Atomic Bomb and the Citizens of Nagasaki," p. 42.

30. Committee for the Compilation of Materials, *Hiroshima and Nagasaki*, pp. 508–13, 593–94; Koschmann, "Postwar Democracy," pp. 7–8; Lifton, *Death in Life*, pp. 453–56; Oe, *Hiroshima Notes*, p. 60.

31. Technically, the word *hibakusha* means "explosion–affected persons," but the Japa-

nese use it somewhat more broadly to refer to those who have experienced the Bomb. Lifton, *Death in Life*, pp. 6–7.

32. *Meaning of Survival*, pp. 58–59; Kurino and Kodama, "Study on the Japanese Peace Movement," p. 120; Committee for the Compilation of Materials, *Hiroshima and Nagasaki*, p. 572.

33. "No More Hiroshimas!" (1948) and statement submitted by Shinzo Hamai and Kiyoshi Tanimoto to the World Pacifist Meeting (Oct. 2, 1949), World Peace Day Records; *PN*, Feb. 18, 1949; *Meaning of Survival*, pp. 57, 60–61, 64, 67; Committee for the Compilation of Materials, *Hiroshima and Nagasaki*, pp. xxxix–xl; Kamata and Salaff, "Atomic Bomb and the Citizens of Nagasaki," pp. 43–46.

34. "No More Hiroshimas!" (1948), World Peace Day Records; *PN*, May 21, Aug. 6, Sept. 10, 1948; *Meaning of Survival*, pp. 69–70; Shinzo Hamai, "The Declaration of Peace" (Aug. 6, 1948), Hiroshima Peace Society Records.

35. Lifton, *Death in Life*, pp. 192, 211–52, 270–71; Pacific War Research Society, *Day Man Lost*, pp. 281–83; *Meaning of Survival*, pp. 76–79; Untitled statement by Shinzo Hamai, July 25, 1949, Hiroshima Peace Society Records; *PN*, Sept. 23, 1949.

36. Hersey, *Hiroshima*, pp. 136–39; Committee for the Compilation of Materials, *Hiroshima and Nagasaki*, p. 565; Cousins to Romulo, Nov. 18, 1949, Box 83, Cousins Papers, Los Angeles; Cousins, *Who Speaks for Man?*, pp. 96–97.

37. Bamba and Howes, eds., *Pacifism in Japan*, p. xiv; Stevenson, *Towards a Christian International*, pp. 66–67; Paul M. Sekiya, "The Japanese Fellowship of Reconciliation" (1958), FOR (Japan) Records.

38. Paul Sekiya, "The Japanese Fellowship of Reconciliation" (1958), FOR (Japan) Records; Brittain, *Rebel Passion*, pp. 64, 207–8; David Wurfel, "The Japanese F.O.R. Today," *Fellowship* 21 (July 1955): 8–11; *Peacemaker* [Australia], May 1949.

39. Jodai to Gladys Walser, Mar. 24, May 29, 1951 and "Peaceful World Is Aim of Club" (1952), Reel 80, WILPF (International) Records.

40. Morikatsu Inagaki, "World Federal Government Movement in Japan" (Aug. 9, 1948), and "Tokyo Assembly for World Federation" (1950), Box 16, Committee to Frame a World Constitution Records; "Zodiac," *CC* 1 (June 1948): 440; "Reply to Questionnaire from the United Nations," Box 52, Cousins Papers, Los Angeles; "Federalist Movements in Japan," *CC* 4 (Apr. 1951): 493–94.

41. Morikatsu Inagaki, "World Federal Government Movement in Japan" (Aug. 9, 1948), Box 16, Committee to Frame a World Constitution Records; *Meaning of Survival*, p. 80.

42. *Crusade for World Government Newsletter* (Nov. 1950), Crusade for World Government Records; Morikatsu Inagaki, "World Federal Government Movement in Japan" (Aug. 9, 1948), and "Tokyo Assembly for World Federation" (1950), Box 16, Committee to Frame a World Constitution Records.

43. Motoharu Kimura, "Reflections of a Japanese Physicist," *BAS* 43 (Nov. 1987): 7–8; Pacific War Research Society, *Day Man Lost*, p. 293; Braw, *Atomic Bomb Suppressed*, p. 106; Mitsuo Tokoro to Elisabeth Mann Borgese, Sept. 30, 1949, Box 16, Committee to Frame a World Constitution Records.

44. Nishi, *Unconditional Democracy*, pp. 51–52; *NYT*, Apr. 18, 1950.

45. Stockwin, *Japanese Socialist Party*, pp. 31–37, 41–42; *Nippon Times*, June 16, 1950; Tomiko Kora to A. J. Muste, Apr. 18, 1951, Box 33, Series B, Sayre Papers.

46. John Nevin Sayre, "Japan: Constructing the Future," *Fellowship* 16 (July 1950): 14–15; Gyotsu Sato, "Japan's Struggle for Peace," *Fellowship* 17 (Nov. 1951): 19; Muriel Lester, "Japan," *News Letter*, no. 73 (Dec. 1951), p. 12; Tomiko Kora to International Secretary, WILPF (1950?), Reel 79, WILPF (International) Records.

47. *NYT*, Sept. 27, 1949; "Japanese Reaction to Hydrogen Bomb News," enclosure in Cloyce K. Huston to SecState, Feb. 11, 1950, 711.5611/2-1150, DOS Records.

48. "An Appeal of the Women of Unarmed Japan to the United States Senators" (1952), Reel 80, WILPF (International) Records; Yasumasa Tanaka, "Japanese Attitudes Toward Nuclear Arms," *Public Opinion Quarterly* 34 (1970): 27, 29; Suzuki, "Japanese Attitudes Toward Nuclear Issues," pp. 102–3.

Chapter 4

Epigraph: Cousins, *Modern Man Is Obsolete*, p. 20.

1. This contention is borne out by much of what follows. It is also made in G. A. Borgese, "Of Atomic Fear and Two 'Utopias,' " *CC* 1 (Sept. 1947): 84–85.

2. Robert M. Hutchins, "Peace or War with Russia?" *Bulletin of the Atomic Scientists of Chicago* 1 (Mar. 1, 1946): 2.

3. There was a slight gender gap in this response, albeit a smaller one than on other issues related to World War II. Among respondents, 86 percent of the men and 83 percent of the women expressed approval of the bombing, while 9 percent of the men and 11 percent of the women expressed disapproval. Gallup, ed., *Gallup Poll*, pp. 521–22; Tom W. Smith, "The Polls: Gender and Attitudes Toward Violence," *Public Opinion Quarterly* 48 (Spring 1984): 387.

4. In 1971, a Harris poll found that 64 percent of American respondents viewed the atomic bombing as necessary and proper, while 21 percent thought it wrong. In 1982, another Harris poll found the proper-improper division to be 63 to 26 percent. Cantril, ed., *Public Opinion*, pp. 21, 23; Kramer, Kalick, and Milburn, "Attitudes Toward Nuclear Weapons and Nuclear War," pp. 12–13.

5. Yavenditti, "American Reactions to the Use of Atomic Bombs," pp. 209–17, 303, 308–10, 317–20; Schaffer, *Wings of Judgment*, pp. 154–55; Boyer, *By the Bomb's Early Light*, pp. 182–89.

6. A. J. Muste, "Memorandum on Atomic Bombing" (Aug. 15, 1945), Box 23, FOR (United States) Records; *Catholic Worker*, Sept. 1945.

7. Personal interview with Mercedes M. Randall, Apr. 26, 1965; Randall, *Improper Bostonian*, p. 403; Detzer to Vera Brittain, Oct. 10, 1945, "Women's International League for Peace and Freedom" folder, Brittain Papers; S. Walker, ed., *First One Hundred Days*, p. 15.

8. Yavenditti, "American Reactions to the Use of Atomic Bombs," p. 205; Fleischman, *Norman Thomas*, p. 215; Thomas, *Appeal to the Nations*, p. 18.

9. When the news of the Hiroshima bombing reached him, Einstein reportedly remarked: "Oh, weh!" (Alas!). Eugene Rabinowitch, "Five Years After," *BAS* 7 (Jan. 1951): 3; Linus Pauling, "Notes on Conversation of Linus Pauling with Albert Einstein on 16 November 1954," Pauling Papers; Nathan and Norden, eds., *Einstein on Peace*, p. 308.

10. Asked on television years later if he had "a feeling of accomplishment" at the time of the Hiroshima bombing, Szilard replied: "None whatsoever. . . . We accomplished trouble." Rhodes, *Making of the Atomic Bomb*, pp. 735, 749–50; Szilard to Alfred W. Painter, Aug. 11, 1945, in Weart and Szilard, eds., *Leo Szilard*, p. 230; Szilard to President of the United States, Aug. 13, 1945, Box 73, Szilard Papers; "Excerpt from a Television Interview with Mike Wallace (February 27, 1961)," in Hawkins, Greb, and Szilard, eds., *Toward a Livable World*, p. 337.

11. Discussing the Bomb with A. J. Muste, William Higinbotham, who worked at Los Alamos, expressed his belief that "the way we used it was very shortsighted." Frisch, *What*

Little I Remember, pp. 176–77; A. Smith, *A Peril and a Hope*, pp. 77–78; Higinbotham to Muste, Aug. 4, 1946, Box 15, FAS Records.

12. In 1965, Oppenheimer stated that he believed that "the warning to Japan was completely inadequate" and that Truman's failure to "ask Stalin to carry on further talks with Japan" was "an error." A. Smith, *A Peril and a Hope*, pp. 78–79; W. Laurence, "Would You Make the Bomb Again?", p. 8.

13. Moellering, *Modern War and the American Churches*, p. 55; Yavenditti, "American Reactions to the Use of Atomic Bombs," p. 186; Boyer, *By the Bomb's Early Light*, p. 203. For the view that the majority of Catholic church leaders "approved or were silent," see McNeal, *American Catholic Peace Movement*, pp. 112–15.

14. *NYT*, Aug. 10, 20, 1945; Federal Council of Churches, *Atomic Warfare and the Christian Faith*, pp. 11–12; Boyer, *By the Bomb's Early Light*, p. 202.

15. Hersey, "Hiroshima," pp. 15–68; Luft and Wheeler, "Reaction to John Hersey's 'Hiroshima,'" pp. 135–40; A. Smith, *A Peril and a Hope*, pp. 80–81; Yavenditti, "John Hersey and the American Conscience," pp. 24–49; Yavenditti, "American Reactions to the Use of Atomic Bombs," pp. 359, 362–63.

16. The anthropologist was Robert Redfield. Boyer, *By the Bomb's Early Light*, pp. 7, 13–32; *Congressional Record*, 79th Cong., 1st sess., Appendix, p. A3842.

17. Swing, *In the Name of Sanity*, p. ix; *NYT*, Nov. 14, 1945; "Atomic Force, Its Meaning for Mankind," p. 12.

18. Rabinowitch, "Five Years After," p. 3. See also Lapp, *Atoms and People*, p. 76.

19. Eugene Rabinowitch, "Memo on 'The Impact of Nucleonics'" (July 12, 1945), in Sherwin, *A World Destroyed*, pp. 334–35; "The Atomic Scientists of Chicago," *Bulletin of the Atomic Scientists of Chicago* 1 (Dec. 10, 1945): 1; A. Smith, *A Peril and a Hope*, pp. 92–97, 100–101; John A. Simpson, "Some Personal Notes," *BAS* 37 (Jan. 1981): 27–28.

20. Folder 1, Box 55, FAS Records; W. A. Higinbotham, "The Federation of American Scientists," *BAS* 4 (Jan. 1948): 21; Rotblat, "Movements of Scientists," pp. 117–18; "Members of Federation of American Scientists as of April 9, 1946" and "The Federation of American Scientists" (1946), Box 12, FOR (United States) Records; A. Smith, *A Peril and a Hope*, pp. 203, 235–37, 249–51, 276.

21. Arthur Compton was apparently quite hostile to the idea of the atomic scientists playing a political role. Eugene Rabinowitch to Compton, Oct. 27, 1945, Box 2, Rabinowitch Papers, Albany.

22. The first of the six aims of the new FAS read: "In the particular field of atomic energy, to urge the United States to help initiate and perpetuate an effective and workable system of world control based on full cooperation among all nations." According to Alice Smith, the movement's most painstaking chronicler, its "central theme" was "that the old concepts of defense, either by destroying the attacker or by monopolizing superior weapons, were no longer valid." A. Smith, *A Peril and a Hope*, pp. 236–37, 253.

23. "The Scientists' Organizations," Appendix II to "A Report on a Conference of Scientists Held at Lake Geneva, Wisconsin, June 18–21, 1947," Box 1, Rabinowitch Papers, Albany; A. Smith, *A Peril and a Hope*, pp. 323, 329.

24. "The Scientists' Organizations," Appendix II to "A Report on a Conference of Scientists Held at Lake Geneva, Wisconsin, June 18–21, 1947," Box 1, Rabinowitch Papers, Albany; Eugene Rabinowitch, "Twenty-Five Years Later," *BAS* 26 (June 1970): 4; McCrea and Markle, *Minutes to Midnight*, pp. 50–59.

25. "Report on the Progress of the Committee for Foreign Correspondence," enclosure in A. S. Bishop to Richard C. Tolman, Jan. 21, 1947, Box 32, SASSAE, DOS Records; A. Smith, *A Peril and a Hope*, pp. 331–34.

26. Smith's interpretation of the origins of ECAS gives somewhat less importance to the role of Szilard than does this account. Hans A. Bethe oral history interview, May 8, 9, 1972, pp. 43–44; Joseph Halle Schaffner to Hans Bethe, Jan. 17, 1947, Box 1, ECAS Records, Chicago; Eugene Rabinowitch, "James Franck, 1882–1964, Leo Szilard, 1898–1964," *BAS* 20 (Oct. 1964): 19; A. Smith, *A Peril and a Hope*, pp. 325, 494–95.

27. ECAS press release of May 22, 1946, Box 57, Einstein Papers; ECAS, "The Last Hour Before Midnight" (1947), ECAS Records, Swarthmore; Einstein to Friend, Apr. 22, 1947, Class 710, Russell Archives 1.

28. Oppenheimer, *Open Mind*, p. 88; *NYT*, Dec. 11, 1945; Federation of American (Atomic) Scientists, "Survival Is at Stake," p. 79.

29. "Excerpt from a Television Interview with Mike Wallace (February 27, 1961)," in Hawkins, Greb, and Szilard, eds., *Toward a Livable World*, pp. 337–38.

30. One of his postwar friends, Edward Shils, concluded that Szilard did harbor "some feeling of guilt." Shils believed that Szilard's experience with the Bomb was "one of the reasons" why he gave up physics in the postwar years and took up biology. Moreover, in a whimsical short story he wrote in 1947, Szilard portrayed himself as on trial for his role in producing nuclear weapons. Shils, "Leo Szilard," p. 41; Szilard, "My Trial as a War Criminal."

31. Weisskopf, *Privilege of Being a Physicist*, p. 212; Eugene Rabinowitch, "Ten Years That Changed the World," *BAS* 12 (Jan. 1956): 2. See also A. Smith, *A Peril and a Hope*, pp. 528–29; Robert Oppenheimer, Speech to Association of Los Alamos Scientists, Nov. 2, 1945, in Smith and Weiner, eds., *Robert Oppenheimer*, pp. 318–19.

32. Eugene Rabinowitch, "Must Millions March?" *BAS* 10 (June 1954): 194.

33. Einstein, "Einstein on the Atomic Bomb," pp. 43–45; Einstein, " 'The Real Problem Is in the Hearts of Men,' " p. 7. See also Einstein to Robert Oppenheimer, Sept. 29, 1945, Box 32, Oppenheimer Papers.

34. Linus Pauling, "Atomic Energy and World Government" (Nov. 30, 1945), Pauling Papers; B. Bernstein, "Introduction," p. xl; Harold C. Urey, "Atomic Energy and World Peace," *BAS* 2 (Nov. 1, 1946): 2; H. Brown, *Must Destruction Be Our Destiny?*; Alice Kimball Smith, "The Recognition of Responsibility," *Our Generation Against Nuclear War* 1 (Autumn 1961): 42.

35. Wooley, *Alternatives to Anarchy*, p. 40. For ferment over the concept of world government among the atomic scientists at Oak Ridge, Los Alamos, and Chicago, see "Statement of the Association of Oak Ridge Scientists" (Jan. 13, 1946), Box 137, Cousins Papers, Los Angeles; "Report from Oak Ridge," *CC* 1 (Sept. 1947): 112–13; "Statement of ALAS Policy—November 9, 1945," Box 12, FOR (United States) Records; Association of Los Alamos Scientists, *Our Atomic World*; "Emery Reves on World Government," *Bulletin of the Atomic Scientists of Chicago* 1 (Feb. 1, 1946): 3.

36. A. Smith, *A Peril and a Hope*, pp. 86–87; Leo Szilard, "Address to Atomic Energy Control Conference, University of Chicago, September 21, 1945," in Weart and Szilard, eds., *Leo Szilard*, p. 234; Einstein, "The Way Out," pp. 76–77.

37. Selig Hecht, a member of the ECAS, insisted that "if atomic energy can be completely controlled by an international authority, it will be a great step forward toward the establishment of a world government." J. Robert Oppenheimer, "The International Control of Atomic Energy," *BAS* 1 (June 1, 1946): 1; Higinbotham to Cord Meyer, Jr., Apr. 24, 1947, Box 25, FAS Records; Hecht to A. J. Muste, n.d., Box 12, FOR (United States) Records.

38. "Atomic Scientists Oppose Hasty Legislation on Atomic Bomb" (Oct. 11, 1945), Box 71, Szilard Papers; "The Atomic Scientists Back the McMahon Bill," *Bulletin of the*

Atomic Scientists of Chicago 1 (Feb. 1, 1946): 1, 4–5; A. Smith, *A Peril and a Hope*, pp. 432–33, 531.

39. Szilard thought that at the conference the Americans should argue the Russian case and the Russians the American. His conference idea finally took shape in the Pugwash meetings, which began in the late 1950s, but they did not adopt this creative format. Leo Szilard, Untitled draft for Pugwash meeting (1957), Box 69, and Leo Szilard, "Memorandum on the difficulties of an over-all settlement with Russia," Box 41, Szilard Papers; Weart and Szilard, eds., *Leo Szilard*, p. 224; Shils, "Leo Szilard," p. 37.

40. Wooley, *Alternatives to Anarchy*, p. 9; Urey, "How Does It All Add Up?" p. 58; Federation of American (Atomic) Scientists, "Survival Is at Stake," p. 79.

41. "Scientists Comment on State Department Report," *BAS* 1 (Apr. 15, 1946): 12; "Plans for International Control Take Shape," *BAS* 1 (Apr. 1, 1946): 1; Higinbotham et al. to Baruch, May 15, 1946, Box 43, SASSAE, DOS Records; A. Smith, *A Peril and a Hope*, pp. 461–63.

42. A. Smith, *A Peril and a Hope*, pp. 464–65; Higinbotham to N. A. Whiffen, May 8, 1946, Box 12, FAS Records.

43. A. Smith, *A Peril and a Hope*, pp. 480–86; "A Victory and an Impending Crisis," *BAS* 2 (Aug. 1, 1946): 32; Simpson, "Some Personal Notes," p. 30; Urey to Baruch, July 5, 16, 1946, Box 61, Baruch Papers; Urey to Richard C. Tolman, Oct. 8, 1946, Box 42, SASSAE, DOS Records.

44. Robert E. Marshak et al. to Frederick H. Osborne, Dec. 1, 1947, Box 7, SASSAE, DOS Records. For other FAS and ECAS statements endorsing continued efforts toward international control, see *NYT*, June 30, 1947; "FAS Suggests Working Control Plan to UNAEC," *BAS* 5 (Mar. 1949): 96.

45. Eugene Rabinowitch, "The Narrow Way Out," *BAS* 4 (June 1948): 187; "Statements on the Second Anniversary of Hiroshima," *BAS* 3 (Sept. 1947): 252; J. H. Rush to ECAS, July 17, 1947, Box 15, ECAS Records, Chicago.

46. Resigning from the ECAS, Bethe said he would miss the "personal contact" with its other leaders but would "much prefer" seeing them at professional gatherings than at meetings dealing with "politics." Bethe to J. Halle Schaffner, Oct. 21, Nov. 5, 1946, Apr. 29, 1947, Box 1, and Bethe to Harold Urey, Jan. 5, 1948, Box 21, ECAS Records, Chicago; Bethe to Harrison Brown, June 13, 1947, Box 1, Rabinowitch Papers, Albany.

47. Einstein to Max Born, Mar. 3, 1947, in Born, ed., *Born-Einstein Letters*, p. 158; Einstein to Eugene Rabinowitch, Aug. 18, 1949, in Nathan and Norden, eds., *Einstein on Peace*, p. 514.

48. Higinbotham to Muste, Aug. 5, 1946, Hans Bethe to Muste, Dec. 16, 1946, Harold Urey to Muste, June 10, 1946, Leo Szilard to Muste, Dec. 18, 1946, and Albert Einstein to Muste, Oct. 11, 1947, Box 12, FOR (United States) Records; Robinson, *Abraham Went Out*, pp. 142–43.

49. Norbert Wiener, "A Scientist Rebels," *BAS* 3 (Jan. 1947): 31; Norbert Wiener, "A Rebellious Scientist After Two Years," *BAS* 4 (Nov. 1948): 338–39; Cuthbert Daniel and Arthur M. Squires, "Freedom Demands Responsibility," *BAS* 4 (Oct. 1948): 300–304; Cuthbert Daniel and Arthur M. Squires, "Scientists' Responsibilities on the Way to Peace, and After," *BAS* 5 (Jan. 1949): 27–28, 32.

50. None of the officers of the new group was a leader in the scientists' movement and most were members of the FOR, which played a key role in launching it. Growing gradually, the Society for Social Responsibility in Science claimed an international membership of about 700 by the early 1960s. "Scientists Objecting to War Work Organize," *BAS* 5 (Nov.

1949): 312; Nathan and Norden, eds., *Einstein on Peace*, pp. 525–26; "Scientists Band for Social Responsibility," *Fellowship* 15 (Nov. 1949): 22; Robinson, *Abraham Went Out*, pp. 143–44.

51. Although much of the postwar exodus from the Manhattan project reflected the desire of scientists to return to their universities, some at least were fed up with military employment or dismayed by the atomic arms race. In mid-1946, physicist Lee DuBridge told readers of the *Bulletin* that some of the top scientists who had worked for the Manhattan project had "refused to participate" in the Bikini tests "because of their grave doubts of the value or propriety" of these ventures. Hans Bethe to A. J. Muste, Dec. 16, 1946, and Einstein to Muste, Oct. 11, 1947, Box 12, FOR (United States) Records; Lee A. DuBridge, "What About the Bikini Tests?" *BAS* 1 (May 15, 1946): 7.

52. Szilard made the case in different versions of the same article, published as Leo Szilard, "Calling for a Crusade," *BAS* 3 (Apr.–May 1947): 102–6, 125; Szilard, "Physicist Invades Politics," pp. 7–8, 31–34.

53. "Statement of the Lake Geneva Conference of Scientists" (June 21, 1947), Box 1, Rabinowitch Papers, Albany; "Statement of the Emergency Committee of Atomic Scientists" (June 30, 1947), Box 57, Einstein Papers; Hawkins, Greb, and Szilard, eds., *Toward a Livable World*, p. 4.

54. "Minutes of the Conference on Atomic Energy and World Cooperation held at Princeton, New Jersey—November 28–30, 1947," Box 1, Rabinowitch Papers, Albany.

55. "A Policy for Survival," *BAS* 4 (June 1948): 176, 188; Anjin Mebane to Horace Kelland, May 14, 1948, Box 13 and Harrison Brown to Drs. Gustavson et al., July 21, 1948, Box 3, ECAS Records, Chicago.

56. Weisskopf to Einstein, May 12, 1948, Box 57, Einstein Papers; Bethe to E. Everet Minett, Nov. 3, 1947, Box 15, and Urey to Bethe, Jan. 9, 1948, Box 1, ECAS Records, Chicago.

57. Muller to Harrison Brown, Sept. 2, 1948, Box 2, and Brown to Cord Meyer, Jr., Jan. 21, 1948, Box 13, ECAS Records, Chicago; Linus Pauling to Brown, Nov. 22, 1948, Pauling Papers; Szilard to Einstein, May 4, 1948, Box 7, Szilard Papers; Harold C. Urey, "Atomic Energy Control Is Impossible Without World Government," *BAS* 4 (Dec. 1948): 365–66.

58. Clifford Grobstein and A. H. Shapley, "The Federation of American Scientists," *BAS* 7 (Jan. 1951): 23; "Press Release of the Council of the Federation of American Scientists" (Feb. 5, 1950), Pauling Papers; *NYT*, Feb. 6, 1950.

59. Bethe, who had been asked to head the theoretical component of the H-Bomb effort, credited Victor Weisskopf with convincing him to reject the offer and condemn the project. Bethe oral history interview, May 8–9, 1972, pp. 23–28; *PN*, Feb. 10, 1950.

60. "The Facts About the Hydrogen Bomb," *BAS* 6 (Apr. 1950): 106–9, 126; B. Bernstein, "Introduction," p. xlii; Pauling to author, Dec. 15, 1987; Linus Pauling, *The Ultimate Decision* (May 1950), brochure enclosed in Pauling to author, Jan. 25, 1988.

61. *NYT*, Feb. 13, 1950. These statements greatly irritated the scientists who championed the H-Bomb. See, for example, *FRUS, 1950*, 1: 200–201.

62. Robert M. Hutchins, "1950," *CC* 1 (July 1947): 1; *NYT*, Oct. 10, 1945.

63. From the start, Clark had believed that control of the Bomb raised the question of developing a "really effective world government." Bantell, "Origins of the World Government Movement," pp. 20–30; *NYT*, Oct. 17, 1945; Clark to Henry Stimson, Oct. 2, 1945, Reel 114, Stimson Papers.

64. W. T. Holliday, "World Law or World Anarchy" (address to the Texas State Bar luncheon, July 1, 1948), Box 50, Cousins Papers, Los Angeles; "One Planet," p. 45; Reuther to

Elisabeth Mann Borgese, July 19, 1950, Box 13, ECAS Records, Chicago; "Signals Green?" *World Government News* 6 (Feb. 1948): 7.

65. Van Doren to Friend, Sept. 1945, Box 12, FOR (United States) Records; "One Planet," p. 45; White, *Wild Flag*, p. 188; Mumford to Frank Olmstead, Mar. 6, 1946, Box 18, War Resisters League Records.

66. Swing, *In the Name of Sanity*, pp. vii–viii.

67. Cousins, *Who Speaks for Man?* pp. 14–15; Cousins, *Modern Man Is Obsolete*, pp. 8, 12, 23.

68. *NYT*, Aug. 26, 1945; Cousins to Raymond Swing, Nov. 23, 1945, Box 70, and "One World or None" (Apr. 19, 1948), Box 49, Cousins Papers, Los Angeles; Norman Cousins and Thomas Finletter, "A Beginning for Sanity," *BAS* 2 (July 1, 1946): 11–12; *Meaning of Survival*, p. 94.

69. Cousins's editorial was also widely reprinted and reportedly reached 40 million readers in this fashion. Lianne Keeney to Tamara Mamedov, May 15, 1959, Box 208, Cousins Papers, Los Angeles; McCrea and Markle, *Minutes to Midnight*, p. 73.

70. Wooley, *Alternatives to Anarchy*, p. 42; Hutchins to Barbara Allee, Aug. 14, 1945, Box 7, Hutchins Papers; *NYT*, Aug. 13, 1945; "Atomic Force, Its Meaning for Mankind," p. 12.

71. Hutchins, *Atomic Bomb Versus Civilization*, p. 10. See also Hutchins, "1950," *CC* 1 (July 1947): 1–2.

72. "Brief History of the Committee," *CC* 1 (July 1947): 11–12; McKeon and Borgese to Hutchins, Sept. 16, 1945, Box 12, Hutchins Papers.

73. "Brief History of the Committee," pp. 15–22; "Preliminary Draft of a World Constitution," *CC* 1 (Mar. 1948): 325–46; Chloe R. Fox, "Federalists '49," *CC* 3 (Nov. 1949): 187.

74. Baratta, "Bygone 'One World,'" pp. 252–57; Cranston, "Strengthening of the U.N. Charter," p. 197.

75. "One Planet," pp. 44–45; "Americans United and the 'Atomic Age Dinner,'" Box 70, Cousins Papers, Los Angeles; *NYT*, Feb. 22, 23, 24, 1947; George T. Peck, "Who Are the United World Federalists?" *CC* 1 (July 1947): 28.

76. United World Federalists, *Unity and Diversity*, pp. 1, 4; "UWF's Birthday Marks Half a Decade of Progress," *Federalist* 1 (Feb. 1952): 6; Wooley, *Alternatives to Anarchy*, pp. 29–34, 38; Meyer, *Facing Reality*, pp. 5–44; Meyer, *Peace or Anarchy*, pp. 3–6.

77. Peck, "Who Are the United World Federalists?" p. 28; "Federalists '47," *CC* 1 (Feb. 1948): 309–10; Schuman, *Commonwealth of Man*, p. 440.

78. Elisabeth Mann Borgese to Robert M. Hutchins, Apr. 29, 1948, Box 12, Hutchins Papers; de Rusett, *Strengthening the Framework*, pp. 88–89; Wooley, *Alternatives to Anarchy*, pp. 26, 43–44.

79. Culbertson, *Total Peace*, pp. 3–10; Wooley, *Alternatives to Anarchy*, pp. 44–46.

80. Mildred M. Riorden Blake and Mark Van Doren to Harold Urey, Nov. 21, 1945, Box 25, FAS Records; A. Smith, *A Peril and a Hope*, pp. 102, 494; "Emery Reves on World Government," *Bulletin of the Atomic Scientists of Chicago* 1 (Feb. 1, 1946): 3.

81. Cord Meyer, Jr., "The Search for Security" (Apr. 19, 1947), Box 25, FAS Records; Meyer, *Facing Reality*, pp. 47–48.

82. Reves to Einstein, Sept. 1945, in Nathan and Norden, eds., *Einstein on Peace*, pp. 337–38; Ulric Bell to David Lilienthal, May 14, 1946, Box 191, Oppenheimer Papers.

83. Cousins and Finletter, "A Beginning for Sanity," pp. 13–14; Meyer, "What Are the Chances?" pp. 42–45; Cord Meyer, Jr., "Hope and Illusion" (May 29, 1946), Box 41, SASSAE, DOS Records.

84. Americans United for World Government also supported the Baruch Plan. *NYT*,

June 23, 1946; Ulric Bell to Richard C. Tolman, July 8, 1946, Box 32, SASSAE, DOS Records.

85. Hutchins to Szilard, Dec. 17, 1946, Box 5, Hutchins Papers; United World Federalists, "New Soviet Atom Plan Rejected by Western Powers" (Oct. 8, 1948), Box 49, Cousins Papers, Los Angeles; Meyer, *Facing Reality*, p. 49; Meyer to Higinbotham, Apr. 30, 1947, Box 25, FAS Records.

86. National Executive Council of UWF, "Policy Statement on Hydrogen Bomb" (Feb. 5, 1950), Box 70, Cousins Papers, Los Angeles; *NYT*, Mar. 26, 1950.

87. Kahler to Bethe, Mar. 23, 1950, Box 1, Kahler Papers; Robert M. Hutchins and G. A. Borgese, "January 31, 1950," *CC* 3 (Mar. 1950): 395.

88. "Council Notes," *World Government News* 7 (July 1949): 7; de Rusett, *Strengthening the Framework*, p. 89; Cord Meyer, Jr., "A Progress Report on World Federation," *BAS* 5 (Oct. 1949): 281.

89. UWF, "We're in the middle . . . and proud of it" (1950), Box 52, and "Executive Department Reports, January 1–March 31, 1949, Field Department," Box 48, Cousins Papers, Los Angeles; "World Opinion on World Government," *CC* 1 (Sept. 1947): 101–3; Wooley, *Alternatives to Anarchy*, pp. 47–48; *Monde Fédéré*, Oct. 1948.

90. Wooley, *Alternatives to Anarchy*, pp. 46–47.

91. Sponsors in the House included Abraham Ribicoff, Christian Herter, John F. Kennedy, Gerald Ford, Mike Mansfield, Jacob Javits, and Henry Jackson. In the Senate, they included Hubert Humphrey, Wayne Morse, and Claude Pepper. *New York Herald Tribune*, June 8, 1949; "UWF's Birthday Marks Half a Decade of Progress," *Federalist* 1 (Feb. 1952): 6; Baratta, *Strengthening the United Nations*, p. 136.

92. Buchanan and Cantril, *How Nations See Each Other*, p. 62; Cottrell and Eberhart, *American Opinion on World Affairs*, p. 129; Wooley, *Alternatives to Anarchy*, p. 48.

93. Meyer, "A Progress Report on World Federation," pp. 281–82; Mangone, *Idea and Practice of World Government*, p. 31. For two works by leading advocates of world government that develop the theme of America's pioneering role, see Nash, *It Must Be Done Again*; Van Doren, *Great Rehearsal*.

94. Wittner, *Rebels Against War*, pp. 34–61, 97–124; "Membership Committee, 1942–1947" folder, Box 4, War Resisters League Records; Minutes of a meeting of the International Council, WRI, July 26–29, 1947, Box 2, WRI Records; Mildred Scott Olmsted, "Report of the Administrative Secretary" (Nov. 19, 1948), Box 13, WILPF (United States) Records.

95. "Memberships and Contributions" (1948), Box 13, WILPF (United States) Records; John M. Swomley, Jr., "Report of Associate Secretary" (May 16, 1949), Box 3, and "Membership Statistics" (1954), Box 4, FOR (United States) Records; Olson, "Peace and the American Community," p. 189.

96. "Excerpts of Comments Received from Members Unable to Attend Executive Committee Meeting of August 24, 1945," Box 2, War Resisters League Records; *Conscientious Objector*, Dec. 1945; "The Role of the Pacifist in the Atomic Age," *Fellowship* 12 (Sept. 1946): 149; Muste to John M. Swomley, Jr., Aug. 20, 1945, Box 11, FOR (United States) Records.

97. Macdonald, Editorial, *Politics* 2 (Aug. 1945): 225; Swomley to Muste, Aug. 7, 1945, Box 11, FOR (United States) Records; "The Victory of Violence," *Pacifica Views* 3 (Aug. 31, 1945): 4. See also "How to Live with the Atom," *Fellowship* 12 (July 1946): 120; Muste, *Not by Might*, p. 201.

98. Winston Dancis to Jessie Wallace Hughan, May 6, 1946, Box 3, War Resisters League Records; Minutes of a meeting of the International Council, WRI, July 26–29, 1947, Box 2, WRI Records; "The Atomic Bomb and Its Message to You" (1945), Box 30, WILPF (United States) Records.

99. Minutes of the Executive Committee meeting, War Resisters League, Nov. 28, 1945, and "The Atomic Bomb" (Feb. 11, 1946), Box 2, War Resisters League Records; "National Board Resolutions Re: Dropping Atomic Bombs on Obsolete Warships," Box 4, WILPF (United States) Records; *NYT*, May 6, 1946.

100. Minutes of the FOR Executive Committee meeting, Nov. 22, 1946, Box 3, and Muste to Vernon Nash, Sept. 7, 1945, Box 9, FOR (United States) Records; Muste, *Not by Might*, p. 3.

101. *NYT*, July 18, 1949; Hennacy, *Autobiography of a Catholic Anarchist*, pp. 145–51; Jack, "Action for Peace," p. 23.

102. Muste to Einstein, May 28, 1946, and Muste to Louis Ridenour, Dec. 18, 1946, Box 12, FOR (United States) Records; Muste, *Not by Might*, pp. 178–96; Rustin, *"In Apprehension How Like a God!"*, p. 15.

103. Muste to Staff Members, Jan. 15, 1946, and Muste to John Swomley and Alfred Hassler, Nov. 21, 1946, Box 12, FOR (United States) Records.

104. FOR, "Draft Statement on San Francisco Conference" (June 29, 1945), Box 3, and Vernon Nash to Muste, Oct. 9, Nov. 22, 1945, Box 9, FOR (United States) Records; Frances Rose Ransom to Audrey Jump, Apr. 3, 1948, Box 17, and Tracy D. Mygatt to Ransom, Jan. 15, 1948, Box 18, War Resisters League Records; "National Board Resolutions Re: Post War World," Box 4, WILPF (United States) Records; Freeman, *Quakers and Peace*, pp. 58–59.

105. "The Role of the Pacifist in the Atomic Age," p. 150. For similar statements by Sayre, see "Notes on Informal Conference, October 4, 1946," Box 6, FOR (United States) Records; John Nevin Sayre, "Europe Revisited," *Fellowship* 12 (June 1946): 95.

106. Abraham Kaufman to Julien Cornell, Oct. 13, 1946, Box 14, War Resisters League Records; Frederick J. Libby to Syracuse Peace Council, Jan. 24, 1946, and to J. B. Th. Hugenholtz, July 9, 1946, Box 9, FOR (United States) Records; Philip E. Jacob, "Peacemaking Without World Government," *CC* 3 (May 1950): 538–41.

107. A. J. Muste, "World Government—Panacea or Promise?" *Fellowship* 12 (Nov. 1946): 177–79; Muste to Dorothy Thompson, Dec. 30, 1946, Box 11, FOR (United States) Records; personal interview with A. J. Muste, June 2, 1966; Freeman, *Quakers and Peace*, p. 58.

108. In 1948, for example, the WILPF National Board voted to cooperate actively with the United World Federalists and the American Association for the United Nations toward the creation of a world government. Muste to Richard Gregg, June 4, 1947, Box 11, FOR (United States) Records; "The Role of the Pacifist in the Atomic Age," p. 150; Roy Kepler to J. L. Manning, Dec. 15, 1948, Box 18, War Resisters League Records; "Summary of Board Meeting Minutes, February 13, 1948," Box 13, WILPF (United States) Records.

109. Minutes of the FOR Executive Committee meeting, Mar. 12, Apr. 9, 1946, Box 3, FOR (United States) Records; Pickett, *For More Than Bread*, pp. 211–59.

110. Vivien Roodenko to Allen Early, Sept. 24, 1948, Box 15, War Resisters League Records; "Swomley, John" folder, Box 11, FOR (United States) Records; Wittner, *Rebels Against War*, pp. 162–64.

111. Peacemakers, "Refuse to Register," Box 8, Section C4, Allen Papers; *Catholic Worker*, May 1946.

112. Each, he noted, said to the other: "I don't trust you and will not take any chances, but I ask you to trust me and take the chances which that involves." Muste to Wallace, Sept. 26, 1945, Box 12, and Muste to Felix Morley, Aug. 1, 1946, Box 9, FOR (United States) Records.

113. *PN*, Jan. 31, Feb. 7, 14, 1947.

114. Muste to Fellow-Minister, Feb. 2, 1950, Box 24, FOR (United States) Records;

"WRL Statement on the Hydrogen Bomb" (1950), Box 10, Series B, War Resisters League Records; *NYT*, Feb. 12, 1950; *Peacemaker* [United States], Mar. 15, 1950.

115. "We Must Draw the Line Now" (1950), Box 28, FOR (United States) Records; *Peacemaker* [United States], Apr. 25, 1950; *Washington Post*, Apr. 7, 1950; Muste, *Gandhi and the H-Bomb*, pp. 12, 18, 20.

116. *NYT*, July 15, Sept. 29, 1946; *New York Herald Tribune*, Dec. 30, 1947; Markowitz, *Rise and Fall of the People's Century*, pp. 124–303.

117. Thomas to Baruch, Oct. 10, 1946, and enclosure, Box 61, Baruch Papers; *NYT*, Oct. 24, 1948, Feb. 17, 1950.

118. Federal Council of Churches, *Atomic Warfare and the Christian Faith*, pp. 13–14; Boyer, *By the Bomb's Early Light*, p. 229; McNeal, *American Catholic Peace Movement*, pp. 123–24.

119. "Thirty Christian Theologians. . . ." (Feb. 1950), Box 24, FOR (United States) Records; *NYT*, Mar. 8, 1946, Apr. 11, May 25, 1950; Hiebert, *Impact of Atomic Energy*, p. 268.

120. In September 1945, 52 percent thought people "better off" and 22 percent "worse off" because of nuclear fission. Gallup, ed., *Gallup Poll*, pp. 527, 680; "The Quarter's Polls," *Public Opinion Quarterly* 11 (Summer 1947): 278; Hazel Gaudet Erskine, "The Polls: Atomic Weapons and Nuclear Energy," *Public Opinion Quarterly* 27 (Summer 1963): 178–79.

121. Two-thirds of Americans polled in the summer of 1946 agreed that there was a "real danger" that atomic weapons would be used against the United States. "The Quarter's Polls," *Public Opinion Quarterly* 10 (Summer 1946): 247; "The Quarter's Polls," *Public Opinion Quarterly* 11 (Summer 1947): 278; Cottrell and Eberhart, *American Opinion on World Affairs*, p. 24.

122. Gallup, ed., *Gallup Poll*, pp. 797–98, 869; Erskine, "The Polls," pp. 156–57, 182–83.

123. Gallup, ed., *Gallup Poll*, p. 571; Erskine, "The Polls," p. 184.

124. Gallup, ed., *Gallup Poll*, pp. 578, 613, 680; Cantril, ed., *Public Opinion*, p. 25; Erskine, "The Polls," p. 168.

125. "The Quarter's Polls," *Public Opinion Quarterly* 10 (Summer 1946): 247; Erskine, "The Polls," pp. 165, 168.

126. Erskine, "The Polls," pp. 165–67; "The Quarter's Polls," *Public Opinion Quarterly* 10 (Winter 1946–47): 618; "One Planet," p. 44.

127. In his edited book on public opinion during this era, Gallup records this question somewhat differently: "Do you think we should try to work out an agreement with Russia to control the atom bomb and the hydrogen bomb?" Furthermore, he indicates that the response to this question in February was 68 to 23 percent. "Public Opinion on the Question of New Approaches to the Atomic Problem" (Feb. 14, 1950), Box 7, SASSAE, DOS Records; Erskine, "The Polls," p. 171; Gallup, ed., *Gallup Poll*, p. 895.

Chapter 5

Epigraph: Brittain to H. Rollin, Aug. 9, 1945, "Replies, August 1945" folder, Brittain Papers.

1. Vera Brittain, the best-known figure on the Bombing Restriction Committee, wrote to one of its stalwarts on August 9 that "the use of the bomb without previously warning the Japanese what to expect . . . makes hypocritical nonsense of all the American wails about Pearl Harbor and of their claims to discriminate between 'targets.' " "The Atomic Bomb," *Christian Pacifist*, no. 45 (Sept. 1945), p. 653; Brittain [or Corder Catchpool] to Hubert

Peet, Aug. 9, 1945, and Brittain to Corder Catchpool, Aug. 9, 1945, "Replies, August 1945" folder, Brittain Papers. For additional indications of pacifist disgust with the bombing, see Corder Catchpool to Brittain, Aug. 28, 1945, "Catchpool, Corder" folder, Brittain Papers; Brittain, *Testament of Experience*, p. 375.

2. *NYT*, Aug. 9, 10, 14, 1945; *PN*, Aug. 24, 31, 1945; Stucky, *August 6, 1945*, p. 102.

3. Hazel Gaudet Erskine, "The Polls: Atomic Weapons and Nuclear Energy," *Public Opinion Quarterly* 27 (Summer 1963): 180; Dorsey Gassaway Fisher to SecState, Sept. 22, 1945, 811.2423/9-2245, DOS Records; Stucky, *August 6, 1945*, pp. 101–3; Ormrod, "Churches and the Nuclear Arms Race," p. 196.

4. Woolf, "Britain in the Atomic Age," pp. 12–13; *NYT*, Aug. 20, 1945.

5. In August 1945, Wells was preoccupied with the Hiroshima and Nagasaki bombings. *PN*, Nov. 23, 1945; H. G. Wells, *Mind at the End of Its Tether*, p. 4; D. Smith, *H. G. Wells*, p. 602.

6. *Times* (London), Aug. 7, 8, 16, 1945; *PN*, Aug. 24, 1945.

7. S. Walker, ed., *First One Hundred Days*, p. 12; *NYT*, Aug. 23, 1945; Brittain to John Nevin Sayre, Aug. 30, 1945, "Replies, August 1945" folder, Brittain Papers. For Brittain's background as a pacifist, see Bennett, "Vera Brittain and the Peace Pledge Union."

8. Gallup, ed., *Gallup International Public Opinion Polls: Great Britain*, pp. 115, 132.

9. By contrast, the figures in the United States were as follows: more good, 42 percent; more harm, 23 percent. Yavenditti, "American Reactions," pp. 357–58; "The Quarter's Polls," *Public Opinion Quarterly* 13 (Spring 1949): 155.

10. S. Walker, ed., *First One Hundred Days*, p. 41; "Speak for England."

11. Responding to a Gallup poll of September 1946, 50 percent of Britons said that their country should "turn over her armed forces, with all atom bomb materials, to a world parliament," providing that other leading nations did so; 27 percent disagreed. "The Quarter's Polls," *Public Opinion Quarterly* 10 (Spring 1946): 104; Gallup, ed., *Gallup International Public Opinion Polls: Great Britain*, pp. 115, 139.

12. Gowing, *Independence and Deterrence*, 1: 53; Gertrude S. Hooker, "James Burnham's World," *CC* 1 (July 1947): 34; Driver, *Disarmers*, p. 16; Myers, "Failure of Protest Against Postwar British Defense Policy," p. 242.

13. Gowing, *Independence and Deterrence*, 1: 51–55; Pierre, *Nuclear Politics*, p. 78; Clement Attlee to Winston Churchill, Sept. 28, 1945, and Churchill to Attlee, Oct. 6, 1945, PREM 8/113, Prime Minister's Records.

14. Ceadel, *Pacifism in Britain*, pp. 169–312; "Peace Pledge Union" (1958), Box 1, PPU Records; Sybil Morrison to Vera Brittain, Nov. 17, 1948, "Peace Pledge Union 1948" folder, Brittain Papers; Hinton, *Protests and Visions*, pp. 102–3, 129–30.

15. Minutes of the General Committee Meeting, British FOR, June 19–20, 1945, Reel 2, FOR (Great Britain) Records; *PN*, Aug. 13, 1948; Ceadel, *Pacifism in Britain*, p. 212; *Peacemaker* [Australia], Nov. 1947.

16. *PN*, Aug. 10, 17, 1945; Brittain, *Rebel Passion*, p. 222.

17. *PN*, Aug. 31, Dec. 28, 1945; "The Atomic Bomb," *Christian Pacifist*, no. 45 (Sept. 1945), p. 654.

18. *PN*, Aug. 31, 1945; National Peace Council, "Britain and the Peace" (Nov. 19, 1945), Box 4, National Peace Council Records.

19. *PN*, Aug. 24, Sept. 7, 1945; Corder Catchpool to Vera Brittain, Sept. 1, 1945, "Catchpool, Corder" folder, Brittain Papers.

20. Minutes of the Executive Committee meeting, British FOR, Oct. 15, 1947, Reel 5, and Minutes of the General Committee meeting, British FOR, Apr. 13–14, 1948, Reel 2, FOR (Great Britain) Records; *PN*, Apr. 2, 16, 30, 1948, Jan. 14, 1949.

364 Notes to Pages 86–90

21. *PN*, Jan. 28, June 24, 1949; Driver, *Disarmers*, pp. 20–21.

22. Minutes of the Executive Committee meeting, British FOR, Jan. 21, 1948, Reel 5, FOR (Great Britain) Records; Alex Comfort, *Civil Defense: What You Should Do Now!* (1950), and *You and the Atom Bomb* (1951), Box 1, PPU Records; *PN*, Oct. 28, 1949, Dec. 8, 1950.

23. *PN*, Jan. 3, 31, Mar. 14, 21, 1947; "A Generous Act," *Christian Pacifist*, no. 55 (July 1946), p. 881; "Counter Proposals," *Christian Pacifist*, no. 55 (July 1946), pp. 881–82.

24. *PN*, Nov. 12, 1948, Sept. 30, 1949. Murry's stormy departure from *Peace News* and from the PPU is discussed in Rigby, "Peace News," pp. 11–12.

25. Minutes of the Executive Committee meeting, British FOR, Oct. 19, 1949, Reel 5, FOR (Great Britain) Records; Brittain to Stuart Morris, Sept. 25, 1949, "Replies, September 1949" folder, Brittain Papers; *PN*, Sept. 30, 1949.

26. The Friends Peace Committee, in a letter to the press, stated that no candidate should be elected to Parliament who did not favor "calling a halt to this mad race to suicide." *PN*, Feb. 10, 1950; PPU, "The H-Bomb" (1950), Box 3, WRI Records; "The H-Bomb," *One World* 3 (Feb.–Mar. 1950): 114.

27. In 1949, Brittain attributed the PPU's decline to "the postwar fatigue and reaction which affects us all," the internal disturbance caused by John Middleton Murry, and the age, exhaustion, or illness of postwar chairs. *PN*, Apr. 25, Dec. 12, 1947, Dec. 24, 1948, Feb. 25, Apr. 14, 1949; Clifford H. MacQuire, "Concerning the Fellowship," *Reconciliation* [Great Britain] 27 (Feb. 1950): 782; Brittain to Mr. Maddever, June 21, 1949, "Replies June 1949" folder, Brittain Papers.

28. *PN*, Sept. 28, 1945. For the draining effect of that campaign, see Sybil Morrison to Vera Brittain, June 1, 1951, "Peace Pledge Union 1951" folder, Brittain Papers.

29. See, for example, *You Are One of 14,022 'Live' Members of the PPU* (1946), Box 1, PPU Records; Minutes of the Executive Committee meeting, British FOR, Sept. 20, Nov. 20, 1945, Reel 5, FOR (Great Britain) Records; and *Peace News* from 1945 to 1951.

30. "Dresden," *Reconciliation* [Great Britain] 27 (Mar. 1950): 787–88; *PN*, Feb. 23, 1951. See also Morrison, *I Renounce War*, pp. 70–71; Wood, *Deeper Challenge of the Atom Bomb*, p. 5.

31. Personal interview with Joseph Rotblat, July 12, 1990; Peierls, *Bird of Passage*, pp. 203, 282; J. Sayers et al. to Clement Attlee, Sept. 19, 1945, PREM 8/114, Prime Minister's Records.

32. *PN*, Dec. 5, 1947; A. Smith, *A Peril and a Hope*, p. 205; H. W. B. Skinner to Einstein, Apr. 22, 1947, Box 57, Einstein Papers.

33. Personal interview with Joseph Rotblat, July 12, 1990; Joseph Rotblat, "Leaving the Bomb Project," *BAS* 41 (Aug. 1985): 19.

34. Minutes of the meeting of the Atomic Scientists' Committee, Feb. 23, Mar. 8, 1946, and minutes of the meeting of the Association of Atomic Scientists Provisional Committee, Mar. 16, 1946, Box 8, FAS Records; J. A. Simpson, "A Scientist's Visit to England and France," *BAS* 1 (Apr. 1, 1946): 17; Rotblat, "Movements of Scientists," p. 121; R. E. Peierls, "The British Atomic Scientists' Association," *BAS* 6 (Feb. 1950): 59.

35. Personal interview with Joseph Rotblat, July 12, 1990; Gowing, *Independence and Deterrence*, 1: 50; Peierls, *Bird of Passage*, p. 283; Harold C. Urey to Richard Tolman, Dec. 24, 1946, Box 42, SASSAE, DOS Records.

36. Oliver Johnson to Einstein, Feb. 6, 1948, Box 12, ECAS Records, Chicago; "Annual General Meeting," *Atomic Scientists' News* 1, n.s. (Sept. 1951): 26; Rotblat, "Movements of Scientists," p. 122; Peierls, "The British Atomic Scientists' Association," p. 59; P. E. Hodgson, "The British Atomic Scientists' Association, 1946–59," *BAS* 15 (Nov. 1959): 393.

37. Atomic Scientists' Committee of Great Britain, "Memo to the UN Atomic Energy Commission," *BAS* 1 (June 1, 1946): 6; A. Smith, *A Peril and a Hope*, p. 460; Oliphant to Oppenheimer, May 1, 1946, Box 53, Oppenheimer Papers.

38. Edward A. Shils, "The Atomic Bomb and the Veto on Sanctions," *BAS* 3 (Feb. 1947): 62; Untitled memo from the British Association of Scientific Workers (Oct. 17, 1946), Box 8, FAS Records; D. Russell, *Tamarisk Tree 3*, p. 61; "Statements on the Second Anniversary of Hiroshima," *BAS* 3 (Sept. 1947): 235.

39. "A Compromise Suggestion by the British Association of Scientific Workers," *BAS* 2 (Oct. 1, 1946): 29; Association of Scientific Workers, "The International Control of Atomic Energy" (Aug. 1947), Class 560, Russell Archives 1; "British Atomic Scientists' Proposals for International Control of Atomic Energy," *BAS* 3 (Feb. 1947): 42–43, 49.

40. "Statements on the Second Anniversary of Hiroshima" *BAS* 3 (Sept. 1947): 235; Council of the Atomic Scientists' Association, "The International Control of Atomic Energy" (July 1948), Box 7, SASSAE, DOS Records; R. E. Peierls, "The President's Report," *Atomic Scientists' News* 3 (July 1949): 4.

41. Sir William Penney, who directed the Bomb project, was not an ASA member. Gowing, *Independence and Deterrence*, 2: 25–28, 205–6; Goldberg, "Atomic Origins," p. 426.

42. Gowing, *Independence and Deterrence*, 1: 184, 2: 10–11; Pierre, *Nuclear Politics*, p. 74; personal interview with Joseph Rotblat, July 12, 1990.

43. In "a long private talk" with Massey, a leading pacifist found him "deeply troubled by the urgency of the [atomic] problem and the apathy of this country. He and Professor Mott believe that we should not make atom bombs in Great Britain." H. S. W. Massey, "An English Physicist Considers His Obligations," *BAS* 4 (Nov. 1948): 339–40; N. F. Mott, "International Control of Atomic Energy," *Atomic Scientists' News* 1 (Sept. 17, 1947): 25; N. F. Mott, "Can Atomic Weapons Keep the Peace?" *BAS* 5 (Jan. 1949): 11–12; Joyce Gordon to F. L. T. Graham-Harrison, May 6, 1948, PREM 8/906, Prime Minister's Records.

44. "National Peace Council Conference," *Atomic Scientists' News* 1 (June 4, 1948): 180–81; "Scientists Urge End of Arms Race," *Fellowship* 16 (Dec. 1950): 19; *PN*, Apr. 7, 1950; "Defence Impossible," *Reconciliation* [Great Britain] 27 (May 1950): 835.

45. *PN*, Dec. 19, 1947, Dec. 3, 1948, Feb. 11, 1949; *Humanity*, no. 12 (Dec. 1948), p. 19; Schuman, *Commonwealth of Man*, pp. 434–35.

46. "One World," *Christian Pacifist*, no. 54 (June 1946), p. 863; *PN*, Oct. 21, 1949.

47. *Manchester Guardian*, Nov. 7, 1945; *NYT*, Nov. 29, 1945; B. Russell, *Has Man a Future?* pp. 21–24.

48. Bertrand Russell, "The Atomic Bomb and the Prevention of War," *BAS* 2 (Oct. 1, 1946): 19–21; Clark, *Life of Bertrand Russell*, pp. 521–27.

49. Clark, *Life of Bertrand Russell*, pp. 527–29; *PN*, Dec. 12, 1947; Russell to A. Bietenholz-Gerhard, Mar. 2, 1961, Class 640, Russell Archives 1; B. Russell, *Common Sense and Nuclear Warfare*, pp. 89–90.

50. *NYT*, Mar. 9, 1947; B. Russell, *Towards World Government*; N. B. Foot to Russell, Sept. 25, 1947, Class 560, Russell Archives 1.

51. Baratta, "Bygone 'One World,' " pp. 284–85, 288; Wooley, *Alternatives to Anarchy*, pp. 53–54; Schuman, *Commonwealth of Man*, p. 440; Crusade for World Government, "Newsletter for Overseas" (Mar. 14, 1948), *Crusade Contact* 1 (Feb.–Mar. 1949), and *Crusade Contact* 1 (Apr. 1949), Crusade for World Government Records.

52. *PN*, Oct. 24, 1947, Feb. 11, 1949; A. Lilienthal, *Which Way to World Government?*, p. 23; Laursen, *Federalism and World Order*, p. 37.

53. A. Lilienthal, *Which Way to World Government?*, p. 19; *PN*, Mar. 10, Aug. 18, 1950;

Crusade for World Government, "Newsletter for Overseas" (Mar. 14, 1948), Crusade for World Government Records.

54. Harris Wofford, Jr., "World Government in the British Elections," *CC* 3 (June 1950): 602–7; A. Lilienthal, *Which Way to World Government?*, p. 23.

55. The British FOR officially declared its "warm support for all action towards world unity" and its "conviction that only in some measure of World Government can progress be made out of the present international anarchy." It also distributed handbills for an event sponsored by the Crusade for World Government. Nevertheless, it remained wary of the "military power" that might be used by a world federation and refused to affiliate with the WMWFG. *PN*, Aug. 31, 1945, Jan. 30, Apr. 9, 30, Dec. 3, 1948, Jan. 7, 1949; Minutes of the General Committee meetings, British FOR, Dec. 31, 1946, Jan. 1, 1947, Apr. 13–14, Sept. 7–8, 1948, Reel 2, FOR (Great Britain) Records; "World Government," *Reconciliation* [Great Britain] 26 (Mar. 1949): 514.

56. *PN*, Aug. 6, 1948, Mar. 31, 1950; "Reply to Questionnaire from the United Nations," Box 52, Cousins Papers, Los Angeles; Buchanan and Cantril, *How Nations See Each Other*, p. 62.

57. Minutes of the General Committee meeting, British FOR, Dec. 30–31, 1947, Reel 2, and minutes of the Executive Committee meeting, British FOR, Mar. 17, 1948, Reel 5, FOR (Great Britain) Records; *PN*, Aug. 12, Oct. 7, 1949, Aug. 11, 1950.

58. *PN*, June 6, 27, 1947, Aug. 6, 1948; *NYT*, June 30, 1946.

59. E. Norman, "Churches and the Peace Movement," p. 269; Ormrod, "Churches and the Nuclear Arms Race," p. 206; *NYT*, May 3, 1946, July 20, 1947; *PN*, Apr. 28, 1950.

60. Gallup, ed., *Gallup International Public Opinion Polls: Great Britain*, p. 210; *NYT*, Oct. 2, 1949; "Archbishop of York," *Reconciliation* [Great Britain] 27 (Mar. 1950): 786.

61. Gallup, ed., *Gallup International Public Opinion Polls: Great Britain*, p. 224; External Research Staff, DOS, "Views of Western European Nations on Use of the Atomic Bomb" (Oct. 16, 1950), p. 2, Box 7, SASSAE, DOS Records.

62. *PN*, Feb. 10, 1950; *NYT*, Dec. 1, 1950; Holmes to SecState, Dec. 1, 1950, 711.5611/12-150, DOS Records.

63. External Research Staff, DOS, "Views of Western European Nations on Use of the Atomic Bomb" (Oct. 16, 1950), pp. 3–4, and Office of Intelligence Research, DOS, "Survey of Western European Opinion on the Atom Bomb as an Immoral Weapon" (Feb. 13, 1951), p. 1, Box 7, SASSAE, DOS Records.

64. "The Quarter's Polls," *Public Opinion Quarterly* 9 (Winter 1945–46): 537–38; "The Quarter's Polls," *Public Opinion Quarterly* 10 (Summer 1946): 247.

65. "The Atomic Bomb Demands That War Be Abolished," Box 1, FOR (Canada) Records, Toronto; "The Challenge of the Atom," *Reconciliation* [Canada] 2 (Dec. 1945): 1–2; Minutes of the meeting of the Toronto members of the National Council, Canadian FOR, June 18, 1946, Box 5, Series B, Sayre Papers.

66. Carlyle A. King, "Five Minutes to Twelve," *Reconciliation* [Canada] 3 (Feb.–Mar. 1947): 3; J. Lavell Smith, untitled sermon (1948), Box 1, Smith Papers.

67. "Reduction of Arms Is Not Enough," *Reconciliation* [Canada] 3 (Dec. 1946): 1–2; "Timely Books and Pamphlets" (1946), FOR (Canada) Records, Swarthmore; FOR, "Pacifist Strategy and Program in the Atomic Era" (1947), Box 1, FOR (Canada) Records, Toronto; Socknat, *Witness Against War*, p. 286.

68. Minutes of the National Council meeting, Canadian FOR, Mar. 24, 1950, Box 1, FOR (Canada) Records, Toronto; *Friends' Service News*, no. 36 (May 1951), p. 3; "Canadian F.O.R. and the International Situation" (Dec. 26, 1950), Box 6, Series B, Sayre Papers.

69. "Peace—Is Our Goal" (1946), FOR (Canada) Records, Swarthmore. See also Min-

utes of the meeting of the Toronto members of the National Council, Canadian FOR, Apr. 1, 1946, Box 5, Series B, Sayre Papers; Albert G. Watson, "Our Task Is Not Impossible" (June 1947), Box 1, FOR (Canada) Records, Toronto; Socknat, *Witness Against War*, pp. 284–88.

70. Socknat, "Dilemma of Canadian Pacifists," pp. 2–8; Albert G. Watson, "Our Task Is Not Impossible" (June 1947), Box 1, FOR (Canada) Records, Toronto; Roberts, "Women's Peace Activism in Canada," pp. 292, 295; J. J. Brown, "Pacifism After Hiroshima," *Reconciliation* [Canada] 3 (July 1946): 9–11.

71. Epstein, "Canada," pp. 171–76.

72. Yavenditti, "American Reactions," pp. 357–58; Members of the U.K. and Canadian Scientific Staff to C. R. Attlee and Mackenzie King, Nov. 9, 1945, "The C.A.Sc.W. and the Atomic Bomb," *Canadian Scientist* 1 (Dec. 1945): 2, 6–7, Florence Armstrong to M. Phillips, June 14, 1946, and W. A. Higinbotham to Victor Weisskopf, May 16, 1946, Box 12, FAS Records.

73. Pattie Tanner, "The Case for the United Nations," *Reconciliation* [Canada] 3 (Feb.–Mar. 1947): 6–7; Lewis Duncan, "The Case for World Government," *Reconciliation* [Canada] 3 (Feb.–Mar. 1947): 7–8; World Government Association, "World Government for a People's Peace" (July 1946), Box 2, FOR (Canada) Records, Toronto; "Reply to Questionnaire from the United Nations," Box 52, Cousins Papers, Los Angeles; W. M. Sheehan, "Foreword," *Canadian World Federalist*, no. 1 (Jan.–Feb 1961), p. 1.

74. The Rev. James M. Finlay, the FOR chair, served on the Advisory Council of one world government group. "Reduction of Arms Is Not Enough," *Reconciliation* [Canada] 3 (Dec. 1946): 1–2; "Pacifist Strategy and Program in the Atomic Era" (1947), Box 1, and World Government Association, "World Government for a People's Peace" (July 1946), Box 2, FOR (Canada) Records, Toronto.

75. *World Opinion* 1 (Sept. 1946): 3; *World Government Highlights*, p. 40; SD/GEN/ 29, July 29, 1949, Bureau of International Organization Affairs, DOS Records.

76. Saunders and Summy, *Australian Peace Movement*, pp. 28, 31; Gilbert and Jordan, "Traditions of Dissent," pp. 345, 354; Eleanor M. Moore to Vera Brittain, Mar. 5, 1942, "Moore, Eleanor M." folder, Brittain Papers; *Peacemaker* [Australia], Sept. 1959.

77. *Peacemaker* [Australia], Sept. 1945; Summy, "Australian Peace Council," pp. 233–34.

78. *Peacemaker* [Australia], Sept. 1945, Jan., Feb. 1946. See also Summy and Saunders, "Disarmament and the Australian Peace Movement," p. 24.

79. *Peacemaker* [Australia], Nov. 1949, Mar. 1950.

80. Minutes of a meeting of the International Council, WRI, July 26–29, 1947, Box 2, WRI Records; David Purnell, "Australian Quakers and Peace, 1900–1963," Australian Quaker Peace Committee Records; *Peacemaker* [Australia], Mar. 1948; Moore, *Quest for Peace*, pp. 157–59.

81. According to the *Peacemaker*, "there was a strong feeling that, in the light of the atom bomb, the proposition must be faced." Moore, *Quest for Peace*, pp. 160–61; Saunders and Summy, *Australian Peace Movement*, p. 31; *Peacemaker* [Australia], Mar. 1947, Mar. 1948, Mar. 1949.

82. Summy and Saunders, "Disarmament and the Australian Peace Movement," pp. 24–25; Moore, *Quest for Peace*, pp. 150–51, 154; Buchanan and Cantril, *How Nations See Each Other*, p. 62; "Reply to Questionnaire from the United Nations," Box 52, Cousins Papers, Los Angeles.

83. R. C. Traill to Secretary, FAS, June 25, 1946, and W. A. Higinbotham to Traill, n.d., Box 12, FAS Records; *Peacemaker* [Australia], Nov. 1947.

84. Cockburn and Ellyard, *Oliphant*, pp. 124–35, 144–45, 153–54, 158–59; *Peace-

maker [Australia], Mar. 1947; *NYT*, Aug. 3, 7, 1950; M. L. Oliphant, "Western Control Means Eastern Supremacy," *BAS* 4 (Dec. 1948): 365.

85. Moore, *Quest for Peace*, p. 151; "News from National Sections," *Pax International* 17 (Jan.–Feb. 1951): 5; *Civil Defence: What YOU Should Do Now!* (1951), Federal Pacifist Council Records; "World Peace Day (Monday, 6th August, 1951)" and untitled statement (1952), Reel 54, WILPF (International) Records.

86. *Peacemaker* [Australia], May 1947; *PN*, May 30, 1947; Charles Duguid, *The Rocket Range, Aborigines and War* (1947), pp. 1–16, and David G. Stead, *Destroy the Rocket Project Now or It Will Destroy You* (1947), Rocket Range Protest Committee Records; Moore, *Quest for Peace*, pp. 152–53.

87. In November 1948 attitudes in Australia were more negative than in the United States but more positive than on the continent of Europe. Yavenditti, "American Reactions," pp. 357–58; "The Quarter's Polls," *Public Opinion Quarterly* 10 (Winter 1946–47): 603; "World Opinion," *International Journal of Opinion and Attitude Research* 1 (Sept. 1947): 128; "The Quarter's Polls," *Public Opinion Quarterly* 13 (Spring 1949): 155.

88. "The Quarter's Polls," *Public Opinion Quarterly* 10 (Spring 1946): 104, 115; "World Opinion," *International Journal of Opinion and Attitude Research* 3 (Summer 1949): 285; Gallup, ed., *Gallup Poll*, p. 937.

89. N. Taylor, *Home Front*, pp. 177–205; Crane, *I Can Do No Other*, pp. 108–202; Burton, *Testament of Peace*, n.p.; Brittain, *Rebel Passion*, pp. 193–94.

90. Grant, *Out in the Cold*, pp. 12, 241–52; *News Letter*, no. 52 (Sept. 1946), p. 8; Minutes of a meeting of the International Council, WRI, July 26–29, 1947, Box 2, WRI Records; Emily Gibson to Gertrude Baer, Feb. 12, 1946, Reel 80, WILPF (International) Records; Clements, *Back from the Brink*, pp. 96–98.

91. *New Zealand Christian Pacifist*, Nov. 1945; Colin Marshall Curtis to FAS, Mar. 2, 1948, Box 48, FAS Records; Grant, *Out in the Cold*, p. 251. For other signs of pacifist concern with the Bomb, see *New Zealand Christian Pacifist*, Oct. 1945, Jan. 1946.

92. *PN*, Sept. 10, 1948; A. C. Barrington, "Responsible for the World," *Fellowship* 15 (Mar. 1949): 5–7; *New Zealand Christian Pacifist*, Sept. 1950.

93. *PN*, Aug. 5, 19, 26, 1949; *New Zealand Christian Pacifist*, Aug. 1949; "New Zealand Pacifists Meet Mob Violence," *Fellowship* 16 (Feb. 1950): 27.

94. Clements, *Back from the Brink*, pp. 13–14, 16–17, 20–21; N. Taylor, *Home Front*, p. 1264.

95. "Reply to Questionnaire from the United Nations," Box 52, Cousins Papers, Los Angeles; *Crusade for World Government Newsletter*, Oct. 1950, Crusade for World Government Records.

Chapter 6

Epigraph: "Hiroshima—und doch keine Einsicht!" *Volk und Friede*, no. 6 (Aug. 1948), p. 1, Deutsche Friedensgesellschaft Records.

1. Gallup, ed., *Gallup International Public Opinion Polls: France*, pp. 35, 41.

2. See, for example, G. A. Borgese, "Of Atomic Fear and Two 'Utopias,' " *CC* 1 (Sept. 1947): 84–85; R. E. Marshak, "European Scientists and the Atomic Bomb," *CC* 2 (Nov. 1948): 130.

3. Stucky, *August 6, 1945*, p. 99; "The Quarter's Polls," *Public Opinion Quarterly* 10 (Spring 1946): 105; *NYT*, Aug. 14, Oct. 29, 1945.

4. Howorth, *France*, pp. 14–16; Borgese, "Of Atomic Fear," p. 84.

5. Lottman, *Albert Camus*, p. 362; S. Walker, ed., *First One Hundred Days*, pp. 17–18; Stucky, *August 6, 1945*, p. 99.

6. Caldwell, "French Socialists," pp. 53–55, 189–90; Howorth, *France*, pp. 34–37.

7. *NYT*, Mar. 9, 1947; Weart, *Scientists in Power*, p. 239; Gallup, ed., *Gallup International Public Opinion Polls: France*, pp. 95, 126.

8. N. Ingram, *Politics of Dissent*; Defrasne, *Le pacifisme*, pp. 92–113; N. Ingram, "Ambivalence in the Post–World War II French Peace Movement," pp. 6–7.

9. *PN*, Jan. 24, 1947; Minutes of the International FOR Council meeting, Mar. 23–29, 1946, p. 9, Box 5, Series C, and Jacques Martin letter of Jan. 20, 1946, quoted in Ben Fuson to editor of *Fellowship*, Feb. 6, 1946, Box 8, Series B, Sayre Papers.

10. Minutes of the meeting of the International Council, WRI, Dec. 28–31, 1946, Box 1, WRI Records; Beaton, *Twenty Years' Work*, pp. 22–23; Brittain, *Rebel Passion*, p. 63; *PN*, Jan. 24, 1947.

11. *PN*, Aug. 8, 1947, May 14, 1948; André Trocmé, "Report on Activities, 1950–51" (Aug. 1951), Box 10, Series B, Sayre Papers; Andrée Jouve, "France and Neutrality" (Oct. 1950), Reel 63, WILPF (International) Records; N. Ingram, "Ambivalence in the Post–World War II French Peace Movement," pp. 11–12, 14.

12. Minutes of the meeting of the European Executive Committee, International FOR, Sept. 23–26, 1946, Box 5, Series C, and André Trocmé to John Nevin Sayre, Nov. 12, 1950, Box 10, Series B, Sayre Papers; John Nevin Sayre, "Pacifist Christianity in Europe," *Fellowship* 12 (July 1946): 115.

13. Symptomatically, in the aftermath of World War II, the heroes of the resistance and the leaders of the Free French were praised lavishly in France, but there was little notice of Trocmé and the villagers of Le Chambon. The international pacifist school that Trocmé founded there before the war and that sheltered so many refugees during that conflict almost came to an end for lack of money and interest. Hallie, *Lest Innocent Blood Be Shed*.

14. Trocmé wrote in 1950 that he was "convinced that world federalism is the constructive plan towards which the constructive forces of pacifists should be directed." Magda Trocmé, "A New Life Beginning," *Fellowship* 16 (July 1950): 23; *Fédéralisme et Non-Violence: Troisième Consultation Fraternelle du Chambon* (1949), Mouvement International de la Réconciliation Records; A. Trocmé to John Nevin Sayre, June 15, 1950, Box 10, Series B, Sayre Papers.

15. Lew Kowarski, "Atomic Research in France," *BAS* 2 (Oct. 1, 1946): 25; "Statements on the Second Anniversary of Hiroshima," *BAS* 3 (Sept. 1947): 235–36; Lew Kowarski, "Atomic Energy Developments in France," *BAS* 4 (May 1948): 139.

16. Victor Weisskopf, "Report on the Visa Situation" (Apr. 1952), Box 77, Oppenheimer Papers; Weart, *Scientists in Power*, p. 232; E. Grillot, "Reminiscences on the First Decade," *Scientific World*, Anniversary Number (1966), pp. 13–14.

17. Association Française des Travailleurs Scientifiques, "The Problem of Atomic Energy" (Nov. 5, 1945), and P. Bonet-Maury to M. Phillips, June 22, 1946, Box 5, FAS Records.

18. P. Bonet-Maury to M. Phillips, July 9, 1946, Box 5, FAS Records; Marcel Golden to Einstein, May 27, 1947, Box 57, Einstein Papers; Oliver Johnson to Einstein, Feb. 6, 1948, Box 12, ECAS Records, Chicago.

19. A. Smith, *A Peril and a Hope*, p. 485; "Communications from French Scientists," *BAS* 4 (Oct. 1948): 309–11.

20. Frédéric Joliot-Curie, "France and Atomic Energy," *BAS* 1 (May 1, 1946): 5; *NYT*, May 14, Nov. 1, 1946; Goldsmith, *Frédéric Joliot-Curie*, pp. 138–39.

21. This subject is treated at length in Chapters 10 and 11.

22. E. A. Gullion, "Report on Article by Joliot-Curie on Atomic Energy Development in France" (July 7, 1947), Box 47, SASSAE, DOS Records.

23. Goldsmith, *Frédéric Joliot-Curie*, pp. 158–59; Weart, *Scientists in Power*, p. 249; "Joliot-Curie and the Atomic Secrets," *BAS* 5 (Apr. 1949): 109–10, 126.

24. Marçais, *Destruction atomique ou gouvernement mondial*. Others included Aron and Marc, *Principes du fédéralisme*; de Man, *Au delà du nationalisme, vers un gouvernement mondial*; Gandolphe, *Système de paix et de securité mondiale*.

25. Schuman, *Commonwealth of Man*, p. 440; Henry Usborne, "Newsletter for Overseas" (Mar. 14, 1948), Crusade for World Government Records; G. Davis, *World Is My Country*, p. 51; "The Conference Day by Day," joint number of *Parlement*, *Across Frontiers*, and *Weltstaat*, Apr. 1950, p. 9; "Reply to Questionnaire from the United Nations," Box 52, Cousins Papers, Los Angeles.

26. Buchanan and Cantril, *How Nations See Each Other*, p. 62; SD/GEN/29, July 29, 1949, Bureau of International Organization Affairs, DOS Records; "Zodiac," *CC* 1 (Feb. 1948): 319.

27. G. Davis, *World Is My Country*, pp. 14–38; *NYT*, Sept. 13, 1948; Wooley, *Alternatives to Anarchy*, p. 54; Defrasne, *Le pacifisme*, p. 116.

28. G. Davis, *World Is My Country*, pp. 36–50, 57–62; "I Am a Citizen of the World" (1953), United States Miscellaneous Peace Material, 1950–54; *PN*, Dec. 17, 1948.

29. Georges Altman, "Don Quixote Is Right," reprinted in *Humanity*, no. 12 (Dec. 1948), pp. 17–19; Albert Camus, "On Behalf of Garry Davis," *CC* 2 (May 1949): 370–72; del Vayo, "On the First 'Citizen of the World,' " p. 18; *PN*, Mar. 4, 1949; *World Government News* 7 (Jan. 1949): 6–8 and (July 1949): 10–12; "The Little Man," pp. 21–22; Andrée Jouve, "The Garry Davis Movement" (Dec. 12, 1948), Davis Papers; G. Davis, *World Is My Country*, pp. 63–79.

30. For indications that some peace activists remained skeptical of Davis, see *PN*, Feb. 18, 1949; Carl-Erik Almström to Elisabeth Mann Borgese, June 14, 1949, Box 1, WMWFG Records.

31. Elisabeth Mann Borgese, "Report from Paris," *CC* 2 (May 1949): 392; International Registry of World Citizens to Friends, Jan. 1950, Davis Papers.

32. "World Opinion," *International Journal of Opinion and Attitude Research* 4 (Fall 1950): 448; *PN*, June 22, 1951; "Zodiac," *CC* 3 (Apr. 1950): 504.

33. *PN*, Feb. 11, 18, 1949; Patrick Armstrong, "International Highspots," *Humanity* (Aug. 1950), pp. 415–16.

34. Bourdet, "Way to European Independence," p. 12; Salvin, "Neutralism in France," pp. 285, 289–90, 296; Caute, *Communism and the French Intellectuals*, pp. 175, 249–50.

35. David Bruce to SecState, Oct. 31, 1949, Box 34, SASSAE, DOS Records; *NYT*, Oct. 2, 1949.

36. Caldwell, "French Socialists," p. 63; Theresa L. Hildebrand, "To Close the Chasm," *CC* 4 (Aug. 1950): 49; *FRUS, 1950*, 1: 57.

37. External Research Staff, DOS, "Views of Western European Nations on Use of the Atomic Bomb" (Oct. 16, 1950), pp. 2–3, and Office of Intelligence Research, DOS, "Survey of Western European Opinion of the Atom Bomb as an Immoral Weapon" (Feb. 13, 1951), pp. 6–7, Box 7, SASSAE, DOS Records.

38. *NYT*, Dec. 1, 1950; Truman, *Years of Trial and Hope*, p. 395; Office of Intelligence Research, DOS, "Survey of Western European Opinion of the Atom Bomb as an Immoral Weapon" (Feb. 13, 1951), p. 6, Box 7, SASSAE, DOS Records.

39. Riesenberger, *Geschichte der Friedensbewegung in Deutschland*, pp. 248–51;

Brock, *Twentieth Century Pacifism*, pp. 206–7; Holl, "German Pacifists in Exile," pp. 167–78; Scholl, *White Rose*; Sayre, "Pacifist Christianity in Europe," p. 116; Minutes of the meeting of the International FOR Council, Mar. 23–29, 1946, pp. 11–12, Box 5, Series C, Sayre Papers.

40. Fritz Küster, "The German Peace Society," *One World* 2 (July 1947): 7–8; Henry Holm, "The Pacifist Movement in Berlin," *Fellowship* 14 (May 1948): 19–20; Theodore Michaltscheff to Frances Ransom, May 22, 1947, Box 4, WRI Records.

41. F. Siegmund-Schültze to John Nevin Sayre, Mar. 19, 1949, Box 17, Series B, Sayre Papers; *News Letter*, no. 64 (Sept. 1949), pp. 11–12; *PN*, Mar. 28, 1947; Theodore Michaltscheff, "Germany: The Conquered," *Fellowship* 16 (July 1950): 5.

42. Donat, "Friedrich (Fritz) Heinrich Christoph Küster," p. 531; *PN*, Mar. 28, 1947; Grossman, "Peace Movements in Germany," pp. 300–301.

43. "Programm der Deutschen Friedensgesellschaft" (Mar. 1946), "Letzte Warnung der Atom-Physiker," *Der Neue Weg*, no. 3 (Aug. 1948), p. 1, and "Bedenke: Jede Kugel trifft nicht—aber jede Atombombe" (1948), Deutsche Friedensgesellschaft Records.

44. Magda Hoppstock-Huth to the International Congress of WILPF, Aug. 4–9, 1946, Reel 66, WILPF (International) Records; *PN*, Jan. 10, Mar. 28, July 4, 1947, Jan. 9, 1948, Jan. 21, Aug. 26, 1949, June 30, 1950; Brittain, *Rebel Passion*, pp. 124–25.

45. O. Hahn, *My Life*, pp. 170, 184, 232–33; Max von Laue, "The World Needs New Ethical Standards," *BAS* 4 (Nov. 1948): 337–38.

46. Oliver Johnson to Einstein, Feb. 6, 1948, Box 12, ECAS Records, Chicago; Rotblat, "Movements of Scientists," pp. 123–24.

47. "The Conference Day by Day," joint issue of *Parlement, Across Frontiers*, and *Weltstaat*, Apr. 1950, p. 8; Martha Hommes to Andrée Jouve, Dec. 28, 1948, Reel 66, WILPF (International) Records; *PN*, Jan. 21, 1949.

48. G. Bernstein, "World Government—Progress Report," p. 662; Henry Usborne, "Newsletter for Overseas" (Mar. 14, 1948), Crusade for World Government Records; "Reply to Questionnaire from the United Nations," Box 52, Cousins Papers, Los Angeles.

49. G. Davis, *World Is My Country*, p. 91; Buchanan and Cantril, *How Nations See Each Other*, p. 62; "Zodiac," *CC* 3 (Sept. 1949): 111; Hans Lamm, "An Opinion Poll in Western Germany," *CC* 3 (Sept. 1949): 92.

50. Merritt and Merritt, eds., *Public Opinion in Occupied Germany*, p. 187; Merritt and Merritt, eds., *Public Opinion in Semisovereign Germany*, p. 20.

51. *PN*, Mar. 24, 1950; Hübner-Funk and Schefold, "Challenge of Youth in the Federal Republic of Germany," p. 232; Brittain, *Rebel Passion*, p. 63; Cioc, *Pax Atomica*, pp. 12–13; *NYT*, Dec. 12, 1950; Otto, " 'Ohne mich!'-Bewegung." For a more positive youth perspective on peace, see "German Youth Appeals," *One World* 1 (Nov. 1946): 92–93; *Peacemaker* [Australia], Aug. 1948.

52. Rupp, *Ausserparlamentarische Opposition in der Ära Adenauer*, pp. 46–56; Drummond, *German Social Democrats in Opposition*, pp. 35, 37–41; *PN*, Oct. 17, 1947.

53. Mushaben, "Cycles of Peace Protest in West Germany," p. 27; F. Siegmund-Schültze to John Nevin Sayre, Oct. 23, 1950, Box 17, and "Ecumenical Biography: Niemoeller, Martin" (Feb. 1962), Box 16, Series B, Sayre Papers; "Niemöller Urges German Neutrality," *Fellowship* 16 (July 1950): 31; Noormann, "Martin Niemöller."

54. Kaspar Mayr to John Nevin Sayre, Jan. 14, July 1, 1951, Box 2, Series B, Sayre Papers; Scharrer, "War and Peace and the German Church," pp. 282–83; Cioc, *Pax Atomica*, p. 18.

55. Salvin, "Neutralism in Germany," pp. 306–8.

56. *PN*, Oct. 20, Nov. 17, 1950; WRI News Release no. 39 (Nov. 1, 1950), Box 3, WRI

Records; "Deutsche Friedensgesellschaft-Internationale der Kriegsdienstgegner" (1974), Internationale der Kriegsdienstgegner Records; Magda Hoppstock-Huth to Vera Brittain, Jan. 1, 1949, "Hoppstock-Huth, Magda" folder, Brittain Papers.

57. "Nie wieder Hiroshima!" (1948), Deutsche Friedensgesellschaft Records; *PN*, Aug. 13, 1948; Lilly Jaeger to Anne Bloch, Jan. 7, 1949, and enclosed newspaper clipping, Reel 66, WILPF (International) Records.

58. "Am 6. August 1945 vernichtete eine Atombombe Hiroshima" (1949) and Theodore Michaltscheff, "No More Hiroshima Meeting in Hamburg" (1949), World Peace Day Records; Michaltscheff, "Germany," p. 6; *PN*, Sept. 23, 1949.

59. *PN*, Aug. 18, 1950.

60. External Research Staff, DOS, "Views of Western European Nations on Use of the Atomic Bomb" (Oct. 16, 1950), pp. 2–3, and Office of Intelligence Research, DOS, "Survey of Western European Opinion on the Atom Bomb as an Immoral Weapon" (Feb. 13, 1951), p. 9, Box 7, SASSAE, DOS Records.

61. *PN*, May 9, 1947, Sept. 3, 1948, Aug. 26, Sept. 23, 30, 1949; "Terzo Convegno per l'opposizione alla guerra e per l'obbiezione di coscienza" (1948), Magda Trocmé, "Italy's Other Peace Conference" (Nov. 13, 1947), and Sandro Sarti to John Nevin Sayre, Oct. 28, 1947, Box 32, Series B, Sayre Papers. For the tiny scale of Italy's postwar pacifist groups, see Brittain, *Rebel Passion*, p. 164; Anne L. Bloch to Maria Remiddi, May 12, 1949, Reel 79, WILPF (International) Records; Asta Brügelmann to Vera Brittain, Nov. 28, 1947, "Brugelmann, Asta" folder, Brittain Papers.

62. Drake, "Aldo Capitini"; *PN*, Sept. 30, 1949; Magda Trocmé, "Report on My Trip to Italy" (Feb. 11, 1947), Box 11, and Magda Trocmé, "Italy's Other Peace Conference" (Nov. 13, 1947), Sandro Sarti to John Nevin Sayre, Oct. 28, 1947, and Aldo Capitini, "Non-Violence: Its Principles and Methods" (Oct. 12, 1951), Box 32, Series B, Sayre Papers.

63. In the summer of 1950, the parent organization, the WMWFG, was "uncertain" about this group's membership; its five other affiliates in Italy had a total of only 4,115 members. Buchanan and Cantril, *How Nations See Each Other*, p. 62; "Zodiac," *CC* 3 (Sept. 1949): 111; *World Government Highlights*, p. 41; Giovanni Pioli, "Peace Work in Italy," *One World* 2 (Nov. 1947): 74; "Reply to Questionnaire from the United Nations" Box 52, Cousins Papers, Los Angeles.

64. *Crusade Contact* 1 (April 1949): 4, Crusade for World Government Records; "World Government Crusade," p. 103; *World Government Highlights*, p. 41.

65. Sandro Sarti to John Nevin Sayre, Oct. 28, 1947, Box 32, Series B, Sayre Papers. Numerous Italian world federalist tracts appeared in these years, including Gostoli, *Per una migliore organizzazione del mondo*; Modigliani and Berardi, *L'Organizzazione della pace, del punto di vista giuridico*.

66. Alan Kirk to SecState, Aug. 14, 1945, 811.2423/8-1445, and Harold Tittmann to SecState, Sept. 7, 1945, 811.2423/9-745, DOS Records; S. Walker, ed., *First One Hundred Days*, p. 12; "Pope and the Bomb."

67. Fermi, *Atoms in the Family*, p. 245; External Research Staff, DOS, "Views of Western European Nations on Use of the Atomic Bomb" (Oct. 16, 1950), p. 2, and Office of Intelligence Research, DOS, "Survey of Western European Opinion on the Atom Bomb as an Immoral Weapon" (Feb. 13, 1951), p. 14, Box 7, SASSAE, DOS Records.

68. *NYT*, Sept. 25, 1949, May 28, Dec. 1, 1950; Office of Intelligence Research, DOS, "Survey of Western European Opinion on the Atom Bomb as an Immoral Weapon" (Feb. 13, 1951), p. 14, and External Research Staff, DOS, "Views of Western European Nations on Use of the Atomic Bomb" (Oct. 16, 1950), p. 3, Box 7, SASSAE, DOS Records.

Chapter 7

Epigraph: J. B. Th. Hugenholtz, "Kerk en Vrede," *Christian Pacifist*, no. 51 (Mar. 1946), pp. 801–2.

1. John Nevin Sayre, "Europe Revisited," *Fellowship* 12 (June 1946): 94–95.

2. Eyvind Tew, "Scandinavian News," *One World* 2 (Aug. 1947): 25; Office of Intelligence Research, DOS, "Survey of Western European Opinion on the Atom Bomb as an Immoral Weapon" (Feb. 13, 1951), Box 7, SASSAE, DOS Records.

3. Jonassen, *Resistance in Denmark*, pp. 3–7; Brittain, *Testament of Experience*, p. 394; Minutes of the International FOR Council meeting, Mar. 23–29, 1946, p. 9, Box 5, Series C, Sayre Papers; Foster, *Women for All Seasons*, p. 23; Vera Brittain, "W.R.I. talk" (Jan. 1946), "War Resisters International" folder, Brittain Papers.

4. Minutes of the meeting of the International Council, WRI, Dec. 28–31, 1946, Box 1, and minutes of the meeting of the International Council, WRI, July 26–29, 1947, Box 2, WRI Records; *PN*, Aug. 26, 1949, Nov. 24, 1950.

5. Margrethe Thorborg to John Nevin Sayre, Jan. 1, 1946, Box 8, Series B, Sayre Papers; John Nevin Sayre, "Pacifist Christianity in Europe," *Fellowship* 12 (July 1946): 114; Brittain, *Rebel Passion*, pp. 172–73.

6. Else Zeuthen to Vera Brittain, Jan. 25, 1946, "Zeuthen, Else" folder, Brittain Papers; "Correction to the report sent by Mrs. Fanny Arnskov" (Nov. 12, 1948), Reel 60, WILPF (International) Records; "News from Sections," *Pax International* 16 (Mar.–Apr. 1950): 2.

7. Else Zeuthen to the international chairs, WILPF, Mar. 23, 1946, and Kvindernes Internationale Liga for Fred og Frihed, "Arbejdsprogram 1949–51," Reel 60, WILPF (International) Records.

8. "Verdens Forenede Stater Paa Vesterbro," *Billed Bladet* (Oct. 25, 1949), pp. 3–6, Denmark Miscellaneous Peace Material; "Zodiac," *CC* 2 (July 1949): 480; Patrick Armstrong, "International Highspots," *Humanity*, Aug. 1950, 415. Two Danish world government tracts of the time are Bendix, *Vi og verdenskatastrofen*; Een Verden, *Een verden eller ingen*.

9. Henry Usborne, "Newsletter for Overseas" (Mar. 14, 1948), and "Danish Town 'Mundialised,'" *Crusade for World Government Newsletter* (Nov. 1950), Crusade for World Government Records; "Zodiac," *CC* 3 (Sept. 1949): 108–9.

10. "Verdens Forenede Stater Paa Vesterbro," *Billed Bladet* (Oct. 25, 1949), pp. 3–6, Danish Miscellaneous Peace Material.

11. J. Branner Jespersen to ECAS, Jan. 7, 1949, and E. Toft-Nielsen to Anjin Mebane, Jan. 27, 1949, Box 18, ECAS Records, Chicago.

12. Birgit Schiotz to the Executive Committee, WILPF, Oct. 7, 1949, Reel 81, WILPF (International) Records; A. Bohr, "War Years," p. 214; Gowing, "Niels Bohr and Nuclear Weapons," p. 275; *Times* (London), Aug. 11, 1945.

13. Bohr to Oppenheimer, Nov. 9, 1945, Box 21, Oppenheimer Papers; N. Bohr, "A Challenge to Civilization"; N. Bohr, "Science and Civilization." For other indications of what one of Bohr's students called his "intense preoccupation" with the Bomb, see Pais, "Reminiscences from the Post-war Years," p. 216; Gowing, *Britain and Atomic Energy*, pp. 365–66.

14. Marvel to SecState, Apr. 23, 1946, Box 191, Oppenheimer Papers; Bohr to Baruch, June 1, 1946, Box 61, Baruch Papers.

15. Robert Oppenheimer to George Marshall, May 20, 1948, and "Memorandum of Conversation" (Apr. 26, 1948), Box 77, SASSAE, DOS Records; Bohr to Oppenheimer,

Oct. 5, 1947, and Bohr to Marshall, June 10, 1948, Box 21, Oppenheimer Papers; Gowing, "Niels Bohr and Nuclear Weapons," p. 276.

16. Stucky, *August 6, 1945*, p. 112; "The Quarter's Polls," *Public Opinion Quarterly* 13 (Spring 1949): 155; External Research Staff, DOS, "Views of Western European Nations on Use of the Atomic Bomb" (Oct. 16, 1950), p. 2, Box 7, SASSAE, DOS Records.

17. Office of Intelligence Research, DOS, "Survey of Western European Opinion on the Atom Bomb as an Immoral Weapon" (Feb. 13, 1951), p. 12, and External Research Staff, DOS, "Views of Western European Nations on Use of the Atomic Bomb" (Oct. 16, 1950), p. 3, Box 7, SASSAE, DOS Records; Butterworth to SecState, Dec. 1, 1950, 711.5611/ 12-150, DOS Records.

18. Substantial majorities supported the atomic bombing of Japan in nations aligned with the United States during World War II (e.g., Canada, France, and Great Britain), while in enemy nations substantial majorities opposed the atomic bombing (e.g., Italy and Germany). In Sweden, a neutral power, support for the action fell in between.

19. Vera Brittain, "W.R.I. talk" (Jan. 1946), "War Resisters International" folder, Brittain Papers; Andersson and Lindkvist, "Peace Movement in Sweden," p. 31; Lindkvist, "Mobilization Peaks and Declines," pp. 155–56.

20. Minutes of the meeting of the European Executive Committee, International FOR, Sept. 23–26, 1946, and minutes of the International FOR Council meeting, Mar. 23–29, 1946, pp. 12–13, Box 5, Series C, Sayre Papers; Minutes of a meeting of the International Council, WRI, July 26–29, 1947, Box 2, WRI Records; Sayre, "Pacifist Christianity," p. 113.

21. "Report from Sweden" (1946), Reel 84, WILPF (International) Records; "News from National Sections," *Pax International* 17 (Jan.–Feb. 1951): 7; *PN*, Jan. 2, 1948; Lindkvist, "Mobilization Peaks and Declines," p. 156.

22. Fogelström, *Kampen för fred*, p. 234; Naima Sahlbom to Kathleen Innes, Aug. 28, 1945, Reel 84, WILPF (International) Records.

23. "Declaration accepted at the meeting of the Central Board of the Swedish section" (1946?), Reel 84, WILPF (International) Records; Stahle, *Internationella Kvinnoförbundet för Fred och Frihet*, p. 25; Fogelström, *Kampen för fred*, p. 238.

24. Lindkvist, "Mobilization Peaks and Declines," p. 156. For a collection of articles showing Swedish thought on world federation during World War II, see Enander et al., eds., *Riktlinjer för en världsfederation, ett inlägg i diskussionen om världens framtid*. For a postwar work on world government, see Holm, *FN och världsfederalismen*.

25. "Zodiac," *CC* 2 (July 1949): 480; Henry Usborne, "Newsletter for Overseas" (Mar. 14, 1948), Crusade for World Government Records; *PN*, Sept. 17, 1948, Jan. 7, 1949.

26. "Reply to Questionnaire from the United Nations," Box 52, Cousins Papers, Los Angeles; "Zodiac," *CC* 2 (July 1949): 480; "Zodiac," *CC* 3 (June 1950): 616; *PN*, Apr. 27, 1951.

27. Hugh S. Cumming, Jr., to SecState, Dec. 9, 1947, 811.2423/12-947, and Matthews to SecState, Mar. 18, 1948, 811.2423/3-1848, DOS Records; Fogelström, *Kampen för fred*, p. 240.

28. Robert-Akesson to Annalee Stewart, Nov. 7, 1946, Reel 50, and Birgitta Bellander to the Presidents, WILPF, Reel 84, WILPF (International) Records; Robert-Akesson to Friend, Aug. 30, 1947, Swedish Peace Campaign Committee Records.

29. Robert-Akesson, "Proclamation II" (1948) and Robert-Akesson, "International Peace Propaganda Campaign" (1949), Swedish Peace Campaign Committee Records; *PN*, Sept. 23, 1949.

30. " 'Peace' is not a popular word," one pacifist complained in August 1945. " 'Preach peace to the Germans' folk are likely to say." Another reported: "In many ways, opinion

in general has moved away from a pacifistic standpoint." Haagerup, "Nordic Peace Movements," p. 159; Myrtle Wright to Barbara Duncan Harris and Kathleen Innes, Aug. 20, 1945, and Sigrid Helliesen Lund to Gertrude Baer, Oct. 30, 1945, Reel 81, WILPF (International) Records.

31. Lund, *Resistance in Norway*; Sigrid Helliesen Lund to Gertrude Baer, Feb. 14, Oct. 30, 1945, Reel 81, WILPF (International) Records; Foster, *Women for All Seasons*, pp. 22–23; *PN*, Aug. 8, 1947.

32. Myrtle Wright to Percy Bartlett, Mar. 11, 1950, Box 37, Series B, Sayre Papers; Aasney Alnaes to Anne Bloch, Mar. 14, 1949, Reel 81, WILPF (International) Records; "News from Sections," *Pax International* 16 (Mar.–Apr. 1950): 3; "News from National Sections," *Pax International* 17 (Jan.–Feb. 1951): 6–7.

33. Sigrid Helliesen Lund to Gertrude Baer, Oct. 30, 1945, WILPF (International) Records; Edwin Listor to John Nevin Sayre, Dec. 12, 1945, and "The Norwegian Peace Council" (n.d.), Box 37, Series B, and minutes of the International FOR Council meeting, Mar. 23–29, 1946, p. 8, Box 5, Series C, Sayre Papers; *PN*, Apr. 6, 1951.

34. *News Letter*, no. 62 (Mar. 1949), pp. 1–3; Foster, *Women for All Seasons*, pp. 26–27; Marie Lous-Mohr to Mrs. McCorkel, May 22, 1950, Reel 51, WILPF (International) Records; Myrtle Wright, "Norway: Sold American," *Fellowship* 16 (July 1950): 3–4; Myrtle Wright to Percy Bartlett, Mar. 11, 1950, Box 37, Series B, Sayre Papers.

35. "Zodiac," *CC* 2 (July 1949): 480; Henry Usborne, "Newsletter for Overseas" (Mar. 14, 1948), Crusade for World Government Records; "Reply to Questionnaire from the United Nations," Box 52, Cousins Papers, Los Angeles; Buchanan and Cantril, *How Nations See Each Other*, p. 62.

36. Ole Olden to Percy Bartlett, May 23, 1950, Box 37, Series B, Sayre Papers; Aasny Alnaes, "Report of the Norwegian Section—November 1948," Reel 81, WILPF (International) Records.

37. Marie Lous-Mohr to Emily G. Balch, Sept. 17, 1947, Reel 50, and Birgit Schiotz to the Executive Committee, WILPF, Oct. 7, 1949, Aasny Alnaes, "Report of the Norwegian Section—November 1948," "Report of the Norwegian Section on the Problem of Norway's Joining the Atlantic Union," and "Norway's Political, Social, and Economic Development, 1946–49" (1949), Reel 81, WILPF (International) Records; *PN*, Aug. 12, 1949.

38. Marselis C. Parsons, Jr., to SecState, Feb. 16, 1950, 711.5611/2-1650, and Villard to SecState, Feb. 27, 1950, 711.5611/2-2750, DOS Records; Office of Intelligence Research, DOS, "Survey of Western European Opinion on the Atom Bomb as an Immoral Weapon" (Feb. 13, 1951), pp. 12–13, Box 7, SASSAE, DOS Records.

39. Verkuil, *De grote illusie*, pp. 10–15; Beaton, *Twenty Years' Work*, pp. 20–22; Minutes of the International FOR meeting, Mar. 23–29, 1946, pp. 9–10, Box 5, Series C, Sayre Papers; Sayre, "Pacifist Christianity," p. 115; J. B. Hugenholtz, "Peace Action in Holland," *One World* 1 (Aug. 1946): 44.

40. Hugenholtz argued that the nationalist and militarist spirit engendered by the war rendered the Dutch less accessible to the pacifist message, a point made independently by Vera Brittain, who visited Holland at the end of the war. *News Letter*, no. 55 (June 1947), p. 6; Vera Brittain, "W.R.I. talk" (Jan. 1946), "War Resisters International" folder, Brittain Papers; Brittain, *Testament of Experience*, p. 387.

41. J. Repelaer van Driel to Gertrude Baer and Clara Ragaz, Nov. 24, 1945, and C. Ramondt-Hirschmann to Anne Bloch, Nov. 5, 1948, Reel 75, WILPF (International) Records.

42. Krijn Strijd, "Kerk en Vrede," *News Letter*, no. 64 (September 1949), p. 9; J. B. Hugenholtz, "Peace Action in Holland," *One World* 1 (Aug. 1946): 44; van den Dungen, "Johannes Bernardus Theodorus Hugenholtz," pp. 431–32.

43. C. Ramondt-Hirschmann to Anne Bloch, Nov. 19, 1948, Reel 75, WILPF (International) Records; Percy W. Bartlett, "International News," *Reconciliation* [Great Britain] 27 (Dec. 1950): 1011.

44. "Dutch Christians Protest," *Reconciliation* [Great Britain] 27 (July 1950): 884; Hugenholtz to John Nevin Sayre, Dec. 28, 1945, June 17, 1950, and Hugenholtz to Einstein, Nov. 2, 1945, Box 36, Series B, Sayre Papers.

45. *PN*, Jan. 10, 17, Aug. 1, 1947, Jan. 21, 1949; *News Letter*, no. 62 (Mar. 1949), pp. 6–9; *Peacemaker* [Australia], June 1949, May 1961; Brittain, *Rebel Passion*, p. 166; Verkuil, *De grote illusie*, p. 23.

46. Oliver Johnson to Einstein, Feb. 6, 1948, Box 12, ECAS Records, Chicago; M. Minnaert, "Opinions of Dutch Scientists About the International Control of Atomic Energy," *Atomic Scientists' News* 1 (1947–48?): 84–86; "Opinions on Atomic Energy from the Netherlands," *BAS* 4 (Mar. 1948): 87; "A Letter from Europe," *BAS* 4 (Jan. 1948): 6.

47. See, for example, Knös, *Wereld federatie van alle landen met nationale ontwapening en internationale politiemacht*; Brent, *Federatie van de wereld*.

48. Henry Usborne, "Newsletter for Overseas" (Mar. 14, 1948), Crusade for World Government Records; Illegible to Bertrand Russell, Oct. 7, 1947, Class 560, Russell Archives 1; G. Bernstein, "World Government—Progress Report," p. 662; Buchanan and Cantril, *How Nations See Each Other*, p. 62.

49. "Reply to Questionnaire from the United Nations," Box 52, Cousins Papers, Los Angeles; Minutes of the meetings of the World Citizens' International Secretariat, Dec. 31, 1950, Jan. 1, 1951, Davis Papers.

50. Verkuil, *De grote illusie*, pp. 34–37.

51. Office of Intelligence Research, DOS, "Survey of Western European Opinion on the Atom Bomb as an Immoral Weapon" (Feb. 13, 1951), p. 11, Box 7, SASSAE, DOS Records.

52. "The Quarter's Polls," *Public Opinion Quarterly* 13 (Spring 1949): 155; Robert Coe to SecState, Feb. 2, 1950, 711.5611/2-250, DOS Records.

53. Brittain, *Rebel Passion*, pp. 164, 181; Anne Bloch to Madame Leruitte, June 14, 1949, Reel 57, WILPF (International) Records; Lubelski-Bernard, "Hem Day," p. 398; Minutes of the meeting of the International Council, WRI, July 26–29, 1947, Box 2, WRI Records; *PN*, Aug. 26, 1949.

54. See, for example, Haesaerts, *L'état mondiale, essai de synthèse politique*.

55. "World Government Crusade," p. 103; "Zodiac," *CC* 3 (Apr. 1950): 504; *World Government Highlights*, p. 40.

56. "Reply to Questionnaire from the United Nations," Box 52, Cousins Papers, Los Angeles; G. Davis, *World Is My Country*, p. 65; A. Lilienthal, *Which Way to World Government?*, p. 22.

57. "Feuille 'Paratomic' Coforces" (1948), "Plan d'Action 'Coforces'" (1948), and "Congrès de l'Union Fédérale" (1948), Reel 57, WILPF (International) Records.

58. Office of Intelligence Research, DOS, "Survey of Western European Opinion on the Atom Bomb as an Immoral Weapon" (Feb. 13, 1951), p. 11, Box 7, SASSAE, DOS Records; *NYT*, Oct. 2, 1949.

59. "A Short Notice on the Swiss Peace Council" (Mar. 2, 1946), Conseil Suisse des Associations pour la Paix Records; Brassel and Tanner, "Zur Geschichte der Friedensbewegung in der Schweiz," p. 59; Minutes of the meeting of the International Council, WRI, Dec. 28–31, 1946, Box 1, WRI Records; *PN*, Aug. 8, 1947, Mar. 19, 1948; Leander, "Die Friedensbewegung in der Schweiz (1945 bis 1980)," pp. 12–14.

60. *Krieg oder Frieden Heute: Erklärung der Arbeitsgemeinschaft entschiedener Friedensvereinigungen* (Sept. 1950), Reel 88, WILPF (International) Records; "An Impor-

tant Swiss Initiative," *Pax et Libertas* 17 (Nov.–Dec. 1951): 8. See also Cammett, "Jules Humbert-Droz," pp. 438–39.

61. Baratta, *Strengthening the United Nations*, p. 156; Bourquin, *Vers une nouvelle société des nations*; *World Government Highlights*, p. 42.

62. Minutes of the meetings of the World Citizens' International Secretariat, Dec. 31, 1950, Jan. 1, 1951, Davis Papers; "The Conference Day by Day," joint issue of *Parlement, Across Frontiers*, and *Weltstaat*, Apr. 1950, p. 8; de Rougement, *Last Trump*, pp. 145–46.

63. Maislinger, "Peace Movement in a Neutral Country," p. 60; Kaspar Mayr, "Interim Report" (Aug. 26, 1949), Box 2, Series B, Sayre Papers.

64. *PN*, Nov. 4, 1949; Osterreichische Friedensgesellschaft, *Denkschrift an die österreichische Bundesregierung über die Wiederaufrüstung Österreichs* (May 1947), Reel 56, WILPF (International) Records.

65. Minutes of a meeting of the International Council, WRI, July 26–29, 1947, Box 2, WRI Records; Kaspar Mayr, "Interim Report" (Aug. 26, 1949), Box 2, Series B, Sayre Papers; "News from Sections," *Pax International* 16 (Mar.–Apr. 1950): 1.

66. *PN*, May 27, Nov. 4, 1949.

67. "Reply to Questionnaire from the United Nations," Box 52, Cousins Papers, Los Angeles; *Crusade Contact* 1 (Apr. 1949): 4, Crusade for World Government Records; Hilde Haslbrunner and Mela Deutsch-Brady to Andrée Jouve, Dec. 30, 1948, Reel 56, WILPF (International) Records.

68. R. Laurence, "Johannes Ude"; Wilhelm Scharf to John Nevin Sayre, Jan. 8, 1947, Box 1, Series B, Sayre Papers; "No More Hiroshimas!" (1948), World Peace Day Records.

69. Erhardt to SecState, Feb. 7, 1950, 711.5611/2-750, DOS Records.

70. Fellner, "Hans Thirring"; V. F. Weisskopf, Review of *Die Geschichte der Atom-Bombe*, *BAS* 4 (Apr. 1948): 105; Hans Thirring, *Stellungnahme zum Pariser Weltfriedenskongress* (1949), pp. 3–6, Oesterreichische Friedensgesellschaft Records.

71. Kaspar Mayr, "Interim Report" (Aug. 26, 1949), Box 2, Series B, Sayre Papers; Office of Intelligence Research, DOS, "Survey of Western European Opinion on the Atom Bomb as an Immoral Weapon" (Feb. 13, 1951), p. 10, Box 7, SASSAE, DOS Records.

72. "Editorial," *Pax* (Easter 1949), p. 1; "February Report," *Pax* (Easter 1950), p. 23.

73. R. M. Beaudry to SecState, Nov. 12, 1946, 811.2423/11-1246, Henry Clinton Reed to SecState, Mar. 3, 1950, 711.5611/3-350, and Henry Clinton Reed to SecState, Feb. 7, 1950, 711.5611/2-750, DOS Records.

74. Office of Intelligence Research, DOS, "Survey of Western European Opinion on the Atom Bomb as an Immoral Weapon" (Feb. 13, 1951), p. 16, Box 7, SASSAE, DOS Records; John Wesley Jones to SecState, Feb. 9, 1950, 711.5611/2-950, DOS Records.

Chapter 8

Epigraph: Iyer, ed., *Moral and Political Writings*, 2: 455.

1. Stevenson, *Towards a Christian International*, pp. 56–57; Brock, *Twentieth Century Pacifism*, pp. 105–6; *News Letter*, no. 66 (Mar. 1950), p. 8.

2. The letter originally appeared on Nov. 26, 1947, in the Soviet *New Times*, signed by Sergei Vavilov, A. N. Frumkin, A. F. Joffe, and A. N. Semyonov. "Open Letter to Dr. Einstein—From Four Soviet Scientists," *BAS* 4 (Feb. 1948): 34, 37–38.

3. Einstein himself defended his position in Albert Einstein, "A Reply to the Soviet Scientists," *BAS* 4 (Feb. 1948): 35–37.

4. I. I. Beliakevich to Committee of Foreign Correspondence, June 10, 1947, enclosure in E. E. Minett to the Trustees and Officers, ECAS, Sept. 15, 1947, Pauling Papers; Kurcha-

tov, "Preface," in Lebedinsky, ed., *What Russian Scientists Say About Fallout*, p. 11; Orlov, *Dangerous Thoughts*, p. 98.

5. Personal interview with Sergei Kapitza, June 28, 1990; Z. Medvedev, *Soviet Science*, pp. 46–47, 50–52.

6. Klose, *Russia and the Russians*, pp. 142–43; Sakharov, *Memoirs*, pp. 97, 100, 116, 577.

7. Telephone interview with Pavel Litvinov, Oct. 7, 1990; "Atomic Energy Control Literature Reaches Russian Scientists" (Dec. 7, 1946), Box 12, ECAS Records, Chicago.

8. Sakharov, *Memoirs*, pp. 108, 125.

9. *NYT*, July 11, 1956; Kramish, *Atomic Energy in the Soviet Union*, pp. 105, 109–10.

10. Personal interview with Sergei Kapitza, June 28, 1990; "Peter Kapitsa: The Scientist Who Talked Back to Stalin," *BAS* 46 (Apr. 1990): 27–32; Holloway, "The Scientist and the Tyrant," pp. 24–25; Kapitza, *Experiment, Theory, Practice*, p. xxiv.

11. Years later, Kapitza told Herbert York, an American physicist, that his refusal to work on the Bomb was not based on "political or moral reasons." Instead, he believed that "since your country had the bomb, my country would have to have it too." Kapitza to Khrushchev, Sept. 22, 1955, in "Peter Kapitsa," p. 32; Sakharov, *Memoirs*, p. 302; York, *Advisors*, p. 38; personal interview with Sergei Kapitza, June 28, 1990.

12. *NYT*, June 24, 1946, Sept. 26, 1949; Weart, *Nuclear Fear*, pp. 117, 136; personal interview with Anatoly Belyayev, June 27, 1990.

13. Alan Kirk to SecState, Oct. 5, 1949, Box 34, SASSAE, DOS Records.

14. Amelia Kurlandska to John Nevin Sayre, Aug. 28, 1947, Box 38, Series B, and minutes of the European Executive Committee, International FOR, Sept. 23–26, 1946, Box 5, Series C, Sayre Papers; Minutes of a meeting of the International Council, WRI, July 26–29, 1947, Box 2, WRI Records; *PN*, Aug. 8, 1947; Vera Bednarova to Friends, July 13, 1947, and Vera Bednarova, "La rapport de la W.I.L.P.F. section Brno/Tchécoslovaquie" (Jan. 1, 1948), Reel 60, WILPF (International) Records.

15. Beaton, *Twenty Years' Work*, pp. 24–25; Brittain, *Rebel Passion*, pp. 143–45; *PN*, June 24, 1955; John Nevin Sayre, "Pacifist Christianity in Europe," *Fellowship* 12 (July 1946): 115; Minutes of the International FOR Council meeting, Mar. 23–29, 1946, Box 5, Series C, Sayre Papers.

16. Oliver Johnson to Einstein, Feb. 6, 1948, Box 12, ECAS Records, Chicago; "A Scientist Speaks for the Small Nations," *BAS* 4 (Feb. 1948): 62.

17. Peter Krehel, "Report from Central and Eastern Europe," *CC* 2 (Nov. 1948): 133–34; *PN*, June 30, 1950; "Zodiac," *CC* 3 (Sept. 1949): 112; "Zodiac," *CC* 2 (Oct. 1948): 120.

18. This issue is addressed at greater length in Chapter 16.

19. *PN*, Dec. 16, 1949; *New Zealand Christian Pacifist*, July 1952; Merritt and Merritt, eds., *Public Opinion in Semisovereign Germany*, pp. 141–42; Allen, *Germany East*, p. 93.

20. Brittain, *Rebel Passion*, pp. 64, 101–2; Francisco E. Estrello, "The Fellowship of Reconciliation in Mexico: Annual Report, August 1946–July 1947," Fraternidad de Reconciliacion y Paz en Mexico Records; *News Letter*, no. 62 (Mar. 1949), p. 15.

21. *News Letter*, no. 59 (June 1948), p. 11; "Regional Conference Organized by the Argentine Section in February and March 1946," Argentina WRI Records; *PN*, Aug. 8, 1947, Aug. 26, 1949; "News from National Sections," *Pax International* 17 (Jan.–Feb. 1951): 6; Brittain, *Rebel Passion*, pp. 195–96.

22. *Hindustan Times*, Aug. 7, 1949, World Peace Day Records; *PN*, Sept. 23, 1949.

23. Minutes of the meeting of the International Council, WRI, Dec. 28–31, 1946, Box 1, WRI Records; *PN*, Aug. 11, 1950; Brittain, *Rebel Passion*, p. 214; Vera Brittain to A. J. Muste, Feb. 16, 1950, "Replies, February 1950" folder, Brittain Papers.

24. K. K. Chandy, "The Fellowship of Reconciliation in India" (1980), FOR (India) Records; "Condensation of Report of K. K. Chandy on the Indian Fellowship of Reconciliation" and Minutes of Indian FOR working committee meetings of June 16, July 21, Oct. 20, 1951, Box 30, and Charles C. Raven, "My Visit to the East" (Mar. 14, 1956), Box 29, Series B, Sayre Papers; Brittain, *Rebel Passion*, pp. 215–17.

25. Iyer, ed., *Moral and Political Writings*, 2: 455, 457; Fischer, ed., *Essential Gandhi*, pp. 335–36. See also *Mahatma Gandhi on Nuclear Arms*; *NYT*, July 8, 1946; *PN*, Oct. 10, 1947.

26. In a thoughtful report on the WMWFG in 1952, one world federalist wrote: "The newly arising nations of the under developed areas of Asia and Africa strenuously oppose transferring governmental powers in the economic and social fields to an international authority. Conscious of their newly won nationalism they will take no risk of new foreign domination through a world government of broad powers." They were also wary, he claimed, of freezing the status quo because of their opposition to colonialism. Harry Hollins III to Norman Cousins, Oct. 1952, Box 54, Cousins Papers, Los Angeles.

27. See, for example, Arce, *Ahora*; Torre Espinosa, *Un mundo nuevo, estados unidas del mundo*; Vergara Robles, *Panamérica en la orbita universal*.

28. Pierre Hovelaque, "World Federalism and Latin America," *CC* 3 (June 1950): 567–70; *PN*, June 18, 1948, Dec. 2, 1949; *Pacifismo*, Dec. 1949; "The Conference Day by Day," joint issue of *Parlement, Across Frontiers*, and *Weltstaat*, Apr. 1950, p. 8; "Reply to Questionnaire from the United Nations," Box 52, Cousins Papers, Los Angeles.

29. Buchanan and Cantril, *How Nations See Each Other*, p. 62; Firuz Kazemzadeh, "Middle East: What of the Night?" *CC* 4 (Apr. 1951): 491–92; "Reply to Questionnaire from the United Nations," Box 52, Cousins Papers, Los Angeles; "Federal Movement Spreading in Turkey," Press Release no. 10 (Sept. 9, 1948), Crusade for World Government Records.

30. "African Letters," *CC* 3 (Summer 1949): 70–71; Eyo Ita, "Africa and One World," *CC* 4 (Apr. 1951): 495.

31. Marguerite Wardlow, "The Indian Approach," *CC* 4 (Apr. 1951): 482–83; "Indian Socialists and World Government," *CC* 3 (Apr. 1950): 495; "Zodiac," *CC* 4 (Aug. 1950): 56; Cord Meyer, Jr., "A Progress Report on World Federation," *BAS* 5 (Oct. 1949): 282. Indian world federalist tracts of the time include Bhalerao, *A Plea, Urgent Entreaty, for World Government*; Chaudhuri, *A Constitution for World Government*; Radhakrishnan, *Is This Peace?*

32. Sal Gene Marzullo, "Letter from the Philippines," *CC* 2 (June 1949): 434–35; Sal Gene Marzullo, "Report from the Philippines," *CC* 3 (Nov. 1949): 195–98; "Reply to Questionnaire from the United Nations," Box 52, Cousins Papers, Los Angeles.

33. Rafael Grinfeld to National Committee on Atomic Information, July 23, 1946, Box 16, FAS Records.

34. "Statement issued by the Science Society of China" (Dec. 31, 1945), "Statement issued by the Natural Science Society of China and the Chinese Association of Scientific Workers" (Jan. 3, 1946), and "Statement on Control of Atomic Energy issued by the Council of the Chinese Physical Society" (Jan. 12, 1946), Box 12, and "Proclamation of the Joint Annual Conference of Seven Chinese Scientific Societies 1947" and H. C. Zen and Y. T. Loo to William Higinbotham, Oct. 15, 1947, Box 16, FAS Records.

35. S. Walker, ed., *First One Hundred Days*, p. 17; Stucky, *August 6, 1945*, p. 111; John M. Cabot to SecState, Aug. 14, 1945, 811.2423/8-1445, and E.G.T. to SecState, Sept. 6, 1945, 811.2423/9-645, DOS Records.

36. From Colombia, the U.S. embassy reported that the bulk of press reaction to the atomic bomb "seemed to indicate considerable fear over the possible consequences of the

employment of this weapon in another world war." W.A.W. to SecState, Aug. 14, 1945, 811.2423/8-1445, and John C. Wiley to SecState, Aug. 24, 1945, 811.2423/8-2445, DOS Records.

37. Frank P. Corrigan to SecState, Aug. 14, 1945, 811.2423/8-1445, DOS Records; "World Opinion," *International Journal of Opinion and Attitude Research* I (Sept. 1947): 141.

38. Huddle to SecState, Sept. 28, 1949, Wiley to SecState, Sept. 28, Oct. 11, 1949, Thurston to SecState, Sept. 27, 1949, and Strong to SecState, Oct. 9, 1949, Box 34, SAS-SAE, DOS Records.

39. Cowen to SecState, Sept. 28, 1949, Merrell to SecState, Sept. 28, 1949, Pinkerton to SecState, Oct. 11, 1949, Hill to SecState, Sept. 29, 1949, Waynick to SecState, Sept. 26, 1949, Streeper to SecState, Oct. 13, 1949, and Harrison to SecState, Sept. 28, 1949, Box 34, SASSAE, DOS Records; *NYT*, Oct. 2, 1949.

40. Donovan to SecState, Feb. 16, 1950, 711.5611/2-1650, Griffis to SecState, Feb. 6, 1950, 711.5611/2-650, Strong to SecState, Feb. 11, 1950, 711.5611/2-1150, and James Webb, Jr., to SecState, Feb. 19, 1950, 711.5611/2-1950, DOS Records.

Chapter 9

Epigraph: *NYT*, Feb. 25, 1950.

1. Bussey and Tims, *Women's International League for Peace and Freedom*, pp. 192–93, 202; Gertrude Bussey, Marie Lous-Mohr, and Agnes Stapledon to Vera Brittain, Oct. 4, 1949, "Women's International League for Peace and Freedom" folder, Brittain Papers; *PN*, Aug. 13, 1948.

2. *News Letter*, no. 61 (Dec. 1948), p. 6; Minutes of the Executive Committee meeting, British FOR, Oct. 19, 1949, Reel 5, FOR (Great Britain) Records; Bussey and Tims, *Women's International League for Peace and Freedom*, p. 207; Emily G. Balch to the International Executive Committee, May 4, 1951, Reel 51, WILPF (International) Records.

3. Minutes of the National Council meeting, United States FOR, May 29–31, 1947, Box 3, FOR (United States) Records; Rajendra Prasad, "Sevagram Pacifist Conference," *One World* 3 (Apr.–May 1949): 40–42; *Sevagram Pacifist Conference* (Calcutta, 1949), pp. 4–5, 14–16, World Pacifist Meeting Records; Brittain, *Testament of Experience*, pp. 460–71; *PN*, Dec. 9, 16, 23, 30, 1949, Jan. 6, 13, 1950.

4. Vera Brittain, "Message for Hiroshima Day Meeting" (1950), "Replies, August 1950" folder, Brittain Papers; Brittain, *Search After Sunrise*, pp. 83–84; "Reports of World Pacifist Meeting, December 1949," Box 32, Series B, Sayre Papers.

5. Grace Rhoads, "The World Pacifist Meeting," *Pax International* 16 (Mar.–Apr. 1950):4; Brittain, *Search After Sunrise*, p. 78; Beauson Tseng to Friend, Sept. 15, 1950, "Tseng, Beauson" folder, and Muste to Vera Brittain, Jan. 19, 1950, "Muste, A. J." folder, Brittain Papers.

6. Henry A. Boorse, "Two International Scientific Meetings in England," *BAS* 2 (Sept. 1, 1946): 6; J. H. Rush, "Summary of Council Sessions of the Federation of American Scientists, N.Y. City, Sept. 22, 23, 1946," *BAS* 2 (Oct. 1, 1946): 25; A. Smith, *A Peril and a Hope*, pp. 337–38.

7. A. Smith, *A Peril and a Hope*, p. 338; W. A. Higinbotham to Paul Doty, Nov. 12, 1946, Jan. 17, 1947, Box 65, FAS Records.

8. Rabinowitch to John [Simpson?], Feb. 11, 1946, Box 2, Rabinowitch Papers, Albany; J. H. Rush to Paul Doty, Jan. 19, 1947, Box 65, FAS Records.

9. Leo Szilard " 'A Letter in the Open' (Draft of an Article, August 31, 1950)," in

Hawkins, Greb, and Szilard, eds., *Toward a Livable World*, pp. 111–12; Szilard to Charles Bohlen, June 16, 1960, Box 19, Szilard Papers.

10. "Report on the Progress of the Committee for Foreign Correspondence," enclosure in A. S. Bishop to Richard Tolman, Jan. 21, 1947, Box 32, SASSAE, DOS Records.

11. Peierls to President, FAS, Mar. 24, 1950, and Higinbotham to Peierls, July 14, 1950, Box 28, FAS Records; "Atomic Bull Session," *FAS Newsletter*, Oct. 24, 1950, p. 3; William A. Higinbotham, "Scientists Discuss War and Peace," *BAS* 6 (Nov. 1950): 350.

12. Pais, "Reminiscences from the Post-war Years," pp. 224–25; Rozental, "The Forties and the Fifties," p. 177; N. Bohr, *Open Letter to the United Nations*.

13. A. Bohr, "War Years," p. 213; "The Political Youth in Denmark on Professor Niels Bohr's Open Letter to the United Nations" (June 16, 1950) and David Hill to Allen Shapley, June 21, 1950, Box 28, FAS Records; Gowing, "Niels Bohr and Nuclear Weapons," p. 277.

14. Aage Bohr to Robert Oppenheimer, June 27, 1950, Box 20, Peierls to the Editor, *Manchester Guardian*, June 17, 1950, Box 57, and Higinbotham to Robert Oppenheimer, July 4, 1950, Box 120, Oppenheimer Papers; Aage Bohr to A. H. Shapley, June 26, 1950, and David Hill to Shapley, June 21, 1950, Box 28, FAS Records; William A. Higinbotham, "Scientists Discuss War and Peace," *BAS* 6 (Nov. 1950): 350.

15. Laursen, *Federalism and World Order*, pp. 2–9, 23–26, 39–56; *PN*, Sept. 5, 1947, Sept. 17, 1948; de Rusett, *Strengthening the Framework*, pp. 71–77; Schuman, *Commonwealth of Man*, pp. 443–45; *World Federalism: 10th Anniversary Congress* (Aug. 1957), p. 8, World Association of World Federalists Records.

16. A. Lilienthal, *Which Way to World Government?*, pp. 26, 43–45; A. R. Brent, "Right Road to European Federation," *CC* 1 (May 1948): 371–73; Egon von Kamarasy, "Survey of European Federalism," *CC* 2 (Mar. 1949): 304–8; de Rusett, *Strengthening the Framework*, pp. 82–83.

17. "Reply to Questionnaire from the United Nations," Box 52, Cousins Papers, Los Angeles. Slightly different figures are given in *PN*, June 30, 1950.

18. Laursen, *Federalism and World Order*, pp. 23–26, 74–77, 91–92; *PN*, Sept. 16, 1949. For additional antinuclear rhetoric, see "Presidential Address for Peoples' World Convention Conference" (Dec. 30, 1950), Box 2, WMWFG Records; *Christian Science Monitor*, Sept. 25, 1948; *Humanity*, Aug. 1950, pp. 398–99.

19. "Subject for action . . ." (1950), Crusade for World Government Records.

20. For discussion of these issues, see A. Lilienthal, *Which Way to World Government?*, pp. 26–28; "Atlantic Pacific?" *World Government News*, Jan. 1949, pp. 8–9; *Humanity*, no. 12 (Dec. 1948), p. 16; Elisabeth Mann Borgese to John Boyd Orr, Feb. 22, 1950, Mar. 13, 1951, Box 2, WMWFG Records; Harris Wofford, "Montreux: World Movement in Microcosm," *CC* 1 (Nov. 1947): 161–63; "Zodiac," *CC* 3 (Oct. 1949): 164–66; Elisabeth Mann Borgese, "Stockholm: Turning Point," *CC* 3 (Dec. 1949): 231–34; Laursen, *Federalism and World Order*, pp. 79–90.

21. Davis to Elisabeth Mann Borgese, Box 10, Committee to Frame a World Constitution Records; Boyd Orr to Elisabeth Mann Borgese, Mar. 2, 1950, Box 2, WMWFG Records.

22. G. A. Borgese, "A Report on Europe," *CC* 2 (Dec. 1948): 163–65; E. M. Borgese to Robert M. Hutchins, Sept. 14, 1948, Box 13, Hutchins Papers; "Reply to Questionnaire from the United Nations," Box 52, and Harry Hollins III to Norman Cousins, Oct. 1952, Box 54, Cousins Papers, Los Angeles.

23. "Reply to Questionnaire from the United Nations," Box 52, Cousins Papers, Los Angeles; Laursen, *Federalism and World Order*, p. 73; Buchanan and Cantril, *How Nations See Each Other*, p. 62.

24. "World Opinion on World Government," *CC* 1 (Sept. 1947): 101–3; "World Opinion on World Government," *CC* 1 (Aug. 1947): 69–71; *PN*, Apr. 20, 1951.

25. *Pacifismo*, Dec. 1949; "Taking Bearings," *CC* 4 (Apr. 1951): 449; "Geneva, 1950," *CC* 4 (Mar. 1951): 432; Baratta, *Strengthening the United Nations*, pp. 7, 82.

26. John Nevin Sayre, "Pacifism at Amsterdam," *Fellowship* 14 (Nov. 1948): 1–2; John Nevin Sayre, "Can War Be Just?" *News Letter*, no. 62 (Mar. 1949), p. 16.

27. *NYT*, Feb. 25, 1950; Hiebert, *Impact of Atomic Energy*, p. 242.

28. For secret reassurances to the U.S. government by Catholic prelates, see Tittmann to SecState, Oct. 25, 1945, 811.2423/10-2545, and Robert E. Wilson to SecState, Feb. 13, 1951, 711.5611/2-1351, DOS Records.

29. Musto, *Catholic Peace Tradition*, pp. 184–86; *NYT*, Feb. 9, 1948, Sept. 25, 1949; Office of Intelligence Research, DOS, "Survey of Western European Opinion on the Atom Bomb as an Immoral Weapon" (Feb. 13, 1951), pp. 14–15, Box 7, SASSAE, DOS Records.

30. Bernard Lalande, "The Development of Pax Christi International from 1945–1965," pp. 1–2, and "A Dialogue with Eileen Egan," Pax Christi International Records; Musto, *Catholic Peace Tradition*, p. 260; Zahn, *War, Conscience and Dissent*, pp. 91–93.

31. "Peace Front Among Buddhists," *Fellowship* 17 (Dec. 1951): 21.

32. These divisions among peace organizations are discussed at greater length in the preceding chapters covering national movements. For the WRI's qualms about world government, see Grace M. Beaton, Letter to Sections, Jan. 31, 1949, Box 3, WRI Records; *PN*, Aug. 26, 1949.

33. See, for example, Emily G. Balch to Miss Josephy, Sept. 23, 1946, Reel 50, WILPF (International) Records.

34. Nora Bremerstent to the Head-office, Geneva, June 21, 1950, and Mrs. Roy McCorkel to Bremerstent, June 23, 1950, Reel 60, WILPF (International) Records.

35. Homer Jack, "April 21, 1952: Interview with Albert Einstein in Princeton, New Jersey," Box 54, Series IVB, Jack Papers; "Dedication to Gandhi," *Monde Fédéré*, Oct. 1948.

36. "I.L.C.O.P.," *News Letter*, no. 66 (Mar. 1950), pp. 12–13; "Report on the Meeting of the World Union of Peace Organizations . . . March 24–25, 1949" and "Brief Statement Concerning ILCOP," Box 12, International Peace Bureau Records.

37. Denis Barritt, "Peace Movements Face the Atomic Challenge," *Pax* (Christmas 1949), pp. 17–20.

38. *PN*, Aug. 5, Sept. 23, 1949; "Observe August 6 Throughout the World," *Fellowship* 16 (July 1950): 25.

39. Huxley to Frank Olmstead, July 21, 1946, Box 16, War Resisters League Records.

Chapter 10

Epigraph: Frédéric Joliot-Curie, "Pour une action commune des peuples de toutes les Nations" (Apr. 1949), in Joliot-Curie, *Cinq années de lutte*, p. 32.

1. Truman, *Year of Decisions*, p. 416; *Daily Worker* (London), Aug. 14, 1945.

2. *Daily Worker* (London), Aug. 7, 9, 11, 14, 1945.

3. Kramish, *Atomic Energy in the Soviet Union*, p. 88; Ewer, *Communists on Peace*, p. 32; Caute, *Communism and the French Intellectuals*, p. 192; "Communist Party and the Bomb," p. 3.

4. Penner, *Canadian Communism*, pp. 207–8; *Daily Worker* (New York), Aug. 8, 1945.

5. Clark, *J.B.S.*, pp. 166, 189; Werskey, *Visible College*, p. 74; Bernal, "New Frontier of the Mind."

6. *Daily Worker* (London), Aug. 13, 1945; *Daily Worker* (New York), Aug. 13, 1945.

7. *Daily Worker* (New York), Nov. 21, 1946; *Daily Worker* (London), Aug. 7, 1952; "Communist Party and the Bomb," p. 3.

8. Werskey, *Visible College*, pp. 39–41, 212–37, 266; "J. D. Bernal: The Man of Science and Peace," *Peace Courier* 2 (Sept.–Oct. 1971): 8; Goldsmith, *Frédéric Joliot-Curie*, pp. 174–75.

9. *The World Federation of Scientific Workers*, pp. 9–10, Box 65, FAS Records; Henry A. Boorse, "Report on International Scientific Conferences Held in England, July, 1946" (Oct. 1, 1946), Box 7, SASSAE, DOS Records; Goldsmith, *Frédéric Joliot-Curie*, pp. 175–76.

10. Paul Doty to W. A. Higinbotham, Jan. 4, 1947, Box 65, FAS Records; Henry A. Boorse, "Report on International Scientific Conferences Held in England, July, 1946" (Oct. 1, 1946), Box 7, SASSAE, DOS Records.

11. J. H. Rush to Paul Doty, Jan. 19, 1947, Box 65, FAS Records. See also Thorfin Hogness to Joseph Halle Schaffner, Oct. 11, 1946, Box 2, ECAS Records, Chicago; Herbert L. Anderson to W. A. Higinbotham, Oct. 30, 1946, Harold C. Urey to Higinbotham, Oct. 30, 1946, and Higinbotham to Doty, Jan. 17, 1947, Box 65, FAS Records.

12. Werskey, *Visible College*, pp. 276–79; Goldsmith, *Frédéric Joliot-Curie*, pp. 176–81, 188; Wooster, "Some Recollections of the W.F.S.W.," pp. 26–27; Joliot-Curie, "Pour une action commune des peuples de toutes les Nations" (Apr. 1949), in Joliot-Curie, *Cinq années de lutte*, pp. 28–29; Rotblat, "Movements of Scientists," pp. 127–28.

13. Huxley, "Intellect at Wroclaw"; Martin, "Hyenas and Other Reptiles"; *PN*, Sept. 10, 1948.

14. A. J. P. Taylor, Letter to the Editor, *New Statesman and Nation* 36 (Sept. 18, 1948): 239; Turski and Zdanowski, *Peace Movement*, pp. 20–21; "Dr. Huxley Issues a Personal Statement on the World Congress of Intellectuals" (Sept. 2, 1948), Box 86, Einstein Papers.

15. Julian Huxley, "Speech delivered on the third day of the Wroclaw Congress of Intellectuals" (Sept. 3, 1948), Box 86, Einstein Papers; A. J. P. Taylor, *Personal History*, pp. 192–93; Turski and Zdanowski, *Peace Movement*, pp. 22–23; Caute, *Fellow-Travellers*, p. 290.

16. This account, originally provided by Einstein, was confirmed by Polish intellectuals at a 1988 commemorative meeting sponsored by the Polish Peace Committee, which subsequently printed his original address. Einstein to Czeslaw Milosz, Sept. 4, 1948, and Einstein to Julian Huxley, Sept. 14, 1948, Box 86, Einstein Papers; Nathan and Norden, eds., *Einstein on Peace*, pp. 492–93; *Polish Peace Committee Newsletter* (1988), pp. 5–8, 22–26.

17. Forrester, *Fifteen Years of Peace Fronts*, p. 2; Shulman, *Stalin's Foreign Policy Reappraised*, pp. 85–87, 89; Huxley, "Intellect at Wroclaw," p. 327; Bernal to Kingsley Martin, Sept. 7, 1948, Box 85, Bernal Papers.

18. Goldsmith, *Frédéric Joliot-Curie*, pp. 184, 186; Biquard, *Frédéric Joliot-Curie*, p. 100; Shulman, *Stalin's Foreign Policy Reappraised*, pp. 92, 94.

19. Joliot-Curie's references to the Atlantic Pact and the "revolt of the peoples" were included in contemporary coverage by the *New York Times* but vanished by 1954, when he had the speech published. Legendre, "Quand les intellectuels partaient en guerre froide (avril 1949)"; Shulman, *Stalin's Foreign Policy Reappraised*, pp. 97–98; Claudin, *Communist Movement*, p. 577; *NYT*, Apr. 21, 1949; Joliot-Curie, "Pour une action commune des peuples de toutes les Nations" (Apr. 1949), in Joliot-Curie, *Cinq années de lutte*, pp. 15, 17, 19, 26.

20. In his biographical study of Robeson, Martin Duberman has claimed that Robeson was misquoted in the press. *NYT*, Apr. 21, 1949; Paul Robeson, *For Freedom and Peace* (1949), p. 13, Box 2, Robeson Papers; Duberman, *Paul Robeson*, p. 342.

21. *NYT*, Apr. 22, 24, 1949; MacKenzie, "Paris Dovecote," p. 425; "World Congress

for Peace," p. 7. Not all of this appears in the official record of the conference, *Le Congrès Mondial des Partisans de la Paix, Paris-Prague, 20–25 Avril 1949 (Documentation)*, WPC Records.

22. Jean Genêt, on hand for the Buffalo Stadium rally, reported: "The stadium seats fifty thousand, and the crowd was estimated next day by *L'Humanité* at five hundred thousand, probably an enthusiastic typographical error." Du Bois, though, continued to use the 500,000 figure. W. E. B. Du Bois, "My Case" (Nov. 1, 1951), Box 2, Robeson Papers; Du Bois, *Autobiography*, p. 350; *NYT*, Apr. 25, 26, 1949; Genêt, "Letter from Paris" (May 7, 1949), p. 99.

23. Genêt, "Letter from Paris" (May 7, 1949), p. 100.

24. A dispatch in the *New York Times* recounted the incident differently but made the same point: "Harvey Moore, an English lawyer representing the International Association of Jurists . . . suggested the conference should be ready for a compromise in the Chinese war. To this suggestion the congress bellowed 'no.' 'Well, if we were for peace,' said Mr. Moore, 'we should be ready to accept a compromise.' The congress once again dissented." Turski and Zdanowski, *Peace Movement*, p. 33; *NYT*, Apr. 24, 1949.

25. *NYT*, Apr. 23, 24, 1949; "World Federalism vs. Communism," *CC* 2 (July 1949): 441; " 'Partisans' Bar Garry Davis as Speaker at Paris Congress" (Apr. 23, 1949), Davis Papers.

26. W. E. B. Du Bois, "My Case" (Nov. 1, 1951), Box 2, Robeson Papers; Claudin, *Communist Movement*, p. 578.

27. *Izvestia*, Apr. 30, 1949, and *Pravda*, Apr. 30, 1949, in *CDSP* 1 (May 31, 1949): 39; Joliot-Curie, "World-Wide Movement Against the Atomic Peril," p. 37; "World Congress for Peace," p. 4.

28. *Pravda*, Oct. 24, Nov. 1, 1949, in *CDSP* 1 (Dec. 6, 1949): 16–17; *NYT*, Oct. 29, 31, 1949; Shulman, *Stalin's Foreign Policy Reappraised*, p. 132.

29. *Pravda*, Oct. 2, 1949, in *CDSP* 1 (Nov. 8, 1949): 17; "Defense of Peace and the Struggle Against the Warmongers."

30. "Defense of Peace and the Struggle Against the Warmongers."

31. Claudin, *Communist Movement*, p. 583.

32. Shulman, *Stalin's Foreign Policy Reappraised*, pp. 80–81; Myrdal, *Game of Disarmament*, p. 379. See also Kissinger, *Nuclear Weapons and Foreign Policy*, pp. 372–78.

33. Inga Beskow to Gertrude Bussey, Mar. 3, 1947, Reel 84, WILPF (International) Records; Bernal to Kingsley Martin, Sept. 7, 1948, Box 85, Bernal Papers; *PN*, Nov. 23, 1951.

34. The wording of the Stockholm Peace Appeal varied slightly depending on the time and place of circulation. I have drawn upon the original wording adopted at Stockholm. Joliot-Curie, "Nous exigeons l'interdiction absolue de l'arme atomique" (Mar. 1950), in Joliot-Curie, *Cinq années de lutte*, pp. 48, 55; Biquard, *Frédéric Joliot-Curie*, pp. 103–4; J. Endicott, ed., *Best of Jim Endicott*, p. 55; *FRUS, 1950*, 4: 276–77.

35. Claudin, *Communist Movement*, p. 580; Shulman, *Stalin's Foreign Policy Reappraised*, p. 133; *Pravda*, Mar. 21, 1950, in *CDSP* 2 (May 6, 1950): 21.

36. Claudin, *Communist Movement*, p. 578; Shulman, *Stalin's Foreign Policy Reappraised*, p. 133; *NYT*, Aug. 5, 13, 1950, Dec. 11, 1951; *FRUS, 1950*, 4: 326–28.

37. *Pravda*, July 10, 1950, in *CDSP* 2 (Aug. 26, 1950): 27; *PN*, Aug. 25, 1950; *NYT*, Aug. 19, 1950; Shulman, *Stalin's Foreign Policy Reappraised*, p. 155.

38. *NYT*, Nov. 19, 1950; "Peace Will Win," *Poland Today* 6 (Jan. 1951): 2, Poland Miscellaneous Peace Material; Biquard, *Frédéric Joliot-Curie*, p. 105; Shulman, *Stalin's Foreign Policy Reappraised*, p. 156.

39. *NYT*, Nov. 18, 19, 23, 1950; "Resolution Adopted by the Partisans of Peace in Warsaw, November 1950," in Carlyle, ed., *Documents on International Affairs*, pp. 145–48; *Second World Congress of the Defenders of Peace, Warsaw, 16–22 November, 1950* (1950), British Peace Committee Records.

40. Shulman, *Stalin's Foreign Policy Reappraised*, pp. 155–56; Claudin, *Communist Movement*, p. 579; *NYT*, Feb. 26, 1951; *Second Session of the World Peace Council, Vienna, November 1–7, 1951 (Reports and Documents)*, WPC Records; F. Joliot-Curie to all Peace Committees and Friends of Peace, Aug. 25, 1952, Box 12, Robeson Papers.

41. Forrester, *Fifteen Years*, pp. 21–22; Shulman, *Stalin's Foreign Policy Reappraised*, p. 188; Robert J. Havighurst et al. to Joliot-Curie, Apr. 24, 1952, enclosure in "Note to LP from Himself" (July 11, 1952), Pauling Papers; Biquard, *Frédéric Joliot-Curie*, p. 113.

42. One WPC brochure publicized "confessions" by U.S. airmen such as "How I was Forced to Take Part in the Inhuman Bacteriological Warfare Launched by the U.S. Wall Street" and "The Truth About How American Imperialism Launched Germ Warfare." Goldsmith, *Frédéric Joliot-Curie*, pp. 190–91; Joliot-Curie to Austin, May 3, 1952, in Joliot-Curie, *Cinq années de lutte*, pp. 151–56; Caute, *Fellow-Travellers*, p. 302; Joliot-Curie, "Après le retour de la Commission Scientifique de Chine et de Corée" (Oct. 10, 1952), in Joliot-Curie, *Cinq années de lutte*, pp. 210–16; WPC, *Statements by Two Captured U.S. Air Force Officers on Their Participation in Germ Warfare in Korea* (1952), Box 12, Robeson Papers.

43. "Reports of World Pacifist Meeting, December 1949," pp. 10–12, Box 32, Series B, Sayre Papers.

44. Bussey and Tims, *Women's International League for Peace and Freedom*, p. 196; Gertrude Baer to Mary Broun, Oct. 21, 1955, Reel 54, WILPF (International) Records.

45. Harold F. Bing and Grace M. Beaton to WRI Council and Sections, Feb. 1, 1951, Box 3, WRI Records. See also Beaton to WRI Sections, Nov. 28, 1950, with enclosures, Box 3, WRI Records.

46. Brittain, *Rebel Passion*, p. 66. See also Percy W. Bartlett, "Stockholm and Sheffield," *News Letter*, no. 69 (Dec. 1950), pp. 4–5.

47. Minutes of the General Committee meeting, British FOR, Apr. 5–6, 1951, Reel 2, and Clifford H. Macquire, "The World Peace Council—Vienna, Oct. 31 to November 6" (1951), Reel 5, FOR (Great Britain) Records.

48. Lonsdale to Gertrude Woker, Jan. 10, 1953, Reel 88, WILPF (International) Records; Einstein to Jacques Hadamard, Apr. 7, 1949, in Nathan and Norden, eds., *Einstein on Peace*, p. 512. See also Einstein to Julian Huxley, Sept. 14, 1948, Box 86, Einstein Papers.

49. Goldsmith, *Frédéric Joliot-Curie*, p. 233; "The Stockholm Appeal" and "Professor Niels Bohr's answer through Ritzau's Bureau" (June 14, 1950), Box 28, FAS Records.

50. Frédéric Joliot-Curie, "A Proposal Toward the Elimination of the Atomic Weapon," *BAS* 6 (June 1950): 166–67; Eugene Rabinowitch, "The Three Points of Professor Joliot-Curie," *BAS* 6 (June 1950): 163–65; *FAS Newsletter*, Oct. 24, 1950, p. 3.

51. Usborne to Harold C. Urey, July 7, 1947, Box 57, Einstein Papers; "World Federalism vs. Communism," *CC* 2 (July 1949): 441–44; Paul Shipman Andrews, "Report on the Rome Congress Situation" (Mar. 26, 1951), Box 1, WMWFG Records; Schuman, *Commonwealth of Man*, pp. 445–46.

52. *NYT*, Apr. 23, 1949, July 6, 1950, Apr. 11, 1951; Flannery, ed., *Pattern for Peace*, p. 244.

53. *NYT*, June 4, Aug. 24, 29, Nov. 5, 1950; "Workers Launch Peace Program" (Mar. 2, 1951), Reel 84, WILPF (International) Records.

54. Joliot-Curie, "La coexistence pacifique de systèmes économiques et politiques dif-

férents est possible" (Nov. 1950), in Joliot-Curie, *Cinq années de lutte*, p. 92; *Second World Peace Congress: Warsaw, November 16–22, 1950 (Reports and Documents)*, p. 7, Box 12, Robeson Papers.

55. Although not a Communist party member, Johnson was a staunch supporter of the Soviet Union and advocate of Communism who consequently became known as the "Red Dean." Montagu, *Plot Against Peace*, p. 104; Johnson, *Searching for Light*, p. 285; *NYT*, Oct. 23, 1966.

Chapter 11

Epigraph: *Britain for Peace: Report of the British Peace Congress, London, October 22–23, 1949* (1949), British Peace Committee Records.

1. Tiersky, *French Communism*, pp. 96–138; Wall, *French Communism*, pp. 19–29; Howorth, *France*, p. 13; Caute, *Communism and the French Intellectuals*, p. 156.

2. Wall, *French Communism*, pp. 77–78, Shulman, *Stalin's Foreign Policy Reappraised*, pp. 85–91; Tiersky, *French Communism*, pp. 219–21; Defrasne, *Le pacifisme*, p. 114.

3. Bourdet, "Rebirth of a Peace Movement," p. 193; Wall, *French Communism*, pp. 97–98; *NYT*, Oct. 3, 1949; Genêt, "Letter from Paris" (June 10, 1950), pp. 96–97.

4. *World Government News*, Jan. 1949, p. 7; Caffery to SecState, Apr. 7, 1949, 800.00B/4-649, DOS Records; Bourdet, "Peace and Politics"; David Rousset and Georges Altman to Eleanor Roosevelt, Apr. 7, 1949, Box 3814, Eleanor Roosevelt Papers.

5. *PN*, May 13, 1949; *NYT*, Apr. 21, 22, May 1, 1949; Caffery to SecState, May 2, 1949, 800.00B/5-249, DOS Records; G. Davis, *World Is My Country*, pp. 87–89.

6. Roser to John Nevin Sayre, Nov. 27, 1950, Trocmé to John Nevin Sayre, Dec. 19, 1950, and André Trocmé, "Report on Activities, 1950–51" (Aug. 1951), Box 10, Series B, Sayre Papers; Caldwell, "French Socialists," pp. 64–65.

7. *NYT*, June 20, 1950; Barrat, "Peace, Peace, When There Is No Peace," pp. 455–57.

8. Of all French newspapers, only *L'Humanité* applauded the development of the Soviet Bomb. *NYT*, Sept. 25, 1949; Caldwell, "French Socialists," pp. 59–62.

9. Tiersky, *French Communism*, p. 221; Caute, *Communism and the French Intellectuals*, p. 187; Salvin, "Neutralism in France," p. 300.

10. Howorth, *France*, pp. 26–27; Wall, *French Communism*, p. 136, 144–48; Shulman, *Stalin's Foreign Policy Reappraised*, pp. 135–36.

11. Goldsmith, *Frédéric Joliot-Curie*, pp. 157–61; Weart, *Scientists in Power*, pp. 257–60; *NYT*, Apr. 29, 1950.

12. Goldsmith, *Frédéric Joliot-Curie*, pp. 161–63; Weart, *Scientists in Power*, pp. 259–60.

13. Lewis and Xue, *China Builds the Bomb*, pp. 36, 38.

14. Defrasne, *Le pacifisme*, p. 115; N. Ingram, "Ambivalence in the Post–World War II French Peace Movement," p. 10.

15. *PN*, Apr. 8, Sept. 30, Oct. 7, 1949; *NYT*, June 14, 1948, Mar. 25, 1949.

16. Minutes of the Executive Committee meeting, British FOR, July 20, 1949, Reel 5, FOR (Great Britain) Records; *NYT*, Mar. 25, Sept. 24, 1949.

17. *Britain for Peace: Report of the British Peace Congress, London, October 22–23, 1949* (1949), British Peace Committee Records; *PN*, Oct. 28, 1949.

18. For a very laudatory account of the Peace Partisans' conference of 1949, written and published by the British Peace Committee, see *Six Hundred Millions for Peace: A Report on the World Congress for Peace, Paris, April 20th to 25th, 1949* (1949), British Peace Committee Records.

19. *Britain for Peace: Report of the British Peace Congress, London, October 22–23, 1949* (1949), British Peace Committee Records; Bernal to Linus Pauling, Feb. 15, 1950, Pauling Papers.

20. *PN*, Apr. 7, 1950; *To Live in Peace* 1 (May 1950): 1, British Peace Committee Records. See also *The Peace Petition* (June 1950), British Peace Committee Records.

21. *NYT*, May 8, 1950; *PN*, July 28, 1950.

22. Johnson, *Searching for Light*, pp. 178, 180, 190–91, 324–28; *PN*, May 20, 1949. For additional information on Johnson's support for Communism and the Soviet Union, see *NYT*, Oct. 23, 1966.

23. The "facts" on Western "bacteriological warfare" in Korea, Montagu claimed, "cannot be disputed and can all be demonstrated." Montagu, *Plot Against Peace*, pp. 19–20, 33, 70–71, 117, 119.

24. *PN*, Nov. 24, 1950; Minnion and Bolsover, eds., *CND Story*, p. 11.

25. Speaking in Moscow on August 27, 1949, Bernal had declared: "In capitalist countries the direction of science is in the hands of those whose only aim is to destroy and torture people so that their own profits may be secured for some years longer." Forrester, *Fifteen Years*, p. 2; *NYT*, Nov. 5, 1949.

26. *NYT*, June 29, 1950; *PN*, June 2, 23, 1950; Liddington, *Long Road to Greenham*, pp. 172–73; Hinton, *Protests and Visions*, p. 151.

27. D. Russell, *Tamarisk Tree 3*, p. 64; Priestley, "Open Letter to a Russian Colleague."

28. "Statement issued by the National Council of the Peace Pledge Union on 26th Sept. 1948," "Peace Pledge Union 1947" folder, Frank Lea to Vera Brittain, Nov. 18, 1948, "Peace News 1948" folder, and Sybil Morrison to Brittain, Nov. 20, 1948, "Peace Pledge Union 1948" folder, Brittain Papers; *PN*, Dec. 3, 1948.

29. Brittain to Lea, Nov. 19, 1948, and Brittain to Morrison, Nov. 19, 1948, "Replies, November 1948" folder, Lea to Brittain, Nov. 18, 1948, "Peace News 1948" folder, and Brittain to Reginald Sorensen, Feb. 16, 1949, "Replies, February 1949" folder, Brittain Papers.

30. *PN*, Nov. 19, 26, 1948, Apr. 29, Dec. 9, 1949, June 2, 1950; Reginald Sorensen to Vera Brittain, Feb. 14, 1949, "Sorensen, Reginald" folder, Brittain Papers; Morrison, *I Renounce War*, p. 84.

31. "Peace Pledge Union Manifesto on Its Attitude Towards the Communist Party and the British Peace Committee" (June 21, 1950), enclosure in Grace M. Beaton to WRI Sections, Nov. 28, 1950, Box 3, WRI Records; *PN*, June 30, 1950.

32. *PN*, July 14, 21, Aug. 25, 1950.

33. Minutes of the General Committee meeting, British FOR, June 27–28, 1950, Reel 2, FOR (Great Britain) Records; *News Letter*, no. 68 (Sept. 1950), p. 9.

34. "Crusade for World Government Newsletter" (Nov. 1950), Crusade for World Government Records; Barbara Duncan Harris to Emily G. Balch, Oct. 24, 1950, Reel 51, WILPF (International) Records.

35. Although it refused to send a representative to the Sheffield conference, the FOR also protested the British government's denial of visas to foreign delegates. *PN*, Oct. 20, 1950, June 1, 15, 1951; Minutes of the Executive Committee meeting, British FOR, Oct. 18, Nov. 15, 1950, Reel 5, FOR (Great Britain) Records.

36. Schmidt, *Henry A. Wallace*; A. J. Muste, "A Vote for Wallace Will Be—A Vote for the Communists," *Fellowship* 14 (July 1948): 7; Seidler, *Norman Thomas*, pp. 231–33; Thomas to Mr. and Mrs. Edward S. Allen, June 28, 1948, Box 54, Thomas Papers; Johnpoll, *Pacifist's Progress*, pp. 235–37.

37. Stanley K. Bigman, "The 'New Internationalism' Under Attack," *Public Opin-*

ion Quarterly 14 (Summer 1950): 239; *Daily Worker* (New York), Dec. 22, 1945; Wooley, *Alternatives to Anarchy*, p. 76.

38. The following year, in a letter to party members, Communist party secretary Eugene Dennis declared that "points one to the end of the agenda in every leading committee and club must be linked with . . . an all-out struggle and campaign against the Truman and Mac-Arthur war policies." Shannon, *Decline of American Communism*, pp. 203–4; *Daily Worker* (New York), June 11, 1950; *NYT*, Apr. 28, 1951.

39. Du Bois, *In Battle for Peace*, pp. 34–35, 42; *Peacegram*, May 31, 1950; W. E. B. Du Bois, "My Case" (Nov. 1, 1951), Box 2, and minutes of the Executive Board meeting, Peace Information Center, Oct. 12, 1950, Box 12, Robeson Papers.

40. *Daily Worker* (New York), Mar. 16, 1951; Roy, *Communism and the Churches*, pp. 215–20; Richardson to Du Bois, Dec. 19, 1952, Box 12, Robeson Papers.

41. *NYT*, Aug. 3, 12, 1950.

42. *NYT*, July 22, Aug. 13, 24, 1950; Peace Information Center, "Prominent Americans Call for Outlawing Atomic Warfare" (Aug. 14, 1950), Peace Information Center Records; Du Bois, *Autobiography*, p. 357.

43. *NYT*, Sept. 7, 12, 1949; "Towards a Mid-Century Conference for Peace, May 29, 30, 1950," Box 24, WILPF (United States) Records; *Peacemaker* [United States], July 11, 1950; "Mid-Century Conference for Peace, Program" (1950), Box 5, Section C4, Allen Papers; Shulman, *Stalin's Foreign Policy Reappraised*, pp. 92–93; Lash, "Weekend at the Waldorf," p. 12.

44. *Daily Worker* (New York), Sept. 26, 1949; Du Bois to Acheson, July 14, 1950, Peace Information Center Records; Du Bois, *I Take My Stand for Peace*, pp. 7–8; Du Bois, *In Battle for Peace*, p. 162. For the very different attitude that Du Bois had toward the Soviet Union, see, for example, Du Bois to H. Ryerson-Decker, Mar. 30, 1950, in Aptheker, ed., *Correspondence of W. E. B. Du Bois*, 3: 282.

45. *NYT*, Sept. 10, 1949, Mar. 9, 1950.

46. Du Bois, in turn, denounced "Rogge the Rat" and "Wallace the Weasel." *NYT*, July 22, Aug. 17, 19, Nov. 20, 23, 1950; Du Bois, *In Battle for Peace*, pp. 109–18.

47. "We had quite a party," Shapley recalled. *PN*, Apr. 14, 1949; Macdonald, "Waldorf Conference"; *NYT*, Mar. 27, 1949; Lash, "Weekend at the Waldorf," pp. 13–14; Harlow Shapley oral history interview, p. 156.

48. Cousins to Shapley, Dec. 28, 1948, Box 77, and Cousins, untitled memo (1949) and Cousins to William P. Maloney, Apr. 4, 1949, Box 98, Cousins Papers, Los Angeles; "Report on Recent Cultural and Scientific Conference for World Peace" (July 21, 1949), 800.00B/7-2149, DOS Records; *NYT*, Mar. 26, 1949; Cousins, "Tell the Folks Back Home."

49. Holmes to Cousins, Mar. 28, 1949, Box 98, Cousins Papers, Los Angeles; Thomas to S. Ralph Harlow, Aug. 31, 1950, Box 60, Thomas Papers; Interim Administrative Committee meeting (#1), June 26, 1950, Box 2, War Resisters League Records; "Notes by A. J. Muste to Draft Statement on 'The Peace Movement and United Fronts'" (June 27, 1950), Box 3, FOR (United States) Records.

50. Mildred Olmsted to Emily G. Balch, Oct. 18, 1950, Reel 51, WILPF (International) Records; Sidney Aberman to Joliot-Curie, Nov. 3, 1950, enclosure in Grace M. Beaton to WRI Sections, Nov. 28, 1950, Box 3, WRI Records.

51. "Peace Fronts Today" (May 1951), Box 4, FOR (United States) Records. See also Minutes of FOR National Council Meeting of May 30–31, 1951, p. 7, and John M. Swomley, Jr., to F. Siegmund-Schültze, Dec. 3, 1953, Box 4, FOR (United States) Records; Roy, *Communism and the Churches*, p. 219.

52. See, for example, Helen Hamer to Cousins, Apr. 1, 1949, Toni Noel to Cousins,

Apr. 1, 1949, and Ray Bowen to Cousins, Apr. 7, 1949, Box 98, Cousins Papers, Los Angeles.

53. *NYT*, May 22, 1950; Wooley, *Alternatives to Anarchy*, p. 71; Branch and Chapter Letter #57 (Sept. 21, 1950), Box 52, Cousins Papers, Los Angeles.

54. Weisskopf to Shapley, Mar. 11, 1949, Box 77, Oppenheimer Papers; Einstein to Joliot-Curie, Nov. 3, 1950, Box 88, Einstein Papers.

55. Pauling to Milton Burton, Feb. 28, 1949, Pauling and Du Bois to Sponsors, American Continental Congress for World Peace, July 26, 1949, and Pauling to Frank Aydelotte, May 21, 1952, Pauling Papers; Pauling to the author, Jan. 25, 1988.

56. Linus Pauling, "Man—An Irrational Animal" (Speech at Western Continental Congress for Peace, Mexico City, Sept. 5, 1949), and Pauling to Frank Aydelotte, May 21, 1952, Pauling Papers; *NYT*, Sept. 7, 1949.

57. Starobin, *American Communism in Crisis*, p. 304.

Chapter 12

Epigraph: Overstreet and Windmiller, *Communism in India*, p. 413.

1. Penner, *Canadian Communism*, pp. 219–21, 226; Weisbord, *Strangest Dream*, pp. 144–94; Avakumovic, *Communist Party in Canada*, pp. 182–83.

2. S. Endicott, *James G. Endicott*, pp. 72–256, 261–64; Socknat, *Witness Against War*, pp. 289–90; Socknat, "Dilemma of Canadian Pacifists," pp. 9–10; J. Endicott, ed., *Best of Jim Endicott*, pp. 18–23, 25–27; Link, *Labor-Religion Prophet*, pp. 142–43; "The Canadian Peace Congress, 1948 to 1978," Canadian Peace Congress Records, Toronto.

3. Minutes of the Canadian FOR National Council meeting of Oct. 22, 1948, Box 2, FOR (Canada) Records, Toronto; James G. Endicott, "An Address to the Toronto Peace Conference" (Dec. 3, 1948), Box 6, Series B, Sayre Papers; Socknat, "Dilemma of Canadian Pacifists," pp. 10–15; "Revised Draft Resolution to the Canadian Peace Congress," Canadian Peace Congress Records, Swarthmore.

4. S. Endicott, *James G. Endicott*, pp. 266–72; *Pravda*, Mar. 9, 1950, in *CDSP* 2 (Apr. 29, 1950): 19; Avakumovic, *Communist Party in Canada*, pp. 184–85.

5. S. Endicott, *James G. Endicott*, pp. 293–98, 303–5; Moffatt, *History of the Canadian Peace Movement*, pp. 73–74, 77; James Endicott, "The Peoples Are Going Forward to Peace" (Aug. 31, 1952), Toronto Peace Association Records.

6. "First National F.O.R. Conference Since 1941 Discusses Role of Pacifism in Atomic Age," *Fellowship* 12 (Oct. 1946): 168–69; Socknat, "Dilemma of Canadian Pacifists," pp. 9–10.

7. Socknat, *Witness Against War*, pp. 290, 295; Socknat, "Dilemma of Canadian Pacifists," pp. 14–16; Minutes of the Canadian FOR National Council meetings of Oct. 22, Dec. 17, 1948, Feb. 4, 1949, Box 2, FOR (Canada) Records, Toronto; Endicott to Ella Lediard, Nov. 15, 1952, Box 5, Series B, Sayre Papers.

8. S. Endicott, *James G. Endicott*, pp. 269–70, 277, 286, 288, 296; "The Canadian Peace Congress, 1948 to 1978," Canadian Peace Congress Records, Toronto; Johnson, *Searching for Light*, p. 280; Avakumovic, *Communist Party in Canada*, pp. 185–86.

9. Davidson, *Communist Party of Australia*, pp. 103–4; Summy, "Australian Peace Council," pp. 234–35; Saunders and Summy, *Australian Peace Movement*, p. 32.

10. Forrester, *Fifteen Years*, p. 3; Saunders and Summy, *Australian Peace Movement*, p. 32; "Peace Movement Grows in Australia," *Peace* 1 (Apr. 1950): 10.

11. "Peace Movement Grows in Australia," p. 10; "The Story of a Mighty Challenge

Against War," *Peace* 1 (June 1950): 7–10; Davidson, *Communist Party of Australia*, p. 105; Summy, "Australian Peace Council," pp. 241–43.

12. Saunders and Summy, *Australian Peace Movement*, p. 32; Summy, "Australian Peace Council," pp. 237, 257.

13. Davidson, *Communist Party of Australia*, pp. 105–43; Albinski, *Politics and Foreign Policy in Australia*, p. 103; Summy, "Australian Peace Council," pp. 237–38, 257; Street, *Truth or Repose*, pp. 307, 314–23; Forrester, *Fifteen Years*, p. 12.

14. Davidson, *Communist Party of Australia*, pp. 105–6; Summy, "Australian Peace Council," p. 241; "By Way of Contrast," *Working for Peace*, no. 5 (Sept. 20, 1950), n.p., and "Peace Is Within Our Grasp," Australian Peace Council Records.

15. "Extracts from the Speeches of the Dean of Canterbury (Dr. Hewlett Johnson) at the Australian Peace Congress," *Peace* 1 (June 1950), n.p.; Forrester, *Fifteen Years*, pp. 13–17, 21–22.

16. Saunders and Summy, *Australian Peace Movement*, p. 32; "Press Has Shown Its Hostility to Urge for Peace," *Peace* 1 (Apr. 1950): 11; *NYT*, Apr. 17, 1950.

17. Summy and Saunders, "Disarmament and the Australian Peace Movement," p. 27; "The A.L.P. Imposes a 'Ban,' " *Peace* 1 (Apr. 1950): 11; *You Can't Ban Peace* (Melbourne: Australian Peace Council, 1950), Australian Peace Council Records.

18. An Australian WILPF leaflet of the time declared that the proposal to outlaw the Communist party "is a threat to all we stand for" and urged Australians to oppose the proposal in the nationwide referendum. *Peacemaker* [Australia], Jan. 1950; "Maintain Freedom! Vote: No!" Reel 54, WILPF (International) Records.

19. Summy, "Australian Peace Council," p. 241; *Peacemaker* [Australia], Sept., Oct., Nov. 1950.

20. *NYT*, Dec. 28, 1949, Aug. 6, 1950, Jan. 5, Nov. 26, 1951; Johnson, *Searching for Light*, p. 275.

21. Andersson and Lindkvist, "Peace Movement in Sweden," pp. 11–12; Lutz, "Ellenor Andrea Andreen," p. 25; *Izvestia*, July 20, 1950, in *CDSP* 2 (Sept. 2, 1950): 32; *FRUS, 1950*, 4: 277–78.

22. *NYT*, July 22, 1950; Else Zeuthen to Gertrude Baer, Jan. 28, 1951, Reel 60, WILPF (International) Records; David Hill to Allen Shapley, June 21, 1950, Box 28, FAS Records; "Professor Niels Bohr's answer through Ritzau's Bureau" (June 14, 1950), Box 77, SASSAE, DOS Records.

23. Verkuil, *De grote illusie*, pp. 24–29.

24. Brassel and Tanner, "Zur Geschichte der Friedensbewegung in der Schweiz," pp. 60–61; "The Swiss Peace Movement in the Struggle for Peace and International Solidarity," *Peace Courier* 15 (May 1984): 2.

25. Lamot, "Peace Movement in Belgium," p. 212; Mark Heirman to the author, Mar. 10, 1989.

26. Peristerakis, "To Elliniko Kinima Eirinis," p. 67.

27. *Pravda*, July 20, 1950, in *CDSP* 2 (Sept. 2, 1950): 32; "In Germany," *News Letter*, no. 67 (June 1950), p. 10.

28. One writer on the Austrian peace movement, Gerhard Jordan, puts the number of signers at nearly a million. Jordan, "Peace Activities in Austria Since 1945"; *NYT*, June 11, 1950; Maislinger, "Peace Movement in a Neutral Country," p. 60.

29. *Pravda*, May 22, 1950, in *CDSP* 2 (July 8, 1950): 23; Kodama, "Red vs. Green," p. 6; von Bonsdorff, "Peace Movement in Nordic Countries," pp. 218–19.

30. Scalapino, *Japanese Communist Movement*, pp. 83, 117; Committee for the Compilation of Materials, *Hiroshima and Nagasaki*, p. 573; Suzuki, "Declining Role of Ideology

in Citizens' Movements," p. 124; Japan Council Against A and H Bombs, *Documentary Photographs*, pp. 11–12.

31. *Izvestia*, Aug. 17, 1950, in *CDSP* 2 (Sept. 30, 1950): 29–30; *NYT*, Sept. 10, 1949, Dec. 12, 1950. For an illustration of the appeal of Communist-led peace ventures to Third World peoples, disgusted with Western racism and colonialism, see Blackman, "Letter to an English Intellectual."

32. Overstreet and Windmiller, *Communism in India*, pp. 412–13; *Pravda* and *Izvestia*, Nov. 27, 1949, in *CDSP* 1 (Jan. 3, 1950): 19.

33. Overstreet and Windmiller, *Communism in India*, pp. 413–14; "Worthy of Note."

34. Masani, *Communist Party of India*, pp. 102–3; Overstreet and Windmiller, *Communism in India*, pp. 413–17.

35. Kautsky, *Moscow and the Communist Party of India*, p. 133; Overstreet and Windmiller, *Communism in India*, p. 418; Masani, *Communist Party of India*, pp. 126–27; *Peace and the Indian People: Resolutions of All-India Peace Convention, Bombay, May 11–13, 1951* (1951), India Miscellaneous Peace Material.

36. Overstreet and Windmiller, *Communism in India*, pp. 418–19; Masani, *Communist Party of India*, pp. 127–28; *Peace and the Indian People: Resolutions of All-India Peace Convention, Bombay, May 11–13, 1951* (1951), India Miscellaneous Peace Material; *NYT*, May 15, 1951.

37. *PN*, June 16, 1950; Verkuil, *De grote illusie*, pp. 29–30; Brassel and Tanner, "Zur Geschichte der Friedensbewegung in der Schweiz," p. 61.

38. Fanny Arnskov to Gertrude Baer, Nov. 7, 1950, Else Zeuthen to Gertrude Baer, Nov. 13, 1950, Jan. 28, 1951, and "Report from the Danish Section in 1952," Reel 60, WILPF (International) Records.

39. *New Zealand Christian Pacifist*, Nov. 1950, Feb., Dec. 1951.

40. *PN*, Nov. 24, 1950; "Germany," WRI News Release No. 39 (Nov. 1, 1950), Box 3, WRI Records.

41. Deutsche Friedensgesellschaft to Friends, Sept. 29, 1950, Deutsche Friedensgesellschaft Records; *PN*, Aug. 18, 1950.

42. Gunnar Bellander to Friends, Nov. 1950, Sweden Miscellaneous Peace Material; *PN*, Jan. 5, 1951; Lindkvist, "Mobilization Peaks and Declines," p. 157.

43. Taipale, "Peace Movement in Finland," pp. 20, 29; Kalemaa, "Felix Iversen"; "News from Sections," *Pax International* 16 (Mar.–Apr. 1950): 2.

44. "Statement No. 4," enclosure in Grace M. Beaton to WRI Sections, Nov. 28, 1950, Box 3, WRI Records; *PN*, Aug. 18, 1950; Hans Thirring, *Stellungnahme zum Pariser Weltfriedenskongress* (May 4, 1949), pp. 6–7, Oesterreichische Friedensgesellschaft Records; *NYT*, June 12, 1950.

Chapter 13

Epigraph: *Pravda*, June 30, 1950, in *CDSP* 2 (Aug. 12, 1950): 18.

1. Ehrenburg, *Post-War Years*, p. 148; *Pravda*, July 7, 1949, in *CDSP* 1 (Aug. 9, 1949): 47–48; *NYT*, Aug. 26, 28, 1949; *Izvestia*, Aug. 30, 1949, in *CDSP* 1 (Oct. 4, 1949): 36.

2. *Pravda*, Sept. 7, 1949, in *CDSP* 1 (Oct. 11, 1949): 75; *Izvestia*, Aug. 28, 1949, in *CDSP* 1 (Sept. 27, 1949): 36.

3. Years later, Ehrenburg reported that the Soviet delegation at Stockholm had been "deeply moved" by the appeal and was "the first to sign it." He did not mention, however, that—as James Endicott later revealed—he wrote the document. Ehrenburg, *Post-War Years*, p. 189; J. Endicott, ed., *Best of Jim Endicott*, p. 55.

4. *Pravda*, June 20, 1950, in *CDSP* 2 (Aug. 12, 1950): 15–16; *NYT*, June 20, 1950.

5. *Pravda*, June 24, 29, 30, 1950, in *CDSP* 2 (Aug. 12, 1950): 17–19.

6. *Pravda*, July 1, 5, 1950, in *CDSP* 2 (Aug. 19, 1950): 36; *Pravda*, July 11, 12, 1950, *CDSP* 2 (Aug. 26, 1950): 45–46.

7. *Izvestia*, July 1, 1950, and *Pravda*, July 6, 1950, in *CDSP* 2 (Aug. 19, 1950): 36–37; *Pravda*, July 11, 1950, in *CDSP* 2 (Aug. 26, 1950): 45; *Pravda*, Aug. 16, 1950, in *CDSP* 2 (Sept. 30, 1950): 44.

8. *Pravda*, July 16, 1950, in *CDSP* 2 (Sept. 2, 1950): 39; *Izvestia*, Aug. 17, 1950, in *CDSP* 2 (Sept. 30, 1950): 44; *Pravda*, July 26, 1950, in *CDSP* 2 (Sept. 9, 1950): 41; *Pravda*, July 12, 1950, in *CDSP* 2 (Aug. 26, 1950): 47.

9. *Izvestia*, July 28, 1950, in *CDSP* 2 (Sept. 9, 1950): 41.

10. *Pravda*, July 11, 1950, in *CDSP* 2 (Aug. 26, 1950): 46; *Literaturnaya gazeta*, July 27, 1950, in *CDSP* 2 (Sept. 30, 1950): 29.

11. Extract from a speech by N. A. Bulganin, Vice Chair of the Council of Ministers, Nov. 6, 1950, in Carlyle, ed., *Documents on International Affairs*, pp. 144–45; "Communiqué of the U.S.S.R. Committee for Peace."

12. For Ehrenburg's account of his work for the Communist-led peace movement, see Ehrenburg, *Post-War Years*, pp. 133–342. Two of his speeches delivered in Great Britain during 1950 are found in Ehrenburg, *Peace Is Everybody's Business* (July 1950), British Peace Committee Records.

13. *Pravda*, Feb. 26, 1950, in *CDSP* 2 (Apr. 22, 1950): 16–17; *Pravda*, Sept. 27, 1950, in *CDSP* 2 (Nov. 11, 1950): 29–30.

14. *Pravda*, Mar. 29, 1950, in *CDSP* 2 (May 13, 1950): 16; *Pravda*, July 27, 1950, in *CDSP* 2 (Sept. 9, 1950): 27.

15. *Pravda*, Sept. 3, 1950, in *CDSP* 2 (Oct. 21, 1950): 26–27; *Pravda*, Mar. 12, 1950, in *CDSP* 2 (Apr. 29, 1950): 22.

16. *NYT*, Oct. 3, 1949, Nov. 3, 4, 1951.

17. "One Planet," p. 44; *Pravda*, Mar. 12, 1950, in *CDSP* 2 (Apr. 29, 1950): 22.

18. The other "warmongers" listed by the Soviet composer were André Malraux, André Gide, and Upton Sinclair. *Pravda*, May 1, 1950, in *CDSP* 2 (June 17, 1950): 34–35; *Izvestia*, July 6, 1950, in *CDSP* 2 (Aug. 19, 1950): 37.

19. *NYT*, Aug. 27, 1949; *Izvestia*, Mar. 12, 1950, in *CDSP* 2 (Apr. 29, 1950): 20; *Literaturnaya gazeta*, Aug. 12, 1950, in *CDSP* 2 (Sept. 30, 1950): 28.

20. *NYT*, Mar. 23, 1949; Ehrenburg, *Post-War Years*, pp. 133–34; "A Visit to the Soviet Peace Committee," *Peace Courier*, no. 1 (1989), p. 8.

21. Caute, *Fellow-Travellers*, pp. 293–97; Khrushchev, *Khrushchev Remembers: The Last Testament*, pp. 77–79; Cohen, "Stalin Question Since Stalin," p. 26.

22. Khrushchev, *Khrushchev Remembers: The Last Testament*, pp. 74–75; "Fadeyev's Suicide."

23. Weart, *Nuclear Fear*, pp. 117–18.

24. *Izvestia*, June 18, 1949, in *CDSP* 1 (July 19, 1949): 30.

25. *PN*, June 16, 1950, May 11, 1951.

26. Ewer, *Communists on Peace*, pp. 22, 35; Vinokurov, "Peace Movement in the People's Democracies," p. 12.

27. Turski and Zdanowski, *Peace Movement*, pp. 31, 37–38.

28. Ibid., pp. 7, 42–43; *NYT*, May 24, 1950.

29. Turski and Zdanowski, *Peace Movement*, pp. 43–44; Vinokurov, "Peace Movement in the People's Democracies," p. 10.

30. *NYT*, June 21, 1950; Turski and Zdanowski, *Peace Movement*, pp. 40–42.

31. Turski and Zdanowski, *Peace Movement*, pp. 45–47, 57–60.

32. *What's the GDR All About?*, p. 21; Schlaga, "Peace Movement as a Party's Tool?" p. 130; *NYT*, Oct. 2, 3, 1949.

33. Schlaga, "Peace Movement as a Party's Tool?" pp. 130–31; WRI News Release No. 33 (June 6, 1950), Box 5, WRI Records.

34. *PN*, June 16, 1950; *Pravda*, Apr. 12, 1950, in *CDSP* 2 (May 27, 1950): 20.

35. "Growing Fight for Peace," p. 1; *PN*, Oct. 27, 1950, Sept. 21, 1951.

36. *NYT*, Oct. 3, 1949, Nov. 13, 1950.

37. Christopher Tang to John Nevin Sayre, Nov. 20, 1961, and Francis P. Jones, "The Church in Communist China," Box 6, and Muriel Lester to Percy Bartlett, Apr. 1954, Box 7, Series B, Sayre Papers.

38. *New Zealand Christian Pacifist*, July 1952; *PN*, Aug. 18, 1950.

39. Premysl Pitter, "Why I Fled from Czechoslovakia," WRI News Release (Nov. 23, 1951), Box 3, WRI Records.

40. Brittain, *Search After Sunrise*, p. 162; *PN*, Aug. 18, 1950.

41. Root, "All in the Name of Peace," pp. 1130–31; Johnson, *Searching for Light*, pp. 324–28.

42. Root, "All in the Name of Peace," pp. 1130–31; Roy, *Communism and the Churches*, p. 212.

43. *NYT*, Aug. 26, 1949, Aug. 7, 1950; Schlaga "Peace Movement as a Party's Tool?" p. 132; Root, "All in the Name of Peace," pp. 1130–31.

44. Root, "All in the Name of Peace," pp. 1130–31; *NYT*, Aug. 12, 1950, June 5, 1951.

45. *Izvestia*, June 16, 1950, and *Pravda*, June 20, 1950, in *CDSP* 2 (Aug. 5, 1950): 32–33; *NYT*, June 20, 21, 1950; Root, "All in the Name of Peace," p. 1131.

Chapter 14

Epigraph: State of the Union address, Jan. 7, 1953. *Public Papers: Truman, 1952–53*, p. 1125.

1. Acheson, *Present at the Creation*, p. 4.

2. Eben Ayers Diary, Aug. 8, 1945, Ayers Papers.

3. Samuel McCrea Cavert to Truman, Aug. 9, 1945, and Truman to Cavert, Aug. 11, 1945, OF 692A, White House Central Files, 1945–53, Truman Papers.

4. In fact, the U.S. government did not have additional atomic bombs in its stockpile at the time. Millis, ed., *Forrestal Diaries*, pp. 83–84; Blum, ed., *Price of Vision*, p. 474; Rusk, *As I Saw It*, p. 126.

5. Szilard to Robert M. Hutchins, Aug. 29, 1945, and K. D. Nichols to Szilard, n.d., Box 73, Szilard Papers; James S. Murray to Szilard, Aug. 27, 28, 1945, in Weart and Szilard, eds., *Leo Szilard*, pp. 216–20.

6. Yavenditti, "John Hersey and the American Conscience," p. 27; Barton J. Bernstein, "Nuclear Deception: The U.S. Record," *BAS* 42 (Aug.–Sept. 1986): 40.

7. Boyer, *By the Bomb's Early Light*, p. 193; Truman to Acheson, May 7, 1946, Box 201, Subject File, President's Secretary's Files, 1945–53, Truman Papers; Miller, *Plain Speaking*, pp. 227–31.

8. B. Bernstein, "Roosevelt, Truman, and the Atomic Bomb," pp. 62–65; *FRUS, 1945*, 2: 41–43.

9. Acheson, *Present at the Creation*, pp. 113, 123–25; Truman, *Year of Decisions*, pp. 524–28; Dean Acheson, "Memorandum Requested by the President" (Sept. 25, 1945),

and Vannevar Bush, "Memorandum" (Sept. 25, 1945), Box 199, Subject File, President's Secretary's Files, 1945–53, Truman Papers.

10. *Public Papers: Truman, 1945*, pp. 212–13, 365–66, 381; Truman, *Year of Decisions*, pp. 522–23.

11. *Public Papers: Truman, 1945*, pp. 472–75; Hewlett and Anderson, *New World*, pp. 461–66.

12. Fyke Farmer, "Memorandum of conference between Fyke Farmer of Nashville, Tennessee, and President Harry S. Truman at the White House on Thursday, October 11, 1945," Box 177, Oppenheimer Papers; Culbertson to Truman, Sept. 17, 1945, and C. G. Ross to Culbertson, Sept. 20, 1945, OF 692A, White House Central Files, Truman Papers; Samuel I. Rosenman, "Memorandum for the President" (Dec. 27, 1945), with Truman's handwritten notation, Box 200, Subject File-NSC-Atomic, President's Secretary's Files, Truman Papers.

13. D. Lilienthal, *Atomic Energy Years*, p. 10; Acheson, *Present at the Creation*, pp. 151–53; B. Bernstein, "Quest for Security," pp. 1030–32.

14. Weisskopf to J. Halle Schaffner, Nov. 1, 1946, Box 2, ECAS Records, Chicago; Lilienthal to Hutchins, Apr. 17, 1946, Box 7, Hutchins Papers; John Hancock, "Memorandum for Files" (May 1, 1946), Box 52, Baruch Papers; A. Smith, *A Peril and a Hope*, pp. 457–59; Acheson, *Present at the Creation*, p. 154; Baratta, "Was the Baruch Plan a Proposal of World Government?" pp. 597–98.

15. In October 1945, Oppenheimer told Einstein that he and his "immediate colleagues" thought the Bomb was "focusing more sharply the attention of the public on the dangers of international anarchy" and "providing a new and specific point of discussion where agreement might be less difficult to achieve." J. R. Oppenheimer, "Atomic Explosives" (Apr. 6, 1946), Box 52, Baruch Papers; Oppenheimer to Einstein, Oct. 10, 1945, Box 32, Oppenheimer Papers.

16. Acheson, *Present at the Creation*, pp. 154–55; D. Lilienthal, *Atomic Energy Years*, p. 30; Baruch, *Baruch*, p. 364.

17. Baruch to Herbert Marks, Oct. 27, 1947, Box 61, "Notes on Bernard M. Baruch," Box 58, and Baruch to Truman, Mar. 26, 1946, Box 52, Baruch Papers.

18. Baruch to Herbert Bayard Swope, June 16, 1947, Box 58, and John Hancock, "Memorandum of Meeting of May 30, 1946, in the State Department," Box 52, Baruch Papers; *FRUS, 1946*, 1: 802–6.

19. Baruch, "Draft" (May 7, 1946), Baruch, untitled memo (May 22, 1946), and "Draft of Mr. Baruch's talk to JFB" (May 26, 1946), Box 52, Baruch Papers; Baratta, "Was the Baruch Plan a Proposal of World Government?" pp. 599–602.

20. *FRUS, 1946*, 1: 860, 982–83; Baruch to Norman Thomas, Oct. 18, 1946, Box 61, Baruch Papers; D. Lilienthal, *Atomic Energy Years*, pp. 42–43; Baruch to John Vorys, Aug. 2, 1946, Oct. 10, 1949, in "Atomic Control or World Government," *CC* 3 (Feb. 1950): 358–59.

21. Baruch to Byrnes, Mar. 13, 1946, and Baruch to Eisenhower, May 24, 1946, Box 52, Baruch Papers; Acheson, *Present at the Creation*, p. 155; Leffler, *Preponderance of Power*, p. 115.

22. Baruch also accused Acheson of recording his telephone conversations, a charge Acheson denied. In fact, Baruch secretly recorded Acheson's. Acheson, *Present at the Creation*, pp. 156, 216; Baruch to Leonard Carmichael, Jan. 15, 1947, Box 61, and Baruch to Acheson, Aug. 21, 1946, and Acheson to Baruch, Aug. 23, 1946, Box 58, Baruch Papers.

23. Lilienthal, Acheson, and even Byrnes were distressed by Baruch's U.N. message.

U.S. Department of State, *United States Atomic Energy Proposals*; D. Lilienthal, *Atomic Energy Years*, pp. 58–59.

24. Truman, *Years of Trial and Hope*, pp. 10–11; Truman to Baruch, July 10, 1946, and Baruch to Truman, July 2, 1946, "Baruch, Bernard M." folder, General File, President's Secretary's Files, 1945–53, Truman Papers; B. Bernstein, "Quest for Security," pp. 1037–44; Mark Oliphant, "Three Men and the Bomb," *BAS* 45 (Mar. 1989): 42.

25. D. Lilienthal, *Atomic Energy Years*, pp. 123, 571; "BMB Incidental Notes" (June 3, 1946), Box 52, Baruch Papers; Herken, *Winning Weapon*, pp. 98–99.

26. Seaborg, *Stemming the Tide*, pp. 25–26; Rosenberg, "American Atomic Strategy," pp. 65–66; Hancock to Norman Thomas, Nov. 20, 1946, Box 42, SASSAE, DOS Records; *FRUS, 1947*, 1: 336; *FRUS, 1949*, 1: 481; Rhodes, *Making of the Atomic Bomb*, p. 769.

27. Osborn oral history interview, July 10, 1974, pp. 42–47.

28. Osborn started out with the same uncompromising attitude. When he began his service, he recalled, "I had no illusion about the Russians at all, and I was inclined to agree right away that they were not going to accept any plan by which foreigners . . . would have a free chance to inspect their country." Osborn, UNAEC Diary, July 24, 1947, Box 2, Osborn to whom it may concern, Mar. 11, 1952, and untitled notes for Oct. 4, 5, 13, 1948, Box 1, Osborn Papers; Osborn to Albert Gotlieb, Mar. 30, 1949, Box 7, SASSAE, DOS Records; Osborn oral history interview, July 10, 1974, pp. 44–45.

29. George Kennan, head of the State Department's Policy Planning Staff, wondered by late 1949 and early 1950 if the U.S. government was interested in international control of nuclear weapons, for "we were basing our defense posture on such weapons, and were intending to make first use of them." D. Lilienthal, *Atomic Energy Years*, pp. 464, 615; Rosenberg, "American Atomic Strategy," p. 75; *FRUS, 1949*, 1: 192–95; McGeorge Bundy to Robert Oppenheimer, Dec. 1, 1952, Box 191, Oppenheimer Papers; Kennan, *Memoirs*, pp. 471–74.

30. Acheson, *Present at the Creation*, pp. 320–21; *FRUS, 1949*, 1: 464–66; George C. Spiegel, "Memorandum for the Files" (Nov. 8, 1951), and William C. Foster, "Memorandum for the Secretary of State" (Dec. 31, 1951), Box 51, SASSAE, DOS Records.

31. Strauss, *Men and Decisions*, pp. 216–24, 350–51; York, *Advisors*, p. 45; *FRUS, 1949*, 1: 595–99.

32. Some years later, Enrico Fermi recalled that his "opinion at that time was that one should try to outlaw the thing before it was born." Another GAC member, Hartley Rowe, thought that people could not "go from one engine of destruction to another, each of them a thousand times greater in potential destruction, and still retain any normal perspective in regard to their relationships with other countries and also in relationship with peace." *FRUS, 1949*, 1: 569–73; York, *Advisors*, pp. 46–56; U.S. Atomic Energy Commission, *In the Matter of J. Robert Oppenheimer*, pp. 395, 510.

33. Lilienthal noted in his diary on November 6 that "just as the A-bomb obscured our view and gave a false sense of security, we are in danger of falling into the same error again in discussion" of the H-Bomb: "some cheap, easy way out." *FRUS, 1949*, 1: 576–85; Hewlett and Duncan, *Atomic Shield*, pp. 385–91; D. Lilienthal, *Atomic Energy Years*, p. 591.

34. Truman, *Years of Trial and Hope*, pp. 308–9; Acheson, *Present at the Creation*, pp. 344–49; Rosenberg, "American Atomic Strategy," pp. 82–84; *FRUS, 1950*, 1: 505–11; D. Lilienthal, *Atomic Energy Years*, pp. 632–33.

35. Acheson, *Present at the Creation*, pp. 377–79; *Hydrogen Bomb*; Pfau, *No Sacrifice Too Great*, p. 134; Leffler, *Preponderance of Power*, pp. 452–53; Weart, *Nuclear Fear*, p. 145; Divine, *Blowing on the Wind*, p. 16.

36. Osborn, UNAEC Diary, June 3, 1947, Box 3, Osborn Papers; Herken, *Winning Weapon*, pp. 258–59; D. Lilienthal, *Atomic Energy Years*, p. 391.

37. Millis, ed., *Forrestal Diaries*, p. 487; S. Everett Gleason, "Memorandum for the President" (Oct. 23, 1952), Box 202, Subject File, President's Secretary's Files, 1945–53, Truman Papers; D. Lilienthal, *Atomic Energy Years*, pp. 473–74.

38. *FRUS, 1949*, 1: 507; *FRUS, 1950*, 1: 22–24; Kennan to Eugene Rabinowitch, Sept. 11, 1956, Box 31, Kennan Papers; Acheson, *Present at the Creation*, p. 347; Minutes of Cabinet Defence Committee Meeting of Dec. 7, 1949, 23 (7), Cabinet Defence Committee Records.

39. This secret account coincides with the public account in Truman's memoirs. British Cabinet meeting of Dec. 12, 1950, 85 (3), CAB 128, Cabinet Records; Truman, *Years of Trial and Hope*, pp. 395–96, 410–11.

40. "Memorandum of Conversation" (June 25, 1950), "Memorandum of Conversation" (Dec. 1, 1950), and "Memorandum of Conversation" (Dec. 27, 1950), Box 65, Acheson Papers.

41. Truman wrote that the furor over his "atomic bomb" remarks at the press conference demonstrated "just how sensitive and on edge the world had become." John K. Emmerson to Dean Rusk, Nov. 8, 1950, 711.5611/11-850, and Satterthwaite to SecState, Dec. 7, 1950, 711.5611/12-750, DOS Records; Truman, *Years of Trial and Hope*, pp. 394–96.

42. Anders, ed., *Forging the Atomic Shield*, p. 137; Seaborg, *Stemming the Tide*, p. 29; "Memorandum of Conversation" (May 25, 1951), 711.5611/5-2551, DOS Records.

43. Pogue, *George C. Marshall*, p. 488; Herken, *Winning Weapon*, pp. 333–34.

44. Dean Rusk, then a State Department official, recalled that, after Chinese Communist military advances in Korea, "Truman's own military advisers told him that the only strategy which could possibly affect the situation in Korea would be the mass destruction of Chinese cities with nuclear weapons. That option was never seriously considered since Truman refused to go down that trail." Truman, "Memorandum" (Apr. 24, 1954), in Ferrell, ed., *Off the Record*, p. 304; Rusk, *As I Saw It*, p. 170.

45. *NYT*, Feb. 3, 1958.

46. Thomas F. Farrell to Baruch, Sept. 3, 1946, Box 38, SASSAE, DOS Records; Baruch to Forrestal, Sept. 10, 1946, and Forrestal to Baruch, Sept. 16, 1946, Box 62, Baruch Papers.

47. Truman claimed that he told Stimson to "straighten out the record." Truman to Karl T. Compton, Dec. 16, 1946, OF 692A, White House Central Files, 1945–53, Truman Papers; Truman to Stimson, Dec. 31, 1946, Reel 116, Stimson Papers.

48. Stimson, "Decision to Use the Atomic Bomb," pp. 97–107; "Message for Lowell Thomas from Mr. Bundy" (Feb. 6, 1947), Reel 116, Stimson Papers.

49. In the months before the Hiroshima bombing, most estimates by U.S. military planners ranged between 20,000 and 46,000 American combat deaths if an invasion of Japan took place. Some top military officers (particularly in the navy) argued that neither an invasion nor use of the Bomb was necessary to secure Japan's surrender. Nevertheless, in his memoirs, Truman claimed that the atomic bombing of Japan saved 500,000 American lives, a figure he sometimes raised to 1,000,000. Clearly, the vastly inflated figures produced by Truman, like those marshaled by Stimson, had more to do with postwar rationalization than with wartime reality. Miles, "Hiroshima," pp. 121–40; Barton J. Bernstein, "A Postwar Myth: 500,000 U.S. Lives Saved," *BAS* 42 (June-July 1986): 38–40; Truman, *Year of Decisions*, p. 121.

50. Stimson told Secretary of State George Marshall that Conant "begged me to write such an article to try to clear the air. He was afraid that the misrepresentations were getting a foothold on the educators of the coming generation." Some four decades later, McGeorge

Bundy, the ghostwriter of the piece, stated that "it was intended to demonstrate that the bomb was not used without a searching consideration of alternatives"—something that, in retrospect, he conceded had not taken place. Stimson to Felix Frankfurter, Dec. 12, 1946, Stimson to Truman, Jan. 7, 1947, and Stimson to Marshall, Jan. 28, 1947, Reel 116, Stimson Papers; Bundy, *Danger and Survival*, pp. 92–93.

51. Truman told Stimson that "it clarifies the situation very well" and reported that "all the people around the White House were highly pleased with it." Marshall to Stimson, Jan. 22, 1947, Acheson to Stimson, Jan. 25, 1947, Truman to Stimson, Jan. 26, Feb. 4, 1947, and Byrnes to Stimson, Jan. 28, 1947, Reel 116, Stimson Papers.

52. Conant to Bundy, Nov. 30, 1946, Conant to Stimson, Jan. 22, 1947, Bush to Stimson, Feb. 3, 1947, and Stimson to Baruch, Jan. 20, 1947, Reel 116, Stimson Papers.

53. This point is developed in Chapter 3.

54. Lifton, *Death in Life*, pp. 281–82; *PN*, Aug. 13, 1948, Aug. 18, 1950.

55. "Many of the scientists . . . want us to tell everything," Baruch complained in late June 1946. Baruch to Norman M. Smith, Mar. 3, 1947, Box 61, Baruch to David Lilienthal, June 7, 1949, Sept. 23, 1947, Box 63, "Notes on Bernard M. Baruch" (1949), Box 58, and Baruch to Ralph Coghlan, June 30, 1946, Box 61, Baruch Papers.

56. In a *New York Herald Tribune* editorial arranged by Osborn, the newspaper accused the ECAS of "dangerous misconceptions" and of showing "high contempt" for the United Nations. Frederick H. Osborn, "The World Debate: Man vs. the State," *Freedom & Union*, Jan. 1948, p. 22; Osborn, UNAEC Diary, June 30, 1947, Box 2, Osborn Papers; *New York Herald Tribune*, July 1, 1947.

57. Kennan to Francis Russell, Aug. 23, 1946, Box 27, Acheson Papers.

58. In 1947, the ECAS tried again to arrange a meeting of American and Soviet scientists. This time, committee members decided not to ask the State Department for permission but to approach Andrei Gromyko, the Soviet delegate to the U.N. Security Council. After two interviews with Gromyko, the latter informed them that Moscow had rejected the proposal. Leo Szilard, " 'A Letter in the Open' (Draft of an Article, August 31, 1950)," in Hawkins, Greb, and Szilard, eds., *Toward a Livable World*, pp. 111–12; Szilard to Charles Bohlen, June 16, 1960, Box 19, Szilard Papers.

59. Groves, *Now It Can Be Told*, p. 410; Groves to Robert Hutchins, Sept. 15, 1945, Box 9, Szilard Papers; Arthur H. Frye, Jr., to K. D. Nichols, May 15, 1946, and Groves to the District Engineer, July 8, 1946, "201 (Szilard, Leo)" folder, Manhattan Engineering District Records; interview with Leslie R. Groves, Nov. 7, 1967, in Ermenc, ed., *Atomic Bomb Scientists*, pp. 244–47.

60. Lilienthal to Hyman Goldsmith and Eugene Rabinowitch, Jan. 1, 1948, Box 2, Rabinowitch Papers, Albany; Lapp, *Atoms and People*, pp. 109–10; Weart, *Nuclear Fear*, p. 180.

61. John M. Hancock, "Meeting—April 5, 1946," Box 52, Baruch Papers; Oppenheimer to Einstein, Apr. 18, 1947, Oppenheimer to Harrison Brown, Mar. 5, 1948, Box 32, and Oppenheimer to Higinbotham, May 20, 1947, Box 120, Oppenheimer Papers.

62. Victor F. Weisskopf, "Report on the Visa Situation" (Apr. 1952), Box 77, Oppenheimer Papers; interview with Lew Kowarski, Mar. 16, 1970, in Ermenc, ed., *Atomic Bomb Scientists*, p. 197; François de Rose to Frederick Osborn, Oct. 26, 1949, and Frederick Osborn to Joseph Chase, Oct. 26, 1949, Box 7, SASSAE, DOS Records; *FRUS, 1949*, 1: 466; Peierls, *Bird of Passage*, pp. 321–22.

63. Oliphant continued to enjoy great prestige as Australia's top nuclear physicist and in 1971 was appointed governor of South Australia. Cockburn and Ellyard, *Oliphant*, pp. 188–95.

64. U.S. Senate, Select Committee to Study Governmental Operations with Respect to Intelligence Activities, *Final Report*, 3: 437–38; "McCarthy's New Accusations," *BAS* 6 (Nov. 1950): 352; Harold C. Urey, "Needed: Less Witch Hunting and More Work," *BAS* 5 (Oct. 1949): 265; Weart, *Nuclear Fear*, p. 121. See also Schrecker, *No Ivory Tower*, pp. 130–31, 138–60; Grodzins and Rabinowitch, eds., *Atomic Age*, pp. 393–493.

65. Szilard had earlier sought information from the Department of Justice as to any legal barriers to publication of the letter, but—at the urging of the State Department, which did not want to encourage him—the attorney general refused to give him any advice. Only after the publication of the "Letter to Stalin" in the December 1947 issue of the *BAS* did the Justice Department begin "determining whether the matter . . . constitutes a violation of the Logan Act." Robert Lovett to Tom Clark, Nov. 11, 1947, Acting Attorney General to Szilard, Nov. 11, 1947, and Jack D. Neal to E. A. Gullion, Jan. 13, 1948, Box 42, SASSAE, DOS Records.

66. Herken, *Winning Weapon*, p. 322; Pfau, *No Sacrifice Too Great*, p. 117.

67. Although the authors expressed their support for the president's decision to build the Bomb, they also portrayed the critics sympathetically and concluded gloomily: "The two sides of the world are, or soon will be, like two men with pistols loaded, cocked, and pointed at each other's heads." Personal interview with Ralph Lapp, June 28, 1987; David Bruce, "Memorandum for the President" (Oct. 16, 1952), Box 39, Confidential File, White House Central Files, Truman Papers; Alsop and Lapp, "Inside Story of Our First Hydrogen Bomb," pp. 29, 150–54.

68. John M. Hancock to Baruch, Dec. 18, 1947, Box 62, Baruch Papers; *FRUS, 1947*, 1: 487–89; Schwartz, "F.B.I. and Dr. Einstein," pp. 168–73.

69. E. A. Gullion, "Memorandum of Conversation" (Apr. 26, 1948), and Marshall to Bernard Baruch, May 26, 1948, Box 77, SASSAE, DOS Records; *FRUS, 1948*, 1: 388–89.

70. *FRUS, 1950*, 1: 76–77, 101–2; George W. Perkins to SecState, June 26, 1950, and Henry S. Villard, "Memorandum of Conversation" (Nov. 18, 1950), Box 77, SASSAE, DOS Records; Groves to Robert Oppenheimer, Dec. 7, 1964, Box 36, Oppenheimer Papers.

71. D. Norman, ed., *Nehru*, 2: 264; *NYT*, Oct. 20, 1949, July 8, 1950; Donovan to SecState, Feb. 16, 1950, 711.5611/2-1650, DOS Records.

72. Sybil Morrison to Secretary, May 26, 1953, "Peace Pledge Union 1953" folder, and Morris to Vera Brittain, June 17, 1953, "Morris, Stuart" folder, Brittain Papers; Morrison, *I Renounce War*, pp. 86–87.

73. Tolman to John Hancock, May 21, 1946, Box 42, SASSAE, DOS Records; "Telephone Conversation Between Mr. Baruch and Dean Acheson, November 26, 1946" and Baruch to Meyer, May 31, 1947, Box 58, Baruch Papers.

74. Frederick Osborn, "International Control of Atomic Energy: Speech at New York University" (Jan. 12, 1949), Box 77, SASSAE, DOS Records; Osborn to Silas Axtell, Apr. 11, 1950, Box 1, Osborn Papers.

75. Welles, "Atomic Bomb and World Government," pp. 39–42; Marshall, "A Federal World Government Now?" pp. 201, 203.

76. Cord Meyer, Jr., to Clayton, Mar. 16, 1948, Clayton to Mrs. Kennard Weddell, Jan. 10, 1949, and Clayton to Meyer, Jan. 18, 1949, Box 82, and Clayton to Earl E. Hart, Mar. 7, 1949, Box 68, Clayton Papers; George V. Allen, "Memorandum of Conversation" (Apr. 12, 1949), Box 64, Acheson Papers.

77. "World Government and Revisionist Movements" (July 29, 1949), SD/GEN/30, Bureau of International Organization Affairs, DOS Records.

78. G. A. Borgese, "Third Year," *CC* 3 (Aug. 1949): 1–2; G. A. Borgese to Austin, Aug. 17, 1949, Box 13, Hutchins Papers; Minutes of the meeting of the National Political

Committee, United World Federalists, Aug. 11, 1949, Box 48, Cousins Papers, Los Angeles.

79. "American Congress and World Federation," *CC* 4 (Aug. 1950): 5–33; Wooley, *Alternatives to Anarchy*, pp. 56–57; Meyer, *Facing Reality*, p. 64; Acheson to Meyer, Apr. 27, 1951, Box 36, Acheson Papers.

80. UWF Branch and Chapter Letter, No. 19 (Jan. 27, 1948), Box 50, and Norman Cousins to Marion Lovekin, Mar. 11, 1948, Box 49, Cousins Papers, Los Angeles; Matthew Connelly to Richard J. Hughes, Feb. 2, 1948, OF 1466A, White House Central Files, Truman Papers.

81. Meyer to Truman, Aug. 18, 1948, R. D. Muir to William D. Hassett, Aug. 26, 1948, and Hassett to Meyer, Aug. 30, 1948, OF 1466, White House Central Files, Truman Papers; Truman to Cousins, Feb. 10, 1948, Cousins Papers, Beverly Hills.

82. United World Federalists, "Correspondence Bulletin" (Oct. 22, 1948), Box 49, Cousins Papers, Los Angeles; Meyer, *Facing Reality*, p. 45.

83. In 1952, Truman sent a friendly letter to UWF on its fifth anniversary. That same year, when Cousins suggested that he help prepare a farewell address for Truman, the president proved agreeable. Truman to Alan Cranston, Feb. 11, 1952, Box 54, Cousins Papers, Los Angeles; Truman to Cousins, Aug. 14, 1952, Cousins Papers, Beverly Hills.

84. Wooley, *Alternatives to Anarchy*, p. 74; Minutes of the Political Committee meeting, United World Federalists, May 3, 1949, Box 48, Cousins Papers, Los Angeles; "Book Burning," *Federalist* 3 (Oct. 1953): 8; Wittner, *Rebels Against War*, pp. 221–22.

85. Secretary Acheson thought this would be the best course of action "from a propaganda point of view." J. Edgar Hoover to the Attorney General, Mar. 11, 1949, 800.00B/3-1449, "For the President from Secretary Acheson" (Mar. 14, 1949), with handwritten approval added by Harry Truman, 800.00B/3-1849, and Acheson to All Missions in Other American Republics, Mar. 16, 1949, 800.00B/3-1449, DOS Records.

86. In the aftermath of the non-Communist peace rally, the U.S. ambassador complained that most speakers failed to adopt the "proper perspective," but he still thought the event a "step in [the] right direction." Caffery to SecState, Mar. 14, 1949, 800.00B/3-1449, Acheson to American Embassy, Paris, Mar. 29, 1949, 800.00B/3-2949, Caffery to SecState, Apr. 6, 1949, and Acheson to American Embassy, Paris, Apr. 8, 1949, 800.00B/4-649, Acheson to Riddleberger, Apr. 12, 1949, 800.00B/4-2149, and Caffery to SecState, May 2, 1949, 800.00B/5-249, DOS Records.

87. Among its members were Pablo Picasso and the Rev. Hewlett Johnson. *FRUS, 1950*, 4: 270–71; "Delegates from World Congress of Partisans of Peace Refused Entry"; *NYT*, Mar. 4, 1950.

88. The U.S. government succeeded in getting the British government to block plans for a proposed Communist-led peace conference at Sheffield, which, consequently, was canceled. The Danish government, however, proved more obdurate. *FRUS, 1950*, 4: 328–31; *FRUS, 1951*, 4: 1252.

89. *FRUS, 1949*, 5: 812–15, 824–26, 836–51; *FRUS, 1950*, 4: 297–301, 309–11, 320–26; "World Peace Council," SD/A/245, Sept. 11, 1951, Bureau of International Organization Affairs, DOS Records; *FRUS, 1951*, 4: 1246–50.

90. Acheson, "Achieving a Community Sense Among Free Nations," p. 16; *NYT*, July 13, 1950.

91. U.S. House of Representatives, Committee on Un-American Activities, *The Communist "Peace" Petition Campaign*, p. 1; U.S. House of Representatives, Committee on Un-American Activities, *Report on the Communist "Peace" Offensive*, p. 32; *NYT*, July 14, 1950, Apr. 5, 1951.

92. Duberman, *Paul Robeson*, pp. 388–89; Caute, *Great Fear*, pp. 247–48.

93. Peace Information Center, Organization Letter #7 (Aug. 25, 1950), Peace Information Center Records; *NYT*, Feb. 10, Nov. 21, 1951; Du Bois, *Autobiography*, pp. 364–65, 379, 385–86; W. E. B. Du Bois, "My Case" (Nov. 1, 1951), Box 2, Robeson Papers; Du Bois, *In Battle for Peace*, pp. 55, 64, 192.

94. Pauling stated that he had associated himself "in a smaller or larger way with every peace movement that has come to my attention" and that he believed in working for peace with both non-Communists and Communists. "Affidavit by Linus Pauling with Reference to Allegations Contained in a Letter from the Department of State, dated 19 July 1954" (Sept. 3, 1954) and "Statement by Linus Pauling" (Apr. 5, 1951), Pauling Papers; Pauling to the author, Dec. 15, 1987.

95. "Statement by Linus Pauling" (Nov. 14, 1950), notarized statement by Pauling (June 20, 1952), "Statement by Linus Pauling" (Jan. 4, 1953), Pauling to William D. Patton, Nov. 26, 1955, R. B. Shipley to Pauling, July 19, Oct. 1, 1954, Pauling Papers.

96. R. B. Shipley to Pauling, Feb. 14, Apr. 18, 1952, Linus Pauling, "The Department of State and the Structure of Proteins" (1952), Pauling to SecState, Sept. 3, 1954, and Charles Saltzman to Pauling, Nov. 19, 1954, Pauling Papers; "Roadblocks to a World Traveler."

97. D.M.M. to District Inspector, District "C," Bureau of Criminal Investigation, Sidney, N.Y., Oct. 19, 1957, Sept. 23, 1958, Case No. 499, Box 10, Non-Criminal Investigation Case Files, New York State Division of State Police Records.

98. *FRUS, 1948*, 1: 627; R. Gordon Arneson, "Memorandum for the Secretary" (June 16, 1950), 711.5611/6-1650, and Truman to Acheson, Feb. 14, 1950, 711.5611/2-1450, DOS Records.

99. J. W. Swihart to Russell and Hardy, Jan. 31, 1950, 711.5611/1-3150, DOS Records; *FRUS, 1950*, 1: 88–93.

100. *FRUS, 1950*, 1: 107; *FRUS, 1952–1954*, 2: 869–72.

101. *Public Papers: Truman, 1952–53*, p. 1125.

102. Stimson Diary, May 14, 1945; Truman, *Year of Decisions*, p. 421; Truman to Acheson, Mar. 17, 1954, Box 166, Acheson Papers.

Chapter 15

Epigraphs: Bullock, *Ernest Bevin*, p. 352; Kramish, *Atomic Energy in the Soviet Union*, pp. 89–90.

1. As early as August 8, Attlee had written Truman that the attack on Hiroshima "has now demonstrated to the world that a new factor pregnant with immense possibilities for good or evil has come into existence. Thoughtful people already realize that there must be a revaluation of policies and a readjustment of international relations." He added: "I believe that our two nations are profoundly convinced that if civilization is to endure and progress, war must be banished forever." Clement Attlee, "The Atomic Bomb" (Aug. 28, 1945), PREM 8/116, Prime Minister's Records; Attlee to Truman, Aug. 8, 1945, Box 83, SASSAE, DOS Records.

2. Gowing, *Independence and Deterrence*, 1: 64–66; Attlee to Truman, Sept. 25, 1945, ibid., pp. 78–81; Truman, *Year of Decisions*, pp. 534–35.

3. H. Freeman Matthews, "British Attitudes Toward Control of the Atomic Bomb" (Nov. 7, 1945), Box 83, SASSAE, DOS Records; *PN*, Sept. 28, 1945; Baratta, "Bygone 'One World,'" pp. 291, 294–95. For confirmation that the British government felt domestic pressures for action, see Attlee to Truman, Oct. 16, 1945, Box 83, SASSAE, DOS Records.

4. Gormly, "Washington Declaration," pp. 131–43; "Atomic Energy," Byrnes Papers; Gowing, *Independence and Deterrence*, 1: 72–77, 82–84.

5. Until the last, Baruch remained uncertain that the British would vote for his proposal at the United Nations. Gowing, *Independence and Deterrence*, 1: 90–91, 164; "Extract from Verbatim Record of Lord Attlee's Television Interview (The Listener, January 22, 1959)," FO 371/140435, Foreign Office Records; Schwarz, *Speculator*, pp. 504–5.

6. Bullock, *Ernest Bevin*, p. 352; Harris, *Attlee*, p. 288. See also Pierre, *Nuclear Politics*, pp. 73–77, 81; Gowing, *Independence and Deterrence*, 1: 183–85, 209, 2: 499–500.

7. P. M. S. Blackett, "Atomic Energy: An Immediate Policy for Great Britain" (Nov. 5, 1945), PREM 8/115, Prime Minister's Records; Gowing, *Independence and Deterrence*, 1: 115, 183–84.

8. E. S. Jacob to Attlee, Nov. 12, 1945, and Attlee's minute of Nov. 6, 1945, PREM 8/115, Prime Minister's Records; Gowing, *Independence and Deterrence*, 1: 115–16, 172.

9. Tizard to Defense Minister, Sept. 26, 1949, PREM 8/1101, Prime Minister's Records; Gowing, *Independence and Deterrence*, 1: 123, 229–31.

10. Pierre, *Nuclear Politics*, p. 79; Millis, ed., *Forrestal Diaries*, p. 491; John H. Bruins to SecState, Dec. 15, 1950, 741.5611/12-1550, DOS Records; Gowing, *Independence and Deterrence*, 1: 449–50.

11. *NYT*, Aug. 20, 1945; Barton Bernstein, "A Postwar Myth: 500,000 U.S. Lives Saved," *BAS* 42 (June–July 1986): 38; Churchill, *Triumph and Tragedy*, pp. 638–39.

12. Gowing, *Independence and Deterrence*, 1: 19–20, 24, 210, 212–13; Myrdal, *Game of Disarmament*, p. 162.

13. G. R. Strauss to Attlee, Nov. 25, 1949, and Attlee to Strauss, Nov. 27, 1949, PREM 8/1093, Prime Minister's Records.

14. Harris, *Attlee*, p. 291; Gowing, *Britain and Atomic Energy*, p. 133; *NYT*, Oct. 6, 1950.

15. Stucky, *August 6, 1945*, p. 108; "Statements on the Second Anniversary of Hiroshima," *BAS* 3 (Sept. 1947): 235.

16. J. D. Cockcroft to R. E. France, Sept. 6, 1951, AB 16/52, Atomic Energy Authority Records; L. N. Helsby to Attlee, Oct. 14, 1947, PREM 8/910, Prime Minister's Records.

17. Attlee to John Wilmot, Sept. 30, 1947, Wilmot to Attlee, Sept. 30, 1947, and Attlee to Wilmot, Oct. 1, 1947, PREM 8/910, Prime Minister's Records.

18. G. R. Strauss to Attlee, Oct. 13, 1947, L. N. Helsby to Attlee, Oct. 14, 1947, A. V. Alexander to Attlee, Oct. 18, 1947, and J.L.P. to J. M. Wilson, Oct. 21, 1947, PREM 8/910, Prime Minister's Records; Joseph Rotblat to D. E. H. Peirson, Nov. 1, 1948, AB 16/401, Atomic Energy Authority Records.

19. Anonymous to J. D. Cockcroft, Jan. 9, 1948, AB 16/401, Atomic Energy Authority Records; Rotblat to Attlee, Mar. 9, 1948, Richard F. Wood to J. L. Pumphrey, Mar. 12, 1948, John Henniker to Pumphrey, Mar. 16, 1948, Pumphrey to Rotblat, Mar. 16, 1948, PREM 8/910, Prime Minister's Records.

20. Minute by D. E. H. Peirson of Apr. 5, 1948, and G. R. Strauss to Rotblat, Apr. 21, 1948, AB 16/401, Atomic Energy Authority Records.

21. Grant to SecState, June 7, 1949, 800.00B/6-749, DOS Records; Minutes of British Cabinet meeting of Sept. 6, 1950, 56(3), CAB 128, Cabinet Records.

22. *NYT*, Oct. 6, 1950; D. Russell, *Tamarisk Tree 3*, pp. 133–34.

23. *Times* (London), Nov. 2, 1950; *NYT*, Nov. 2, 1950.

24. D. Russell, *Tamarisk Tree 3*, pp. 131–32; *FRUS, 1950*, 4: 328–32; British Cabinet meeting of Nov. 9, 1950, 72(8), CAB 128, Cabinet Records.

25. British Cabinet meeting of Nov. 30, 1950, 80(1), CAB 128, Cabinet Records; Acheson, *Present at the Creation*, pp. 478–79, 484.

26. Gowing, *Independence and Deterrence*, 1: 315–16, 414.

27. Holloway, "Entering the Nuclear Arms Race," pp. 183–87; Holloway, *Soviet Union and the Arms Race*, pp. 19–20. See also Joint Atomic Energy Intelligence Committee, "Status of the Soviet Atomic Energy Program" (July 4, 1950), Box 200, Subject File, President's Secretary's Files, 1945–53, Truman Papers; Bundy, *Danger and Survival*, p. 50.

28. Khrushchev, *Khrushchev Remembers: The Last Testament*, pp. 11, 46, 58; Khrushchev, *Khrushchev Remembers: The Glasnost Tapes*, pp. 69, 100–101. See also W. Averell Harriman to SecState, Nov. 27, 1945, Box 83, SASSAE, DOS Records.

29. York, *Advisors*, pp. 32–37; R. Medvedev and Z. Medvedev, *Khrushchev*, pp. 38–39; *Los Angeles Times*, Aug. 26, 1984; Holloway, *Soviet Union and the Arms Race*, pp. 20–23.

30. Holloway, *Soviet Union and the Arms Race*, pp. 24–27. See also Sakharov, *Memoirs*, pp. 99–100.

31. Kramish, *Atomic Energy in the Soviet Union*, pp. 87–88; Herken, *Winning Weapon*, pp. 48–49, 77; *NYT*, Sept. 25, 1946.

32. "The Soviet Press and the Atom Bomb," *U.S.S.R. Fact Sheet* 1 (July 29, 1946): 1, Box 43, SASSAE, DOS Records; Kissinger, *Nuclear Weapons and Foreign Policy*, p. 365; Alan Kirk to SecState, Jan. 23, 1950, 711.5611/1-2350, DOS Records; Gouré, *Civil Defense in the Soviet Union*, p. 8.

33. B. Bernstein, "Roosevelt, Truman, and the Atomic Bomb," p. 64; Holloway, *Soviet Union and the Arms Race*, pp. 27–28.

34. Beker, *Disarmament Without Order*, p. 21; D. Lilienthal, *Atomic Energy Years*, p. 75.

35. Andrei Gromyko, "The Russian Proposal for International Control," *BAS* 2 (July 1, 1946): 8–10; Potyarkin and Kortunov, eds., *USSR Proposes Disarmament*, pp. 106–14; *NYT*, Oct. 30, Nov. 30, 1946, Feb. 15, 1947, Jan. 30, 1948.

36. For speculations along these lines, see "News in Brief," *BAS* 6 (June 1950): 192; Grodzins and Rabinowitch, eds., *Atomic Age*, p. 5; Bloomfield, Clemens, and Griffiths, *Khrushchev and the Arms Race*, p. 10; Seaborg, *Stemming the Tide*, p. 68.

37. Rusk, *As I Saw It*, p. 139.

38. D. Lilienthal, *Atomic Energy Years*, p. 75; Osborn oral history interview, pp. 49, 59–61.

39. *NYT*, Sept. 25, 1949; *Pravda*, Jan. 16, 1950, in *CDSP* 2 (Mar. 13, 1950): 21; *Pravda*, Nov. 6, 1949, in *CDSP* 1 (Nov. 22, 1949): 7.

40. *NYT*, Oct. 31, 1950; Alan Kirk to SecState, Oct. 6, 1951, Box 7, SASSAE, DOS Records.

41. *PN*, July 22, 1949, May 12, 1950; *NYT*, Aug. 31, 1948, July 8, Aug. 10, 1949, Oct. 17, 18, 1950; "Zodiac," *CC* 3 (July 1950): 670–71.

42. *Pravda*, Apr. 14, 1949, in *CDSP* 1 (May 10, 1949): 36; "Anti-War Front"; *Pravda*, May 13, 1950, in *CDSP* 2 (July 1, 1950): 20.

43. *NYT*, Aug. 13, 1950; *Pravda*, May 28, 1950, in *CDSP* 2 (July 15, 1950): 23; "Peace Front Is Invincible."

44. *Pravda*, Sept. 23, 1950, in *CDSP* 2 (Nov. 4, 1950): 40–41; *Pravda*, Aug. 25, 1950, in *CDSP* 2 (Oct. 7, 1950): 39; *Pravda*, Aug. 28, 1950, in *CDSP* 2 (Oct. 14, 1950): 30–31; *NYT*, Aug. 25, 1951.

45. "International Stalin Peace Prizes"; *NYT*, Dec. 21, 1949, Apr. 7, 1951; Johnson, *Searching for Light*, p. 286; J. Endicott, ed., *Best of Jim Endicott*, pp. 91–92.

46. *Pravda*, Nov. 6, 1949, in *CDSP* 1 (Nov. 22, 1949): 6; *Pravda*, July 16, 1950, in *CDSP* 2 (Sept. 2, 1950): 31.

47. Bussey and Tims, *Women's International League for Peace and Freedom*, p. 197;

Izvestia, July 1, 1950, in *CDSP* 2 (Aug. 19, 1950): 28. For earlier attacks on Jehovah's Witnesses, see *Izvestia*, June 16, 1950, in *CDSP* 2 (Aug. 5, 1950): 32–33.

48. *Pravda*, May 28, 1950, in *CDSP* 2 (July 15, 1950): 24.

49. Nogee, *Soviet Policy Towards International Control of Atomic Energy*, p. 31; Smith to SecState, June 26, 1946, 811.2423/6-2646, DOS Records; *NYT*, June 30, 1946; Graham, *Science and Philosophy in the Soviet Union*, p. 74.

50. *NYT*, Nov. 21, 1948, July 15, 1951; "Open Letter to Dr. Einstein—From Four Soviet Physicists," *BAS* 4 (Feb. 1948): 37; *Pravda*, Aug. 8, 1950, in *CDSP* 2 (Sept. 23, 1950): 25; Graham, *Science and Philosophy in the Soviet Union*, pp. 114–15, 303.

51. The Soviet campaign against "cosmopolitanism," which began in January 1949, was launched on Stalin's personal initiative. Although the term "cosmopolitan" was usually applied to Jews, it referred more generally to persons who seemed suspiciously internationalist or unpatriotic. *NYT*, Nov. 25, 1948; "Attack Is Extended to Atomic Physics," *BAS* 4 (Dec. 1948): 371; Peter Krehel, "More on Cosmopolitanism in the U.S.S.R.," *CC* 2 (June 1949): 435–36; W. Hahn, *Postwar Soviet Politics*, pp. 118–22. See also Sakharov, *Memoirs*, p. 123.

52. Robert G. Hooker, Jr., to Arneson, Mar. 8, 1949, Box 54, SASSAE, DOS Records; Harrison Brown to Pierre Auger et al., Mar. 16, 1948, and Brown to George C. Marshall, Mar. 15, 1948, Box 16, ECAS Records, Chicago; Szilard to Dean Rusk, ca. Dec. 1949, Box 16, Szilard Papers.

53. Baratta, "Bygone 'One World,' " pp. 298, 303–4; "World Opinion on World Government," *CC* 1 (July 1947): 29; Goodman, "Soviet Union and World Government," p. 232.

54. "General Reactions," *CC* 2 (Aug. 1948): 34; Goodman, "Soviet Union and World Government," p. 233. See also Baratta, *Strengthening the United Nations*, p. 184.

55. Stanley K. Bigman, "The 'New Internationalism' Under Attack," *Public Opinion Quarterly* 14 (Summer 1950): 239; "Constitutional Survey—VIII," *CC* 2 (Jan. 1949): 229–32; *Pravda*, Apr. 7, 1949, in *CDSP* 1 (May 3, 1949): 25.

56. Goodman, "Soviet Union and World Government," pp. 243–48; "Pravda's Peeve," *World Government News* 7 (June 1949): 21; *Izvestia*, June 8, 1950, in *CDSP* 2 (July 22, 1950): 24. See also G. Davis, *World Is My Country*, pp. 55–56.

57. D. Russell, *Tamarisk Tree 3*, pp. 92–93; "Peace Front Is Invincible," p. 2.

58. *NYT*, Nov. 20, 1950; *Pravda*, Mar. 27, 1949, in *CDSP* 1 (Apr. 26, 1949): 24; Caute, *Communism and the French Intellectuals*, p. 187.

59. *Pravda*, July 24, 26, 1950, in *CDSP* 2 (Sept. 9, 1950): 28–29.

60. *Literaturnaya gazeta*, May 17, 1950, in *CDSP* 2 (July 8, 1950): 22.

Chapter 16

Epigraph: *NYT*, July 8, 1950.

1. Epstein, *Canada and Nuclear Weapons*, pp. 1–3.

2. S. Walker, ed., *First One Hundred Days*, p. 19; Goldsmith, *Frédéric Joliot-Curie*, p. 144; Scheinman, *Atomic Energy Policy in France*, p. 20; Goldschmidt, *Atomic Adventure*, p. 60; *World Government Highlights*, p. 41.

3. "Notes on Bernard M. Baruch," Box 58, Baruch Papers.

4. Epstein, *Canada and Nuclear Weapons*, pp. 2–3; Edwards, "Canada's Nuclear Industry," p. 125.

5. *FRUS, 1950*, 1: 61, 100–101, 561.

6. Goldschmidt, "France," pp. 58–60; Weart, *Scientists in Power*, pp. 216–17, 235–36, 263–65, 272.

7. Jules Moch oral history interview, p. 24; *FRUS, 1950*, 1: 56–57, 80–81.

8. Peter Axel, "News in Brief," *BAS* 7 (Jan. 1951): 30; *FRUS, 1950*, 1: 115; Office of Intelligence Research, DOS, "Survey of Western European Opinion on the Atom Bomb as an Immoral Weapon" (Feb. 13, 1951), p. 12, Box 7, SASSAE, DOS Records.

9. Eyvind Tew, "Scandinavian News," *One World* 2 (Aug. 1947): 25; John Nevin Sayre, "Pacifist Christianity in Europe," *Fellowship* 12 (July 1946): 114; Myrtle Wright, "Norway: Sold American," *Fellowship* 16 (July 1950): 2–3.

10. *FRUS, 1950*, 1: 76–79.

11. *PN*, Sept. 15, 1950, Aug. 10, 1951; Furtado, ed., *Turkey*, p. 9.

12. Wittner, *American Intervention in Greece*, p. 144; *PN*, Aug. 26, 1949, Aug. 10, 1951; Bourdet, "Way to European Independence," p. 12.

13. John Swomley to staff members, Oct. 16, 1951, Box 13, Series B, Sayre Papers; "German Pacifists Face Persecution," *Fellowship* 17 (Dec. 1951): 21.

14. Jean Laffitte to Friends, Apr. 20, 1951, Box 12, Robeson Papers; *NYT*, Nov. 17, 1950, Apr. 9, 1951; Peristerakis, "To Elliniko Kinima Eirinis," pp. 66–71.

15. S. Endicott, *James G. Endicott*, pp. 274–75, 286; Weisbord, *Strangest Dream*, pp. 199–200. For the much milder reaction in Norway, see Villard to SecState, Mar. 2, 1950, 711.5611/3-250, and Theodore B. Olson to SecState, Apr. 18, 1950, 711.5611/4-1850, DOS Records.

16. Robert P. Terrill to Gordon Arneson, Nov. 23, 1949, Box 47, SASSAE, DOS Records; Weart, *Scientists in Power*, pp. 240–42, 249–50; Scheinman, *Atomic Energy Policy in France*, pp. 41–42; Kowarski oral history interview, p. 207.

17. Weart, *Scientists in Power*, pp. 260–61; Scheinman, *Atomic Energy Policy in France*, pp. 43–44; *NYT*, Apr. 29, 1950; Kowarski oral history interview, pp. 207–10; interview with Lew Kowarski, in Ermenc, ed., *Atomic Bomb Scientists*, pp. 196–98.

18. Rudolf E. Schoenfeld to SecState, Jan. 12, 1949, 811.2423/1-1249, and Gallman to SecState, Feb. 7, 1950, 711.5611/2-750, DOS Records.

19. McConaughy to SecState, Sept. 29, 1949, and Clubb to SecState, Oct. 5, 1949, Box 34, SASSAE, DOS Records.

20. Cochran to SecState, Sept. 29, 1949, Heath to SecState, Oct. 1, 1949, and Schoenfeld to SecState, Oct. 13, 1949, Box 34, SASSAE, DOS Records; *NYT*, Sept. 27, Oct. 2, 1949; Ewer, *Communists on Peace*, pp. 32–33.

21. *PN*, July 16, 1948; Ewer, *Communists on Peace*, p. 22.

22. *PN*, Aug. 18, 1950; Stanley K. Bigman, "The 'New Internationalism' Under Attack," *Public Opinion Quarterly* 14 (Summer 1950): 239.

23. Grace Beaton, International Council Communication No. 379, Mar. 11, 1948, Box 2, WRI Records.

24. Bussey and Tims, *Women's International League for Peace and Freedom*, pp. 195–96; Olga Fierz to John Nevin Sayre, Apr. 28, 1950, Jan Kucera to Ernest Best, Oct. 11, 1956, and Sayre to Harold Weaver, June 12, 1959, Box 8, Series B, Sayre Papers.

25. Allen P. Lovejoy to John Nevin Sayre, June 19, 1950, Box 6, and Christopher Tang to Sayre, Dec. 14, 1951, Box 7, Series B, Sayre Papers.

26. *PN*, Aug. 26, 1949, Sept. 29, 1950; "German Pacifists Face Prosecution," *Fellowship* 17 (Dec. 1951): 21; *Peacemaker* [Australia], Aug. 1949; John Swomley to staff members, Oct. 16, 1951, Box 13, Series B, Sayre Papers; Cord Meyer, Jr., "A Progress Report on World Federation," *BAS* 5 (Oct. 1949): 282.

27. Premysl Pitter, "Why I Fled from Czechoslovakia," WRI News Release of Nov. 23, 1951, Box 3, WRI Records; Olga Fierz, "Rescue of the Germans," *Fellowship* 22 (Mar. 1956): 21; *PN*, Dec. 7, 1951.

28. Brittain, *Rebel Passion*, p. 145; Premysl Pitter, "Why I Fled from Czechoslovakia," WRI News Release of Nov. 23, 1951, Box 3, WRI Records; Premysl Pitter to Lewis Maclachlan, Feb. 12, 1952, Box 8, Series B, Sayre Papers.

29. *Yugoslav Newsletter*, July 6, 1951, Nov. 1951, Yugoslavia Miscellaneous Peace Material; Marija Vilfan to Library of the Peace Palace, Dec. 15, 1951, Portefeuille No. 25, Publications Pacifistes et Internationales Parus Après 1940.

30. Wahlbäck, *Roots of Swedish Neutrality*, pp. 76–79; Andrén, *Power-Balance and Non-Alignment*, pp. 53–72; Jervas, *Sweden Between the Power Blocs*, pp. 11–12; Einhorn, *National Security and Domestic Politics in Post-War Denmark*, pp. 13, 21.

31. Fehrm, "Sweden," pp. 213–14; Reiss, *Without the Bomb*, pp. 39–44.

32. Office of Intelligence Research, DOS, "Survey of Western European Opinion on the Atom Bomb as an Immoral Weapon" (Feb. 13, 1951), p. 12, Box 7, SASSAE, DOS Records; Matthews to SecState, Mar. 23, 1950, 758.5611/3-2350, DOS Records.

33. Allison, *Finland's Relations with the Soviet Union*, pp. 12–37; Nevakivi, "Finland and the Cold War," p. 215.

34. Bamba and Howes, eds., *Pacifism in Japan*, pp. 31–32; Schonberger, *Aftermath of War*, pp. 240–78; Harries and Harries, *Sheathing the Sword*, pp. 220–57; George, "Japan and the United States," pp. 237–96.

35. Nevakivi, "Finland and the Cold War," p. 215.

36. *FRUS, 1950*, 4: 278; *NYT*, July 22, Aug. 29, 1950; *Pravda*, Sept. 30, 1950, in *CDSP* 2 (Nov. 11, 1950): 13.

37. "News from National Sections," *Pax International* 17 (Jan.–Feb. 1951): 7; *Meaning of Survival*, pp. 86, 96.

38. *PN*, Oct. 8, 1948; *Yugoslav Newsletter*, Nov. 1951, Yugoslavia Miscellaneous Peace Material.

39. *NYT*, Nov. 6, 1949; "Zodiac," *CC* 3 (Dec. 1949): 278.

40. *FRUS, 1950*, 1: 116; Peter Axel, "News in Brief," *BAS* 7 (Jan. 1951): 30; *PN*, Nov. 17, 1950.

41. Norman, ed., *Nehru*, 2: 264; *NYT*, Oct. 20, 1949; Donovan to SecState, Feb. 16, 1950, 711.5611/2-1650, DOS Records.

42. *NYT*, Dec. 7, 1950; *PN*, Mar. 30, 1951. See also Nehru and Cousins, *Talks with Nehru*, pp. 45–46.

43. SD/GEN/29, July 29, 1949, Bureau of International Organization Affairs, DOS Records; Bantell, "Origins of the World Government Movement," p. 31; "News in Brief," *BAS* 6 (June 1950): 191.

44. Kimche, *Afro-Asian Movement*, pp. 214–16; Norman, ed., *Nehru*, 2: 398–99. See also Nehru and Cousins, *Talks with Nehru*, p. 40.

45. For some illustrations of these points, see, for example, Clara Ragaz to Louisa Jaques, Sept. 2, 1946, Reel 50, WILPF (International) Records; Brittain, *Search After Sunrise*, pp. 26–32, 136–37, 265.

46. In a 1952 interview, Einstein said that "he felt that Nehru was a fit successor to Gandhi . . . and that he is holding high Gandhi's standards in India's role in the United Nations and in the world." Bantell, "Origins of the World Government Movement," p. 34; Cousins to Romulo, Nov. 8, 1949, Box 83, Cousins Papers, Los Angeles; Nehru and Cousins, *Talks with Nehru*; Gerald Bailey to Vera Brittain, Apr. 19, 1948, "National Peace Council" folder, Brittain Papers; Homer Jack, "April 21, 1952: Interview with Albert Einstein in Princeton, New Jersey," Box 54, Series IVB, Jack Papers. See also Brittain, *Search After Sunrise*, pp. 270–71.

Chapter 17

Epigraph: Borgese to Erich Kahler, Sept. 16, 1950, Box 1, Kahler Papers.

1. Thomas, *Appeal to the Nations*, pp. 42–46; Mildred Fahrni to James Finlay et al., Apr. 25, 1951, Box 1, FOR (Canada) Records, Toronto; Eugene Rabinowitch, "Five Years After," *BAS* 7 (Jan. 1951): 5; Sakharov, *Memoirs*, p. 164.

2. *NYT*, Apr. 1, Sept. 24, 1949; *Daily Express*, July 26, 1950, quoted in "Today Britain Prepares Her 'Defence,' " *Humanity*, Aug. 1950, p. 399.

3. Ormrod, "Churches and the Nuclear Arms Race," pp. 194–98; Gallup, ed., *Gallup International Public Opinion Polls: Great Britain*, p. 263; Reginald Sorensen, "Great Britain: The Labour Government Now," *Fellowship* 16 (July 1950): 13. See also Groom, *British Thinking About Nuclear Weapons*, pp. 196–97.

4. Caldwell, "French Socialists," pp. 190–91; Gallup, ed., *Gallup International Public Opinion Polls: France*, p. 160.

5. Merritt and Merritt, eds., *Public Opinion in Semisovereign Germany*, pp. 20, 95–97, 102, 111, 124, 130; Scharrer, "War and Peace and the German Church," p. 283; Mushaben, "Cycles of Peace Protest in West Germany," p. 27.

6. External Research Staff, DOS, "Views of Western European Nations on Use of the Atomic Bomb" (Oct. 16, 1950), Box 7, SASSAE, DOS Records; Merritt and Merritt, eds., *Public Opinion in Semisovereign Germany*, pp. 98, 127.

7. U.S. government surveys in October and November 1950 found that only 9 percent of Germans in the American zone held strict pacifist views. André Trocmé to John Nevin Sayre, Dec. 19, 1950, Box 10, Series B, Sayre Papers; Cioc, *Pax Atomica*, pp. 20–21; Merritt and Merritt, eds., *Public Opinion in Semisovereign Germany*, p. 101.

8. According to a State Department study, this was "in striking contrast" to the attitudes of West Europeans, who consistently opposed future use of the Bomb. Only in Great Britain was there a fairly even split on the question of its use. Yergin, *Shattered Peace*, p. 285; Boyer, *By the Bomb's Early Light*, pp. 335–39; Gallup, ed., *Gallup Poll*, pp. 839, 895, 929; External Research Staff, DOS, "Views of Western European Nations on Use of the Atomic Bomb" (Oct. 16, 1950), pp. 4, 7, Box 7, SASSAE, DOS Records.

9. Einstein to Born, Sept. 15, 1950, in Born, ed., *Born-Einstein Letters*, pp. 187–88; William O. Douglas, "An Obligation to History," *CC* 4 (Jan. 1951): 281.

10. Of this 51 percent, about one out of five qualified their response. Even so, in September 1950, only 28 percent had desired to "use the atom bomb in Korea." Hewlett and Duncan, *Atomic Shield*, p. 548; York, *Making Weapons, Talking Peace*, p. 51; Boyer, *By the Bomb's Early Light*, pp. 340, 347; "Churchmen Sanction Possible Use of Bomb," *Fellowship* 17 (Jan. 1951): 24; Gallup, ed., *Gallup Poll*, pp. 938, 1027.

11. G. A. Borgese, "Of Common Cause," *CC* 4 (June 1951): 562.

12. The speakers included Laurence Housman, Alex Comfort, and Vera Brittain (authors); Michael Tippett (composer); and Dame Sybil Thorndike (actress). André Trocmé to John Nevin Sayre, Box 10, Series B, Sayre Papers; Morrison, *I Renounce War*, p. 86; *PN*, Jan. 21, 28, Dec. 16, 1949.

13. Minutes of the International Secretariat of World Citizens meetings of Dec. 31, 1950 and Jan. 1, 1951, Davis Papers; "Thought Needed," *CC* 4 (Apr. 1951): 501; "This Critical Hour," *CC* 4 (June 1951): 613; Wooley, *Alternatives to Anarchy*, p. 61.

14. Cranston added: "The worse the international situation becomes, the more urgently federalists feel they must get world government before World War III breaks out. The worse the international situation becomes, the more hopelessly non-federalists respond that we cannot get world government." "Taking Bearings," *CC* 4 (Apr. 1951): 449; Alan Cranston, "To Fill the Vacancy," *CC* 4 (Apr. 1951): 451.

15. Leo Szilard, "Can We Have International Control of Atomic Energy?" *BAS* 6 (Jan. 1950): 64–65.

16. Szilard to Linus Pauling, Feb. 8, 1950, and Pauling to Szilard, Feb. 1, 1950, Box 15; Szilard to Einstein, Feb. 24, 1950, Box 7; and Szilard to Stringfellow Barr, Apr. 24, 1950, Box 4, Szilard Papers.

17. Theresa L. Hildebrand, "To Close the Chasm," *CC* 4 (Aug. 1950): 49; Hans Thirring, "Who Is an Aggressor?" *BAS* 9 (Mar. 1953): 68–72, 96.

18. Harold C. Urey, "An Alternative Course for the Control of Atomic Energy," *BAS* 3 (June 1947): 139–42; " 'The Atlantic Community Faces the Bomb' (Radio Discussion, September 25, 1949)," in Hawkins, Greb, and Szilard, eds., *Toward a Livable World*, pp. 57–58; Harold C. Urey, "Should America Build the H-Bomb?" *BAS* 6 (Mar. 1950): 72–73; A. Smith, *A Peril and a Hope*, pp. 503–4.

19. Wooley, *Alternatives to Anarchy*, pp. 92–115, 120–21; de Rusett, *Strengthening the Framework*, pp. 96–97; Baratta, *Strengthening the United Nations*, p. 121. For material on the extensive activities and influence of the AUC, see Clayton Papers, Boxes 68–69, 84–87.

20. Cherwell insisted: "Scientists wishing to express political views should join frankly political organizations." "Annual General Meeting," *Atomic Scientists' News* 1 [n.s.] (Sept. 1951): 24–26; personal interview with Joseph Rotblat, July 12, 1990.

21. Thomas to A. J. Muste, Jan. 15, 1951, Box 62, and Thomas to Richard Harrington, Aug. 23, 1950, Box 60, Thomas Papers; personal interview with Norman Thomas, Oct. 4, 1966.

22. Alfred Hassler, "Cops in Korea," *Fellowship* 16 (Sept. 1950): 4; "Interim Administrative Committee" (Aug. 7, 1950), Box 2, War Resisters League Records; Shannon, *Decline of American Communism*, pp. 211–13.

23. "Branch and Chapter Letter," no. 57 (Sept. 21, 1950), Box 52, and United World Federalists, "Declaration of American Purpose" (Nov. 22, 1950), Box 51, Cousins Papers, Los Angeles. For other indications of support for the war by America's world government advocates, see Wooley, *Alternatives to Anarchy*, pp. 70–72, 80; "Grim Lesson," *World Government News* 8 (Sept. 1950): 3–5; Albert Guerard, "The Meaning of Victory," *CC* 4 (Nov. 1950): 169–70.

24. *PN*, Aug. 18, 1950; Stockwin, *Japanese Socialist Party*, pp. 44–48, 70; Office of Intelligence Research, DOS, "Survey of Western European Opinion on the Atom Bomb as an Immoral Weapon" (Feb. 13, 1951), p. 15, Box 7, SASSAE, DOS Records.

25. Personal interview with Norman Thomas, Oct. 4, 1966; United World Federalists, "Declaration of American Purpose" (Nov. 22, 1950), Box 51, Cousins Papers, Los Angeles. See also Guerard, "Meaning of Victory," pp. 170–71; Elisabeth Mann Borgese to Henry Usborne, Dec. 18, 1950, Box 9, WMWFG Records.

26. Cousins to Dean Acheson, Dec. 14, 1950, Box 62, Acheson Papers; Cousins to Einstein, Aug. 8, 1950, Box 87, Einstein Papers; Cousins to Paul Reese, June 12, 1951, Box 48, Cousins Papers, Los Angeles; Cousins, *Who Speaks for Man?* pp. 255–318.

27. Baratta, "Bygone 'One World,' " p. 484; "UWF's Birthday Marks Half a Decade of Progress," *Federalist* 1 (Feb. 1952): 6–7; Elisabeth Mann Borgese, "1950: World Movement at the Divide," *CC* 4 (Dec. 1950): 226–27.

28. Michael Howard, "Korean Signpost," *Humanity*, Aug. 1950, pp. 383–86; Usborne to Elisabeth Mann Borgese, Dec. 28, 1950, Box 9, WMWFG Records.

29. Edward Teller, "Atomic Scientists Have Two Responsibilities," *BAS* 3 (Dec. 1947): 355–56; A. Smith, *A Peril and a Hope*, p. 504; Teller, *Legacy of Hiroshima*, pp. 62–76.

30. Meyer was assigned to the Office of Policy Coordination, which handled the CIA's covert operations. Meyer, *Facing Reality*, pp. 55–57, 63–65; Wooley, *Alternatives to Anarchy*, pp. 57–58.

31. Caute, *Communism and the French Intellectuals*, pp. 251–55; Caute, *Fellow-Travellers*, p. 293. For some of Sartre's pro-Soviet essays, published in *Les Temps Modernes* during the early 1950s, see Sartre, *Communists and Peace*.

32. F. Siegmund-Schültze to John Nevin Sayre, Oct. 23, 1950, Box 17, Series B, Sayre Papers; *PN*, Aug. 3, 1951; Ueda, "Tabata Shinobu," p. 240.

33. Leo Szilard, "Shall We Face the Facts?" *BAS* 5 (Oct. 1949): 269–73; Einstein to Norman Cousins, Aug. 2, 1950, Box 87, Einstein Papers.

34. Frank J. Gordon, "A Brief History of the Women's International League for Peace and Freedom" (1981), p. 6, WILPF International Office Records; Minutes of the Executive Committee meeting, British FOR, July 19, 1950, Reel 5, FOR (Great Britain) Records; N. Ingram, "Ambivalence in the Post–World War II French Peace Movement," p. 13; "Canadian F.O.R. Statement on Korea" (Aug. 1950), Box 1, FOR (Canada) Records, Toronto.

35. Helene Stahelin to Lester Pearson, Feb. 25, 1953, Reel 88, WILPF (International) Records; Leander, "Die Friedensbewegung," pp. 73–83; Clements, *Back from the Brink*, p. 98.

36. K. Ingram, *Fifty Years*, p. 21; "Copy of letter sent to American press agencies and representatives in Great Britain" (Jan. 23, 1951), Box 4, National Peace Council Records; Wittner, *Rebels Against War*, pp. 202–3; FOR, *Meaning of Korea*, n.p.

37. Siegmund-Schültze to John Nevin Sayre, Oct. 23, 1950, Box 17, Series B, Sayre Papers; McCrea and Markle, "Atomic Scientists and Protest," p. 225; "To Our Readers," *BAS* 5 (Oct. 1949): 261.

38. This phenomenon is reported extensively in *Peace News* after the beginning of the Korean War. The three-quarter-page headline appears in the Jan. 12, 1951, issue. See also "N.P.C. Notes and News," *One World* 4 (Dec. 1950–Jan. 1951): 12–13.

39. Morrison, *I Renounce War*, pp. 83–84.

40. Committee for the Compilation of Materials, *Hiroshima and Nagasaki*, pp. 574–75; Tano Jodai to Agnes Stapledon, Oct. 12, 1953, Reel 79, WILPF (International) Records; *PN*, Aug. 3, 1951.

41. Brittain, "Changes in the Peace Movement," p. 261. Brittain says much the same thing in her *Testament of Experience*, p. 438.

42. "Report of F.o.R. Work in Argentina" (July 1957), Box 1, Series B, Sayre Papers; Brittain, *Rebel Passion*, p. 66; *News Letter*, no. 69 (Dec. 1950), p. 7.

43. Mildred Fahrni to James Finlay et al., Apr. 25, 1951, Box 1, FOR (Canada) Records, Toronto; Mildred Scott Olmsted, "Report of the National Administrative Secretary" (Nov. 1950), Box 13, WILPF (United States) Records.

44. Noting that the Canadian FOR secretary had just been accused of preaching Communism, a leading Canadian pacifist concluded: "The very use of the word 'peace' is to attach a stigma to the one who uses it." Howorth, *France*, p. 18; Andersson and Lindkvist, "Peace Movement in Sweden," pp. 11–12; Kaspar Mayr, "Interim Report" (Aug. 26, 1949), Box 2, Series B, Sayre Papers; James M. Finlay to John F. Davidson, Feb. 14, 1951, Box 1, FOR (Canada) Records, Toronto.

45. The National Peace Council took this same tack in 1951, noting that it had "no connection whatsoever with the Communist peace campaign." "Civil Defense" (1950), Box 1, PPU Records; "Copy of letter sent to American press agencies and representatives in Great Britain" (Jan. 23, 1951), Box 4, National Peace Council Records.

46. "Report of the Swedish section May 1951," Reel 84, WILPF (International) Records; K. Ingram, *Fifty Years*, p. 21; A. Smith, *A Peril and a Hope*, p. 523; "Is Peace a Bad Word?" (1950), Box 28, FOR (United States) Records.

47. Helen Strong to Dorothy Robinson, Sept. 12, 1951, Reel 54, WILPF (International)

Records; "A Red Is a Red Is a Red," *CC* 4 (Dec. 1950): 280; "Red," *Fellowship* 16 (Nov. 1950): 1; personal interview with James Peck, Apr. 21, 1966.

48. *PN*, Nov. 10, 24, Dec. 29, 1950; *New Zealand Christian Pacifist*, Feb. 1951.

49. "Report of the Norwegian Section of WILPF, June 1950–April 1951," Reel 81, "Report from the Swedish Section of the WILPF, July 1950," Reel 84, and "Report of the Danish Section" (July 1950), WILPF (International) Records; Roberts, "Women's Peace Activism in Canada," p. 295; Bussey and Tims, *Women's International League for Peace and Freedom*, p. 196.

50. Stanley K. Bigman, "The 'New Internationalism' Under Attack," *Public Opinion Quarterly* 14 (Summer 1950): 235–61; Wooley, *Alternatives to Anarchy*, pp. 72–74; "The Myth That Threatened One American Town," *Federalist* 3 (Apr. 1953): 8–10.

51. "Opposition Renews Attacks on Scattered Fronts," *Federalist* 1 (Jan. 1952): 6; Stanley Platt to Norman Cousins, Oct. 5, 1952, Box 54, Cousins Papers, Los Angeles.

52. Cranston would later become U.S. senator from California. Swing, *"Good Evening!"* pp. 244, 262, 264, 276–81; "The Myth That Threatened One American Town," p. 10; Wooley, *Alternatives to Anarchy*, p. 73. See also Cranston to Members of the National Executive Council, UWF, Mar. 1, 1950, Box 52, Cousins Papers, Los Angeles; Meyer, *Facing Reality*, p. 51.

53. Köszegi and Szent-Ivanyi, "A Struggle Around an Idea," p. 117.

54. This point is dealt with in Chapters 10–13.

55. See, for example, *PN*, June 23, July 14, 21, Aug. 25, 1950, Aug. 10, 1951; Lillian Westell to John Nevin Sayre, Nov. 23, 1954, Box 5, Series B, Sayre Papers; Marie Lous-Mohr to Emily G. Balch, Oct. 23, 1950, Reel 51, WILPF (International) Records.

56. For disputes over these questions, see *PN*, June 2, 1950; *Peacemaker* [United States] 2 (July 11, 1950): 4; "Executive Committee Minutes" (Nov. 9, 1950), Abraham Kaufman to Sidney Aberman, Nov. 10, 1950, and Frieda Lazarus to Aberman, Jan. 8, 1951, Box 2, War Resisters League Records.

57. Else Zeuthen to Gertrude Baer, Oct. 31, 1950, Reel 60, WILPF (International) Records; "Packet on Infiltration and Attack, issued by the National Board of the WIL" (1953?), Box 31, WILPF (United States) Records.

58. Agnes Stapledon to Gertrude Baer, Apr. 28, 1951, Reel 51, WILPF (International) Records; Bussey and Tims, *Women's International League for Peace and Freedom*, pp. 196–97, 214.

59. A. Smith, *A Peril and a Hope*, pp. ix, 498; John A. Simpson, "Some Personal Notes," *BAS* 37 (Jan. 1981): 30; Roy Kepler, "Report on Country-Wide Trip" (1949), p. 6, Box 11, War Resisters League Records; *PN*, Jan. 13, 1950.

60. A. C. Barrington to Vera Brittain, July 22, 1951, "Barrington, A. C." folder, Brittain Papers; "Report on F.O.R. Retreat, Pendle Hill, April 12–14, 1951," Box 4, FOR (United States) Records.

61. In 1946, Szilard had changed fields, from physics to biology. A. Smith, *A Peril and a Hope*, p. 499; Szilard to Bohr, Nov. 7, 1950, in Feld and Szilard, eds., *Collected Works of Leo Szilard*, p. xix.

62. Lifton discusses "psychic numbing" in two of his books, *Death in Life*, pp. 500–510 and *Boundaries*, pp. 26–34.

63. *PN*, Jan. 30, 1948, May 11, 1951.

64. Weart, *Nuclear Fear*, pp. 134–35; "Foreign Reaction to Announcement of Atomic Explosion" (1949), Box 201, Subject File, President's Secretary's Files, 1945–53, Truman Papers.

65. Douvan and Withey, "Some Attitudinal Consequences of Atomic Energy"; Cottrell

and Eberhart, *American Opinion on World Affairs*, pp. 18, 27–29, 104; Hazel Gaudet Erskine, "The Polls: Atomic Weapons and Nuclear Energy," *Public Opinion Quarterly* 27 (Summer 1963): 158, 161.

66. Boyer, *By the Bomb's Early Light*, pp. 293–333.

67. Einstein and Szilard wanted its remaining funds turned over to the American Friends Service Committee. But the other members prevailed and the money went to the *BAS*. A. S. Bishop to Einstein, Mar. 27, 1948, Box 12, and Harrison Brown to H. J. Muller et al., Nov. 15, 1948, Box 21, ECAS Records, Chicago; A. Smith, *A Peril and a Hope*, pp. 507–11; Einstein to Brown, June 12, 1951, Box 57, Einstein Papers.

68. A. Smith, *A Peril and a Hope*, pp. 511–13; Alice Kimball Smith, "The Recognition of Responsibility," *Our Generation Against Nuclear War* 1 (Autumn 1961): 44; "To Our Readers," *BAS* 5 (Oct. 1949): 261.

69. P. F. D. Shaw, "The Future of the Atomic Scientists' Association," *Atomic Scientists' Journal* 3 (Jan. 1954): 149–51; Peierls, *Bird of Passage*, p. 284.

70. Wooley, *Alternatives to Anarchy*, pp. 60–61, 78, 80–81; Borgese to Erich Kahler, Sept. 16, Oct. 6, 1950, Box 1, Kahler Papers. See also "This Critical Hour," *CC* 4 (June 1951): 613.

71. "Geneva 1950," *CC* 4 (Mar. 1951): 432–40; *PN*, Jan. 19, 1951; Schuman, *Commonwealth of Man*, pp. 439–43; Usborne to Elisabeth Mann Borgese, n.d., Box 9, WMWFG Records.

72. G. Davis, *World Is My Country*, pp. 90–244; *NYT*, Oct. 2, 1950; "Garry Davis Changes His Mind," *Fellowship* 16 (Nov. 1950): 27; André Trocmé to A. J. Muste, June 23, 1950, and Minutes of the International Secretariat of World Citizens meetings of Dec. 31, 1950, and Jan. 31, 1951, Davis Papers.

73. *PN*, Dec. 2, 1949; *Meaning of Survival*, p. 295.

74. Personal interview with Ralph DiGia, Apr. 21, 1966; "Membership Statistics" (1954) and "Preliminary Report for Discussion Purposes" (Apr. 1956), Box 4, FOR (United States) Records; "Contributions 1953," Box 14, WILPF (United States) Records.

75. Verkuil, *De grote illusie*, pp. 7, 36–40, 42.

76. Brassel and Tanner, "Zur Geschichte der Friedensbewegung in der Schweiz," pp. 61–62; Leander, "Die Friedensbewegung," pp. 14–18; Bussey and Tims, *Women's International League for Peace and Freedom*, p. 214; Lindkvist, "Mobilization Peaks and Declines," p. 157; "French and British Pacifists Convene," *Fellowship* 17 (Oct. 1951): 24.

77. Thirring, "Who Is an Aggressor?" pp. 72, 96.

78. " 'The Atlantic Community Faces the Bomb' (Radio Discussion, September 25, 1949)," in Hawkins, Greb, and Szilard, eds., *Toward a Livable World*, p. 56.

Conclusion and Epilogue

Epigraph: "The Role of the Pacifist in the Atomic Age," *Fellowship* 12 (Sept. 1946): 150.

1. For some observations on the peace movement's traditional appeal to these constituencies, see Wittner, "Peace Movements and Foreign Policy," p. 364; Elshtain, *Women and War*; Reardon, *Sexism and the War System*.

2. These factors are discussed in Ceadel, *Thinking About Peace and War*, pp. 136–37, 176–84; Wittner, "Peace Movements and Foreign Policy," p. 364.

3. D. Smith, *H. G. Wells*, p. 458.

4. For a discussion of the complex interaction between a peace movement, public opinion, and policymakers in a different context, see Small, *Johnson, Nixon, and the Doves*, pp. 225–34.

5. Bernal to Erich Fromm, Nov. 20, 1961, Box 39, Muste Papers.

6. Claudin, *Communist Movement*, p. 582.

7. Some thoughts on this issue can be found in Wittner, "Peace Movements and Foreign Policy," pp. 356–58, 363.

8. Morrison, *I Renounce War*, pp. 74–75; Eugene Rabinowitch, "Five Years After," *BAS* 7 (Jan. 1951): 4.

9. A Soviet account, written in 1986, is more modest, maintaining that "the resolute Soviet stand [for disarmament] and the anti-nuclear public movement were important factors due to which Washington dared not use nuclear weapons on a global scale." Turski and Zdanowski, *Peace Movement*, p. 75; Montagu, *Plot Against Peace*, p. 112; "Stockholm Appeal's 25th Anniversary," *Peace Courier* 6 (Feb.–Mar. 1975): 1; Potyarkin and Kortunov, eds., *USSR Proposes Disarmament*, p. 101.

10. In 1947, when the clock made its appearance on the cover of the *Bulletin*, the editors set it at seven minutes to midnight. Seaborg, *Kennedy, Khrushchev, and the Test Ban*, facing p. 145.

11. Eugene Rabinowitch, "Living With H-Bombs," *BAS* 11 (Jan. 1955): 5; Grodzins and Rabinowitch, eds., *Atomic Age*, p. 7.

12. de Madariaga, *Disarmament*, pp. 42, 254, 258.

Bibliography

Manuscript Sources

Dean G. Acheson Papers, Harry S. Truman Library, Independence, Mo.

Aldrig mere Krig Records, Swarthmore College Peace Collection, Swarthmore, Pa. (hereafter SCPC)

Devere Allen Papers, SCPC

Argentina War Resisters International Section Records, SCPC

Asociacion Pacifista Argentina Records, SCPC

Atomic Bomb File, Franklin D. Roosevelt Library, Hyde Park, N.Y.

Atomic Energy Authority Records, Public Record Office, Kew, Great Britain

Australian Peace Council Records, SCPC

Australian Quaker Peace Committee Records, Australian Quaker Peace Committee Office, Victoria, Australia

Eben A. Ayers Papers, Harry S. Truman Library, Independence, Mo.

Bernard M. Baruch Papers, Seeley Mudd Library, Princeton University, Princeton, N.J.

J. Desmond Bernal Papers, University Library, Cambridge University, Cambridge, Great Britain

Max Born–Bertrand Russell Correspondence, Mills Memorial Library, McMaster University, Hamilton, Ontario, Canada

British Peace Committee Records, SCPC

Vera Brittain Papers, Mills Memorial Library, McMaster University, Hamilton, Ontario, Canada

James F. Byrnes Papers, Robert Muldrow Cooper Library, Clemson University, Clemson, S.C.

Cabinet Defence Committee Records, Public Record Office, Kew, Great Britain

Cabinet Records, Public Record Office, Kew, Great Britain

Canadian Peace Congress Records, Canadian Peace Congress Office, Toronto, Ontario, Canada; SCPC

William L. Clayton Papers, Harry S. Truman Library, Independence, Mo.

Clark M. Clifford Papers, Harry S. Truman Library, Independence, Mo.

Committee to Frame a World Constitution Records, Joseph Regenstein Library, University of
    Chicago, Chicago, Ill.
Conseil Suisse des Associations pour la Paix Records, SCPC
Norman Cousins Papers, Norman Cousins Home, Beverly Hills, Calif.; University Research
    Library, University of California, Los Angeles, Calif.
Crusade for World Government Records, SCPC
Garry Davis Papers, SCPC
Denmark Miscellaneous Peace Material, SCPC
Department of State Records, National Archives, Washington, D.C.
    Bureau of International Organization Affairs and Its Predecessors, 1945–75
    Central Decimal File
    Special Assistant to the Secretary of State for Atomic Energy, 1944–52
Deutsche Friedensgesellschaft Records, SCPC
Allen W. Dulles Papers, Seeley Mudd Library, Princeton University, Princeton, N.J.
Albert Einstein Papers, Seeley Mudd Library, Princeton University, Princeton, N.J.
Emergency Committee of Atomic Scientists Records, Joseph Regenstein Library, University
    of Chicago, Chicago, Ill.; SCPC
Federal Pacifist Council Records, SCPC
Federation of American Scientists Records, Joseph Regenstein Library, University of Chi-
    cago, Chicago, Ill.
Fellowship of Reconciliation (Canada) Records, SCPC; United Church Archives, Victoria
    University, University of Toronto, Toronto, Ontario, Canada
Fellowship of Reconciliation (Great Britain) Records, British Library of Political and Eco-
    nomic Science, London, Great Britain (microfilm)
Fellowship of Reconciliation (India) Records, Fellowship of Reconciliation (India) Office,
    Kottayam, India
Fellowship of Reconciliation (Japan) Records, SCPC
Fellowship of Reconciliation (United States) Records, SCPC
Foreign Office Records, Public Record Office, Kew, Great Britain
Fraternidad de Reconciliacion y Paz en Mexico Records, SCPC
Leslie R. Groves Papers, National Archives, Washington, D.C.
Hiroshima Peace Society Records, SCPC
Robert Maynard Hutchins Papers, Joseph Regenstein Library, University of Chicago, Chi-
    cago, Ill.
India Miscellaneous Peace Material, SCPC
International Fellowship of Reconciliation Records, SCPC
International Peace Bureau Records, SCPC
Internationale der Kriegsdienstgegner Records, SCPC
Homer Jack Papers, SCPC
Erich Kahler Papers, University Library, State University of New York, Albany, N.Y.
George F. Kennan Papers, Seeley Mudd Library, Princeton University, Princeton, N.J.
David E. Lilienthal Papers, Seeley Mudd Library, Princeton University, Princeton, N.J.
Manhattan Engineering District Records, National Archives, Washington, D.C.
Edmondo Marcucci Papers, SCPC
Miscellaneous Historical Documents, Harry S. Truman Library, Independence, Mo.
Mouvement International de la Réconciliation Records, SCPC
A. J. Muste Papers, SCPC
National Peace Council (Great Britain) Records, SCPC

Non-Criminal Investigation Case Files, New York State Division of State Police Records, New York State Archives, Albany, N.Y.

Oesterreichische Friedensgesellschaft Records, SCPC

J. Robert Oppenheimer Papers, Library of Congress, Washington, D.C.

Frederick Osborn Papers, Harry S. Truman Library, Independence, Mo.

Linus and Ava Helen Pauling Papers, Kerr Library, Oregon State University, Corvallis, Ore.

Pax Christi International Records, Pax Christi International Office, Antwerp, Belgium

Peace Information Center Records, SCPC

Peace Pledge Union (Great Britain) Records, SCPC

Poland Miscellaneous Peace Material, SCPC

Prime Minister's Records, Public Record Office, Kew, Great Britain

Publications Pacifistes et Internationales Parus Après 1940, Library, Peace Palace, The Hague, Netherlands

Eugene I. Rabinowitch Papers, Joseph Regenstein Library, University of Chicago, Chicago, Ill.; University Library, State University of New York, Albany, N.Y.

Paul Robeson Papers, Schomburg Collection, New York Public Library, New York, N.Y.

Rocket Range Protest Committee Records, SCPC

Eleanor Roosevelt Papers, Franklin D. Roosevelt Library, Hyde Park, N.Y.

Franklin D. Roosevelt Papers, Franklin D. Roosevelt Library, Hyde Park, N.Y.

Bertrand Russell Archives 1, Mills Memorial Library, McMaster University, Hamilton, Ontario, Canada

John Nevin Sayre Papers, SCPC

J. Lavell Smith Papers, United Church Archives, Victoria University, University of Toronto, Toronto, Ontario, Canada

Henry L. Stimson Diary, Sterling Library, Yale University, New Haven, Conn.

Henry L. Stimson Papers, Sterling Library, Yale University, New Haven, Conn. (microfilm)

Sweden Miscellaneous Peace Material, SCPC

Swedish Peace Campaign Committee Records, SCPC

Switzerland Miscellaneous Peace Material, SCPC

Leo Szilard Papers, Central University Library, University of California, San Diego, Calif.

Norman M. Thomas Papers, Main Branch, New York Public Library, New York, N.Y.

John Toland Papers, Franklin D. Roosevelt Library, Hyde Park, N.Y.

Toronto Peace Association Records, Mills Memorial Library, McMaster University, Hamilton, Ontario, Canada

André and Magda Trocmé Papers, SCPC

Harry S. Truman, Papers as President of the United States, Harry S. Truman Library, Independence, Mo.

President's Secretary's Files, 1945–53 (General File, Subject File)

White House Central Files, 1945–53 (Confidential File, General File, Official File, President's Personal File)

United States Miscellaneous Peace Material, SCPC

War Resisters' International Records, SCPC

War Resisters League Records, SCPC

Women's International League for Peace and Freedom (International) Records, SCPC (microfilm)

Women's International League for Peace and Freedom (International Office) Records, Women's International League for Peace and Freedom Office, Geneva, Switzerland

Women's International League for Peace and Freedom (United States) Records, SCPC

World Association of World Federalists Records, SCPC
World Movement for World Federal Government Records, Joseph Regenstein Library, University of Chicago, Chicago, Ill.
World Pacifist Meeting Records, SCPC
World Peace Council Records, SCPC
World Peace Day Records, SCPC
Yugoslavia Miscellaneous Peace Material, SCPC

Interviews

Interviews Conducted by the Author
   Anatoly A. Belyayev, June 27, 1990
   Ralph DiGia, April 21, 1966
   Sergei Kapitza, June 28, 1990
   Ralph E. Lapp, June 28, 1987
   Pavel Litvinov, October 7, 1990
   A. J. Muste, June 2, 1966
   James Peck, April 21, 1966
   Mercedes M. Randall, April 26, 1965
   Joseph Rotblat, July 12, 1990
   Norman M. Thomas, October 4, 1966
Oral History Interviews
   American Institute of Physics, Niels Bohr Library, New York, N.Y.
      Hans A. Bethe
      James Chadwick
      Lew Kowarski
      Harlow Shapley
      Hideki Yukawa
   Harry S. Truman Library, Independence, Mo.
      Jules Moch
      Frederick Osborn

Peace Movement Periodicals

Atomic Scientists' Journal (Atomic Scientists' Association, London)
Atomic Scientists' News (Atomic Scientists' Association, London)
Bulletin of the Atomic Scientists (Independent, Chicago)
Bulletin of the Atomic Scientists of Chicago (Atomic Scientists of Chicago, Chicago)
Canadian World Federalist (World Federalists of Canada, Ottawa)
Catholic Worker (Catholic Worker, New York City)
Christian Pacifist (Fellowship of Reconciliation [Great Britain], London)
Common Cause (Committee to Frame a World Constitution, Chicago)
Conscientious Objector (War Resisters League et al., New York City)
FAS Newsletter (Federation of American Scientists, Washington, D.C.)
Federalist (United World Federalists, Washington, D.C.)
Fellowship (Fellowship of Reconciliation [United States], New York City)
Freedom & Union (Federal Union, Washington, D.C.)
Friends' Service News (Canadian Friends Service Committee, Toronto)
Humanity (Crusade for World Government, Glasgow)

Information Bulletin (Yugoslav League for Peace, Independence, and Equality of Peoples, Belgrade)
Monde Fédéré (World Movement for World Federal Government, Geneva)
News Letter (International Fellowship of Reconciliation, London)
New Zealand Christian Pacifist (New Zealand Christian Pacifist Society, Auckland)
One World (National Peace Council, London)
Our Generation Against Nuclear War (Combined Universities Campaign for Nuclear Disarmament, Montreal)
Pacifica Views (Independent, Glendora, Calif.)
Pacifismo (Asociacion Pacifista Argentina, Cordoba)
Pax (Irish Anti-War Crusade, later Irish Pacifist Movement, Dublin)
Pax et Libertas (Women's International League for Peace and Freedom, Geneva)
Pax International (Women's International League for Peace and Freedom, Geneva)
Peace (Australian Peace Council, Melbourne)
Peace Action (New South Wales Peace Committee, Sydney)
Peace Courier (World Peace Council, Helsinki)
Peacegram (Peace Information Center, New York City)
Peacemaker (Federal Pacifist Council, Melbourne)
Peacemaker (Peacemakers, Yellow Springs, Ohio)
Peace News (Peace Pledge Union, London)
Polish Peace Committee Newsletter (Polish Peace Committee, Warsaw)
Reconciliation (Fellowship of Reconciliation [Canada], Toronto)
Reconciliation (Fellowship of Reconciliation [Great Britain], London)
World Government News (United World Federalists, later Independent, New York City)

Other Sources

Abrams, Ray H. "The Churches and the Clergy in World War II." *Annals of the American Academy of Political and Social Science* 256 (Mar. 1948): 110–19.
Acheson, Dean. "Achieving a Community Sense Among Free Nations—A Step Toward World Order." *Department of State Bulletin* 23 (July 3, 1950): 14–17, 38.
———. *Present at the Creation: My Years in the State Department*. New York: Norton, 1969.
Adenauer, Konrad. *Memoirs, 1945–53*. Chicago: Henry Regnery, 1966.
"Against American Aggression in Asia." *New Times*, no. 31 (1950), pp. 9–10.
Albinski, Henry S. *Politics and Foreign Policy in Australia: The Impact of Vietnam and Conscription*. Durham, N.C.: Duke University Press, 1970.
Allen, Bruce. *Germany East: Dissent and Opposition*. Montreal: Black Rose Books, 1989.
Allison, Roy. *Finland's Relations with the Soviet Union, 1944–84*. London: Macmillan, 1985.
Alsop, Stewart, and Ralph Lapp. "The Inside Story of Our First Hydrogen Bomb." *Saturday Evening Post* 225 (Oct. 25, 1952): 29, 150–54.
Ambrose, Stephen E. *Eisenhower*. 2 vols. New York: Simon & Schuster, 1983, 1984.
"Americans Urged to Reject and Expose False Motives of 'Peace Pilgrimage' of the 'American Peace Crusade.'" *Department of State Bulletin* 24 (Mar. 5, 1951): 368–69.
Anders, Roger M., ed. *Forging the Atomic Shield: Excerpts from the Office Diary of Gordon E. Dean*. Chapel Hill: University of North Carolina Press, 1987.
Andersson, Jan, and Kent Lindkvist. "The Peace Movement in Sweden," pp. 5–32 in Werner Kaltefleiter and Robert L. Pfaltzgraff, eds., *The Peace Movements in Europe and the United States*. London: Croom Helm, 1985.
Andrén, Nils. *Power-Balance and Non-Alignment: A Perspective on Swedish Foreign Policy*. Stockholm: Almqvist & Wiksell, 1967.

"The Anti-War Front." *New Times*, no. 26 (June 22, 1949), pp. 1–2.

Aptheker, Herbert, ed. *The Correspondence of W. E. B. Du Bois* Vol. 3, *Selections, 1944–1963*. Amherst: University of Massachusetts Press, 1978.

Arce, José. *Ahora*. Madrid: Espasa-Calpe, 1950.

Aron, Robert, and Alexandre Marc. *Principes du fédéralisme*. Paris: Le Portulan, 1948.

Asada, Sadao. "Japanese Perceptions of the A-Bomb Decision, 1945–1980," pp. 199–219 in Joe C. Dixon, ed., *The American Military in the Far East*. Washington, D.C.: U.S. Government Printing Office, 1980.

Association of Los Alamos Scientists. *Our Atomic World*. Albuquerque: University of New Mexico Press, 1946.

"Atomic Force, Its Meaning for Mankind." *University of Chicago Round Table*, no. 386 (Aug. 12, 1945), pp. 1–12.

Avakumovic, Ivan. *The Communist Party in Canada: A History*. Toronto: McClelland & Stewart, 1975.

Badash, Lawrence, Elizabeth Hodes, and Adolph Tiddens. "Nuclear Fission: Reaction to the Discovery in 1939." *Proceedings of the American Philosophical Society* 130 (June 1986): 196–231.

Bainton, Roland H. *Christian Attitudes Toward War and Peace*. New York: Abingdon Press, 1960.

Bamba, Nobuya, and John F. Howes, eds. *Pacifism in Japan: The Christian and Socialist Tradition*. Vancouver: University of British Columbia Press, 1978.

Bantell, John F. "The Origins of the World Government Movement: The Dublin Conference and After." *Research Studies* 42 (Mar. 1974): 20–35.

Baratta, Joseph Preston. "Bygone 'One World': The Origin and Opportunity of the World Government Movement, 1937–1947." Ph.D. diss., Boston University, 1982.

———. "The International History of the World Federalist Movement." *Peace and Change* 14 (Oct. 1989): 372–403.

———. *Strengthening the United Nations: A Bibliography on U.N. Reform and World Federalism*. New York: Greenwood Press, 1987.

———. "Was the Baruch Plan a Proposal of World Government?" *International History Review* 7 (Nov. 1985): 592–621.

Barrat, Robert. "Peace, Peace, When There Is No Peace." *Commonweal* 52 (Aug. 18, 1950): 455–58.

Baruch, Bernard M. *Baruch: The Public Years*. New York: Holt, Rinehart and Winston, 1960.

Beales, Arthur C. F. *The History of Peace*. London: G. Bell, 1931.

Beaton, Grace M. *Twenty Years' Work in the War Resisters' International*. Enfield, Middlesex: War Resisters' International, 1945.

Beker, Avi. *Disarmament Without Order: The Politics of Disarmament at the United Nations*. Westport, Conn.: Greenwood Press, 1985.

Belilos, Léon. *Unir les hommes*. Paris: La Colombe, 1956.

Bendix, Karen S. *Vi og verdenskatastrofen: Generalopgor med tider og tilstande*. Copenhagen: Nyt nordisk forlag, 1946.

Bennett, Yvonne Aleksandra. "Vera Brittain and the Peace Pledge Union: Women and Peace," pp. 192–213 in Ruth Roach Pierson, ed., *Women and Peace: Theoretical, Historical and Practical Perspectives*. London: Croom Helm, 1987.

Bernal, J. D. "New Frontier of the Mind." *New Statesman and Nation* 30 (Aug. 18, 1945): 104.

Bernstein, Barton J. "Introduction," pp. xvii–lxxiv in Helen Hawkins, G. Allen Greb, and Gertrud Weiss Szilard, eds., *Toward a Livable World: Leo Szilard and the Crusade for Nuclear Arms Control*. Cambridge, Mass.: MIT Press, 1987.

————. "The Quest for Security: American Foreign Policy and International Control of Atomic Energy, 1942–1946." *Journal of American History* 60 (Mar. 1974): 1003–44.

————. "Roosevelt, Truman, and the Atomic Bomb: A Reinterpretation." *Political Science Quarterly* 90 (Spring 1975): 23–69.

Bernstein, George A. "World Government—Progress Report." *Nation* 166 (June 12, 1948): 660–62.

Beyerchen, Alan D. *Scientists Under Hitler: Politics and the Physics Community in the Third Reich*. New Haven: Yale University Press, 1977.

Bhalerao, M. R. *A Plea, Urgent Entreaty, for World Government*. Lashkar, India: Gwalior, 1950.

Biquard, Pierre. *Frédéric Joliot-Curie*. New York: Paul S. Eriksson, 1966.

Blackman, Peter. "Letter to an English Intellectual." *New Statesman and Nation* 36 (Dec. 11, 1948): 519–20.

Bloomfield, Lincoln, Walter C. Clemens, Jr., and Franklyn Griffiths. *Khrushchev and the Arms Race: Soviet Interests in Arms Control and Disarmament, 1954–1964*. Cambridge, Mass.: MIT Press, 1966.

Blum, John M., ed. *The Price of Vision: The Diary of Henry A. Wallace, 1942–1946*. Boston: Houghton Mifflin, 1973.

Blumberg, Stanley A., and Gwinn Owens. *Energy and Conflict: The Life and Times of Edward Teller*. New York: G. P. Putnam's Sons, 1976.

Bohr, Aage. "The War Years and the Prospects Raised by the Atomic Weapons," pp. 191–214 in Stefan Rozental, ed., *Niels Bohr: His Life and Work as Seen by His Friends and Colleagues*. New York: Interscience Publishers, 1967.

Bohr, Niels. "A Challenge to Civilization." *Science* 102 (Oct. 12, 1945): 363–64.

————. *Open Letter to the United Nations, June 9th, 1950*. Copenhagen: J. H. Schultz Forlag, 1950.

————. "Science and Civilization," pp. ix–x in Dexter Masters and Katherine Way, eds., *One World or None*. New York: McGraw-Hill, 1946.

Born, Max, ed. *The Born-Einstein Letters*. New York: Macmillan, 1971.

Bourdet, Claude. "Peace and Politics." *Nation* 168 (Apr. 30, 1949): 489.

————. "The Rebirth of a Peace Movement," pp. 190–201 in Jolyon Howorth and Patricia Chilton, eds., *Defense and Dissent in Contemporary France*. London: Croom Helm, 1984.

————. "The Way to European Independence." *New Reasoner*, no. 5 (Summer 1958), pp. 12–24.

Bourquin, Maurice. *Vers une nouvelle société des nations*. Neuchâtel: Editions de la Baconnière, 1945.

Bowman, Rufus D. *The Church of the Brethren and War, 1708–1941*. Elgin, Ill.: Brethren Publishing House, 1944.

Boyer, Paul. *By the Bomb's Early Light*. New York: Pantheon Books, 1985.

Brassel, Ruedi, and Jakob Tanner. "Zur Geschichte der Friedensbewegung in der Schweiz," pp. 17–90 in Thomas Bein, Ruedi Brassel, and Martin Leuenberger, eds., *Handbuch Frieden Schweiz*. Basel: Z-Verlag, 1986.

Braw, Monica. *The Atomic Bomb Suppressed: American Censorship in Japan, 1945–1949*. Malmo, Sweden: Liber Förlag, 1986.

Brent, Abraham Rodrigues. *Federatie van de wereld*. Leiden: H. E. Stenfert Kroese, 1950.

Brinton, Howard H. *Sources of the Quaker Peace Testimony*. Wallingford, Pa.: Pendle Hill Historical Studies, 1942.

Brittain, Vera. "Changes in the Peace Movement," pp. 260–64 in Paul Berry and Alan

Bishop, eds., *Testament of a Generation: The Journalism of Vera Brittain and Winifred Holtby*. London: Virago Press, 1985.

———. *The Rebel Passion: A Short History of Some Pioneer Peace-makers*. London: Allen & Unwin, 1964.

———. *Search After Sunrise*. London: Macmillan, 1951.

———. *Testament of Experience*. New York: Macmillan, 1957.

Brock, Peter. *Pacifism in Europe to 1914*. Princeton: Princeton University Press, 1972.

———. *Pacifism in the United States, from the Colonial Era to the First World War*. Princeton: Princeton University Press, 1968.

———. *Twentieth Century Pacifism*. New York: Van Nostrand Reinhold, 1970.

Brown, Harrison. *Must Destruction Be Our Destiny?* New York: Simon & Schuster, 1946.

Brown, Seyom. *The Causes and Prevention of War*. New York: St. Martin's Press, 1987.

Bryant, Arthur. *Triumph in the West*. Garden City, N.Y.: Doubleday, 1959.

Buchanan, William, and Hadley Cantril. *How Nations See Each Other: A Study in Public Opinion*. Urbana: University of Illinois Press, 1953.

Bullock, Alan. *Ernest Bevin: Foreign Secretary, 1945–1951*. London: Heinemann, 1983.

Bundy, McGeorge. *Danger and Survival*. New York: Random House, 1988.

Burton, Ormond. *A Testament of Peace*. Levin: New Zealand Christian Pacifist Society, 1965.

Bussey, Gertrude, and Margaret Tims. *Women's International League for Peace and Freedom, 1915–1965: A Record of Fifty Years' Work*. London: Allen & Unwin, 1965.

Byrnes, James F. *All in One Lifetime*. New York: Harper & Brothers, 1958.

Caldwell, Bill S. III. "The French Socialists' Attitudes Toward the Use of Nuclear Weapons, 1945–1978." Ph.D. diss., University of Georgia, 1980.

Cammett, John M. "Jules Humbert-Droz," pp. 437–39 in Harold Josephson, ed., *Biographical Dictionary of Modern Peace Leaders*. Westport, Conn.: Greenwood Press, 1985.

Cantril, Hadley, ed. *Public Opinion, 1935–1946*. Princeton, N.J.: Princeton University Press, 1951.

Carlyle, Margaret, ed. *Documents on International Affairs, 1949–1950*. London: Oxford University Press, 1953.

Caute, David. *Communism and the French Intellectuals, 1914–1960*. New York: Macmillan, 1964.

———. *The Fellow-Travellers: A Postscript to the Enlightenment*. New York: Macmillan, 1973.

———. *The Great Fear: The Anti-Communist Purge Under Truman and Eisenhower*. New York: Simon & Schuster, 1979.

Ceadel, Martin. *Pacifism in Britain, 1914–1945: The Defining of a Faith*. Oxford: Clarendon Press, 1980.

———. *Thinking About Peace and War*. New York: Oxford University Press, 1989.

Chatfield, Charles. *For Peace and Justice: Pacifism in America, 1914–1941*. Knoxville: University of Tennessee Press, 1971.

Chaudhuri, Sanjib. *A Constitution for World Government*. Calcutta: Bhupal Chandra Dutta Art Press, 1950.

Churchill, Winston S. *The Gathering Storm*. Boston: Houghton Mifflin, 1948.

———. *Triumph and Tragedy*. Boston: Houghton Mifflin, 1953.

Cioc, Mark. *Pax Atomica: The Nuclear Defense Debate in West Germany During the Adenauer Era*. New York: Columbia University Press, 1988.

Clark, Ronald W. *The Birth of the Bomb*. New York: Horizon Press, 1961.

———. *Einstein: The Life and Times*. New York: Harry N. Abrams, 1984.

———. *J.B.S.: A Biography of J. B. S. Haldane*. London: Oxford University Press, 1968.

———. *The Life of Bertrand Russell*. London: Jonathan Cape and Weidenfeld & Nicolson, 1975.

Claudin, Fernando. *The Communist Movement: From Comintern to Cominform.* New York: Monthly Review Press, 1975.

Clements, Kevin. *Back from the Brink: The Creation of a Nuclear-Free New Zealand.* Wellington: Allen & Unwin/Port Nicholson Press, 1988.

Cockburn, Stewart, and David Ellyard. *Oliphant.* Adelaide: Axiom Books, 1981.

Cockcroft, John. "Kapitza at the Cavendish." *New Scientist*, no. 421 (Dec. 10, 1964), pp. 739–40.

Cohen, Stephen F. "The Stalin Question Since Stalin," pp. 22–50 in Stephen Cohen, ed., *An End to Silence: Uncensored Opinion in the Soviet Union.* New York: Norton, 1982.

Committee for the Compilation of Materials on Damage Caused by the Atomic Bombs in Hiroshima and Nagasaki. *Hiroshima and Nagasaki: The Physical, Medical, and Social Effects of the Atomic Bombings.* New York: Basic Books, 1981.

"Communiqué of the U.S.S.R. Committee for Peace." *New Times*, no. 32 (1950), p. 3.

"The Communist Party and the Bomb." *Socialist Review* 4 (Oct. 1954): 3, 5.

Compton, Arthur Holly. *Atomic Quest.* New York: Oxford University Press, 1956.

Cooper, Sandi E. *Patriotic Pacifism: Waging War on War in Europe, 1815–1914.* New York: Oxford University Press, 1991.

Coox, Alvin D. "Evidences of Antimilitarism in Prewar and Wartime Japan." *Pacific Affairs* 46 (Winter 1973–74): 502–14.

Cottrell, Leonard S., Jr., and Sylvia Eberhart. *American Opinion on World Affairs in the Atomic Age.* New York: Greenwood Press, 1969.

Cousins, Norman. "The Case of Robert Maynard Hutchins." *Saturday Review of Literature* 31 (May 1, 1948): 18–19.

——— . *Modern Man Is Obsolete.* New York: Viking Press, 1945.

——— . "Tell the Folks Back Home." *Saturday Review of Literature* 32 (Apr. 9, 1949): 20–22.

——— . *Who Speaks for Man?* New York: Macmillan, 1953.

Crane, Ernest. *I Can Do No Other: A Biography of Ormond Burton.* Auckland: Hodder and Stoughton, 1986.

——— . "Ormond Edward Burton," pp. 128–29 in Harold Josephson, ed., *Biographical Dictionary of Modern Peace Leaders.* Westport, Conn.: Greenwood Press, 1985.

Cranston, Alan. "The Strengthening of the U.N. Charter." *Political Quarterly* 17 (July–Sept. 1946): 187–200.

Culbertson, Ely. *Total Peace: What Makes Wars and How to Organize Peace.* Garden City, N.Y.: Doubleday, Doran, 1943.

Curti, Merle E. *Peace or War: The American Struggle, 1636–1936.* New York: Norton, 1936.

Dallin, Alexander, et al. *The Soviet Union and Disarmament.* New York: Frederick A. Praeger, 1964.

Davidson, Alastair. *The Communist Party of Australia: A Short History.* Stanford, Calif.: Hoover Institution Press, 1969.

Davis, Garry. *The World Is My Country.* New York: G. P. Putnam's Sons, 1961.

Davis, Nuel Pharr. *Lawrence and Oppenheimer.* New York: Simon & Schuster, 1968.

DeBenedetti, Charles. *Origins of the Modern American Peace Movement, 1915–1929.* Millwood, N.Y.: KTO Press, 1978.

——— . *The Peace Reform in American History.* Bloomington: Indiana University Press, 1980.

"Defense of Peace and the Struggle Against the Warmongers." *For a Lasting Peace, for a People's Democracy!* no. 28 (Nov. 29, 1949), p. 1.

Defrasne, Jean. *Le pacifisme.* Paris: Presses Universitaires de France, 1983.

del Vayo, J. A. "On the First 'Citizen of the World.' " *Nation* 168 (Jan. 1, 1949): 18.

"Delegates from World Congress of Partisans of Peace Refused Entry to U.S." *Department of State Bulletin* 22 (Mar. 13, 1950): 400–402.

de Madariaga, Salvador. *Disarmament*. New York: Coward-McCann, 1929.

de Man, Henri. *Au delà du nationalisme, vers un gouvernement mondial*. Geneva: Editions du Cheval ailé, 1946.

de Rougement, Denis. *The Last Trump*. Garden City, N.Y.: Doubleday, 1947.

de Rusett, Alan. *Strengthening the Framework of Peace*. London: Royal Institute of International Affairs, 1950.

Dickson, Lovat. *H. G. Wells: His Turbulent Life and Times*. New York: Atheneum, 1969.

Divine, Robert A. *Blowing on the Wind: The Nuclear Test Ban Debate, 1954–1960*. New York: Oxford University Press, 1978.

Donat, Helmut. "Das Andere Deutschland," pp. 26–29 in Helmut Donat and Karl Holl, eds., *Die Friedensbewegung: Organisierter Pazifismus in Deutschland, Österreich und in der Schweiz*. Düsseldorf: ECON Taschenbuch Verlag, 1983.

———. "Friedrich (Fritz) Heinrich Cristoph Küster," pp. 529–32 in Harold Josephson, ed., *Biographical Dictionary of Modern Peace Leaders*. Westport, Conn.: Greenwood Press, 1985.

Douvan, Elizabeth, and Stephen B. Withey. "Some Attitudinal Consequences of Atomic Energy." *Annals of the American Academy of Political and Social Science* 290 (Nov. 1953): 108–17.

Dower, John W. "Science, Society, and the Japanese Atomic Bomb Project During World War Two." *Bulletin of Concerned Asian Scholars* 10 (Apr.–June 1978): 41–54.

———. *War Without Mercy: Race and Power in the Pacific War*. New York: Pantheon Books, 1986.

Drake, Richard. "Aldo Capitini," pp. 140–41 in Harold Josephson, ed., *Biographical Dictionary of Modern Peace Leaders*. Westport, Conn: Greenwood Press, 1985.

Driver, Christopher. *The Disarmers: A Study in Protest*. London: Hodder & Stoughton, 1964.

Drummond, Gordon D. *The German Social Democrats in Opposition, 1949–1960*. Norman: University of Oklahoma Press, 1982.

Duberman, Martin Bauml. *Paul Robeson*. New York: Knopf, 1988.

Du Bois, William E. B. *The Autobiography of W. E. B. Du Bois*. New York: International Publishers, 1969.

———. *I Take My Stand for Peace*. New York: Masses & Mainstream, 1951.

———. *In Battle for Peace: The Story of My 83rd Birthday*. New York: Masses & Mainstream, 1952.

Dyer, Gwynne. *War*. Homewood, Ill.: Dorsey Press, 1985.

Earle, Edward Mead. "H. G. Wells: British Patriot in Search of a World State." *World Politics* 2 (Jan. 1950): 181–208.

Edwards, Gordon. "Canada's Nuclear Industry and the Myth of the Peaceful Atom," pp. 122–70 in Ernie Regehr and Simon Rosenblum, eds., *Canada and the Nuclear Arms Race*. Toronto: James Lorimer, 1983.

Een Verden. *Een verden eller ingen*. Copenhagen: Samlerens forlag, 1949.

Ehrenburg, Ilya. *Post-War Years, 1945–1954*. Cleveland: World, 1967.

Einhorn, Eric S. *National Security and Domestic Politics in Post-War Denmark: Some Principal Issues, 1945–1961*. Odense, Denmark: Odense University Press, 1975.

Einstein, Albert. "Einstein on the Atomic Bomb." *Atlantic Monthly* 176 (Nov. 1945): 43–45.

———. " 'The Real Problem Is in the Hearts of Men.' " *New York Times Magazine*, June 23, 1946, pp. 7, 42–44.

———. "The Way Out," pp. 76–77 in Dexter Masters and Katherine Way, eds., *One World or None*. New York: McGraw-Hill, 1946.

Eisenhower, Dwight D. *Crusade in Europe*. Garden City, N.Y.: Doubleday, 1948.

———. *Mandate for Change, 1953–1956*. Garden City, N.Y.: Doubleday, 1963.

Elshtain, Jean Bethke. *Women and War*. New York: Basic Books, 1987.

Enander, Mauriz, et al., eds. *Riktlinjer för en världsfederation, ett inlägg i diskussionen om världens framtid*. Stockholm: Natur och Kultur, 1945.

Endicott, James G., ed. *The Best of Jim Endicott*. Toronto: NC Press, 1982.

Endicott, Stephen. *James G. Endicott: Rebel Out of China*. Toronto: University of Toronto Press, 1980.

Epstein, William. "Canada," pp. 171–84 in Jozef Goldblat, ed., *Non-Proliferation: The Why and the Wherefore*. London: Taylor & Francis, 1985.

———. *Canada and Nuclear Weapons*. Waterloo, Ontario: Project Ploughshares, 1985.

Ermenc, Joseph J., ed. *Atomic Bomb Scientists: Memoirs, 1939–1945*. Westport, Conn.: Meckler, 1989.

Ewer, W. N. *Communists on Peace*. London: Batchworth Press, 1953.

"Fadeyev's Suicide," pp. 115–16 in Stephen Cohen, ed., *An End to Silence: Uncensored Opinion in the Soviet Union*. New York: Norton, 1982.

Federal Council of the Churches of Christ in America, Commission on the Relations of the Church to the War in the Light of the Christian Faith. *Atomic Warfare and the Christian Faith*. New York: N.p., 1946.

Federation of American (Atomic) Scientists. "Survival Is at Stake," p. 79 in Dexter Masters and Katherine Way, eds., *One World or None*. New York: McGraw-Hill, 1946.

Fehrm, Martin. "Sweden," pp. 213–20 in Jozef Goldblat, ed., *Non-Proliferation: The Why and the Wherefore*. London: Taylor & Francis, 1985.

Feld, Bernard. "Leo Szilard, Scientist for All Seasons." *Social Research* 51 (Autumn 1984): 675–90.

Feld, Bernard, and Gertrud Weiss Szilard, eds. *The Collected Works of Leo Szilard: Scientific Papers*. London: MIT Press, 1972.

Fellner, Fritz. "Hans Thirring," pp. 386–87 in Helmut Donat and Karl Holl, eds., *Die Friedensbewegung: Organisierter Pazifismus in Deutschland, Österreich und in der Schweiz*. Düsseldorf: ECON Taschenbuch Verlag, 1983.

Fellowship of Reconciliation. *The Meaning of Korea*. New York: Fellowship of Reconciliation, 1950.

Ferguson, John. *War and Peace in the World's Religions*. New York: Oxford University Press, 1978.

Fermi, Laura. *Atoms in the Family*. Chicago: University of Chicago Press, 1954.

Ferrell, Robert H., ed. *Off the Record: The Private Papers of Harry S. Truman*. New York: Harper & Row, 1980.

"Fifth Column in Paris." *Economist* 156 (Apr. 30, 1949): 780–81.

Fischer, Louis, ed. *The Essential Gandhi: An Anthology*. New York: Random House, 1962.

Flannery, Harry W., ed. *Pattern for Peace: Catholic Statements on International Order*. Westminster, Md.: Newman Press, 1962.

Fleischman, Harry. *Norman Thomas: A Biography*. New York: Norton, 1964.

Fogelström, Per Anders. *Kampen för fred*. Stockholm: Bonniers, 1971.

Forrester, J. P. *Fifteen Years of Peace Fronts*. Sydney: McHugh Printery, 1964.

Forty Years for Peace: A History of the Fellowship of Reconciliation, 1914–1954. New York: Fellowship of Reconciliation, 1954.

Foster, Catherine. *Women for All Seasons: The Story of the Women's International League for Peace and Freedom*. Athens: University of Georgia Press, 1989.

Franck, James, et al. "A Report to the Secretary of War," pp. 19–27 in Morton Grodzins and Eugene Rabinowitch, eds., *The Atomic Age*. New York: Basic Books, 1963.

Franklin, H. Bruce. *War Stars: The Superweapon and the American Imagination*. New York: Oxford University Press, 1988.

Freeman, Ruth. *Quakers and Peace*. Ithaca, N.Y.: Pacifist Research Bureau, 1947.

Frisch, Otto R. *What Little I Remember*. Cambridge, Eng.: Cambridge University Press, 1979.

Furtado, Jean, ed. *Turkey: Peace on Trial*. London: European Nuclear Disarmament and Merlin Press, 1983.

Gallup, George H., ed. *The Gallup International Public Opinion Polls: France 1939, 1944–1975*. New York: Random House, 1976.

———. *The Gallup International Public Opinion Polls: Great Britain, 1937–1975*. New York: Random House, 1976.

———. *The Gallup Poll: Public Opinion, 1935–1971*. 3 vols. New York: Random House, 1972.

Gandolphe, Maurice. *Système de paix et de securité mondiale: Universalisme exécutoire, paix organique, équilibre vital, droit des hommes*. Paris: Editions inter-nationales, 1949.

Genêt, Jean. "Letter from Paris." *New Yorker* 25 (May 7, 1949): 96–102.

———. "Letter from Paris." *New Yorker* 26 (June 10, 1950): 92–97.

George, Aurelia. "Japan and the United States: Dependent Ally or Equal Partner?" pp. 237–96 in J. A. A. Stockwin, ed., *Dynamic and Immobilist Politics in Japan*. Honolulu: University of Hawaii Press, 1988.

Gilbert, Alan D., and Ann-Mari Jordan. "Traditions of Dissent," pp. 338–65 in M. McKernan and M. Browne, eds., *Australia: Two Centuries of War and Peace*. Canberra: Australian War Memorial and Allen & Unwin, 1988.

Gillie, D. R. "Whose Peace?" *Spectator* 182 (May 6, 1949): 599–600.

Giovannitti, Len, and Fred Freed. *The Decision to Drop the Bomb*. New York: Coward-McCann, 1965.

Goldberg, Alfred. "The Atomic Origins of the British Nuclear Deterrent." *International Affairs* 40 (July 1964): 409–29.

Goldschmidt, Bertrand. *The Atomic Adventure*. Oxford: Pergamon Press, 1964.

———. "France," pp. 57–71 in Jozef Goldblat, ed., *Non-Proliferation: The Why and the Wherefore*. London: Taylor & Francis, 1985.

Goldsmith, Maurice. *Frédéric Joliot-Curie*. London: Lawrence & Wishart, 1976.

Golovin, I. N. *I. V. Kurchatov: A Socialist-Realist Biography of the Soviet Nuclear Scientist*. Bloomington, Ind.: Selbstverlag Press, 1968.

Gombin, Richard. *Les socialistes et la guerre*. Paris: Mouton, 1970.

Goodman, Elliott R. "The Soviet Union and World Government." *Journal of Politics* 15 (May 1953): 231–53.

Gordon, Michael R. *Conflict and Consensus in Labour's Foreign Policy, 1914–1965*. Stanford, Calif.: Stanford University Press, 1969.

Gormly, James L. "The Washington Declaration and the 'Poor Relation': Anglo-American Atomic Diplomacy, 1945–46." *Diplomatic History* 8 (Spring 1984): 125–43.

Gostoli, Antonio. *Per una migliore organizzazione del mondo*. Milan: Gastaldi, 1950.

Gouré, Leon. *Civil Defense in the Soviet Union*. Berkeley: University of California Press, 1962.

Gowing, Margaret. *Britain and Atomic Energy, 1939–1945*. London: Macmillan, 1964.

———. *Independence and Deterrence: Britain and Atomic Energy, 1945–1952*. 2 vols. New York: St. Martin's Press, 1974.

———. "Niels Bohr and Nuclear Weapons," pp. 266–77 in A. P. French and P. J. Kennedy, eds., *Niels Bohr: A Centenary Volume*. Cambridge, Mass.: Harvard University Press, 1985.

Graham, Loren R. *Science and Philosophy in the Soviet Union*. New York: Knopf, 1972.

Grant, David. *Out in the Cold: Pacifists and Conscientious Objectors in New Zealand During World War II*. Auckland: Reed Methuen, 1986.

Gressel, H. "Johannes Ude," pp. 391–92 in Helmut Donat and Karl Holl, eds., *Die Friedensbewegung: Organisierter Pazifismus in Deutschland, Österreich und in der Schweiz*. Düsseldorf: ECON Taschenbuch Verlag, 1983.

Grillot, E. "Reminiscences on the First Decade." *Scientific World*, Anniversary Number (1966), pp. 13–16.

Grodzins, Morton, and Eugene Rabinowitch, eds. *The Atomic Age: Scientists in World Affairs*. New York: Basic Books, 1963.

Groom, A. J. R. *British Thinking About Nuclear Weapons*. London: Frances Pinter, 1974.

Grossman, Kurt R. "Peace Movements in Germany." *South Atlantic Quarterly* 49 (July 1950): 292–302.

Groves, Leslie R. *Now It Can Be Told*. New York: Da Capo Press, 1975.

"The Growing Fight for Peace." *New Times*, no. 14 (Mar. 30, 1949), pp. 1–3.

Haagerup, Niels Jorgen. "The Nordic Peace Movements," pp. 144–65 in Walter Laqueur and Robert Hunter, eds., *European Peace Movements and the Future of the Western Alliance*. New Brunswick, N.J.: Transaction Books, 1985.

Haesaerts, Paul. *L'état mondiale, essai de synthèse politique*. Brussels: Jaric, 1948.

Hahn, Otto. *My Life: The Autobiography of a Scientist*. New York: Herder & Herder, 1970.

Hahn, Werner G. *Postwar Soviet Politics: The Fall of Zhdanov and the Defeat of Moderation, 1946–53*. Ithaca, N.Y.: Cornell University Press, 1982.

Hallie, Philip P. *Lest Innocent Blood Be Shed*. New York: Harper & Row, 1979.

Harries, Meirion, and Susie Harries. *Sheathing the Sword: The Demilitarization of Japan*. London: Hamish Hamilton, 1987.

Harris, Kenneth. *Attlee*. London: Weidenfeld & Nicolson, 1982.

Hawkins, Helen S., G. Allen Greb, and Gertrud Weiss Szilard, eds., *Toward a Livable World: Leo Szilard and the Crusade for Nuclear Arms Control*. Cambridge, Mass.: MIT Press, 1987.

Heisenberg, Elisabeth. *Inner Exile*. Boston: Birkhäuser, 1984.

Heisenberg, Werner. "Research in Germany on the Technical Application of Atomic Energy." *Nature* 160 (Aug. 16, 1947): 211–15.

Hennacy, Ammon. *Autobiography of a Catholic Anarchist*. New York: Catholic Worker Press, 1954.

Herken, Gregg. *The Winning Weapon: The Atomic Bomb in the Cold War, 1945–1950*. New York: Vintage Books, 1982.

Hersey, John. *Hiroshima*. New York: Vintage Books, 1989.

———. "Hiroshima." *New Yorker* 22 (Aug. 31, 1946): 15–68.

Hershberger, Guy Franklin. *War, Peace, and Nonresistance*. Scottdale, Pa.: Herald Press, 1944.

Hewlett, Richard G., and Oscar E. Anderson, Jr. *The New World, 1939–1949*. University Park: Pennsylvania State University Press, 1962.

Hewlett, Richard G., and Francis Duncan. *Atomic Shield, 1947–1952*. University Park: Pennsylvania State University Press, 1969.

Hiebert, Erwin N. *The Impact of Atomic Energy*. Newton, Kan.: Faith and Life Press, 1961.

Hinton, James. *Protests and Visions: Peace Politics in Twentieth-Century Britain*. London: Hutchinson Radius, 1989.

Hirst, Margaret. *Quakers in Peace and War*. London: Swarthmore Press, 1923.

Holl, Karl. "German Pacifists in Exile, 1933–1940," pp. 165–83 in Charles Chatfield and Peter van den Dungen, eds., *Peace Movements and Political Cultures*. Knoxville: University of Tennessee Press, 1988.

Holl, Karl, and Wolfram Wette, eds. *Pazifismus in der Weimarer Republik*. Paderborn: Ferdinand Schöningh, 1981.

Holloway, David. "Entering the Nuclear Arms Race: The Soviet Decision to Build the Atomic Bomb, 1939–45." *Social Studies of Science* 11 (May 1981): 159–97.

———. "The Scientist and the Tyrant." *New York Review of Books* 37 (Mar. 1, 1990): 23–25.

———. *The Soviet Union and the Arms Race*. New Haven, Conn.: Yale University Press, 1983.

Holm, Torsten. *FN och världsfederalismen*. Stockholm: Informationsbyran Mellanfolkligt Samarbete för Fred, 1949.

Howorth, Jolyon. *France: The Politics of Peace*. London: Merlin Press, 1984.

Hübner-Funk, Sibylle, and Werner Schefold. "The Challenge of Youth in the Federal Republic of Germany: No Future Without Peace." *Prospects* 14, no. 2 (1984): 231–36.

Hutchins, Robert M. *The Atomic Bomb Versus Civilization*. Washington, D.C.: Human Events, 1945.

Huxley, Julian. "Intellect at Wroclaw." *Spectator* 181 (Sept. 10, 1948): 326–27.

The Hydrogen Bomb: A Plan for Atomic Peace: Speech of Hon. Brien McMahon . . . February 2, 1950. Washington, D.C.: U.S. Government Printing Office, 1950.

Ienaga, Saburo. *The Pacific War: World War II and the Japanese, 1931–1945*. New York: Pantheon Books, 1978.

Ingram, Kenneth. *Fifty Years of the National Peace Council, 1908–1958*. London: National Peace Council, 1958.

Ingram, Norman. "Ambivalence in the Post–World War II French Peace Movement (1946–1952)." Paper presented at the Conference on the Pacifist Impulse in Historical Perspective, University of Toronto, Toronto, Canada, May 12, 1991.

———. *The Politics of Dissent: Pacifism in France, 1919–1939*. Oxford: Clarendon Press, 1991.

"The International Stalin Peace Prizes." *New Times*, no. 2 (Jan. 8, 1950), pp. 1–3.

Irving, David. *The German Atomic Bomb: The History of Nuclear Research in Nazi Germany*. New York: Simon & Schuster, 1967.

Iyer, Raghavan, ed. *The Moral and Political Writings of Mahatma Gandhi*. 2 vols. Oxford: Clarendon Press, 1986.

Jack, Homer A. "Action for Peace." *Progressive* 15 (Feb. 1951): 23.

Japan Council Against A and H Bombs. *Documentary Photographs, 1945–1985: For a World Free of Nuclear Weapons*. Tokyo: Japan Council Against A and H Bombs, 1986.

Jervas, Gunnar. *Sweden Between the Power Blocs: A New Strategic Position?* Uppsala: Swedish Institute, 1986.

Johnpoll, Bernard K. *Pacifist's Progress: Norman Thomas and the Decline of American Socialism*. Chicago: Quadrangle Books, 1970.

Johnson, Hewlett. *Searching for Light: An Autobiography*. London: Michael Joseph, 1968.

Joliot-Curie, Frédéric. *Cinq années de lutte pour la Paix*. Paris: Editions "Défense de la Paix," 1954.

———. "The World-wide Movement Against the Atomic Peril." *Scientific World* 2, no. 4 (1958): 36–39.

Jonassen, Hagbard. *Resistance in Denmark*. Enfield, Middlesex: War Resisters' International, 1945.

Jones, R. V. "Meetings in Wartime and After," pp. 278–87 in A. P. French and P. J. Kennedy, eds., *Niels Bohr: A Centenary Volume*. Cambridge, Mass.: Harvard University Press, 1985.

Jordan, Gerhard. "Peace Activities in Austria Since 1945." Paper presented at the American-

European Consultation on Peace Research in History, Stadtschlaining, Austria, Aug. 1986.

Josephson, Harold. "Albert Einstein: The Search for World Order," pp. 122–46 in Charles DeBenedetti, ed., *Peace Heroes in Twentieth-Century America*. Bloomington: Indiana University Press, 1986.

Jungk, Robert. *Brighter Than a Thousand Suns: A Personal History of the Atomic Scientists.* New York: Harcourt, Brace, 1958.

Kalemaa, Kalevi. "Felix Iversen," pp. 448–49 in Harold Josephson, ed., *Biographical Dictionary of Modern Peace Leaders*. Westport, Conn.: Greenwood Press, 1985.

Kamata, Sadao, and Stephen Salaff. "The Atomic Bomb and the Citizens of Nagasaki." *Bulletin of Concerned Asian Scholars* 14 (Apr.–June 1982): 38–50.

Kapitza, Peter L. *Experiment, Theory, Practice: Articles and Addresses*. Dordrecht, Holland: D. Reidel, 1980.

Kautsky, John H. *Moscow and the Communist Party of India*. Boston: Technology Press of MIT, 1956.

Kennan, George F. *Memoirs, 1925–1950*. Boston: Little, Brown, 1967.

Kevles, Daniel J. *The Physicists*. New York: Alfred A. Knopf, 1978.

Khrushchev, Nikita. *Khrushchev Remembers*. Boston: Little, Brown, 1970.

——. *Khrushchev Remembers: The Glasnost Tapes*. Boston: Little, Brown, 1990.

——. *Khrushchev Remembers: The Last Testament*. Boston: Little, Brown, 1974.

Kimche, David. *The Afro-Asian Movement: Ideology and Foreign Policy of the Third World.* Jerusalem: Israel Universities Press, 1973.

King, Ernest J., and Walter Muir Whitehill. *Fleet Admiral King*. New York: Norton, 1952.

Kissinger, Henry A. *Nuclear Weapons and Foreign Policy*. New York: Harper & Brothers, 1957.

Klose, Kevin. *Russia and the Russians: Inside the Closed Society*. New York: Norton, 1984.

Knebel, Fletcher, and Charles W. Bailey. "The Fight Over the A-Bomb." *Look* 27 (Aug. 13, 1963): 19–23.

Knös, Gunnar. *Wereld federatie van alle landen met nationale ontwapening en internationale politiemacht: vier radiolezingen*. Utrecht: W. de Haan, 1946.

Kodama, Katsuya. "Red vs. Green: A Comparative Study on Peace Movements in Japan, Denmark, and Finland." Paper presented at the Lund Conference on Peace Movements, Lund, Sweden, Aug. 1987.

Koschmann, J. Victor. "Postwar Democracy and Japanese Ban-the-Bomb Movements." Unpublished paper.

Köszegi, Ferenc, and Istvan Szent-Ivanyi. "A Struggle Around an Idea: The Peace Movement in Hungary." *New Society* 62 (Oct. 21, 1982): 115–20 and (Oct. 28, 1982): 163–64.

Kramer, Bernard M., S. Michael Kalick, and Michael Milburn. "Attitudes Toward Nuclear Weapons and Nuclear War, 1945–1982." *Journal of Social Issues* 39 (Spring 1983): 7–24.

Kramish, Arnold. *Atomic Energy in the Soviet Union*. Stanford, Calif.: Stanford University Press, 1959.

Kuehl, Warren F. *Seeking World Order: The United States and International Organization to 1920*. Nashville: Vanderbilt University Press, 1969.

Kurino, Ohtori, and Katsuya Kodama. "A Study on the Japanese Peace Movement," pp. 119–27 in Katsuya Kodama and Unto Vesa, eds., *Towards a Comparative Analysis of Peace Movements*. Hants, Eng.: Dartmouth Publishing Company, 1990.

Lamont, Lansing. *Day of Trinity*. New York: Atheneum, 1965.

Lamot, Marc. "Peace Movement in Belgium," pp. 212–14 in Ervin Laszlo and Jong Youl Yoo, eds., *World Encyclopedia of Peace*, vol. 2. Oxford: Pergamon Press, 1986.

Lapp, Ralph E. Address to the luncheon meeting of the Conference on Peace Research in History, U.S. Naval Academy, Annapolis, Md., June 25, 1987.

———. *Atoms and People*. New York: Harper & Brothers, 1956.

Lash, Joseph P. "Weekend at the Waldorf." *New Republic* 120 (Apr. 18, 1949): 10–14.

Laurence, Richard R. "Johannes Ude," pp. 973–74 in Harold Josephson, ed., *Biographical Dictionary of Modern Peace Leaders*. Westport, Conn.: Greenwood Press, 1985.

Laurence, William L. *Men and Atoms: The Discovery, the Uses and the Future of Atomic Energy*. New York: Simon & Schuster, 1959.

———. "Would You Make the Bomb Again?" *New York Times Magazine*, Aug. 1, 1965, pp. 8–9.

Laursen, Finn. *Federalism and World Order: Compendium II*. Copenhagen: World Federalist Youth, 1972.

Leahy, William D. *I Was There*. New York: McGraw-Hill, 1950.

Leander, Amherd. "Die Friedensbewegung in der Schweiz (1945 bis 1980)." Lizentiats-arbeit, Historical Institute, University of Bern, Bern, Switzerland, 1984.

Lebedinsky, A. V., ed. *What Russian Scientists Say About Fallout*. New York: Collier Books, 1962.

Leffler, Melvin P. *A Preponderance of Power: National Security, the Truman Administration, and the Cold War*. Stanford, Calif.: Stanford University Press, 1992.

Legendre, Bernard. "Quand les intellectuels partaient en guerre froide (avril 1949)." *Histoire*, no. 11 (1979), pp. 79–80.

Lewis, John Wilson, and Xue Litai. *China Builds the Bomb*. Stanford, Calif.: Stanford University Press, 1988.

Liddington, Jill. *The Long Road to Greenham: Feminism and Anti-Militarism in Britain Since 1820*. London: Virago Press, 1989.

Lifton, Robert J. *Boundaries: Psychological Man in Revolution*. New York: Random House, 1970.

———. *Death in Life: Survivors of Hiroshima*. New York: Simon & Schuster, 1967.

———. *History and Human Survival*. New York: Vintage Books, 1971.

Lilienthal, Alfred M. *Which Way to World Government?* New York: Foreign Policy Association, 1950.

Lilienthal, David E. *The Atomic Energy Years, 1945–1950*. New York: Harper & Row, 1964.

Lindkvist, Kent. "Mobilization Peaks and Declines of the Swedish Peace Movement," pp. 147–67 in Katsuya Kodama and Unto Vesa, eds., *Towards a Comparative Analysis of Peace Movements*. Hants, Eng.: Dartmouth Publishing Company, 1990.

Link, Eugene P. *Labor-Religion Prophet: The Times and Life of Harry F. Ward*. Boulder, Colo.: Westview Press, 1984.

"The Little Man." *Time* 53 (Jan. 10, 1949): 21–22.

Lottman, Herbert R. *Albert Camus: A Biography*. Garden City, N.Y.: Doubleday, 1979.

Lubelski-Bernard, Nadine. "Hem Day," pp. 397–98 in Harold Josephson, ed., *Biographical Dictionary of Modern Peace Leaders*. Westport, Conn.: Greenwood Press, 1985.

Luft, John, and W. M. Wheeler. "Reaction to John Hersey's 'Hiroshima.' " *Journal of Social Psychology* 28 (1948): 135–40.

Lund, Diderich. *Resistance in Norway*. New York: War Resisters League, 1945.

Lutz, Howard T. "Ellenor Andrea Andreen," pp. 24–26 in Harold Josephson, ed., *Biographical Dictionary of Modern Peace Leaders*. Westport, Conn.: Greenwood Press, 1985.

Macdonald, Dwight. Editorial. *Politics* 2 (Aug. 1945): 225.

———. *Memoirs of a Revolutionist: Essays in Political Criticism*. New York: Farrar, Straus and Cudahy, 1957.

———. "The Waldorf Conference." *Politics* 6 (Winter 1949), special insert, 32A–32D.

MacKenzie, Norman. "The Paris Dovecote." *New Statesman and Nation* 37 (Apr. 30, 1949): 425–26.

Mahatma Gandhi on Nuclear Arms. New Delhi: Gandhi Peace Foundation, 1963.

Maislinger, Andreas. "The Peace Movement in a Neutral Country: On the Subject of the New Peace Movement in Austria." *Wiener Blätter zur Friedensforschung*, no. 42–43 (May 1985), pp. 57–68.

Mangone, Gerard J. *The Idea and Practice of World Government*. New York: Columbia University Press, 1951.

Marçais, Henri. *Destruction atomique ou gouvernement mondial: Discours aux élus du peuple français par Henri Marçais et ses camarades*. Paris: Citoyens du monde, 1950.

Mark, Eduard. " 'Today Has Been a Historical One': Harry S. Truman's Diary of the Potsdam Conference." *Diplomatic History* 4 (Summer 1980): 317–26.

Markowitz, Norman D. *The Rise and Fall of the People's Century: Henry A. Wallace and American Liberalism, 1941–1948*. New York: Free Press, 1973.

Marshall, George C. "A Federal World Government Now?" *Congressional Digest* 27 (Aug.– Sept. 1948): 201, 203.

Martin, Kingsley. "Hyenas and Other Reptiles." *New Statesman and Nation* 36 (Sept. 4, 1948): 187–88.

Masani, M. R. *The Communist Party of India*. New York: Macmillan, 1954.

McCrea, Frances B., and Gerald E. Markle. "Atomic Scientists and Protest," pp. 219– 33 in Leonard Kriesberg, ed., *Research in Social Movements, Conflict, and Change*. Greenwich, Conn.: JAI, 1989.

———. *Minutes to Midnight: Nuclear Weapons Protest in America*. Newbury Park, Calif.: Sage, 1989.

McElheny, Victor K. "Kapitsa to Visit England." *Science* 152 (May 6, 1966): 744.

McNeal, Patricia F. *The American Catholic Peace Movement, 1928–1972*. New York: Arno Press, 1978.

McNelly, Theodore H. " 'Induced Revolution': The Policy and Process of Constitutional Reform in Occupied Japan," pp. 76–106 in Robert E. Ward and Sakamoto Yoshikazu, eds., *Democratizing Japan: The Allied Occupation*. Honolulu: University of Hawaii Press, 1987.

The Meaning of Survival: Hiroshima's 36 Year Commitment to Peace. Hiroshima: Chugoku Shimbun and the Hiroshima International Cultural Foundation, 1983.

Medvedev, Roy. *Khrushchev*. Oxford: Basil Blackwell, 1982.

Medvedev, Roy, and Zhores A. Medvedev. *Khrushchev: The Years in Power*. New York: Columbia University Press, 1976.

Medvedev, Zhores A. *Soviet Science*. New York: Norton, 1978.

Merritt, Anna J., and Richard L. Merritt, eds. *Public Opinion in Occupied Germany: The OMGUS Surveys, 1945–1949*. Urbana: University of Illinois Press, 1970.

———. *Public Opinion in Semisovereign Germany: The HICOG Surveys, 1949–1955*. Urbana: University of Illinois Press, 1980.

Meyer, Cord, Jr. *Facing Reality: From World Federalism to the CIA*. New York: Harper & Row, 1980.

———. *Peace or Anarchy*. Boston: Little, Brown, 1947.

———. "What Are the Chances?" *Atlantic Monthly* 178 (July 1946): 42–45.

Miles, Rufus E., Jr. "Hiroshima: The Strange Myth of Half a Million American Lives Saved." *International Security* 10 (Fall 1985): 121–40.

Miller, Merle. *Plain Speaking: An Oral Biography of Harry S. Truman*. New York: Berkley Publishing, 1974.

Millis, Walter, ed. *The Forrestal Diaries*. New York: Viking Press, 1951.

Minnion, John, and Philip Bolsover, eds. *The CND Story*. London: Allison & Busby, 1983.

Modigliani, Edoardo, and Andrea Berardi. *L'Organizzazione della pace, dal punto di vista giuridico*. Verona: M. Lecce, 1947.

Moellering, Ralph Luther. *Modern War and the American Churches*. New York: American Press, 1957.

Moffatt, Gary. *History of the Canadian Peace Movement Until 1969*. St. Catherines, Ontario, Canada: Grapevine Press, 1969.

Montagu, Ivor. *Plot Against Peace*. New York: International Publishers, 1953.

Moore, Eleanor M. *The Quest for Peace*. Melbourne: Wilke, 1949.

Morrison, Sybil. *I Renounce War: The Story of the Peace Pledge Union*. London: Sheppard Press, 1962.

Mushaben, Joyce Marie. "Cycles of Peace Protest in West Germany: Experiences from Three Decades." *West European Politics* 8 (Jan. 1985): 24–40.

Muste, A. J. *Gandhi and the H-Bomb*. New York: Fellowship Publications, 1950.

——— . *Not by Might*. New York: Harper & Brothers, 1947.

Musto, Ronald G. *The Catholic Peace Tradition*. Maryknoll, N.Y.: Orbis Books, 1986.

Myers, Frank E. "The Failure of Protest Against Postwar British Defense Policy," pp. 240–64 in Sol Wank, ed., *Doves and Diplomats: Foreign Offices and Peace Movements in Europe and America in the Twentieth Century*. Westport, Conn.: Greenwood Press, 1978.

Myrdal, Alva. *The Game of Disarmament: How the United States and Russia Run the Arms Race*. New York: Pantheon Books, 1976.

Nash, Vernon. *It Must Be Done Again: Thirteen American States Point the Way for the Nations Now*. New York: Union Press, 1948.

Nathan, Otto, and Heinz Norden, eds. *Einstein on Peace*. New York: Schocken Books, 1968.

Nehru, Jawaharlal, and Norman Cousins. *Talks with Nehru*. New York: John Day, 1951.

Nevakivi, Jukka. "Finland and the Cold War." *Scandinavian Journal of History* 10, no. 3 (1985): 211–24.

Nishi, Toshio. *Unconditional Democracy: Education and Politics in Occupied Japan*. Stanford, Calif.: Hoover Institution Press, 1982.

Noelle, Elisabeth, and Erich Peter Neumann, eds. *The Germans: Public Opinion Polls, 1947–1966*. Allensbach: Verlag für Demoskopie, 1967.

Nogee, Joseph L. *Soviet Policy Towards International Control of Atomic Energy*. Notre Dame, Ind.: University of Notre Dame Press, 1961.

Noorman, H. "Martin Niemöller," pp. 283–84 in Helmut Donat and Karl Holl, eds., *Die Friedensbewegung: Organisierter Pazifismus in Deutschland, Österreich und in der Schweiz*. Düsseldorf: ECON Taschenbuch Verlag, 1983.

Norman, Dorothy, ed. *Nehru: The First Sixty Years*. 2 vols. New York: John Day, 1965.

Norman, Edward. "The Churches and the Peace Movement: The British Experience," pp. 260–72 in Walter Laqueur and Robert Hunter, eds., *European Peace Movements and the Future of the Western Alliance*. New Brunswick, N.J.: Transaction Books, 1985.

Oe, Kenzaburo. *Hiroshima Notes*. Tokyo: YMCA Press, 1981.

Ohnishi, Hitoshi. "The Peace Movement in Japan." *International Peace Research Newsletter* 21 (1983): 26–33.

Olson, Theodore W. "Peace and the American Community: A Manual for Instructors in a Work and Study Program for Peace Interns." New York, 1963. Mimeographed.

"One Planet: America Ponders the Vision of a Federation of the World." *Newsweek* 28 (Oct. 14, 1946): 44–45.

Oppenheimer, J. Robert. *The Open Mind*. New York: Simon & Schuster, 1955.

Orlov, Yuri. *Dangerous Thoughts: Memoirs of a Russian Life*. New York: William Morrow, 1991.

Ormrod, David. "The Churches and the Nuclear Arms Race," pp. 189–220 in Richard Taylor and Nigel Young, eds., *Campaigns for Peace: British Peace Movements in the Twentieth Century*. Manchester: Manchester University Press, 1987.

Otto, Karl A. " 'Ohne mich!'-Bewegung," pp. 292–93 in Helmut Donat and Karl Holl, eds., *Die Friedensbewegung: Organisierter Pazifismus in Deutschland, Österreich und in der Schweiz*. Düsseldorf: ECON Taschenbuch Verlag, 1983.

Overstreet, Gene D., and Marshall Windmiller. *Communism in India*. Berkeley: University of California Press, 1960.

Pacific War Research Society. *The Day Man Lost*. Tokyo: Kodansha International, 1982.

Pais, Abraham. "Reminiscences from the Post-war Years," pp. 215–26 in Stefan Rozental, ed., *Niels Bohr: His Life and Work as Seen by His Friends and Colleagues*. New York: Interscience Publishers, 1967.

Parry, Albert. *Peter Kapitsa on Life and Science*. New York: Macmillan, 1968.

"The Peace Front Is Invincible." *New Times*, no. 17 (Apr. 20, 1949), pp. 1–2.

"Peace Movement in the People's Democracies." *New Times*, no. 36 (1950), pp. 10–12.

Peierls, Rudolf. *Bird of Passage: Recollections of a Physicist*. Princeton: Princeton University Press, 1985.

Penner, Norman. *Canadian Communism: The Stalin Years and Beyond*. Toronto: Methuen, 1988.

Peristerakis, Michalis N. "To Elliniko Kinima Eirinis." Ph.D. diss., Panteios University, Athens, 1988.

Pfau, Richard. *No Sacrifice Too Great: The Life of Lewis L. Strauss*. Charlottesville: University Press of Virginia, 1984.

Pickett, Clarence E. *For More Than Bread*. Boston: Little, Brown, 1953.

Piehl, Mel. *Breaking Bread: The Catholic Worker and the Origin of Catholic Radicalism in America*. Philadelphia: Temple University Press, 1982.

Pierre, Andrew J. *Nuclear Politics: The British Experience with an Independent Strategic Force, 1939–1970*. London: Oxford University Press, 1972.

Pogue, Forrest C. *George C. Marshall: Statesman, 1945–1959*. New York: Viking Press, 1987.

"The Pope and the Bomb: He Denies Disapproving." *Newsweek* 26 (Aug. 20, 1945): 76–77.

Potyarkin, Y., and S. Kortunov, eds. *The USSR Proposes Disarmament, 1920s-1980s*. Moscow: Progress Publishers, 1986.

Powell, C. F. "Nuclear Weapons and the Federation." *Scientific World* 8, no. 1 (1964): 3–4.

Priestley, J. B. "Open Letter to a Russian Colleague." *New Statesman and Nation* 39 (Apr. 22, 1950): 451.

Public Papers of the Presidents of the United States: Harry S. Truman, 1945. Washington, D.C.: U.S. Government Printing Office, 1961.

Public Papers of the Presidents of the United States: Harry S. Truman, 1952–53. Washington, D.C.: U.S. Government Printing Office, 1966.

Radhakrishnan, Sarvepalli. *Is This Peace?* Bombay: Hind Kitabs, 1945.

Randall, Mercedes M. *Improper Bostonian: Emily Greene Balch*. New York: Twayne, 1964.

Reardon, Betty A. *Sexism and the War System*. New York: Teachers College Press, 1985.

Reiss, Mitchell. *Without the Bomb: The Politics of Nuclear Nonproliferation*. New York: Columbia University Press, 1988.

Reves, Emery. *The Anatomy of Peace*. New York: Harper & Brothers, 1945.

Rhodes, Richard. *The Making of the Atomic Bomb*. New York: Simon & Schuster, 1986.

Riesenberger, Dieter. *Geschichte der Friedensbewegung in Deutschland*. Göttingen: Vandenhoeck & Ruprecht, 1985.

Rigby, Andrew. "Peace News, 1936–1986: An Overview," pp. 7–26 in Gail Chester and Andrew Rigby, eds., *Articles of Peace*. Bridport, Dorset: Prism Press, 1986.

"Roadblocks to a World Traveler." *Chemical and Engineering News* 33 (Nov. 28, 1955): 5156–57.

Roberts, Barbara. "Women's Peace Activism in Canada," pp. 276–308 in Linda Kealey and Joan Sangster, eds., *Beyond the Vote: Canadian Women and Politics*. Toronto: University of Toronto Press, 1989.

Robinson, Jo Ann. *Abraham Went Out: A Biography of A. J. Muste*. Philadelphia: Temple University Press, 1981.

Root, Robert. "All in the Name of Peace." *Christian Century* 67 (Sept. 27, 1950): 1130–31.

Rosenberg, David Alan. "American Atomic Strategy and the Hydrogen Bomb Decision." *Journal of American History* 66 (June 1979): 62–87.

Rotblat, Joseph. "Movements of Scientists Against the Arms Race," pp. 115–57 in Joseph Rotblat, ed., *Scientists, the Arms Race and Disarmament: A UNESCO/Pugwash Symposium*. London: Taylor & Francis, 1982.

Roy, Ralph Lord. *Communism and the Churches*. New York: Harcourt, Brace, 1960.

Rozental, Stefan. "The Forties and the Fifties," pp. 149–90 in Stefan Rozental, ed., *Niels Bohr: His Life and Work as Seen by His Friends and Colleagues*. New York: Interscience Publishers, 1967.

Rubin, Jay. "From Wholesomeness to Decadence: The Censorship of Literature Under the Allied Occupation." *Journal of Japanese Studies* 11 (Winter 1985): 71–103.

Rupp, Hans K. *Ausserparlamentarische Opposition in der Ära Adenauer: Der Kampf gegen die Atombewaffnung in den fünfziger Jahren*. Cologne: Pahl-Rugenstein, 1970.

Rusk, Dean. *As I Saw It*. New York: Penguin Books, 1990.

Russell, Bertrand. *Common Sense and Nuclear Warfare*. London: Allen & Unwin, 1959.

———. *Has Man a Future?* New York: Simon & Schuster, 1962.

———. *Towards World Government*. London: New Commonwealth, 1948.

Russell, Dora. *The Tamarisk Tree 3: Challenge to the Cold War*. London: Virago Press, 1985.

Russell, Francis H. "Where We Stand Today." *Department of State Bulletin* 23 (July 17, 1950): 112–17.

Rustin, Bayard. *"In Apprehension How Like a God!"* Philadelphia: Young Friends Movement of the Philadelphia Yearly Meetings, 1948.

Sakharov, Andrei. *Memoirs*. New York: Knopf, 1990.

Salvin, Marina. "Neutralism in France." *International Conciliation*, no. 472 (June 1951), pp. 285–303.

———. "Neutralism in Germany." *International Conciliation*, no. 472 (June 1951), pp. 304–18.

Sartre, Jean-Paul. *The Communists and Peace*. New York: George Braziller, 1968.

Saunders, Malcolm, and Ralph Summy. *The Australian Peace Movement: A Short History*. Canberra: Peace Research Centre, Australian National University, 1986.

———. "One Hundred Years of an Australian Peace Movement, 1885–1984: Part II: From the Second World War to Vietnam and Beyond." *Peace and Change* 10 (Fall–Winter 1984): 57–75.

———. "Salient Themes of the Australian Peace Movement: An Historical Perspective." *Social Alternatives* 3 (Oct. 1982): 23–32.

Scalapino, Robert A. *The Japanese Communist Movement, 1920–1966*. Berkeley: University of California Press, 1967.

Schaffer, Ronald. *Wings of Judgment: American Bombing in World War II*. New York: Oxford University Press, 1988.

Scharrer, Siegfried. "War and Peace and the German Church," pp. 273–317 in Walter Laqueur and Robert Hunter, eds., *European Peace Movements and the Future of the Western Alliance*. New Brunswick, N.J.: Transaction Books, 1985.

Scheinman, Lawrence. *Atomic Energy Policy in France Under the Fourth Republic*. Princeton: Princeton University Press, 1965.

Schlaga, Rüdiger. "Peace Movement as a Party's Tool? The Peace Council of the German Democratic Republic," pp. 129–46 in Katsuya Kodama and Unto Vesa, eds., *Towards a Comparative Analysis of Peace Movements*. Hants, Eng.: Dartmouth Publishing Company, 1990.

Schmidt, Karl M. *Henry A. Wallace: Quixotic Crusade, 1948*. Syracuse: Syracuse University Press, 1960.

Scholl, Inge. *The White Rose: Munich, 1942–1943*. Middletown, Conn.: Wesleyan University Press, 1983.

Schonberger, Howard B. *Aftermath of War: Americans and the Remaking of Japan, 1945–1952*. Kent, Ohio: Kent State University Press, 1989.

Schrecker, Ellen. *No Ivory Tower: McCarthyism and the Universities*. New York: Oxford University Press, 1988.

Schuman, Frederick L. *The Commonwealth of Man*. New York: Knopf, 1952.

Schwartz, Richard Alan. "The F.B.I. and Dr. Einstein." *Nation* 237 (Sept. 3–10, 1983): 168–73.

Schwarz, Jordan A. *The Speculator: Bernard M. Baruch in Washington, 1917–1965*. Chapel Hill: University of North Carolina Press, 1981.

Seaborg, Glenn T. *Kennedy, Khrushchev, and the Test Ban*. Berkeley: University of California Press, 1981.

———. *Stemming the Tide: Arms Control in the Johnson Years*. Lexington, Mass.: Lexington Books, 1987.

Seidler, Murray B. *Norman Thomas: Respectable Rebel*. Syracuse: Syracuse University Press, 1961.

Shannon, David A. *The Decline of American Communism*. New York: Harcourt, Brace, 1959.

Shapley, Deborah. "Nuclear Weapons History: Japan's Wartime Bomb Projects Revealed." *Science* 199 (Jan. 13, 1978): 152–57.

Sherwin, Martin J. *A World Destroyed: Hiroshima and the Origins of the Arms Race*. New York: Vintage Books, 1987.

Shils, Edward. "Leo Szilard: A Memoir." *Encounter* 23 (Dec. 1964): 35–41.

Shoenberg, David. "Kapitza, Fact and Fiction." *Intelligence and National Security* 3 (Oct. 1988): 49–61.

Shulman, Marshall D. *Stalin's Foreign Policy Reappraised*. New York: Atheneum, 1966.

Small, Melvin. *Johnson, Nixon, and the Doves*. New Brunswick, N.J.: Rutgers University Press, 1988.

Smith, Alice Kimball. *A Peril and a Hope: The Scientists' Movement in America, 1945–47*. Chicago: University of Chicago Press, 1965.

Smith, Alice Kimball, and Charles Weiner, eds. *Robert Oppenheimer: Letters and Recollections*. Cambridge, Mass.: Harvard University Press, 1980.

Smith, David C. *H. G. Wells: Desperately Mortal*. New Haven, Conn.: Yale University Press, 1986.

Socknat, Thomas P. "The Dilemma of Canadian Pacifists During the Early Cold War Years." Paper presented at the Conference on the Pacifist Impulse in Historical Perspective, University of Toronto, Toronto, Canada, May 12, 1991.

———. *Witness Against War: Pacifism in Canada, 1900–1945*. Toronto: University of Toronto Press, 1987.

"Soviet World-Peace Appeal Called Propaganda Trick." *Department of State Bulletin* 23 (July 24, 1950): 131.

"Speak for England." *New Statesman and Nation* 30 (Aug. 18, 1945): 101.

Speer, Albert. *Inside the Third Reich*. New York: Macmillan, 1970.

Stahle, Elisabeth. *Internationella Kvinnoförbundet för Fred och Frihet*. Stockholm: IKFF, 1988.

Starobin, Joseph R. *American Communism in Crisis, 1943–1957*. Cambridge, Mass.: Harvard University Press, 1972.

Stevenson, Lilian. *Towards a Christian International: The Story of the International Fellowship of Reconciliation*. London: International Fellowship of Reconciliation, 1941.

Stimson, Henry L. "The Decision to Use the Atomic Bomb." *Harper's* 194 (Feb. 1947): 97–107.

Stimson, Henry L., and McGeorge Bundy. *On Active Service in Peace and War*. New York: Harper & Brothers, 1948.

Stockwin, J. A. A. *The Japanese Socialist Party and Neutralism*. Carlton: Melbourne University Press, 1968.

Strauss, Lewis L. *Men and Decisions*. Garden City, N.Y.: Doubleday, 1962.

Street, Jessie M. G. *Truth or Repose*. Sydney: Australasian Book Society, 1966.

Streit, Clarence K. *Union Now*. New York: Harper & Brothers, 1939.

Strickland, Donald A. *Scientists in Politics: The Atomic Scientists Movement, 1945–46*. West Lafayette, Ind.: Purdue University Studies, 1968.

Stucky, Harley J. *August 6, 1945—The Impact of Atomic Energy*. New York: American Press, 1964.

Summy, Ralph. "The Australian Peace Council and the Anticommunist Milieu, 1949–1965," pp. 233–64 in Charles Chatfield and Peter van den Dungen, eds., *Peace Movements and Political Cultures*. Knoxville: University of Tennessee Press, 1988.

Summy, Ralph, and Malcolm Saunders. "Disarmament and the Australian Peace Movement: A Brief History." *World Review* 26 (Dec. 1987): 15–52.

Suzuki, Sunao. "The Declining Role of Ideology in Citizens' Movements." *Japan Quarterly* 23 (Apr.–June 1976): 121–26.

———. "Japanese Attitudes Toward Nuclear Issues," in Japan Peace Research Group, ed., *Peace Research in Japan* (1974–75), pp. 99–117.

Swing, Raymond Gram. *"Good Evening!": A Professional Memoir*. New York: Harcourt, Brace, and World, 1964.

———. *In the Name of Sanity*. New York: Harper & Brothers, 1946.

Szilard, Leo. "Can We Avert an Arms Race by an Inspection System?" pp. 61–65 in Dexter Masters and Katherine Way, eds., *One World or None*. New York: McGraw-Hill, 1946.

———. "My Trial as a War Criminal," pp. 75–86 in Leo Szilard, ed., *The Voice of the Dolphins and Other Stories*. New York: Simon & Schuster, 1961 (reissued: Stanford, Calif.: Stanford University Press, 1992).

———. "A Personal History of the Atomic Bomb." *University of Chicago Round Table*, no. 601 (Sept. 25, 1949), pp. 14–16.

———. "The Physicist Invades Politics." *Saturday Review of Literature* 30 (May 3, 1947): 7–8, 31–34.

Taipale, Ilkka. "The Peace Movement in Finland," pp. 17–49 in Kimmo Kiljunen, Folke Sundman, and Ilkka Taipale, eds., *Finnish Peace Making*. Helsinki: Peace Union of Finland, 1987.

Taylor, A. J. P. *A Personal History*. London: Hamish Hamilton, 1983.

Taylor, A. J. P., et al. Letter to the Editor. *New Statesman and Nation* 36 (Sept. 4, 1948): 195.

Taylor, Nancy M. *The Home Front*. Wellington: Government Printer, 1986.

Teller, Edward. *Energy: From Heaven and Earth*. San Francisco: W. H. Freeman, 1979.

Teller, Edward, with Allen Brown. *The Legacy of Hiroshima*. Garden City, N.Y.: Doubleday, 1962.

Thomas, Norman M. *Appeal to the Nations*. New York: Henry Holt, 1947.

Thurlow, Setsuko. "The Atomic Bombing of Hiroshima and Nagasaki: The Role of Women in the Japanese Peace Movement," pp. 225–35 in Ruth Roach Pierson, ed., *Women and Peace: Theoretical, Historical and Practical Perspectives*. London: Croom Helm, 1987.

Tiersky, Ronald. *French Communism, 1920–1972*. New York: Columbia University Press, 1974.

Torre Espinosa, Adolfo. *Un mundo nuevo, estados unidas del mundo*. Mérida, Mexico: N.p., 1945.

Truman, Harry S. *Year of Decisions*. Garden City, N.Y.: Doubleday, 1955.

——— . *Years of Trial and Hope*. Garden City, N.Y.: Doubleday, 1956.

Tsurumi, Kazuko. *Social Change and the Individual: Japan Before and After Defeat in World War II*. Princeton: Princeton University Press, 1970.

Tsurumi, Shunsuke. *An Intellectual History of Wartime Japan, 1931–1945*. London: Routledge & Kegan Paul, 1986.

Turski, Marian, and Henryk Zdanowski. *The Peace Movement: People and Facts*. N.p., Poland: Interpress Publishers, 1976.

Ueda, Katsumi. "Tabata Shinobu: Defender of the Peace Constitution," pp. 221–49 in Nobuya Bamba and John F. Howes, eds., *Pacifism in Japan: The Christian and Socialist Tradition*. Vancouver: University of British Columbia Press, 1978.

United World Federalists. *Unity and Diversity*. New York: World Government House, [1947?].

Urey, Harold C. "How Does It All Add Up?" pp. 58–60 in Dexter Masters and Katherine Way, eds., *One World or None*. New York: McGraw-Hill, 1946.

U.S. Atomic Energy Commission. *In the Matter of J. Robert Oppenheimer*. Cambridge, Mass.: MIT Press, 1971.

U.S. Department of State. *Foreign Relations of the United States*. Annual volumes, 1946–51. Washington, D.C.: U.S. Government Printing Office, 1972–85.

——— . *The International Control of Atomic Energy: Policy at the Crossroads*. Washington, D.C.: U.S. Government Printing Office, 1948.

——— . *United States Atomic Energy Proposals: Statement of the United States Policy on Control of Atomic Energy as Presented by Bernard M. Baruch, Esq., to the United Nations Atomic Energy Commission June 14, 1946*. Washington, D.C.: U.S. Government Printing Office, 1946.

U.S. House of Representatives, Committee on Un-American Activities. *The Communist "Peace" Petition Campaign*. 81st Cong., 2d sess. Washington, D.C.: U.S. Government Printing Office, 1950.

——— . *Report on the Communist "Peace" Offensive: A Campaign to Disarm and Defeat the United States*. 82d Cong., 1st sess. Washington, D.C.: U.S. Government Printing Office, 1951.

U.S. Senate, Select Committee to Study Governmental Operations with Respect to Intelligence Activities. *Final Report: Book III, Supplementary Detailed Staff Reports on Intelligence Activities and the Rights of Americans*. 94th Cong., 2d sess. Washington, D.C.: U.S. Government Printing Office, 1976.

U.S. Strategic Bombing Survey. *The Effects of Atomic Bombs on Hiroshima and Nagasaki*. Washington, D.C.: U.S. Government Printing Office, 1946.

——— . *Japan's Struggle to End the War*. Washington, D.C.: U.S. Government Printing Office, 1946.

van den Dungen, Peter. "Johannes Bernardus Theodorus Hugenholtz," pp. 430–32 in Harold Josephson, ed., *Biographical Dictionary of Modern Peace Leaders*. Westport, Conn.: Greenwood Press, 1985.

Van Doren, Carl. *The Great Rehearsal*. New York: Viking Press, 1948.

Van Kirk, Walter. *Religion Renounces War*. Chicago: Willett, Clark, 1934.

Vergara Robles, Enrique. *Panamérica en la orbita universal*. Santiago, Chile: Imprenta universitaria, 1945.

Verkuil, I. D. *De grote illusie: De Nederlandse vredesbeweging na 1945*. Utrecht: HES, 1988.

Vinokurov, P. "Peace Movement in the People's Democracies." *New Times*, no. 36 (1950), p. 12.

von Bonsdorff, Göran. "Peace Movement in Nordic Countries," pp. 218–19 in Ervin Laszlo and Jong Youl Yoo, eds., *World Encyclopedia of Peace*, vol. 2. Oxford: Pergamon Press, 1986.

Wagar, W. Warren. *H. G. Wells and the World State*. New Haven, Conn.: Yale University Press, 1961.

Wahlbäck, Krister. *The Roots of Swedish Neutrality*. Uppsala: Swedish Institute, 1986.

Walker, Mark. "Uranium Machines, Nuclear Explosives, and National Socialism: The German Quest for Nuclear Power, 1939–1949." Ph.D. diss., Princeton University, 1987.

Walker, Sydnor H., ed. *The First One Hundred Days of the Atomic Age*. New York: Woodrow Wilson Foundation, 1945.

Wall, Irwin M. *French Communism in the Era of Stalin: The Quest for Unity and Integration*. Westport, Conn.: Greenwood Press, 1983.

Weart, Spencer R. *Nuclear Fear: A History of Images*. Cambridge, Mass.: Harvard University Press, 1988.

——— . *Scientists in Power*. Cambridge, Mass.: Harvard University Press, 1979.

——— . "Scientists with a Secret." *Physics Today* 29 (Feb. 1976): 23–30.

Weart, Spencer R., and Gertrud Weiss Szilard, eds. *Leo Szilard: His Version of the Facts*. Cambridge, Mass.: MIT Press, 1978.

Weisbord, Merrily. *The Strangest Dream: Canadian Communists, the Spy Trials, and the Cold War*. Toronto: Lester & Orpen Dennys, 1983.

Weisskopf, Victor F. *The Privilege of Being a Physicist*. New York: W. H. Freeman, 1989.

Welles, Sumner. "The Atomic Bomb and World Government." *Atlantic Monthly* 177 (January 1946): 39–42.

Wells, G. P., ed. *H. G. Wells in Love*. London: Faber & Faber, 1984.

Wells, H. G. *Mind at the End of Its Tether*. New York: Didier, 1946.

——— . *The Open Conspiracy: Blue Prints for a World Revolution*. Garden City, N.Y.: Doubleday, Doran, 1928.

——— . *The World Set Free*. New York: Dutton, 1914.

Werskey, Gary. *The Visible College*. London: Allen Lane, 1978.

What's the GDR All About? Berlin: Panorama DDR, 1989.

White, Elwyn Brooks. *The Wild Flag*. Boston: Houghton Mifflin, 1946.

Williams, Robert Chadwell. *Klaus Fuchs, Atom Spy*. Cambridge, Mass.: Harvard University Press, 1987.

Willkie, Wendell. *One World*. New York: Simon & Schuster, 1943.

Wittner, Lawrence S. *American Intervention in Greece, 1943–1949*. New York: Columbia University Press, 1982.

——— . "Peace Movements and Foreign Policy: The Challenge to Diplomatic Historians." *Diplomatic History* 11 (Fall 1987): 355–70.

——— . *Rebels Against War: The American Peace Movement, 1933–1983*. Philadelphia: Temple University Press, 1984.

————. "The Transnational Movement Against Nuclear Weapons: A Preliminary Survey," pp. 265–94 in Charles Chatfield and Peter van den Dungen, eds., *Peace Movements and Political Cultures*. Knoxville: University of Tennessee Press, 1988.

Wood, Alex. *The Deeper Challenge of the Atom Bomb*. London: Peace News, 1946.

Wooley, Wesley T. *Alternatives to Anarchy: American Supranationalism Since World War II*. Bloomington: Indiana University Press, 1988.

Woolf, Leonard. "Britain in the Atomic Age." *Political Quarterly* 17 (Jan.–Mar. 1946): 12–24.

Wooster, W. A. "Some Recollections of the W.F.S.W." *Scientific World*, Anniversary Number (1966), pp. 26–29.

"The World Congress for Peace." *New Times*, no. 18 (Apr. 27, 1949), pp. 4–8.

"The World Government Crusade." *Christian Century* 65 (Jan. 28, 1948): 102–4.

World Government Highlights. Washington, D.C.: United World Federalists of the District of Columbia, 1948.

"World Government Sought by 1955." *Christian Century* 64 (Oct. 8, 1947): 1196.

"World Opinion." *International Journal of Opinion and Attitude Research* 1 (Sept. 1947): 127–52.

"World Opinion." *International Journal of Opinion and Attitude Research* 3 (Summer 1949): 285–303.

"World Opinion." *International Journal of Opinion and Attitude Research* 4 (Fall 1950): 444–70.

"Worthy of Note." *New Times*, no. 36 (1950), p. 11.

Wright, Quincy. *A Study of War*. Chicago: University of Chicago Press, 1965.

Wynner, Edith, and Georgia Lloyd. *Searchlight on Peace Plans*. New York: E. P. Dutton, 1949.

Yavenditti, Michael J. "American Reactions to the Use of Atomic Bombs on Japan, 1945–1947." Ph.D. diss., University of California, Berkeley, 1970.

————. "John Hersey and the American Conscience: The Reception of 'Hiroshima.' " *Pacific Historical Review* 43 (Feb. 1974): 24–49.

Yergin, Daniel. *Shattered Peace: The Origins of the Cold War and the National Security State*. Boston: Houghton Mifflin, 1977.

York, Herbert F. *The Advisors: Oppenheimer, Teller, and the Superbomb*. San Francisco: W. H. Freeman, 1976.

————. *Making Weapons, Talking Peace: A Physicist's Odyssey from Hiroshima to Geneva*. New York: Basic Books, 1987.

Zahn, Gordon C. *War, Conscience and Dissent*. New York: Hawthorn Books, 1967.

Zhukov, Georgi K. *The Memoirs of Marshal Zhukov*. New York: Delacorte Press, 1971.

Index

In this index "f" after a number indicates a separate reference on the next page, and "ff" indicates separate references on the next two pages. A continuous discussion over two or more pages is indicated by a span of numbers. *Passim* is used for a cluster of references in close but not consecutive sequence.

Library of Congress Cataloging-in-Publication Data

Wittner, Lawrence S.
  The struggle against the bomb / Lawrence S. Wittner.
    p.   cm. — (Stanford nuclear age series)
  Includes bibliographical references and index.
  Contents: v. 1. One world or none: A history of the world nuclear disarmament movement
  through 1953
  ISBN 0-8047-2141-6 (v. 1 : acid-free paper) :
    1. Nuclear disarmament—History. 2. Antinuclear movement—History.   I. Title.
  II. Series.
JX1974.7.W575   1993
327.1′74′09—dc20   92-28026
                                                                            CIP

∞ This book is printed on acid-free paper